Fuzzy Reasoning
and its Applications

Computers and People Series

Edited by

B. R. GAINES

The series is concerned with all aspects of man-computer relationships, including interaction, interfacing, modelling and artificial intelligence. Books are interdisciplinary, communicating results derived in one area of study to workers in another. Applied, experimental, theoretical and tutorial studies are included.

Fuzzy Reasoning and its Applications

Edited by
DR. E. H. MAMDANI
Department of Electrical Engineering
Queen Mary College, London
PROFESSOR B. R. GAINES
Centre for Man—Computer Studies
Barbican, London

1981

ACADEMIC PRESS
A Subsidiary of Harcourt Brace Jovanovich, Publishers
London • New York • Toronto • Sydney • San Francisco

ACADEMIC PRESS INC. (LONDON) LTD.
24–28 Oval Road
London NW1

United States Edition published by
ACADEMIC PRESS INC.
111 Fifth Avenue
New York, New York 10003

British Library Cataloguing in Publication Data
Fuzzy reasoning and its applications.—(Computers and people series)
 1. Fuzzy sets
 I. Mamdani, E. H.   II. Gaines, B. R.
 511.3   QA248

ISBN 0–12–467750–9

LCCCN 81–67148

Printed by J. W. Arrowsmith Ltd.
Bristol BS3 2NT

Contributors' Addresses

ASSILIAN, S., c/o Dr. E. H. Mamdani, Department of Electrical Engineering, Queen Mary College, Mile End Road, London E1 4NS

BAINBRIDGE, L., Department of Psychology, University of Reading, Whiteknights, Reading, RG6 2AL

BALDWIN, J. F., Department of Engineering Maths, University of Bristol, Bristol, BS8 1TH

BANDLER, W., Department of Mathematics, University of Essex, Wivenhoe Park, Colchester, CO4 3SQ

CHILAUSKY, R. L., Department of Computer Science, University of Illinois at Urbana–Champaign, Urbana, Illinois 61801

ESHRAGH, F., c/o Dr. E. H. Mamdani, Department of Electrical Engineering, Queen Mary College, Mile End Road, London E1 4NS

GAINES, B. R., Centre for Man–Computer Studies, Barbican, London EC2

GILES, R., Department of Mathematics and Statistics, Queen's University, Kingston, Ontario, Canada K1L 3N6

GOGUEN, J. A., Computer Science Department, University of California, 5151 State University Drive, Los Angeles, California 90032, USA

KING, P. J., Warren Spring Laboratory, Gunnels Wood Road, Stevenage, Herts.

KLINGER, A., Data Structure and Display Co., Los Angeles, California, USA

KOHOUT, L. J., Department of Computer Science, Brunel University, Uxbridge, Middlesex UB8 3PH

LARSEN, P. M., Electric Power Engineering Department, Technical University of Denmark, DK-2800 Lyngby, Denmark

MAMDANI, E. H., Department of Electrical Engineering, Queen Mary College, Mile End Road, London E1 4NS

MICHALSKI, R. S., Department of Computer Science, University of Illinois at Urbana–Champaign, Urbana, Illinois 61801, U.S.A.

RHODES, M. L., Computer Science Department, University of California at Los Angeles, 5151 State University Drive, Los Angeles, California 90032, U.S.A.

SCHEFE, P., Fachbereich Informatik, Universität Hamburg, 2 Hamburg 13, Schulüterstrasse 66–72, Hamburg, West Germany

UMBERS, I, Warren Spring Laboratory, Gunnels Wood Road, Stevenage, Herts.

WENSTØP, F., Bedriftsøkonomisk Institutt, Frysjaveien 33c, Oslo 8, Norway.

ZADEH, L., Electronics Research Laboratory, College of Engineering, University of California, Berkeley, CA 94720, U.S.A.

Preface

In this book we have gathered together a selection of papers that have all previously appeared in the International Journal of Man–Machine Studies. This collection represents, in our opinion, a unique contribution to the theory and application of fuzzy sets which deserves the attention of those interested in the field. The Journal itself has played a leading role during the past few years in disseminating research work in the field. Other equally good papers that have appeared in the Journal have had to be omitted. Those included here, however, present a coherent picture on Linguistic Fuzzy Reasoning and its Applications, particularly the application to the control of industrial processes. Their original inclusion in the Journal reflected our own interest and thus our aim in this book is to paint this picture in the words of other research workers by highlighting the link through the introductory chapter. It is worth mentioning also that many of the papers were originally presented at Workshops that we, the editors, organised at Queen Mary College in London on the subject of Fuzzy Reasoning and its Applications.

March 1981

E. H. MAMDANI
B. R. GAINES

Contents

PART I

PRUF—a meaning representation language for natural languages
L. A. ZADEH

Concept Representation in Natural and Artificial Languages: Axioms, Extensions and Applications for Fuzzy Sets
J. A. GOGUEN Jr.

Lukasiewicz Logic and Fuzzy Set Theory
R. GILES

Knowledge acquisition by encoding expert rules versus computer induction from examples: a case study involving soybean pathology
R. S. MICHALSKI and R. L. CHILAUSKY

Conversational text input for modifying graphics facial images
M. L. RHODES and A. KLINGER

Logical Foundations for Database Systems
B. R. GAINES

PART III

Introduction

An alternative title to this book could well have been *Fundamentals of Expert Systems* as the main concern in all the papers included here is the computerisation of human derived knowledge. This is a rapidly growing area of artificial intelligence in which Fuzzy Reasoning has an obvious application. All the applications considered in this book deal with problems in Expert Systems to some extent. Our intention in the rest of this chapter is to give a commentary on the material included in the text. To simplify matters we have divided the book into three parts. Part I deals mainly with the philosophical aspects of Fuzzy Reasoning and Fuzzy Logic. Part II is on applications dealing with fuzzy data and Part III on application to process control.

Fuzzy Reasoning and Fuzzy Logic

To put Fuzzy Logic in its proper prospective, a reader could not do better than start by carefully studying Susan Haack's book entitled 'Philosophy of Logics'. She points out that logic is about valid arguments and has to reflect human discourse; thus, semantic aspects are far more important than algebraic ones. To us the moral in this is that while the latter may appeal to a computer scientist who can thus implement the various linguistic terms (connectives, adjectives, etc.) operationally, he must not do this without due regard to what it all means.

It is this concern with meaning which also suggests that two valued logics— propositional and predicate—are not sufficient to capture all semantic aspects of language. Haack supports the notion of a variety of logics in contrast to Quine who believes in the uniqueness of predicate calculus (Quine, incidentally, has a booklet entitled 'Philosophy of Logic'—note the use of the plural in Haack's title). Haack, thus, gives the following classification of logics.

Classical Aristotelian Sentence (propositional) Quantified (predicate)	2 valued
Modal logics Deontic logic Tense logic Epistemic logic Etc.	Extended logics

Multiple Valued Logics
  Lukasiewicz
  Kleene
  and so on . . .
Intuitionistic Logic
	Deviant

To this we would add Probabilistic Logic and Fuzzy Logic although Haack, herself, would probably not support this.

In sentence logic, the chief semantic definitions are embodied in the truth tables; the terms being defined being logical connectives such as AND, OR, NOT etc. The philosophical issues in predicate calculus concern the things being quantified. What things exist? How do we know they exist? etc. In language there are in fact more quantifiers than the existential and the universal quantifiers used in predicated logic. For example, *some*, *almost all*, *most* and so on. These are characteristically fuzzy and do appear in fuzzy logic.

Extended logics are used to distinguish different types of sentences: past and future tense in Tense Logic; necessarily true from possibly true in Modal Logic and so on. Clearly modality is the main issue that fuzzy logic also attempts to deal with. Degrees of possibility and probability are issues of modality; but, in fuzzy and probability logics, these are handled through multi-valuedness, rather than through extension. However, those interested in fuzzy logic would also do well to study Modal Logic in detail.

Modality is only one of the many meanings that can be ascribed to multiple values; these can be used to interpret other semantics as well, such as truth. Therefore, while classical logicians sometimes consider truth values such as: TRUE, FALSE and UNKNOWN or UNDECIDABLE, they regard these last as epistemic extensions and do not consider that truth itself is a matter of degree. Many system scientists would strongly disagree with this by saying that modified truth values such as QUITE TRUE, SLIGHTLY TRUE, VERY TRUE etc. all mean different degrees of truth. Perhaps at this stage we should say that there is 'probably some truth' in both sides of this argument!

Zadeh's view is that ordinary language has many types of fuzziness: those of truth, possibility, probability and so on. In his paper which begins Part I of this book, he describes a Schema for interpreting fuzzy statements of ordinary language. This is followed by an older paper by Goguen in which he shows that the category of concepts is identical to the category of fuzzy sets. Giles' paper describes an interesting way of interpreting a multiple-valued logic which deserves greater attention. Baldwin also gives a variant of fuzzy logic. Wenstøp's paper produced here was the first to give an account of a computational method of dealing with linguistic modifiers such as VERY, SLIGHTLY, MORE OR LESS and so on. Other modifications followed from Wenstøp's work and one of these is described in the paper by Eshragh and Mamdani. Finally, Part I of the book ends with Schefe's paper which makes some critical points about fuzzy reasoning.

Two of the papers in Part II of the book, while they mainly deal with application studies, also deal with important theoretical matters. These are the papers by Bandler and Kohout and by Michalski. Below we shall look at the background to the theoretical issues of semantics in multi-valued logic that they raise. To explain this, first note that in two-valued sentence logic, we can write down 16 different truth tables of two arguments. If these are examined carefully, then one finds unique candidates to represent the meaning of the various logical connectives that we use in ordinary language such as AND, IMPLICATION, EQUIVALENCE etc. However, note that even here we find two types of OR's defined: the Inclusive and the Exclusive variety.

This means that the truth table for $\bar{A} \vee B$ should be taken not as the definitive meaning of IMPLICATION but merely as one of the 16 truth tables that comes nearest in meaning to the intuitive notion of this connective. The same applies to Modus Ponens. If one knew that either A OR B is true and one was further told that A is not true (i.e. $\bar{A}$

is true) then one can conclude that B must be true. Now because IMPLICATION is $\bar{A} \vee B$, then by complementing A in the above reasoning Modus Ponens follows: given $A \rightarrow B$, and A we can conclude B.

In infinitely valued multi-valued logic, one should not be surprised to find a large number of functions as possible candidates to represent the meaning of each of the logical connectives, especially one such as IMPLICATION which has been a source of much philosophical discussion. In fuzzy logic research, many papers have been published on the proper mathematical form for the various logical connectives. Bandler and Kohout's in Part II of the book, lists several different implication-like functions. It is worth noting that the non-uniqueness of these functions for a given logical connective almost certainly reflects the different shades of meaning these connectives have in ordinary language. For example, in ordinary language, entailment, implication and the construct 'If A then B' are almost never used interchangeably. They all mean different things and, in particular, the latter is usually reserved to indicate causal connection.

Both extended and deviant logics in Haacks' list are modifications of two-valued sentence logic. Thus, just as sentence logic is quantified to give predicate calculus, both extended and deviant logics can, and have, also been quantified. Michalski's paper, also included in Part II of this book, uses a quantified multi-valued logic to model statements in an expert system. Fuzzy logic is also a form of quantified multi-valued logic, but there are also differences between Michalski's logic and fuzzy logic, as can be seen by trying to substitute the latter in Michalski's work. The reason that this cannot be done has a great deal to do with the way the universe of discourse is explicated in fuzzy logic.

Applications of Fuzzy Reasoning

Fuzzy logic, as opposed to any other branch of fuzzy mathematics, is primarily designed to represent knowledge. We assume here that this knowledge will be in a linguistic form, and also that the exercise must not be merely intellectual but must also be operationally powerful so that computers can be used. The *knowledge* is derived from *experts*, and the database of this knowledge thus created is to be used to make decisions. Expert Systems and Knowledge Engineering are thus rapidly growing areas of systems engineering and artificial intelligence.

Early work in this area used predicate calculus to model the reasoning process. There is a growing realisation that exactness, closure and completeness are not important and may even be a hindrance in powerful decision making. Thus, in many systems the data is often fuzzy and incomplete. Furthermore, if the size of the database is limited then criteria for including a data item maybe both arbitrary and fuzzy. In general, decision algorithms based on completeness and working to satisfy crisp criteria are often too long to be practical and in such circumstances plausible reasoning can be used to advantage. This then is the unifying motivation behind research into fuzzy reasoning and its applications.

Fuzzy reasoning theory aims to provide a model for implementing a knowledge-based system. However, we have already seen that language has many ambiguities that can only be resolved by a very sophisticated system. Such a system does not as yet exist. The applications reported here all have slightly different theoretical foundations but they do illustrate what is required. They are thus useful not only as successful application studies in themselves, but also serve as motivation for the theoretician.

Both Part II and Part III of this book deal with applications. The papers in Part III deal exclusively with control applications. We have already seen that two of the papers in Part II also have a strong theoretical contribution. Rhodes and Klinger describe a typical problem in which fuzzy reasoning may be usefully employed. Gaines' paper on the other hand, takes a more general look at the problem of fuzzy databases, thereby providing a foundation for that particular area of work.

Part III of the book contains papers on the application of fuzzy reasoning to process control. This work has opened up a new approach in process control. The traditional techniques in process control always begin with the development of a mathematical model of the process to be controlled. A mathematical approach is the adopted to obtain the controller of the process. In the expert system type approach using fuzzy reasoning, described in Part III of this book, the control to be carried out is obtained in a linguistic form from a skilled operator. The original work, and other studies resulting from this are described in two papers by Mamdani. Such an approach is ideally suited for complex processes such as cement kilns. An industrial controller for cement kilns is described in Larsen's paper.

One of the main problems in this application and, in fact, with all expert systems, is how to obtain the knowledge from an expert. Such knowledge, especially where an acquired skill is to be described, is often intuitive, and thus not easily articulated. The problems are dealt with in the papers by Bainbridge and Umbers.

PRUF—a meaning representation language for natural languages†

L. A. ZADEH

Computer Science Division, Department of Electrical Engineering and Computer Sciences and the Electronics Research Laboratory, University of California, Berkeley, CA 94720, U.S.A.

(*Received 18 October 1977*)

PRUF—an acronym for Possibilistic Relational Universal Fuzzy—is a meaning representation language for natural languages which departs from the conventional approaches to the theory of meaning in several important respects.

First, a basic assumption underlying PRUF is that the imprecision that is intrinsic in natural languages is, for the most part, possibilistic rather than probabilistic in nature. Thus, a proposition such as "Richard is tall" translates in PRUF into a possibility distribution of the variable Height (Richard), which associates with each value of the variable a number in the interval [0,1] representing the possibility that Height (Richard) could assume the value in question. More generally, a proposition, p, translates into a procedure, P, which returns a possibility distribution, Π^p, with P and Π^p representing, respectively, the *meaning* of p and the *information* conveyed by p. In this sense, the concept of a possibility distribution replaces that of truth as a foundation for the representation of meaning in natural languages.

Second, the logic underlying PRUF is not a two-valued or multivalued logic, but a fuzzy logic, FL, in which the truth-values are linguistic, that is, are of the form *true, not true, very true, more or less true, not very true*, etc., with each such truth-value representing a fuzzy subset of the unit interval. The truth-value of a proposition is defined as its compatibility with a reference proposition, so that given two propositions p and r, one can compute the truth of p *relative to* r.

Third, the quantifiers in PRUF—like the truth-values—are allowed to be linguistic, i.e. may be expressed as *most, many, few, some, not very many, almost all*, etc. Based on the concept of the cardinality of a fuzzy set, such quantifiers are given a concrete interpretation which makes it possible to translate into PRUF propositions exemplified by "Many tall men are much taller than most men," "All tall women are blonde is not very true," etc.

The translation rules in PRUF are of four basic types: Type I—pertaining to modification; Type II—pertaining to composition; Type III—pertaining to quantification; and Type IV—pertaining to qualification and, in particular, to truth qualification, probability qualification and possibility qualification.

The concepts of semantic equivalence and semantic entailment in PRUF provide a basis for question-answering and inference from fuzzy premises. In addition to serving as a foundation for approximate reasoning, PRUF may be employed as a language for the representation of imprecise knowledge and as a means of precisiation of fuzzy propositions expressed in a natural language.

1. Introduction

In a decade or so from now—when the performance of natural language understanding and question-answering systems will certainly be much more impressive than it is today—it may well be hard to comprehend why linguists, philosophers, logicians and

---

†To Professor I. M. Gel'fand, who had suggested—a decade ago—the application of the theory of fuzzy sets to natural languages.

cognitive scientists have been so reluctant to come to grips with the reality of the pervasive imprecision of natural languages and have persisted so long in trying to fit their theories of syntax, semantics and knowledge representation into the rigid conceptual mold of two-valued logic.†

A fact that puts this issue into a sharper perspective is that almost any sentence drawn at random from a text in a natural language is likely to contain one or more words that have a fuzzy‡ denotation—that is, are labels of classes in which the transition from membership to non-membership is gradual rather than abrupt. This is true, for example, of the italicized words in the simple propositions "John is *tall*," "May has *dark* hair," and "May is *much younger* than John," as well as in the somewhat more complex and yet commonplace propositions exemplified by: "*Most* Frenchmen are not *blond*," "It is *very true* that *many* Swedes are *tall*," "It is *quite possible* than *many wealthy* Americans have *high* blood pressure," and "It is *probably quite true* that *most* X's are *much larger* than *most* Y's."

The numerous meaning representation, knowledge representation and query representation languages which have been described in the literature§—prominent among which are semantic networks, predicate calculi, relation algebra, Montague grammar, conceptual dependency graphs, logical networks, AIMDS, ALPHA, CONVERSE, DEDUCE, DILOS, HAM-RPM, HANSA, ILL, KRL, KRS, LIFER, LSP, LUNAR, MAPL, MEANINGEX, MERLIN, OWL, PHILQAI, PLANES, QUEL, REL, REQUEST, SAM, SCHOLAR, SEQUEL, SQUARE and TORUS—are not oriented toward the representation of fuzzy propositions, that is, propositions containing labels of fuzzy sets and hence have no facilities for semantic—as opposed to syntactic—inference from fuzzy premises.‖ However, facilities for the representation and execution of fuzzy instructions are available in the programming languages FUZZY (LeFaivre, 1974), FLOU and FSTDS (Noguchi, Umano, Mizumoto & Tanaka, 1976, 1977) and in the system modelling language of Fellinger (1974).

To clarify this remark, it should be noted that, although a fuzzy proposition such as "Herb is tall," may be—and frequently is—represented in predicate notation as Tall (Herb), such a representation presupposes that Tall is a predicate which partitions a collection of individuals, U, into two disjoint classes: those for which Tall(Herb) is true and those for which Tall(Herb) is false. One could, of course, interpret Tall as a predicate in a multivalued logic—in which case the extension of Tall would be a fuzzy subset of U—but even such more general representations cannot cope with quantified or qualified propositions of the form "Most tall men are fat," "It is very true that X is much larger than Y," "It is quite possible that if X is large then it is very likely that Y is small," etc.

In earlier papers (Zadeh, 1973, 1975*a, b, c*, 1976*a, b*; Bellman & Zadeh, 1976), we

†An incisive discussion of this and related issues may be found in Gaines (1976*b*).

‡Although the terms *fuzzy* and *vague* are frequently used interchangeably in the literature, there is, in fact, a significant difference between them. Specifically, a proposition, *p*, is *fuzzy* if it contains words which are labels of fuzzy sets; and *p* is *vague* if it is both fuzzy and insufficiently specific for a particular purpose. For example, "Bob will be back in a few minutes" is fuzzy, while "Bob will be back sometime" is vague if it is insufficiently informative as a basis for a decision. Thus, the vagueness of a proposition is a decision-dependent characteristic whereas its fuzziness is not.

§A list of representative papers and books dealing with the subject of meaning representation languages and related issues is presented in the appended bibliography.

‖Semantic inference differs from syntactic inference in that it involves the meaning of premises while syntactic inference involves only their surface structure.

have argued that traditional logical systems are intrinsically unsuited for the manipulation of fuzzy knowledge—which is the type of knowledge that underlies natural languages as well as most of human reasoning—and have proposed a fuzzy logic, FL, as a model for approximate reasoning. In this logic, the truth-values are *linguistic*, i.e. of the form *true, not true, very true, not very true, more or less true, not very true and not very false* etc., with each truth-value representing a fuzzy subset of the unit interval. In effect, the fuzziness of the truth-values of FL provides a mechanism for the association of imprecise truth-values with imprecise propositions expressed in a natural language, and thereby endows FL with a capability for modeling the type of qualitative reasoning which humans employ in uncertain and/or fuzzy environments.

More recently, the introduction of the concept of a possibility distribution (Zadeh, 1977*a, b*) has clarified the role of the concept of a fuzzy restriction† in approximate reasoning, and has provided a basis for the development of a meaning representation language named PRUF (an acronym for *P*ossibilistic‡ *R*elational *U*niversal *F*uzzy) in which—in a significant departure from tradition—it is the concept of a possibility distribution, as opposed to truth, that plays the primary role.

The conceptual structure of PRUF is based on the premise that, in sharp contrast to formal and programming languages, natural languages are intrinsically incapable of precise characterization on either the syntactic or semantic level. In the first place, the pressure for brevity of discourse tends to make natural languages *maximally ambiguous* in the sense that the level of ambiguity in human communication is usually near the limit of what is disambiguable through the use of an external body of knowledge which is shared by the parties in discourse.

Second, a significant fraction of sentences in a natural language cannot be characterized as strictly grammatical or ungrammatical. As is well known, the problem of partial grammaticality is accentuated in the case of sentences which are partially nonsensical in the real world but not necessarily in an imaginary world. Thus, a realistic grammar for a natural language should associate with each sentence its degree of grammaticality— rather than merely generate the sentences which are completely grammatical. The issue of partial grammaticality has the effect of greatly complicating the problem of automatic translation from a natural language into a meaning representation language— which is an important aspect of Montague-type grammars (Montague, 1974; Partee, 1976*b*).

Third, as was alluded to already, a word in a natural language is usually a summary of a complex, multifaceted concept which is incapable of precise characterization. For this reason, the denotation of a word is generally a fuzzy—rather than non-fuzzy—subset of a universe of discourse. For example, if U is a collection of individuals, the denotation of the term *young man* in U is a fuzzy subset of U which is characterized by a membership function $\mu_{young\ man} : U \rightarrow [0,1]$, which associates with each individual u in U the degree— on the scale from 0 to 1—to which u is a young man. When necessary or expedient, this degree or, equivalently, the grade of membership, $\mu_{young}(u)$, may be expressed in linguistic

---

†A *fuzzy restriction* is a fuzzy set which serves as an elastic constraint on the values that may be assigned to a variable. A variable which is associated with a fuzzy restriction or, equivalently, with a possibility distribution, is a *fuzzy variable*.

‡The term "possibilistic" was coined by Gaines & Kohout (1975). The concept of a possibility distribution is distinct from that of possibility in modal logic and related areas (Hughes & Cresswell, 1968; N. Rescher, 1975).

terms such as *high, not high, very high, not very high, low, more or less low*, etc., with each such term representing a fuzzy subset of the unit interval. In this case, the denotation of *young man* is a fuzzy set of Type 2, i.e. a fuzzy set with a fuzzy membership function.†

In essence, PRUF bears the same relation to FL that predicate calculus does to two-valued logic. Thus, it serves to translate a set of premises expressed in a natural language into expressions in PRUF to which the rules of inference in FL (or PRUF) may be applied, yielding other expressions in PRUF which upon retranslation become the conclusions inferred from the original premises. More generally, PRUF may be used as a basis for question-answering systems in which the knowledge-base contains imprecise data, i.e. propositions expressed in a natural or synthetic language which translate into a collection of possibility and/or probability distributions of a set of variables.

Typically, a simple proposition such as "John is young," translates in PRUF into what will be referred to as a *possibility assignment equation* of the form

$$\Pi_{Age(John)} = YOUNG \qquad (1.1)$$

in which YOUNG—the denotation of young—is a fuzzy subset of the interval [0,100], and $\Pi_{Age\ (John)}$ is the possibility distribution of the variable Age(John). What (1.1) implies is that, if on the scale from 0 to 1, the degree to which a numerical age, say 30, is compatible with YOUNG is 0·7, then the possibility that John's age is 30 is also equal to 0·7. Equivalently, (1.1) may be expressed as

$$JOHN[\Pi_{Age} = YOUNG] \qquad (1.2)$$

in which JOHN is the name of a relation which characterizes John and Age is an attribute of John which is particularized by the assignment of the fuzzy set YOUNG to its possibility distribution.

In general, an expression in PRUF may be viewed as a procedure which acts on a set of possibly fuzzy relations in a database and computes the possibility distribution of a set of variables. Thus, if p is a proposition in a natural language which translates into an expression P in PRUF, and Π^p is the possibility distribution returned by P, then P may be interpreted as the *meaning of p* while Π^p is the *information conveyed* by p.‡ The significance of these notions will be discussed in greater detail in section 3.

The main constituents of PRUF are (a) a collection of translation rules, and (b) a set of rules of inference.§ For the present, at least, the translation rules in PRUF are human-use oriented in that they do not provide a system for an automatic translation from a natural language into PRUF. However, by subordinating the objective of automatic translation to that of achieving a greater power of expressiveness, PRUF provides a system for the translation of a far larger subset of a natural language than is possible with the systems based on two-valued logic. Eventually, it may be possible to achieve the goal of machine translation into PRUF of a fairly wide variety of expressions in a natural language. It is not likely, however, that this goal could be attained through

---

†Expositions of the relevant aspects of the theory of fuzzy sets may be found in the books and papers noted in the bibliography, especially Kaufmann (1975), Negoita & Ralescu (1975), and Zadeh, Fu, Tanaka & Shimura (1975).

‡In effect, P and Π^p are the counterparts of the concepts of *intension* and *extension* in language theories based on two-valued logic (Cresswell, 1973; Linsky, 1971; Miller & Johnson-Laird, 1976).

§The rules of inference in PRUF and their application to approximate reasoning are described in a companion paper (Zadeh, 1977b).

the employment of algorithms of the conventional type in translation programs. Rather, it is probable that recourse would have to be made to the use of fuzzy logic for the representation of imprecise contextual knowledge as well as for the characterization and execution of fuzzy instructions in translation algorithms.

At present, PRUF is still in its initial stages of development and hence our exposition of it in the present paper is informal in nature, with no pretense at definiteness or completeness. Thus, our limited aim in what follows is to explain the principal ideas underlying PRUF; to describe a set of basic translation rules which can serve as a point of departure for the development of other, more specialized, rules; and to illustrate the use of translation rules by relatively simple examples. We shall not consider the translation of imperative propositions nor the issues relating to the implementation of interactive connectives, reserving these and other important topics for subsequent papers.

In the following sections, our exposition of PRUF begins with an outline of some of the basic properties of the concept of a possibility distribution and its role in the representation of the meaning of fuzzy propositions. In section 3, we consider a number of basic concepts underlying PRUF, among them those of possibility assignment equation, fuzzy set descriptor, proposition, question, database, meaning, information, semantic equivalence, semantic entailment and definition.

Section 4 is devoted to the formalization of translation rules of Type I (modification), Type II (composition) and Type III (quantification). In addition, a translation rule for relations is derived as a corollary of rules of Type II, and a rule for forming the negation of a fuzzy proposition is formulated.

The concept of truth is defined in section 5 as a measure of the compatibility of two fuzzy propositions, one of which acts as a reference proposition for the other. Based on this conception of truth, a translation rule for truth-qualified propositions is developed in section 6. In addition, translation rules for probability-qualified and possibility-qualified propositions are established, and the concept of semantic equivalence is employed to derive several meaning-perserving transformations of fuzzy propositions. Finally, in section 7 a number of examples illustrating the application of various translation rules—both singly and in combination—are presented.

2. The concept of a possibility distribution and its role in PRUF

A basic assumption underlying PRUF is that the imprecision that is intrinsic in natural languages is, in the main, possibilistic rather than probabilistic in nature.

As will be seen presently, the rationale for this assumption rests on the fact that most of the words in a natural language have fuzzy rather than non-fuzzy denotation. A conspicuous exception to this assertion are the terms in mathematics. Even in mathematics, however, there are concepts that are fuzzy, e.g. the concept of a sparse matrix, stiff differential equation, approximate equality, etc. More significantly, almost all mathematical concepts become fuzzy as soon as one leaves the idealized universe of mathematical constructs and comes in contact with the reality of pervasive ill-definedness, irreducible uncertainty and finiteness of computational resources.

To understand the relation between fuzziness and possibility,† it is convenient to consider initially a simple non-fuzzy proposition such as‡

---

†A more detailed account of this and other issues related to the concept of a possibility distribution may be found in Zadeh (1977a).

‡The symbol $\triangleq$ stands for "is defined to be" or "denotes."

$$p \triangleq X \text{ is an integer in the interval } [0,5].$$

Clearly, what this proposition asserts is that (a) it is possible for any integer in the interval [0,5] to be a value of X, and (b) it is not possible for any integer outside of this interval to be a value of X.

For our purposes, it is expedient to reword this assertion in a form that admits of extension to fuzzy propositions. More specifically, in the absence of any information regarding X other than that conveyed by p, we shall assert that: p induces a *possibility distribution* Π_x which associates with each integer u in [0,5] the possibility that u could be a value of X. Thus,

$$\text{Poss}\{X=u\}=1 \text{ for } 0\leq u\leq 5$$

and

$$\text{Poss}\{X=u\}=0 \text{ for } u<0 \text{ or } u>5$$

where $\text{Poss}\{X=u\}$ is an abbreviation for "The possibility that X may assume the value u." For the proposition in question the possibility distribution Π_x is *uniform* in the sense that the possibility-values are equal to unity for u in [0,5] and zero elsewhere.

Next, let us consider a proposition q which may be viewed as a fuzzified version of p, namely,

$$q \triangleq X \text{ is a small integer}$$

where "small integer" is the label of a fuzzy set defined by, say,†

$$\text{SMALL INTEGER} = 1/0 + 1/1 + 0.8/2 + 0.6/3 + 0.4/4 + 0.2/5 \qquad (2.1)$$

in which + denotes the union rather than the arithmetic sum and a fuzzy singleton of the form 0·6/3 signifies that the grade of membership of the integer 3 in the fuzzy set SMALL INTEGER—or, equivalently, the *compatibility* of 3 with SMALL INTEGER— is 0·6.

At this juncture, we can make use of the simple idea behind our interpretation of p to formulate what might be called the *possibility postulate*—a postulate which may be used as a basis for a possibilistic intepretation of fuzzy propositions. In application to q, it may be stated as follows.

Possibility postulate. In the absence of any information regarding X other than that conveyed by the proposition $q \triangleq X$ is a small integer, q induces a possibility distribution Π_x which equates the possibility of X taking a value u to the grade of membership of u in the fuzzy set SMALL INTEGER. Thus

$$\text{Poss}\{X=0\}=\text{Poss}\{X=1\}=1$$
$$\text{Poss}\{X=2\}=0.8$$
$$\text{Poss}\{X=3\}=0.6$$
$$\text{Poss}\{X=4\}=0.4$$
$$\text{Poss}\{X=5\}=0.2$$

†To differentiate between a label and its denotation, we express the latter in upper case symbols. To simplify the notation, this convention will not be adhered to strictly where the distinction can be inferred from the context.

and

$$\text{Poss}\{X=u\}=0 \text{ for } u<0 \text{ or } u>5.$$

More generally, the postulate asserts that if X is a variable which takes values in U and F is a fuzzy subset of U, then the proposition

$$q \triangleq X \text{ is } F \tag{2.2}$$

induces a possibility distribution Π_X *which is equal to* F, *i.e.*

$$\Pi_X=F \tag{2.3}$$

implying that

$$\text{Poss}\{X=u\}=\mu_F(u), \quad u \in U \tag{2.4}$$

where $\mu_F: U \to [0,1]$ is the membership function of F, and $\mu_F(u)$ is the grade of membership of u in F.

In essence, then, the possibility distribution of X is a fuzzy set which serves to define the possibility that X could assume any specified value u in U. The function $\pi_X: U \to [0,1]$ which is equal to μ_F and which associates with each $u \in U$ the possibility that X could take u as its value is called the *possibility distribution function* associated with X. In this connection, it is important to note that the possibility distribution defined by (2.3) depends on the definition of F and hence is purely subjective in nature.

We shall refer to (2.3) as the *possibility assignment equation* because it signifies that the proposition "X is F" translates into the assignment of a fuzzy set F to the possibility distribution of X. More generally, the possibility assignment equation corresponding to a proposition of the form "N is F," where F is a fuzzy subset of a universe of discourse U, and N is the name of (a) a variable, (b) a fuzzy set, (c) a proposition, or (d) an object, may be expressed as

$$\Pi_{X(N)}=F \tag{2.5}$$

or, more simply,

$$\Pi_X=F \tag{2.6}$$

where X is either N itself (when N is a variable) or a variable that is explicit or implicit in N, with X taking values in U. For example, in the case of the proposition "Nora is young," $N \triangleq \text{Nora}$, $X=\text{Age(Nora)}$, $U=[0,100]$ and

$$\text{Nora is young} \to \Pi_{\text{Age(Nora)}}=\text{YOUNG} \tag{2.7}$$

where the symbol $\to$ stands for "translates into."

Since the concept of a possibility distribution is closely related to that of a fuzzy set,† possibility distributions may be manipulated by the rules applying to such sets. In what follows, we shall discuss briefly some of the basic rules of this kind, focusing our attention only on those aspects of possibility distributions which are of direct relevance to PRUF.

---

†Strictly speaking, the concept of a possibility distribution is coextensive with that of a fuzzy restriction rather than a fuzzy set (Zadeh, 1973, 1975b).

POSSIBILITY *VS.* PROBABILITY

Intuitively, possibility relates to our perception of the degree of feasibility or ease of attainment, whereas probability is associated with the degree of likelihood, belief, frequency or proportion. All possibilities are subjective, as are most probabilities.[†] In general, probabilistic information is not as readily available as possibilistic information and is more difficult to manipulate.

Mathematically, the distinction between probability and possibility manifests itself in the different rules which govern their combinations, especially under the union. Thus, if A is a non-fuzzy subset of U, and Π_X is the possibility distribution induced by the proposition "N is F," then the *possibility measure*,[‡] $\Pi(A)$, of A is defined as the supremum of μ_F over A, i.e.

$$\Pi(A) \triangleq \text{Poss}\{X \in A\} = \text{Sup}_{u \in A} \mu_F(u) \tag{2.8}$$

and, more generally, if A is a fuzzy subset of U,

$$\Pi(A) = \text{Poss}\{X \text{ is } A\} = \text{Sup}_u(\mu_A(u) \wedge \mu_F(u)) \tag{2.9}$$

where μ_A is the membership function of A and $\wedge \triangleq$ min.

From the definition of $\Pi(A)$, it follows at once that the possibility measure of the union of two arbitrary subsets of U is given by

$$\Pi(A \cup B) = \Pi(A) \Pi \vee (B) \tag{2.10}$$

where $\vee \triangleq$ max. Thus, possibility measure does not have the basic additivity property of probability measure, namely,

$$P(A \cup B) = P(A) + P(B) \text{ if A and B are disjoint}$$

where $P(A)$ and $P(B)$ are the probability measures of A and B, respectively, and $+$ is the arithmetic sum.

An essential aspect of the concept of possibility is that it does not involve the notion of repeated or replicated experimentation and hence is nonstatistical in nature. Indeed, the importance of the concept of possibility stems from the fact that much—perhaps most—of human decision-making is based on information that is possibilistic rather than probabilistic in nature.[§]

POSSIBILITY DISTRIBUTIONS *VS.* FUZZY SETS

Although there is a close connection between the concept of a possibility distribution

---

[†]There are eminent authorities in probability theory (DeFinetti, 1974) who maintain that all probabilities are subjective.

[‡]The possibility measure defined by (2.8) is a special case of the more general concept of a fuzzy measure defined by Sugeno (1974) and Terano & Sugeno (1975).

[§]In many realistic decision processes it is impracticable or impossible to obtain objective probabilistic information in the quantitative form that is needed for the application of statistical decision theory. Thus, the probabilities that are actually used in much of human decision-making are (a) subjective, and (b) linguistic (in the sense defined in Zadeh, 1975). Characterization of linguistic probabilities is related to the issue of probability qualification, which is discussed in section 6. A more detailed discussion of linguistic probabilities may be found in Nguyen (1976*a*).

and that of a fuzzy set, there is also a significant difference between the two that must be clearly understood.

To illustrate the point by a simple example which involves a non-fuzzy set and a uniform possibility distribution, consider a variable labeled Sister(Dedre) to which we assign a set, as in

$$\text{Sister(Dedre)} = \text{Sue} + \text{Jane} + \text{Lorraine} \qquad (2.11)$$

or a possibility distribution, as in

$$\Pi_{\text{Sister(Dedre)}} = \text{Sue} + \text{Jane} + \text{Lorraine} \qquad (2.12)$$

where + denotes the union. Now, the meaning of (2.11) is that Sue, Jane and Lorraine are sisters of Dedre. By contrast, the meaning of (2.12) is that the sister of Dedre is Sue *or* Jane *or* Lorraine, where *or* is the exclusive or. In effect, (2.12) signifies that there is uncertainty in our knowledge of who is the sister of Dedre, with the possibility that it is Sue being unity, and likewise for Jane and Lorraine. In the case of (2.11), on the other hand, we are certain that Sue, Jane and Lorraine are all sisters of Dedre. Thus, the set {Sue, Jane, Lorraine} plays the role of a possibility distribution in (2.12) but not in (2.11).

Usually, it is clear from the context whether or not a fuzzy (or non-fuzzy) set should be interpreted as a possibility distribution. A difficulty arises, however, when a relation contains a possibility distribution, as is exemplified by the relation RESIDENT whose tableau is shown in Table 2.1.

TABLE 2.1

Resident	Subject	Location
	Jack	New Rochelle
	Jack	White Plains
	Ralph	New Rochelle
	Ralph	Tarrytown

In this case, the rows above the dotted line represent a relation in the sense that Jack resides both in New Rochelle and in White Plains. On the other hand, the rows below the dotted line represent a possibility distribution associated with the location of residence of Ralph, meaning that Ralph resides either in New Rochelle *or* in Tarrytown, but not both. It should be noted parenthetically that there is no provision for dealing with this kind of ambiguity in the conventional representations of relational models of data because the concept of a possibility distribution and the related issue of data uncertainty have not been an object of concern in the analysis of database management systems.

REPRESENTATION BY STANDARD FUNCTIONS

In the manipulation of possibility distributions, it is convenient to be able to express the membership function of a fuzzy subset of the real line as a standard function whose parameters may be adjusted to fit a given membership function in an approximate fashion. A standard function of this type is the S-function, which is a piecewise quadratic function defined by the equations:

$$S(u;\alpha,\beta,\gamma)=0 \qquad\qquad \text{for } u \le \alpha \qquad\qquad (2.13)$$

$$=2\left(\frac{u-\alpha}{\gamma-\alpha}\right)^2 \qquad \alpha \le u \le \beta$$

$$=1-2\left(\frac{u-\gamma}{\gamma-\alpha}\right)^2 \quad \text{for } \beta \le u \le \gamma$$

$$=1 \qquad\qquad\qquad \text{for } u \ge \gamma$$

in which the parameter $\beta \triangleq (\alpha+\gamma)/2$ is the *crossover* point, i.e. the value of u at which $S(u;\alpha,\beta,\gamma)=0\cdot5$. Other types of standard functions which are advantageous when the arithmetic operations of addition, multiplication and division have to be performed on fuzzy numbers, are (i) piecewise linear (triangular) functions, and (ii) exponential (bell-shaped) functions. A discussion of these functions and their applications may be found in Nahmias (1976) and Mizumoto & Tanaka (1976).

There are two special types of possibility distributions which will be encountered in later sections. One is the *unity* possibility distribution, which is denoted by I and is defined by

$$\pi_I(u)=1 \text{ for } u \in U \qquad\qquad (2.14)$$

where π_I is the possibility distribution function of I. The other, which is defined on the unit interval, is the *unitary* possibility distribution (or the *unitary fuzzy set* or the *unitor*, for short), which is denoted by $\perp$ and is defined by

$$\pi_\perp(v)=v \text{ for } v \in [0,1]. \qquad\qquad (2.15)$$

In the particular case where a truth-value in FL is the unitary fuzzy set, it will be referred to as the *unitary* truth-value. On denoting this truth-value by u-true, we have

$$\mu_{u\text{-true}}(v) \triangleq v, \ v \in [0,1]. \qquad\qquad (2.16)$$

PROJECTION AND MARGINAL POSSIBILITY DISTRIBUTIONS

The possibility distributions with which we shall be concerned in the following sections are, in general, n-ary distributions denoted by $\Pi_{(X_1, \dots, X_n)}$, where $X_1, \dots, X_n$ are variables—or, equivalently, *attributes*—taking values in their respective universes of discourse $U_1, \dots, U_n$.† As a simple example in which $n=2$, consider the proposition "John is a big man," in which BIG MAN is a fuzzy relation F defined by Table 2.2, with the variables Height and Weight expressed in centimeters and kilograms, respectively.

The relation in question may also be expressed as a linear form

$$\text{BIG MAN}=0\cdot5/(165,60)+0\cdot6/(170,60)+ \ \dots \ +1/(180,80)+ \ \dots \qquad (2.17)$$

---

†When it is necessary to place in evidence that X takes values in U (i.e. the domain of X is U), we shall express the domain of X as U(X) or, where no confusion can arise, as X (see (2.23)).

TABLE 2.2

BIG MAN	Height	Weight	μ
	165	60	0·5
	170	60	0·6
	175	60	0·7
	170	65	0·75
	—	—	—
	180	70	0·9
	175	75	0·9
	180	75	0·95
	180	80	1
	185	75	1

in which a term such as 0·6/(170,60) signifies that the grade of membership of the pair (170,60) in the relation BIG MAN—or, equivalently, its compatibility with the relation BIG MAN—is 0·6.

The possibility postulate implies that the proposition "John is a big man" induces a binary possibility distribution $\Pi_{(Weight(John), Height(John))}$ whose tableau is identical with Table 2.2 except that the label of the last column is changed from μ to π in order to signify that the compatibility-values in that column assume the role of possibility-values. What this means is that, by inducing the possibility distribution $\Pi_{(Height(John),Weight(John))}$, the proposition "John is a big man" implies that the possibility that John's height and weight are, say, 170 cm and 60 kg, respectively, is 0·6.

It should be noted that, in general, the entries in a relation F need not be numbers, as they are in Table 2.2. Thus, the entries may be pointers to—or identifiers of—physical or abstract objects. For example, the u's in the relation CUP shown in Table 2.3:

TABLE 2.3

CUP	Identifier	μ
	u_1	0·8
	u_2	0·9
	u_3	1·0
	u_4	0·2

may be pictures of cups of various forms. In this case, given the relation CUP, the proposition "X is a cup" induces a possibility distribution Π_X such that Poss$\{X=u_1\}=$ 0·8 and likewise for other rows in the table.

In the translation of expressions in a natural language into PRUF, there are two operations on possibility distributions (or fuzzy relations) that play a particularly important role: *projection* and *particularization*.

Specifically, let $X \triangleq (X_1, \ldots, X_n)$ be a fuzzy variable which is associated with a possibility distribution $\Pi_{(X_1, \ldots, X_n)}$ or, more simply, Π_X, with the understanding that Π_X is an *n*-ary fuzzy relation in the Cartesian product, $U = U_1 \times \ldots \times U_n$, of the universes of discourse associated with $X_1, \ldots, X_n$. We assume that Π_X is characterized

by its possibility distribution function—or, equivalently, membership function—
$\pi_{(X_1, \ldots, X_n)}$ (or π_X, for short).

A variable of the form

$$X_{(s)} \triangleq (X_{i_1}, \ldots, X_{i_k}), \tag{2.18}$$

where $s \triangleq (i_1, \ldots, i_k)$ is a subsequence of the index sequence $(1, \ldots, n)$, constitutes a *subvariable* of $X \triangleq (X_1, \ldots, X_n)$. By analogy with the concept of a marginal probability distribution, the *marginal possibility distribution* associated with $X_{(s)}$ is defined by

$$\Pi_{X_{(s)}} = \text{Proj}_{U_{(s)}} \Pi_{(X_1, \ldots, X_n)}, \tag{2.19}$$

where $U_{(s)} \triangleq U_{i_1} \times \ldots \times U_{i_k}$, and the operation of projection is defined—in terms of possibility distribution functions—by

$$\pi_{X_{(s)}}(u_{(s)}) = \text{Sup}_{u_{(s')}} \pi_X(u_1, \ldots, u_n), \tag{2.20}$$

where $u_{(s)} \triangleq (u_{i_1}, \ldots, u_{i_k})$ and $u_{(s')} \triangleq (u_{j_1}, \ldots, u_{j_l})$, with s' denoting the index sequence complementary to s (e.g. if $n=5$ and $s=(2,3)$, then $(s')=(1,4,5)$). For example, for $n=2$ and $s=(2)$, (2.20) yields

$$\pi_{X_2}(u_2) = \text{Sup}_{u_1} \pi_{(X_1, X_2)}(u_1, u_2) \tag{2.21}$$

as the expression for the marginal possibility distribution function of X_2.

The operation of projection is very easy to perform when Π_X is expressed as a linear form. As an illustration, assume that $U_1 = U_2 = a + b$, or, more conventionally, $\{a,b\}$, and

$$\Pi_{(X_1, X_2)} = 0{\cdot}8aa + 0{\cdot}6ab + 0{\cdot}4ba + 0{\cdot}2bb \tag{2.22}$$

in which a term of the form $0{\cdot}6ab$ signifies that

$$\text{Poss}\{X_1 = a, X_2 = b\} = 0{\cdot}6.$$

To obtain the projection of Π_X on, say, U_2 it is sufficient to replace the value of X_1 in each term in (2.22) by the null string Λ. Thus†

$$\begin{aligned}\text{Proj}_{U_2} \Pi_{(X_1, X_2)} &= 0{\cdot}8a + 0{\cdot}6b + 0{\cdot}4a + 0{\cdot}2b \\ &= 0{\cdot}8a + 0{\cdot}6b.\end{aligned}$$

To simplify the notation, it is convenient—as is done in SQUARE (Boyce *et al.*, 1974)— to omit the word Proj in (2.19) and interpret $U_{(s)}$ as $X_{i_1} \times \ldots \times X_{i_k}$ (see footnote on p. 404). Thus,

$$\text{Proj}_{U_{(s)}} \Pi_{(X_1, \ldots, X_n)} \triangleq_{U_{(s)}} \Pi_{(X_1, \ldots, X_n)} \triangleq x_{i_1} \times \cdots \times x_{i_k} \Pi_{(X_1, \ldots, X_n)}. \tag{2.23}$$

---

†If r and s are two tuples and α and β are their respective possibilities, then $\alpha r + \beta r = (\alpha \vee \beta)r$. Additional details may be found in Zadeh (1977a).

In some applications, it is convenient to have at one's disposal not only the operation of projection, as defined by (2.20), but also its *dual, conjunctive projection*,† which is defined by (2.20) with Sup replaced by Inf. It is easy to verify that the latter can be expressed in terms of the former as

$$\overline{\text{Proj}}_{U_{(s)}}\Pi_{(X_1, \ldots, X_n)} = (\text{Proj}_{U_{(s)}}\Pi'_{(X_1, \ldots, X_n)})' \tag{2.24}$$

in which $\overline{\text{Proj}}$ stands for conjunctive projection and ′ denotes the complement, where the complement of a fuzzy set F in U is a fuzzy set F′ defined by

$$\mu_{F'}(u) = 1 - \mu_F(u), \; u \in U. \tag{2.25}$$

PARTICULARIZATION

Informally, by the *particularization* of a fuzzy relation or a possibility distribution which is associated with a variable $X \triangleq (X_1, \ldots, X_n)$, is meant the effect of specification of the possibility distributions of one or more subvariables of X. In the theory of non-fuzzy relations, the resulting relation is commonly referred to as a *restriction* of the original relation; and, in the particular case where the values of some of the constituent variables are specified, the degenerate restriction becomes a *section* of the original relation.

Particularization in PRUF may be viewed as the result of forming the conjunction of a proposition of the form "X is F," where X is an *n*-ary variable, $X \triangleq (X_1, \ldots, X_n)$, with particularizing propositions of the form "$X_{(s)}$ is G," where $X_{(s)}$ is a subvariable of X, and F and G are fuzzy subsets of $U \triangleq U_1 \times \ldots \times U_n$ and $U_{(s)} = U_{i_1} \times \ldots \times U_{i_k}$, respectively.

More specifically, let $\Pi_X \triangleq \Pi_{(X_1, \ldots, X_n)} = F$ and $\Pi_{X_{(s)}} \triangleq \Pi_{(X_{i_1}, \ldots, X_{i_k})} = G$ be the possibility distributions induced by the propositions "X is F" and "$X_{(s)}$ is G," respectively. By definition, the *particularization of* Π_X *by* $X_{(s)} = G$ (or, equivalently, of F by G) is denoted by $\Pi_X[\Pi_{X_{(s)}} = G]$ (or $F[\Pi_{X_{(s)}} = G]$) and is defined as the intersection‡ of F and G, i.e.

$$\Pi_X[\Pi_{X_{(s)}} = G] = F \cap \overline{G}, \tag{2.26}$$

where $\overline{G}$ is the cylindrical extension of G, i.e. the cylindrical fuzzy set in $U_1 \times \ldots \times U_n$ whose projection on $U_{(s)}$ is G and whose membership function is expressed by

$$\mu_{\overline{G}}(u_1, \ldots, u_n) \triangleq \mu_G(u_{i_1}, \ldots, u_{i_k}), \quad (u_1, \ldots, u_n) \in U_1 \times \ldots \times U_n. \tag{2.27}$$

As a simple illustration, assume that $U_1 = U_2 = U_3 = a + b$,

$$\Pi_{(X_1, X_2, X_3)} = 0 \cdot 8aab + 0 \cdot 6baa + 0 \cdot 1bab + 1bbb \tag{2.28}$$

and

$$\Pi_{(X_1, X_2)} = G = 0 \cdot 5aa + 0 \cdot 2ba + 0 \cdot 3bb.$$

---

†A more detailed discussion of conjunctive projections may be found in Zadeh (1966). It should be noted that the concept of a conjunctive projection is related to that of a conjunctive mapping in SQUARE (Boyce *et al.*, 1974) and to universal quantification in multivalued logic (Rescher, 1969).

‡If A and B are fuzzy subsets of U, their *intersection* is defined by $\mu_{A \cap B}(u) = \mu_A(u) \wedge \mu_B(u)$, $u \in U$. Thus, $\mu_{F \cap \overline{G}}(u_1, \ldots, u_n) = \mu_F(u_1, \ldots, u_n) \wedge \mu_G(u_{i_1}, \ldots, u_{i_k})$. Dually, the *union* of A and B is denoted as A+B (or $A \cup B$) and is defined by $\mu_{A+B}(u) \triangleq \mu_A(u) \vee \mu_B(u)$. ($\vee \triangleq$ max and $\wedge \triangleq$ min.)

In this case

$$\overline{G}=0\cdot5aaa+0\cdot5aab+0\cdot2baa+0\cdot2bab+0\cdot3bba+0\cdot3bbb$$
$$F\cap\overline{G}=0\cdot5aab+0\cdot2baa+0\cdot1bab+0\cdot3bbb$$

and hence

$$\Pi_{(x_1,\,x_2,\,x_3)}[\Pi_{(x_1,\,x_2)}=G]=0\cdot5aab+0\cdot2baa+0\cdot1bab+0\cdot3bbb.$$

As will be seen in section 4, the right-hand member of (2.26) represents the possibility distribution induced by the conjunction of "X is F" and "$X_{(s)}$ is G," that is, the proposition "X is F and $X_{(s)}$ is G". It is for this reason that the particularized possibility distribution $\Pi_X[\Pi_{X_{(s)}}=G]$ may be viewed as the possibility distribution induced by the proposition "X is F and $X_{(s)}$ is G".

In cases in which more than one subvariable is particularized, e.g. the particularizing propositions are "$X_{(s)}$ is G," and "$X_{(r)}$ is H," the particularized possibility distribution will be expressed as

$$\Pi_X[\Pi_{X_{(s)}}=G;\ \Pi_{X_{(r)}}=H]. \tag{2.29}$$

Furthermore, particularization may be *nested*, as in

$$\Pi_X[\Pi_{X_{(s)}}=G[\Pi_{Y_{(t)}}=J]] \tag{2.30}$$

where the particularizing relation G is, in turn, particularized by the proposition "$Y_{(t)}$ is J," where $Y_{(t)}$ is a subvariable of the variable associated with G.

It is of interest to observe that, as its name implies, particularization involves an imposition of a restriction on the values that may be assumed by a variable. However, by dualizing the definition of particularization as expressed by (2.26), that is, by replacing the intersection with the union the opposite effect is achieved, with the resulting possibility distribution corresponding to the disjunction of "X is F" and "$X_{(s)}$ is G". We shall not make an explicit use of the dual of particularization in the present paper.

As a simple illustration of particularization, consider the proposition $p \triangleq$ John is big, where BIG is defined by Table 2.2, and assume that the particularizing proposition is $q \triangleq$ John is tall, in which TALL is defined by Table 2.4.

The assertion "John is big" may be expressed equivalently as "Size(John) is big," which is of the form "X is F," with X $\triangleq$ Size(John) and F $\triangleq$ BIG. Similarly, "John is tall" may be expressed as "Height(John) is tall," or, equivalently, Y is G, where Y $\triangleq$ Height (John) and G $\triangleq$ TALL.

TABLE 2.4

TALL	Height	μ
	165	0·6
	170	0·7
	175	0·8
	180	0·9
	185	1

TABLE 2.5

BIG($\Pi_{Height} = $TALL)	Height	Weight	μ
	165	60	0·5
	170	60	0·6
	175	60	0·7
	170	65	0·7
	—	—	—
	180	70	0·9
	175	75	0·8
	180	75	0·9
	180	80	0·9
	185	75	1

Using (2.26), the tableau of the particularized relation BIG[$\Pi_{Height} = $TALL] is readily found to be given by Table 2.5.

The value of μ for a typical row in this table, say for (Height = 180, Weight = 75), is obtained by computing the minimum of the values of μ for the corresponding rows in BIG and TALL (i.e. (180,75) in BIG and (180) in TALL). As is pointed out in section 4, this mode of combination of μ's corresponds to *non-interactive* conjunction, which is assumed to be a standard default definition of conjunction in PRUF. However, PRUF allows any definition of conjunction which is specified by the user to be employed in place of the standard definition.

As an additional example, consider the particularized possibility distribution (see (2.23))

$$\text{PROFESSOR[Name} = \text{Simon; Sex} = \text{Male;}$$
$$\Pi_{Age} = {}_{\mu \times Age2}\text{APPROXIMATELY[Age1} = 45]] \qquad (2.31)$$

which describes a subset of a set of professors whose name is Simon, who are male and who are approximately 45 years old. In this case, the possibility distribution of the variable Age is a particularized relation APPROXIMATELY in which the first variable, Age1, is set equal to 45, and which is projected on the Cartesian product of U(μ) and U(Age2), yielding the fuzzy set of values of Age which are approximately equal to 45.

It should be noted that some of the attributes in (2.31) (e.g. Name) are assigned single values, while others—whose values are uncertain—are associated with possibility distributions. As will be seen in the following sections, this is typical of the particularized possibility distributions arising in the translation of expressions in a natural language into PRUF.

Expressions of the form (2.31) are similar in appearance to the commonly employed semantic network, query language and predicate calculus representations of propositions in a natural language. An essential difference, however, lies in the use of possibility distributions in (2.31) for the characterization of the values of fuzzy variables and in the concrete specification of the manner in which possibility distributions and fuzzy relations are modified by particularization and other operations which will be described in sections 4 and 6.

3. Basic concepts underlying translation into PRUF

The concept of a possibility distribution provides a natural point of departure for the formalization of many other concepts which underlie the translation of expressions in a natural language into PRUF. We shall present a brief exposition of several such concepts in this section, without aiming at the construction of an embracing formal framework.

In speaking somewhat vaguely of expressions in a natural language, what we have in mind is a variety of syntactic, semantic and pragmatic forms exemplified by sentences, propositions, phrases, clauses, questions, commands, exclamations, etc. In what follows, we shall restrict our attention to expressions which are (a) fuzzy propositions (or assertions); (b) fuzzy questions; and (c) what will be referred to as *fuzzy set descriptors* or simply *descriptors*.

PROPOSITIONS

Basically, a fuzzy proposition may be regarded as an expression which translates into a possibility assignment equation in PRUF. This is analogous to characterizing a non-fuzzy proposition as an expression which translates into a well-formed formula (or, equivalently, a closed sentence) in predicate calculus.

The types of fuzzy propositions to which our analysis will apply are exemplified by the following. (Italics place in evidence the words that have fuzzy denotation.)

Ronald is *more or less young*	(3.1)
Miriam was *very rich*	(3.2)
Harry *loves* Ann	(3.3)
X is *much smaller* than Y	(3.4)
X and Y are *approximately equal*	(3.5)
If X is *large* then Y is *small*	(3.6)
Most Swedes are *blond*	(3.7)
Many men are *much taller* than *most men*	(3.8)
Most Swedes are *tall* is *not very true*	(3.9)
The man in the *dark* suit is *walking slowly toward* the door	(3.10)
Susanna gave *several expensive* presents to each of her *close friends*	(3.11)
If X is *much greater* than Y then (Z is *small* is *very probable*)	(3.12)
If X is *much greater* than Y then (Z is *small* is *quite possible*)	(3.13)

In these examples, propositions (3.9), (3.12) and (3.13) are, respectively, truth qualified, probability qualified and possibility qualified; propositions (3.7), (3.8), (3.9) and (3.11) contain fuzzy quantifiers; and proposition (3.10) contains a fuzzy relative clause.

FUZZY SET DESCRIPTORS

Informally, a fuzzy set descriptor or simply a descriptor is an expression which is a label of a fuzzy set or a characterization of a fuzzy set in terms of other fuzzy sets. Simple examples of fuzzy set descriptors in English are

Very tall man	(3.14)
Tall man wearing a brown hat	(3.15)
The dishes on the table	(3.16)

Small integer	(3.17)
Numbers which are much larger than 10	(3.18)
Most	(3.19)
All	(3.20)
Several	(3.21)
Many tall women	(3.22)
Above the table	(3.23)
Much taller than	(3.24)

A descriptor differs from a proposition in that it translates, in general, into a fuzzy relation rather than a possibility distribution or a possibility assignment equation. In this connection, it should be noted that a non-fuzzy descriptor (i.e. a description of a non-fuzzy set) would, in general, translate into an open sentence (i.e. a formula with free variables) in predicate calculus. However, while the distinction between open and closed sentences is sharply drawn in predicate calculus, the distinction between fuzzy propositions and fuzzy set descriptors is somewhat blurred in PRUF.

QUESTIONS

For the purposes of translation into PRUF, a question will be assumed to be expressed in the form B is ?A, where B is the body of the question —e.g., How tall is Vera—and A indicates the form of an admissible answer, which might be (a) a possibility distribution or, as a special case, an element of a universe of discourse; (b) a truth-value; (c) a probability-value; and (d) a possibility-value. To differentiate between these cases, A will be expressed as Π in (a) and, more particularly, as α when a numerical value of an attribute is desired; as τ in (b); as λ in (c); and as ω in (d).

To simplify the treatment of questions, we shall employ the artifice of translating into PRUF not the question itself but rather the answer to it, which, in general, would have the form of a fuzzy proposition. As an illustration,

How tall is Tom?$\Pi\rightarrow$Tom is ?Π	(3.25)
How tall is Tom ?$\alpha\rightarrow$Tom is ?α tall	(3.26)
Where does Tom live$\rightarrow$Tom lives in ?α	(3.27)
Is it true that Fran is blonde$\rightarrow$Fran is blonde is ?τ	(3.28)
Is it likely that X is small$\rightarrow$X is small is ?λ	(3.29)
Is it possible that (Jan is tall is false)$\rightarrow$(Jan is tall is false) is ?ω	(3.30)

In this way, the translation of questions stated in a natural language may be carried out by the application of translation rules for fuzzy propositions, thus making it unnecessary to have separate rules for questions.

POSSIBILITY ASSIGNMENT EQUATIONS

The concept of a possibility assignment equation and its role in the translation of propositions in a natural language into PRUF have been discussed briefly in section 2. In what follows, we shall focus our attention on several additional aspects of this concept which relate to the translation rules which will be formulated in sections 4 and 6.

As was stated earlier, a proposition of the form $p \triangleq N$ is F in which N is the name of (a) a variable, (b) a fuzzy set, (c) a proposition, or (d) an object, and F is a fuzzy subset of a universe of discourse U, translates, in general, into a possibility assignment equation of the form

$$\Pi_{X(N)} = F \qquad (3.31)$$

or, more simply,

$$\Pi_X = F \qquad (3.32)$$

where X is a variable taking values in U, with X being either N itself (when N is a variable) or a variable that is explicit or implicit in N.

To place in evidence that (3.32) is a translation of "N is F," we write

$$p \triangleq N \text{ is } F \rightarrow \Pi_X = F \qquad (3.33)$$

and, conversely,

$$p \triangleq N \text{ is } F \leftarrow \Pi_X = F \qquad (3.34)$$

with the left-hand member of (3.34) referred to as a *retranslation* of its right-hand member.

In general, the variable X is an *n*-ary variable which may be expressed as $X \triangleq (X_1, \ldots, X_n)$, with $X_1, \ldots, X_n$ varying over $U_1, \ldots, U_n$, respectively. In some instances, the identification of the X_i and F is quite straightforward; in others, it may be a highly non-trivial task requiring a great deal of contextual knowledge.† For this reason, the identification of the X_i is difficult to formulate as a mechanical process. However, as is usually the case in translation processes, the problem can be greatly simplified by a decomposition of *p* into simpler constituent expressions, translating each expression separately, and then combining the results. The translation rules formulated in sections 4 and 6 are intended to serve this purpose.

In general, a constituent variable, X_i, has a nested structure of the form

$$X_i = \text{Attribute name(Part name(Part name} \ldots \text{(N)))} \qquad (3.35)$$

which is similar to the structure of selectors in the Vienna Definition Language (Lucas *et al.*, 1968; Wegner, 1972). As a simple illustration,

$$\text{Myrna is blonde} \rightarrow \Pi_{\text{Color(Hair(Myrna))}} = \text{BLONDE} \qquad (3.36)$$

where Color(Hair(Myrna)) is a nested variable of the form (3.35) and BLONDE is the fuzzy denotation of blonde in the universe of discourse which is associated with the proposition in question.

A problem that arises in some cases relates to the lack of an appropriate attribute name. For example, to express the translation of "Manuel is kind," in the form (3.33), we need a designation in English for the attribute which takes "kind" as a value. When such a name is not available in a language, it will be denoted by the symbol A, with a subscript if necessary, to indicate that "kind" is a value of A. However, what is really needed in cases like this is a possibly algorithmic definition of the concept represented

---

†In one form or another, this problem arises in all meaning representation languages. However, it is a much more difficult problem in machine–oriented languages than in PRUF, because in PRUF the task of identifying the X_i is assumed to be performed by a human.

by A which decomposes it into simpler concepts for which appropriate names are available.

In the foregoing examples, N represents the name of an object, e.g. the name of a person. More generally, N may be a descriptor, which is usually expressed as a relative clause, as in

$$\text{The man standing near the door is tall.} \qquad (3.37)$$

N may also be a proposition, as in

$$\text{Lucia is tall is false.} \qquad (3.38)$$

In (3.37), $N \triangleq$ The man standing in the door, while in (3.38), $N \triangleq$ Lucia is tall and $X(N)$ is the truth-value of the proposition "Lucia is tall".

An important point concerning propositions of the form "N is F" which can be clarified at this juncture, is that "N is F" should be regarded not as a restricted class of propositions, but as a canonical form for all propositions which admit of translation into a possibility assignment equation†. Thus, if p is any proposition such that

$$p \rightarrow \Pi_X = F \qquad (3.39)$$

then upon retranslation it may be expressed as "X is F," which is of the form "N is F".

As an illustration, the proposition "Paul was rich," may be translated as

$$\text{Paul was rich} \rightarrow \Pi_{(\text{Wealth(Paul), Time})} = \text{RICH} \times \text{PAST} \qquad (3.40)$$

where (Wealth(Paul),Time) is a binary variable whose first component is the wealth of Paul (expressed as net worth) and the second component is the time at which net worth is assessed; RICH is a fuzzy subset of U(Wealth); PAST is a fuzzy subset of the time-interval extending from the present into the past; and RICH×PAST is the Cartesian product‡ of RICH and PAST.

Similarly, the proposition "X and Y are approximately equal," where X and Y are real numbers, may be translated as

$$\text{X and Y are approximately equal} \rightarrow \Pi_{(X, Y)} = \text{APPROXIMATELY EQUAL} \quad (3.41)$$

where APPROXIMATELY EQUAL is a fuzzy relation in R^2. Upon retranslation, (3.41) yields the equivalent proposition

$$\text{(X,Y) is approximately equal} \qquad (3.42)$$

which, though ungrammatical, is in canonical form.

†This is equivalent to saying that "N is F" is a canonical form for all propositions which can be expressed in the form "N is F" through the application of a meaning-preserving transformation. Such transformations will be defined later in this section in connection with the concept of semantic equivalence.

‡If A and B are fuzzy subsets of U and V, respectively, their *Cartesian product* is defined by $\mu_{A \times B}(u,v) \triangleq \mu_A(u) \wedge \mu_B(v)$, $u \in U$, $v \in V$.

A related issue which concerns the form of possibility assignment equations is that, in general, such equations may be expressed equivalently in the form of possibility distributions. More specifically, if we have

$$N \text{ is } F \rightarrow \Pi_X = F \qquad (3.43)$$

then the possibility assignment equation in (3.43) may be expressed as a possibility distribution (labeled N) of the variable X(N), with the tableau of N having the form:

TABLE 3.1

N	X(N)	π
	u_1	π_1
	u_2	π_2
	.	.
	u_n	π_n

where the π_i are the possibility-values of the u_i.

As a simple illustration, in the translation

$$\text{Brian is tall} \rightarrow \Pi_{\text{Height(Brian)}} = \text{TALL} \qquad (3.44)$$

where TALL is a fuzzy set defined by, say,

$$\text{TALL} = 0 \cdot 5/160 + 0 \cdot 6/165 + 0 \cdot 7/170 + 0 \cdot 8/175 + 0 \cdot 9/180 + 1/185 \qquad (3.45)$$

the possibility assignment equation may be replaced by the possibility distribution

BRIAN	Height	π
	160	0·5
	165	0·6
	170	0·7
	175	0·8
	180	0·9
	185	1·0

which in turn may be expressed as the particularized possibility distribution

$$\text{BRIAN}[\Pi_{\text{Height}} = \text{TALL}] \qquad (3.46)$$

on the understanding that, initially,

$$\Pi_{\text{BRIAN}} = I; \qquad (3.47)$$

that is, BRIAN is a unity possibility distribution with

$$\pi_{\text{BRIAN}}(u) = 1 \text{ for } u \in U. \tag{3.48}$$

It is this equivalence between (3.44) and (3.46) that forms the basis for the statement made in section 1 regarding the equivalence of (1.1) and (1.2).

DEFINITION

All natural languages provide a mechanism for defining a concept in terms of other concepts and, more particularly, for designating a complex descriptor by a single label. Consequently, it is essential to have a facility for this purpose in every meaning representation language, including PRUF.†

A somewhat subtle issue that arises in this connection in PRUF relates to the need for normalizing‡ the translation of the definiens into PRUF. As an illustration of this point, suppose that the descriptor *middle-aged* is defined as

$$\text{middle-aged} \triangleq \text{not young and not old.} \tag{3.49}$$

Now, as will be seen in section 5, the translation of the right-hand member of (3.49) is expressed by

$$\text{not young and not old} \rightarrow \text{YOUNG}' \cap \text{OLD}' \tag{3.50}$$

where YOUNG and OLD are the translations of young and old, respectively, and ' denotes the complement. Consequently, for some definitions of YOUNG and OLD the definition of *middle-aged* by (3.49) would result in a subnormal fuzzy set, which would imply that there does not exist any individual who is middle-aged to the degree 1.

While this may be in accord with one's intuition in some cases, it may be counter-intuitive in others. Thus, to clarify the intent of the definition, it is necessary to indicate whether or not the definiens is to be normalized.§ For this purpose, the notation

$$\text{definiendum} \triangleq \text{Norm(definiens)} \tag{3.51}$$

e.g.

$$\text{middle-aged} \triangleq \text{Norm(not young and not old)} \tag{3.52}$$

may be employed to indicate that the translation of the definiens ought to be normalized.

EXPRESSIONS IN PRUF

Expressions in PRUF are not rigidly defined, as they are in formal, programming and machine-oriented meaning representation languages. Typically, an expression in PRUF may assume the following forms.

†Concept definition plays a particularly important role in conceptual dependency graphs (Schank, 1973), in which a small number of primitive concepts are used as basic building blocks for more complex concepts.

‡A fuzzy set F is *normal* if and only if $\text{Sup}_u \, \mu_F(u) = 1$. If F is *subnormal*, it may be normalized by dividing μ_F by $\text{Sup}_u \, \mu_F(u)$. Thus, the membership function of normalized F, Norm(F), is given by
$$\mu_{\text{Norm}(F)}(u) \triangleq \mu_F(u)/\text{Sup}_u \, \mu_F(u).$$

§The need for normalization was suggested by some examples brought to the author's attention by P. Kay (U.C., Berkeley) and W. Kempton (U.T., San Antonio). (See Kay 1975).)

(a) A label of a fuzzy relation or a possibility distribution. Examples: CUP, BIG MAN, APPROXIMATELY EQUAL.

(b) A particularized fuzzy relation or a possibility distribution. Examples:

$$\text{CUP}[\Pi_{\text{Color}}=\text{RED}; \text{Weight}=35 \text{ gr}] \qquad (3.53)$$

$$\text{CAR}[\text{Make}=\text{Ford}; \Pi_{\text{Size(Trunk)}}=\text{BIG};$$
$$\Pi_{\text{Weight}}=_{\mu\times\text{Weight2}}\text{APPROXIMATELY}[\text{Weight1}=1500 \text{ kg}]].$$

(c) A possibility assignment equation. Examples:

$$\Pi_{\text{Height(Valentina)}}=\text{TALL} \qquad (3.54)$$

$$\Pi_{X}=\text{CUP}[\Pi_{\text{Color}}=\text{RED}; \text{Weight}=35 \text{ gr}].$$

(d) A definition. Examples:

$$F \triangleq H + G[\Pi_{X(s)}=K] \qquad (3.55)$$

where $+$ denotes the union, H is a fuzzy relation and $G[\Pi_{X(s)}=K]$ is a particularized fuzzy relation

$$F\triangleq\text{HOUSE}[\Pi_{\text{Color}}=\text{GREY}; \Pi_{\text{Price}}=\text{HIGH}] \qquad (3.56)$$

which defines a fuzzy set of houses which are grey in color and high-priced.

(e) A procedure—expressed in a natural, algorithmic or programming language—for computing a fuzzy relation or a possibility distribution. Examples: examples (t), (u) and (v) in section 7.

In general, a fuzzy set descriptor will translate into an expression of the form (a), (b) or (d), while a fuzzy proposition will usually translate into (b), (c) or (d). In all these cases, an expression in PRUF may be viewed as a procedure which—given a set of relations in a database—returns a fuzzy relation, a possibility distribution or a possibility assignment equation.†

DATABASE, MEANING AND INFORMATION

By a *relational database* or, simply, a *database* in the context of PRUF is meant a collection, $\mathscr{D}$, of fuzzy, time-varying relations which may be characterized in various ways, e.g. by tables, predicates, recognition algorithms, generation algorithms, etc. A simple self-explanatory example of a database, $\mathscr{D}$, consisting of fixed (i.e. time-invariant) relations POPULATION, YOUNG and RESEMBLANCE is shown in Table 3.2. What is implicit in this representation is that each of the variables (i.e. attributes) which appear as column headings, is associated with a specified universe of discourse (i.e. a domain). For example, the universe of discourse associated with the variable Name in POPULATION is given by

$$U(\text{Name})=\text{Codd}+\text{King}+\text{Chen}+\text{Chang}. \qquad (3.57)$$

---

†It should be noted that an expression in PRUF may also be interpreted as a probability—rather than possibility—manipulating procedure. Because of the need for normalization, operations on probability distributions are, in general, more complex than the corresponding operations on possibility distributions.

In general, two variables which have the same name but appear in different tables may be associated with different universes of discourse.

The relations YOUNG and RESEMBLANCE in Table 3.2 are *purely extensional*† in the sense that YOUNG and RESEMBLANCE are defined directly

TABLE 3.2

POPULATION	Name	RESEMBLANCE	Name1	Name2	μ
	Codd		Codd	King	0·8
	King		Codd	Chen	0·6
	Chen		Codd	Chang	0·6
	Chang		King	Chen	0·5
			. . .	. . .	. . .
			Chang	Chen	0·8

YOUNG	Name	μ
	Codd	0·7
	King	0·9
	Chen	0·8
	Chang	0·9

as fuzzy subsets of POPULATION and not through a procedure which would allow the computation of YOUNG and RESEMBLANCE for any given POPULATION. To illustrate the point, if POPULATION and YOUNG were defined as shown in Table 3.3, then it would be possible to compute the fuzzy subset YOUNG of any given POPULATION by employing the procedure expressed by

$$YOUNG =_{\mu \times Name} POPULATION[\Pi_{Age} = YOUNG] \qquad (3.58)$$

TABLE 3.3

POPULATION	Name	Age	YOUNG	Age	μ
	Codd	45		30	0·8
	King	31		31	0·75
	Chen	42		32	0·70
	Chang	33		33	0·60
				. . .	. . .
				42	0·4
				45	0·3

†In the theories of language based on two-valued logic (Linsky, 1971; Quine, 1970a; Cresswell, 1973) the dividing line between *extensional* and *intensional* is sharply drawn. This is not the case in PRUF—in which there are levels of intensionality (or, equivalently, levels of procedural generality), with pure extensionality constituting one extreme. This issue will be discussed in greater detail in a forthcoming paper.

where YOUNG in the right-hand member is a fuzzy subset of U(Age), and μ is implicit in POPULATION.

Since an expression in PRUF is a procedure, it involves, in general, not the relations in the database but only their *frames*.† In addition, an expression in PRUF may involve the names of universes of discourse and/or their Cartesian products; the names of some of the relation elements; and possibly the values of some attributes of the relations in the database (e.g. the number of rows).

As an illustration, the *frame of the database* shown in Table 3.2 (i.e. the collection of frames of its constituent relations) is comprised of:

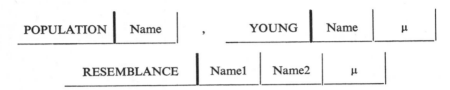

Correspondingly, an expression in PRUF such as

$$_{μ×Name1} RESEMBLANCE[Name2 = King] \qquad (3.59)$$

represents a procedure which returns the fuzzy subset of POPULATION comprising names of individuals who resemble King.

Ultimately, each of the symbols or names in a database is assumed to be defined ostensively (Lyons, 1968) or, equivalently, by exemplification; that is, by pointing or otherwise focussing on a real or abstract object and indicating the degree—on the scale from 0 to 1—to which it is compatible with the symbol in question. In this sense, then, a database may viewed as an interface with an external world which might be real or abstract or a combination of the two.‡

In general, the correspondence between a database and an external world is difficult to formalize because the universe of discourse associated with an external world comprises not just a model of that world, say M, but also the set of fuzzy subsets of M, the set of fuzzy subsets of fuzzy subsets of M, etc. To illustrate this point, it is relatively easy to define by exemplification the denotation of *red*, which is a fuzzy subset of M; much more difficult to define the concept of *color*, which is a subset of $\mathscr{P}(M)$, the set of fuzzy subsets of M; and much much more difficult to define the concept of *attribute*, which is a subset of $\mathscr{P}(\mathscr{P}(M))$ (Zadeh, 1971*b*).

Viewed in this perspective, the issues related to the correspondence between a database and an external world are similar to those which arise in pattern recognition and are even harder to formulate and resolve within a formal framework. As a direct consequence of this difficulty, a complete formalization of the concept of *meaning* does not appear to be an attainable goal in the foreseeable future.

In the context of PRUF, the concept of meaning is defined in a somewhat restricted way, as follows:

---

†By the *frame* of a relation is meant its name and column headings (i.e. the names of variables or, equivalently, attributes). The rest of the relation (i.e. the table without column headings) is its *body*.

‡In this sense, the concept of a database is related to that of a possible world in possible world semantics and modal logic (Kripke, 1963; Hughes & Cresswell, 1968; Partee, 1976*a*).

Let e be an expression in a natural language and let E be its translation into PRUF, i.e.

$$e \to E \tag{3.60}$$

and, more particularly,

$$p \to P \tag{3.61}$$

if e is a proposition; and

$$d \to D \tag{3.62}$$

if e is a descriptor. To illustrate:

$$\text{cup} \to \text{CUP} \tag{3.63}$$

$$\text{red cup} \to \text{CUP}[\Pi_{\text{Color}} = \text{RED}] \tag{3.64}$$

$$\text{George is young} \to \Pi_{\text{Age(George)}} = \text{YOUNG} \tag{3.65}$$

or, equivalently,

$$\text{George is young} \to \text{GEORGE}[\Pi_{\text{Age}} = \text{YOUNG}]. \tag{3.66}$$

Stated informally, the procedure, E, may be viewed as the *meaning* of e in the sense that, if $e \triangleq d$, then for any given database $\mathscr{D}$ on which D is defined, D computes (or returns) a fuzzy relation F^d which is a fuzzy denotation (or extension) of d in its universe of discourse (which may be different from $\mathscr{D}$). Similarly, if $e \triangleq p$, then P is a procedure which, for any given database $\mathscr{D}$ on which P is defined, computes a possibility distribution Π^p. This distribution, then, may be regarded as the *information* conveyed by p.† In particular, if Π^p is the possibility distribution of a variable X and $X_{(s)}$ is a subvariable of X, then the *information conveyed by p about* $X_{(s)}$ is given by the projection of Π^p on $U_{(s)}$. When it is necessary to indicate that Π^p is the result of acting with P on a particular database $\mathscr{D}$, Π^p will be referred to as the possibility distribution induced by p (or the information conveyed by p) in application to $\mathscr{D}$.

As an illustration, consider the proposition

$$p \triangleq \text{Mike recently lived near Boston} \tag{3.67}$$

which in PRUF translates into

$$\text{RESIDENCE}[\text{Subject} = \text{Mike}; \Pi_{\text{Time}} = \text{RECENT PAST};$$
$$\Pi_{\text{Location}} = {}_{\mu \times \text{City1}} \text{NEAR}[\text{City2} = \text{Boston}]] \tag{3.68}$$

where NEAR is a fuzzy relation with the frame

NEAR	City1	City2	μ

,

RECENT PAST is a fuzzy relation with the frame

RECENT PAST	Time	μ

---

†It should be noted that a non-probabilistic measure of information was introduced by Kampe de Feriet & Forte (1967, 1977). In the present paper, however, our concern is with the information itself, which is represented by a possibility distribution, rather than with its measure, which is a real number.

(in which Time is expressed in years counting from the present to the past), and $_{\mu \times City1}$NEAR[City2 = Boston] is the fuzzy set of cities which are near Boston. Given a database, $\mathscr{D}$, (3.68) would return a possibility distribution such as shown (in a partially tabulated form) in Table 3.4, in which

TABLE 3.4

RESIDENCE	Subject	Location	Time	π
	Mike	Cambridge	1	1
	Mike	Cambridge	2	0·8
	Mike	Cambridge	3	0·6
	Mike	Wayland	1	0·9
	Mike	Wayland	2	0·8
	. . .	. . .	. . .	. . .

the third row, for example, signifies that the possibility that Mike lived in Cambridge 3 years ago is 0·6. In this example, (3.68) constitutes the meaning of p, while the possibility distribution whose tableau is given by Table 3.4 is the information conveyed by p.

In addition to representing the meaning of an expression, e, in a natural language, the corresponding expression, E, in PRUF may be viewed as its *deep structure*—not in the technical sense employed in the literature of linguistics (Chomsky, 1965, 1971)—but in the sense of being dependent not on the surface structure of e but on its meaning. This implies that the form of E is independent of the natural language in which e is expressed, thus providing the basis for referring to PRUF as a universal language. The same can be said, of course, of most of the meaning representation languages that have been described in the literature.

Another characteristic of PRUF that is worthy of mention is that it is an *intentional*† language in the sense that an expression in PRUF is supposed to convey the intended rather than the literal meaning of the corresponding expression in a natural language. For example, if the proposition $p \triangleq$ John is no genius is intended to mean that $q \triangleq$ John is dumb, then the translation of p into PRUF would be that of q rather than p itself. As an example illustrating a somewhat different point, consider the proposition

$$p \triangleq \text{Alla has red hair.} \tag{3.69}$$

In PRUF, its translation could be expressed in one of two ways:

(a) $\qquad\qquad$ Alla has red hair $\rightarrow \Pi_{Color(\,Hair(Alla))} = \varphi$ $\qquad\qquad$ (3.70)

where φ is an identifier of the color that is commonly referred to as *red* in the case of hair; or

(b) $\qquad\qquad$ Alla has red hair $\rightarrow \Pi_{Color(\,Hair(Alla))} = \text{RED}^f$ $\qquad\qquad$ (3.71)

---

†A thorough discussion of the concept of intentionality may be found in Grice (1968) and Searle (1971).

in which the superscript f (standing for *footnote*) points to a non-standard definition of RED which must be used in (3.71). The same convention is employed, more generally, whenever a non-standard definition of any entity in an expression in PRUF must be employed.

SEMANTIC EQUIVALENCE AND SEMANTIC ENTAILMENT

The concepts of semantic equivalence and semantic entailment are two closely related concepts in PRUF which play an important role in fuzzy logic and approximate reasoning.

Informally, let p and q be a pair of expressions in a natural language and let Π^p and Π^q be the possibility distributions (or the fuzzy relations) induced by p and q in application to a database $\mathcal{D}$. Then, we shall say that p and q are *semantically equivalent*, expressed as

$$p \leftrightarrow q, \qquad (3.72)$$

if and only if $\Pi^p = \Pi^q$. Furthermore, if (3.72) holds for all databases,† the semantic equivalence between p and q is said to be *strong*.‡ Thus, the definition of strong semantic equivalence implies that p and q have the same meaning if and only if they are strongly semantically equivalent. In this sense, then, any transformation which maps p into q is *meaning-preserving*.

To illustrate, as will be seen in section 6, the propositions

$$p \triangleq \text{Jeanne is tall is true} \qquad (3.73)$$

and

$$q \triangleq \text{Jeanne is not tall is false} \qquad (3.74)$$

in which *false* is the antonym of *true*, i.e.

$$\mu_{\text{FALSE}}(v) = \mu_{\text{TRUE}}(1-v), \quad v \in [0,1] \qquad (3.75)$$

are semantically equivalent no matter how TALL and TRUE are defined. Consequently, p and q are strongly semantically equivalent and hence have the same meaning. On the other hand, the propositions

$$p \triangleq \text{Jeanne is tall is very true} \qquad (3.76)$$

and

$$q \triangleq \text{Jeanne is very tall} \qquad (3.77)$$

can be shown to be semantically equivalent when TRUE is the unitary fuzzy set (see (2.15)), that is

$$\mu_{\text{TRUE}}(v) = v, \quad v \in [0,1]$$

but not when TRUE is an arbitrary fuzzy subset of [0,1]. Consequently, p and q are not strongly semantically equivalent.

---

†Generally, "all databases" should be interpreted as all databases which are related in a specified way to a reference database. This is analogous to the role of the alternativeness relation in possible world semantics (Hughes & Cresswell, 1968).

‡The concept of strong semantic equivalence as defined here reduces to that of semantic equivalence in predicate logic (see Lyndon, 1966) when p and q are non-fuzzy propositions.

Usually, it is clear from the context whether a semantic equivalence is or is not strong. When it is necessary to place in evidence that a semantic equivalence is strong, it will be denoted by $s\leftrightarrow$. Correspondingly, if the equality between Π^p and Π^q is approximate in nature, the approximate semantic equivalence between p and q will be expressed as $p\ a\leftrightarrow q$.

While the concept of semantic equivalence relates to the equality of possibility distributions (or fuzzy relations), that of *semantic entailment* relates to inclusion.† More specifically, on denoting the assertion "p semantically entails q (or q is semantically entailed by p)," by $p\mapsto q$, we have

$$p\mapsto q \text{ iff } \Pi^p \subset \Pi^q \tag{3.78}$$

where Π^p and Π^q are the possibility distributions induced by the propositions p and q, respectively.

As in the case of semantic equivalence, semantic entailment is *strong* if the relation $\mapsto$ holds for all databases. For example, as will be seen in section 4, the possibility distribution induced by the proposition "Gary is very tall" is contained in that induced by "Gary is tall" no matter how TALL is defined. Consequently, we can assert that

$$\text{Gary is very tall } s\mapsto \text{Gary is tall} \tag{3.79}$$

where $s\mapsto$ denotes strong semantic entailment. On the other hand, the validity of the semantic entailment

$$\text{Gary is very tall}\mapsto \text{Gary is not short} \tag{3.80}$$

depends on the definitions of *tall* and *short*, and hence (3.80) does not represent strong semantic entailment.

As was stated earlier, the concepts of semantic equivalence and semantic entailment play an important role in fuzzy logic and approximate reasoning (Zadeh, 1977*b*). In the present paper, we shall make use of the concept of semantic equivalence in sections 4 and 6 to derive several useful meaning-preserving transformations.

4. Translation rules of Types I, II and III

To facilitate the translation of expressions in a natural language into PRUF, it is desirable to have a stock of translation rules which may be applied singly or in combination to yield an expression, E, in PRUF, which is a translation of a given expression, e, in a natural language.

The translation rules which apply to descriptors may readily be deduced from the corresponding rules for propositions. Consequently, we shall restrict our attention in the sequel to the translation of propositions.

The translation rules for propositions may be divided into several basic categories, the more important of which are the following:

    Type I.   Rules pertaining to modification.
    Type II.   Rules pertaining to composition.

---

†If A and B are fuzzy subsets of U, then $A \subset B$ iff $\mu_A(u) \leq \mu_B(u)$, $u \in U$.

Type III.   Rules pertaining to quantification.
Type IV.   Rules pertaining to qualification.

Simple examples of propositions to which the rules in question apply are the following:

Type I.   X is very small   (4.1)
              X is much larger than Y   (4.2)
              Eleanor was very upset   (4.3)
              The man with the blond hair is very tall   (4.4)

Type II.   X is small and Y is large (conjunctive composition)   (4.5)
              X is small or Y is large (disjunctive composition)   (4.6)
              If X is small then Y is large   (4.7)
                 (conditional composition)
              If X is small then Y is large else Y is very large   (4.8)
                 (conditional and conjunctive composition)

Type III.   Most Swedes are tall   (4.9)
              Many men are much taller than most men   (4.10)
              Most tall men are very intelligent   (4.11)

Type IV.   Abe is young is not very true   (4.12)
                 (truth qualification)
              Abe is young is quite probable   (4.13)
                 (probability qualification)
              Abe is young is almost impossible   (4.14)
                 (possibility qualification)

Rules of Types I, II and III will be discussed in this section. Rules of Type IV will be discussed in section 6, following an exposition of the concepts of consistency, compatibility and truth in section 5.

Translation rules in PRUF are generally expressed in a conditional format exemplified by

If $p \to P$ (4.15)
then $p^+ \to P^+$

where p^+ and P^+ are modifications of p and P, respectively. In effect, a rule expressed in this form states that if in a certain context p translates into P, then in the *same context* a specified modification of p, p^+, translates into a specified modification of P, P^+. In this way, the rule makes it explicit that the translation of a modified proposition, p^+, depends on the translation of p. The simpler notation employed in (4.28) conveys the same information, but does so less explicitly.

RULES OF TYPE I

A basic rule of Type I is the *modifier rule*, which may be stated as follows.
  If the proposition

$$p \triangleq N \text{ is } F \qquad (4.16)$$

translates into the possibility assignment equation (see (3.31))

$$\Pi_{(x_1, \ldots, x_n)} = F \qquad (4.17)$$

then the translation of the modified proposition

$$p^+ \triangleq N \text{ is } mF \qquad (4.18)$$

where m is a modifier such as *not, very, more or less, quite, extremely*, etc., is given by

$$N \text{ is } mF \rightarrow \Pi_{(x_1, \ldots, x_n)} = F^+ \qquad (4.19)$$

where F^+ is a modification of F induced by m. In particular:

    (a)   if $m \triangleq$ not, then $F^+ = F' \triangleq$ complement of F;   (4.20)
    (b)   if $m \triangleq$ very, then $F^+ = F^2$, where†   (4.21)

$$F^2 = \int_U \mu_F^2(u)/u; \qquad (4.22)$$

    (c)   if $m \triangleq$ more or less, then $F^+ = \sqrt{F}$ where   (4.23)

$$\sqrt{F} = \int_U \sqrt{\mu_F(u)}/u; \qquad (4.24)$$

or, alternatively,

$$F^+ = \int_U \mu_F(u)K(u) \qquad (4.25)$$

where $K(u)$ is the kernel of *more or less*.‡

    As a simple illustration of (4.21), let p be the proposition "Lisa is young," where YOUNG is a fuzzy subset of the interval [0,100] whose membership function is expressed in terms of the S-function (2.13) as (omitting the arguments of μ and S):

$$\mu_{YOUNG} = 1 - S(25,35,45). \qquad (4.26)$$

Then, the translation of "Lisa is very young" is given by

$$\text{Lisa is very young} \rightarrow \Pi_{Age(Lisa)} = YOUNG^2 \qquad (4.27)$$

where

$$\mu_{YOUNG}^2 = (1 - S(25,35,45))^2.$$

---

†The "integral" representation of a fuzzy set in the form $F = \int_U \mu_F(u)/u$ signifies that F is a union of the fuzzy singletons $\mu_F(u)/u$, $u \in U$, where μ_F is the membership function of F. Thus, (4.22) means that the membership function of F^2 is the square of that of F.

‡More detailed discussions of various types of modifiers may be found in Zadeh (1972a, 1975c), Lakoff (1973a,b), Wenstop (1975, 1976), Mizumoto *et al.* (1977), Hersh & Caramazza (1976), and other papers listed in the bibliography. It is important to note that (4.21) and (4.23) should be regarded merely as standardized default definitions which may be replaced, if necessary, by the user-supplied definitions.

Note that we can bypass the conditional format of the translation rule (4.16) and assert directly that

$$\text{Lisa is very young} \to \Pi_{\text{Age(Lisa)}} = \text{YOUNG}^2 \qquad (4.28)$$

on the understanding that YOUNG is the denotation of *young* in the context in which the proposition "Lisa is very young" is asserted. As was stated earlier, the conditional format serves the purpose of making this understanding more explicit.

In some cases, a modifier such as *very* may be implicit rather than explicit in a proposition. Consider, for example, the proposition

$$p \triangleq \text{Vera and Pat are close friends.} \qquad (4.29)$$

As an approximation, p may be assumed to be semantically equivalent to

$$q = \text{Vera and Pat are friends}^2 \qquad (4.30)$$

so that (using (4.22)) the translation of p may be expressed as (see (7.21))

$$\pi(\text{FRIENDS}) = \mu \text{FRIENDS}^2[\text{Name1} = \text{Vera}; \text{Name2} = \text{Pat}] \qquad (4.31)$$

where $\pi(\text{FRIENDS})$ is the possibility of the relation FRIENDS in $\mathscr{D}$. Thus, what (4.31) implies is that the relation FRIENDS in $\mathscr{D}$ is such that

$$\Pi_X = \perp^2 \qquad (4.32)$$

where

$$X \triangleq {}_\mu \text{FRIENDS}[\text{Name1} = \text{Vera}; \text{Name2} = \text{Pat}] \qquad (4.33)$$

and $\perp$ is the unitor defined by (2.15).

RULES OF TYPE II

Translation rules of Type II pertain to the translation of propositions of the form

$$p = q * r \qquad (4.34)$$

where $*$ denotes an operation of composition, e.g. conjunction (and), disjunction (or), implication (if . . . then), etc.

Under the assumption that the operation of composition is non-interactive (Bellman & Zadeh, 1976),† the rules in question may be stated as follows.

If

$$q \triangleq M \text{ is } F \to \Pi_{(X_1, \ldots, X_m)} = F$$

and   (4.35)

$$r \triangleq N \text{ is } G \to \Pi_{(Y_1, \ldots, Y_n)} = G$$

---

†Informally, a binary operation $*$ on real numbers u, v is *non-interactive* if an increase in the value of u (or v) cannot be compensated by a decrease in the value of v (or u). It should be understood that the non-interactive definitions of *and* and *or* in (4.36) and (4.37) may be replaced, if necessary, by user-supplied interactive definitions.

then

(a)   M is F and N is $G \rightarrow \Pi_{(X_1, \ldots, X_m, Y_1, \ldots, Y_n)} = \overline{F} \cap \overline{G}$ (4.36)
$$= F \times G$$

(b)   M is F or N is $G \rightarrow \Pi_{(X_1, \ldots, X_m, Y_1, \ldots, Y_n)} = \overline{F} + \overline{G}$ (4.37)

and

(c_1) If M is F then N is $G \rightarrow \Pi_{(X_1, \ldots, X_m, Y_1, \ldots, Y_n)} = \overline{F}' \oplus \overline{G}$ (4.38)

or

(c_2) If M is F then N is $G \rightarrow \Pi_{(X_1, \ldots, X_m, Y_1, \ldots, Y_n)} = F \times G + F' \times V$ (4.39)

where F and G are fuzzy subsets of $U \triangleq U_1 \times \ldots \times U_n$ and $V = V_1 \times \ldots \times V_n$, respectively; $\overline{F}'$ and $\overline{G}$ are the cylindrical extensions of F' and G, i.e.

$$\overline{F}' = F' \times V \tag{4.40}$$

$$\overline{G} = U \times G; \tag{4.41}$$

$F \times G$ is the Cartesian product of F and G which may be expressed as $\overline{F} \cap \overline{G}$ and is defined by

$$\mu_{F \times G}(u,v) = \mu_F(u) \wedge \mu_G(v), \quad u \in U, \quad v \in V; \tag{4.42}$$

$+$ is the union and $\oplus$ is the bounded-sum, i.e.

$$\mu_{\overline{F}' \oplus \overline{G}}(u,v) = 1 \wedge (1 - \mu_F(u) + \mu_G(v)) \tag{4.43}$$

where $u \triangleq (u_1, \ldots, u_n)$, $v \triangleq (v_1, \ldots, v_n)$, $\wedge \triangleq \min$, $+ \triangleq$ arithmetic sum and $- \triangleq$ arithmetic difference.† Note that there are two distinct rules for the conditional composition, (c_1) and (c_2). Of these, (c_1) is consistent with the definition of implication in Łukasiewicz's $Ł_{Aleph_1}$ logic (Rescher, 1969), while (c_2)—in consequence of (4.53)—corresponds to the relation expressed by the table:

TABLE 4.1

M	N
F	G
F'	V

As a very simple illustration, assume, as in Zadeh (1977b), that $U = V = 1 + 2 + 3$, $M \triangleq X$, $N \triangleq Y$,

$$F \triangleq SMALL \triangleq 1/1 + 0·6/2 + 0·1/3 \tag{4.44}$$

and

$$G \triangleq LARGE \triangleq 0·1/1 + 0·6/2 + 1/3. \tag{4.45}$$

†If the variables $X \triangleq (X_1, \ldots, X_n)$ and $Y \triangleq (Y_1, \ldots, Y_n)$ have a subvariable, say Z, in common, i.e. $X \triangleq (S,Z)$ and $Y \triangleq (T,Z)$, then F and G should be interpreted as cylindrical extensions of F and G in $U(S) \times U(T) \times U(Z)$ rather than in $U(X) \times U(Y)$, where U(S), U(T) and U(Z) denote, respectively, the universes in which S, T and Z take their values. Additionally, the possibility distributions in (7.38) and (7.39) should be interpreted, in a strict sense, as conditional distributions.

Then (4.36), (4.37), (4.38) and (4.39) yield

X is small and Y is large $\rightarrow$ (4.46)
$$\Pi_{(X,Y)}=0\cdot1/(1,1)+0\cdot6/(1,2)+1/(1,3)+0\cdot1/(2,1)+0\cdot6/(2,2)+0\cdot6/(2,3)$$
$$+0\cdot1/(3,1)+0\cdot1/(3,2)+0\cdot1/(3,3)$$

X is small or Y is large $\rightarrow$ (4.47)
$$\Pi_{(X,Y)}=1/(1,1)+1/(1,2)+1/(1,3)+0\cdot6/(2,1)+0\cdot6/(2,2)+1/(2,3)+0\cdot1/(3,1)$$
$$+0\cdot6/(3,2)+1/(3,3)$$

If X is small then Y is large $\rightarrow$ (4.48)
$$\Pi_{(X,Y)}=0\cdot1/(1,1)+0\cdot6/(1,2)+1/(1,3)+0\cdot5/(2,1)+1/(2,2)+1/(2,3)$$
$$+1/(3,1)+1/(3,2)+1/(3,3)$$

If X is small then Y is large $\rightarrow$ (4.49)
$$\Pi_{(X,Y)}=0\cdot1/(1,1)+0\cdot6/(1,2)+1/(1,3)+0\cdot4/(2,1)+0\cdot6/(2,2)+0\cdot6/(2,3)$$
$$+0\cdot9/(3,1)+0\cdot9/(3,2)+0\cdot9/(3,3)$$

The rules stated above may be employed in combination, yielding a variety of corollary rules which are of use in the translation of more complex forms of composite propositions and descriptors. Among the basic rules of this type are the following.

(d) If M is F then N is G else N is H   (4.50)

$$\rightarrow\Pi_{(X_1,\ldots,X_m,Y_1,\ldots,Y_n)}=(\overline{F}'\oplus\overline{G})\cap(\overline{F}\oplus\overline{H})$$

where $F\subset U\triangleq U_1\times\ldots\times U_m$ and $G,H\subset V\triangleq V_1\times\ldots\times V_n$. This rule follows from the semantic equivalence:

If M is F then N is G else N is H   (4.51)
$$\leftrightarrow(\text{If M is F then N is G}) \text{ and } (\text{If M is not F then N is H})$$

and the application of (a) and (c_1).

(e) *Translation rule for relations*
Consider a relation, R, whose tableau is of the form shown in Table 4.2.

TABLE 4.2

R	X_1	X_2	$\ldots$	X_n
	F_{11}	F_{12}	$\ldots$	F_{1n}
	$\ldots$	$\ldots$	$\ldots$	$\ldots$
	F_{m1}	$\ldots$	$\ldots$	F_{mn}

in which the F_{ij} are fuzzy subsets of the U_j, respectively. On interpreting R as

$$R = X_1 \text{ is } F_{11} \text{ and } X_2 \text{ is } F_{12} \text{ and } \ldots \text{ and } X_n \text{ is } F_{1n} \text{ or} \qquad (4.52)$$
$$X_1 \text{ is } F_{21} \text{ and } X_2 \text{ is } F_{22} \text{ and } \ldots \text{ and } X_n \text{ is } F_{2n} \text{ or } \ldots \text{ or}$$
$$X_1 \text{ is } F_{m1} \text{ and } X_2 \text{ is } F_{m2} \text{ and } \ldots \text{ and } X_n \text{ is } F_{mn}$$

it follows from (a) and (b) that

$$R \to F_{11} \times \ldots \times F_{1n} + \ldots + F_{m1} \times \ldots \times F_{mn} \qquad (4.53)$$

which will be referred to as the *tableau rule*. This rule plays an important role in applications to pattern recognition, decision analysis, medical diagnosis and related areas, in which binary relations are employed to describe the features of a class of objects (Zadeh, 1976*a,b*).

As a simple illustration, consider the relation defined by Table 4.3

TABLE 4.3

X	Y
small	large
very small	not very large
not small	very small

in which X and Y are real-valued variables and

$$\text{small} \to \text{SMALL}$$
$$\text{large} \to \text{LARGE}$$

where SMALL and LARGE are specified fuzzy subsets of the real line.
First, by the application of (4.20) and (4.21), we have

$$\text{very small} \to \text{SMALL}^2 \qquad (4.54)$$
$$\text{not small} \to \text{SMALL}' \qquad (4.55)$$
$$\text{not very large} \to (\text{LARGE}^2)'. \qquad (4.56)$$

Then, on applying (4.53), we obtain

$$R \to \text{SMALL} \times \text{LARGE} + (\text{SMALL}^2) \times (\text{LARGE}^2)' + \text{SMALL}' \times \text{SMALL}^2$$

which is the desired translation of the relation in question.

LINGUISTIC VARIABLES

The modifier rule in combination with the translation rules for conjunctive and disjunctive compositions provides a simple method for the translation of linguistic values of so-called *linguistic variables* (Zadeh, 1973, 1975*c*).

Informally, a *linguistic variable* is a variable whose *linguistic values* are words or sentences in a natural or synthetic language, with each such value being a label of a fuzzy subset of a universe of discourse. For example, a variable such as Age may be viewed both as a numerical variable ranging over, say, the interval [0,150], and as a linguistic variable which can take the values *young, not young, very young, not very young, quite young, old, not very young and not very old*, etc. Each of these values may be interpreted as a label of a fuzzy subset of the universe of discourse U=[0,150], whose base variable, *u*, is the generic numerical value of Age.

Typically, the values of a linguistic variable such as Age are built up of one or more *primary terms* (which are the labels of *primary fuzzy sets*†), together with a collection of modifiers which allow a composite linguistic value to be generated from the primary terms through the use of conjunctions and disjunctions. Usually the number of primary terms is two, with one being an antonym of the other. For example, in the case of Age, the primary terms are *young* and *old*, with *old* being the antonym of *young*.

Using the translation rules (4.20), (4.21), (4.36) and (4.37) in combination, the linguistic values of a linguistic variable such as Age may be translated by inspection. To illustrate, suppose that the primary terms *young* and *old* are defined by

$$\mu_{YOUNG} = 1 - S(20,30,40) \tag{4.57}$$

and

$$\mu_{OLD} = S(40,55,70). \tag{4.58}$$

Then

$$\text{not very young} \rightarrow (YOUNG^2)' \tag{4.59}$$

and

$$\text{not very young and not very old} \rightarrow (YOUNG^2)' \cap (OLD^2)' \tag{4.60}$$

and thus

$$\text{John is not very young} \rightarrow \Pi_{Age(John)} = (YOUNG^2)' \tag{4.61}$$

where

$$\mu_{(YOUNG^2)'} = 1 - (1 - S(20,30,40))^2. \tag{4.62}$$

The problem of finding a linguistic value of Age whose meaning approximates to a given fuzzy subset of U is an instance of the problem of *linguistic approximation* (Zadeh, 1975c; Wenstop, 1975; Procyk, 1976). We shall not discuss in the present paper the ways in which this non-trivial problem can be approached, but will assume that linguistic approximation is implicit in the retranslation of a possibility distribution into a proposition expressed in a natural language.

RULES OF TYPE III

Translation rules of Type III pertain to the translation of propositions of the general form

$$p \triangleq QN \text{ are } F \tag{4.63}$$

where N is the descriptor of a possibly fuzzy set, Q is a fuzzy quantifier (e.g. *most, many, few, some, almost all*, etc.) and F is a fuzzy subset of U. Simple examples of (4.63) are:

$$\text{Most Swedes are tall} \tag{4.64}$$

†Such sets play a role which is somewhat analogous to that of physical units.

$$\text{Many tall men are fat} \tag{4.65}$$

$$\text{Some men are much taller than most men.} \tag{4.66}$$

In general, a fuzzy quantifier is a fuzzy subset of the set of integers, the unit interval or the real line. For example, we may have

$$\text{SEVERAL} \triangleq 0 \cdot 2/3 + 0 \cdot 6/4 + 1/5 + 1/6 + 0 \cdot 6/7 + 0 \cdot 2/8 \tag{4.67}$$

$$\text{MOST} \triangleq \int_0^1 S(u; 0 \cdot 5, 0 \cdot 7, 0 \cdot 9)/u \tag{4.68}$$

(which means that MOST is a fuzzy subset of the unit interval whose membership function is given by $S(0 \cdot 5, 0 \cdot 7, 0 \cdot 9)$) and

$$\text{LARGE NUMBER} \triangleq \int_0^\infty (1 + (\tfrac{u}{100})^{-2})^{-1}/u. \tag{4.69}$$

In order to be able to translate propositions of the form (4.63), it is necessary to define the *cardinality* of a fuzzy set, i.e. the number (or the proportion) of elements of U which are in F. Strictly speaking, the cardinality of a fuzzy set should be a fuzzy number, which could be defined as in Zadeh (1977b). It is simpler, however, to deal with the *power* of a fuzzy set (DeLuca & Termini, 1972), which in the case of a fuzzy set with a finite support† is defined by‡

$$|F| \triangleq \sum_i \mu_F(u_i), \quad u_i \in \text{Support of F} \tag{4.70}$$

where $\mu_F(u_i)$, $i = 1, \ldots, N$, is the grade of membership of u_i in F and $\sum$ denotes the arithmetic sum. For example, for the fuzzy set SMALL defined by

$$\text{SMALL} \triangleq 1/0 + 1/1 + 0 \cdot 8/2 + 0 \cdot 6/3 + 0 \cdot 4/4 + 0 \cdot 2/5 \tag{4.71}$$

we have

$$|F| = 1 + 1 + 0 \cdot 8 + 0 \cdot 6 + 0 \cdot 4 + 0 \cdot 2 = 4.$$

In the sequel, we shall usually employ the more explicit notation Count(F) to represent the power of F, with the understanding that F should be treated as a bag§ rather than a set. Furthermore, the notation Prop(F/G) will be used to represent the "proportion" of F in G, i.e.

$$\text{Prop}\{F/G\} \triangleq \frac{\text{Count}(F \cap G)}{\text{Count}(G)} \tag{4.72}$$

†The *support* of a fuzzy subset F of U is the set of all points in U at which $\mu_F(u) > 0$.

‡For some applications, it is necessary to eliminate from the count those elements of F whose grade of membership falls below a specified threshold. This is equivalent to replacing F in (4.70) with $F \cap \Gamma$, where Γ is a fuzzy or non-fuzzy set which induces the desired threshold.

§The elements of a bag need not be distinct. For example, the collection of integers {2,3,5,3,5} is a bag if {2,3,5,3,5} ≠ {2,3,5}.

and more explicitly

$$\text{Prop}\{F/G\} = \frac{\sum_i (\mu_F(u_i) \wedge \mu_G(u_i))}{\sum_j \mu_G(u_j)} \tag{4.73}$$

where the summation ranges over the values of i for which $u_i \in$ Support of $F \cap$ Support of G. In particular, if $G \triangleq U \triangleq$ finite non-fuzzy set, then (4.73) becomes

$$\text{Prop}\{F/U\} = \frac{1}{N} \sum_{i=1}^N \mu_F(u_i) \tag{4.74}$$

where N is the cardinality of U. For convenience, the number $\text{Prop}\{F/U\}$ will be referred to as the *relative cardinality* of F expressed as

$$\text{Prop}(F) \triangleq \text{Prop}\{F/U\} = \frac{1}{N} \sum_{i=1}^N \mu_F(u_i). \tag{4.75}$$

As N increases and U becomes a continuum, the expression for the power of F tends in the limit to that of the *additive measure* of F (Zadeh, 1968; Sugeno, 1974), which may be regarded as a continuous analog of the proportion of the elements of U which are "in" F. More specifically, if $\rho(u)$ is a density function defined on U, the measure in question is defined by†

$$\text{Prop}(F) = \int_U \rho(u) \mu_F(u) du. \tag{4.76}$$

For example, if $\rho(u)du$ is the proportion of Swedes whose height lies in the interval $[u, u+du]$, then the proportion of tall Swedes is given by

$$\text{Prop(tall Swedes)} = \int_0^{200} \rho(u) \mu_{\text{TALL}}(u) du \tag{4.77}$$

where μ_{TALL} is the membership function of *tall* and height is assumed to be measured in centimeters.

In a similar fashion, the expression for $\text{Prop}\{F/G\}$ tends in the limit to that of the *relative measure* of F in G, which is defined by

$$\text{Prop}(F/G) \triangleq \frac{\int_{U \times V} \rho(u,v)(\mu_F(u) \wedge \mu_G(v)) du dv}{\int_V \rho(v) \mu_G(v) dv} \tag{4.78}$$

where $\rho(u,v)$ is a density function defined on $U \times V$ and

$$\rho(v) = \int_U \rho(u,v) du. \tag{4.79}$$

---

†We employ the notation Prop(F) even in the continuous case to make clearer the intuitive meaning of measure.

For example, if $F \triangleq$ TALL MEN and $G \triangleq$ FAT MEN, (4.78) becomes

$$\text{Prop\{TALL MEN/FAT MEN\}} = \frac{\displaystyle\int_{[0,200] \times [0,100]} \rho(u,v)\mu_{TALL}(u) \wedge \mu_{FAT}(v) du dv}{\displaystyle\int_{[0,100]} \rho(v)\mu_{FAT}(v) dv} \qquad (4.80)$$

where $\rho(u,v)dudv$ is the proportion of men whose height lies in the interval $[u,u+du]$ and whose weight lies in the interval $[v,v+dv]$.

The above definitions provide the basis for the *quantifier rule* for the translation of propositions of the form "QN are F". More specifically, assuming for simplicity that N is a descriptor of a non-fuzzy set, the rule in question may be stated as follows.

If $U = \{u_1, \ldots, u_N\}$ and

$$N \text{ is } F \rightarrow \Pi_X = F \qquad (4.81)$$

then

$$QN \text{ are } F \rightarrow \Pi_{\text{Count}(F)} = Q \qquad (4.82)$$

and, if U is a continuum,

$$QN \text{ are } F \rightarrow \Pi_{\text{Prop}(F)} = Q \qquad (4.83)$$

which implies the more explicit rule

$$QN \text{ are } F \rightarrow \pi(\rho) = \mu_Q\left(\int_U \rho(u)\mu_F(u) du\right) \qquad (4.84)$$

where $\rho(u)du$ is the proportion of X's whose value lies in the interval $[u,u+du]$, $\pi(\rho)$ is the possibility of ρ, and μ_Q and μ_F are the membership functions of Q and F, respectively.

As a simple illustration, if MOST and TALL are defined by (4.68) and $\mu_{TALL} = S(160,170,180)$, respectively, then

$$\text{Most men are tall} \rightarrow \pi(\rho) = S\left(\int_0^{200} \rho(u)S(u;160,1970,180)du; 0\cdot5, 0\cdot7, 0\cdot9\right) \qquad (4.85)$$

where $\rho(u)du$ is the proportion of men whose height (in cm) is in the interval $[u,u+du]$. Thus, the proposition "Most men are tall" induces a possibility distribution of the height density function ρ which is expressed by the right-hand member of (4.85).

MODIFIER RULE FOR PROPOSITIONS

The modifier rule which was stated earlier in this section (4.16) provides a basis for the formulation of a more general modifier rule which applies to propositions and which leads to a rule for transforming the negation of a proposition into a semantically equivalent form in which the negation has a smaller scope.

The *modifier rule for propositions* may be stated as follows.

If a proposition p translates into a procedure P, i.e.

$$p \rightarrow P \qquad (4.86)$$

and P returns a possibility distribution Π^p in application to a database $\mathscr{D}$, then mp, where m is a modifier, is semantically equivalent to a retranslation of mP, i.e.

$$mp \leftrightarrow q \qquad (4.87)$$

where

$$q \leftarrow mP. \qquad (4.88)$$

In (4.88), mP is understood to be a procedure which returns (in application to $\mathscr{D}$):

$$(\Pi^p)' \text{ if } m \triangleq \text{not} \qquad (4.89)$$

$$(\Pi^p)^2 \text{ if } m \triangleq \text{very} \qquad (4.90)$$

and

$$(\Pi^p)^{0\cdot5} \text{ if } m \triangleq \text{more or less.} \qquad (4.91)$$

For simplicity, the possibility distribution defined by (4.89), (4.90) and (4.91) will be denoted as $m\Pi^p$.

On applying this rule to a proposition of the form $p \triangleq N$ is F and making use of the translation rules (4.20), (4.21), (4.23), (4.36), (4.37) and (4.87), we obtain the following general forms of (strong) semantic equivalence:

(a)
$$m(\text{N is F}) \leftrightarrow \text{N is } m\text{F} \qquad (4.92)$$

and, in particular,

$$\text{not(N is F)} \leftrightarrow \text{N is not F} \qquad (4.93)$$

$$\text{very(N is F)} \leftrightarrow \text{N is very F} \qquad (4.94)$$

$$\text{more or less(N is F)} \leftrightarrow \text{N is more or less F.} \qquad (4.95)$$

(b)
$$m(\text{M is F and N is G}) \leftrightarrow (\text{X,Y}) \text{ is } m(\text{F} \times \text{G}) \qquad (4.96)$$

and, in particular (in virtue of (4.20), (4.36) and 4.37)),

$$\text{not(M is F and N is G)} \leftrightarrow (\text{X,Y}) \text{ is } (\text{F} \times \text{G})' \qquad (4.97)$$
$$\leftrightarrow (\text{X,Y}) \text{ is } \overline{\text{F}}' + \overline{\text{G}}' \qquad (4.98)$$
$$\leftrightarrow \text{M is not F or N is not G} \qquad (4.99)$$
$$\text{very(M is F and N is G)} \leftrightarrow \text{M is very F and N is very G} \qquad (4.100)$$
$$\text{more or less(M is F and N is G)} \leftrightarrow \text{M is more or less F and N is}$$
$$\text{more or less G} \qquad (4.101)$$

and dually for disjunctive composition.

(c)
$$m(\text{QN are F}) \leftrightarrow (m\text{Q})\text{N are F} \qquad (4.102)$$

and, in particular,

$$\text{not(QN are F)} \leftrightarrow (\text{not Q})\text{N are F} \qquad (4.103)$$

which may be regarded as a generalization of the standard negation rules in predicate calculus, viz.

$$\daleth (\forall x)F(x)\leftarrow\to(\exists x)\daleth F(x),\tag{4.104}$$

$$\daleth (\exists x)F(x)\leftarrow\to(\forall x)\daleth F(x).\tag{4.105}$$

To see the connection between (4.104), say, and (4.102), we first note that, in consequence of (4.84), we can assert the semantic equivalence

$$QN \text{ are } F\leftarrow\to\text{ant } Q \text{ are not } F\tag{4.106}$$

where ant Q, the antonym of Q, is defined by

$$\mu_{\text{ant } Q}(v)=\mu_Q(1-v),\quad v\in[0,1].\tag{4.107}$$

Thus, on combining (4.103) and (4.106), we have

$$\text{not}(QN \text{ are } F)\leftarrow\to(\text{ant}(\text{not } Q))N \text{ are not } F\tag{4.108}$$

which for $Q\triangleq$ all gives

$$\text{not}(\text{all } N \text{ are } F)\leftarrow\to(\text{ant}(\text{not all}))N \text{ are not } F.\tag{4.109}$$

Then, the right-hand member of (4.109) may be expressed as

$$\text{not}(\text{all } N \text{ are } F)\leftarrow\to\text{some } N \text{ are not } F\tag{4.110}$$

if we assume that

$$\text{some}\triangleq\text{ant}(\text{not all}).\tag{4.111}$$

In a similar fashion, the modifier rule for propositions may be employed to derive the negation rules for qualified propositions of the form $q\triangleq p$ is γ, where γ is a truth-value, a probability-value, or a possibility-value. Rules of this type will be formulated in section 5.

5. Consistency, compatibility and truth

Our aim in this section is to lay the groundwork for the translation of truth-qualified propositions of the form "p is τ," where τ is a linguistic truth-value. To this end, we shall have to introduce two related concepts—consistency and compatibility—in terms of which the *relative* truth of a proposition p with respect to a reference proposition r may be defined.

The concept of truth has traditionally been accorded a central place in logic and philosophy of language. In recent years, it has also come to play a primary role in the theory of meaning—especially in Montague grammar and possible world semantics.

By contrast, it is the concept of a possibility distribution rather than truth that serves as a basis for the definition of meaning as well as other primary concepts in fuzzy logic and PRUF. Thus, as we shall see in the sequel, the concept of truth in PRUF serves in the main as a mechanism for assessing the consistency or compatibility of a pair of propositions rather than—as in classical logic—as an indicator of the correspondence between a proposition and "reality".

CONSISTENCY AND COMPATIBILITY

Let p and q be two propositions of the form $p \triangleq N$ is F and $q \triangleq N$ is G, which translate, respectively, into

$$p \triangleq N \text{ is } F \rightarrow \Pi^p{}_{(X_1, \ldots, X_n)} = F \tag{5.1}$$

and

$$q \triangleq N \text{ is } G \rightarrow \Pi^q{}_{(X_1, \ldots, X_n)} = G \tag{5.2}$$

where $(X_1, \ldots, X_n)$ takes values in U. Intuitive considerations suggest that the *consistency* of p with q (or vice versa) be defined as the possibility that "N is F" given that "N is G" (or vice versa). Thus, making use of (2.9), we have

$$\text{Cons}\{N \text{ is } F, N \text{ is } G\} \triangleq \text{Poss}\{N \text{ is } F \mid N \text{ is } G\} \tag{5.3}$$
$$= \underset{u \in U}{\text{Sup}} \ (\mu_F(u) \wedge \mu_G(u))$$

where $u \triangleq (u_1, \ldots, u_n)$ denotes the generic value of $(X_1, \ldots, X_n)$, and μ_F and μ_G are the membership functions of F and G, respectively.

As a simple illustration, assume that

$$p \triangleq N \text{ is a small integer} \tag{5.4}$$

$$q \triangleq N \text{ is not a small integer} \tag{5.5}$$

where

$$\text{SMALL INTEGER} \triangleq 1/0 + 1/1 + 0 \cdot 8/2 + 0 \cdot 6/3 + 0 \cdot 4/4 + 0 \cdot 2/5. \tag{5.6}$$

In this case, $\text{Cons}\{p, q\} = 0 \cdot 4$.

As a less simple example, consider the propositions

$$p \triangleq \text{Most men are tall} \tag{5.7}$$

and

$$q \triangleq \text{Most men are short} \tag{5.8}$$

which translate into (see (4.84))

$$\pi^p(\rho) = \mu_{MOST}\left(\int_0^{200} \rho(u) \mu_{TALL}(u) du \right) \tag{5.9}$$

and

$$\pi^q(\rho) = \mu_{MOST}\left(\int_0^{200} \rho(u) \mu_{SHORT}(u) du \right). \tag{5.10}$$

In this case, assuming that μ_{MOST} is a monotone function, we have

$$\text{Cons}\{p, q\} = \mu_{MOST}\left(\underset{\rho}{\text{Sup}}\left((\int_0^{200} \rho(u) \mu_{TALL}(u) du) \wedge (\int_0^{200} \rho(u) \mu_{SHORT}(u) du) \right) \right). \tag{5.11}$$

If q is assumed to be a *reference* proposition, which we shall denote by r, then the *truth of p relative to r* could be defined as the consistency of p with r. It appears to be more appropriate, however, to define the truth of p relative to r through the concept of *compatibility* rather than consistency. More specifically, assume that the reference proposition r is of the form

$$r \triangleq N \text{ is } u \tag{5.12}$$

where u is an element of U. Then, by definition,

$$\text{Comp}\{N \text{ is } u/N \text{ is } F\} \triangleq \mu_F(u) \tag{5.13}$$

which coincides with the definition of $\text{Poss}\{X \text{ is } u | N \text{ is } F\}$ (see (2.4)) as well as with the definition of the consistency of "N is u" with "N is F". However, when the reference proposition is of the form $r \triangleq N$ is G, the definitions of compatibility and consistency cease to coincide. More specifically, by employing the extension principle,[†] (5.13) becomes

$$\text{Comp}\{N \text{ is } G/N \text{ is } F\} = \mu_F(G) \tag{5.14}$$
$$= \int_{[0,1]} \mu_G(u)/\mu_F(u)$$

in which the right-hand member is the union over the unit interval of the fuzzy singletons $\mu_G(u)/\mu_F(u)$. Thus, (5.14) signifies that the compatibility of "N is G" with "N is F" is a fuzzy subset of $[0,1]$ defined by (5.14).

The concept of compatibility as defined by (5.14) provides the basis for the following definition of Truth.

Truth. Let p be a proposition of the form "N is F," and let r be a reference proposition, $r \triangleq N$ is G, where F and G are subsets of U. Then, the *truth*, τ, of p *relative to r* is defined as the compatibility of r with p, i.e.

$$\tau \triangleq \text{Tr}\{N \text{ is } F/N \text{ is } G\} \triangleq \text{Comp}\{N \text{ is } G/N \text{ is } F\} \tag{5.15}$$
$$\triangleq \mu_F(G)$$
$$\triangleq \int_{[0,1]} \mu_G(u)/\mu_F(u).$$

It should be noted that τ, as defined by (5.15), is a fuzzy subset of the unit interval, implying that a linguistic truth-value may be regarded as a linguistic approximation to the subset defined by (5.15).

A more explicit expression for τ which follows at once from (5.15) is:

$$\mu_\tau(v) = \text{Max}_u \mu_G(u), \quad v \in [0,1] \tag{5.16}$$

subject to

$$\mu_F(u) = v.$$

[†]The extension principle (Zadeh, 1975c) serves to extend the definition of a mapping $f : U \to V$ to the set of fuzzy subsets of U. Thus, $f(F) \triangleq \int_U \mu_F(u)/f(u)$, where $f(F)$ and $f(u)$ are, respectively, the images of F and u in V.

Thus, if μ_F is 1–1, then the membership function of τ may be expressed in terms of those of F and G as

$$\mu_\tau(v) = \mu_G(\mu_F^{-1}(v)). \tag{5.17}$$

Another immediate consequence of (5.15) is that the truth-value of p relative to itself is given by

$$\mu_\tau(v) = v$$

rather than unity. Thus, in virtue of (2.15), we have

$$Tr\{N \text{ is } F/N \text{ is } F\} = \bot \tag{5.18}$$
$$= u\text{-true}.$$

As an illustration of (5.15), assume that

$$p \triangleq N \text{ is not small} \tag{5.19}$$

and

$$r \triangleq N \text{ is small} \tag{5.20}$$

where SMALL is defined by (5.6). Then, (5.15) yields

$$\tau = 1/0 + 0{\cdot}8/0{\cdot}2 + 0{\cdot}6/0{\cdot}4 + 0{\cdot}4/0{\cdot}6 + 0{\cdot}2/0{\cdot}8 \tag{5.21}$$

which may be regarded as a discretized version of the antonym of u-true (see (4.107)). Thus,

$$Tr\{N \text{ is not small}/N \text{ is small}\} = \text{ant } u\text{-true} \tag{5.22}$$

which, as will be seen later, is a special case of the strong semantic equivalence

$$Tr\{N \text{ is } F/N \text{ is not } F\} = \text{ant } u\text{-true}. \tag{5.23}$$

As can be seen from the foregoing discussion, in our definition of the truth-value of a proposition p, τ serves as a measure of the compatibility of p with a reference proposition r. To use this definition as a basis for the translation of truth-qualified propositions, we adopt the following postulate.

Postulate. A truth-qualified proposition of the form "p is τ" is semantically equivalent to the reference proposition, r, relative to which

$$Tr\{p/r\} = \tau. \tag{5.24}$$

We shall use this postulate in the following section to establish translation rules for truth-qualified propositions.

6. Translation rules of Type IV

Our concern in this section is with the translation of qualified propositions of the form $q \triangleq p$ is γ, where γ might be a truth-value, a probability-value, a possibility-value or, more generally, the value of some specified propositional function, i.e. a function from the space of propositions (or n-tuples of propositions) to the set of fuzzy subsets of the unit interval.

Typically, a translation rule of Type IV may be viewed as an answer to the following question: Suppose that a proposition p induces a possibility distribution Π^p. What, then, is the possibility distribution induced by the qualified proposition $q \triangleq p$ is γ, where γ is a specified truth-value, probability-value or possibility-value?

In what follows, we shall state the translation rules pertaining to (a) truth qualification; (b) probability qualification; and (c) possibility qualification. These are the principal modes of qualification which are of more or less universal use in natural languages.

RULE FOR TRUTH QUALIFICATION

Let p be a proposition of the form

$$p \triangleq N \text{ is } F \tag{6.1}$$

and let q be a truth-qualified version of p expressed as

$$q \triangleq N \text{ is } F \text{ is } \tau \tag{6.2}$$

where τ is a linguistic truth-value. As was stated in section 5, q is semantically equivalent to the reference proposition r, i.e.

$$N \text{ is } F \text{ is } \tau \leftrightarrow N \text{ is } G \tag{6.3}$$

where F, G and τ are related by

$$\tau = \mu_F(G). \tag{6.4}$$

Equation (6.4) states that τ is the image of G under the mapping $\mu_F : U \to [0,1]$. Consequently (Zadeh, 1965), the expression for the membership function of G in terms of those of τ and F is given by

$$\mu_G(u) = \mu_\tau(\mu_F(u)). \tag{6.5}$$

Using this result, the rule for truth qualification may be stated as follows.
If

$$N \text{ is } F \to \Pi_X = F \tag{6.6}$$

then

$$N \text{ is } F \text{ is } \tau \to \Pi_X = F^+ \tag{6.7}$$

where

$$\mu_{F^+}(u) = \mu_\tau(\mu_F(u)). \tag{6.8}$$

In particular, if τ is the unitary truth-value, that is,

$$\tau = u\text{-true} \tag{6.9}$$

where

$$\mu_{u\text{-true}}(v) = v, \quad v \in [0,1] \tag{6.10}$$

then

$$N \text{ is } F \text{ is } u\text{-true} \to N \text{ is } F. \tag{6.11}$$

As an illustration of (6.5), if

$$q \triangleq N \text{ is small is very true} \tag{6.12}$$

where

$$\mu_{\text{SMALL}} = 1 - S(5,10,15), \quad u \in [0,\infty) \tag{6.13}$$

and

$$\mu_{\text{TRUE}} = S(0 \cdot 6, 0 \cdot 8, 1 \cdot 0) \tag{6.14}$$

then

$$q \to \pi_X(u) = S^2(1 - S(u;5,10,15);0 \cdot 6,0 \cdot 8,1 \cdot 0). \tag{6.15}$$

RULE FOR PROBABILITY QUALIFICATION

Let p be a proposition of the form (6.1) and let q be a probability-qualified version of p expressed as

$$q \triangleq N \text{ is F is } \lambda \tag{6.16}$$

where λ is a linguistic probability-value such as probable, very probable, not very probable, or, equivalently, likely, very likely, not very likely, etc.

We shall assume that q is semantically equivalent to the proposition

$$\text{Prob}\{N \text{ is F}\} \text{ is } \lambda \tag{6.17}$$

in which $p \triangleq N$ is F is interpreted as a fuzzy event (Zadeh, 1968). More specifically, let $p(u)du$ be the probability that $X \in [u, u+du]$, where $X \triangleq X(N)$. Then

$$\text{Prob}\{N \text{ is F}\} = \int_U p(u)\mu_F(u)du \tag{6.18}$$

and hence (6.17) implies that

$$\Pi_{\int_U p(u)\mu_F(u)du} = \lambda. \tag{6.19}$$

Equation (6.19) provides the basis for the following statement of the rule for probability qualification.

If

$$N \text{ is F} \to \Pi_X = F \tag{6.20}$$

then

$$N \text{ is F is } \lambda \to \Pi_{\int_U p(u)\mu_F(u)du} = \lambda \tag{6.21}$$

or more explicitly

$$\pi(p(\cdot)) = \mu_\lambda\left(\int_U p(u)\mu_F(u)du\right) \tag{6.22}$$

where $\pi(p(\cdot))$ is the possibility of the probability density function $p(\cdot)$.

As an illustration of (6.22), assume that

$$q \triangleq N \text{ is small is likely} \tag{6.23}$$

where LIKELY is defined by

$$\mu_{LIKELY}=(0\cdot7,0\cdot8,0\cdot9) \tag{6.24}$$

and SMALL is given by (6.13). Then

$$N \text{ is small is likely} \rightarrow \pi(p(\cdot)) = \int_0^\infty p(u)(1-S(u;5,10,15))du. \tag{6.25}$$

Note that in this case the proposition in question induces a possibility distribution of the probability density of $X \triangleq N$.

RULE FOR POSSIBILITY QUALIFICATION

Our concern here is with the translation of possibility-qualified propositions of the form

$$q \triangleq N \text{ is F is } \omega \tag{6.26}$$

where ω is a linguistic possibility-value such as *quite possible, very possible, almost impossible*, etc., with each such value representing a fuzzy subset of the unit interval.

By analogy with our interpretation of probability-qualified propositions, q may be interpreted as

$$N \text{ is F is } \omega \leftrightarrow \text{Poss}\{X \text{ is F}\} \text{ is } \omega \tag{6.27}$$

which implies that

$$\Pi_{\text{Poss}\{X \text{ is F}\}} = \omega. \tag{6.28}$$

Now suppose that we wish to find a fuzzy set G such that

$$N \text{ is F is } \omega \leftrightarrow N \text{ is } G. \tag{6.29}$$

Then, from the definition of possibility measure (2.9), we have

$$\text{Poss}\{N \text{ is F} | N \text{ is } G\} = \sup_u(\mu_F(u) \wedge \mu_G(u)) \tag{6.30}$$

and hence

$$N \text{ is F is } \omega \rightarrow \pi(\mu_G(\cdot)) = \mu_\omega\left(\sup_u(\mu_F(u) \wedge \mu_G(u))\right) \tag{6.31}$$

where μ_ω is the membership function of ω. Note that (6.31) is analogous to the translation rule for probability-qualified propositions (6.22).†

Although the interpretation expressed by (6.31) is consistent with (6.22), it is of interest to consider alternative interpretations which are not in the spirit of (6.28). One such interpretation which may be employed as a basis for possibility qualification is the following.

Assume that $\omega \triangleq 1$-possible (i.e. $\mu_\omega(v)=1$ for $v=1$ and $\mu_\omega(v)=0$ for $v \in [0,1)$), and let

$$p \triangleq N \text{ is F} \rightarrow \Pi_X = F. \tag{6.32}$$

†A more detailed discussion of this issue may be found in Zadeh (1977a).

Then

$$q \triangleq N \text{ is F is 1-possible} \rightarrow \Pi_X = G \qquad (6.33)$$

where G is a fuzzy set of Type 2† which has an interval-valued membership function defined by

$$\mu_G(u) = [\mu_F(u),1], \quad u \in U \qquad (6.34)$$

with the understanding that (6.34) implies that $\text{Poss}\{X=u\}$ may be any number in the interval $[\mu_F(u),1]$.

More generally, if $\omega \triangleq \alpha$-possible (i.e. $\mu_\omega(v)=\alpha$ for $v=1$ and $\mu_\omega(v)=0$ for $v \in [0,1)$), then

$$N \text{ is F is } \alpha\text{-possible} \rightarrow \Pi_X = G \qquad (6.35)$$

where G is a fuzzy set of Type 2 defined by

$$\mu_G(u) = [\alpha \wedge \mu_G(u), \alpha \oplus (1-\mu_F(u))], \quad u \in U \qquad (6.36)$$

and $\oplus$ denotes the bounded sum (see (4.43)). The rules expressed by (6.33) and (6.35) should be regarded as provisional in nature, since further experience in the use of possibility distributions may suggest other, more appropriate, interpretations of the concept of possibility qualification.

MODIFIER RULES FOR QUALIFIED PROPOSITIONS

As in the case of translation rules of Types I, II and III, the modifier rule for propositions may be applied to translation rules of Type IV to yield, among others, the negation rule for qualified propositions. In what follows, we shall restrict our attention to the application of this rule to truth-qualified propositions.

Specifically, on applying the modifier rule for propositions to (6.7), we obtain the following general form of strong semantic equivalence

$$m(N \text{ is F is } \tau) \leftrightarrow N \text{ is F is } m\tau \qquad (6.37)$$

which implies that

$$\text{not}(N \text{ is F is } \tau) \leftrightarrow N \text{ is F is not } \tau \qquad (6.38)$$

$$\text{very}(N \text{ is F is } \tau) \leftrightarrow N \text{ is F is very } \tau \qquad (6.39)$$

and

$$\text{more or less}(N \text{ is F is } \tau) \leftrightarrow N \text{ is F is more or less } \tau. \qquad (6.40)$$

On the other hand, from (6.7) it also follows that

$$N \text{ is not F is } \tau \leftrightarrow N \text{ is F is ant } \tau \qquad (6.41)$$

where ant τ is the antonym of τ. Thus, for example,

$$\text{false} \triangleq \text{ant true} \qquad (6.42)$$

†A fuzzy set F is of Type 2 if, for each $u \in U$, $\mu_F(u)$ is a fuzzy subset of Type 1, i.e. $\mu_{\mu_F(u)} : [0,1] \rightarrow [0,1]$.

i.e.

$$\mu_{FALSE}(v) = \mu_{TRUE}(1-v), \quad v \in [0,1] \tag{6.43}$$

where FALSE and TRUE are the fuzzy denotations of false and true, respectively. Similarly, from (6.7) it follows that

$$N \text{ is very } F \text{ is } \tau \leftrightarrow N \text{ is } F \text{ is } ^{0\cdot5}\tau \tag{6.44}$$

where the "left square-root" of τ is defined by

$$\mu_{0\cdot5\tau}(v) \triangleq \mu_\tau(v^2), \quad v \in [0,1] \tag{6.45}$$

and, more generally, for a "left-exponent" α,

$$\mu_{\alpha_\tau}(v) \triangleq u_\tau(v^{1/\alpha}), \quad v \in [0,1]. \tag{6.46}$$

On applying these rules in combination to a proposition such as "Barbara is not very rich," we are led to the following chain of semantically equivalent propositions:

Barbara is not very rich	(6.47)
Barbara is not very rich is u-true	(6.48)
Barbara is very rich is ant u-true	(6.49)
Barbara is rich is $^{0\cdot5}$(ant u-true)	(6.50)

where

$$\mu_{0\cdot5(\text{ant } u\text{-true})}(v) = 1 - v^2. \tag{6.51}$$

If *true* is assumed to be approximately semantically equivalent to *u-true*, the last proposition in the chain may be approximated by

$$\text{Barbara is rich is not very true.} \tag{6.52}$$

Thus, if we know that "Barbara is not very rich," then by using the chain of reasoning represented by (6.48), (6.49), (6.50) and (6.52), we can assert that an approximate answer to the question "Is Barbara rich?τ" is "not very true".

This example provides a very simple illustration of a combined use of the concepts of semantic equivalence and truth qualification for the purpose of deduction of an approximate answer to a given question, given a knowledge base consisting of a collection of fuzzy propositions. Additional illustrations relating to the application of PRUF to approximate reasoning may be found in Zadeh (1977*b*).

7. Examples of translation into PRUF

As was stated earlier, the translation rules formulated in the preceding sections are intended to serve as an aid to a human user in the translation of propositions (or descriptors) expressed in a natural language into PRUF. The use of the rules in question is illustrated by the following examples, with the understanding that, in general, in the translation of an expression, *e*, in a natural language into an expression, E, in PRUF,

E is a procedure whose form depends on the frame of the database and hence is not unique.

For convenience of the reader, the notation employed in the examples is summarized below.

In a translation $e \rightarrow E$, if w is a word in e then its correspondent, W, in E is the name of a relation in $\mathscr{D}$ (the database).

$F \triangleq$ fuzzy relation with membership function μ_F

$\Pi_X \triangleq$ possibility distribution of the variable X

$\pi_X \triangleq$ possibility distribution function of Π_X (or X) ((2.2 *et seq.*)

$F[\Pi_{X_{(s)}} = G] \triangleq$ fuzzy relation F which is particularized by the proposition "$X_{(s)}$ is G," where $X_{(s)}$ is a subvariable of the variable, X, associated with F (2.26)

$x_{i_1} \times \cdots \times x_{i_k} \ F \triangleq$ Proj F on $U_{i_1} \times \ldots \times U_{i_k}$, $U_{i_k} \triangleq U_{i_k}(X_{i_k})$ (2.23)

$F^2 \triangleq$ square of F (4.21)

$\sqrt{F} \triangleq$ square root of F (4.24)

$+ \triangleq$ union or arithmetic sum

$\vee \triangleq$ max

$\wedge \triangleq$ min

$' \triangleq$ complement (2.25)

$\cap \triangleq$ intersection (footnote on p. 407)

$\times \triangleq$ Cartesian product (footnote on p. 413)

$\oplus \triangleq$ bounded sum (4.43)

$\perp \triangleq$ unitor (2.15)

$\text{Count}(F) \triangleq$ Cardinality (power) of F (4.70)

$\text{Prop}(F) \triangleq \text{Count}(F)/$Cardinality of universe of discourse (4.75)

$\text{Prop}(F/G) \triangleq \text{Count}(F \cap G)/\text{Count}(G)$ (4.73)

$\text{Name}_i \triangleq$ Name of ith object in a population

$\text{Support}(F) \triangleq$ set of all points u in U for which $\mu_F(u) > 0$

$U(X) \triangleq$ universe of discourse associated with X

Example (a)

$$\text{Ed is 30 years old} \rightarrow \text{Age(Ed)} = 30 \tag{7.1}$$

$$\text{Ed is young} \rightarrow \Pi_{\text{Age(Ed)}} = \text{YOUNG} \tag{7.2}$$

$$\text{Ed is not very young} \rightarrow \Pi_{\text{Age(Ed)}} = (\text{YOUNG}^2)', \tag{7.3}$$

where the frame of YOUNG is

YOUNG	Age	μ

Alternatively,

$$\text{Ed is young} \rightarrow \text{ED}[\Pi_{\text{Age}} = \text{YOUNG}]. \tag{7.4}$$

Example (b)

$$\text{Sally is very intelligent} \rightarrow \Pi_X = \perp^2, \tag{7.5}$$

where

$$X \triangleq_\mu \text{INTELLIGENT}[\text{Name} = \text{Sally}] \tag{7.6}$$

(that is, X is the degree of intelligence of Sally in the table

INTELLIGENT	Name	μ

).

Note that (7.5) implies that

$$\pi(X) = X^2, \quad X \in [0,1]. \tag{7.7}$$

Example (c)

    Edith is tall and blonde $\rightarrow \Pi_{(\text{Height}(\text{Edith}), \text{Color}(\text{Hair}(\text{Edith})))} = \text{TALL} \times \text{BLONDE}$. (7.8)

Alternatively,

    Edith is tall and blonde $\rightarrow \text{EDITH}[\Pi_{\text{Height}} = \text{TALL}; \Pi_{\text{Color}(\text{Hair})} = \text{BLONDE}]$. (7.9)

Example (d)

$$A \ man \ is \ tall \rightarrow \Pi_{\text{Height}(X)} = \text{TALL} \tag{7.10}$$

where X is the name of the tallest man in the relation

POPULATION	Name	Height

.

Equivalently,

$$A \ man \ is \ tall \rightarrow \Pi_{\text{Height}(\text{Name}_1)} = \text{TALL}$$
$$\text{or } \Pi_{\text{Height}(\text{Name}_2)} = \text{TALL} \tag{7.11}$$
$$\ldots\ldots\ldots\ldots\ldots$$
$$\text{or } \Pi_{\text{Height}(\text{Name}_N)} = \text{TALL}$$

Example (e)

$$All \ men \ are \ tall \rightarrow \Pi_{\text{Height}(X)} = \text{TALL} \tag{7.12}$$

where X is the name of the shortest man in the relation

POPULATION	Name	Height

.

Equivalently,

$$All \ men \ are \ tall \rightarrow \Pi_{\text{Height}(\text{Name}_1)} = \text{TALL} \tag{7.13}$$
$$\ldots\ldots\ldots\ldots\ldots$$
$$\Pi_{\text{Height}(\text{Name}_N)} = \text{TALL}$$

Example (f)

$$Most \ men \ are \ tall. \tag{7.14}$$

Case 1. The frame of $\mathscr{D}$ is comprised of

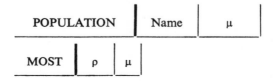

POPULATION	Name	μ

MOST	ρ	μ

where μ_i in POPULATION is the degree to which Name$_i$ is TALL, and μ_j in MOST is the degree to which ρ_j is compatible with MOST. Then

$$Most\ men\ are\ tall \rightarrow \Pi_{Prop(TALL)} = MOST \qquad (7.15)$$

where

$$Prop(TALL) = \frac{\sum_i{}_\mu POPULATION[Name = Name_i]}{Count(POPULATION)}. \qquad (7.16)$$

Case 2. The frame of $\mathscr{D}$ is comprised of

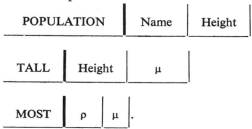

In this case, the translation is still expressed by (7.15), but with Prop(TALL) given by

$$Prop(TALL) = \frac{\sum_i{}_\mu TALL[Height = {}_{Height}POPULATION[Name = Name_i]]}{Count(POPULATION)}. \qquad (7.17)$$

Example (g)

$$Three\ tall\ men \rightarrow \mu(X) = Min_i\ \mu_i \quad for\ Name_i \in Support(X)\ and \qquad (7.18)$$
$$Count(Support(X)) = 3$$
$$= 0 \quad otherwise$$

where X is a fuzzy subset of

POPULATION	Name	μ

and μ_i is the degree to which Name$_i$ is tall. The left-hand member of (7.18) is a descriptor, while the right-hand member defines the membership function of a fuzzy subset of the fuzzy power set of $_{Name}$POPULATION (i.e. the set of all fuzzy subsets of the names of individuals in POPULATION).

More generally,

$$Several\ tall\ men \rightarrow \mu(X) = Min_i \mu_i \wedge \mu_{SEVERAL}(Count(Support(X))) \qquad (7.19)$$

where, as in (7.18), Min$_i$ is taken over all i such that Name$_i \in$ Support(X).

Example (h)

$$Expensive\ red\ car\ with\ big\ trunk \rightarrow \qquad (7.20)$$
$$CAR[\Pi_{Price} = EXPENSIVE;\ \Pi_{Color} = RED;\ \Pi_{Size(Trunk)} = BIG].$$

Example (*i*)
$$John\ loves\ Pat \rightarrow \Pi_X = \perp \qquad (7.21)$$
where
$$X \underset{\mu}{\triangleq} LOVES(Name1 = John;\ Name2 = Pat), \qquad (7.22)$$

with the right-hand member of (7.21) implying that

$$\pi(X) = X. \qquad (7.23)$$

It should be noted that in the special case where LOVES is a non-fuzzy relation, (7.21) reduces to the conventional predicate representation LOVES(John,Pat).

Example (*j*)
$$John\ loves\ someone \rightarrow \Pi_X = \perp \qquad (7.24)$$
where
$$\mu_i \underset{\mu}{\triangleq} LOVES[Name1 = John;\ Name2 = Name_i] \qquad (7.25)$$
$$\triangleq degree\ to\ which\ John\ loves\ Name_i$$
and
$$X \triangleq Max_i\ \mu_i. \qquad (7.26)$$

Note that when LOVES is a non-fuzzy relation, (7.24) reduces to $(\exists y)LOVES(John, y)$.

Example (*k*)
$$John\ loves\ everyone \rightarrow \Pi_X = \perp \qquad (7.27)$$
where
$$X \triangleq Min_i\ \mu_i \qquad (7.28)$$
and μ_i is expressed by (7.25).

Example (*l*)
$$Someone\ loves\ someone \rightarrow \Pi_X = \perp \qquad (7.29)$$
where
$$X = Max_{i,j}\ \mu_{ij} \qquad (7.30)$$
and μ_{ij} is expressed by

$$\mu_{ij} \underset{\mu}{\triangleq} LOVES[Name1 = Name_i;\ Name2 = Name_j]. \qquad (7.31)$$

Example (*m*)
$$Someone\ loves\ everyone \rightarrow \Pi_X = \perp \qquad (7.32)$$
where
$$X \triangleq Max_i\ Min_j\ \mu_{ij} \qquad (7.33)$$
and μ_{ij} is given by (7.31).

Example (*n*)
$$Jill\ has\ many\ friends \rightarrow \Pi_X = MANY \qquad (7.34)$$
where
$$X \triangleq Count(_{\mu \times Name2}FRIENDS(Name1 = Jill)). \qquad (7.35)$$

Note that the argument of Count is the fuzzy set of friends of Jill.

Example (o)

$$\text{The man near the door is young} \rightarrow \Pi_{\text{Age}(N)} = \text{YOUNG} \qquad (7.36)$$

where

$$N = \text{MAN} \cap_{\mu \times \text{Object1}} \text{NEAR}[\text{Object2} = \text{DOOR}]. \qquad (7.37)$$

Implicit in (7.37) is the assumption that the descriptor "The man near the door" identifies a man uniquely. The frame of MAN is

MAN	Name

Example (p)

$$\text{Kent was walking slowly toward the door} \rightarrow \text{WALKING}[\text{Name} = \text{Kent}; \qquad (7.38)$$
$$\Pi_{\text{Speed}} = \text{SLOW}; \ \Pi_{\text{Time}} = \text{PAST}; \ \Pi_{\text{Direction}} = \text{TOWARD}(\text{Object} = \text{DOOR})].$$

Example (q)

$$\text{Herta is not very tall is very true} \rightarrow \qquad (7.39)$$
$$\pi_{\text{Height}(\text{Herta})}(u) = \mu^2_{\text{TRUE}}(1 - \mu^2_{\text{TALL}}(u)), \quad u \in [0,200]$$

where the frames are

TRUE	v	μ

TALL	Height	μ

$v \in [0,1].$

Example (r)

$$\text{Carole is very intelligent is very likely.} \qquad (7.40)$$

Let

$$v \triangleq_{\mu} \text{INTELLIGENT}[\text{Name} = \text{Carole}] \qquad (7.41)$$

i.e. v is the degree to which Carole is intelligent, and the frame of INTELLIGENT is assumed to be

INTELLIGENT	Name	μ

Then (see (7.5))

$$\text{Carole is very intelligent} \rightarrow \Pi_v = \perp^2 \qquad (7.42)$$

in which the right-hand member is equivalent to

$$\pi(v) = v^2. \qquad (7.43)$$

Next, let

$$X = \int_0^1 p(v)v^2 \, dv \qquad (7.44)$$

where $p(v)dv$ is the probability that Carole's degree of intelligence falls in the interval $[v, v+dv]$. Then, using the translation rule for probability qualification, we obtain

(Carole is very intelligent) is very likely $\rightarrow \Pi_X = \text{LIKELY}^2$ (7.45)

in which the right-hand member is equivalent to

$$\pi(p(\cdot)) = \mu^2_{\text{LIKELY}}\left(\int_0^1 p(v)v^2 dv\right)$$ (7.46)

and the frame of LIKELY is

LIKELY	p	μ

$p \in [0,1]$. Expressed in this form, the translation defines a possibility distribution of the probability density function $p(\cdot)$.

Example (s)

X is small is very true is likely $\rightarrow$

$$\pi(p(\cdot)) = \mu_{\text{LIKELY}}\left(\int_0^\infty p(u)\mu^2_{\text{TRUE}}(\mu_{\text{SMALL}}(u))du\right)$$ (7.47)

where $U \triangleq [0,\infty)$ and $p(u)du \triangleq \text{Prob}\{X \in [u, u+du]\}$. As in the previous example, (7.47) defines a possibility distribution of the probability density function of X.

Example (t)

Men who are much taller than most men $\rightarrow$ F   (7.48)

where the fuzzy subset F of POPULATION is computed by the following procedure. (For simplicity, the procedure is stated in plain English.)
   Assume that the frame of $\mathscr{D}$ is comprised of:

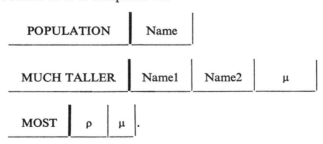

1. Compute
    $F_i \triangleq _{\mu \times \text{Name2}}\text{MUCH TALLER}[\text{Name1} = \text{Name}_i]$
       $\triangleq$ fuzzy set of men in relation to whom Name_i is much taller.

2. Compute the relative cardinality of F_i, i.e.

$$\text{Prop}(F_i) = \frac{\text{Count}(F_i)}{\text{Count}(\text{POPULATION})}.$$ (7.49)

3. Compute
$$\delta_i \triangleq \mu_{\text{MOST}}(\text{Prop}(F_i))$$ (7.50)
$\triangleq$ degree to which Name$_i$ is much taller than most men.

4. The fuzzy set of men who are much taller than most men is given by
$$F = \delta_1/\text{Name}_1 + \ldots + \delta_N/\text{Name}_N$$ (7.51)

where $+$ denotes the union and $\text{Name}_1, \ldots, \text{Name}_N$ are the elements of U(Name) in POPULATION. Alternatively, assume that the frame of $\mathscr{D}$ is comprised of:

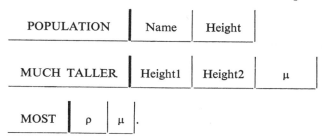

POPULATION	Name	Height	

MUCH TALLER	Height1	Height2	μ

MOST	ρ	μ

In this case, the procedure assumes the following form.
1. Compute
$$h_i \triangleq \text{Height}(\text{Name}_i) = \ _{\text{Height}}\text{POPULATION}[\text{Name}=\text{Name}_i].$$ (7.52)
2. Compute
$$\gamma_{ij} = \text{MUCH TALLER}[\text{Height1}=h_i; \text{Height2}=h_j]$$ (7.53)
$\triangleq$ degree to which Name$_i$ is much taller than Name$_j$.
3. Compute the fuzzy set
$$F_i = \gamma_{i1}/\text{Name}_1 + \ldots + \gamma_{iN}/\text{Name}_N$$ (7.54)
$\triangleq$ fuzzy set of men in relation to whom Name$_i$ is much taller.
4. Same as Step 3 in previous procedure.
5. Same as Step 4 in previous procedure.

Example (u)
$$\textit{Many men are much taller than most men} \to \pi(\text{POPULATION}) = \mu_G$$ (7.55)

where μ_G is computed by the following procedure.
Assume that the frame of $\mathscr{D}$ is comprised of

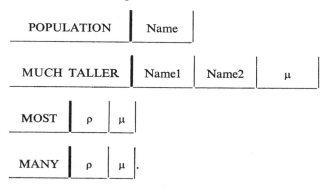

POPULATION	Name		

MUCH TALLER	Name1	Name2	μ

MOST	ρ	μ

MANY	ρ	μ

1. Compute F as in Example (t).
2. Compute
   $\gamma = \text{Prop}(F)$
   $\triangleq$ Proportion of men who are much taller than most men.
3. The possibility of the relation POPULATION is given by

$$\pi(\text{POPULATION}) = {}_{\mu}\text{MANY}[\rho = \gamma] \qquad (7.56)$$

in which the right-hand member defines μ_G.

Example (v)

> *Beth gave several big apples to each of her close friends* $\rightarrow \pi(\text{GAVE}) = \mu_G$. (7.57)

The following procedure computes μ_G on the assumption that the frame of $\mathscr{D}$ is comprised of:

GAVE	Giver	Receiver	Object

BIG	Object	μ

FRIEND	Name1	Name2	μ

SEVERAL	ρ	μ

1. Compute
   $G_i \triangleq {}_{\text{Object}}\text{GAVE}[\text{Giver} = \text{Beth}; \text{Receiver} = \text{Name}_i]$ (7.58)
   $\triangleq$ Set of objects received from Beth by Name_i.
2. Compute
   $H = \text{BIG}[\text{Object} = \text{APPLE}]$ (7.59)
   $\triangleq$ fuzzy set of big apples.
3. Compute
   $K = G_i \cap H$ (7.60)
   $\triangleq$ fuzzy set of big apples received from Beth by Name_i.
4. Compute
   $\gamma_i = {}_{\mu}\text{SEVERAL}[\rho = \text{Count}(K)]$ (7.61)
   $\triangleq$ degree to which Name_i received several big apples from Beth.
5. Compute
   $\delta_i = {}_{\mu}\text{FRIEND}^2[\text{Name1} = \text{Beth}; \text{Name2} = \text{Name}_i]$ (7.62)
   $\triangle$ degree to which Name_i is a close friend of Beth.
6. Compute
   $\sigma_i \triangleq 1 \wedge (1 - \delta_i + \gamma_i)$ (7.63)
   $\triangleq$ degree to which (If Name_i is a close friend of Beth then Name_i received several big apples from Beth).

7. Compute

$$\pi(\text{GAVE}) \triangleq \text{Min}_i \, \sigma_i \qquad (7.64)$$

$\triangleq$ degree to which all close friends of Beth received from her several big apples.

It should be noted that when the translation of a proposition, p, into PRUF requires the execution of a procedure, P, which cannot be expressed as a relatively simple expression in PRUF—as is true of Examples (t), (u) and (v)—the relationship between p and P ceases to be transparent. A higher degree of transparency in cases of this type may be achieved through the introduction into PRUF of higher-level constructions relating to quantification, qualification, particularization and definition. This and other issues concerning the translation of more complex propositions than those considered here will be treated in subsequent papers.

8. Concluding remarks

In essence, PRUF may be regarded as a relation-manipulating language which serves the purposes of (a) precisiation of expressions in a natural language; (b) exhibiting their logical structure; and (c) providing a system for the characterization of the meaning of a proposition by a procedure which acts on a collection of fuzzy relations in a database and returns a possibility distribution.

By serving these purposes, PRUF provides a basis for a formalization of approximate reasoning. More specifically, through the use of PRUF, a set of imprecise premises expressed in a natural or synthetic language may be translated into possibility distributions to which the rules of inference in FL (or PRUF) may be applied, yielding other possibility distributions which upon retranslation lead to approximate consequents of the original premises. In this respect, PRUF plays the same role in relation to fuzzy premises and fuzzy conclusions that predicate calculus does in relation to non-fuzzy premises and non-fuzzy conclusions.

An important aspect of PRUF is a concomitant of its break with the long-standing tradition in logic, linguistics and philosophy of language—the tradition of employing the concept of truth as a foundation for theories of meaning. By adopting instead the concept of a possibility distribution as its point of departure, PRUF permits a uniform treatment of truth-qualification, probability-qualification and possibility-qualification of fuzzy propositions and thereby clarifies the roles played by the concepts of truth, probability and possibility not only in logic and language theory, but also in information analysis, decision analysis and related application areas.

As was stated in the Introduction, our exposition of PRUF in the preceding sections is neither definitive nor complete. There are many issues that remain to be explored, the most complex of which is that of automatic translation from a natural language into PRUF. However, to view this issue in a proper perspective, it must be recognized that the existing systems for automatic translation from a small subset of a natural language into a meaning representation language (and especially, a query language) have very narrow versatility since they are limited in their use to highly restricted domains of semantic discourse and human concept comprehension.

Although PRUF is still in its initial stages of development, its somewhat unconventional conceptual framework puts into a different perspective many of the long-standing issues in language theory and knowledge representation, expecially those pertaining to vagueness, uncertainty and inference from fuzzy propositions. By so doing, PRUF points a way toward the conception of question-answering systems having the capability to act on imprecise, incomplete or unreliable information which is resident in a database. To implement such systems, however, we shall need (a) a better system of linguistic modifiers than those that are available in natural languages, and (b) special-purpose hardware that is oriented toward the storage and manipulation of fuzzy rather than non-fuzzy data.

I wish to thank Barbara Cerny, Christian Freksa and Lucia Vaina for reading the manuscript and offering helpful criticisms. I also wish to acknowledge stimulating discussions with Zoltan Domotor, Brian Gaines, Ellen Hisdal, Hung Nguyen, Paul Kay, Elie Sanchez, Pat Suppes and Hans Zimmermann on various issues related to those considered in this paper. This research was supported by National Science Foundation Grant MCS77–07568 and Naval Electronic Systems Command Contract N00039–77–C–0022.

References

AIZERMAN, M. A. (1976). Fuzzy sets, fuzzy proofs and certain unsolved problems in the theory of automatic control. *Avtomatika i Telemehanika*, 171–177.

ANDERSON, J. & BOWER, G. (1973). *Human Associative Memory*. Washington, D.C.: Winston.

BALLMER, T. T. (1976). Fuzzy punctuation or the continuum of grammaticality. *Electronics Research Laboratory Memo M-590*. University of California, Berkeley.

BAR-HILLEL, Y. (1964). *Language and Information*. Reading, Mass.: Addison-Wesley.

BELLINGER, D. (1972). *Degree Words*. The Hague: Mouton.

BELLMAN, R. E. & GIERTZ, M. (1973). On the analytic formalism of the theory of fuzzy sets. *Information Sciences*, **5**, 149–156.

BELLMAN, R. E. & ZADEH, L. A. (1976). Local and fuzzy logics. *Electronics Research Laboratory Memorandum M-584*. University of California, Berkeley. In EPSTEIN, G., Ed., *Modern Uses of Multiple-Valued Logic*. Dordrecht: D. Reidel, pp. 103–165.

BEZDEK, J. D. & DUNN, J. C. (1975). Optimal fuzzy partitions: a heuristic for estimating the parameters in a mixture of normal distributions. *IEEE Transactions on Computers*, **C-24**, 835–838.

BIERWISCH, M. (1970). Semantics. In LYONS, J., Ed., *New Horizons in Linguistics*. Baltimore: Penguin.

BISS, K., CHIEN, K. & STAHL, F. (1971). R2—a natural language question–answering system. *Proceedings of the Fall Joint Computer Conference*, **38**, 303–308.

BLACK, M. (1963). Reasoning with loose concepts. *Dialogue*, **2**, 1–12.

BOBROW, D. G. (1977). A panel on knowledge representation. *Proceedings of the Fifth International Conference on Artificial Intelligence*, M.I.T., Cambridge, Mass., pp. 983–992.

BOBROW, D. & COLLINS, A., Eds (1975). *Representation and Understanding*. New York: Academic Press.

BOBROW, D. G. & WINOGRAD, T. (1977). An overview of KRL, a knowledge representation language. *Cognitive Science*, **1**, 3–46.

BOYCE, R. F., CHAMBERLIN, D. D., KING, W. F. III & HAMMER, M. M. (1974). Specifying queries as relational expressions. In KLIMBIE, J. W. & KOFFEMAN, K. L., Eds, *Data Base Management*. Amsterdam: North-Holland, pp. 169–176.

BRACCHI, G., FEDELI, A. & PAOLINI, P. (1972). A multilevel relational model for data base management systems. In KLIMBIE, J. W. & KOFFEMAN, K. L., Eds, *Data Base Management*. Amsterdam: North-Holland, pp. 211–223.

BRACHMAN, R. J. (1977). What's in a concept: structural foundations for semantic networks. *International Journal of Man–Machine Studies*, **9**, 127–152.

BRIABRIN, V. M. & POSPELOV, D. A. (1977). DILOS—Dialog system for information retrieval, computation and logical inference. In MICHIE, D., Ed., *Machine Intelligence*, **19**. New York: American Elsevier.

BRIABRIN, V. M. & SENIN, G. V. (1977). Natural language processing within a restricted context. *Proceedings of the International Workshop on Natural Language for Interactions with Data Bases*, IIASA, Vienna.

CARBONELL, J. R. & COLLINS, A. M. (1973). Natural semantics in artificial intelligence. *Proceedings of the Third Joint Conference on Artificial Intelligence*, Stanford University, Stanford, pp. 344–351.

CARLSTROM, I. F. (1975). Truth and entailment for a vague quantifier. *Synthese*, **30**, 461–495.

CARNAP, R. (1937). *The Logical Syntax of Language*. New York: Harcourt, Brace & World.

CHAMBERLIN, D. D. & BOYCE, R. F. (1974). SEQUEL: a structured English query language. *Proceedings of the ACM SIGMOD Workshop on Data Description, Access and Control*, pp. 249–264.

CHANG, C. L. (1975). Interpretation and execution of fuzzy programs. In ZADEH, L. A. *et al.* (1975), op. cit., pp. 191–218.

CHANG, C. L. (1976). DEDUCE—a deductive query language for relational data bases. In CHEN, C. H., Ed., *Pattern Recognition and Artificial Intelligence*. New York: Academic Press pp. 108–134.

CHANG, S. K. & KE, J. S. (1976). Database skeleton and its application to fuzzy query translation. Dept of Information Engineering, University of Illinois, Chicago, Illinois.

CHANG, S. S. L. (1972). Fuzzy mathematics, man and his environment. *IEEE Transactions on Systems, Man and Cybernetics*, **SMC-2**, 92–93.

CHARNIAK, E. (1972). Toward a model of children's story comprehension. *AITR-266*. Artificial Intelligence Laboratory, M.I.T., Cambridge, Mass.

CHARNIAK, E. (1973). Context and the reference problem. In RUSTIN, R. (1973), op. cit.

CHARNIAK, E. (1975). Organization and inference in a frame-like system of common sense knowledge. In SCHANK, R. & NASH-WEBBER, B. L., Eds, *Theoretical Issues in Natural Language Processing*. Cambridge.

CHOMSKY, N. (1957). *Syntactic Structures*. The Hague: Mouton.

CHOMSKY, N. (1965). *Aspects of the Theory of Syntax*. Cambridge, Mass.: M.I.T. Press.

CHOMSKY, N. (1971). Deep structure, surface structure, and semantic interpretation. In STEINBERG, D. D. & JAKOBOVITS, L. A., Eds, *Semantics: An Interdisciplinary Reader in Philosophy, Linguistics and Psychology*. Cambridge: Cambridge University Press.

CLIFF, N. (1959). Adverbs as multipliers. *Psychology Review*, **66**, 27–44.

CODD, E. F. (1971). A data base sublanguage founded on the relational calculus. *Proceedings of the ACM SIGFIDET Workshop on Data Description, Access and Control*, pp. 35–68.

CODD, E. F. (1974). Seven steps to rendezvous with the casual user. In KLIMBIE, J. W. & KOFFEMAN, K. L., Eds, *Data Base Managemment*. Amsterdam: North-Holland, pp. 179–199.

CRESSWELL, M. J. (1973). *Logics and Languages*. London: Methuen.

DAMERAU, F. J. (1975). On fuzzy adjectives. *Memorandum RC 5340*. IBM Research Laboratory, Yorktown Heights, N.Y.

DAVIDSON, D. (1964). The method of extension and intension. In SCHILPP, Ed., *The Philosophy of Rudolf Carnap*. La Salle, Illinois: Open Court, pp. 311–350.

DAVIDSON, D. (1967). Truth and meaning. *Synthese*, **17**, 304–323.

DEFINETTI, B. (1974). *Probability Theory*. New York: Wiley.

DELUCA, A. & TERMINI, S. (1972a). A definition of a non-probabilistic entropy in the setting of fuzzy sets theory. *Information and Control*, **20**, 301–312.

DELUCA, A. & TERMINI, S. (1972b). Algebraic properties of fuzzy sets. *Journal of Mathematical Analysis and Applications*, **40**, 373–386.

DIMITROV, V. D. (1975). Efficient governing hymanistic systems by fuzzy instructions. *Third International Congress of General Systems and Cybernetics*, Bucarest.

DREYFUSS, G. R., KOCHEN, M., ROBINSON, J. & BADRE, A. N. (1975). On the psycholinguistic reality of fuzzy sets. In GROSSMAN, R. E., SAN, L. J. & VANCE, T. J., Eds, *Functionalism*. Chicago, Illinois: University of Chicago Press.

DUDA, R. O., HART, P. E., NILSSON, N. & SUTHERLAND, G. L. (1977). Semantic network representations in rule-based inference systems. *Technical Note 136*. Artificial Intelligence Center, Stanford Research Institute, Menlo Park, Calif. In WATERMAN, D. A. & HAYES-ROTH, F., Eds, *Pattern-directed Inference Systems*. New York: Academic Press, to appear.

EVANS, G. & McDOWELL, J. (1976). *Truth and Meaning*. Oxford: Clarendon Press.

FELLINGER, W. L. (1974). Specifications for a fuzzy systems modelling language. Ph.D. thesis. Oregon State University, Corvallis.

FILLMORE, C. J. (1968). The case for case. In BACH, E. & HARMS, R. T., Eds, *Universals in Linguistic Theory*. New York: Holt, Rinehart & Winston.

FINE, K. (1975). Vagueness, truth and logic. *Synthese*, **30**, 265–300.

FODOR, J. A. (1975). *The Language of Thought*. New York: Crowell.

FODOR, J. A. & KATZ, J. J., Eds (1964). *The Structure of Language: Readings in the Philosophy of Language*. Englewood Cliffs, N.J.: Prentice-Hall.

FREDERIKSEN, C. (1975). Representing logical and semantic structure of knowledge acquired from discourse. *Cognitive Psychology*, **7**, 371–458.

GAINES, B. R. (1976*a*). General fuzzy logics. *Proceedings of the Third European Meeting on Cybernetics and Systems Research*, Vienna.

GAINES, B. R. (1976*b*). Foundations of fuzzy reasoning. *International Journal of Man–Machine Studies*, **6**, 623–668.

GAINES, B. R. & KOHOUT, L. J. (1975). Possible automata. *Proceedings of International Symposium on Multiple-Valued Logic*, Bloomington, Indiana, pp. 183–196.

GAINES, B. R. & KOHOUT, L. J. (1977). The fuzzy decade: a bibliography of fuzzy systems and closely related topics. *International Journal of Man–Machine Studies*, **9**, 1–68.

GILES, R. (1976). Łukasiewicz logic and fuzzy set theory. *International Journal of Man–Machine Studies*, **8**, 313–327.

GOGUEN, J. A. (1969). The logic of inexact concepts. *Synthese*, **19**, 325–373.

GOGUEN, J. A. (1974). Concept representation in natural and artificial languages: axioms, extension and applications for fuzzy sets. *International Journal of Man–Machine Studies*, **6**, 513–561.

GOLDSTEIN, I. & PAPERT, S. (1977). Artificial intelligence, language and the study of knowledge. *Cognitive Science*, **1**, 84–123.

GOTTINGER, H. W. (1973). Toward a fuzzy reasoning in the behavioral science. *Cybernetica*, **2**, 113–135.

GREENWOOD, D. (1957). *Truth and Meaning*. New York: Philosophical Library.

GRICE, H. P. (1968). Utterer's meaning, sentence-meaning and word-meaning. *Foundations of Language*, **4**, 225–242.

HAACK, S. (1974). *Deviant Logic*. Cambridge: Cambridge University Press.

HAACK, S. (1976). The pragmatist theory of truth. *British Journal of the Philosophy of Science*, **27**, 231–249.

HAMACHER, H. (1976). On logical connectives of fuzzy statements and their affiliated truth functions. *Proceedings of the Third European Meeting on Cybernetics and Systems Research*, Vienna.

HARRIS, J. I. (1974*a*). Fuzzy implication—comments on a paper by Zadeh. DOAE Research Working Paper, Ministry of Defence, Byfleet, Surrey, U.K.

HARRIS, J. I. (1974*b*). Fuzzy sets: how to be imprecise precisely. DOAE Research Working Paper, Ministry of Defense, Byfleet, Surrey, U.K.

HELD, G. D. & STONEBRAKER, M. R. (1975). Storage structures and access methods in the relational data base management system INGRES. *Proceedings of ACM Pacific Meeting* 1975, pp. 26–33.

HELD, G. D., STONEBRAKER, M. R. & WONG, E. (1975). INGRES—a relational data base system. *Proceedings AFIPS-National Computer Conference*, **44**, 409–416.

HENDRIX, G. G. (1975). Expanding the utility of semantic networks through partitioning. *Advance Papers of the Fourth International Joint Conference on Artificial Intelligence Tbilisi, 1975*, pp. 115–121.

HENDRIX, G. G. (1977). The LIFER manual. *Technical Note 138*. Stanford Research Institute, Menlo Park, California.

HENDRIX, G. G., THOMPSON, C. W. & SLOCUM, J. (1973). Language processing via canonical verbs and semantics models. *Proceedings of the Third Joint International Conference on Artificial Intelligence*, Stanford, pp. 262–269.

HERSH, H. M. & CARAMAZZA, A. (1976). A fuzzy set approach to modifiers and vagueness in natural language. *Journal of Experimental Psychology*, **105**, 254–276.

HINTIKKA, J. (1967). Individuals, possible worlds and epistemic logic, *Nous*, **1**, 33–62.

HUGHES, G. E. & CRESSWELL, M. J. (1968). *An Introduction to Modal Logic*. London: Methuen.

INAGAKI, Y. & FUKUMURA, F. (1975). On the description of fuzzy meaning of context-free language. In ZADEH, L. A. *et al.* (1975), op. cit., pp. 301–328.

JACOBSON, R., Ed. (1961). *On the Structure of Language and Its Mathematical Aspects.* Providence, R.I.: American Mathematical Society.

JOSHI, A. K. & ROSENSCHEIN, S. J. (1976). Some problems of inferencing: relation of inferencing to decomposition of predicates. *Proceedings of International Conference on Computational Linguistics*, Ottawa, Canada.

JOUAULT, J. P. & LUAN, P. M. (1975). Application des concepts flous a la programmation en languages quasi-naturels. Inst. Inf. d'Entreprise, C.N.A.M., Paris.

KAMPÉ DE FERIET, J. (1977). Mesure de l'information fournie par un évenement. In PICARD, C. F., Ed., *Structures de l'Information*. Paris: Centre National de la Recherche Scientifique, University of Pierre and Marie Curie, pp. 1–30.

KAMPÉ DE FERIET, J. & FORTE, B. (1967). Information et probabilité. *Comptes Rendus, Academy of Sciences (Paris)*, **265A**, 142–146, 350–353.

KATZ, J. J. (1964). Analyticity and contradiction in natural language. In FODOR, J. A. & KATZ, J. J. (1964), op. cit.

KATZ, J. J. (1966). *The Philosophy of Language*. New York: Harper & Row.

KATZ, J. J. (1967). Recent issues in semantic theory. *Foundations of Language*, **3**, 124–194.

KAUFMANN, A. (1973). *Introduction to the Theory of Fuzzy Subsets, Vol. 1, Elements of Basic Theory*. Paris: Masson and Co. English translation. New York: Academic Press.

KAUFMANN, A. (1975a). *Introduction to the Theory of Fuzzy Subsets, Vol. 2. Applications to Linguistics, Logic and Semantics*. Paris: Masson and Co.

KAUFMANN, A. (1975b). *Introduction to the Theory of Fuzzy Subsets, Vol. 3. Applications to Classification and Pattern Recognition, Automata and Systems and Choice of Criteria*. Paris: Masson and Co.

KAY, P. (1975). A model-theoretic approach to folk taxonomy. *Social Science Information*, **14**, 151–166.

KELLOGG, C. H., BURGER, J., DILLER, T. & FOGT, K. (1971). The CONVERSE natural language data management system: current status and plans. *Proceedings of ACM Symposium on Information Storage and Retrieval*, University of Maryland, College Park, pp. 33–46.

KHATCHADOURIAN, H. (1965). Vagueness, meaning and absurdity. *American Philosophical Quarterly*, **2**, 119–129.

KLEIN, S. (1973). Automatic inference of semantic deep structure rules in generative semantic grammars. *Technical Report No. 180*. Computer Science Department, University of Wisconsin, Madison.

KLING, R. (1974). Fuzzy PLANNER: reasoning with inexact concepts in a procedural problem-solving language. *Journal of Cybernetics*, **4**, 105–122.

KNEALE, W. C. (1972). Propositions and truth in natural languages. *Mind*, **81**, 225–243.

KNUTH, D. E. (1968). Semantics of context-free languages. *Mathematical Systems Theory*, **2**, 127–145.

KOCHEN, M. & BADRE, A. N. (1974). On the precision of adjectives which denote fuzzy sets. *Journal of Cybernetics*, **4**, 49–59.

KRIPKE, S. (1963). Semantical analysis of modal logic I. *Zeitschrift für Mathematische Logik und Grundlagen der Mathematik*, **9**, 67–96.

KRIPKE, S. (1971). Naming and necessity. In DAVIDSON, D. & HARMAN, G., Eds, *Semantics of Natural Languages*. Dordrecht, Holland: D. Reidel.

KUHNS, J. L. (1967). Answering questions by computer. *Memorandum RM-5428-PR*. Rand Corporation, Santa Monica, California.

LABOV, W. (1973). The boundaries of words and their meanings. In BAILEY, C.-J. N. & SHUY, R. W., Eds, *New Ways of Analyzing Variation in English, Vol. 1*. Washington: Georgetown University Press.

LAKOFF, G. (1971). Linguistics and natural logic. In DAVIDSON, D. & HARDMAN, G., Eds, *Semantics of Natural Languages*. Dordrecht, Holland: D. Reidel.

LAKOFF, G. (1973a). Hedges: a study in meaning criteria and the logic of fuzzy concepts. *Journal of Philosophical Logic*, **2**, 458–508. In HOCKNEY, D., HARPER, W. & FREED, B., Eds, *Contemporary Research in Philosophical Logic and Linguistic Semantics*. Dordrecht, Holland: D. Riedel, pp. 221–271.

LAKOFF, G. (1973b). Fuzzy grammar and the performance/competence terminology game. *Proceedings of Meeting of Chicago Linguistics Society*, pp. 271–291.

LAMBERT, K. & VAN FRAASSEN, B. C. (1970). Meaning relations, possible objects and possible worlds. *Philosophical Problems in Logic*, 1–19.

LEE, E. T. (1972). Fuzzy languages and their relation to automata. *Ph.D. thesis*. Department of Electrical Engineering and Computer Sciences, University of California, Berkeley.

LEE, E. T. & CHANG, C. L. (1971). Some properties of fuzzy logic. *Information and Control*, **19**, 417–431.

LEE, E. T. & ZADEH, L. A. (1969). Note on fuzzy languages. *Information Sciences*, **1**, 421–434.

LEFAIVRE, R. A. (1974a). FUZZY: a programming language for fuzzy problem solving. *Technical Report 202*. Department of Computer Science, University of Wisconsin, Madison.

LEFAIVRE, R. A. (1974b). The representation of fuzzy knowledge. *Journal of Cybernetics*, **4**, 57–66.

LEHNERT, W. (1977). Human and computational question answering. *Cognitive Science*, **1**, 47–73.

LEWIS, D. K. (1970). General semantics. *Synthese*, **22**, 18–67.

LEWIS, P. M., ROSENKRANTZ, D. J. & STEARNS, R. E. (1974). Attributed translations. *Journal of Computer and System Sciences*, **9**, 279–307.

LINSKY, L. (1971). *Reference and Modality*. London: Oxford University Press.

LUCAS, P. *et al.* (1968). Method and notation for the formal definition of programming languages. *Report TR 25.087*. IBM Laboratory, Vienna.

LYNDON, R. C. (1966). *Notes on Logic*. New York: D. Van Nostrand.

LYONS, J. (1968). *Introduction to Theoretical Linguistics*. Cambridge: Cambridge University Press.

MACHINA, K. F. (1972). Vague predicates. *American Philosophical Quarterly*, **9**, 225–233.

MAMDANI, E. H. (1976). Advances in the linguistic synthesis of fuzzy controllers. *International Journal of Man–Machine Studies*, **8**, 669–678.

MAMDANI, E. H. & ASSILIAN, S. (1975). An experiment in linguistic synthesis with a fuzzy logic controller. *International Journal of Man–Machine Studies*, **7**, 1–13.

MARINOS, P. N. (1969). Fuzzy logic and its application to switching systems. *IEEE Transactions on Electronic Computers*, **EC-18**, 343–348.

MARTIN, W. A. (1973). Translation of English into MAPL using Winograd's syntax, state transition networks, and a semantic case grammar. *M.I.T. APG Internal Memo 11*. Project MAC, M.I.T., Cambridge, Mass.

MCCARTHY, J. & HAYES, P. (1969). Some philosophical problems from the standpoint of artificial intelligence. In MICHIE, D. & MELTZER, B., Eds, *Machine Intelligence 4*. Edinburgh University Press, pp. 463–502.

MCDERMOTT, D. V. (1974). Assimilation of new information by a natural language-understanding system. *AI TR-291*. M.I.T.

MESEGUER, J. & SOLS, I. (1975). Fuzzy semantics in higher order logic and universal algebra. University of Zaragoza, Spain.

MILLER, G. A. & JOHNSON-LAIRD, P. N. (1976). *Language and Perception*. Cambridge: Harvard University Press.

MINSKY, M. (1975). A framework for representing knowledge. In WINSTON, P., Ed., *The Psychology of Computer Vision*. New York: McGraw-Hill.

MISHELEVICH, D. J. (1971). MEANINGEX—a computer-based semantic parse approach to the analysis of meaning. *Proceedings of Fall Joint Computer Conference*, **39**, 271–280.

MIZUMOTO, M., UMANO, M. & TANAKA, K. (1977). Implementation of a fuzzy-set-theoretic data structure system. *Third International Conference on Very Large Data Bases*, Tokyo, Japan, 6–8 October 1977. *ACM Transactions on Data Base Systems*, to appear.

MIZUMOTO, M. & TANAKA, K. (1976). Algebraic properties of fuzzy numbers. *Proceedings of the International Conference on Cybernetics and Society*, Washington, D.C., pp. 559–563.

MOISIL, G. C. (1975). Lectures on the logic of fuzzy reasoning. *Scientific Editions*. Bucarest.

MONTAGUE, R. (1974). *Formal Philosophy (Selected Papers)*. New Haven: Yale University Press.

MONTGOMERY, C. A. (1972). Is natural language an unnatural query language? *Proceedings of ACM National Conference*, New York, pp. 1075–1078.

MOORE, J. & NEWELL, A. (1973). How can MERLIN understand? In GREGG, L., Ed., *Knowledge and Cognition*. Hillsdale, N.J.: Lawrence Erlbaum Associates.

MYLOUPOULOS, J., BORGIDA, A., COHEN, P., ROUSSOPOULOS, N., TSOTSOS, J. & WONG, H. (1976). TORUS: a step towards bridging the gap between data bases and the casual user. *Information Systems*, **2**, 49–64.

MYLOUPOULOS, J., SCHUSTER, S. A. & TSICHRITZIS, D. C. (1975). A multi-level relational system. *Proceedings of AFIPS-National Computer Conference*, **44**, 403–408.

NAGAO, M. & TSUJII, J.-I. (1977). Programs for natural language processing. *Information Processing Society of Japan*, **18**(1), 63–75.

NAHMIAS, S. (1976). Fuzzy variables. *Technical Report 33*. Department of Industrial Engineering, Systems Management Engineering and Operations Research, University of Pittsburgh.

NALIMOV, V. V. (1974). *Probabilistic Model of Language*. Moscow: Moscow State University.

NASH-WEBBER, B. (1975). The role of semantics in automatic speech understanding. In BOBROW, D. G. & COLLINS, A. M. (1975), op. cit., pp. 351–383.

NEGOITA, C. V. & RALESCU, D. A. (1975). *Applications of Fuzzy Sets to Systems Analysis*. Basel, Stuttgart: Birkhauser Verlag.

NEWELL, A. & SIMON, H. A. (1972). *Human Problem Solving*. Englewood Cliffs, N.J.: Prentice-Hall.

NGUYEN, H. T. (1976a). On fuzziness and linguistic probabilities. *Memorandum M-595*. Electronics Research Laboratory, University of California, Berkeley.

NGUYEN, H. T. (1976b). A note on the extension principle for fuzzy sets. *Memorandum M-611*. Electronics Research Laboratory, University of California, Berkeley.

NOGUCHI, K., UMANO, M., MIZUMOTO, M. & TANAKA, K. (1976). Implementation of fuzzy artificial intelligence language FLOU. *Technical Report on Automation and Language of IECE*.

NORMAN, D. A., RUMELHART, D. E. & LNR RESEARCH GROUP. *Explorations in Cognition*. San Francisco: W. H. Freeman.

PAL, S. K. & MAJUMDAR, D. D. (1977). Fuzzy sets and decision-making approaches in vowel and speaker recognition. *IEEE Transactions on Systems, Man and Cybernetics*, **SMC-7**, 625–629.

PARSONS, C. (1974). Informal axiomatization, formalization and the concept of truth. *Synthese*, **27**, 27–47.

PARTEE, B. (1976a). Possible world semantics and linguistic theory. Department of Linguistics, University of Massachusetts, Amherst. *Monist*, to appear.

PARTEE, B. (1976b). *Montague Grammar*. New York: Academic Press.

PARTEE, B. (1977). Montague grammar, mental representations and reality. *Proceedings of the Symposium on Philosophy and Grammar*, University of Uppsala, Uppsala, Sweden, to appear.

PETRICK, S. R. (1973). Semantic interpretation in the REQUEST system. *IBM Research Report RC4457*. IBM Research Center, Yorktown Heights, New York.

PROCYK, T. J. (1976). Linguistic representation of fuzzy variables. Fuzzy Logic Working Group, Queen Mary College, London, U.K.

PUTNAM, H. (1975). The meaning of "meaning." In GUNDERSON, K., Ed., *Language, Mind and Knowledge*. Minneapolis, Minn.: University of Minnesota Press.

PUTNAM, H. (1976). *Meaning and Truth*. Sherman Lectures, University College, London, U.K.

PYOTROVSKII, R. G., BEKTAYEV, K. B. & PYOTROVSKAYA, A. A. (1977). *Mathematical Linguistics*. Moscow: Higher Education Press.

QUILLIAN, M. R. (1968). Semantic memory. In MINSKY, M., Ed., *Semantic Information Processing*. Cambridge: M.I.T. Press.

QUINE, W. V. (1970a). *Philosophy of Logic*. Englewood Cliffs, N.J.: Prentice-Hall.

QUINE, W. V. (1970b). Methodological reflections on current linguistic theory. *Synthese*, **21**, 387–398.

RESCHER, N. (1969). *Many-Valued Logic*. New York: McGraw-Hill.

RESCHER, N. (1973). *The Coherence Theory of Truth*. Oxford: Oxford University Press.

RESCHER, N. (1975). *Theory of Possibility*. Pittsburgh: University of Pittsburgh Press.

RIEGER, B. (1976). Fuzzy structural semantics. *Proceedings of Third European Meeting on Cybernetics and Systems Research*, Vienna.

RIEGER, C. (1976). An organization of knowledge for problem solving and language comprehension. *Artificial Intelligence*, **7**, 89–127.

RÖDDER, W. (1975). On "and" and "or" connectives in fuzzy set theory. Institute for Operations Research, Technical University of Aachen.

ROSCH, E. (1973). On the internal structure of perceptual and semantic categories. In MOORE, T. M., Ed., *Cognitive Development and the Acquisition of Language*. New York: Academic Press.

ROSCH, E. (1975). Cognitive representations of semantic categories. *Journal of Experimental Psychology: General*, **104**, 192–233.

ROSS, J. R. (1970). A note on implicit comparatives. *Linguistic Inquiry*, **1**, 363–366.

ROUSSOPOULOS, N. D. (1976). A semantic network model of data bases. Department of Computer Science, University of Toronto, Canada.

RUSTIN, R., Ed. (1973). *Courant Computer Science Symposium 8: Natural Language Processing*. New York: Algorithmics Press.

SAGER, N. (1977). Natural language analysis and processing. In BELZER, J., HOLZMAN, A. G. & KENT, A., Eds. New York: Marcel Dekker, to appear.

SANCHEZ, E. (1974). Fuzzy relations. Faculty of Medicine, University of Marseille, France.

SANCHEZ, E. (1977). On possibility qualification in natural languages. *Electronics Research Laboratory Memorandum M77/28*. University of California, Berkeley.

SANDEWALL, E. (1970). Formal methods in the design of question-answering systems. *Report No. 28*. Uppsala University, Sweden.

SANFORD, D. H. (1975). Borderline logic. *American Philosophical Quarterly*, **12**, 29–39.

SANTOS, E. (1970). Fuzzy algorithms. *Information and Control*, **17**, 326–339.

SCHANK, R. C. (1973). Identification of conceptualizations underlying natural language. In SCHANK, R. & COLBY, K., Eds, *Computer Models of Thought and Language*. Englewood Cliffs, N.J.: Prentice-Hall.

SCHANK, R. C., Ed. (1975). *Conceptual Information Processing*. Amsterdam: North-Holland.

SCHOTCH, P. K. (1975). Fuzzy modal logic. *Proceedings of International Symposium on Multiple-Valued Logic*. University of Indiana, Bloomington, pp. 176–182.

SCHUBERT, L. K. (1972). Extending the expressive power of semantic networks. *Artificial Intelligence*, **2**, 163–198.

SEARLE, J., Ed. (1971). *The Philosophy of Language*. Oxford: Oxford University Press.

SHAUMJAN, S. K. (1965). *Structural Linguistics*. Moscow: Nauka.

SHIMURA, M. (1975). An approach to pattern recognition and associative memories using fuzzy logic. In ZADEH, L. A. *et al.* (1975), op. cit., pp. 449–476.

SHORTLIFFE, E. (1976). *MYCIN: Computer-based Medical Consultations*. New York: American Elsevier.

SHORTLIFFE, E. H. & BUCHANAN, B. G. (1975). A model of inexact reasoning in medicine. *Mathematical Biosciences*, **23**, 351–379.

SIMMONS, R. F. (1973). Semantic networks, their computation and use for understanding English sentences. In SCHANK, R. & COLBY, K., Eds, *Computer Models of Thought and Language*. Englewood Cliffs, N.J.: Prentice-Hall, pp. 63–113.

SIMON, H. A. (1973). The structure of ill structured problems. *Artificial Intelligence*, **4**, 181–201.

SIMON, H. A. & SIKLOSSY, L. (1972). *Representation and Meaning: Experiments with Information Processing Systems*. Englewood Cliffs, N.J.: Prentice-Hall.

SIY, P. & CHEN, C. S. (1974). Fuzzy logic for handwritten numerical character recognition. *IEEE Transactions on Systems, Man and Cybernetics*, **SMC-4**, 570–575.

SLOMAN, A. (1971). Interactions between philosophy and artificial intelligence: the role of intuition and non-logical reasoning in intelligence. *Artificial Intelligence*, **2**, 209–225.

SRIDHARAN, M. J. (1976). A frame-based system for reasoning about actions. *Technical Report CBM-TM-56*. Department of Computer Science, Rutgers University, New Brunswick, N.J.

STAAL, J. F. (1969). Formal logic and natural languages. *Foundations of Language*, **5**, 256–284.

STALNAKER, R. (1970). Probability and conditionals. *Philosophical Science*, **37**, 64–80.

STITCH, S. P. (1975). Logical form and natural language. *Philosophical Studies*, **28**, 397–418.

STONEBRAKER, M. R., WONG E. & KREPS, P. (1976). The design and implementation of INGRES. *ACM Transactions on Database Systems*, **1**, 189–222.

SUGENO, M. (1974). Theory of fuzzy integrals and its applications. *Ph.D. thesis*. Tokyo Institute of Technology, Japan.

SUGENO, M. & TERANO, T. (1977). A model of learning based on fuzzy information. *Kybernetes*, **6**, 157–166.

SUPPES, P. (1974a). The axiomatic method in the empirical sciences. In HENKIN, J., Ed., *Proceedings of the Tarski Symposium*. Rhode Island: American Mathematical Society.

SUPPES, P. (1974b). Probabilistic metaphysics. *Filofiska Studier nr. 22*. Uppsala University, Sweden.

SUPPES, P. (1976). Elimination of quantifiers in the semantics of natural languages by use of extended relation algebras. *Revue Internationale de Philosophie*, **117–118**, 243–259.

SUSSMAN, G. (1973). *A Computational Model of Skill Acquisition*. Amsterdam: North-Holland.

TAMURA, S. & TANAKA, K. (1973). Learning of fuzzy formal language. *IEEE Transactions on Systems, Man and Cybernetics*, **SMC-3**, 98–102.

TARSKI, A. (1956). *Logic, Semantics, Metamathmatics*. Oxford: Clarendon Press.

TERANO, T. & SUGENO, M. (1975). Conditional fuzzy measures and their applications. In ZADEH, L. A. *et al.* (1975), op.cit., pp. 151–170.

THOMPSON, F. P., LOCKEMANN, P. C., DOSTERT, B. H. & DEVERILL, R. (1969). REL: a rapidly extensible language system. *Proceedings of the 24th ACM National Conference*, New York, pp. 399–417.

THORNE, J. P., BRATLEY, P. & DEWAR, H. (1968). The syntactic analysis of English by machine. In MICHIE, D., Ed., *Machine Intelligence 3*. New York: American Elsevier.

ULLMANN, S. (1962). *Semantics: An Introduction to the Science of Meaning*. Oxford: Blackwell.

URAGAMI, M., MIZUMOTO, M. & TANAKA, K. (1976). Fuzzy robot controls. *Journal of Cybernetics*, **6**, 39–64.

VAN FRAASSEN, B. C. (1971). *Formal Semantics and Logic*. New York: Macmillan.

WALTZ, D. L. (1977). Natural language interfaces. *SIGART Newsletter*, **61**, 16–65.

WASON, P. C. & JOHNSON-LAIRD, P. N. (1972). *Psychology of Reasoning: Structure and Content*. Cambridge, Mass.: Harvard University Press.

WECHSLER, H. (1975). Applications of fuzzy logic to medical diagnosis. *Proceedings of International Symposium on Multiple-valued Logic*, University of Indiana, Bloomington, pp. 162–174.

WEGNER, P. (1972). The Vienna definition language. *ACM Computing Surveys*, **4**, 5–63.

WENSTØP, F. (1975). Application of linguistic variables in the analysis of organizations. *Ph.D. thesis*. School of Business Administration, University of California, Berkeley.

WENSTØP, F. (1976). Deductive verbal models of organizations. *International Journal of Man–Machine Studies*, **8**, 293–311.

WHEELER, S. C. (1975). Reference and vagueness. *Synthese*, **30**, 367–380.

WILKS, Y. (1974). Natural language understanding systems within the AI paradigm. *SAIL Memo AIM-237*. Stanford University.

WINOGRAD, T. (1972). *Understanding Natural Language*. New York: Academic Press.

WINSTON, P. (1975). Learning structural descriptions from examples. In WINSTON, P., Ed., *The Psychology of Computer Vision*. New York: McGraw-Hill.

WOODS, W. A. (1973). Progress in natural language understanding—an application to lunar geology. *Proceedings AFIPS-National Computer Conference*, **42**, 441–450.

WOODS, W. A. (1975). What is in a link: foundations for semantic networks. In BOBROW, D. B. & COLLINS, A. (1975), op. cit., pp. 35–82.

WOODS, W. A., KAPLAN, R. M. & NASH-WEBBER, B. (1972). The lunar sciences natural language information system. Cambridge, Mass.: Bolt, Beranek & Newman.

WRIGHT, C. (1975). On the coherence of vague predicates. *Synthese*, **30**, 325–365.

ZADEH, L. A. (1966). Shadows of fuzzy sets. *Probl. Transmission Inf.* (in Russian), **2**, 37–44.
ZADEH, L. A. (1968a). Probability measures of fuzzy events. *Journal of Mathematical Analysis and Applications*, **23**, 421–427.
ZADEH, L. A. (1968b). Fuzzy algorithms. *Information and Control*, **12**, 94–102.
ZADEH, L. A. (1971a). Similarity relations and fuzzy orderings. *Information Sciences*, **3**, 177–200.
ZADEH, L. A. (1971b). Quantitative fuzzy semantics. *Information Sciences*, **3**, 159–176.
ZADEH, L. A. (1972a). A fuzzy-set-theoretic interpretation of linguistic hedges. *Journal of Cybernetics*, **2**, 4–34.
ZADEH, L. A. (1972b). Fuzzy languages and their relation to human and machine intelligence. *Proceedings of International Conference on Man and Computer*, Bordeaux, France, pp. 130–165. Basel: S. Karger.
ZADEH, L. A. (1973). Outline of a new approach to the analysis of complex systems and decision processes. *IEEE Transactions on Systems, Man and Cybernetics*, **SMC-3**, 28–44.
ZADEH, L. A. (1975a). Fuzzy logic and approximate reasoning (in memory of Grigore Moisil). *Synthese*, **30**, 407–428.
ZADEH, L. A. (1975b). Calculus of fuzzy restrictions. In ZADEH, L. A. *et al.* (1975), op. cit., pp. 1–39.
ZADEH, L. A. (1975c). The concept of a linguistic variable and its application to approximate reasoning, Part I. *Information Sciences*, **8**, 199–249; Part II, *Information Sciences*, **8**, 301–357; Part III, *Information Sciences*, **9**, 43–80.
ZADEH, L. A. (1976a). A fuzzy-algorithmic approach to the definition of complex or imprecise concepts. *International Journal of Man–Machine Studies*, **8**, 249–291.
ZADEH, L. A. (1976b). Fuzzy sets and their application to pattern classification and cluster analysis. *Memorandum M-607*. Electronics Research Laboratory, University of California, Berkeley. In VAN RYZIN, J., Ed., *Classification and Clustering*. New York: Academic Press, pp. 251–299.
ZADEH, L. A. (1977a). Fuzzy sets as a basis for a theory of possibility. *Memorandum M77/12*. Electronics Research Laboratory, University of California, Berkeley. In *Fuzzy Sets and Systems*, **1**, 3–28.
ZADEH, L. A. (1977b). A theory of approximate reasoning. *Memorandum M77/58*. Electronics Research Laboratory, University of California, Berkeley.
ZADEH, L. A., FU, K. S., TANAKA, K. & SHIMURA,. M. (1975). *Fuzzy Sets and Their Application to Cognitive and Decision Processes*. New York: Academic Press.
ZIMMERMANN, H. J. (1974). Optimization in fuzzy environments. Institute for Operations Research, Technical University of Aachen.
ZIMMERMANN, H. J. (1978). Fuzzy programming and linear programming with several objective functions. *Fuzzy Sets and Systems*, **1**, 45–56.

Concept Representation in Natural and Artificial Languages: Axioms, Extensions and Applications for Fuzzy Sets

Joseph A. Goguen, Jr.*

Computer Science Department, University of California at Los Angeles, California, U.S.A., and
Naropa Institute, Boulder, Colorado, U.S.A.

(*Received 11 July 1973*)

This paper reports research related to mathematics, philosophy, computer science and linguistics. It gives a system of axioms for a relatively simple form of fuzzy set theory, and uses these axioms to consider the accuracy of representing concepts in various ways by fuzzy sets. By-products of this approach include a number of new operations and laws for fuzzy sets, parallel to those for ordinary sets, and a demonstration that all the basic operations are intrinsically determined. In addition, the paper explores both hierarchical and algorithmic extensions of fuzzy sets, and then applications to problems in natural language semantics and combinatorics. Finally, the paper returns to the problem of representing concepts, and discusses some implications for artificial intelligence.

1. The Problem of Foundations for Fuzzy Set Theory

The large and rapidly growing literature on fuzzy sets (almost one hundred papers at the time of this writing) with its very diverse applications [complexity (Tsichritzis, 1969), control theory (Zadeh, 1965b), linguistics (Lee & Zadeh, 1969), information (Zadeh, 1968b), logic (Goguen, 1968), pattern recognition (Zadeh, 1968a), philosophy (Goguen, 1969b), switching theory (Marinos, 1969), automata (Mizumoto, Toyoda & Tanaka, 1969), algorithms (Zadeh, 1968a), learning (Wee & Fu, 1969), topology (Goguen), systems (Zadeh, 1969), artificial intelligence (Goguen, 1972), and especially natural language semantics (Goguen, 1969b; Reddy, 1972)] suggests that some careful attention to foundations would be valuable, particularly since the basic definitions have been attacked, for example, by Watanabe (1969):

*Written while the author was a Research Fellow in the Mathematical Sciences at IBM Thomas J. Watson Research Center, Yorktown Heights, New York, U.S.A., on leave from the Committee on Information Sciences, University of Chicago, Chicago, Illinois.

67

Zadeh's theory of fuzzy set . . . . uses from the beginning the notions of set conjunction, disjunction, etc., as if they were already known to us. His determination of the values at the membership function for conjunction and disjunction is arbitrary.

Moreover, our look at foundations reveals a number of useful new operations (e.g. product, image, inverse image, and exponential) parallel to the corresponding basic operations in ordinary set theory; shows that these operations satisfy many of the same basic laws as in ordinary set theory; and opens up new applications to combinatorics and language theory by various extensions the notion of fuzzy set (see sections 6 and 7). The applications to language are particularly interesting as a bridge between linguistics, philosophy, artificial intelligence, computer science, and mathematics (see section 8).

It is not immediately obvious how to construct a foundation for fuzzy set theory which meets Watanabe's criticism. Zadeh's (1965a, 1965b) first papers give the impression of distinguishing between a fuzzy set A and its "grade of membership" μ_A, an assignment of truth values in the unit interval [0,1] to points. Operations on fuzzy sets, such as union, are defined directly from these membership functions, e.g. by

$$\mu_{A \cup B}(x) = \max \{\mu_A(x), \mu_B(x)\},$$

which does not make it explicitly clear that such definitions are intrinsically natural. Any appearance of a lack of rigor is easily dispelled by defining a fuzzy set to be a function $A : X \rightarrow [0,1]$ either directly as in Goguen (1967), or indirectly as a set of ordered pairs $<x, \mu_A(x)>$ as in Zadeh (1971). This clearly embeds fuzzy set theory into any ordinary set theory, and thus into ordinary rigorous mathematics. It also has some additional advantages: The "universe of discourse" X of A is made explicit, and need not be fixed (Goguen, 1967, 1969b); and the possibility of replacing [0,1] by some more general structure V, such as a completely distributive lattice, a "closg" (Goguen, 1967), or a semiring (Arbib, 1970), becomes more attractive. But the set operations do not appear very much less arbitrary.

Ideally we would like a foundation for fuzzy sets which is independent of ordinary set theory, which justifies the intuitive identification of fuzzy sets with (inexact) concepts, and in which the familiar set operations are uniquely and inevitably determined. These desires are clearly though not explicitly expressed in Zadeh (1965a), and they are all satisfied by the system given in this paper.

Attempts to give axioms parallel to those of some standard system of set theory such as Zermello–Fraenkel (Schoenfield, 1967), do not seem promising.

One might allow assertions such as "$x \varepsilon A$" to be infinite valued (in the set [0,1]), so that the metalanguage would be infinite valued; or one might axiomatize the class of functions $A : X \to V$, say by using a ternary two-valued "degree" relation $D(A, x, v)$, true iff $A(x) = v$, as in Chapin (1971). The difficulty with such systems is in showing categoricity, i.e. that their only model is in fact the universe of fuzzy sets. As far as I know, this has not been done for any other axiomatization so far announced, but it is a main result for the system of this paper.

If it is unpromising to generalize standard set theories, what unusual set theories might be promising? Perhaps the original von Neumann (1961) axioms; but we have actually used as a paradigm Lawvere's (1964) relatively unknown axiomatization of sets in the language of category theory. This approach has a number of advantages: (1) In contrast to ordinary axiom systems for ordinary sets, which cannot be categorical,[1] and are not even known to be consistent, we show categoricity, and use in our proof only such ordinary mathematics as any foundation for mathematics must be expected to support.[2] (2) We characterize not only the class of fuzzy sets, but the category of fuzzy sets, which also includes the "morphisms" or transformations of the sets. (3) The axioms can be thought of as asserting the existence, but not the form, of certain basic constructions on fuzzy sets; however, the form of these constructions is uniquely determined in the context of a standard model for the axioms, and this serves to justify Zadeh's definitions of union, etc. (see section 4). (4) A number of basic laws interrelating the various set operations follow automatically from their mere existence as categorical constructions. (5) In fact, looking for categorical constructions yields a number of new basic operations for fuzzy sets (such as product and exponential), which can be expected to be just as important in this theory as their analogues are for ordinary sets. (6) And finally, the axioms are all plausible assertions about concepts, so that categoricity of the axioms plus the fact that fuzzy sets satisfy them gives an equivalence of concepts and fuzzy sets and thus justifies the representation of concepts by fuzzy sets.

1 "Categorical" in the model-theoretic sense means uniquely determined (up to isomorphism) by the axioms. Zermello–Fraenkel and related systems use only first order axioms, and therefore by the Lowenhein–Skolem theorem have models of all (infinite) cardinalities, including countable models. One speaks of "nonstandard" models in this connection, and clearly does not have categoricity (Schoenfield, 1967).

2 For example, everything we do can be formalized in Gödel–Bernays set theory, in the general style of MacLane (1971). There are also several other embeddings of category theory into standard axiomatic systems, but this does not concern us. This approach does not guarantee consistency, but it entitles us to feel that our system is about as secure as the rest of ordinary mathematics; in any case, our system will not collapse if some particular foundation happens to be inconsistent.

It may surprise the reader not familiar with both standard and categorical foundations, that we can do things for fuzzy sets which cannot be done for ordinary sets with ordinary set theory.[3] This comes from the special appropriateness of categorical methods for foundational problems with fuzzy sets. Since a category is an abstract embodiment of a structure, axioms on categories are conditions on the types of structure which can be embodied. For example, we can assume our category C has unions without assuming anything about the form of these unions. Indeed, not all types of structure admit unions in their categories, and among those which do we see a wide variety of forms. I do not know of any way to make such "formless existence assumptions" except through the sort of structural characterization of operations given by category theory. We will show that when a sufficient number of such structural assumptions are imposed on C, it must essentially be the category of fuzzy sets. A category is itself an algebraic object, and theorems that a certain algebra is characterized by certain axioms, are not unfamiliar in mathematics. For example, there are several axiomatic characterizations of the real number system.

There are other uses for our axioms. Using the argument that concepts satisfy the axioms and therefore can be represented by fuzzy sets, we can prove things about concepts from things about fuzzy sets. For example, any laws satisfied by the operations on fuzzy sets (such as commutativity for union) transfer to the algebra of concepts (in this case, to commutativity for the disjunction of concepts).

Section 6 here discusses extended notions of fuzzy sets, some of which are particularly appropriate for applications to the semantics of natural language (see also Goguen, 1969b and Reddy, 1972). The algorithmic or programming approach toward fuzzy hierarchical structures in subsection 6(2) is not only practically oriented, but is also particularly relevant to the philosophical discussion of the nature of concepts given later. Section 7 considers extensions of fuzzy sets appropriate to "multisets" and related combinatorial topics, and in particular aspects of the theory of formal (i.e. artificial) languages. Finally, section 8 discusses the relationship of these matters to the field called "artificial intelligence", as well as to practical reasoning with inexact concepts.

This paper assumes some familiarity with categorical algebra. However, sufficient material for following our general meaning is contained in the

3 This refers to proving categoricity. Actually, the sense in which we prove categoricity is as an "equivalence" of categories, rather than an isomorphism. Equivalence is the proper notion of structural identity for most category-theoretic purposes. One advantage it has over the model-theoretic categoricity is in not requiring equal cardinality for equivalent categories. See definition 3.

Appendix (section 9) along with references to more detailed works. The paper is technically self-contained as far as fuzzy sets are concerned; but some previous exposure will be helpful for motivation. We include a fairly complete bibliography (up to about 1972).

The reader is warned that foundational questions necessarily involve some philosophizing. Moreover, many issues taken for granted in ordinary set theory have to be discussed anew here, and from an unfamiliar viewpoint. Because these matters are perhaps less easily reconstructed by the reader, and to shorten the text, we have given them more emphasis than the technical mathematical proofs.

We write "iff" as an abbreviation for "if and only if". The results (propositions, theorems, etc.) are numbered sequentially throughout the paper; and so are the major definitions, but separately from the results.

The reader might want to skim or even skip section 3, which contains the most technical categorical material. He might also want to look over the Appendix before reading the rest of the paper, and then consult it as he proceeds. The most esoteric matters have been confined to footnotes.

2. Fuzzy Sets

Definition 1. Let V be a partially ordered set (hereafter abbreviated *poset*). Then a *V-set* is a function $A : X \to V$ from a set X to V. X is called the *carrier* or *universe* of A, and V is called the *truth set* of A. $A(x)$ is the degree of membership of the point x in the V-set A.

This degree of membership may take various partially ordered values intermediate to "in" and "out". The classical truth set for fuzzy sets is the unit interval $[0,1]$; see Zadeh (1965a) and Chang (1963). For the most part, we shall consider Vs which are completely distributive lattices (abbreviated cdls), i.e. complete lattices satisfying the complete distributive laws,

$$a \wedge \vee_i b_i = \vee_i (a \wedge b_i) \text{ and } a \vee \wedge_i b_i = \wedge_i (a \vee b_i),$$

for all a, $b_i \varepsilon V$ with $i \varepsilon I$, an arbitrary index set. We will see that complete distributivity is needed to obtain many (though not all) desirable properties of fuzzy sets.

The fuzzy set "structure" is an assignment of a value in V to each point in an underlying set X. This can be visualized in the "graph" of the assignment, the subset $\{<x,v> | x \varepsilon X, f(x) = v\}$ of the product $X \times V$. A transformation of the underlying set (or carrier) aspect of fuzzy set structure is of course a set mapping of the carriers. So if $A : X \to V$ and $B : Y \to V$ are V-sets, a morphism $A \to B$ should have an underlying set mapping $f : X \to Y$. This function will preserve the order structure iff the induced map $f \times V : X \times V \to Y \times V$

(mapping $<x,v>$ to $<f(x),v>$) takes A into B; that is, iff whenever $<x,a>$ is in the graph of A, the induced point $<f(x),b>$ has lower value than the corresponding point $<f(x),b>$ in the graph of B; i.e. iff $A(x){\leqslant}B(f(x))$ for all $x\varepsilon X$. Let us state this basic concept formally.

Definition 2. A *morphism* $A{\rightarrow}B$ of *V*-sets $A : X{\rightarrow}V$ and $B : Y{\rightarrow}V$ is a triple $<A,f,B>$, where $f : X{\rightarrow}Y$ is a function such that $A(x){\leqslant}B(f(x))$ for all $x\varepsilon X$.

It is easily verified that this gives rise to a category **Set**(V) *of V*-sets, using ordinary composition of functions.[4] As with the category **Set** of ordinary sets (see the Appendix), one formally defines a morphism as a triple, so that its domain A and codomain B come with it; but one writes $f : A{\rightarrow}B$, or $A\xrightarrow{f}B$, or even just f, rather than $<A,f,B>$.

If V is the one point poset **1**, then *V*-sets are[5] just ordinary sets and their morphisms are just ordinary set mappings; i.e. **Set(1)** $=$ **Set**. If V is the two point simply ordered poset $\mathbf{2} = \{0,1\}$ with $0{<}1$, then *V*-sets are[5] "pairs of sets" as used in topology (i.e. a set and a subset) and *V*-set morphisms are set maps which take the domain subset into the codomain subset, again as in topology. Setting $V = \mathbf{3} = \{0,1,2\}$, $0{<}1{<}2$, gives "triples of sets" (i.e. a set, a subset, and a subsubset) with the appropriate subset preserving morphisms, again as in topology. In general, a *V*-set can be thought of as a set with a family of subsets, and a *V*-set morphism as a map of the sets which preserves the ordering of the families of subsets; one might then call a *V*-set a "*V*-tuple of sets". The case $V = [0,1]$ gives a "continuous chain of subsets". If $A : X{\rightarrow}V$ is a *V*-set and $v\varepsilon V$, let $A_v = \{x\varepsilon X | A(x){\leqslant}v\}$, the "$v$-level set" of A. Also let $B : Y{\rightarrow}V$. Then $F : X{\rightarrow}Y$ is a *V*-set morphism $A{\rightarrow}B$ iff $f(A_v) \subseteq B_v$ for all $v\varepsilon V$, where $f(A_v) = \{f(x) | x\varepsilon A_v\}$ is the set image of A_v under f.

In summary, for many interesting special examples of *V*-sets, the natural morphisms agree with our definition 2; and the intuitive idea behind these examples allows us to visualize *V*-sets for any V so that the structure preserving mappings are clearly as given in definition 2. Getting the correct notion of morphism is essential for getting the right category of fuzzy sets, and this is important to us because it is the entire category **Set**(V) which we characterize.

As a further check on the definition of morphism for *V*-sets, let us see

---

4 We can assume the objects and maps in **Set**(V) are from within some ordinary set theory, such as Gödel–Bernays, if we want to be formal here. See also footnote 2, and the sentence to which it is attached.

5 Actually, **Set(1)** and **Set** are isomorphic but unequal categories. However, in the present philosophical context, such a close relationship can be considered tantamount to equality. Similarly for **Set(2)** and pairs of sets.

whether sub-V-sets, in the categorical sense, have a reasonable form. In general, a "subobject" of an object A in a category C is an equivalence class of monics with codomain A, where $m_i : A_i \to A$, for $i = 1,2$, are equivalent[6] iff there are $f : A_1 \to A_2$ and $g : A_2 \to A_1$ such that $m_2 f = m_1$ and $m_1 g = m_2$. Denote the class of all subjects of A by $\underline{P}(A)$, the (generalized) power poset[7] of A, $\underline{P}(A)$ is partially ordered by the extension to equivalence classes of the relation: $m_1 \leqslant m_2$ iff there is an $f : A_1 \to A_2$ such that $m_2 f = m_1$. We sometimes loosely write $A_1 \leqslant A_2$. Note f is unique if it exists.

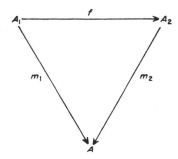

Proposition 1. A V-set morphism $f : A_1 \to A$ is monic iff the underlying set map $f : X_1 \to X$ is monic. Moreover $\underline{P}(A)$ is (isomorphic to) the set of all $A_1 : X_1 \to V$ where the carrier X_1 of A_1 is a subset of X and $A_1(x) \leqslant A(x)$ for all $x \varepsilon X_1$.

This corresponds exactly to the notion of subset given earlier in Goguen (1969b) for J-sets, and in Zadeh (1969a) for $X_1 = X$. If $L = 1$, it gives the usual notion of subset, and if $L = 2$ or 3 the appropriate notion of subpair or subtriple.

3. Axioms for Fuzzy Sets

This section states the axioms which will be shown (in section 4) to hold for $\mathbf{Set}(V)$. Of course, these axioms actually characterize $\mathbf{Set}(V)$. Although we rely on the Appendix for the basic formal categorical terminology, for the reader's convenience much is also defined here in the context where it arises. Section 5 interprets the axioms for the category of concepts. The axioms are stated for a fixed but arbitrary category C, in the usual style of axiomatic systems.

6 It follows that f,g are mutually inverse isomorphisms, and that this really is an equivalence relation (Mitchell, 1965; Goguen, 1973a).

7 If the category C is not sufficiently well-behaved, some $\underline{P}(A)$ might actually be partially ordered "classes" (in the sense of Gödel–Bernays set theory) rather than sets; but this is of little importance to us in this paper.

Axiom 1. **C** has initial and terminal objects, denoted $\varnothing$ and T respectively.

In a category with an initial object $\varnothing$, every object A has a least subobject, namely the unique morphism $\varnothing \to A$; thus each $\underline{P}(A)$ has a least element, which we also denote $\varnothing$.

A category **C** *has images*, iff each morphism $f : A \to B$ factors as qi through a (unique) smallest subobject $f(A) \overset{i}{\hookrightarrow} B$, of B, called the *image* of f, and often denoted $f(A)$ for short. If A_1 is a subobject of A, $f(A_1)$ denotes the image of the composite $A_1 \to A \overset{f}{\to} B$; and we say **C** has *associative images* iff given $A \overset{f}{\to} B$ and $B \overset{g}{\to} C$, we have $g(f(A)) = (fg)(A)$, noting that $f(A)$ is a subobject of B.

Axiom 2. **C** has associative images.

We say a category **C** is *cdl-ordered* iff for each object A in **C**, $\underline{P}(A)$ is a cdl. Least upper and greatest lower bounds in $\underline{P}(A)$ are called *unions* and *intersections* of subobjects of A, as is entirely natural, and the usual notations $\cup$ and $\cap$ are used.[8] Any cdl L is *pseudo-complemented*, with *pseudo-complement* given by $a' = \bigvee \{x \mid x \wedge a = \varnothing\}$, for $a \varepsilon L$ and $\varnothing$ the minimum element. An atom in a poset is an element $a \neq \varnothing$ such that $\varnothing \leqslant b \leqslant a$ implies $b = \varnothing$ or $b = a$. We say that a cdl L is *disjointed* iff for each pair a, b of unequal atoms in L, $a' \vee b' = T$, the maximum element. A category is *disjointedly cdl-ordered* iff each $\underline{P}(A)$ is a disjointed cdl.

Axiom 3. **C** is disjointedly cdl-ordered.

Notice that the assertion that each $\underline{P}(A)$ in **C** has (lattice theoretic) unions and intersections says nothing whatsoever about the form which they have, say in terms of formulae for particular representations for subobjects.

A collection $A_i \to A$, $i \varepsilon I$, of subobjects in a category with initial object $\varnothing$ is called *disjoint* iff $A_i \cap A_j = \varnothing$ for all distinct $i, j \varepsilon I$. We say a category has *disjoint unions* iff each disjoint collection of subobjects has a union.

A *co-product* in **C** of objects A_i (called *summands*) for each $i \varepsilon I$, if it exists, is an object A in **C**, denoted $\underline{\amalg}_{i \varepsilon I} A_i$, together with morphisms $j_i : A_i \to A$, called *injections*, such that given morphisms $k_i : A_i \to B$ in **C** for each $i \varepsilon I$. there is a unique morphism $m : A \to B$ such that $j_i m = k_i$ for all $i \varepsilon I$. A binary coproduct of A_1 and A_2 will be written $A_1 + A_2$.

Axiom 4. **C** has coproducts which are disjoint unions; and conversely, each disjoint union in **C** is the coproduct of its summands.

8 There is actually a "universal" sense of unions and intersections of subobjects in a category, which is strictly stronger than the "lattice theoretic" sense we have given in the text; see Mitchell (1965) for the definitions. Usually the two agree; and certainly in our case they do. Our axioms refer only to the lattice theoretic sense, but some proofs use the (easily established) fact that these also satisfy the "universal" definitions.

An object P in a category $\mathbf{C}$ is *monic* iff each morphism $P \rightarrow A$ in $\mathbf{C}$ is monic; P is called *atomic monic* iff P is monic, each subobject, $P \rightarrow A$ in $\underline{P}(A)$ is atomic, and for $A \neq \varnothing$, there is always at least one morphism $P \rightarrow A$. An object P is a *generator* in $\mathbf{C}$ iff whenever $f, g : A \rightarrow B$ are unequal morphisms in $\mathbf{C}$, there is a morphism $m : P \rightarrow A$ such that $mf \neq mg;$ and we say P is *projective* iff for each epic $f : A \rightarrow B$ and morphism $m : P \rightarrow B$, there is a morphism $m' : P \rightarrow A$ such that $m'f = m$.

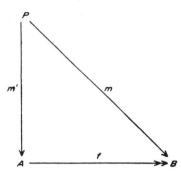

Axiom 5. $\mathbf{C}$ has an atomic monic projective generator P.

Our final axiom asserts a form of nontriviality.

Axiom 6. $P + P$ is not isomorphic to P in $\mathbf{C}$.

Without this axiom, it would have been possible to have a one object category $|\mathbf{C}| = \{P\}$ satisfying the axioms.

We are now able to assert that these axioms really are entirely satisfactory. The main result uses the following notion of "essential sameness".

Definition 3. Categories $\mathbf{C}$ and $\mathbf{D}$ are *equivalent* iff there is a functor $F : \mathbf{C} \rightarrow \mathbf{D}$ such that for each pair C, C' of objects in $\mathbf{C}$, the restriction $F_{C,C'}$ of F to $\mathbf{C}[C, C']$ is a (set) isomorphism to $\mathbf{D}[FC, FC']$; and for each object D in $\mathbf{D}$, there is some C in $\mathbf{C}$ such that $F(C)$ is isomorphic to D (more briefly, iff there is an $F : \mathbf{C} \rightarrow \mathbf{D}$ which is faithful, full, and representative).

Intuitively, equivalence means $\mathbf{C}$ and $\mathbf{D}$ differ only in the numbers of isomorphic copies of the objects they have.

Theorem 2. Any category $\mathbf{C}$ satisfying the above six axioms is equivalent to a category $\mathbf{Set}(V)$ for a cdl V, uniquely determined up to isomorphism.

The next section shows in some detail that the category $\mathbf{Set}(V)$ of V-fuzzy sets satisfies these axioms. The converse is much more difficult and important because it shows categoricity of the axioms. The proof is discussed in Goguen (1968 and 1969a). Another consequence of this result is that anything which is true of fuzzy sets and is preserved under equivalence is provable directly from just the axioms. This is a stronger assertion than it may seem to be. For, any universal construction, i.e. anything defined by a universal property, or equivalently by an adjoint situation, is preserved under equivalence, and (as far as we know) every important construction is universal (though not always in an obvious way). In particular, all the constructions mentioned above (in connection with theorem 2) are universal [see MacLane (1971) or MacLane & Birkhoff (1967) for many further examples]. Moreover, the basic laws (associative, distributive, etc.) which govern these constructions are preserved under equivalence, and are therefore provable from the axioms.

Perhaps the most interesting consequence of the axioms is that we don't need to prove things preserved under equivalence directly from the axioms for a category C satisfying them, but can instead verify them in the particular category $Set(V)$, which may be much easier. We can use this to establish facts about concepts, once we believe that they satisfy the axioms.

There are some things not preserved under equivalence; for example, equality. Thus, we have validity of certain laws only up to isomorphism. In particular, the nature of the elements of the carrier is not uniquely determined under equivalence; but only the cardinality of the carrier is. However, there is a tricky way to force equality of carriers under an isomorphism, related to some extended categories of fuzzy sets needed for certain applications to linguistics; see section 6. Moreover, many laws hold, often with equality, just because of the universal nature of the constructions; see section 4.

There are systems of axioms which are simpler (in a sense), and presumably permit simpler proofs of categoricity. However, our axioms have been chosen to be very weak, and to be as illuminating as possible in connection with the discussion of concepts. More powerful axiom systems would in general be harder to defend as assertions about concepts. For example, our axioms assume nothing about products of objects, yet it surprisingly follows that any category satisfying our axioms does have a product for any set of objects.

Although our use of categorical axioms seems to be novel as a method in philosophy and linguistics,[9] it is not so in pure mathematics. Lawvere (1964)

9 We hope this method may serve as a prototype for a new research method in other "soft" sciences, such as psychology, where it can be difficult to obtain detailed internal data, even though many high-level structural facts are available; first express the structural facts categorically; then examine the consequences for lower level data. In fortunate cases, a representation theorem may be possible; but even in less fortunate cases, useful information might be obtained this way. A category theoretic approach to structure in some ways parallels the system theoretic approach to scientific research, in which one obtains information about objects' structures by observation of their mutual relations and interactions.

gave the first category theoretic axiomatization, for sets, and proved a result of the same general type as our theorem 2. In fact, our result can be specialized to give a new axiomatization for **Set** (just assume in addition that $P = T$). Similar results have been given for categories of set-valued functors (Bunge, 1966) and topological spaces (Schlomink, 1967).

4. Operations and Laws for Fuzzy Sets

In this section we show that **Set**(V), for V a cdl, satisfies the axioms of the previous section; we also show that **Set**(V) has considerable structure not mentioned in the axioms, including certain additional operations and many algebraic laws for these operations. We first give the long-promised justification of Zadeh's definitions of union and intersection. This is done by showing that Zadeh's explicit formulae give constructions for the union and intersection of subobjects. As a preliminary, for any poset V with maximum element T, let T also denote the V-set with one point carrier **1** and value $T \varepsilon V$ on that point. Note that T is a terminal object in **Set**(V), since for any V-set $A : X \rightarrow V$, there is exactly one set map $u : X \rightarrow \mathbf{1}$, and it satisfies $A(x) \leqslant T(u(x)) = T$ for all $x \varepsilon X$.

Proposition 3. If V is a [complete] lattice with maximum and minimum elements, and if A is a V-set, then $\underline{P}(A)$ is also a [complete] lattice with maximum and minimum elements. For a finite [arbitrary] index set I and $A_i \varepsilon \underline{P}(A)$ with carrier X_i (for $i \varepsilon I$), union is given by $(\bigcup_{i \varepsilon I} A_i) (x) = \vee \{A_i(x) | x \varepsilon X_i$ for some $i \varepsilon I\}$ with carrier $\bigcup_{i \varepsilon I} X_i$; and intersection is given by $(\cap_i A_i)(x) = \wedge \{A_i(x) | i \varepsilon I\}$ with carrier $\bigcup_{i \varepsilon I} X_i$. If V is also distributive or completely distributive, so is each $\underline{P}(A)$. In fact, V has one of these structures iff $\underline{P}(T)$ does.

Thus, the standard definitions of union and intersection for fuzzy sets are not merely natural, they are forced upon us by the structure of fuzzy sets if we admit, as I think I must, that our definition of morphism is correct at least for subobject inclusions, and that the lattice theoretic criteria for union and intersection are right. We now similarly clarify and justify a number of other constructions.

Proposition 4. If V is complete, then **Set**(V) has associative images. In fact for $f : A \rightarrow B$ and $A_0 \subseteq A$ (with the carrier of A_0, A, B being respectively X_0, X, Y), $f(A_0)$ has carrier $f(X_0)$ and values $f(A)(y) = \vee \{A(x) | y = f(x)\}$, for $y \varepsilon f(X)$. Of course $f(A) \rightarrow B$ is the set inclusion $f(X_0) \rightarrow Y$.

Images generalize Zadeh's notion of shadow (Zadeh, 1966).

Proposition 5. For any poset V, **Set**(V) has coproducts over arbitrary index sets I. In fact, the coproduct $\underline{\amalg}_i A_i$ of V-sets A_i with carriers X_i has carrier the set coproduct $\underline{\amalg}_i X_i = \{<x_i,i> \mid x_i \varepsilon X_i\}$ with values $(\underline{\amalg}_i A_i)(<x_i,i>) = A_i(x_i)$ for $x_i \varepsilon X_i$, and injections $j_i : A_i \to \underline{\amalg}_i A_i$ given by the set injections $j_i : X_i \to \underline{\amalg}_i X_i$ sending x to $<x,i>$. These injections are monics in **Set**(V), and in fact $\underline{\amalg}_i A_i$ is a disjoint union $\bigcup_i A_i$ of the subobjects $j_i : A_i \to \underline{\amalg}_i A_i$. For any I, whenever A is a disjoint union $_i \bigcup A_i$ of subobjects in $\underline{P}(A)$, A is also the coproduct $\underline{\amalg}_i A_i$ of the A_i with the subobject **monics** $A_i \to \bigcup_i A_i = A$ as injections.

Proposition 6. Let V be a poset with minimum element $\varnothing$, and define $P : \mathbf{1} \to V$ to have value $\varnothing$ on the one point of $\mathbf{1}$. Then P is an atomic projective generator.

The above results contain among them everything needed to verify the six axioms for **Set**(V) with V a cdl; we now give the explicit forms for some further universal constructions. Note that in each case, we make fairly weak assumptions about the structure of V, so that we know **Set**(V) is a pretty reasonable category even if V is only a lattice.

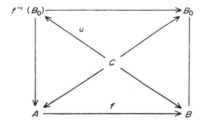

Proposition 7. If V has finite [arbitrary] greatest lower bounds, then any finite [arbitrary] family $<A_i>_{i\epsilon I}$ of V-sets has a product $\Pi_i A_i$, with carrier the set product of carriers, $\Pi_i X_i$, values $(\Pi_i A_i)(x) = \wedge_i A_i(x_i)$ for $x = (x_i) \varepsilon \Pi_i X_i$, and projections given by the set projections $\Pi_i X_i \to X_j$.

Products are defined categorically in the Appendix, and should play as important a role in fuzzy set theory and its applications as they do in ordinary set theory and its applications; see Goguen (1974) for some uses in fuzzy topology. If $I = \{0,1\}$, we will denote the binary product $\Pi_{i\epsilon\{0,1\}}A_i$ by $A_0 \times A_i$, as in the usual set theory.

Recall that the *inverse image* of a subobject $B_0 \subseteq B$ under a morphism $f : A \to B$ (if it exists) is a subobject $f^{-1}(B_0) \subseteq A$ such that the restriction of f to $f^{-1}(B_0)$ factors through B_0, and if $C \to A$, $C \to B_0$ are such that $C \to A \xrightarrow{f} B = C \to B_0 \xrightarrow{\subseteq} B$, then there is a unique $C \xrightarrow{u} f^{-1}(B_0)$ such that the above diagram commutes (more succinctly put, $f^{-1}(B_0)$ is the pullback of $B_0 \to B$ along f). An image $f(A)$ of $f : A \to B$ in a category is said to be *epic* iff in the factorization $A \to f(A) \xrightarrow{\subseteq} B$, the morphism $A \to f(A)$ is epic. Equalizers, and coproducts of morphisms, are relatively less important concepts, and are defined in the Appendix.

Proposition 8. Let V be any poset. Then for any $B_0 \subseteq B$ and $f : A \to B$ in **Set**(V), the inverse image $f^{-1}(B_0)$ exists, and is given by $f^{-1}(B_0)(x) = B_0$ $(f(x))$, for x in its carrier $f^{-1}(Y_0)$, where Y_0 is the carrier of B_0. Images in **Set**(V) are epic whenever they exist. Moreover, **Set**(V) has equalizers, and coproducts of monic morphisms are always monic.

One advantage of a category theoretic approach to operations is that a large number of laws are known to hold automatically whenever constructions exist which satisfy the universal properties. We temporarily depart from studying the existence and form of constructions in **Set**(V) to summarize some of these laws, stating them for the special case at hand. Proofs may be found in (Goguen, 1968).

Proposition 9. If V is a complete lattice, then unions and intersections in **Set**(V) each satisfy (generalized infinitary) commutative and associative laws. In particular, let $I = \bigcup_{j \in J} I_j$ be a union of sets, and let A_i be subobjects of A for $i \in I$. Then $\bigcap_{j \in J}(\bigcap_{i \in I_j} A_i) = \bigcap_{i \in I} A_i$; and similarly for unions. The general distributive laws hold if V is a cdl. Let $f : A \to B$, Then $f(\bigcup_i A_i) = \bigcup_i f(A_i)$, and for $B_i \subseteq B$ for $i \in I$, $f^{-1}(\bigcup_i B_i) = \bigcup_i f^{-1}(B_i)$. Finally $g^{-1}(f^{-1}(C_0)) = (gf)^{-1}(C_0)$, for $A \xrightarrow{g} B \xrightarrow{f} C$ and $C_0 \subseteq C$.

It is also true in **Set**(V), for V complete, that $f^{-1}(\bigcup_i B_i) = \bigcup_i f^{-1}(B_i)$, as is easily checked. We do not include this in the above proposition because it does not follow from any well-known general result about inverse images and unions. The assertions of proposition 9 actually depend on the fact that unions and intersections exist in a somewhat stronger than lattice theoretic sense.[8] Mitchell (1965) may be consulted for this, as well as for the general version of the following.

Proposition 10. Let V be a complete lattice, and let $f : A \to B$ in **Set**(V). Then images and inverse images under f give rise to a Galois connection between $\underline{P}(A)$ and $\underline{P}(B)$; in particular, for $A_0 \subseteq A_1 \subseteq A$ and $B_0 \subseteq B_1 \subseteq B$, the following hold:

$$(1)\ f(A_0) \subseteq f(A_1).$$
$$(2)\ f^{-1}(B_0) \subseteq f^{-1}(B_1).$$
$$(3)\ A_0 \subseteq f^{-1}f(A_0).$$
$$(4)\ B_0 \subseteq ff^{-1}(B_0).$$
$$(5)\ f(A_0) = ff^{-1}f(A_0).$$
$$(6)\ f^{-1}(B_0) = f^{-1}ff^{-1}(B_0).$$

We now consider some further operations on $\mathbf{Set}(V)$, and will return to their properties later. An exponential for objects A and B in a category [such as $\mathbf{Set}(V)$] with Cartesian product $\times$, if it exists, is an object B^A with a morphism $e : A \times B^A \to B$ called *evaluation* such that for any other object C and morphism $f : A \times C \to B$, there is a unique $h : C \to B^A$ such that $(A \times h)e = f$. One further preliminary to the next result. If V is a cdl, it has a *Brouwerian implication* operation, given for $a, b \varepsilon V$ by $a \to b = \vee \{x \mid a \wedge x \leqslant b\}$; this operation may also exist more generally, as characterized by the "adjointness" condition $x \leqslant (a \to b)$ iff $x \wedge a \leqslant b$ (see Goguen, 1969b for further discussion). Call V a "Brouwerian lattice" iff it is a lattice with a binary operation $\to$ satisfying the above condition.

Proposition 11. If V is a complete Brouwerian lattice, then $\mathbf{Set}(V)$ has exponentials,[10] given for $A : X \to V$, $B : Y \to V$ by $B^A(f) = \Lambda_{x \varepsilon X}(A(x) \to B(f(x)))$, for $f \varepsilon Y^X$, the set of all functions from X to Y, which is taken to be the carrier of B^A; evaluation $e : A \times B^A \to B$ has carrier $X \times Y^X \to Y$ given by $e(x, f) = f(x)$.

Now let $\mathbf{C\ell}$ denote the category whose objects are complete lattices, and whose morphisms are supremum preserving functions.

Proposition 12. When V is a complete lattice, the power poset construction defines a functor $\underline{P} : \mathbf{Set}(V) \to \mathbf{C\ell}$, with $\underline{P}(A)$ as before, and for $f : A \to B$, $\underline{P}(f) : \underline{P}(A) \to \underline{P}(B)$ by sending $A_0 \subseteq A$ to $f(A_0) \subseteq B$. This functor preserves unions (by proposition 9), and if f is monic, it also preserves intersections. In particular, if $A_0 \subseteq A$, then $\underline{P}(A_0)$ is a sublattice of $\underline{P}(A)$.

There are a number of basic laws in ordinary set theory which take the form of natural isomorphisms rather than equalities. For example, if A, B, C are sets, one has $(A \times B) \times C \cong A \times (B \times C)$, under the bijective correspondence $<<a, b>, c> \leftrightarrow <a, <b, c>>$; but one does not have equality (unless one of the sets is $\varnothing$). Quite a number of such laws follow from the existence of constructions having the standard universal property. We state a number of these for the case at hand, $\mathbf{Set}(V)$. Recall that binary coproducts are written with "$+$".

Proposition 13. If V is a cdl, then the following natural isomorphisms exist in $\mathbf{Set}(V)$:

$$(1) \quad (A \times B) \times C \cong A \times (B \times C)$$

---

10 We thank Dana Scott for pointing out and correcting an error in our earlier result on exponentials in Goguen, 1968. Also note that proposition 11 holds for finite sets with V a "Brouwerian semilattice", a poset with finite greatest lower bounds, and $\to$ satisfying the adjointness condition.

$$(2) \quad A \times B \cong B \times A$$
$$(3) \quad (A+B)+C \cong A+(B+C)$$
$$(4) \quad A+B \cong B+A$$
$$(5) \quad T \times A \cong A \cong A \times T$$
$$(6) \quad \emptyset +A \cong A \cong A+\emptyset$$
$$(7) \quad (A \times B)^c \cong A^c \times B^c$$
$$(8) \quad A^{B+C} \cong A^B \times A^c$$
$$(9) \quad f^{-1}(A \times B) \cong f^{-1}(A) \times f^{-1}(B)$$

Obviously, most of these isomorphisms hold somewhat more generally: for example (1) and (2) only need V to have finite greatest lower bounds; and (3), (4), (5), and (6) require nothing at all. A number of the properties we have been considering are summarized in the following result, for whose terminology we refer to the Appendix.

Theorem 14. If V is a complete lattice, then **Set**(V) is a complete and co-complete category. If V is a cdl, **Set**(V) is Cartesian closed.

We finally mention that the dual of proposition 1 holds: a fuzzy set morphism is epic iff its carrier is, and quotient objects correspond bijectively with quotient sets having larger V-values.

5. Representing Concepts

This section presents the argument that concepts are represented by fuzzy sets. The procedure is to argue that the category **C** of concepts satisfies the six axioms of theorem 2; it then follows that **C** is equivalent to **Set**(V) for some cdl V, and this is the representation result.

The category **C** of concepts has concepts as objects, and has "modellings", "metaphors", or "simplifications" of one concept to a subconcept of another as morphisms. Clearly, there is an "identity" modelling of any concept by itself; and obviously we can compose two modellings or metaphors to obtain a third "composite" modelling. Moreover, this operation is evidently associative. Thus, **C** satisfies all the conditions for being a category.

We do not need precise concepts of "concept" and "modelling of concepts" to consider **C**. "Concept" and "modelling" are "undefined terms". In fact, our method is *axiomatic*,[11] and requires only the acceptance of certain general properties of concepts and modelling; these properties involve no commitment to any specific descriptive theory of concepts. On the contrary,

11 Our use of "axiom" can be compared to that of the ancients: a self-evident truth, in this case about concepts. Actually, some of the assertions here are less than self-evident as will be seen.

we wish to deduce things about the internal structure of representations for concepts finally at the end of the argument. In discussing the assumed properties of concepts, we shall draw upon intuitions about language and thought, on the traditions of Western culture, and on intuitions about exact concepts, as they stand codified in properties of the category **Set** of sets. For sets are the "extensive" (or "finger-pointing") forms of the traditional exact concepts as they are used in modern mathematics and science.

Notice that while morphisms in **C** may preserve the "structure of concepts", whatever that may be, they do not generally preserve the "meaning" in any sense. For example, particular concepts[12] of "red" and "blue", say R and B, may have the same structure in the strong sense of being isomorphic, in that a simple invertible translation of frequency will convert one into the other; but obviously they have quite distinct meanings. This is not different from the situation in **Set** for exact concepts: two sets are isomorphic iff they have the same cardinality; and the nature of the elements is immaterial. This fact renders useless neither set theory nor the category of sets. It merely means that if we wish to keep track of elements, we have to use some notion other than set isomorphism.

Substructures are generally given by monomorphisms, and this is also the case for subconcepts. For the defining concellation law for $m : B \to C$ in **C** says that two distinct modellings of some concept A into B remain distinct when viewed as modellings of A into C through composition with m. This is just what a (purely structural) notion of subconcept should do.

In forming $\underline{P}(C)$ we identify equivalent monomorphisms. If all goes well— and we argue that it does—there will be one and only one subobject for each subconcept in the conventional meaning-preserving sense. Equivalence classes of monics correspond to possible substructures. Thus R and B, "red" and "blue", are distinct subobjects of C, "color"; and B', in which "blue" is described by wavelengths rather than frequencies, is equivalent to B. The preceding discussion is not part of any axiom; it is intended to be a explication of the meaning, here in the language of concepts, of certain general categorical concepts.

In our everyday thinking we easily combine arbitrary collections of subconcepts of a concept by "and" and "or" ("It was red or blue". "It was red and blue".), and we intuitively expect the distributive law to hold. This is axiom 3, except for disjointedness, which we discuss later.

12 Notice that we speak of "a particular concept" of "red", rather than "the concept" of "red", for we believe that different individuals quite likely have somewhat different concepts; and clearly different "color recognition" machines can be constructed to embody different concepts, by their discriminating different frequencies.

A morphism $f : A \rightarrow B$ gives a subobject of B which models A "without exteraneous parts" iff f factors through a (unique smallest) subobject of B. i.e. iff **C** has *images*.[13] Images will not match our intuitive sense unless they are also "associative". This is axiom 2.

We certainly have a "null" or "empty" concept which is a subconcept of every concept in a unique way (the existence of more than one inclusion $\varnothing \rightarrow A$ would imply $\varnothing$ had non-trivial structure). There is a concept "something", denoted T, into which any concept can be modelled in exactly one way[14] (again, more than one arrow $A \rightarrow T$ would give T too much structure). $\varnothing$ and T are the "initial" and "terminal" objects of axiom 1.

The "disjoint union" of concepts A and B is a third concept C such that $A \vee B = C$ and $A \wedge B = \varnothing$ in the lattice $\underline{P}(C)$. Alternatively, C should be the "smallest" concept modelling A and B, in the sense made precise by co-product. When extended to arbitrary collections of summands, this is axiom 4.

Axiom 5 is an "atomic hypothesis" of the sort so common and useful in Western science: the atoms of a concept A are the morphisms $P \rightarrow A$, or equivalently since P is monic, the atoms in $\underline{P}(A)$. P is the smallest object with just one atom. That P is a projective generator just means there are lots of useful models of P in other concepts, i.e. concepts have enough atoms. It might seem that we should postulate more than one type of atom. But because in this axiomatization we are concerned with the structure of concepts rather than their meaning, axiom 5 only says that all atoms have isomorphic structure; i.e. there could be more than one type of atom as far as meaning is concerned, but as far as structure is concerned, we are assuming they are all isomorphic to some (arbitrary given) single one, P.

Axiom 6 just says there is a two atom concept, surely an innocuous assumption.

The disjointedness condition of axiom 3 is really another part of the atomic hypothesis: we would not want to call $x, y \varepsilon \underline{P}(A)$ "atoms" unless (assuming $x \neq y$) the parts x', y' of A disjoint from them were big enough so that when put back together they gave all of A, i.e. $x' \vee y' = A$ in $\underline{P}(A)$.

This concludes our argument that the axioms of theorem 2 are satisfied by the category **C** of concepts. If it is accepted, then **C** is equivalent to **Set**(V) for some cdl V, and all categorical, i.e. all structural, aspects of concepts are represented by fuzzy sets. In most applications, there is no difficulty about actually choosing carriers and truth sets for fuzzy sets (Bellman, Kalaba &

---

13 We are forming an "image" whenever we ignore extraneous parts of a metaphorical embedding into a complex concept.

14 Saunders MacLane has suggested calling this concept "God".

Zadeh, 1966; Goguen, 1972), so that our "structurally oriented" argument poses no practical difficulties.

However, the theorem asserts one ultimate cdl V. What is it? We don't know. But probably anything big enough will do for all practical uses; for example $V = J^J$ (where $J = [0,1]$), the set of all uncountable-tuples of elements of the unit interval, should be big enough.

Those who have read Goguen (1967, or 1969b) may wonder why we have not used "closgs" as truth sets, because those papers argue that closgs may be the most appropriate truth sets for concepts (see also section 6.4 following). There is probably a suitable version of theorem 2 for closgs; but it is unnecessary, because every practically interesting closg we know is also a cdl, and the pure lattice structure of V suffices in comparing V-sets.

Our position regarding the above argument that **C** satisfies axioms 1 to 6 is that it is usefully near valid.[15] The argument helps to clarify the sorts of situations in which fuzzy sets are and are not useful representations. In particular, the atomic hypothesis must be plausible in such a situation. In the next section we discuss some more sophisticated types of fuzzification which can be used when atomicity is implausible; however, they all start from **Set**(V) as a first approximation and foundation.

One particularly interesting consequence of the representation is a classification of types of inexactness.[16] For simplicity, assume X is a space (e.g. a topological space) such that it makes sense to assume $A : X \rightarrow V$ is continuous.[17] If $A : X \rightarrow V$ takes any values other than $\varnothing$ and T in V, call A "vague", in that it exhibits "in-between" or "borderline" cases of membership; otherwise, A is "crisp", and each $x \varepsilon X$ is either totally in A or totally out of A. If $A : X \rightarrow V$ has more than one local maximum, call it "ambiguous", in that it is a union of specific "unambiguous" subconcepts, each with exactly one local maximum. If X has more than one point where A is non-zero, we say A has "generality", in that it can refer to more than one entity. Finally, if V is non-simply-ordered, we have the possibility of "ambivalence" or "conflict". For example, if $V = J^2$, it may well happen for $x,y \varepsilon X$ that $A(x) = <1,0>$ while $A(y) = <0,1>$. Then there is no *a priori* ground for declaring that one or the other is more in A, as there is a conflict between two independent criteria for membership in A, given by the first and second co-ordinates. This

---

15 The paper (Goguen, 1969b) contains a general discussion of "near valid" arguments. Suffice it here to say that such a concept is eminently compatible with the theory of fuzzy sets.

16 A somewhat less complete treatment of this topic appears in (Goguen, 1969b).

17 For this we also need a topology for V. When V is a cdl, it has natural topologies; see Birkhoff (1960).

observation seems to be important for many aspects of natural language semantics.

The above classification is in itself inexact. For example, the generality of a V-set should be greater if it has many points with value T than if it has only a few non-zero values, and these are all nearly zero. It may well be ambivalent whether a V-set is more ambiguous or more general. This kind of discussion could be formalized, starting for example with specific measures of generality, ambiguity, vagueness and ambivalence. But probably there is no unique best formalization, because of inherent ambiguity, vagueness, generality, and ambivalence to the concepts of ambiguity, vagueness, generality, and ambivalence.

We should like to particularly emphasize that from the few assumptions about concepts discussed above, all the algebraic results stated in section 4 now follow: we have epic images, inverse images, exponentiation, and products; in fact, we have completeness, cocompleteness, and Cartesian closure for the category of concepts; and we have all the laws of propositions 9, 10, 12, and 13. Of course, we do *not* have the specific formulae for constructions in **C**, but only for the representations in **Set**(V). All this is discussed in more detail in section 7.2.

6. Extensions, with Applications to Natural Language Semantics

There are respects in which fuzzy sets without some sort of elaboration, are inadequate for use in analyzing natural language. This section gives a sequence of extensions of the basic fuzzy set concept into more and more flexible systems suitable for more and more sophisticated language analyses. Its continuation into section 7 describes extensions for treating "multi-sets", combinatorial problems, and the power series approach to context-free languages.

6.1. FUZZY FUZZY SETS

As an approximation to the facts that there are many possible versions of a single concept (for example "red"), and that we may not know which one is being used, consider a fuzzy set $\underset{\sim}{A}$ of fuzzy sets $A : X \to V$, with a fixed universe X, i.e. $\underset{\sim}{A} : V^X \to V$. Think of each $A \, \varepsilon \, V^X$ as a possible version of the concept $\underset{\sim}{A}$, and of the value $\underset{\sim}{A}(A) \, \varepsilon \, V$ as measuring our confidence that it might be A.

For a fixed universe X, the fuzzy fuzzy sets on X are all fuzzy sets on the universe V^X, so that the algebra of all fuzzy fuzzy sets on X is just the algebra of all V-sets on V^X. For any set Z, and cdl V, the set V^Z of all V-sets on Z is also a cdl in a natural way, namely for $A, B \, \varepsilon \, V^Z$ we have: $A \leqslant B$ in V^Z iff

$A(z) \leqslant B(z)$ in V for all $z \varepsilon Z$; $(A \wedge B)(z) = A(z) \wedge B(z)$; and $(A \vee B)(z) = A(z) \vee B(z)$. Thus if V is a cdl, the fuzzy fuzzy sets on X are also a cdl (let $Z = V^x$ in the preceding); for further properties see Goguen (1967).

6.2. HIERARCHIES OF FUZZY SETS AND SEMANTICS

It is natural to extend the idea of a fuzzy set of fuzzy sets to the idea of hierarchies, i.e. fuzzy sets of fuzzy sets of . . . fuzzy sets, for all finite levels.

To avoid awkward notation, let us now write $\mathbf{Set}[X,V]$ for the set of all functions from X to V. Then an n-level fuzzy set is an element of $\mathbf{Set}[\mathbf{Set} [. . . \mathbf{Set}[X,V] . . .,V],V]$, where there are n $\mathbf{Set}$s and n Vs.

Such structures can be represented by trees with leaves in X and "strengths of connection" from V on each edge.

Let us suppose that X consists of the symbols $x_0, x_1, x_2, \ldots$, and that $V = J = [0,1]$, and consider the tree of Fig. 1. The picture uses the conven-

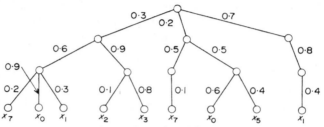

FIG. 1. A three-level fuzzy set.

tion that connections (or memberships) of degree zero are not drawn. Thus, Fig. 1 has five third-level sets, the first of which is $A_{31} : X \to J$, with $A_{31}(x_7) = 0\cdot2$, $A_{31}(x_0) = 0\cdot9$, $A_{31}(x_1) = 0\cdot3$, and $A_{31}(x_i) = 0$ for $i \neq 0,1,7$; it has three second-level sets, the first of which has $A_{21}(A_3) = 0\cdot6$, $A_{21}(A_3) = 0\cdot9$, and $A_{21}(A) = 0$ for all other $A : X \to J$; and so on.

One might think of such a tree as representing a concept in a somewhat more complex sense than any previously described. Thus, the "highest" level sets represent various "simple" concepts which are combined by the lower level sets to give the final complex concept. The modes of combination are by convention, a convenient example being that all odd levels are combined by "or" and all even levels by "and". This leads to an algorithm to check how well some state of the world satisfies the complex concept. In the example of Fig. 1, the formula for computing the truth value of the whole concept from some state $x = \langle x_0, x_1, \ldots \rangle$, under the assumption that each $x_i \varepsilon J$, is

$$0\cdot3[0\cdot6(0\cdot2x_7 \vee 0\cdot9x_0 \vee 0\cdot3x_1) \wedge 0\cdot9(0\cdot1x_1 \vee 0\cdot8x_3)] \vee 0\cdot2[0\cdot5x_7 \wedge 0\cdot5(0\cdot6x_0$$
$$\vee 0\cdot4x_5)] \vee 0\cdot7[0\cdot8(0\cdot4x_1)].$$

For a simpler but purely intuitive and oversimplified example, consider the following concept of "red": either a physical perception is involved and the predominant wave length is between 575 and 675 nm, or else there is a human being who is a communist. More precisely, let x_0 be the degree of "physical perception", f_λ the degree of "predominant wave-length λ" x_1 the degree of "human being", and x_2 of "communist". Then the formula might be

$$(x_0 \wedge \vee_\lambda R(\lambda) \cdot f_\lambda) \vee 0 \cdot 8 (0 \cdot 5 x_1 \wedge 0 \cdot 9 x_2),$$

where $R(\lambda)$ expresses some usual color concept "red". A tree for this concept is given in Fig. 2.

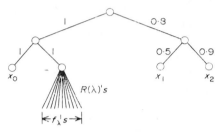

FIG. 2. A concept of "red".

Three ideas are particularly worth isolating from this discussion: (1) a hierarchical fuzzy set can be thought of as specifying an *algorithm* which computes the degree to which the concept holds in a state of the world; (2) the "coefficients" or "weights" given by the fuzzy set memberships express the *relevance* of the various parts of the concept to the whole; (3) three operations on truth values are being used, supremum, infimum, and product ($\vee$, $\wedge$, and $\cdot$).

The idea (1) reflects our view that a reasonable pragmatic approach to natural language semantics arises from computer implementation of algorithms representing concepts (see Goguen, 1972; Reddy, 1972). The idea (2) then becomes useful in determining metaphorical uses or "secondary references" of words, in that it gives a definite ordering to the component concepts, thus facilitating an orderly search for the most prominent. The theory of metaphor which lies behind such a search is that the meaning of some component concept is used for the meaning of the original word (Reddy, 1972). For example, in "The crown has gone hunting", we do not mean literally that "a metallic object worn on the head by a king has gone hunting", but that "the king has gone hunting". In more complex metaphors, the "structure" of some of the component concepts may be used, rather than the concepts themselves, as when one says "this bureaucracy is like a swamp". The idea (3) points toward a more inclusive view of what the truth set V should be; this is explored in section 6.4.

From a computer science point of view, the tree representation is very convenient, as there is a good body of knowledge on how to efficiently store and manipulate trees. But for some purposes in language, "nets" (or graphs) of concepts, representing more complex interactions among components, might be more appropriate, though less efficiently implemented. From the theoretical point of view, the corresponding "abstract systems of fuzzy sets" can be obtained by putting $\mathbf{Set}(V)$ for the category $\mathbf{O}$ of "objects" in the categorical systems theory framework of Goguen (1970). We do not wish to elaborate on this approach here.

6.3. UNIVERSES OF FUZZY SETS

As the preceding subsection makes clear, it can be desirable for a fuzzy set to have its universe of discourse contain other fuzzy sets. Since some concepts can exhibit "self-reference", e.g. is "clear" a clear concept? Is "fuzzy" a fuzzy concept? Is "deep" a deep concept? It may be desirable to consider fuzzy sets which have themselves in their universe of discourse. Methods suitable for this have been given by Scott (1972, 1973), rather like those of Goguen (1970). Scott used his construction to give mathematical models for the λ-calculus and certain computer languages, while Goguen was interested in hierarchically organized systems; one connection between these applications is that programs can be viewed as systems (Goguen, 1973a).

The construction of a universe $D^\infty(X;V)$ with "atomic concepts" in X and truth set V a complete lattice is rather technical, and some readers may want to skip to the next paragraph, which discusses properties of the construction. Hereafter, we feel free to not mention V explicitly in notation. Let $D^0(X) = X$ and let $D^1(X) = V^X$, viewed as a complete lattice in the product ordering (Goguen, 1967). For $n \geqslant 1$, let $D^{n+1}(X) = [D^n(X), V]$, where $[U,V]$ is the complete lattice[18] of all continuous (i.e. $\vee$-preserving) functions from a complete lattice U to another V, with the ordering $\varphi \leqslant \psi$ in $[U,V]$ iff $\varphi(u) \leqslant \psi(u)$ in V for all $u \varepsilon U$. Note that there is a natural inclusion $j_n : D^n(X) \to D^{n+1}(X)$, taking $\varphi \varepsilon D^n(X)$ to its "characteristic function" $j_n(\varphi)$ in $[D^n(X), V]$, $(j_n(\varphi))(\psi) = \top$ (maximum element) if $\psi = \varphi$, and $(j_n(\varphi))(\psi) = \bot$ (minimum element) if $\psi \neq \varphi$ (assuming of course that $\top \neq \bot$ in V). We then define

18 It might be noted that the category with complete lattices as objects and V-preserving maps as morphism is Cartesian closed, and the operation $[\, , \,]$ is its exponential (in the sense of p. 526, section 4).

$D^\infty(X)$ to be the *direct limit* (see the Appendix) of the sequence $D^1(X) \xrightarrow{j_1} D^2(X) \xrightarrow{j_2} D^3(X) \rightarrow \ldots$. Now given $\varphi : D^\infty(X) \rightarrow V$ continuous, we let $\varphi_n = \varphi i_n$, where $i_n : D^n(X) \rightarrow D^\infty(X)$ is the natural direct limit *injections* (see Appendix), and note that φ and $<\varphi_n>_{n \geq 1}$ determine each other uniquely. Finally, we define $j(\varphi)$ to be the point of $D^\infty(X)$ corresponding similarly to the sequence $<j_{n-1}\varphi_n>_{n \geq 1}$, where $j_0 : X \rightarrow V^X$ is again the natural inclusion by characteristic functions. Figure 3 may help visualize this construction. The following can then be shown.

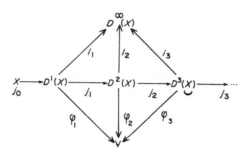

FIG. 3. Diagram for $[D^\infty(X),V]$.

Proposition 15. The function $j : [D^\infty(X),V] \rightarrow D^\infty(X)$ is injective.[19]

Thus every (continuous[19]) fuzzy set on $D^\infty X$ corresponds to an "element" of $D^\infty(X)$, so that $D^\infty(X)$ is a "universe" of V-sets closed under the process of constructing V-sets on it. In particular, every V-set arising in this way (from a V-set on the universe $D^\infty(X)$) is defined on itself in a natural sense. Thus, "self-reference" exists in this universe of concepts. For each n, $D^n(X) \subseteq D^\infty(X)$ is the complete lattice of n-level concepts. It might be noted that from the "tree" viewpoint of section 6.2, some concepts in $D^\infty(X)$ have trees of infinite depth. This may have something to do with our intuitions about the complexity of nestedness of concepts, particularly self-referential concepts.[20]

19 The technicality that $\varphi : D^\infty(X) \rightarrow V$ be continuous is not a severe restriction; most things one might want to consider are continuous. In fact, it is "Scott's thesis" that, in his context of data structures, computable functions always appear as continuous functions.

20 It is clear that in looking up a word in the dictionary, looking up the words used to define it, and so on recursively, one eventually obtains again some earlier word. If we call such words "self-referential", we obtain a rather large class of "self-referential" words, and even more so if one also includes words defined in terms of words defined using themselves. (In fact, since the dictionary is finite and every word must refer to other words, *all* words fall in the last and largest sense of "self-referential").

However, every concept has a best approximation at each finite level, i.e. in each $D^n(X)$.[21]

It is sometimes convenient to consider partial functions on $D^\infty(X)$, for example, if the set $A : D^\infty(X) \to V$ is the characteristic function of some element of $D^n(X)$ for small n, there is little interest in the values of A on deeper concepts. Rather than do the whole construction over for partial functions, we can use the truth set $V^+ = V \cup \{\Lambda\}$, where Λ is some point not in V with ordering $\Lambda < v$, for all $v \varepsilon V$. This gives a complete lattice ordering for V^+. The intuitive interpretation for Λ is "undefined", and $D^\infty(X)$ with V^+ allows functions which are partially "undefined".

These ideas are not so strange as they may first seem. $D^\infty(X)$ is really an almost inevitable outgrowth of the idea of "fuzzy fuzzy" sets. The existence of such a universe was used by M. Reddy in his University of Chicago English Department thesis (1972) on metaphor (following then unpublished remarks of Goguen), and similar, though vaguer, ideas can be discerned in several older philosophical discussions of concepts.

6.4. MORE GENERAL TRUTH SETS

A number of considerations suggest that for many purposes the cdl is too limited a truth set. For one, the previous subsection only assumed that V was a complete lattice in its construction of $D^\infty(X;V)$, and really only needed to assume that directed nets in V had suprema. We saw that many constructions in $\mathbf{Set}(V)$ are fine when V is a lattice, or even a poset, and actually some would be just as fine if V had almost any algebraic structure at all. In the next section we shall see important applications where the natural choice for V is a semiring.

A somewhat different motivation for generalization is our intuition that the truth value of "A and B" should actually decrease with *both* A and B, whatever (non-zero) values they may have. Thus, for $V = J = [0,1]$ with $\wedge =$ min used to model "and", $1/4 \wedge 1 = 1/4 \vee 1/2 = 1/4 \wedge 1/4$, whereas we might feel that $1/4 \wedge 1/4$ should be "less true" than $1/4 \wedge 1$. The obvious way to insure this is to use $\cdot =$ multiplication to model "and". Then $1/4 \cdot 1/4 = 1/16 < 1/4 \cdot 1/2 = 1/8 < 1/4 \cdot 1 = 1/4$, which seems more natural. But what happens to our carefully constructed algebra of concepts? Actually, things remain pretty much the same. The first step is to find an algebraic structure

---

21 From the point of view of the system theoretic construction of Goguen (1970), it is more natural to start with a *category* $\mathbf{C}$ of V-sets than with just V^X (the best category is probably not $\mathbf{Set}(V)$, but one of these described in Goguen (1967) which has fuzziness in the morphisms too). The constructions proceed pretty much as in the text, with $D^1 = \mathbf{C}$, D^2 the category of all nets or "systems" built from $\mathbf{C}$, D^3 the category of all "systems of systems", etc. We shall not give details here.

which includes both J with $\cdot$ and cdls; the next step is to do V-set theory for such Vs.

A "semilattice ordered monoid" is a monoid $<M,\otimes,e>$ with partial order $\leqslant$ having binary suprema such that the distributive laws

$$(a_1 \vee a_2) \otimes b_1 = (a_1 \otimes b_1) \vee (a_2 \otimes b_1) \text{ and}$$
$$a_1 \otimes (b_1 \vee b_2) = (a_1 \otimes b_1) \vee (a_1 \otimes b_2)$$

hold for all $a_i, b_i \,\varepsilon M$. This structure is (right) "residuated" iff $\otimes$ has a right adjoint, i.e. a binary operation $\rightarrow$ on M such that

$$(a \otimes b) \leqslant c \text{ iff } a \leqslant (b \rightarrow c),$$

for all $a, b, c \,\varepsilon M$. A *complete lattice ordered monoid* is a semilattice ordered monoid which has arbitrary suprema and satisfies the complete distributive laws

$$(\vee_i a_i) \otimes b_1 = \vee_i (a_i \otimes b_1)$$
$$a_1 \otimes (\vee_i b_i) = \vee_i (a_1 \otimes b_i)$$

for all index sets, and $a_i, b_i \,\varepsilon M$. It is well-known that a poset with arbitrary suprema is actually a complete lattice (Birkhoff, 1960). Complete lattice ordered monoids are residuated, with $b \rightarrow c = \vee \{a \mid a \otimes b \leqslant c\}$. A complete lattice ordered monoid such that $e = \top$ (i.e. which is "integral") has previously been called a "closg" (Goguen, 1967, 1969b), though "clom" would have been better[22], and is used hereafter. Any cdl is a clom with $\otimes = \wedge$. Moreover, [0,1] with $\otimes = \cdot$ is a clom. Many further examples are given in the references cited. Hereafter we refer to $\otimes$ as "confluence", evoking the generalization of $\cdot$ and $\wedge$ [this word was suggested in Bellman and Zadeh (1970)].

We now briefly discuss the algebra of V-sets where V is a clom. All operations previously defined (except exponential) can stay as they are. But there is a new binary confluence operation on V-sets, $(A \otimes B)(x) = A(x) \otimes B(x)$, for x in the domains of both A and B. We can also define a corresponding new binary "confluential product", $A \# B : X \times Y \rightarrow V$ (for $A : X \rightarrow V$, $B : Y \rightarrow V$) by $A \# B(x,y) = A(x) \otimes B(y)$. The new "exponential" is right adjoint to this product, and is defined by the same formula as before (see proposition 11) but using residuation[23] in V for $\rightarrow$.

Proposition 16. If V is a clom, the results of propositions 1,3 (except the last two sentences), 4, 5, 6, 7 (for the Cartesian product), 8, 9, 10, 11 (for

22 "m" for "monoid" instead of "sg" for "semigroup".

23 This operation might better be called an "internal hom functor", as "exponential" suggests adjointness to the Cartesian product, but we do not want to get into this particular technicality here; see MacLane (1971) for the appropriate discussion.

the confluential product) and 12 all apply directly, as does the first sentence (asserting completeness and cocompleteness) of theorem 14. In proposition 13, either product may be used for assertions (1), (2) and (4), but the Cartesian product must be used in (7) and (8), and (2) is valid for the confluentia product iff ⊗ is commutative in V.

There is presumably a version of the fundamental categoricity result, theorem 2, for cloms, but we have not pursued this matter. The theory of relations sketched in (Goguen, 1967) also pretty well generalizes to the use of cloms as truth sets, as partially indicated there.

7. Semiring Sets, Multisets, and Formal Languages

This section develops some particular properties and applications for fuzzy sets having truth values in a semiring or ordered semiring. Some general theory for such "semiring sets" is given in subsection 7.1, and then applied in subsection 7.2 to the special case of "multisets", which have some interest in connection with combinatorics. Finally subsection 7.3 discusses specifically how these ideas can be used in the theory of formal (i.e. artificial) languages.

7.1. SEMIRING SETS

A *semiring* is a set V with binary operations $+$ and $\cdot$ such that $+$ is associative and commutative, and $\cdot$ is associative and distributes over $+$, i.e.

$$a \cdot (b+c) = (a \cdot b)+(a \cdot c) \text{ and } (a+b) \cdot c = (a \cdot c)+(a \cdot c).$$

A semiring is *unitary* iff $\cdot$ has a unit e and is *commutative* iff $\cdot$ is commutative. An important commutative unitary semiring is the set N of non-negative numbers, with $+$, $\cdot$ as usual and $e = 1$. Of course, any ring is a semiring, in particular the ring Z of all (positive or negative or zero) integers, and $Z[X]$ of all polynomials in indeterminant X with coefficients in Z. Similarly, $N[X]$ is a semiring, but it is not a ring. Any distributive lattice is a commutative semiring with $+ = \vee$ and $\cdot = \wedge$; and therefore any cdl is a unitary commutative semiring with *zero* (meaning $+$ has an identity 0 such that $0 \cdot a = a \cdot 0 = 0$ for all a). Similarly, any clom is a unitary semiring with $+ = \vee$ and $\cdot = \otimes$. It is also *integral*, in the sense that $e \geqslant a$ for all $a \varepsilon V$.

A number of operations can be readily defined for V-sets where V is a semiring. In particular, define $A \cdot B$ by $(A \cdot B)(x) = A(x) \cdot B(x)$ for all x in the carriers of *both* A and B and otherwise undefined; and $A+B$ by $(A+B)(x)$ $= A(x) + B(x)$ for x in the carriers of both, $= A(x)$ for x in the carrier of A only, $= B(x)$ for x in the carrier of B only, and otherwise undefined. Let $\varnothing$ be the unique V-set with carrier $\varnothing$.

Proposition 17. Let V be a semiring. Then

(1) $(A+B)+C = A+(B+C)$ and $(A \cdot B) \cdot C = A \cdot (B \cdot C)$;

(2) $A+B = B+A$;

(3) $A \cdot (B+C) = (A \cdot B)+(A \cdot C)$ and $(A+B) \cdot C = (A \cdot C)+(B \cdot C)$;

(4) if V is commutative, $A \cdot B = B \cdot A$.

(5) $A+\varnothing = \varnothing+A = A$, and $A \cdot \varnothing = \varnothing \cdot A = \varnothing$.

There is no natural unit for $\cdot$ unless the carriers are all a fixed set, X, in which case the constant function $X \to V$ with value e works. We cannot give infinite versions of the $+$ and $\cdot$ operators on V-sets as we did for $\vee$ and $\wedge$ in a cdl, because $+$ and $\cdot$ are not infinitary in V, though they extend to all finite (non-$\varnothing$) sets by associativity. However, there is one infinitary operation we can define, coproduct. We shall have to use a notation different from $A+B$ for the binary case, and we suggest $A \amalg B$. The general definition of co-product is of course identical to that given in proposition 5; it uses no operations from V whatsoever. We can also define a binary product for V-sets, with V a semiring, analogous to that for the previous confluential product, namely $(A \cdot B)(x,y) = A(x) \cdot B(y)$. We would now like to assert, for example, associative laws, in the form of natural isomorphisms, as in proposition 13; but we are unable to at this point, because we lack a suitable definition of morphism for V-sets with V a semiring. In order to give one with the same intuitive significance as that in section 2, V should also have an order structure. In fact, it is generally the case for the semirings which arise in practice, that they are "po-semirings", i.e. have a partial order $\leqslant$ such that $+$ and $\cdot$ are monotone operations. This is certainly the case for N and $N[X]$. For V a po-semiring, we then define morphism of V-sets *exactly* as in definition 2, and obtain the category $\mathbf{Set}(V)$ of V-sets exactly as before, but now enriched by the operations $+$, $\cdot$, and $\#$. This category has coproducts in the cate-gorical sense, given as indicated above. It may also have unions, intersections, products, etc., depending on the richness of the order structure of V, exactly as described in section 4. In addition, we now have the following.

Proposition 18. If V is a po-semiring, then

(1) $A \# (B \# C) \cong (A \# B) \# C$;

(2) If V is commutative, then

$A \# B \cong B \# A$;

(3) $A \amalg (B \amalg C) \cong (A \amalg B) \amalg C$;

(4) $A \amalg B \cong B \amalg A$;

(5) $A \# (B \amalg C) \cong (A \# B) \amalg (A \# C)$ and

$(A \amalg B) \# C \cong (A \# C) \amalg (B \# C)$;

(6) $A \cdot (B \underline{\underline{\shortparallel}} C)$ $\cong$ $(A \cdot B)\underline{\underline{\shortparallel}}(A \cdot C)$ and
$(A\underline{\underline{\shortparallel}}B) \cdot C$ $\cong$ $(A \cdot C)\underline{\underline{\shortparallel}}(B \cdot C)$;

(7) $A+(B\underline{\underline{\shortparallel}}C)$ $\cong$ $(A+B)\underline{\underline{\shortparallel}}(A+C)$ and
$(A\underline{\underline{\shortparallel}}B)+C$ $\cong$ $(A+C)(B+C)$;

(8) $(A+B)\#C$ $\cong$ $A\#C+B\#C$ and
$A\#(B+C)$ $\cong$ $A\#B+A\#C$;

(9) $\varnothing \# A$ $= A\#\varnothing = \varnothing$, and $\varnothing \underline{\underline{\shortparallel}} A \cong A \underline{\underline{\shortparallel}} \varnothing \cong A$.

(10) If $a+b \geqslant a$ for all $a,b \, \varepsilon V$ (for example if V has a "zero" which is both a minimum element and an identity for $+$) then
$A\mathsf{v}(A+B)$ $= A+B$, and $A\wedge(A+B) = A$;

(11) If V is unitary and $B(x) \geqslant e$ for all x in the universe of B, then
$A\mathsf{v}(A \cdot B)$ $= A \cdot B$, and
$A\mathsf{v}(A \cdot B)$ $= A$, provided B is defined whenever A is.

Knuth (1973) calls the laws of (10) and (11) above "absorptive" laws in the special case he studies, $V = P$, the positive integers. They may be taken as asserting these particular v and $\wedge$ exist. We now sketch a proof of the first assertion of (11), the others being more straightforward. Certainly $A\mathsf{v}(A \cdot B) \geqslant (A \cdot B)$, so it suffices to show $(A \cdot B) \geqslant A\mathsf{v}(A \cdot B)$, for which it is sufficient that $(A \cdot B) \geqslant A$. But $B(x) \geqslant e$ implies $A(x) \cdot B(x) \geqslant A(x) \cdot e = A(x)$, as desired. Note that there are "symmetric" versions of these laws; e.g. $(A \cdot B)\mathsf{v}B = A \cdot B$. To obtain further identities it is necessary to make still further assumptions about V. A lattice-ordered semiring is a po-semiring in which the order structure is a lattice, and both $+$ and $\cdot$ distributive over v. For example, N is a lattice-ordered semiring.

Proposition 19. If V is a lattice-ordered semiring, the following additional laws hold for V-sets:

(1) $(A\mathsf{v}B)+C$ $= (A+C) \mathsf{v} (B+C)$, and
$A+(B\mathsf{v}C)$ $= (A+B) \mathsf{v} (A+C)$;

(2) $(A\mathsf{v}B) \cdot C$ $= (A \cdot C) \mathsf{v}(B \cdot C)$, and
$A \cdot (B\mathsf{v}C)$ $= (A \cdot B) \mathsf{v} (A \cdot C)$.

If V is a "dually" lattice ordered semiring, i.e. if $+$ and $\cdot$ distribute over v, then the laws (1), (2) above hold with $\wedge$ substituted for v [denote these laws (1'), and (2')].

(3) $(A\wedge B) \cdot (A\mathsf{v}B) \leqslant (B \cdot A) \mathsf{v} (A \cdot B)$;

(4) $(A\wedge B)+(A\mathsf{v}B) \leqslant (A+B)$, and
if $\cdot$ is commutative then
$(A\wedge B) \cdot (A\mathsf{v}B) \leqslant A \cdot B$;

(5) If V is simply ordered, then equality holds in (4).

Knuth (1973) calls the first law of (5) the "counting law" (for $V = P$, which satisfies the hypothesis). We prove (3) here; following Goguen (1967, p. 154), we check it for elements $a,b \, \varepsilon \, V$: $(a \wedge b) \cdot (a \vee b) = [(a \wedge b) \cdot a] \vee [(a \wedge b) \cdot b]$ $\leqslant (b \cdot a) \vee (a \cdot b)$. In fact, the above propositions include all the laws given by Knuth (1973) for his special case, plus quite a few more; and of course the results are valid in far greater generality than $V = P$. But the case $V = P$ is particularly important, and has a special terminology and notation.

7.2. MULTISETS AND COMBINATORICS

The name "multiset" has been suggested by N. G. deBruijn for a P-set, and it is convenient to use ordinary set notation, slightly extended. Thus, for $X = \{a,b,c\}$, $A : X \to P$ defined by $A(a) = 1$, $A(b) = 3$, and $A(c) = 2$ is denoted simply $\{a,b,b,b,c,c\}$, with repetitions written out, or $\{a, 3 \cdot b, 2 \cdot c\}$ using a variant preferable for large multiplicities. The reader might enjoy rewriting the results of this subsection with this notation for multisets. The special importance of multisets lies in their great convenience in carrying out combinatorial arguments, as shown by many examples in Knuth (1973). The additional operations and laws are given here presumably further extend the usefulness of this technique.

It is suggestive to note that multisets of non-negative integers correspond bijectively with generating functions with non-negative integer coefficients, $A \leftrightarrow \Sigma_{n \in A} z^n$, where $A : N \to P$, in such a way as to take the set operations to familiar power series operations. In fact, it is presumably useful for some more complex combinatorial arguments to have available "multisets" with polynomials, or generating functions, as "degrees of membership", and our results give reasonable set laws for this case too. This paper is not the place to go into any detailed discussion of particular combinatorial problems, but the next subsection does consider one special problem of particular relevance to our general theme.

7.3. FORMAL LANGUAGE THEORY

Chomsky and Schützenberger (1963) show that formal power series (with coefficients in the ring Z of all integers and noncommuting variables) are a useful tool in studying "Chomsky-style" "context-free" formal languages. Shamir (1968) extends many of their results to the case where the coefficients come from an arbitrary commutative ring with identity, and Arbib (1970) extends some of them further to a commutative semiring with identity, so as to also cover the fuzzy languages of Lee and Zadeh (1969). We now briefly outline some of this work in the notation and terminology given in the previous subsection.

Let X be a set of "words" for our language, and let X^* be the set of all finite strings of words from X (i.e. "sentences"), with Λ the empty string (note that X^* is a monoid under concatenation: i.e. the binary operation of juxtaposing strings from X is associative, and has Λ as an identity). The usual notion of a formal language is just a subset A of X^*, the "grammatical" or "acceptable" strings of words. A *fuzzy language* or *V-language* is a V-set $A : X^* \to V$, where $A(x_1 \ldots x_n) \varepsilon V$ is the degree of acceptability of the string $x_1 \ldots x_n$. The usual case then corresponds to $V = \{0,1\} = \{$"out", "in"$\}$. If V is a semiring, $A : X^* \to V$ corresponds to a formal power series with variables the elements of X and coefficients in V. For example, if $V = N$, $X = \{x_1, x_2, x_3\}$, and $A(x_1) = 1$, $A(x_1{}^k x_2) = 2^{k-1}$ for $k \geqslant 1$, with $A(s) = 0$ for all other strings, the corresponding power series is $x_1 + x_2 x_3 + 2 x_2 x_2 x_3 + 4 x_2 x_2 x_2 x_3 + 8 x_2 x_2 x_2 x_2 x_3 + \ldots = x_1 + \sum_{k=1}^{\infty} 2^{k-1} x_2{}^k x_3$. The set of all such formal power series forms a semiring, with operations $+$ and $\cdot$ defined by:

$$\sum_{s \varepsilon X^*} A(s)s + \sum_{s \varepsilon X^*} B(s)s = \sum_{s \varepsilon X^*} (A(s) + B(s))s; \text{ and}$$

$$\left(\sum_{s \varepsilon X^*} A(s)s\right) \cdot \left(\sum_{s \varepsilon X^*} B(s)s\right) = \sum_{s \varepsilon X^*} \left[\sum_{s_1 s_2 = s} A(s_1) \cdot B(s_2)\right]s.$$

That is, the coefficient of s in the power series of $A + B$ is $A(s) + B(s)$; and of $A \cdot B$ is $\sum_{s_1 s_2 = s} A(s_1) \cdot B(s_2)$, where $s_1 s_2 = s$ means that the strings s_1 and s_2 juxtaposed or cancatenated yield s. These operations correspond to the union and concatenation of languages for the usual case $V = \{0,1\}$, and to their various generalizations stated in Arbib (1970), Chomsky and Schützenberger (1963), Lee and Zadeh (1969), and Shamir (1968). In the present context, we would perhaps more sensibly reserve "union" for the case where V has binary suprema, and the operation $\left(\sum_{x \varepsilon X^*} A(s)s\right) \vee \left(\sum_{s \varepsilon X^*} B(s)s\right) = \sum_{s \varepsilon X^*} (A(s) \vee B(s))$ is defined. This terminology is consistent with Lee and Zadeh (1969) and the usual classical case, but not Arbib (1970), who does not treat $+, \cdot, \vee, \wedge$ as potentially separate operations in V.

How very natural the particular lattice-ordered semiring N really is for formal languages becomes clear when formal grammars are also considered. A context-free grammar has productions which take some strings to others, starting symbol (string of length one), and (in most cases) a separate collection of auxiliary symbols (disjoint from X) which help keep track of the grammatical structure (for example, by standing for grammatical classes). Here is a simple example, with no auxiliary symbols, and x_1 as starting symbol,

$$p_1 : x_1 \to x_2 x_3$$
$$p_2 : x_2 \to x_2 x_2$$
$$p_3 : x_3 \to x_2 x_3.$$

Then it is easy to see that the set of strings one can derive from x_1, by replacing occurrences of x_1, x_2, x_3 using the rules p_1, p_2, p_3 respectively, is

$\{x_1\}\cup\{x_2{}^kx_3\,|\,k\geqslant1\}$, an ordinary (formal) language. One expresses more about the nature of this language, however, if one notes that the *number* of ways one can derive a string $s\,\varepsilon\,X^*$ is 2^{k-1} if $s=x_2{}^kx_3$, $k\geqslant1$; is 1 if $s=x_1$; and is 0 for all other $s\,\varepsilon\,X^*$. Thus we have the multiset $\{x_1,x_2,x_3,\ 2\cdot x_2x_2x_3,\ 4\cdot x_2x_2x_2x_3,\ \ldots\}$ which was given before as an example of an N-language.

More precisely now, a *context-free V-grammar* is a quadruple $G=\langle X,N,s_0,P\rangle$, where $S=X\cup N$ is the finite set of symbols, $X=$ the terminal symbols, $N=$ the nonterminal (or auxiliary) symbols, $s_0\,\varepsilon\,S$, and P is a finite set of triples $\langle s,v,s'\rangle$ with $s,s'\,\varepsilon\,S^*$ and $v\,\varepsilon\,V$, written $s\to v\cdot s'$ and called *productions*. The degree of G-grammaticality of $s\,\varepsilon\,X^*$ is $\sum\{v\,|\,x_0{}^*\Rightarrow v\cdot s\}$, where $x^*\Rightarrow v\cdot s'$ in G means that there is a string $s_0\Rightarrow v_1\cdot s_1\Rightarrow v_2\cdot s_2\ldots\Rightarrow v_n\cdot s_n$ such that $s_0=s$, $s_n=s'$, and $v=v_1\cdot v_2\cdot\ldots\cdot v_n$, where $s\Rightarrow v\cdot s'$ means s' is obtained from s by using some production $s_0\to v\cdot s_0{}'$ in P to replace an occurrence of s_0 in s by $s_0{}'$ to obtain s'. For $V=N$, this process applied to an ordinary grammar gives the multiplicities of strings, as in the example worked out above. For $V=[0,1]$, it gives fuzzy languages and grammars, in the sense of Lee and Zadeh (1969), and so on.

If $A_1:X^*\to P$ and $A_2:X^*\to P$ are the P-languages defined by P-grammars G_1 and G_2, then $(A_1+A_2)(s)$ tells the number of ways of deriving $s\,\varepsilon\,X^*$ in the grammar G_1+G_2 obtained by allowing both the rules of G_1 and of G_2; and $(A_1\cdot A_2)(s)$ tells the number of ways of deriving s in the grammar $G_1\cdot G_2$ which derives composite strings s_1s_2 with s_1 from G_1 and s_2, from G_2. However, if one wants to consider ordinary unions and intersections of $\{0,1\}$-languages in the context of P-languages, one will need to have $\vee$ and $\wedge$ available in P.

There are also good reasons for sometimes considering $\#$ and $\underline{\underline{\amalg}}$ of languages. These operations, of course, obey the laws given in the preceding subsection. The various references we have given go on to generalize various of the usual context free language theory, but this exceeds our present purpose, which is merely to show the relevance of V-sets to formal linguistics.

8. Philosophical Discussion and Conclusions

We hope the reader has noticed that the applications and extensions in the previous section support our claim that the representation of concepts by fuzzy sets is usefully near valid. For these extensions and applications to linguistics, semantics, and combinatorics cluster around the central notion of V-set with V a cdl. Of course, the mere existence of useful proper extensions in semantics refutes any strict claim that unextended fuzzy sets completely represent concepts.

8.1. LAWS OF THOUGHT

One of the main fruits of the representation of concepts by V-sets is validity of the algebraic "laws of thought" developed in section 4 for concepts. Because the statement of the laws preceded the argument in section 5 that the axioms of theorem 2 are satisfied by the category C of concepts, it is appropriate to discuss briefly here the significance of these laws as assertions about C. Because their validity depends on the validity of the argument of section 5, they should be about as "usefully near valid" as is the argument itself. Thus, these laws might serve as guides in the construction of practical arguments, but should be employed only with some caution and appropriate attention to the sort of situation in which they might break down. Part of the purpose of this section is to provide preliminary information helpful in this regard. Notice that we precede pretty much the same way with practical reasoning in the "real world"; we do not examine all the ramifications and underpinnings of an argument, but only those which might crucially effect its validity for the purpose at hand.

The results in question begin with proposition 8 in section 4 (previous results in that section verified the axioms themselves); although these results are stated for $\mathbf{Set}(V)$, we know that whatever is preserved under equivalence transfers to C. Thus from proposition 8 we have inverse images, epic images, equalizers, and that coproducts of monics are monic. Inverse images allow one to determine portions of concepts relevant to submetaphors; e.g. if $f : A \rightarrow B$ is a morphism in C (a "metaphor" or "modelling") and $B_0 \subseteq B$ a subconcept of the concept providing the model, then $f^{-1}(B_0) \subseteq A$ is the part of A to which B_0 is relevant. That images are epic says that for a modelling $A \xrightarrow{f} B = A \rightarrow f(A) \subseteq B$, $A \rightarrow f(A)$ is epic, or all of $f(A)$ is "used" by the modelling $A \rightarrow f(A)$. Equalizers give the largest subconcept of B actually used the same way by each of two metaphors $A \rightarrow B$. The coproduct fact means that simultaneous joint consideration of a family $A_i \subseteq B_i$ (for $i \varepsilon I$) of subconcepts gives a joint subconcept $\amalg_i A_i \subseteq \amalg_i B_i$.

The interpretation of proposition 9 is that conjunction and disjunction are associative and commutative operations, even over infinite families of concepts; this result therefore includes associative and commutative laws for the quantifier "there exists", and for the quantifier "for all", as these can be viewed as (possibly infinite) disjunction, and conjunction, respectively. These are familiar "laws of thought" from ordinary logic, as are the distributive laws for binary conjunction and disjunction. In the infinitary case, this gives certain special quantifier laws. Proposition 9 also includes the laws that disjunction commutes with image and conjunction with inverse image, and a composition law for inverse image. The first says (in part) that for a modelling

$f : A \to B$ and subconcepts $A_0, A_1 \subseteq A$, the relevant part of B for the disjunction of A_0 and A_1 is the disjunction of the relevant parts of A_0 and A_1; and a similar law for quantifiers. The interpretation of the other two laws should be evident now. Proposition 10 asserts a Galois connection for the direct and inverse "relevant part of" operators for modellings. Proposition 11 asserts a natural inexact concept structure for the modellings of one concept into another. Proposition 12 asserts a form of naturalness for the lattice of subconcept construction. In particular, if A_0 is a subconcept of A, then the subconcepts of A_0 give rise to subconcepts of A in a way which preserves conjunctions and disjunctions. We leave the reader to work out proposition 13 and theorem 14.

Of course, in order to go really far with a practical guide to reasoning, one needs to have a theory of deduction, that is, of implication. In fact, the pseudo-complement in $\underline{P}(A)$ gives an appropriate operation, and its theory has been developed elsewhere (Goguen, 1969b). Since $\underline{P}(A)$ is a Brouwerian lattice, the laws for implication are essentially those of intuitionistic logic. For example, reasoning by contradiction is not valid. However, things get far more interesting when cloms are used as truth sets. Then deduction is not in general transitive: indeed for $V = [0,1]$, implications have truth values which are combined multiplicatively to yield the truth value of the compound implication, i.e. errors can combine multiplicatively, much as in the theories of measurement and probability. See Goguen (1969b) for further discussion of deduction when the truth set is a clom.

These laws are exact assertions about precise models for concepts, but the laws may not be useful approximations outside the range of validity of the models. This is much like the situation in physics: for example, certain assertions exactly true in the Newtonian theory are empirically useful only when velocities are negligible in comparison with the speed of light. The above "laws of thought" are not, therefore, absolutes in the sense Boole (1854) might have thought, but are serviceable scaffoldings; not masters, but guides.

8.2. EXPERIMENTAL PHILOSOPHY AND ARTIFICIAL INTELLIGENCE

It may be worth going a bit deeper into the ideas behind one of the "extensions", that of representing concepts by algorithms or procedures (see section 6.2), before discussing the validity of the "atomic hypothesis" of axiom 5. There has been considerable thought given to what is "meaning" (see Ryle, 1957). It seems at one time to have been thought, for example (Ryle, 1957) by followers of John Stuart Mill, that the meaning of a word or phrase was a thing which it "denoted" or "referred to". But this cannot account for even so simple a speech act as "Hello!". Wittgenstein (1958) suggested a way out which has been paraphrased as "Don't ask for the meaning, ask for the use." An algorithm, called by a word when it occurs, indeed is an account of how the word is used: for it embodies a "set of rules", in the context of a "supervisor" program which controls its interactions with algorithms for other words; a group of algorithms for words can be combined in this way to give a "global" algorithm for a phrase, a sentence, or a still larger unit. It should be noted, however, that algorithms are "things", "entities", or "objects", in some sense, and that words are then names for the things they "call" or activate; thus those who postulated Platonic entities for meanings may not have been entirely wrong, although they did not of course envisage any such complex or abstract entities. Indeed, an algorithm, in the modern sense of computer science (see, for example, Knuth, 1968) is not merely a "set of rules", but is commonly described by a highly structured text in a specialized "programming language", with a highly specialized and quite precise syntax and semantics of its own. The "algorithm itself" is often thought of as independent of any particular description of it, and is therefore a more abstract entity than any particular program "coded" in a particular language. It is in the "structural nature" of algorithms that they can be combined in the ways we have hinted to form compound algorithms.

This "procedural" or "algorithmic" approach to meaning has something of a behavioral or experimental tinge to it. To test whether we have the meaning of a word right, we can write a program for it, then run it, and see if it works. This requires a particular "semantic context", "test world", or "universe of discourse", hopefully smaller than that of "the world" as humans know it; it also requires a "supervisor" program; and it requires that one have a sufficiently large number of words coded. We hope to carry out, or at least more precisely describe, such a project and a sketch of an appropriate world appears in Goguen (1972). This is a project in what is often called "artificial intelligence", and it suggests a new meaning for the old phrase "experimental philosophy". At least, if philosophy is the study of meanings, or of linguistic usages, or of "the logic of the functionings of expressions" (Ryle, 1957), then the above project is "experimental philosophy" in that it asks for experiments to be performed in testing the correctness of hypotheses about language meanings: namely, can this program understand what I say (about its small world) well enough to answer questions and take appropriate actions?

Most of the material in this paper bears the same relationship to this sense of "experimental philosophy" that theoretical physics bears to experimental physics. Of course, much of the material can also be interpreted as traditional mathematics or philosophy, or as somewhat less traditional artificial intelligence, in the sense of studying data structures which might be used in various programming problems.

We hope that the value of this kind of rigorous scientific approach to these problems now becomes clear. One has a family of very precise models with very precisely knowable properties; one does not give a somewhat vague and flexible description of a "philosophical system", and then hint that it has "other aspects" which can be developed or called upon to resolve whatever "deeper questions" may arise. One tests the models by writing programs and seeing how well they work; and one accepts, rejects, or revises accordingly.

Objections to artificial intelligence are often heard, to the effect that work in this field is *ad hoc*, unscientific, and incapable of exhibiting a sustained and meaningful growth. This has been true of some past work, but the situation seems to be changing. T. Winograd (1971) and others at M.I.T. and Stanford have done some impressive work. Also, there is a large body of relevant work in computer science, although it tends to lack philosophical sophistication. The viewpoint expressed by the following tentative "definition" tends to unify artificial intelligence (as a branch of computer science), aspects of linguistics and psychology, and of philosophy (at least "ordinary language" philosophy).

Definition 4. Artificial intelligence is the scientific study (both experimental and theoretical) of the representation, manipulation, utilization and acquisition of concepts and conceptual systems.

Difficulties with present-day artificial intelligence do not include lack of competence or of good results, but do include lack of a theoretical foundation and coherent rationale for its relation to other subjects. In particular, the adjective "artificial" is in some ways misleading. For not only can results be applied to performance of well-defined mechanical tasks, as in robotics, but also to better understanding the structure of situations in which humans perform, such as language use and other areas in what has traditionally been the province of philosophy.

8.3. THE ATOMIC HYPOTHESIS FOR CONCEPTS

There are at least two ways to approach the question of the validity of axiom 5: directly, from its intuitive content; and indirectly, through its consequences. We have already given the positive side of the direct view of axiom 5 in section 4. We add to this here only that it is hard to see how one could analyze concepts into parts without having atomic parts. On the negative side, our experience in analyzing real situations suggests that it is often possible, perhaps always possible in nonidealized situations, to analyze further and "deeper", to bring out new elements and relationships which are, or might be, relevant; to see further analogies with already partially explored material, and so on. Indeed, it is part of (some versions of) the credo of modern science that there is no final ultimate knowledge, but only the continuing refinement and development of existing knowledge. So perhaps there are no final atomic constituents of concepts. Moreover, it does seem oversimplified to assume that all atomic concepts are isomorphic, and other-wise bear no particular relationships to one another.

By way of indirect examination, we have that though axiom 5 is the most suspect of all the axioms for inexact concepts, still the representation which results from the axioms is interesting and useful. It leads, as I hope section 4 shows, to a considerable richness of structure for operations and laws; it has a number of nontrivial direct applications; and it forms the conceptual basis for a number of others. On the other hand, the representation of concepts directly by V-sets really does not seem to be adequate to handle the sorts of dynamic processes for which models were sketched in the last subsection, or for the sort of hierarchical considerations posed in subsection 6.1. We conclude from this that the axiom is a rough approximation, useful in some situations, suggestive perhaps in others, and finally misleading in still others.

Let us go over one aspect of this argument more carefully. If we imagine **C** as a universe of concepts which are dynamic, hierarchical and interactive, with modelling processes as morphisms, the other axioms do not seem so implausible as the atomic hypothesis. Surely the static concepts $\varnothing$ and T are still in **C,** and the formation of new processes from old in axioms 2 and 4 do not seem very problematic. The nontriviality assertion of axiom 6 is still harmless, and we are left with axioms 3 and 5. Except that it may not be so clear anymore what one ought to mean by subconcepts in the sense of sub-process, cdl ordering does not seem implausible. As already mentioned, disjointedness in axiom 3 is really another part of the atomic hypothesis. This and axiom 5 remain as clearly less compelling. Thus any incredulity with the final representation result must be reflected most strongly upon these assumptions.

It is hard to see how one could otherwise so carefully support the conclusion that the atomic hypothesis is an approximation particularly useful in one-level static situations. We suggest that this technique, of proving a rigorous categorical representation theorem from axioms about a structure, exploring the usefulness of the representation, and then reflecting credit and/or doubt back on the most sensitive hypothesis, should be of utility in other areas of "soft science", particularly psychology and sociology. It would also, of course, be interesting to apply it to other questions in the theory of concepts, or in other areas of philosophy and artificial intelligence.

Before leaving this subject it should be mentioned that the atomic hypothesis we have been exploring is not identical to that first advanced and then refuted by Wittgenstein. Indeed, it could not be identical unless it were part of (a perhaps rigorous mathematical representation of) exactly the same philosophical system. Since Wittgenstein was thinking in the Tractatus (1922) in terms of the logical combination of symbols, there is clearly some difference in viewpoint. Nonetheless, I feel that the same issue is involved, and that Wittgenstein's problem is also illuminated, though it be by reflected light. It might be noted that Wittgenstein's reasons for the inadequacy of his earlier approach are very like the ones discussed here, and in fact deeply influenced the work of this paper. One improvement we wish to claim is greater precision and clarity in some aspects of the argument, particularly the representation theorem, its consequences, and the various more elaborate data structures which were proposed in section 6. These remarks will also apply to the work of a number of other philosophers who have considered these problems from a variety of other points of view.

The general considerations of this subsection point, in my opinion, toward the idea that "meaning" has its "root" in something far deeper. For even if one of our models proves *fully* adequate as an explanation for the *structure* of meaning, this will tell us little or nothing about how words and their meanings came into the possession of human beings; or about how words and meanings seem to grow, almost as living beings, within the matrix of their supporting culture; about how meanings are communicated or shared; about their relationships to human aspirations; or ultimately perhaps, about the nature of man. This is not to deny that the structures discussed in this paper could be useful in such questions, but clearly other ingredients are also involved, and perhaps some aspects truly lie in Wittgenstein's (1922) realm of "that of which one cannot speak".

Appendix

CATEGORY THEORY

This section contains those definitions from category theory which are either more basic or more technical than the general level of the main text. We give only the most essential examples and clarifying discussion, and no results whatsoever. The reader who wants more detailed background is referred to MacLane & Birkhoff (1967), especially chap. XV, for an undergraduate mathematics level algebra oriented approach; to MacLane (1971), Pareigis (1970), or Mitchell (1965) for a graduate mathematics level approach; and to Goguen, Thatcher, Wagner & Wright (1973 and 1974) for a graduate computer science oriented approach (which should also be readable by those with undergraduate level mathematics and/or mathematical logic training).

Definition. A *category* **C** consists of:

(1) a class $|\mathbf{C}|$, whose elements are called *objects*;
(2) a class, denoted **C**, whose elements are called *morphisms*;
(3) functions $\partial_0, \partial_1 : \mathbf{C} \to |\mathbf{C}|$, called *source* and *target* respectively;
(4) a function $1 : |\mathbf{C}| \to \mathbf{C}$ called the *identity function* (we often write 1_A or $1A$ for $1(A)$);
(5) a partial binary function $\circ : \mathbf{C} \times \mathbf{C} \to \mathbf{C}$ called *composition* (note that we write $f \circ g$ or even fg for $\circ(f,g)$)
such that the following axioms hold for $f, g, h \varepsilon \mathbf{C}$ and $A \varepsilon |\mathbf{C}|$:

(1) $\partial_0 1_A = A$ and $\partial_1 1_A = A$;
(2) if $\partial_0 f = A$, then $f \circ 1A = f$, and
    if $\partial_1 f = A$, then $1A \circ f = f$;
(3) if $f \circ g$ is defined, then $\partial_0 f = \partial_1 g$;
(4) if $\partial_0 f = \partial_1 g$ and $\partial_1 g = \partial_0 h$, then both $(f \circ g) \circ h$ and $f \circ (g \circ h)$ are defined and are equal.

The basic intuitive idea is that a category represents a type of mathematical structure by giving the system of objects with that structure and (more importantly) of structure-preserving mappings between those objects. Following some basic facts and conventions about categories, we will discuss in some detail the "category of sets", which represents "discrete" structure. For the moment, we note it has sets as objects and set mappings (i.e. functions) as morphisms. Of course, composition and identities are as usual. In much the same way, there is a "category of groups" with groups as objects and group homomorphisms as morphisms. And similarly, there are categories of vector spaces, fuzzy sets, topological spaces, semigroups, and so on and on.

Fact 1. $\partial_i 1 \partial_j f = \partial_j f$ for all $i, j = 0, 1$.

Proof. Let $\partial_j f = A$. Then $\partial_i 1 \partial_j f = \partial_i 1A = A = \partial_j f$ by axiom (1). $\square$

The source and target functions, ∂_0 and ∂_1, tell where the morphism goes from and to (respectively) while the identity function gives for each object A an identity morphism from A to A. If $f \varepsilon \mathbf{C}$, $\partial_0 f = A$ and $\partial_1 f = B$, it is customary to write $f : A \to B$ or $A \xrightarrow{f} B$ to indicate these facts schematically. Thus $1_A : A \to A$. Sometimes it is convenient to "identify" 1_A with A, so that $1 : |\mathbf{C}| \to \mathbf{C}$ can be thought of as an "inclusion function", and we might write $A : A \to A$.

The collection of all morphisms in **C** from A to B, for $A, B \varepsilon |\mathbf{C}|$, is denoted $\mathbf{C}[A,B]$.

Fact 2. $f \circ g$ is defined iff $\partial_0 f = \partial_1 g$.

Proof. We need only show that $\partial_0 f = \partial_1 g$ implies $f \circ g$ defined, since the converse is axiom (3). Let $h = 1 \partial_0 g$. Then by (4), $(f \circ g) \circ h$ is defined, and in particular, $f \circ g$ is defined. $\square$

Thus for $f : C \to D$ and $g : A \to B$, $f \circ g$ is defined iff $B = C$, and then the "composite arrow" $A \overset{g}{\to} B \overset{f}{\to} D$ equals $A \overset{f \circ g}{\to} D$. The assertion just made for the source and target of the composite require a separate formal justification, given as follows.

Fact 3. If $f \circ g$ is defined, then $\partial_0(f \circ g) = \partial_0 g$ and $\partial_1(f \circ g) = \partial_1 f$.

Proof. By fact 2 [or by axiom (3)], if $f \circ g$ is defined, then $\partial_0 f = \partial_1 g$. Now let $h = 1 \partial_0 g$, and say $\partial_0 g = A$. Then by (4), $(f \circ g) \circ h$ is defined, so that $\partial_1 h = \partial_0(f \circ g)$ by (3) again. But $\partial_1 h = \partial_1 1_A = A$ by (1) (or by fact 1). Therefore $\partial_0(f \circ g) = A = \partial_0 g$, as we wished. On the other hand, by (4), $(1 \partial_1 f) \circ (f \circ g)$ is defined, so $\partial_0 1 \partial_1 f = \partial_1(f \circ g)$. But $\partial_0 1 \partial_1 f = \partial_1 f$, so $\partial_1(fg) = \partial_1 f$. $\square$

Example. Perhaps the most familiar and important category is that of *sets* and functions, denoted **Set**. Thus, $|\textbf{Set}|$ is the class of all sets, and morphisms are triples $<A,f,B>$, where A, B are sets and $f \subseteq A \times B$ satisfies the *functional property*: if $<a,b> \, \varepsilon f$ and $<a,b'> \, \varepsilon f$, then $b = b'$; and for each $a \, \varepsilon A$, there is some $b \, \varepsilon B$ such that $<a,b> \, \varepsilon f$. Of course, we write $A \overset{f}{\to} B$ or $f : A \to B$ rather than $<A,f,B>$; and we write $b = f(a)$ rather than $<a,b> \, \varepsilon f$. Sometimes we even write $a \overset{f}{\to} b$ or $f : a \to b$ for $<a,b> \, \varepsilon f$. We define $\partial_0 <A,f,B> = A$ and $\partial_1 <A,f,B> = B$. Composition is the usual composition of functions, $<B,f,C> \circ <A,g,B> = <A,fg,C>$, where $fg = \{<a,c> \, | \text{ there exists some } b \, \varepsilon B \text{ such that } <b,c> \, \varepsilon f \text{ and } <a,b> \, \varepsilon g\}$. The identity 1_A is the "diagonal function" on A, $<A, \Delta_A, A>$, where $\Delta_A = \{<a,a> \, | \, a \, \varepsilon A\}$. The axioms (1)–(4) are now easily verified.

There are a number of special conditions which morphisms in a fixed category **C** might satisfy, and which play an important role in the general.

Definition. A morphism $f : A \to B$ is *monic* (or is a *monomorphism*) iff for all $g, h : C \to A$, if fg and fh are defined and equal, then $g = h$. Similarly $f : A \to B$ is *epic* (or is an *epimorphism*) iff for all $g, h : B \to C$, if gf and hf are defined and equal, then $g = h$. Finally, $f : A \to B$ is an *isomorphism* iff there is a morphism $g : B \to A$ such that $fg = 1_B$ and $gf = 1_A$. We also say the objects A and B are *isomorphic* if there is an isomorphism $f : A \to B$.

In the category of sets, the monics are exactly the injections, the epics the surjections, and the isomorphisms the bijections, as expected. This is often, but not always, the case in categories where such assertions make sense. There are also certain properties of objects which are of special interest in this paper.

Definition. An object $T \varepsilon |\textbf{C}|$ is *terminal* iff there is exactly one morphism $A \to T$ in **C** for each object A in **C**. Dually, an object $\varnothing$ in **C** in *initial* iff there is exactly one morphism $\varnothing \to A$ in **C** for each $A \varepsilon |\textbf{C}|$.

In **Set,** the empty set $\varnothing$ is initial, and any one point set is terminal. Not every category has terminal (or initial) objects; but the important property of terminal (and initial) objects is their essential uniqueness if they do exist, as expressed in the following.

Fact 4. Any two terminal objects in a category **C** are isomorphic in **C**, and in fact, are isomorphic by a unique isomorphism in **C**.

Proof. Say T and T' are terminal in **C**. Then there are unique morphism $f : T \to T'$ and $g : T' \to T$ in **C**. Moreover, by composition we have morphisms $fg : T' \to T'$ and $gf : T \to T$ in **C**. But we also have morphisms $1_{T'} : T' \to T'$ and $1_T : T \to T$ in **C**. So by uniqueness, $fg = 1_T$, and $gf = 1_{T'}$, thus showing f and g isomorphisms and T, T' isomorphic. ◻

Essentially the same assertion and proof hold for initial objects.

Definition. A *functor* F from a category $\mathbf{C}$ to another $\mathbf{D}$, written $F : \mathbf{C} \rightarrow \mathbf{D}$, consists of a function $|F| : |\mathbf{C}| \rightarrow |\mathbf{D}|$, and for each pair $C, C' \varepsilon |\mathbf{C}|$, a function $F_{CC'} : \mathbf{C}[C,C] \rightarrow \mathbf{D}[|F|C, |F|C']$, such that the following conditions hold:

(1) $F_{CC}(1_C) = 1_{|F|C}$;
(2) if $f : B \rightarrow C$ and $g : A \rightarrow B$ in $\mathbf{C}$, then $F_{AB}(fg) = F_{BC}(f) \circ F_{AB}(g)$.

It is easy to see that the sets $\mathbf{C}[C,C']$ are always disjoint, and that their union is $\mathbf{C}$, the class of all morphisms, so that the collection of functions $F_{CC'}$ defines a "global" function $F : \mathbf{C} \rightarrow \mathbf{D}$ on morphisms. Thus one can omit the subscripts on $F_{CC'}$, and we often shall.

A functor $F : \mathbf{C} \rightarrow \mathbf{D}$ is *full* iff each $F_{CC'}$ is surjective, and is *faithful* iff each $F_{CC'}$ is injective. A functor $F : \mathbf{C} \rightarrow \mathbf{D}$ is *representative* iff each $D \varepsilon |\mathbf{D}|$ is isomorphic to some $F(C)$, for $C \varepsilon |\mathbf{C}|$. A functor which is full, faithful, and representative is an *equivalence* of categories (see also definition 3 of the text). This is in many ways a more interesting and useful notion than isomorphism for categories.

There are quite a number of constructions familiar in many concrete instances which can be defined intrinsically or "categorically". Perhaps the most basic of these is that of (Cartesian) product.

Definition. Let $\mathbf{C}$ be a category and let $<A_i>_{i \varepsilon I}$ be a family of objects in $\mathbf{C}$. Then a (*Cartesian*) *product* of the family in $\mathbf{C}$, if it exists, is an object A in $\mathbf{C}$, denoted $\Pi_{i \varepsilon I} A_i$ or $\Pi_i A_i$, together with a family $<p_i : A \rightarrow A_i>_{i \varepsilon I}$ of morphisms in $\mathbf{C}$, called *projections*, such that if $<q_i : B \rightarrow A_i>_{i \varepsilon I}$ is any other such family, then there is a unique morphism $n : B \rightarrow A$ in $\mathbf{C}$ such that $p_i n = q_i$ for all $i \varepsilon I$.

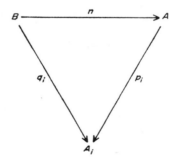

In **Set** the usual Cartesian product with the obvious projections satisfies the conditions of this definition. A very important fact about the above notion of product is that the object defined is uniquely determined up to isomorphism in $\mathbf{C}$, if it exists at all (some categories actually do fail to have products). We could show this fact directly, but it is simpler, and more suggestive for later developments, to go through an auxiliary construction which reduces the situation to that of fact 4.

Given a collection $\underline{A} = <A_i>_{i \varepsilon I}$ of objects in $\mathbf{C}$ (i.e. a function $I \rightarrow |\mathbf{C}|$), let us temporarily call a collection of morphisms $<A_i : A \rightarrow A_i>_{i \varepsilon I}$ a *cone* over $\underline{A}$, with *vertex A*. Then it is reasonable to define a *morphism of cones* over A, $<q_i : B \to A_i>_{i \in I} \to <p_i : A \to A_i>_{i \in I}$ to be a morphism $n : B \to A$ in **C** such that $q_i = p_i n$ for all $i \varepsilon I$.

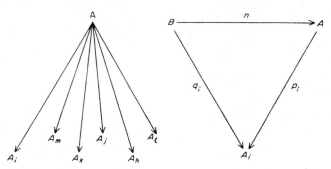

With the obvious definitions of source, target, identity, and composition, this gives rise to a category **C**/A of cones in **C** over A. It is now easy to see that a product of $<A_i>_{i \in I}$ is exactly the same thing as a terminal object in **C**/A. Then fact 4 implies that any two terminal cones are isomorphic, and in particular, so are their vertex objects.

If $<p_i : A \to A_i>_{i \in I}$ is a product of A and $<q_i : B \to A_i>_{i \in I}$ is another cone over A, then the unique cone morphism $B \to A$ is often called the *tupling* of the q_i, and the denoted $[q_i]_{i \in I}$. In case $I = \{0,1\}$, we have *binary* (Cartesian) product, and the notations $A_0 \pi A_1$ or $A_0 \times A_1$ for the product, and $[q_0, q_1]$ for the tupling, are convenient. The analogous notations are used for other finite index sets.

We now use a very similar cone construction to discuss the notion of an *equalizer* of two morphisms $f, g : A \to B$ in a category **C**. In this case, the diagram and cone in question are as below and the condition required for $<e, h>$ to be a

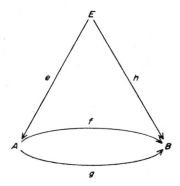

cone over $f, g : A \to B$ is that $ef = eg = h$. (Actually, the h is unnecessary, since it is determined by the other data). A morphism of cones over f, g is a morphism $a : E \to E'$ in **C** such that $e = e'a$ and $h = h'a$ (the latter condition again follows from the former).

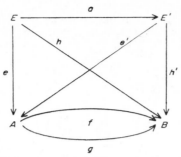

Then a terminal object in the category of cones over $f,g : A \to B$, if it exists, is called an "equalizer" for f and g. It can be shown that the resulting $e : E \to A$ is always monic, and one generally omits the morphism h. In **Set**, the equalizer of $f,g : A \to B$ is the inclusion $\{a \mid f(a) = g(a)\} \subseteq A$ of the subset where f and g are equal into their common source set, A.

A somewhat esoteric looking concept which is nonetheless quite basic to category theory is the following.

Definition. Given functors $F,G : \mathbf{A} \to \mathbf{B}$, a *natural transformation* from F to G is a family $<\eta_A : F(A) \to G(A)>_{A \in |A|}$ of morphisms in **B**, such that for each $a : A \to A'$ in **A**, $\eta_{A'} \circ F(a) = G(a) \circ \eta_A$, i.e. the diagram commutes in **B**. We write $\eta : F \Rightarrow G$ to symbolize this situation. If each η_A is an isomorphism in **B**, η is called a *natural equivalence* or a *natural isomorphism* of the functors F and G.

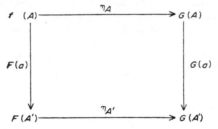

Actually, it is only this last special case which is important in the text. We now give a broad generalization of the notions of product and equalizer previously given, through a suitable generalization of the notion of cone.

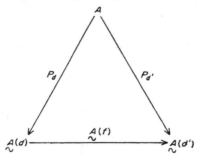

We shall say, without further explanation, that a diagram in **C** is a functor with target **C**. Then a cone in **C** over a diagram $\underline{A} : \mathbf{D} \to \mathbf{C}$ is a collection $<p_d : \underline{A} \to \underline{A}(d)>_{d \epsilon |\mathbf{D}|}$ of morphisms in **C**, such that for each $f : d \to d'$ in **D**, the diagram

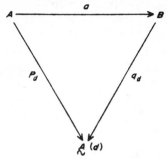

commutes in **C**. A morphism $<p_d : A \to \underline{A}(d)>_{d \epsilon |\mathbf{D}|} \to <q_d : B \to \underline{A}(d)>_{d \epsilon |\mathbf{D}|}$ of cones over $\underline{A}$ is a morphism $a : A \to B$ in **C** such that for all $d \epsilon |\mathbf{D}|$ the diagram commutes in **C**. Denote the category of cones in **C** over $\underline{A}$ by $\mathbf{C}/\underline{A}$. Then a *limit* of $\underline{A} : \mathbf{D} \to \mathbf{C}$ is a terminal object in $\mathbf{C}/\underline{A}$.

Dually, a *co-cone* under $\underline{A}$ is a collection $<j_d : \underline{A}(d) \to A>_{d \epsilon |\mathbf{D}|}$ of morphisms in **C** such that for all $f : d \to d'$ in **D**, the diagram commutes in **C**. A morphism of co-cones under $\underline{A}$ is a morphism $a : A \to B$ in **C** such that for all $d \epsilon |\mathbf{D}|$ the diagram

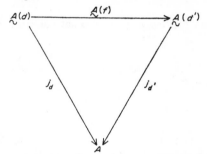

commutes in **C**. The category of co-cones in **C** under $\underline{A}$ is denoted $\underline{A}/\mathbf{C}$, and an initial object in this category is called a *colimit* of $\underline{A}$.

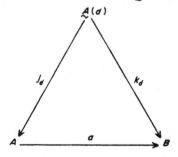

The notion of coproduct given in the text is an example of a colimit, in much the same way that product is an example of limit. One particular notion associated with coproducts is needed in the text, that of the coproduct of two (or more) morphisms in a category $\mathbf{C}$ with coproducts. Let $f : A \rightarrow B$ and $g : C \rightarrow D$ in $\mathbf{C}$. Then $f \amalg g :$ $A \amalg C \rightarrow B \amalg D$ is defined as the unique map from $A \amalg C$ induced by the co-cone under with co-vertex $B \amalg D$ given by

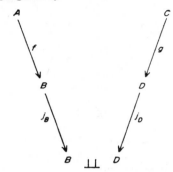

The coproduct of a family $<f_i : A_i \rightarrow B_i>_{i \in I}$ of morphisms is defined analogously using the injections $j_i : B_i \rightarrow \amalg_i B_i$.

Finally, we give some important "regularity" or "niceness" conditions which categories can satisfy.

Definition. A category $\mathbf{C}$ is *complete* if all (small) diagrams in $\mathbf{C}$ have limits, and is *cocomplete* if they all have colimits.

Definition. A category $\mathbf{C}$ is *Cartesian closed* iff it has: a terminal object T; binary (and therefore finite) Cartesian products; and an exponential (this is defined just after proposition 10 in section 4).

References*

ANSCOMBE, G. E. M. (1963). *An Introduction to Wittgenstein's Tractatus* (2nd ed.). London: Harper & Row.

ARBIB, M. A. (1970). Semiring Languages, manuscript. Electrical Engineering Department, Stanford University.

BELLMAN, R., KALABA, R., ZADEH, L. A. (1966). Abstraction and pattern classification. *J. Mathematical Analysis and Applications*, **13**, 1.

BELLMAN, R. G. & ZADEH, L. A. (1970). Decision making in a fuzzy environment. *Management Science*, **17**, B-141.

BELLMAN, R. (1972). Retrospective futurology: a dialogue of civilisations. An interview with J. Wilkinson. Retrospective futurology: some introspective comments, Technical Report No. 72-55, Depts. of Electrical Engineering, Mathematics, and Medicine, University of Southern California.

*This is intended to be a fairly comprehensive bibliography (up to about 1971) of relevant topics in fuzzy logic and category theory, and contains many papers not referenced in the text.

BELLMAN, R. & GIERTZ, M. (1973). On the analytic formalism of the theory of fuzzy sets. *Information Sciences*, **5**, 149.

BIRKHOFF, G. (1960). *Lattice Theory*. Vol. XXV (revised edition). American Mathematical Society Colloquium Publications.

BISHOP, E. (1967). *Foundations of Constructive Analysis*. New York: McGraw-Hill.

BLACK, M. (1937). Vagueness: an exercise in logical analysis. *Phil. Science*, **4**, 427.

BLACK, M. (1963). Reasoning with loose concepts. *Dialogue*, **2**(1), 1.

BLACK, M. (1968). *The Labyrinth of Language*. Praeger.

BOOLE, G. (1854). *An Investigation into the Laws of Thought*. London (paperback edition by Open Court, Chicago, 1940).

BROWN, J. G. (1969). Fuzzy Sets on Boolean Lattices, Report 1957, Ballistic Research Lab., Aberdeen, Maryland.

BROWN, J. G. (1971). A note on fuzzy sets. *Information and Control*, **18**, 32.

BUNGE, M. C. (1966). Categories of Set Valued Functors, Ph.D. Thesis, University of Pennsylvania, Department of Math.

CATON, C. E. (1963) (editor). *Philosphy and Ordinary Language*. Illinois: University of Illinois Press.

CHANG, C. C. (1963). The axiom of comprehension in infinite valued logic. *Mathematica Scandinavica*, **13**, 9.

CHANG, C. C. (1964). Infinite valued logic as a basis for set theory. *Proc. of 1964 International Congress for Logic, Methodology and Philosophy of Science*, North Holland.

CHANG, C. C. & KEISLER, H. J. (1966). *Continuous Model Theory*. Anals of Math. Studies No. 58, Princeton.

CHANG, C. L. (1968). Fuzzy topological spaces. *J. Mathematical Analysis and Applications*, **24**, 182.

CHANG, S. S. L. (1969). Fuzzy dynamic programming and the decision making process. *Proc. 3rd Princeton Conference on Information Science and Systems*, 200.

CHANG, S. K. (1971). Fuzzy programs—theory and applications. *Proc. of Polytechnic Institute of Brooklyn Symposium on Computers and Automata*, 147

CHAPIN, E. W. (1971). An axiomatization of the set theory of Zadeh. *Notices Amer. Math. Soc.*, **687-02-4**, 753.

CHOMSKY, N. & SCHÜTZENBERGER, M. P. (1963). The algebraic theory of context-free languages. In *Computer Programming and Formal Systems*, pp. 118–161. Eds P. Braffort & D. Hirschberg. Amsterdam: North-Holland Co.

CHURCH, A. (1951). A formulation of the logic of sense and denotation. In *Method and Meaning, A Collection of Essays in Honor of Henry M. Sheffer*, pp. 3–24. New York:

COHEN, P. J. (1966). *Set Theory and the Continuums Hypothesis*. New York: W. A. Benjamin Co.

COHEN, P. J. & HIRSCH, R. (1967). Non-cantorian set theory. *Scientific American*, 101.

DELUCA, A. & TERMINI, S. (1972). Algebraic properties of fuzzy sets. *J. Mathematical Analysis and Applications*, **40**, 373.

DELUCA, A. & TERMINI, S. (1972a). A definition of a non-probabilistic entropy in the setting of fuzzy sets theory. *Information and Control*, **20**, 301.

DeLuca, A. & Termini, S. (1972*b*). Algorithmic aspects in the analysis of complex systems, LC/54/71/AL, Laboratorio di Cibernetica del C.N.R., Napoli, Italy.

Eilenberg, S. (1969). The algebraicization of mathematics. In *The Mathematical Sciences, Essays for COSRIMS*. Pp. 153–160. New York: MIT Press.

Eilenberg, S. & MacLane, S. (1945). General theory of natural equivalence. *Trans. Amer. Math. Soc.*, **58**, 231.

Gitman, I. & Levine, M. D. (1970). An algorithm for detecting unimodel fuzzy sets and its applications as a clustering technique. *IEEE Trans. Computers*, **C–19**[7], 583.

Goguen, J. A. (1967). L-fuzzy sets. *J. Mathematical Analysis and Applications*, **18**, 145.

Goguen, J. A. (1968). Categories of fuzzy sets: applications of non-cantorian set theory. Ph.D. Thesis, Department of Mathematics, University of California, Berkeley.

Goguen, J. A. (1969*a*). Categories of L-sets. *Bulletin of the American Mathematical Society*, **75**, 622.

Goguen, J. A. (1969*b*). The logic of inexact concepts. *Synthese*, **19**, 325.

Goguen, J. A. (1969*c*). Representing inexact concepts. ICR quarterly report No. 20, Institute for Computer Research, University of Chicago.

Goguen, J. A. (1970). Mathematical representation of hierarchically organized systems. In *Global Systems Dynamics*. Ed. E. O. Attinger. Pp. 111–29. Berlin: S. Karger.

Goguen, J. A. (1972). Hierarchical inexact data structures in artificial intelligence problems. *Proc. Fifth Hawaii International Conference on Systems Sciences, Honolulu*, 345.

Goguen, J. A. (1973). Systems theory concepts in computer science. *Proc. Sixth Hawaii International Conference on Systems Sciences, Honolulu. Hawaii*, 77.

Goguen, J. A. (1974). The fuzzy tychonoff theorem. *J. Mathematical Analysis and Applications*, **73**, 734.

Goguen, J., Thatcher, J., Wagner, E. & Wright, J. (1973). A junction between computer science and category theory, I: Basic concepts and examples (Part 1). IBM Research Report RC4526.

Goguen, J., Thatcher, J., Wagner, E. & Wright, J. (1974). A junction between computer science and category theory, II: Universal constructions. IBM Research Report (in preparation).

Hirai, H., Asai, K. & Katajima, S. (1968). Fuzzy automaton and its application to learning control systems. *Memo of the Faculty of English* (Osaka City University), **10**, 67.

Hopcroft, J. E. & Ullman, J. D. (1969). *Formal Languages and their Relation to Automata*. Addison-Wesley.

Kling, R. (1973). Fuzzy planner. Technical Report 168, Computer Science Dept., University of Wisconsin.

Knuth, D. E. (1968). *The Art of Computer Programming*. Vol. I, *Fundamental Algorithms*. Addison-Wesley.

Knuth, D. E. (1973). *The Art of Computer Programming*. Vol. III, *Sorting and Searching*. Addison-Wesley.

Körner, S. (1960). *The Philosophy of Mathematics*. New York: Harper Torchbooks.

LAKOFF, G. (1972). Hedges: A study in meaning criteria and the logic of fuzzy concepts, *Chicago Linguistics Society Meeting.*

LAWVERE, F. W. (1964). An elementary theory of the category of sets. *Proc. Nat. Acad. Sci., U.S.A.,* **52,** 1506.

LEE, E. T., ZADEH, L. A. (1969). Note on fuzzy languages. *Information Sciences,* **1,** 421.

LEE, R. C. T. (1972). Fuzzy logic and the resolution principle. *Journal of the Association for Computing Machinery,* **10,** 109.

LIENTZ, B. P. (1972). On time dependent fuzzy sets. *Information Sciences,* **4,** 367.

LINSKY, L. (1959). Reference and referents. In Caton (1963), part previously published in *The Philosphical Review,* **LXVIII,** 515.

MacLANE, S. (1971). *Category Theory for the Working Mathematician.* Berlin: Springer Verlag.

MacLANE, S. & BIRKHOFF, G. (1967). *Algebra.* New York: Macmillan.

MARINOS, P. N. (1969). Fuzzy logic and its application to switching systems. *IEEE Trans. Computers,* **C–18,** 343.

MITCHELL, B. (1965). *Theory of Categories.* New York: Academic Press.

MIZUMOTO, M., TOYODA, J. & TANAKA, K. (1969). Some considerations on fuzzy automata. *Journal of Computer and System Sciences,* **3,** 409.

MIZUMOTO, M., TOYODA, J. & TANAKA, K. (1973). N-fold fuzzy grammars. *Information Sciences,* **5,** 25.

NASU, M. & HONDA, N. (1968). Fuzzy events realized by finite probabilistic automata. *Inf. Control,* **12,** 284.

NASU, M. & HONDA, N. (1969). Mappings induced by PGSM-mappings and some recursively unsolvable problems of finite probabilistic automata. *Information and Control,* **15,** 250.

NASU, M. & HONDA, N. (1968). Fuzzy events realized by finite probabilistic automata. *Information and Control,* **12,** 284.

NASU, M. & HONDA, N. (1969). Mappings induced by PGSM-mappings and some recursively unsolvable problems of finite probabilistic automata. *Information and Control,* **15,** 250.

NEGOITA, C. V. (1973). On the application of the fuzzy sets separation theorem for automatic classification in information retrieval systems. *Information Sciences,* **5,** 279.

NETTO, A. B. (1968). Fuzzy classes. *Notices of the American Mathematical Society,* **68T–H28,** 945.

PAREIGIS, B. (1970). *Categories and Functors.* Academic Press.

PAZ, A. (1967). Fuzzy star functions, probabilistic automata and their approximation by nonprobabilistic automata. *J. Computer & System Sciences,* **1,** 371.

PREPARATA, F. D. & YEH, R. T. (1972). Continuously valued logic. *J. Computer & System Sciences,* **6,** 397.

POSTON, T. (1971). Fuzzy geometry. Doctoral Thesis, University of Warwick, England.

QUINE, W. V. O. (1936). Toward a calculus of concepts. *J. Symbolic Logic,* **1,** 2.

QUINE, W. V. O. (1960). *Word and Object.* New York: MIT Press.

REDDY, M. (1972). Reference and metaphor in human language. English Department Thesis, University of Chicago.

ROSENFELD, A. (1971). Fuzzy groups. *J. Mathematical Analysis and Applications*, **35**, 512.

RUSPINI, E. H. (1969). A new approach to clustering. *Information and Control*, **15**, 22.

RUSPINI, E. H. (1970). Numerical methods for fuzzy clustering. *Information Sciences*, **2**, 319.

RUSSELL, B. (1923). Vagueness. *Australian J. Phil.*, **1**, 84.

RYLE, G. (1957). The theory of meaning. In *British Philosophy in the Mid-century*. Ed. C. A. Mace. Pp. 239–64. London: Allen and Unwin, Ltd.

SANTOS, E. S. (1968). Maximin automata. *Information and Control*, **13**, 363.

SANTOS, E. S. (1969). Maximin sequential-like machines and chains. *Math. Sys. Th.*, **3**, 300–309.

SANTOS, E. S. (1972). Max-product machines. *J. J. Mathematical Analysis and Applications*, **37**, 677.

SANTOS, E. S. & WEE, W. G. (1968). General formulation of sequential machines. *Information and Control*, **12**, 5.

SCHLOMINK, D. I. (1967). A characterization of the category of topological spaces. Ph.D. Dissertation, McGill University.

SCHOENFIELD, J. R. (1967). *Mathematical Logic*. Addison-Wesley.

SCOTT, D. (1970). Outline of a mathematical theory of computation. *Proc. 4th Princeton Conference on Information Science and Systems*.

SCOTT, D. (1972). Continuous lattices. *Proc. of the 1971 Dalhousie Conf.* Springer Lecture Note Series, No. 274. Berlin: Springer Verlag.

SCOTT, D. (1973). Lattice-theoretic models for the λ-calculus (in preparation).

SCOTT, D., SOLOVAY, P. (1968). Boolean valued models for set theory. L.A. Conference Set Theory.

SHAMIR, E. (1968). Algebraic, rational and context-free power series in noncommuting variables. In *Algebraic Theory of Machines, Languages, and Semigroups*. Ed. M. A. Arbib. Pp. 327–41. New York: Academic Press.

SIY, P. & CHEN, C. S. (1972). Minimization of fuzzy functions. *IEEE Trans. on Computers*, 100.

TSICHRITZIS, D. (1969). Fuzzy properties and almost solvable problems. Princeton University, Dept. EE, Comp. Sci. Lab. Technical Report 70.

TSICHRITZIS, D. (1969). Measures on countable sets. Technical Report No. 8, University of Toronto. Dept. of Computer Science.

VON NEUMANN, J. (1961). *Collected Works*. Vol. I. New York: Pergamon Press.

WATANABE, S. (1969). Modified concepts of logic, probability, and information based on generalized continuous characteristic function. *Information and Control*, **15**, 1.

WEE, W. G. (1967). On a generalization of adoptive algorithms and applications of the fuzzy set concept to pattern classification. Ph.D. Thesis, Technical Report TR-EE-67-7, EE Dept., Purdue University, Lafayette, Ind.

WEE, W. G. & FU, K. S. (1969). A formulation of fuzzy automata and its application as a model of learning systems. *IEEE Trans. SSC*, **5**, 215.

WINOGRAD, T. (1971). Procedures as a representation for data in a computer program for understanding natural language. Report A1 TR-17 Artificial Intelligence Lab., MIT.

WITTGENSTEIN, L. (1922). *Tractatus Logico-Philosophicus*. New York and London.

WITTGENSTEIN, L. (1958). *Philosophical Investigations* (2nd ed.). (Trans. G. E. M. Anscombe). Oxford: Blackwell.

WONG, C. K. (1971). Covering properties of fuzzy topological spaces. IBM Research Report, Yorktown Heights, New York.

WONG, C. K. (1973). Fuzzy points and local properties of fuzzy topology. Report IVCDCS-R-73-561. University of Illinois at Urbana-Champaign.

WONG, C. K. (1973). Covering properties of fuzzy topology spaces. *J. Mathematical Analysis and Applications* (in preparation).

WONG, C. K. (1973). Fuzzy topology: product and quotient theorems. *J. Mathematical Analysis and Applications* (in preparation).

YEH, R. T. (1970). A Study of General Systems Using Automata. *Cybernetica*, **13**, 3, 180–194.

YOELI, M. (1961). A note on a generalization of Boolean matrix theory. *Amer. Math. Monthly*, **68**, 552.

ZADEH, L. A. (1963). Optimality and non-scalar-valued performance criteria. *IEEE Trans. Automatic Control*, AC-8, 315.

ZADEH, L. A. (1965a). Fuzzy sets. *Information and Control*, **8**, 338.

ZADEH, L. A. (1965b). Fuzzy sets and systems. *Proc. Symp. Systems Theory*. Pp. 29–37. New York: Polytechnic Press of Polytechnic Inst. of Brooklyn.

ZADEH, L. A. (1966). Shadows of fuzzy sets. *Problems in Transmission of Information*, **2**, 37 (in Russian).

ZADEH, L. A. (1968a). Fuzzy algorithms. *Information and Control*, **12**, 94.

ZADEH, L. A. (1968b). Probability measures of fuzzy events. *J. Mathematical Analysis and Applications*, **23**, 421.

ZADEH, L. A. (1969). Toward of theory of fuzzy systems. ERL Report 69–2, Electronics Research Lab., University of California, Berkeley.

ZADEH, L. A. (1971a). Quantitative fuzzy semantics. *Information and Control*, **3**, 159.

ZADEH, L. A. (1971b). Fuzzy languages and their relation to human and machine intelligence. Memo. ERL-M302, Electronics Research Laboratory, University of California, Berkeley.

ZADEH, L. A. (1971c). Similarity relations and fuzzy orderings. *Information Sciences*, **3**, 338.

ZADEH, L. A. (1972). A fuzzy set—theoretic interpretation of hedges. Memo, Dept. of Electrical Engineering and Computer Science, University of California, Berkeley.

Łukasiewicz logic and fuzzy set theory†

R. GILES

Department of Mathematics, Queen's University, Canada

(*Received 16 May 1975*)

A new form of logic is described, originally developed for the formalization of physical theories, the essential feature being a "fuzzification" of the concept of a proposition. A proposition is not regarded as being necessarily true or false; it is defined not via truth conditions but in terms of a definite commitment that is assumed by the speaker. In the case of an atomic proposition the commitment amounts to a bet on the outcome of some agreed test; for a compound proposition it leads to a dialogue between the speaker and an opponent. The resulting logic corresponds closely to the infinite-valued logic $Ł_{\alpha}$ of Łukasiewicz. In fact, the approach provides a *dialogue interpretation* of $Ł_{\infty}$ and leads to a convenient method for establishing logical identities.

Set theory is then developed, not by taking *set* as a primitive concept but by assuming each set A is determined by a property P characteristic of its members: $A = \{x:P(x)\}$. When this is expressed formally the result can be read in two ways according to whether the underlying logic is classical logic or $Ł_{\infty}$ (with the above interpretation). If the propositions $P(x)$ are classical we get ordinary sets; if they are propositions in the new "fuzzy" sense we get fuzzy sets (*f*-sets). The situation is illustrated by a number of definitions and theorems involving simple operations on *f*-sets. Lastly, the notion of a *convex f-set* is defined, and a simple theorem is stated and proved using $Ł_{\infty}$ and the dialogue method of proof. All statements and proofs are expressed in terms of the new logic. In particular, use of the quantitative notion of "grade of membership" in a fuzzy set is entirely avoided.

1. Introduction

In developing a language for the formalization of physical theories I have been led to abandon ordinary logic in favour of a non-classical logic (Giles, 1974, in press). This logic, defined by means of a dialogue interpretation, reduces with certain mild assumptions to the infinite-valued logic $Ł_{\infty}$ of Łukasiewicz (1930). (With much stronger assumptions—not acceptable in the context of the formalization problem—it reduces further to classical logic.) Now, it turns out that, with this dialogue interpretation, Łukasiewicz logic is exactly appropriate for the formulation of the "fuzzy set theory" first described by Zadeh (1965); indeed, it is not too much to claim that $Ł_{\infty}$ is related to fuzzy set theory exactly as classical logic is related to ordinary set theory.

It is my object here to justify this claim by developing the elements of fuzzy set theory in terms of the new logic. I first give the motivation for this logic, whose essential feature is a new definition of the concept of a proposition. I describe the dialogue interpretation and show how it gives rise to the truth tables of $Ł_{\infty}$ and leads to a new method for establishing logical identities.

We then pass to set theory. Instead of adopting the notion of a set as a primitive concept I assume that each set may be defined in terms of a unary predicate (property)

†The original version of this paper was published in *Proceedings of the 5th International Symposium on Multiple-Valued Logic, IEEE 1975.*

that characterizes its members. When this is expressed formally the result may be read in two ways, according to whether the underlying logic is taken to be classical logic or $Ł_\infty$. (Syntactically, they are identical.) With the former interpretation we get ordinary set theory; with the latter fuzzy set theory. Similar remarks apply to the definitions and theorems characterizing various simple operations and relations involving sets. In the final section this approach is used in giving a brief treatment of convex fuzzy sets, and a simple theorem is stated and proved using $Ł_\infty$ and the dialogue method of proof. In general, however, proofs have been omitted owing to lack of space.

Since Zadeh's original paper a considerable literature has appeared on fuzzy set theory and its applications. It is not appropriate to review this here but I should like to mention three items: first, the work of Goguen (1967, 1968–69), which is similar in spirit to the present paper; secondly, that of Chang, who has developed in detail the algebraic properties of a class of many-valued logics including $Ł_\infty$ (1958) and applied this work to the definition and metamathematical study of a generalized set theory (1965); thirdly, a neglected series of papers by Klaua (1965–1970), which I came across only when the work reported here was essentially complete. Klaua (see especially 1966a) develops a "many-valued set theory" based on Łukasiewicz logic in a manner similar to (but much more sophisticated than) that adopted here. In particular, most of the logical identities given here have been independently obtained by Klaua. His work goes far beyond the present paper in the mathematical development of the subject and deserves much more attention than it appears to have received. Both Klaua and Chang discuss, in different notations, the concepts of "bold" conjunction and disjunction introduced here in section 4, and Klaua applies these to set theory as in section 7.

2. A pragmatic logic

I shall first give the original motivation for the new approach to logic and then describe how it applies to those practical situations which have provided the motivation for the development of fuzzy set theory.

In order to give a precise account of a physical theory it is necessary to describe how the verifiable assertions of the theory are to be interpreted. For this purpose the language employed must include expressions which refer to particular experiments. In fact, it is sufficient to refer only to "elementary experiments", an *elementary* experiment being one which has only two possible outcomes, which we may designate "yes" and "no". For precision it is desirable to use a formal language for this purpose, and it turns out (Giles, in press) that there is a natural way of doing this in which the expressions which designate elementary experiments have the syntactic structure of prime sentences.[†]

At first sight this situation, which is familiar in the case of formalized mathematical theories, seems to accord perfectly with classical logic: one need merely describe a sentence as *true* if the corresponding elementary experiment gives the outcome "yes" and *false* otherwise. However, a serious difficulty immediately arises. Many of the elementary experiments referred to in physical theories are *dispersive*: i.e. they have the property that a repetition of the experiment does not necessarily produce a repetition of the outcome. This is most obvious in the case of quantum mechanics, but it occurs also with other theories, being then usually ascribed to thermal or statistical "fluctuations". To take

---

† A *prime* sentence is one without logical symbols. I use the term "sentence" when referring to the syntactic structure of an expression, and "proposition" when the semantics is in question.

account of this situation it is necessary either to give up interpreting the expressions mentioned above as prime propositions—which turns out to be very unsatisfactory—or to develop some alternative approach to logic which is capable of dealing with the situation. I follow the latter route here.

The changes required are fundamental. We must give up the classical definition of a proposition as "a statement that is either true or false", since the notion of truth is no longer available. What is to be done then? In the case of a *prime* proposition an obvious alternative is as follows.

Definition 1. A *prime proposition* is an expression to which there corresponds a definite elementary experiment. If this experiment is dispersive we call the prime proposition *dispersive*; if not, it is *dispersion-free*.

So far so good. However, to deal with compound propositions we need a new notion of the concept of a proposition itself. To this end we shall be quite realistic. We regard a proposition as a statement made by some speaker. It does not tell us anything about the "world"; at best it informs us about the beliefs of the speaker, and in the case of an irresponsible speaker it may not even do that. What can we do to make the best of this situation? Clearly, we cannot expect a statement to represent *more* than the belief of the speaker, but we can at least try to avoid irresponsibility. Now, in practice irresponsibility is held in check in the following way. He who asserts a proposition incurs a certain *risk*, if only of loss of face, if his assertion should turn out to be unjustified. Indeed, in jurisprudence this aspect is emphasized: in many cases an assertion is considered to entail a legal commitment on the part of the speaker. This suggests a possible solution: Let us try the following definition.

Definition 2. A *proposition* is an expression whose assertion entails a definite commitment on the part of the speaker.

Thus the "meaning" of a proposition is now to be given not by describing conditions for its truth but by assigning some commitment that is assumed by him who asserts it. I shall call such an assignment a *tangible meaning* for the proposition. In order that a prime proposition, as defined above, should be a proposition in this sense we must associate some commitment with its assertion. Since the assertion should surely represent a belief that the corresponding elementary experiment will have outcome "yes" we may suppose that the commitment takes the form of a penalty should a trial of this experiment yield the outcome "no". Conceivably, the penalty could vary arbitrarily from case to case, but for the sake of simplicity we shall assume that it has the form of a constant (negative) utility, which we may for convenience denote by $1.† This gives the following.

Rule 1. He who asserts a prime proposition undertakes to pay $1 should a trial of the corresponding elementary experiment yield the outcome "no".

It is to be understood that when *one* trial has been carried out and the debt (if any) paid then the obligation incurred under Rule 1 has been discharged. Notice that repetition of the assertion increases the commitment and can thus be used to express a stronger belief—a fact well known to young children!

---

†The notion of utility that is introduced here may be left vague, since everything we assume about it is embodied in a basic axiom that is described below (just before Theorem 1). The present informal introduction merely provides motivation for that axiom.

I now interrupt the argument to explain the connection with fuzzy set theory. In the above we have been concerned with the most exact of all sciences, physics. Let us now turn to the opposite extreme, the use of language in ordinary life. Consider an everyday proposition such as "John Smith is tall". Although we may perhaps agree that everyone over 7 ft and no one under 4 ft is tall, it clearly does not conform to normal usage to lay down any particular height and claim that everyone over and no one under that height is tall. Nevertheless, the proposition clearly has a useful meaning. For the clarification of this meaning it is natural to ask how we might decide—for instance to settle a bet—whether "John is tall", with the understanding that "tall" is used in the sense of the man in the street. The obvious answer is to ask the man in the street! We might agree, for instance, on the following procedure: let us go with John Smith into the street and ask the first man we meet whether he considers John tall; his opinion will be considered final. Now this is just an elementary experiment—a well-defined procedure resulting in an outcome, "yes" or "no". Thus with such an agreement the proposition, "John Smith is tall", becomes a "prime proposition" in the sense defined above. Moreover, it is clearly dispersive—repetition of the experiment will not always produce the same outcome. Thus we are faced with just the same situation as arises in the formalization of physical theories.

It seems likely that any proposition framed in common language can be given an exact meaning in the sense of Definition 1 (and in agreement with the intuitive meaning) in a similar way: namely, by laying down a definite procedure of arbitration, involving the selection of and subsequent appeal to an "umpire". Naturally, the umpire need not be the man in the street; perhaps more typically he may be some sort of "expert witness" or possibly a particular individual.

Returning to the main argument, we must now assign a meaning, in accordance with Definition 2, to every compound proposition. As in the classical case it is convenient to use a recursive procedure, explaining the significance of each logical connective by describing the commitment associated with any compound proposition in which it is the main connective in terms of those associated with its components. Of course, the choice of these commitments is a matter for deliberation, the aim being that (a) the meanings assigned to the logical connectives should be acceptable as explications of the corresponding intuitive notions, (b) the language so defined should be of practical value, and (c) this language should reduce (in a suitable sense) to classical logic when applied to dispersion-free propositions.

I now put forward a set of rules in which this procedure is carried out. These rules are to be understood in the following terms. When a speaker makes an assertion it is at first to be regarded as an *offer* to assume the indicated commitment. Any other speaker may respond to this offer, whereupon a debate ensues between these two speakers, in which no other speaker may intervene. The rules govern the conduct of this debate. (We use the usual logical symbols, $\wedge$, $\vee$, $\neg$, $\rightarrow$, $\forall$, $\exists$, denoting respectively "and", "or", "not", "implies", "for all", and "for some".)

Rule 2. Let P and Q be arbitrary sentences.

   (a) He who asserts $P \vee Q$ undertakes to assert either P or Q at his own choice.

   (b) He who asserts $P \wedge Q$ undertakes to assert either P or Q at his opponent's choice.

   (c) He who asserts $P \rightarrow Q$ offers to assert Q if his opponent will assert P.

   (d) To assert $\neg P$ is the same as to assert $P \rightarrow F$, where:

(e) He who asserts F promises to pay his opponent $1. (The symbol F may be regarded as denoting a distinguished prime proposition which always gives outcome "no".)

(f) He who asserts $(\exists xP(x)$ undertakes to assert $P(a)$ for some term a of his own choice.

(g) He who asserts $\forall xP(x)$ undertakes to assert $P(a)$ for some term a chosen by his opponent.

[In (f) and (g) $P(x)$ denotes an open sentence involving a single free variable x and $P(a)$ is the result of replacing x by a.]

The crucial rule is (c). To motivate it consider the case when P and Q are prime propositions. The assertion $P \rightarrow Q$ may then be interpreted as expressing a belief that P is at least as likely as Q to yield outcome "no", an interpretation which accords with classical material implication. In the general case the rule is to be understood in the following terms: If either speaker asserts a proposition of the form $P \rightarrow Q$ then the other speaker must either *admit* it (the assertion is then simply annulled) or *challenge* it by asserting P. In the latter case the first speaker must discharge his obligation by asserting Q, the original assertion then being annulled. An assertion may be challenged only once.

By (d) and (e) the assertion of $\neg P$ amounts to an offer to pay $1 if a trial of P should yield "yes", which is a tangible way of expressing the belief that the outcome will always be "no". The definition of $\vee$ requires no comment. For $\wedge$ observe that although he who asserts $P \wedge Q$ is obliged to assert only one of P and Q he must be prepared to assert either, since he cannot tell which his opponent may choose. The rules for $\exists$ and $\forall$ are natural extensions of those for $\vee$ and $\wedge$.

Through these rules a tangible meaning is assigned to every proposition. In fact, suppose an arbitrary proposition is asserted by one speaker, say "me". The rules then govern an ensuing debate—with "you", say—which ends in a *final position* in which we are each committed to a number of propositions. These propositions are then tried, and the debts incurred under Rules 1 and 2(e) paid.

With dispersive prime propositions the same final position will result in different payments on different occasions. However, depending on my beliefs, there will be certain final positions which seem "acceptable" to me, in that I expect on average a non-negative gain. To reach one of these is, as far as I am concerned, a "win". Thus I will be willing to assert a given proposition P iff ($=$ if and only if) I am able to conduct the ensuing debate in such a way that an acceptable final position is assured. When this is the case we shall say P is true (for me) and write $\models P$.† If several speakers are under consideration we express the statement "P is true for a speaker S" by writing $S \models P$. In this way truth re-enters the theory, albeit only in a subjective form.

As an example, suppose I assert the proposition $P \rightarrow Q$, where P and Q are prime. If you challenge by asserting P then I must reply with Q. The final position so reached may be acceptable to me—for instance if (in my opinion) the probability that P will yield outcome "no" is at least as great as that for Q—and in this case $P \rightarrow Q$ will be true

†The symbol "$\models$" belongs to the metalanguage: $S \models P$ is a proposition in the metalanguage, expressing a property of the proposition P. Since we assume all propositions in the metalanguage are dispersion-free we can use classical logic there, and are not obliged to assign a tangible meaning to $S \models P$. (It is also possible to introduce $\models$ into the primary language, for instance by the following rule: he who asserts $\models P$ agrees either to pay $1 or to assert P n times, where n is any positive integer chosen by his opponent.)

for me: i.e. $\models P \rightarrow Q$. [Note that $Q \vee \neg P$ holds only if I am sure that Q will yield "yes" or that P will yield "no". Thus in this logic $P \rightarrow Q$ and $Q \vee \neg P$ are not equivalent.]

"P is *false*" will mean "$\neg P$ is true": i.e. $\models \neg P$. This is a much stronger statement than $\not\models P$, which denotes "it is not the case that P is true". For instance, a prime proposition P is true for me iff I am *sure* that a trial will yield outcome "yes", and false iff I am *sure* the outcome will be "no". A dispersive proposition is neither true nor false.

To develop the logic that should govern the reasoning of a rational speaker in these circumstances one must give some interpretation of "rationality" in terms of assumptions about the structure of the set A of acceptable final positions. The stronger these assumptions the simpler the resulting logic. As an extreme case we might assume that, for every prime proposition P, either the final position, denoted $\varnothing \mid P$, in which I have asserted P while you have asserted nothing or the position $P \mid F$ in which you have asserted P and I have asserted F is acceptable. (This amounts to saying that either P is true or $\neg P$ is true.) With the addition of certain other assumptions (described below) this leads to a logic which essentially coincides with classical logic. It has the same logical identities and differs only in respect of the interpretation of a proposition (Definition 2). However, in this sense of rationality no rational speaker would recognize any proposition as dispersive, and we have seen that this "classical" attitude is too narrow both for the formalization of physics and for everyday life. At the other extreme we might assume very little about the structure of the set A. This leads to a rich language, but to a relatively complicated logic that is not yet fully worked out. This complication is due to the fact that it is necessary to add to the rules of debate certain principles governing the *order* in which the various outstanding commitments should be discharged.

A reasonable compromise that admits the possibility of dispersive prime propositions but avoids these difficulties of order (in fact, it turns out that the "order of play" makes no difference) is given in Giles (1976) and (in press). The basic axiom may be stated in two parts. (Adopting only the first part leads to the logic just mentioned.) In the first part certain relatively uncontroversial assumptions are put forward: first, if α and β are two acceptable final positions then their "sum", namely that final position in which each speaker's commitment is given by adjoining his commitments in α and β, is also acceptable; secondly, for any prime proposition P, the positions $F \mid P$ and $P \mid \varnothing$ are acceptable, while the position $\varnothing \mid F$ is not acceptable; thirdly, there is an Archimedian postulate which (roughly speaking) asserts that any position which I would be willing to accept on payment of an arbitrarily small fee is itself acceptable. The second part contains a postulate of a more arbitrary nature. For any final position α let $-\alpha$ denote the position obtained by exchanging the roles of the two speakers. Then the postulate asserts: *for any final position α either α or $-\alpha$ (or both) is acceptable.* (This corresponds to a familiar assumption in the foundations of Bayesian statistics.) If the set of final positions acceptable to a speaker satisfies this postulate I shall call the speaker *probability-definite*. The reason for this term is explained below.

The assumption of probability-definiteness is the crucial postulate that leads to Łukasiewicz logic. Indeed, using it (i.e. assuming "I" am probability-definite) one can show the following theorem (Giles, 1976).

Theorem 1. There is a unique function which assigns to each proposition P a *risk value* $\langle P \rangle$ with the following properties. If P and Q are any propositions and $P(x)$ becomes a proposition whenever the variable x is replaced by a term denoting an object, then:

(a) $0 \leq \langle P \rangle \leq 1$;

(b) $\langle P \wedge Q \rangle = \sup\{\langle P \rangle, \langle Q \rangle\}$;

(c) $\langle P \vee Q \rangle = \inf\{\langle P \rangle, \langle Q \rangle\}$;

(d) $\langle P \rightarrow Q \rangle = \sup\{0, \langle Q \rangle - \langle P \rangle\}$;

(e) $\langle \neg P \rangle = 1 - \langle P \rangle$;

(f) $\langle \forall x P(x) \rangle = \sup \langle P(a) \rangle$;

(g) $\langle \exists x P(x) \rangle = \inf \langle P(a) \rangle$;

(h) $\models P$ iff $\langle P \rangle = 0$;

(i) any position is acceptable iff its risk value is non-positive.

In (f) and (g) the sup and inf extend over all constant terms a which may be substituted for the variable x, and for (i) any position a in which I am committed by assertions of propositions $P_1, \ldots, P_m$ and you by $Q_1, \ldots, Q_n$ is assigned the risk value $\langle a \rangle = \Sigma \langle P_i \rangle - \Sigma \langle Q_j \rangle$.

With the substitution $1 - \langle P \rangle =$ truth-value of P, these properties yield the truth tables of the infinite-valued Łukasiewicz logic Ł_∞ (Łukasiewicz & Tarski, 1930; Rescher, 1969) extended to include quantifiers in the natural way.

The risk value of a proposition P may be interpreted as "my" expected loss in asserting P (and my expected gain if you assert P). In particular, if P is a prime proposition $\langle P \rangle$ may be described as the probability (in my opinion) that a trial of the corresponding elementary experiment will give outcome "no", and Theorem 1 may be paraphrased by saying that the speaker (here "I") *behaves as though he assigned to each prime proposition a definite subjective probability of outcome "no"*. This is the reason for the term "probability-definite". Henceforth all speakers will be assumed to be probability-definite.

Let P be a proposition. If, for some speaker S, $\models P$ or $\models \neg P$, i.e. if $\langle P \rangle = 0$ or $\langle P \rangle = 1$, we shall say that the proposition P is *dispersion-free* or *crisp* (for S). Like many semantic notions in this language, crispness is a subjective matter—everyone is entitled to his own opinion. However, if in fact all speakers under consideration are agreed we shall say "P is crisp" without qualification. If every prime proposition is crisp for a certain speaker S then it follows easily by recursion that *every* proposition is crisp for S and properties (b)–(g) in Theorem 1 reduce to the usual truth tables of classical logic. Thus, in so far as the propositions he is prepared to assert are concerned, S behaves as though he were using classical logic. In this way classical logic falls out as a special case.

3. Logical identities

A sentence P which, in virtue of its form, is true for every speaker is called a *logical identity* and we write $\vdash P$. In view of Theorem 1 a sentence can be shown to be a logical identity by computing its risk value for an arbitrary speaker. This method is straightforward but often tedious. There is an alternative procedure, independent of Theorem 1, that is based directly on the dialogue interpretation. Consider, for example, a sentence of the form $P \rightarrow (Q \rightarrow P)$. Suppose I, the *proponent P*, assert this sentence. You, the *opponent O*, may admit it, in which case I have "won", or you may, in the first *move* of the debate, challenge by asserting P whereupon I must reply with $Q \rightarrow P$, thus discharging my original commitment. In move 2 you may admit my new assertion, in which case I win, or challenge it by asserting Q when I reply with P. We have now both asserted P. Since my expected loss due to my assertion is balanced by my expected gain due to your assertion we may in move 3 cancel these assertions. This leaves me with no outstanding commitments and hence certainly in a winning position. It follows that $P\to(Q\to P)$ is a logical identity. The course of debate may be represented as follows:

$$
\begin{array}{lll}
0\ \mathrm{P}\ 1 & & P\to(Q\to P) \\
1\ \mathrm{O}\ 3 & & P \\
1\ \mathrm{P}\ 2 & & Q\to P \\
2\ \mathrm{O} & & Q \\
2\ \mathrm{P}\ 3 & & P
\end{array}
$$

Each proposition is labelled with a symbol denoting the speaker who asserted it. On the left of this symbol is placed the number of the move at which the assertion was made, and on its right the number of the move at which the incurred commitment was discharged. Even in this simple form this dialogue method suffices to establish a large number of logical identities. With a slight embellishment (roughly, "my" right at any time to name any proposition and require that both speakers assert it) it leads to a method by which at least every logical identity not containing quantifiers may be proved (Giles, unpublished).

Various logical identities which we shall need are listed in the following theorem. The derived connective $\leftrightarrow$ used here is defined by the rule: $P\leftrightarrow Q$ is an abbreviation for $(P\to Q)\wedge(Q\to P)$. Whenever $\vdash P\leftrightarrow Q$, the propositions P and Q have equal risk values for every speaker. Such propositions are *logically equivalent*: i.e. one may be replaced by the other in any sentence without affecting its truth.

Theorem 2. Let P, Q, R be any propositions and let $P(a)$ be a proposition for every object a. Then:

(a) $\vdash (P\vee P)\leftrightarrow P$;

(b) $\vdash (P\vee Q)\leftrightarrow(Q\vee P)$;

(c) $\vdash [(P\vee Q)\vee R]\leftrightarrow[P\vee(Q\vee R)]$;

(d) $\vdash [P\vee(Q\wedge R)]\leftrightarrow[(P\vee Q)\wedge(P\vee R)]$;

(e) $\vdash \neg(P\vee Q)\leftrightarrow(\neg P\wedge\neg Q)$;

(f)–(j) the same, exchanging $\wedge$ and $\vee$;

(k) $\vdash P\leftrightarrow\neg\neg P$;

(l) $\vdash [(P\vee Q)\leftrightarrow Q]\leftrightarrow(P\to Q)$;

(m) $\vdash [(P\to R)\wedge(Q\to R)]\leftrightarrow[(P\vee Q)\to R]$;

(n) $\vdash [(R\to P)\wedge(R\to Q)]\leftrightarrow[R\to(P\wedge Q)]$;

(o) $\vdash \neg\forall x P(x)\leftrightarrow\exists x\,\neg P(x)$;

(p) $\vdash \neg\exists x P(x)\leftrightarrow\forall x\,\neg P(x)$;

(q) $\vdash \forall x P(x)\to P(a)$;

(r) $\vdash P(a)\to\exists x P(x)$.

As an illustration of the dialogue method I give the tableau for the proof of (p). The tableau splits at move 1 corresponding to the two options for O.

$$
\begin{array}{ll}
\qquad\qquad \mathrm{O\ P\ 1} & \neg\exists x P(x)\leftrightarrow\forall x\,\neg P(x) \\
\end{array}
$$

1 P 2	$\neg\exists x P(x)\to\forall x\,\neg P(x)$	1 P 2	$\forall x\,\neg P(x)\to\neg\exists x P(x)$
2 O 5	$\neg\exists x P(x)$	2 O 5	$\forall x\,\neg P(x)$
2 P 3	$\forall x\,\neg P(x)$	2 P 3	$\neg\exists x P(x)$
3 P 4	$\neg P(a)$	3 O 4	$\exists x P(x)$
4 O 8	$P(a)$	3 P 8	F

4 P 7	F	4 O 7	$P(a)$
5 P 6	$\exists x P(x)$	5 O 6	$\neg P(a)$
5 O 7	F	6 P 7	$P(a)$
6 P 8	$P(a)$	6 O 8	F

Commentary. By the definition of $\leftrightarrow$ my original assertion is a conjunction of two propositions. At move 1 you select one of these and require me to assert it. (The following refers to the left branch of the tableau.) At move 2 you must (lose or) challenge my assertion by asserting $\neg\exists x P(x)$ and I am obliged to reply with $\forall x \neg P(x)$. By Rule 2(g) you can now (move 3) select any object a and call on me to assert $\neg P(a)$, whereupon you must again challenge (move 4) by asserting $P(a)$ when I reply with F. I now (move 5) challenge your statement in move 2 by asserting $\exists x P(x)$ and you must reply with F. We have now both asserted F and at move 6 these assertions are cancelled. In move 7 I select the same object a and discharge the obligation incurred in move 5 by asserting $P(a)$. We have now both asserted $P(a)$. In move 8 these assertions are cancelled and I am left with no outstanding commitments.

Since a similar discussion applies to the right branch of the tableau the truth of the original assertion is established.

4. Some derived connectives

We have already noted that, in $Ł_\infty$, $Q \vee \neg P$ is a stronger assertion than $P \to Q$. Let us write $P \twoheadrightarrow Q$ as an abbreviation for $Q \vee \neg P$ and call $\twoheadrightarrow$ *bold implication*. Both $\to$ and $\twoheadrightarrow$ reduce for dispersion-free propositions to ordinary classical implication. The latter has thus two natural generalizations in Łukasiewicz logic. The same applies to conjunction and disjunction. We write $P \vee Q$ as an abbreviation for $(\neg P) \to Q$ and call $\vee$ *bold disjunction*. Like $\vee$, $\vee$ is commutative and associative; but it is not idempotent: i.e. $P \vee P$ is not equivalent to P. One finds $\langle P \vee Q \rangle = \sup\{0, \langle P\rangle + \langle Q\rangle - 1\}$, which suggests an alternative and more direct dialogue interpretation: *he who asserts $P \vee Q$ offers to assert both P and Q if his opponent will pay \$1 (or assert F).* We write $P \wedge Q$ as an abbreviation for $\neg(\neg P \vee \neg Q)$ and call $\wedge$ *bold conjunction*. Like $\vee$, $\wedge$ is commutative and associative but not idempotent: $P \wedge P$ is not equivalent to P. One finds $\langle P \wedge Q\rangle = \inf\{1, \langle P\rangle + \langle Q\rangle\}$, giving the direct interpretation: *he who asserts $P \wedge Q$ agrees either to pay \$1 (or assert F) or to assert both P and Q (at his own choice).*

A consideration of truth functions shows that no further equally simple generalizations exist: the classical connectives $\to$, $\wedge$, and $\vee$ have each exactly two simple generalizations in $Ł_\infty$; namely, $\to$ and $\twoheadrightarrow$, $\wedge$ and $\wedge$, and $\vee$ and $\vee$, respectively.

A vast number of logical identities involving these connectives can easily be obtained. Some which we shall need are given in the following theorem.

Theorem 3. For any propositions P, Q, and R:

(a) $\vdash (P \vee Q) \to (P \vee Q)$;

(b) $\vdash (P \wedge Q) \to (P \wedge Q)$;

(c) $\vdash (P \twoheadrightarrow Q) \to (P \to Q)$;

(d) $\vdash [P \wedge (P \to Q)] \to Q$;

(e) $\vdash [(P \wedge Q) \to R] \leftrightarrow [P \to (Q \to R)]$;

(f) $\vdash (P \to Q) \leftrightarrow (Q \vee \neg P)$;

(g) $\vdash (P \twoheadrightarrow Q) \leftrightarrow (Q \vee \neg P)$;

(h) $\vdash \neg(P \vee Q) \leftrightarrow (\neg P \wedge \neg Q)$;

(i) $\vdash \neg(P \wedge Q) \leftrightarrow (\neg P \vee \neg Q)$;

(j) $\vdash [(P \to Q) \wedge (Q \to R)] \to (P \to R)$;

(k) $\vdash [(P \leftrightarrow Q) \wedge (Q \leftrightarrow R)] \to (P \leftrightarrow R)$;

(l) $\vdash P \vee \neg P$ and hence $\vdash \neg(P \wedge \neg P)$;

(m) $\vdash \neg[(P \wedge \neg Q) \wedge Q]$;

(n) $\vdash [(P \wedge \neg Q) \vee (P \wedge Q)] \leftrightarrow P$;

(o) $\vdash [(P \wedge \neg Q) \vee Q] \leftrightarrow (P \vee Q)$;

(p) $\vdash [(P \wedge Q) \wedge (P \wedge R)] \leftrightarrow [P \wedge (Q \wedge R)]$;

(q) $\vdash [(P \wedge Q) \vee (P \wedge R)] \leftrightarrow [P \wedge (Q \vee R)]$.

(a), (b), and (c) show that $\vee$, $\wedge$, and $\twoheadrightarrow$ are "stronger" connectives than V, $\wedge$ and $\rightarrow$ respectively; (d) and (e) give two simple uses of $\wedge$; (f) and (g) show the two forms taken in $Ł_\infty$ by a familiar classical equivalence; (l) is the "principle of the excluded middle", which holds for V although it fails for $\vee$. It can be shown not only that $\wedge$ and V are associative and commutative but also that (like $\wedge$ and $\vee$) they are both distributive with respect to $\underset{\sim}{\wedge}$ and $\vee$; this last property is illustrated by (p) and (q).

To illustrate the dialogue interpretation of $\wedge$ I give a proof of (d):

$$
\begin{array}{llll}
0 & P & 1 & [P \wedge (P \rightarrow Q)] \rightarrow Q \\
1 & O & 2 & P \wedge (P \rightarrow Q) \\
1 & P & 5 & Q \\
2 & O & 4 & P \\
2 & O & 3 & P \rightarrow Q \\
3 & P & 4 & P \\
3 & O & 5 & Q
\end{array}
$$

Commentary. At move 1 you are forced to challenge my assertion by asserting $P \wedge (P \rightarrow Q)$ and I reply with Q. In discharging the obligation you have thus incurred you have a choice; you may assert either F or both P and $P \rightarrow Q$. The first option results in the final position $F | Q$, which is a winning (i.e. acceptable) position for me, so, to avoid losing, you are obliged at move 2 to take the second option. At move 3 I challenge your assertion and you reply in accordance with your commitment. We have now both asserted both P and Q and these assertions are cancelled in moves 4 and 5.

5. Fuzzy sets

It has become customary in mathematics to adopt the notion of a set as a primitive concept. However, much may be said (see, for example, Weyl, 1949, section 2) for the alternative of regarding every set as being determined by a property; indeed, unless it be finite, a set can hardly be given except by naming a property which characterizes its members. Now a *property* is just a (unary) predicate: i.e. a mapping which assigns to each object a proposition. For instance, the set P of prime numbers is determined by the predicate "prime": i.e. by the map which assigns to each number a the proposition "a is prime"—in fact we use the expression "$a \varepsilon P$" simply as an abbreviation for this proposition. Thus to specify any set P amounts to specifying the meaning of the proposition $a \varepsilon P$ for every object a. With this approach our new definition of the meaning of a proposition (Definition 2) automatically gives rise to a new definition of "set". In fact, it turns out that in the general case in which we admit dispersive propositions we arrive exactly at Zadeh's (1965) notion of a "fuzzy set", while if we allow only crisp propositions we obtain as before the classical notion of a set.

From the present viewpoint, then, the concept of a fuzzy set is *prior* to that of a set: a set is simply a special kind of fuzzy set. Certainly, in spite of the terminology, a fuzzy set is not a particular kind of set. To emphasize this situation, and to bring out the analogy between fuzzy set theory with Łukasiewicz logic and ordinary set theory with classical logic I shall use the term "*f*-set" as an abbreviation for "fuzzy set". A *set* now becomes a *crisp f*-set. We thus arrive at the following definition.

Definition 3. An expression A is said to denote an *f-set* whenever a rule is laid down which assigns a proposition, denoted $a \in A$, to every object a. If (for some speaker S) this proposition is crisp for every object a then the f-set is said to be *crisp* (*for* S). A *set* is a crisp f-set. An f-set which is not crisp is *fuzzy*. By "abuse of language" a fuzzy f-set is also referred to as a *fuzzy set*.

If an expression $P(a)$ denotes a proposition for every object a then the f-set $\{x:P(x)\}$ (in which x is any variable) is defined by the stipulation that, for any a, the expression $a\in\{x:P(x)\}$ denotes $P(a)$. $\{x:F\}$ is the empty f-set, denoted $\varnothing$; $\{x:T\}$ is the *universal f-set* denoted I. (T is an abbreviation for $\neg F$, the universally true proposition.) Both $\varnothing$ and I are crisp. $a\notin A$ will be used as an abbreviation for $\neg(a\in A)$.

For practical purposes it is natural to assume that f-sets are distinguishable (for instance syntactically) from objects: i.e., technically, they belong to a different "type". We shall assume for simplicity that objects are all of the same type and call them *points*. With this understanding "$\in$" denotes a binary predicate or *relation* between points and f-sets. But (cf. the remarks at the beginning of this section) it should not be regarded as a set of ordered pairs—rather, it is a map that assigns to any pair (a,A) the proposition $a\in A$. Moreover, in as much as this proposition is in general dispersive, $\in$ is a *fuzzy relation*. We shall meet other fuzzy relations later.

Previous discussions of fuzzy sets have relied on a generalization of the notion of the characteristic function of a set. This concept plays no part here, either in the definitions or in the statements and proofs of theorems. However, it is easily defined. Let A be an f-set and let S be a speaker. Then for each object a the proposition $a\varepsilon A$ has, for S, a definite risk value $\langle a\in A\rangle$. The map which assigns to each a the number $X_A(a) = 1 - \langle a\in A\rangle$ is called the *characteristic function* of A for S. (Naturally, the function X_A is here dependent on the speaker S.)

6. Elementary operations

Our definition of an f-set is formally identical to a valid classical definition of a set. The same applies to the following definitions of some standard operations and relations involving f-sets.

Definition 4. The *intersection* $A\cap B$ and *union* $A\cup B$ of two f-sets A and B are defined to be respectively $\{x:x\in A\wedge x\in B\}$ and $\{x:x\in A\vee x\in B\}$. The *complement* $\sim A$ of A is $\{x:x\notin A\}$. Further, we define the relations $\subset$ and $=$ between f-sets by:

$A\subset B$ is an abbreviation for $\forall x(x\in A\to x\in B)$, and
$A=B$ is an abbreviation for $\forall x(x\in A\leftrightarrow x\in B)$.
$A\not\subset B$ and $A\neq B$ will be used as abbreviations for $\neg A\subset B$ and $\neg A=B$.

Notice that, like $\in$, $\subset$ and $=$ are *fuzzy relations*. The definition of $\subset$, for instance, does not merely describe the circumstances under which $A\subset B$ is true (the necessary and sufficient condition for this is easily seen to be $X_A\leq X_B$, in agreement with Zadeh, 1965), it also associates a definite commitment (and hence a risk value) with the assertion of $A\subset B$ in cases when it is not true. The same applies to $A=B$. It is possible to introduce crisp relations, $\subset_c$ and $=_c$ say, corresponding to $\subset$ and $=$ by writing $A\subset_c B$ for $\models A\subset B$ and $A=_c B$ for $\models A=B$. However, since (in our present formulation) "$\models$" belongs to the metalanguage, so do "$\subset_c$" and "$=_c$". Clearly, any fuzzy predicate can be "crispened" in the same way.

Theorem 4. Let A, B, C be f-sets and let a be a point. Then:

(a) $\vdash A \cup A = A;$

(b) $\vdash A \cup B = B \cup A;$

(c) $\vdash A \cup (B \cup C) = (A \cup B) \cup C;$

(d) $\vdash A \cup (B \cap C) = (A \cup B) \cap (A \cup C);$

(e) $\vdash {\sim}(A \cup B) = {\sim}A \cap {\sim}B;$

(f)–(j) the same exchanging $\cap$ and $\cup;$

(k) $\vdash {\sim}{\sim}A = A;$

(l) $\vdash A \cup B = B \leftrightarrow A \subset B;$

(m) $\vdash (A \subset C \wedge B \subset C) \leftrightarrow A \cup B \subset C;$

(n) $\vdash (C \subset A \wedge C \subset B) \leftrightarrow C \subset A \cap B;$

(o) $\vdash A \subset A;$

(p) $\vdash (A \subset B \wedge B \subset C) \rightarrow A \subset C;$

(q) $\vdash A = A;$

(r) $\vdash A = B \leftrightarrow B = A;$

(s) $\vdash (A = B \wedge B = C) \rightarrow A = C;$

(t) $\vdash A = B \rightarrow (a \in A \leftrightarrow a \in B);$

(u) $\vdash (a \in A \wedge A \subset B) \rightarrow a \in B;$

(v) $\vdash A \neq \varnothing \leftrightarrow \exists x(x \in A).$

(a)–(n) follow easily from the corresponding assertions in Theorem 2. The proofs of (p), (s), and (u) use in addition Theorem 3(j), (k), and (d), respectively. (t) follows immediately from the definition of equality, using Theorem 2(q). The other results are proved with no more difficulty.

As an example, I prove one half of (v):

$$
\begin{array}{llll}
0 & P & 1 & A \neq \varnothing \rightarrow \exists x(x \in A) \\
1 & 0 & 2 & A \neq \varnothing \\
1 & P & 7 & \exists x(x \in A) \\
2 & P & 3 & A = \varnothing \\
2 & 0 & 6 & F \\
3 & P & 4 & a \in A \leftrightarrow a \in \varnothing \\
4 & P & 5 & a \in A \rightarrow a \in \varnothing \\
5 & 0 & 8 & a \in A \\
5 & P & 6 & a \in \varnothing \\
7 & P & 8 & a \in A
\end{array}
$$

Commentary. At move 1 you challenge my initial assertion. At move 2 I challenge you by asserting $A = \varnothing$ and you reply with F. By Definition 4 you may now choose a point a and call upon me to assert (move 3) $a \in A \leftrightarrow a \in \varnothing$. By the definition of $\leftrightarrow$ you may require (move 4) that $\leftrightarrow$ be replaced by $\rightarrow$. You are then again forced to challenge (move 5) by asserting $a \in A$ and I reply with $a \in \varnothing$. By Definition 3, $a \in \varnothing$ is equivalent to $F;$ in move 6 we cancel these assertions. Finally, in move 7 I discharge the obligation incurred in move 1 by asserting $a \in A$, which assertion is then cancelled with your assertion of move 5.

At first sight the relations in Theorem 4 seem very familiar, but one must remember that the underlying logic is $Ł_\infty$ and not classical logic. (m), for instance, not only asserts that $A \cup B \subset_c C$ iff both $A \subset_c C$ and $B \subset_c C$ (the classical characterization of the least upper bound); it also says that the risk in asserting $A \cup B \subset C$ is always equal to the greater of the risks in asserting $A \subset C$ and $B \subset C$. Similarly, (p) does not merely say that if $A \subset_c B$ and $B \subset_c C$ then $A \subset_c C$ (which, along with (o), characterizes a classical partial ordering); it also says that the risk in asserting $A \subset C$ never exceeds the sum of the risks in asserting $A \subset B$ and $B \subset C$.

It is easy to deduce from (t) that if $\vdash A = B$ then A and B are *equivalent* in that they are interchangeable in any proposition; (a)–(j) provide a number of examples of such equivalent f-sets. These identities show that the family of all f-sets is a distributive lattice in the classical sense, the corresponding partial ordering being (in view of (l)) the (crisp) relation which holds between two f-sets A and B if $A \subset B$. However, in spite of (e), (j), and (k), $\sim$ is not a classical complementation, since neither $A \cup \sim A = \mathrm{I}$ nor $A \cap \sim A = \emptyset$ holds in general. What is to be done about this we shall see in the next section.

7. Bold intersection and union

In ordinary set theory two sets A and B are said to be disjoint if $A \cap B = \emptyset$. As Zadeh (1965, p. 35) has observed, this relation is much too strong for practical use in fuzzy set theory; for instance, even A and $\sim A$ are not disjoint in this sense. However, let us consider the classically equivalent condition for disjointness, $A \subset \sim B$. By Definition 4, $A \subset \sim B$ is equivalent to $\forall x (x \in A \to x \notin B)$ which is, by Theorem 3(f), equivalent to $\forall x (x \notin B \lor x \notin A)$ and finally, by Theorem 2(p) and Theorem 3(h), to $\neg \exists x (x \in A \land x \in B)$. But, by Theorem 2(k) and Theorem 4(v), this means $\{x : x \in A \land x \in B\} = \emptyset$. We shall call the f-set mentioned here, which in view of Theorem 3(b) is contained in $A \cap B$, the *bold intersection* $A \cap B$ of A and B. It and the corresponding bold union provide the key to the concepts of disjointness and difference of f-sets.

Definition 5. Let A and B be f-sets. The *bold intersection* $A \cap B$ and *bold union* $A \cup B$ are respectively the f-sets $\{x : x \in A \land x \in B\}$ and $\{x : x \in A \lor x \in B\}$. The sentence "$A$ and B are (*weakly*) *disjoint*", denoted $A \perp B$, is an abbreviation for $A \cap B = \emptyset$. The *difference* $A \backslash B$ of A and B is $A \cap \sim B$.

Of the many logical identities involving these operations, I offer a few that follow easily from Theorem 3, (l)–(q). In the case of crisp f-sets, when the distinction between the two kinds of union and intersection can be ignored, they reduce to familiar classical properties of the complement and difference operation on sets.

Theorem 5. Let A, B, C be any f-sets. Then:

(a) $\vdash A \perp \sim A$: i.e. $A \cap \sim A = \emptyset$;

(b) $\vdash A \cup \sim A = \mathrm{I}$;

(c) $\vdash A \backslash B \perp B$;

(d) $\vdash (A \backslash B) \cup (A \cap B) = A$;

(e) $\vdash (A \backslash B) \cup B = A \cup B$;

(f) $\vdash (A \backslash B) \cap (A \backslash C) = A \backslash (B \cup C)$;

(g) $\vdash (A \backslash B) \cup (A \backslash C) = A \backslash (B \cap C)$.

8. Convex fuzzy sets

As a final illustration of the formulation of fuzzy set theory using Łukasiewicz logic I shall now develop the elements of the theory of convex fuzzy sets.† To this end we assume that the points are the elements of a linear space.‡ Thus there are now two "types" of object, *points* and (real) *numbers*. Particular numbers and variables for numbers will be denoted by Greek letters. Quantification extends only over the indicated type—e.g. $\forall \lambda$ means "for every number λ", while $\forall x$ means "for every point x". Our definition of "A is convex" (abbreviated "A *conv*") is syntactically identical to the classical definition:

†The notion of a convex fuzzy set was introduced by Zadeh in his original paper (1965). It has been discussed also by Brown (1971).

‡Formally this means that the underlying language is enriched by various symbols: for instance binary function symbols for addition and multiplication. The interpretation of these and other nonlogical symbols is *not* to be understood in terms of orthodox mathematical model theory (which begs the question of interpretation in any *practical* sense); instead, we assume that to each symbol there corresponds an *experimental procedure* in such a way that any prime proposition denotes an elementary experiment (Definition 1). (For details see Giles (1974, in press)). For simplicity we assume that any proposition expressing an arithmetic relation between numbers or a linear relation between points is crisp. (By relaxing these requirements one can obtain a theory incorporating "fuzzy points" and even "fuzzy numbers".) We assume also the usual axioms for a linear space: for example $\vdash \forall x \forall y (x + y = y + x)$.

Definition 6. Let A be an f-set in a real linear space. Then A conv is an abbreviation for

$$\forall \lambda\{\lambda\in[0,1]\to\forall x\forall y[(x\in A \wedge y\in A)\to\lambda x+(1-\lambda)y\in A]\}.$$

(Here $[0,1]$ denotes the closed unit interval, a crisp f-set of numbers.) It is easy to show that the condition for the truth of "A conv" agrees with that adopted by Zadeh as the definition of a convex fuzzy set. However, Definition 6 is richer than this: it assigns also a risk value to the assertion A conv in the case when $\not\models A$ conv. Thus one can now speak of "degrees of convexity": for example if $\langle A$ conv$\rangle = 0{\cdot}2$, as for instance when A is the f-set, in a 1-dimensional space, whose characteristic function is sketched in Fig. 1 (cf. Fig. 4 in Zadeh, 1965), then we might say "A is nearly convex", or more precisely "the truth value of 'A is convex' is $0{\cdot}8$".

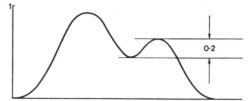

FIG. 1. Characteristic function of a nearly convex f-set.

Zadeh shows that if A and B are convex fuzzy sets then so is $A\cap B$: i.e., in the above notation, if $\models A$ conv and $\models B$ conv then $\models A\cap B$ conv. This result is contained in the following.

Theorem 6. For any f-sets A and B

$$\vdash (A \text{ conv} \wedge B \text{ conv})\to A\cap B \text{ conv}.$$

But this theorem says more than that: it tells us also that the risk in asserting $A\cap B$ conv never exceeds the greater of the risks in asserting A conv and B conv.

In dialogue form the proof of the theorem is as follows:

```
0 P 1   (A conv ∧ B conv)→A∩B conv
1 O 5   A conv ∧ B conv
1 P 2   A∩B conv
2 O 7   a∈[0,1]
2 P 3   ∀x∀y[(x∈A∩B ∧ y∈A∩B)→ax+(1−a)y∈A∩B]
3 O 10  a∈A∩B ∧ b∈A∩B
3 P 4   c∈A∩B
```

Here c is an abbreviation for $aa+(1-a)b$. At this point the tableau splits. We follow one branch; the other is similar:

```
4 P 9   c∈A
5 O 6   A conv
6 P 7   a∈[0,1]
6 O 8   ∀x∀y[(x∈A ∧ y∈A)→ax+(1−a)y∈A]
8 P 12  a∈A ∧ b∈A
8 O 9   c∈A
10 O 11 a∈A ∧ a∈B ∧ b∈A ∧ b∈B
11 O 12 a∈A ∧ b∈A
```

Commentary. If you hope to win you must, at move 1, challenge my initial assertion and I must then reply with $A \cap B$ conv. In accordance with Definition 6 you must now (move 2) choose a particular value a for the variable λ and will lose unless you challenge. At move 3 you must choose particular points a and b and are again forced to challenge. By Definition 4 $c \in A \cap B$ means $c \in A \wedge c \in B$. At move 4 you must choose which assertion I am to make; without loss of generality we may assume you choose the former. At move 5 I refer to your assertion in move 1 and require you to assert A conv. By Definition 6 I may now (move 6) choose the same number a as you chose at move 2, and challenge. Since my assertion here coincides with yours at move 2 these two assertions may be cancelled (move 7). Next (move 8) I choose the same points a and b as you chose at move 3 and challenge again. My assertion in move 4 is now cancelled (move 9) by yours in move 8. In view of the definition of $\cap$ your assertion at move 3 may be expanded as in move 10 (where we omit parentheses in view of the associative law, Theorem 2(h)); and this, in view of the definition of $\wedge$, may be replaced (at my request) by the assertion in move 11. Finally, in move 12, this assertion cancels my assertion in move 8. I am left with no outstanding commitments, and so have reached a winning position. This shows that my original assertion was safe, which proves the theorem.

This work was supported by a grant from the National Research Council of Canada.

References

BROWN, J. G. (1971). A note on fuzzy sets. *Information and Control*, **18**, 32–39.

CHANG, C. C. (1958). Algebraic analysis of many valued logics. *Transactions of the American Mathematical Society*, **88**, 467–490.

CHANG, C. C. (1965). Infinite valued logic as a basis for set theory. *In Proceedings of the 1964 International Congress for Logic, Methodology, and Philosophy of Science*. Amsterdam, London: North Holland.

GILES, R. (1974). A non-classical logic for physics. *Studia Logica*, **33**, 397–415.

GILES, R. (in press). A pragmatic approach to the formalization of empirical theories. To appear in *Proc. Conf. Formal Methods in the Methodology of Empirical Sciences, Warsaw, June,* 1974. Dordrecht, Holland: Reidel, and Warsaw: Ossdineum.

GILES, R. (1976). A logic for subjective belief. In *Foundations of Probability Theory, Statistical Inference, and Statistical Theories of Science*. Vol. 1, 41–72. Dordrecht, Holland: Reidel.

GOGUEN, J. A. (1967). L-fuzzy sets. *Journal of Mathematical Analysis and Applications*, **18**, 145–174.

GOGUEN, J. A. (1968–69). The logic of inexact concepts. *Synthese*, **19**, 325–373.

KLAUA, D. (1965). Uber einen Ansatz zur mehrwertigen Mengenlehre. *Monatsb. Deutsch. Akad. Wiss. Berlin*, **7**, 859–867.

KLAUA, D. (1966a). Uber einen zweiten Ansatz zur mehrwertigen Mengenlehre. *Monatsb. Deutsch. Akad. Wiss. Berlin*, **8**, 161–177.

KLAUA, D. (1966b). Grundbegriffe einer mehrwertigen Mengenlehre. *Monatsb. Deutsch. Akad. Wiss. Berlin*, **8**, 782–802.

KLAUA, D. (1967)a. Ein ansatz zur mehrwertigen Mengenlehre. *Math. Nachr.*, **33**, 273–296.

KLAUA, D. (1967b). Einbettung der klassischen Mengenlehre in die mehrwertige. *Monatsb. Deutsch. Akad. Wiss. Berlin*, **9**, 258–272.

KLAUA, D. (1970). Stetige Gleichmachtigkeiten kontinuierlichwertiger Mengen. *Monatbs. Deutsch. Akad. Wiss. Berlin*, **12**, 749–758.

ŁUKASIEWICZ, J. & TARSKI, A. (1930). Investigations in the sentential calculus. Translation in J. ŁUKASIEWICZ *Selected Works*. Amsterdam: Reidel (1970), and in A. TARSKI *Logic, Semantics, Metamathematics*. Oxford: Clarendon Press (1956).

RESCHER, N. (1969). *Many-valued Logic*. New York: McGraw-Hill.

WEYL, H. (1949). *Philosophy of Mathematics and Natural Science*. Princeton: Princeton Univ. Press.

ZADEH, L. A. (1965). Fuzzy sets. *Information and Control*, **8**, 338–353.

Fuzzy logic and fuzzy reasoning

J. F. BALDWIN

Department of Engineering Mathematics, University of Bristol, Bristol BS8 1TR, U.K.

The concepts of truth value restriction and fuzzy logical relation are used to give a general approach to fuzzy logic and also fuzzy reasoning involving propositions with imprecise or vague description.

1. Introduction

In this paper we use the concepts of truth value restriction and fuzzy logical relation to give a general approach to fuzzy logic and fuzzy reasoning involving propositions with imprecise or vague description. The method of approach described here is a generalisation of that described in Baldwin (1978a, b, c).

The method is equally effective for binary logic analysis and in this case compares favourably with resolution and other methods of simplifying the basic truth table analysis. Binary logic as well as fuzzy logic examples are given to show the power of the method. No particular multi-valued base logic is necessary for the method. For various interpretations of implication see Baldwin & Pilsworth (1978a).

Computational details are not discussed here but relevant algorithms can be found in Baldwin & Guild (1978a). Pencil and paper methods of calculation are easily developed and these are diagrammatically represented in one example. Computation is in general very efficient since most calculations are performed in a simple truth space.

We assume a knowledge of fuzzy set theory (Zadeh, 1965) and the treatment of restriction has been influenced strongly by the treatment given in Zadeh (1975a). The connection with possibility theory is given in Baldwin & Pilsworth (1978b) and an application of the approach for resolving the Fulakros paradox given in Baldwin & Guild (1978b).

Important theorems of fuzzy logic are easily proved using the basic definitions in this paper. We have only included here those theorems which were not proved in Baldwin (1978c) so that this latter paper should be read in conjunction with this one.

A brief review of modelling using algorithmic hierarchical models and feedback is given and an application of the approach to the design of a ship control room can be found in Baldwin & Guild (1978c). The approach can be used for fuzzy decision theory but the concept of optimum decision is more complicated than when using binary logic. This is discussed in Baldwin & Guild (1978d). Present work is concerned with further aspects of modelling using fuzzy logic and fuzzy reasoning as well as the inclusion of fuzzy probabilistic concepts and fuzzy qualifiers.

2. Truth value restrictions and fuzzy logic relations

The concepts of truth value restriction and fuzzy logic relations are fundamental to the approach of fuzzy logical reasoning given below and have been described in Baldwin (1968a, b, c). We will briefly review these concepts and related material in this section.

Let U denote the set of possible truth values, so that for binary logic $U = \{0, 1\}$ where 0 denotes false and 1 true, while for a non denumerably infinite valued logic $U = [0, 1]$.

Definition 2.1. A truth value restriction τ is a subset of U, denoted by $\tau \subset U$, and can be defined by its membership function, χ_τ, which is a mapping

$$\chi_\tau : U \rightarrow \{0, 1\}.$$

Definition 2.2. A fuzzy truth value restriction τ is a fuzzy subset of U, denoted by $\tau \subseteq U$, and can be defined by its membership function, χ_τ, which is a mapping

$$\chi_\tau : U \rightarrow [0, 1]$$

In this paper we will be concerned solely with the case $U = [0, 1]$ for Definition 2.2.

Definition 2.1 is thus relevant to binary logic with $U = \{0, 1\}$ and a non-denumerably infinite valued logic with $U = [0, 1]$ while Definition 2.2 is relevant to fuzzy logic with $U = [0, 1]$. If we add the further restriction that $\chi_\tau(0) + \chi_\tau(1) = 1$ then Definition 2.2 with $U = \{0, 1\}$ is relevant to probability logic.

Special labels can be given to certain truth value restrictions and these labels will be consistent with Zadeh's use of fuzzy quantifiers such as "fairly" and "very". Baldwin (1978c) defines a general family of truth value restrictions although such a set of labels is not necessary to the general methods given below.

Definition 2.3. The truth value restrictions "**true, false,** *unrestricted, impossible, absolutely true* and *absolutely false*" are defined as

$$\chi_{\textbf{true}} \quad (\eta) = \eta; \quad \forall \eta \in U$$

$$\chi_{\textbf{false}} \quad (\eta) = 1 - \eta; \quad \forall \eta \in U$$

$$\chi_{unrestricted} (\eta) = 1; \quad \forall \eta \in U$$
$$\chi_{impossible} \ (\eta) = 0; \quad \forall \eta \in U \qquad ; \quad U = [0, 1]$$

$$\chi_{abs.\ true} \quad (\eta) = \begin{cases} 1 & \text{if } \eta = 1 \\ 0 & \text{otherwise} \end{cases}; \quad \forall \eta \in U$$

$$\chi_{abs.\ false} \quad (\eta) = \begin{cases} 1 & \text{if } \eta = 0 \\ 0 & \text{otherwise} \end{cases}; \quad \forall \eta \in U$$

We can further define **very true** and **very false** as

$$\chi_{\textbf{very true}} (\eta) = \chi_{\textbf{true}}^2 (\eta); \quad \chi_{\textbf{very false}} (\eta) = \chi_{\textbf{false}}^2 (\eta); \quad \forall \eta \in U$$

and **fairly true** and **fairly false** as

$$\chi_{\textbf{fairly true}} (\eta) = \chi_{\textbf{true}}^{1/2} (\eta); \quad \chi_{\textbf{fairly false}} (\eta) = \chi_{\textbf{false}}^{1/2} (\eta); \quad \forall \eta \in U$$

These are shown diagrammatically in Fig. 1.

Definition 2.4. A proposition P can have allocated to it a truth value restriction $\tau \subseteq U$ and we denote this by

$$P \text{ is } \tau \quad \text{or} \quad v(P) = \tau.$$

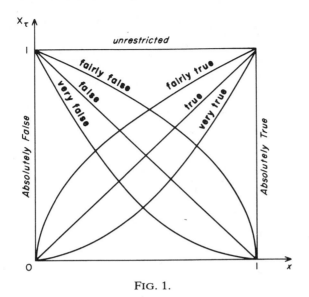

FIG. 1.

The proposition P may take the special form of

$$P: u \text{ is } \mathbf{p}$$

where $\mathbf{p} \subseteq X$, i.e. a fuzzy subset of discourse X and u is a name, object or construct. See Zadeh (1975).

We further require the concept of truth functional modification (T.F.M.) which was first introduced by Zadeh (1975a).

Definition 2.5. If P: (u is $\mathbf{p}$) is τ; $\mathbf{p} \subseteq X$; $\tau \subseteq U$ then an equivalent proposition is

$$P: u \text{ is } \mathbf{p}'; \qquad \mathbf{p}' \subseteq X$$

where

$$\chi_{\mathbf{p}'}(\eta) = \chi_{\tau}(\chi_{\mathbf{p}}(\eta)).$$

We call $\mathbf{p}'$ the truth functional modification of $\mathbf{p}$ given τ and write $\mathbf{p}' = \text{T.F.M. } (\tilde{\mathbf{p}}|\tau)$.

The concept of inverse truth functional modification, I.T.F.M., first introduced by Baldwin (1978a), is introduced by means of the following definition.

Definition 2.6. If P: u is $\mathbf{p}$; $\mathbf{p} \subseteq X$ and further it is known that u is $\mathbf{p}'$; $\mathbf{p}' \subseteq X$ then $\tau = v(P|u \text{ is } \mathbf{p}')$ read as truth value restriction of proposition P given that u is $\mathbf{p}'$, is defined by the membership function

$$\chi_{\tau(\eta)} = \bigvee_{\substack{x \in X \\ \chi_{\mathbf{p}}(x) = \eta}} [\chi_{\mathbf{p}'}(x)]; \quad \forall \eta \in U$$

and the proposition P, given the data u is $\mathbf{p}'$, can be replaced by the proposition P' where

$$P': (u \text{ is } \mathbf{p}) \text{ is } \tau.$$

We can thus write $v(P) = \text{I.T.F.M. } (\mathbf{p}/\mathbf{p}')$.

Definition 2.7. For an atomic proposition P the associated fuzzy logic relation $\mathbf{R} \subseteq U$ is defined by its membership function

$$\chi_{\mathbf{R}}(u) = u; \quad \forall u \in U$$

and further, if

$$P \text{ is } \tau$$

then the associated logic relation is $\mathbf{R}_1 \subseteq U$ where

$$\chi_{\mathbf{R}_1}(u) = \chi_\tau(\chi_{\mathbf{R}}(u)).$$

For a compound proposition $\sum$ involving atoms $P_1, P_2, \ldots, P_n$ the associated logic relation is $\mathbf{R} \subseteq U_1 \times U_2 \times \cdots \times U_n$ where $\chi_{\mathbf{R}}(u_1, u_2, \ldots, u_n)$ is the truth value associated with $\sum$ where $(|P_1| = u_1), (|P_2| = u_2), \ldots, (|P_n| = u_n)$ where $|P_i| = u_i$ signifies that the multi-valued truth value associated with proposition P_i is u_i, and further, if

$$\sum \text{ is } \tau$$

then the associated logic relation is $\mathbf{R}_1 \subseteq U_1 \times U_2 \times \cdots \times U_n$, where

$$\chi_{\mathbf{R}_1}(u_1, \ldots, u_n) = \chi_\tau(\chi_{\mathbf{R}}(u_1, \ldots, u_n)); \quad \forall u_1 \in U_1, \ldots, \forall u_n \in U_n$$

which generalises the concept of T.F.M.

For example

$$\{[(P \text{ and } Q) \text{ is } \tau_1] \supset S\} \text{ is } \tau_2$$

will have the associated fuzzy logic relation $\mathbf{R} \subseteq U_P \times U_Q \times U_S$ where

$$\chi_{\mathbf{R}}(u_1, u_2, u_3) = \chi_{\tau_2}\{(1 - (\chi_{\tau_1}(u_1 \wedge u_2)) + u_3) \wedge 1\}$$

where

$$u_1 \in U_P, \quad u_2 \in U_Q, \quad u_3 \in U_S; \quad U_P = U_Q = U_S = [0, 1].$$

This assumes using as a base logic the non-denumerably infinite multi-valued logic system of Łukasiewicz. Alternative base logics can be used. Various alternatives for defining implication are discussed in Baldwin & Pilsworth (1978*a*).

Definition 2.8. Let $\mathbf{C}$, $\mathbf{D}$, $\mathbf{I}$, $\mathbf{E}$ be fuzzy logic binary relations corresponding to conjunction, disjunction, implication and equivalence and defined by

$$\mathbf{C} \subseteq U_1 \times U_2; \quad \chi_{\mathbf{C}}(x, y) = x \wedge y; \quad \forall x \in U_1 \text{ and } \forall y \in U_2$$

$$\mathbf{D} \subseteq U_1 \times U_2; \quad \chi_{\mathbf{D}}(x, y) = x \vee y; \quad \forall x \in U_1 \text{ and } \forall y \in U_2$$

$$\mathbf{I} \subseteq U_1 \times U_2; \quad \chi_{\mathbf{I}}(x, y) = (1 - x + y) \wedge 1; \quad \forall x \in U_1 \text{ and } \forall y \in U_2$$

$$\mathbf{E} \subseteq U_1 \times U_2; \quad \chi_{\tilde{\mathbf{E}}}(x, y) = (1 - x + y) \wedge (1 - y + x); \quad \forall x \in U_1 \text{ and } \forall y \in U_2$$

where

$$a \wedge b \neq \text{MIN}(a, b) \quad \text{and} \quad a \vee b = \text{MAX}(a, b); \quad U_1 = U_2 = [0, 1].$$

Let $\mathbf{N}$ be a fuzzy logic unary relation associated with negation and defined by

$$\mathbf{N} \subseteq U; \quad \chi_{\mathbf{N}}(x) = 1 - x; \quad \forall x \in U.$$

Definition 2.9. If $\mathbf{R}_1 \subseteq U_1 \times U_2 \times \cdots \times U_n$ is the fuzzy relation corresponding with a compound proposition Σ involving atoms $P_1, P_2, \ldots, P_n$, then the fuzzy relation associated with the proposition

$$\Sigma \text{ is } \tau$$

is given by $\mathbf{R} = \mathbf{R}_1(\tau)$ where

$$\chi_{\mathbf{R}}(u_1, u_2, \ldots, u_n) = \chi_\tau(\chi_{\mathbf{R}_1}(u_1, u_2, \ldots, u_n)).$$

This generalises the concept of T.F.M.

Definition 2.10. The global projection of $\mathbf{R} \subseteq U_1 \times U_2 \times \cdots \times U_n$, denoted by $h(\mathbf{R})$ is defined by

$$h(\mathbf{R}) = \bigvee_{u_1 \in U_1} \bigvee_{u_2 \in U_2} \cdots \bigvee_{u_n \in U_n} \chi_{\mathbf{R}}(u_1, u_2, \ldots, u_n).$$

3. Fuzzy reasoning using fuzzy logic

In this section we will give a generalisation of fuzzy reasoning using truth value restrictions of that given in Baldwin (1978c) and illustrate the power of the method with examples. Computational details will not be dealt with in this paper but some aspects of this can be realised in Baldwin & Guild (1978a).

Definition 3.1. The projection of $\mathbf{R} \subseteq U_1 \times U_2 \times \cdots \times U_n$ on U_i is a fuzzy subset of U_i denoted by $\mathrm{Proj}_{U_i}(\mathbf{R})$ and defined by its membership function

$$\chi_{\mathrm{Proj}_{U_i}(\mathbf{R})}(u_i) = \bigvee_{\left\{\substack{u_j \in U_j \\ j \neq i}\right\}} [\chi_{\mathbf{R}}(u_1, u_2, \ldots, u_n)]; \quad \forall u_i \in U_i.$$

The extension to the case of a projection on to a multi-dimensional subspace is obvious.

Definition 3.2. If $\mathbf{R} \subseteq U_1 \times U_2 \times \cdots \times U_n$ is the fuzzy relation associated with a compound fuzzy logic proposition Σ involving atoms $P_1, P_2, \ldots, P_n$, then the least restrictive fuzzy relation $\mathbf{R}_1 \subseteq U_1, U_2, \ldots, U_n$, for $r < n$, associated with atoms $P_1, P_2, \ldots, P_r$ is defined by

$$\mathbf{R}_1 = \mathrm{Proj}_{U_1 \times U_2 \times \cdots \times U_r}(\mathbf{R})$$

and more specifically the least restrictive truth value for P_i is

$$v(P_i) = \mathrm{Proj}_{U_i}(\mathbf{R}).$$

Furthermore, if a compound fuzzy logic proposition Σ_1 involving atoms $P_1, \ldots, P_r$ has an associated fuzzy relation $\mathbf{R}_2 \subseteq U_1 \times \cdots \times U_r$, then the least restrictive truth value for Σ_1 denoted by $v(\Sigma_1/\Sigma)$ is defined by means of the membership function

$$X_{v(\Sigma_1/\Sigma)}(\eta) = h(\mathbf{R}_2(e_\eta) \cap \mathrm{Proj}_{U_1 \times U_2 \times \cdots \times U_r}(\mathbf{R})); \quad \forall \eta \in U$$

and we term this I.T.F.M. $(\mathbf{R}_2 | \mathbf{R}_1)$ analogous to the atomic proposition case, so that we can write

$$v(\Sigma_1/\Sigma) = \text{I.T.F.M. } (\mathbf{R}_2 | \mathrm{Proj}_{U_1 \times \cdots \times U_r}(\mathbf{R}))$$

where e_n is a singleton truth value restriction defined by

$$\chi_{e_n}(u) = \begin{cases} 1 & \text{if } u = \eta, \\ 0 & \text{otherwise.} \end{cases}$$

Definition 3.3. If $\mathbf{R}_1 \subseteq U_1 \times U_2 \times \cdots \times U_n$ is the fuzzy relation associated with the compound proposition Σ_1 involving atoms $P_1, P_2, \ldots, P_n$ and $\mathbf{R}_2 \subseteq U_1 \times U_2 \times \cdots \times U_n$ is the fuzzy relation associated with the compound proposition Σ_2 involving atoms $P_1, P_2, \ldots, P_n$ and $\mathbf{R}(\tau)$ is the fuzzy relation associated with

$$\Sigma_1 \square \Sigma_2 \text{ is } \tau$$

where $\square$ is a logic connective and $\mathbf{R}_3$ is the fuzzy relation corresponding to $\square$ then

$$\mathbf{R}(\tau) = \mathbf{R}_1 \cap_\square (\tau)\mathbf{R}_2$$

where $\cap_\square (\tau)$ is defined as a generalised intersection with

$$\chi_{\mathbf{R}(\tau)}(u_1, u_2, \ldots, u_n) = \chi_{\mathbf{R}_3(\tau)}(\chi_{\mathbf{R}_1}(u_1, u_2, \ldots, u_n), \chi_{\mathbf{R}_2}(u_1, u_2, \ldots, u_n))$$

It can be noted that

$$\cap_{\text{AND}} (\textbf{true}) = \cap; \qquad \cap_{\text{OR}} (\textbf{true}) = \cup.$$

Definition 3.4. The MAX–$\square$ composition of $\mathbf{R}_1 \subseteq U_1 \times U_2$ and $\mathbf{R}_2 \subseteq U_2 \times U_3$, denoted by $\mathbf{R}_1 \circ_\square \mathbf{R}_2$, is given by

$$\mathbf{R} = \mathbf{R}_1 \circ_\square \mathbf{R}_2; \qquad \mathbf{R} \subseteq U_1 \times U_3$$

where

$$\chi_{\mathbf{R}}(u_1, u_3) = \bigvee_\eta [\chi_{\mathbf{R}_3}\{\chi_{\mathbf{R}_1}(u_1, \eta), \chi_{\mathbf{R}_2}(\eta, u_3)\}]; \quad \forall u_1 \in U_1; \quad \forall u_3 \in U_3$$

where $\mathbf{R}_3$ is the fuzzy relation corresponding to the logic connective $\square$. To obtain the MAX–$\square$ (τ) composition we replace $\mathbf{R}_3$ with $\mathbf{R}_3(\tau)$.

In particular

$$\circ_{\text{AND}} (\textbf{true}) = \circ \quad \text{the MAX–MIN composition.}$$

Theorem 3.1. If $[(P \bullet Q \text{ is } \tau_1) * (Q \square S \text{ is } \tau_2)]$ is τ has the associated fuzzy relation $\mathbf{R} \subseteq U_P \times U_Q \times U_S$ and

$$\mathbf{R}_1 = \text{Proj}_{U_P \times U_S} (\mathbf{R})$$

then

$$\mathbf{R}_1 = \mathbf{R}_\bullet(\tau_1) \circ_* (\tau)\mathbf{R}_\square(\tau_2)$$

where

$$\mathbf{R}_\bullet \subseteq U_P \times U_Q \text{ is the fuzzy relation corresponding to } \bullet$$

and

$$\mathbf{R}_\square \subseteq U_Q \times U_S \text{ is the fuzzy relation corresponding to } \square$$

and $*, \bullet, \square$ are any logic connectives.

Proof. $\mathbf{R} = \mathbf{R}_*(\tau_1) \cap_* (\tau)\mathbf{R}_\square(\tau_2)$ using Definition 3.3 so that

$$\chi_\mathbf{R}(x, y, z) = \chi_{\mathbf{R}_3(\tau)}(\chi_{\mathbf{R}_*(\tau_1)}(x, y), \chi_{\mathbf{R}_\square(\tau_2)}(y, z)); \quad \forall x \in U_P; \quad \forall y \in U_Q; \quad \forall z \in U_S$$

where $\mathbf{R}_3$ is the fuzzy relation corresponding to $*$, and further

$$\chi_{\mathrm{Proj}_{U_P \times U_S}(\mathbf{R})}(x, z) = \bigvee_y [\chi_\mathbf{R}(x, y, z)]; \quad \forall x \in U_P; \quad \forall z \in U_S$$

$$= \bigvee_y [\chi_{\mathbf{R}_3(\tau)}(\chi_{\mathbf{R}_*(\tau_1)}(x, y), \chi_{\mathbf{R}_\square(\tau_2)}(y, z))]$$

$$= \chi_{\mathbf{R}_*(\tau_1) \circ_* (\tau)\mathbf{R}_\square(\tau_2)}.$$

Hence the theorem.

Theorem 3.2. Let $v\{P * Q \text{ is } \tau \mid v(P) \text{ AND } v(Q)) \subseteq U$ represent the fuzzy truth value restriction for the proposition $P * Q$ is τ, where $*$ is any logic connective, when given $v(P)$ and $v(Q)$. Then

$$\chi_{v(P*Q \text{ is }\tau / v(P) \text{ AND } v(Q))}(\eta) = h(\mathbf{R}(e_\eta) \cap (v(P) \times v(Q))); \quad \forall \eta \in U$$

where $\mathbf{R} = \mathbf{R}_1(\tau); \mathbf{R} \subseteq U_P \times U_Q$ and $\mathbf{R}_1$ is the fuzzy logic relation corresponding to $*$; $\mathbf{R}_1 \subseteq U_P \times U_Q$.

Proof. We interpret the given information as

$$((P \text{ is } v(P)) \text{ AND } (Q \text{ is } v(Q))) \text{ is } \mathbf{true}$$

so that the associated fuzzy relation is

$$(v(P) \times U_Q) \cap (U_P \times v(Q)) = v(P) \times v(Q)$$

and hence the theorem follows from Definition 3.2.

In Baldwin (1978c) the various fuzzy logic formulae given in Zadeh (1975b) and Baldwin (1978a), for example

$$\chi_{v(P \text{ AND } Q)}(x) = \bigvee_{\substack{y \wedge z = x \\ y \in U_P; z \in U_Q}} \{\chi_{v(P)}(y) \wedge \chi_{v(Q)}(z)\}; \quad \forall x \in U$$

are derived from this more fundamental definition.

We will now present various examples illustrating the use of these definitions and theorems. In each of the examples a conclusion is drawn from a set of logic propositions. The conclusion takes the form of a least restrictive fuzzy truth value being associated with a given proposition. The least restrictive truth value is chosen since this is the restriction given by the data, i.e. the set of logic propositions. In the case of two-valued logic, if the least restrictive truth value is a single truth value (true or false) then the result will correspond to that found by classical logical analysis. It is important, of course, to use the data in such a way that the most restrictive least restrictive fuzzy truth value restriction is determined. This is discussed further with respect to one of the examples. Furthermore Theorem 3.1 should be used as much as possible to reduce the dimensionality of the computation.

Examples

1. $(P \supset Q \text{ is } \tau_1)$ AND $(P \text{ OR } Q \text{ is } \tau_2)$ is τ.

If the associated fuzzy relation is **R** then

$$\mathbf{R} = \mathbf{I}(\tau_1) \cap_{\text{AND}} (\tau) \mathbf{D}(\tau_2); \qquad \mathbf{R} \subseteq U_P \times U_Q$$

so that

$$v(P) = \text{Proj}_{U_P} (\mathbf{R}) = (\mathbf{I}(\tau_1) \cap_{\text{AND}} (\tau) \mathbf{D}(\tau_2)) \circ \textit{unrestricted.}$$

Similarly

$$v(Q) = \textit{unrestricted} \circ (\mathbf{I}(\tau_1) \cap_{\text{AND}} (\tau) \mathbf{D}(\tau_2)).$$

This and related examples were discussed fully in Baldwin (1978c). In the binary logic case where $\tau_1 = \tau_2 = \tau = abs.\ true$ then $v(P) = \textit{unrestricted}$ and $v(Q) = abs.\ true$; a result which can be checked using truth tables.

2. If $(P \supset Q \text{ is } \tau_1)$ AND $(Q \text{ AND } R \text{ is } \tau_2)$ is τ

then

$$v(P \supset R \text{ is } \tau_3) = \text{I.T.F.M.} \ (\mathbf{I}(\tau_3) | \mathbf{I}(\tau_1) \circ_{\text{AND}} (\tau) \mathbf{C}(\tau_2)).$$

In the binary logic case this example takes the special form of proving the theorem

$$((P \supset Q) \text{ AND } (Q \text{ AND } R)) \supset (P \supset R).$$

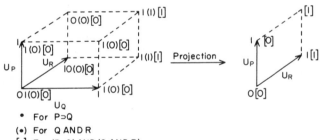

• For P ⊃ Q
(•) For Q AND R
[•] For (P ⊃ Q) AND (Q AND R)

Truth table

P	Q	R	P⊃Q	Q AND R	(P⊃Q)AND(Q AND R)	(P⊃R)
T	T	T	T	T	T	T
T	T	F	F	F	F	F
T	F	T	T	F	F	T
F	T	T	T	T	T	T
T	F	F	F	F	F	F
F	T	F	T	F	F	T
F	F	T	T	F	F	T
F	F	F	T	F	F	T

FIG. 2.

We illustrate fully the working of this example

$$v(P \supset R) = \text{I.T.F.M.} \ (I \,|\, I \circ C)$$

$$I \circ C = U_P{}^0_1 \begin{matrix} U_Q \\ 0 \ \ 1 \\ \begin{bmatrix} 1 & 1 \\ 0 & 1 \end{bmatrix} \end{matrix} \circ U_Q \begin{matrix} U_R \\ \begin{bmatrix} 0 & 0 \\ 0 & 1 \end{bmatrix} \end{matrix} = U_P \begin{matrix} U_R \\ \begin{bmatrix} 0 & 1 \\ 0 & 1 \end{bmatrix} \end{matrix}$$

$$v(P \supset R) = \text{I.T.F.M.} \ \left(\begin{bmatrix} 1 & 1 \\ 0 & 1 \end{bmatrix} \middle| \begin{bmatrix} 0 & 1 \\ 0 & 1 \end{bmatrix} \right) = (0, 1) = \text{True.}$$

A pictorial representation of the alternative three dimensional calculation is shown in Fig. 2 alongside a truth table analysis to which it is equivalent.

3. The following binary logic argument will be shown to be correct

$$\begin{array}{c} \text{B OR A} \\ A \supset C \\ B \supset D \\ \hline \text{C OR D} \end{array}$$

Now

$$v(\text{C OR D}) = \text{I.T.F.M.} \ (D \,|\, (D \circ I)^T \circ I) = \text{true since}$$

$$U_B \begin{matrix} U_A \\ \begin{bmatrix} 0 & 1 \\ 1 & 1 \end{bmatrix} \end{matrix} \circ U_A \begin{matrix} U_C \\ \begin{bmatrix} 1 & 1 \\ 0 & 1 \end{bmatrix} \end{matrix} = U_B \begin{matrix} U_C \\ \begin{bmatrix} 0 & 1 \\ 1 & 1 \end{bmatrix} \end{matrix}$$

$$U_C \begin{matrix} U_B \\ \begin{bmatrix} 0 & 1 \\ 1 & 1 \end{bmatrix} \end{matrix} \circ U_B \begin{matrix} U_D \\ \begin{bmatrix} 1 & 1 \\ 0 & 1 \end{bmatrix} \end{matrix} = U_C \begin{matrix} U_D \\ \begin{bmatrix} 0 & 1 \\ 1 & 1 \end{bmatrix} \end{matrix}$$

therefore C OR D.

4. The following binary logic examples show the need for transposition (T), interchanging row (T_r) and interchanging columns (T_c).

(a) $P \supset Q$

     $\neg R \supset \neg Q$

     $\overline{\neg R \supset \neg P}$

$$v(\neg R \supset \neg P) = \text{I.T.F.M.} \ (I \,|\, ((I \circ (I^T)^T)^T)^T) = \text{True since}$$

$$U_P \begin{matrix} U_Q \\ \begin{bmatrix} 1 & 1 \\ 0 & 1 \end{bmatrix} \end{matrix}; \quad U(\neg R) \begin{matrix} U_{\neg Q} \\ \begin{bmatrix} 1 & 1 \\ 0 & 1 \end{bmatrix} \end{matrix} \text{ therefore } U_R \begin{matrix} U_{\neg Q} \\ \begin{bmatrix} 0 & 1 \\ 1 & 1 \end{bmatrix} \end{matrix} \text{ therefore } U_R \begin{matrix} U_Q \\ \begin{bmatrix} 1 & 0 \\ 1 & 1 \end{bmatrix} \end{matrix} = I^T$$

$$U_P \begin{matrix} U_Q \\ \begin{bmatrix} 1 & 1 \\ 0 & 1 \end{bmatrix} \end{matrix} \circ U_Q \begin{matrix} U_R \\ \begin{bmatrix} 1 & 1 \\ 0 & 1 \end{bmatrix} \end{matrix} = U_P \begin{matrix} U_R \\ \begin{bmatrix} 1 & 1 \\ 0 & 1 \end{bmatrix} \end{matrix} \text{ therefore } U_{\neg P} \begin{matrix} U_R \\ \begin{bmatrix} 0 & 1 \\ 1 & 1 \end{bmatrix} \end{matrix} \text{ therefore } U_{\neg P} \begin{matrix} U_{\neg R} \\ \begin{bmatrix} 1 & 0 \\ 1 & 1 \end{bmatrix} \end{matrix}$$

$$U_{\neg P}$$

therefore $U_{\neg R}\begin{bmatrix}1 & 1\\0 & 1\end{bmatrix}$ therefore $\neg R \supset \neg P$

(b) $\qquad \neg P \supset Q$

$$\underline{\neg R \supset \neg Q}$$;

Find valid conclusion

involving P and R only

Let R_1 denote the fuzzy relation $R_1 \subseteq U_P \times U_R$ then $R_1 = I^{Tr} \circ (I^T)^T = D$, therefore P or R.

5. (1)   P or Q is τ_1
   (2) $\neg P \supset R$ is τ_2
   (3) $R \supset S$ is τ_3
   (4) $Q \supset \neg S$ is τ_4

   Find $v(P)$

In this example we are interpreting the conjunction of the statements (1), (2), (3), (4) as (((1) AND (2) is **true**) AND (3) is **true**) AND (4) is **true**. For determining $v(P)$ we first use (2) and (3) to eliminate R, then the result of this with (4) to eliminate S and the result of this with (1) to produce the fuzzy relation associated with the resulting fuzzy logic statement involving P and Q. We then project onto U_P to determine $v(P)$, so that

$$v(P) = \text{Proj}_{U_P}[\mathbf{D}(\tau_1) \cap ((\mathbf{I}^{T_r}(\tau_2) \circ \mathbf{I}(\tau_3)) \circ (\mathbf{I}^{T_c}(\tau_4))^T]$$

For the special case of binary logic where $\tau_1 = \tau_2 = \tau_3 = \tau_4 = abs.$ *true* then

$$v(P) = abs.\ true \text{ so that P is a valid conclusion.}$$

6. These binary logic examples show the need for transformation to avoid high dimensional calculations.
   (a)   (P AND Q) OR (Q $\supset$ S)
   $\qquad\underline{Q \text{ OR } S}$

   P OR S

We can avoid a three-dimensional truth table analysis by transforming the problem to

$$[(P \text{ AND } Q) \text{ AND } (Q \text{ OR } S)] \quad \text{OR} \quad [(Q \supset S) \text{ AND } (Q \text{ OR } S)].$$

Then

$$v(P \text{ OR } S) = \text{I.T.F.M. } [D|(C \circ D) \cup (U_P \times (\text{Proj}_{U_S}(I \cap D)))] = (0, 1) = abs.\ true$$

since

$$U_P\begin{bmatrix}0&0\\0&1\end{bmatrix} \circ U_Q\begin{bmatrix}0&1\\1&1\end{bmatrix} = U_P\begin{bmatrix}0&0\\1&1\end{bmatrix}$$

$$I \cap D = U_Q\begin{bmatrix}1&1\\0&1\end{bmatrix} \cap U_Q\begin{bmatrix}0&1\\1&1\end{bmatrix} = U_Q\begin{bmatrix}0&1\\0&1\end{bmatrix} \xrightarrow{\text{Proj}} [0\ 1] \xrightarrow[\text{extension}]{\text{cyl.}} U_P\begin{bmatrix}0&1\\0&1\end{bmatrix}$$

so that

$$(C \circ D) \cup (U_P \times (\text{Proj}_{U_S}(I \cap D))) = U_P \begin{bmatrix} 0 & 0 \\ 1 & 1 \end{bmatrix} \cup U_P \begin{bmatrix} 0 & 1 \\ 0 & 1 \end{bmatrix} = U_P \begin{bmatrix} 0 & 1 \\ 1 & 1 \end{bmatrix}.$$

Hence P or S.

(b)   P AND Q ⊃ S
      Q OR S
      P AND S
      _____

      $v(Q) = $ *unrestricted*

We first transform the problem to

$$[(P \supset S) \text{ OR } (Q \supset S)] \text{ AND } (Q \text{ OR } S) \text{ AND } (P \text{ AND } S)$$

and then to

$$[(P \supset S) \text{ AND } (Q \text{ OR } S) \text{ AND } (P \text{ AND } S)] \text{ OR}$$

$$[(Q \supset S) \text{ AND } (Q \text{ OR } S) \text{ AND } (P \text{ AND } S)]$$

so that

$$v(Q) = \text{Proj}_{U_Q} [(I_{P,S} \cap C_{P,S}) \circ D_{S,Q}) \cup ((I_{Q,S} \cap D_{Q,S}) \circ C_{S,P})^T]$$

$$= \textit{unrestricted}$$

where we have used the notation, for example

$$I_{P,S} \text{ signifies } I \subseteq U_P \times U_S.$$

The transformations are necessary to ensure the most restrictive answer; for example if in 6(a) we do not transform and use

$$v(P \text{ or } S) = \text{I.T.F.M.} [D/(D \circ_{OR} I) \cap (\text{Proj}_{U_S}(D) \times U_P)^T] = \textit{unrestricted}$$

and we cannot conclude that P or S is true but only that it could be.

7. (a)   P ⊃ Q is τ
         P is τ_1
         _____

         Therefore $v(Q) = \tau_1 \circ \mathbf{I}(\tau)$

   (b)   P ⊃ Q is τ
         Q is τ_1
         _____

         Therefore $v(P) = \mathbf{I}(\tau) \circ \tau_1$

These two cases with their use for approximate reasoning were discussed in Baldwin (1978*a*) and computational considerations were given in Baldwin & Guild (1978*a*). For example

   (c)   [(u is $\mathbf{p}$) ⊃ (w is $\mathbf{q}$)] is τ; $\mathbf{p}, \mathbf{p}' \subseteq X$; $\mathbf{q} \subseteq Y$; $\tau \subseteq U$
         u is $\mathbf{p}'$
         _____

         Therefore w is $\mathbf{q}'$; $\mathbf{q}' \subseteq Y$

where $\mathbf{q}' = \text{T.F.M.} [\mathbf{q} | \text{I.T.F.M.} (\mathbf{p}/\mathbf{p}') \circ \mathbf{I}(\tau)]$.

As a specific example we can consider

u is **tall** $\supset w$ is **short**
u is **very tall**

---

v (u is **tall**/u is **very tall**) = **very true**

so that $v(w$ is **short**) = **almost fairly true**
so that w is **almost fairly short**
where the calculations and definitions of the various terms are shown in Fig. 3.

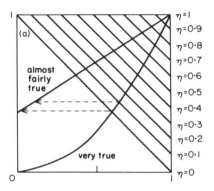

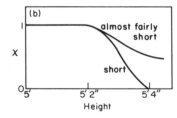
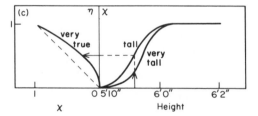

FIG. 3.

Many more examples of this and related type can be found in Baldwin (1978*a, b, c*) and Baldwin & Guild (1978*a, b*).

8. (1)   (P AND Q) $\supset$ R is τ
   (2)   P is τ_1
   (3)   R is τ_2

We have [(P AND Q) $\supset$ R is τ] AND R is τ_2
so that by result 7(b) v(P AND Q) = $\mathbf{I}(\tau) \circ \tau_2$.
We have [P AND Q is $\mathbf{I}(\tau) \circ \tau_2$] AND P is τ_1
so that by result 7(b) v(Q) = $\tau_1 \circ \mathbf{C}(\mathbf{I}(\tau) \circ \tau_2)$.

We can again use this for reasoning with vague statements as the following example illustrates. More detailed examples can be found in Baldwin (1978*b*) where this was termed a "mixed input argument".

$[((u \text{ is } \mathbf{p}) \text{ AND } (v \text{ is } \mathbf{q})) \supset (w \text{ is } \mathbf{r})] \text{ is } \tau; \quad \mathbf{p}, \mathbf{p}' \subseteq X; \quad \mathbf{q} \subseteq Y$
$u \text{ is } \mathbf{p}'$
$w \text{ is } \mathbf{r}' \qquad\qquad\qquad\qquad\qquad ; \quad \mathbf{r}, \mathbf{r}' \subseteq Z; \quad \tau \subseteq U$

Therefore v is $\mathbf{q}'$; $\quad \mathbf{q}' \subseteq Y$
where $\mathbf{q}' = \text{T.F.M.} [\mathbf{q} | \text{I.T.F.M.}(\mathbf{p} | \mathbf{p}') \circ \mathbf{C}(\mathbf{I}(\tau) \circ \text{I.T.F.M.} (\mathbf{r}/\mathbf{r}'))].$

9. The following problem was used as a tutorial example by Raphael (1976) to illustrate the use of Wang's algorithm and the Resolution principle to simplify the proving of theorems in propositional logic. We will solve the problem with the above method and compare this with the other methods given in Fig. 4.

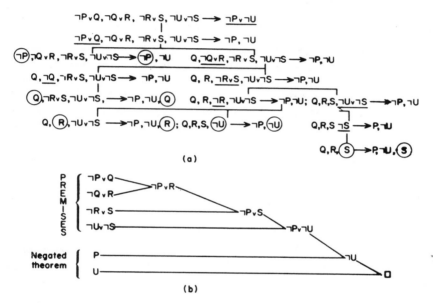

(a)

(b)

FIG. 4(a). Mystery solved by Wang's algorithm. (b) Mystery solved by propositional resolution.

Problem

To prove: If the maid told the truth the butler lied.

The facts: The maid said that she saw the butler in the living room.

The living room adjoins the kitchen. The shot was fired in the kitchen and could be heard in all nearby rooms. The butler, who has good hearing, said he did not hear the shot.
Representation:

Let P: the maid told the truth
   Q: the butler was in the living room
   R: the butler was near the kitchen
   S: the butler heard the shot
   U: the butler told the truth

The example is therefore represented as

$$P \supset Q$$
$$Q \supset R$$
$$R \supset S$$
$$\underline{U \supset \neg S}$$
$$P \supset \neg U$$

Using the method above

$$v(P \supset \neg U) = \text{I.T.F.M. } (I/((I \circ I) \circ (I \circ (I^{T_c})^T))^{T_c}) = abs.\ true.$$

4. Fuzzy algorithms, recursion and feedback structures

Fuzzy algorithms, which for present purposes we will simply think of as a set of propositions involving fuzzy sets as labels, fuzzy relations of the type discussed in section 3 are important in the application of fuzzy set theory. For example concept formulation such as the meaning of "beautiful" can be modelled using fuzzy algorithms or the meaning of a "good decision" resuires a fuzzy algorithmic definition. Each fuzzy algorithm requires a set of inputs and gives rise to an output or outputs. In this formulation inputs and outputs are assumed to be fuzzy subsets of appropriate universes of discourse. More often than not these algorithms are hierarchical in nature where the output of one algorithm is an input of another. In this section we will define such a hierarchical structure using the concept of a recursive fuzzy algorithm.

The fuzzy algorithm

$$\text{Alg } (\mathbf{x} \subseteq X: \pounds; X_1, X_2, \ldots, X_r: \mathbf{i}_1 \subseteq X_1, \mathbf{i}_2 \subseteq X_2, \ldots, i_n \subseteq X_n)$$

computes the fuzzy set $\mathbf{x} \subseteq X$ where $X_1, X_2, \ldots, X_n$ are defined universes of discourse and $\mathbf{i}_1, \mathbf{i}_2, \ldots, \mathbf{i}_n$ are known fuzzy subsets representing inputs and $\pounds$ is a set of propositions of the form discussed in section 3 with terms involving the atomic propositions of the form $\{u_i \text{ is } \mathbf{x}_i; \mathbf{x}_i \subseteq X_i\}$ and $X, X_1, \ldots, X_r$ are the universes of discourse applicable to $\pounds$. The method of computing $\mathbf{x} \subseteq X$ is that given in section 3. $\mathbf{x} \subseteq X$ is termed the output of the algorithm. For example

$$\text{Alg } [\textbf{fatness} \subseteq [0, 1]: \textbf{tall AND fat} \supset \textbf{heavy, short AND thin} \supset \textbf{light etc.};$$

$$[0, 10 \text{ ft}], [0, 25 \text{ stone}]: \sim\!\textbf{6 ft}, \sim\!\textbf{13 stone}]$$

will produce a fuzzy subset defined on $[0, 1]$ representing the "degree of fatness".

Often the inputs of a given algorithm are the outputs of other algorithms giving rise to a recursive structure.

For example

$$\text{Alg } (\mathbf{x} \subseteq X: \pounds; X_1, \ldots, X_r: \text{Alg } (\mathbf{i}_1 \subseteq X_1: \pounds_1; Y_1, \ldots, Y_m : \mathbf{e}_1 \subseteq Y_1, \ldots, e_m \subseteq Y_m))$$

$$\text{Alg } (\mathbf{i}_2 \subseteq X_2: \pounds_2; Z_1, \ldots, Z_n: \mathbf{a}_1 \subseteq Z_1, \ldots, \mathbf{a}_n \subseteq Z_n, \mathbf{i}_3 \subseteq X_3, \ldots, \mathbf{i}_r \subseteq X_r)$$

gives a recursive structure defined by the hierarchical tree in (Fig. 5). We can label an algorithm as

$$\textbf{Label } (X) = \text{Alg } (\textbf{label} \subseteq X: \pounds: \ldots)$$

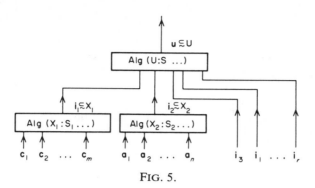

FIG. 5.

where the label takes a description of the output fuzzy subset. For example

Fatness of John ([0, 1]) = Alg (**Fatness** $\subseteq$ [0, 1]: **tall** AND **fat** $\supset$ **heavy**, etc. . . .).

An example of a recursive structural algorithm is

T.V.R. for letter a ([0, 1])

    = Alg ($v(a) \subseteq$ [0, 1]: **letter a** $\supset$ **circular part** AND **included vertical line on right** AND **vertical line NOT too large**; [0, 1], [0, 1], [0, 1]: T.V.R. for circular part ([0, 1]), T.V.R. for included vertical line on right ([0, 1]), T.V.R. for not too large vertical line ([0, 1])), where T.V.R. stands for truth value restriction.

A few examples of concepts which require hierarchical fuzzy algorithmic modelling are given below:

    suitable home for a family of four;
    reasonable area in which to retire;
    politically suitable country in which to live;
    stable society;
    good hop growing soil;
    dangerous criminal;
    good engineering design.

Each of these could be modelled using the above ideas and methods. More generally than not, the modelling will be such that the truth of a given concept will be given as a truth value restriction with a "false characteristic" such as **fairly false**, **very false** etc. For an example of modelling in this way see Baldwin & Guild (1978d).

The form of modelling above can be extended to include "feedback paths" and a "clock time mechanism" giving rise to the concept of a fuzzy automaton which could be used in the fields of control, programming and artificial intelligence. Dynamic systems of fuzzy automaton could be used to model complex industrial processes and such concepts as "stable systems", "stable cycles", could be considered. A more sophisticated form of "world modelling" could be evolved, being able to deal with both precise and vague concepts and information, giving rise to simulations which might be more useful for the control of industrial and economic development than present-day attempts.

Extensions of the above work to include fuzzy probabilistic reasoning and fuzzy qualifiers are being developed.

5. Conclusion

A general approach to fuzzy reasoning, fuzzy logic analysis and fuzzy theorem proving has been given and its application to model building indicated.

References

BALDWIN, J. F. (1978a). A new approach to approximate reasoning using a fuzzy logic. *Research Report EM/FS3*. University of Bristol, Engineering Mathematics Department. To appear in *Fuzzy Sets and Systems*.

BALDWIN, J. F. (1978b). Fuzzy logic and approximate reasoning for mixed input arguments. *Research Report EM/FS4*. University of Bristol, Engineering Mathematics Department.

BALDWIN, J. F. (1978c). A model of fuzzy reasoning and fuzzy logic. *Research Report EM/FS10*. University of Bristol, Engineering Mathematics Department.

BALDWIN, J. F. & GUILD, N. (1978a). Feasible algorithms for approximate reasoning using a fuzzy logic. *Research Report EM/FS8*. University of Bristol, Engineering Mathematics Department.

BALDWIN, J. F. & GUILD, N. (1978b). The resolution of two paradoxes using a fuzzy logic. *Research Report EM/FS11*. University of Bristol, Engineering Mathematics Department.

BALDWIN, J. F. & GUILD, N. (1978c). A model for multi-criterial decision-making using fuzzy logic. *Research Report EM/FS13*. University of Bristol, Engineering Mathematics Department.

BALDWIN, J. F. & GUILD, N. (1978d). Comparison of fuzzy sets on the same decision space. *Research Report EM/FS2*. University of Bristol, Engineering Mathematics Department. To appear in *Fuzzy Sets and Systems*.

BALDWIN, J. F. & PILSWORTH, B. (1978a). Axiomatic approach to implication for approximate reasoning using a fuzzy logic. *Research Report EM/FS9*. University of Bristol, Engineering Mathematics Department.

BALDWIN, J. F. & PILSWORTH, B. (1978b). Fuzzy truth definition of possibility measure for decision classification. *Research Report EN/FS12*. University of Bristol, Engineering Mathematics Department.

RAPHAEL, B. (1976). *The Thinking Computer*. San Francisco: W. H. Freeman.

ZADEH, L. A. (1965). Fuzzy sets. *Information and Control*, **8**, 338–353.

ZADEH, L. A. (1975a). Calculus of fuzzy restrictions. In ZADEH, et al., Eds, *Fuzzy Sets and Their Applications to Cognitive and Decision Processes*. New York: Academic Press.

ZADEH, L. A. (1975b). Fuzzy logic and approximate reasoning. *Synthese*, **30**, 407–428.

Deductive verbal models of organizations

FRED WENSTØP

Bedriftsøkonomisk Institutt, Frysjaveien 33c, Oslo 8, Norway

(*Received 14 October 1975 and in revised form 10 February 1976*)

The idea that loosely defined simulation models of organizational behavior can yield more significant information than conventional precisely defined ones, has been explored. Natural language has been utilized as a medium for this purpose. This has allowed for the values of the variables to be linguistic rather than numerical, and for causal relations between the variables to be formulated verbally rather than mathematically. Such models have been called *verbal models*. A generative grammar is presented which restricts the set of allowed linguistic values and relations in a model specification. This makes it possible to formulate a semantical model based on fuzzy set theory of the words in the vocabulary. The semantical model can be used to calculate the dynamic behavior of verbal models. Thus it becomes possible to infer future behavior of a verbal model, given its linguistically stated initial state. This process was greatly facilitated by implementing the semantical model in an APL-workspace, thus making it possible to write linguistic values and relations directly on a terminal, using a syntax very close to that of natural language. The semantical model would then be automatically activated and respond with the linguistic values of output variables.

A simulation study is presented which shows that verbal models indeed may yield significant information based on rather general premises. This indicates that they may, under certain circumstances, be superior to corresponding conventional simulation models. It is generally concluded that the present approach towards modelling the behavior of complex organizations is not without interesting potentialities.

Introduction

BACKGROUND

During recent years Zadeh's concept of *fuzzy sets* (Zadeh, 1965) has been the object of increasing attention as a potential mathematical tool for the analysis of complex systems.

Fuzzy set theory is essentially a generalization of Boolean algebra which was originally developed by Boole (1854) as an instrument for the semantical analysis of a certain class of propositions. Boolean algebra has as its basis a *semantical model* of the meaning of the connectives "or", "and" and "not". This makes it possible to calculate the truth-values of propositions that are otherwise too complicated to infer by simple unaided reasoning.

Zadeh's approach broadens the area to which these principles can be applied. It becomes possible also to put forward semantic definitions of several words which in natural language are used to approximately characterize both magnitudes (Zadeh, 1972; Lakoff, 1972) and the causal relations between such magnitudes as well. This opens up the possibility of *deductive verbal models*.

THE CONCEPT OF DEDUCTIVE VERBAL MODELS AND THEIR RELATION TO
CONVENTIONAL SIMULATION MODELS

An *organization* will be understood as a dynamic system where human behavior plays an important role. Organizations typically exhibit a very complex behavior and numerous models or theories have been offered in order to explain and/or predict such behavior (March, 1965; March & Simon 1958). Lately, emphasis has been placed on so-called simulation models. Examples are discussed in Forrester (1961), Cyert (1965), Garzo & Yanouzas (1967), to mention just a few.

Traditional simulation models consist of
(a) a set of variables (names of organizational attributes);
(b) a set of mathematical functional relationships between numerical values of the variables (models of causal relations).

Since the variables here take numerical values, we will refer to such models as *numerical (simulation) models*. Numerical models are, by their very construction, *deductive*, in the sense that explicit values of output variables, being implicitly determined by the model and a set of input values, can be derived by simulation or mathematical analysis. The methodological principle which is involved here, is that of *explaining* the output values in terms of a set of more comprehensible causal relations. Being too involved for the human mind, a machine is usually employed to perform the actual *deduction process*.

As a matter of general experience, the powerfulness of numerical simulation models as a tool in this context is somewhat limited and for the following reasons:

(a) In order to be measurable, the variables have to be operationally defined. This tends to limit the free choice of variables and often leads to variable-definitions which are artificial in relation to the intuitive connotations of their names.
(b) The specifications of the mathematical relations usually give the impression of being somewhat arbitrarily chosen. This is so because the general types of relations involved and the parameters specifying them most often must be conjectured with very little empirical support. The effect is to give the models a flavor of unreality.
(c) Because of the immense freedom in selecting parameter values, it is most often difficult or even impossible in practice to get an overall impression of the system's behavior patterns by simulation.

If by a *significant model* we, informally, understand one which can convey believable and important information about the natural system which it is supposed to model, it may be concluded from the above arguments that the significance of numerical simulation models generally tends to be of limited scope. It is also obvious, however, that the three features responsible for this are direct results of the very preciseness of numerical models which is manifested by exact relations between numerical entities.

Thus, precision and significance seem to be competing or *complementary* principles. We are therefore led to believe that the road to go must be to find a method of relaxing the degree of precision which is found in conventional simulation models.

As suggested by Zadeh, one way of achieving this might be to allow the variables in a model to take *linguistic* rather than numerical values. Examples of linguistic values are: "high", "rather high", "not very low", etc. We may also allow causal relations between variables to be stated *verbally*, i.e.: "X becomes somewhat higher than Y if Y is not low". Models which are formulated in this way will be called *verbal models*. Since verbal models are much more approximate and unpretentious than corresponding numerical ones, they should also be more significant since their implications have a more general validity.

The major problem which must be solved once the concept of verbal models is introduced, is how to derive the consequences of their implicitly stated dynamic behavior. We shall show how this can be efficiently done by postulating a *semantic model* based on fuzzy set theory and applying the principle of fuzzy compositional inference (Zadeh, 1973). If this is done, the verbal model becomes *deductive* when it is coupled with the semantic model and we have a *verbal simulation model*.

OUTLINE

We shall here discuss a particular implementation of these ideas. We shall first present a semantical model with an associated grammatical rule which can be used in formulation and simulation of verbal models. We shall thereafter consider a simulation example which is well-suited to illustrate the concept and usefulness of verbal simulation models of organizations.

It should be noted that the present syntactic-semantical system is a first attempt at realizing more concretely the concept of verbal simulation models. It therefore is meant to serve mainly as a practical device which makes possible a closer study of the nature and potentialities of verbal models.

A grammatical frame for verbal models

To be able to apply a semantical model for the analysis of a verbal model, it is necessary to somehow restrict the set of allowed sentences in the verbal model. This is most conveniently done (Zadeh, 1975) by defining a vocabulary and a generative grammar (Chomsky, 1965) which together normatively defines a set of *grammatically correct* sentences.

VOCABULARY

Lexical category	Generic symbol	Category members
Organizational variable	X	any variable-name
Primary term	T	high, low, unknown, undefined
Elementary relation	ER	higher, lower, similar, equal, opposite
Value hedge	HV	very, not, indeed, sortof, rather, moreorless, atleast
Relation hedge	HR	slightly, somewhat, much, considerably, very, not, moreorless, indeed
Connective	C	and, or
Relation evaluator	E	of, than, to
Conditionalizer		if
Comparator		is
Normalizer		value
Value assigner		←
Parentheses		(,)

Here, the set of all *category members* defines the set of words in our *vocabulary*. The *generic symbols* refer to any one of the words in the respective *lexical categories*. Each category is thus a subset of the vocabulary.

GRAMMAR

The words from the vocabulary can be arranged in sequence to form statements, S. S will be called *grammatical* if it can be generated according to the following *production rules:*

(1) S → $X \leftarrow$ value M;   (7) V → (ER E X);
(2) M → (M or M);   (8) V → T;
(3) M → V;   (9) T → (T C T);
(4) M → (V if N);   (10) T → (HV T);
(5) N → (N C N);   (11) ER → (ER C ER);
(6) N → (X is V);   (12) ER → (HR ER);

(13) any generic symbol→one of its category members.

Here, capital letters represent non-terminal symbols. The words from the vocabulary are terminal symbols and cannot be rewritten. They are written with lower case letters. The set of non-terminal symbols consists of the generic symbols of lexical categories plus the symbols M, V and N which actually represent a main statement part, a fuzzy value and a fuzzy truth-value, respectively. These will be explained in the section on semantic models.

If a statement S is grammatical, it will be called a *linguistic assignment statement* since it, in effect, assigns a linguistic value to a variable.

EXAMPLES

Assume that X, Y and Z are names of variables. We can then use the production rules to generate an assignment statement as follows (the rewriting rule which is used at each stage is shown at the right margin):

```
S
X← value M                                                        (1)
X← value V                                                        (3)
X← value T                                                        (8)
X← value (T C T)                                                  (9)
X← value ((HV T) C (HV T))                                       (10)
X← value ((HV T) C (HV (HV T)))                                  (10)
X← value ((not high) and (not (very low)))
```

Stated in a slightly more natural English, the terminal string reads: "X is assigned the value not high and not very low". Without introducing ambiguity we may drop parentheses according to Łukasiewicz' parentheses-free notation (Iverson, 1962). For evaluation, the statements must then be read from the right hand side:

X← value (not high) and not very low.

Two more examples of production trees:

S
X← value M	(1)
X← value M or M	(2)
X← value (V if N) or V if N	(4)
X← value (V if Y is V) or V if Y is V	(6)
X← value (T if Y is T) or T if Y is T	(8)
X← value (T if Y is T) or T if Y is HV T	(10)
X← value (high if Y is low) or low if Y is not low	(13)

S
X← value M	(1)
X← value V	(3)
X← value V if N	(4)
X← value (ER E Y) if N	(7)
X← value (ER E Y) if Z is V	(6)
X← value (ER E Y) if Z is T	(8)
X← value ((HR ER) E Y) if Z is T	(12)
X← value ((somewhat lower) than Y) if Z is low	(13)

After a little practise, it is very easy to write grammatical statements without referring directly to the grammar.

VERBAL MODELS

The concept of verbal models can now be stated more precisely: We shall by a *verbal model* understand simply a list of verbal assignment statements which are ordered so that all independent variables in a given statement have been assigned values in statements preceding it.

A semantical model

Given a verbal model, it is usually not intuitively easy to predict its behavior. This is especially true when feed-back loops are involved since these are difficult for the human mind readily to assimilate.

What we need, therefore, is an automized system which not only understands the meaning behind each assignment statement in the sense that it can make intuitively acceptable inferences from them also in cases which were not explicitly mentioned, but in addition can put this together and thereby calculate the implied dynamic behavior of the total system.

Such a system can be realized by a computerized semantical model based on fuzzy set theory. APL (Iverson, 1962) has been found to be a computer language remarkably suited for this purpose. The present semantical system will therefore be described partly by use of APL-symbols (Gilman & Rose, 1970). Unusual symbols will be explained as they occur.

PRINCIPLES AND BASIC ASSUMPTIONS

We shall model the *meaning* of linguistic values as fuzzy subsets of the appropriate psychological continuum (Torgerson, 1958).

Thus, even in cases where there exists a natural physical continuum, as for instance in the case of the variable "age", we will stick to an assumed mental representation of the physical interval as our universe of discourse. A psychological continuum has the advantage that equidistant points in it are also psychologically equidistant. This means that difficulties which may arise, for instance from manifestations of Weber's law, are avoided.

Hence, organizational variables are treated as linguistic variables in the sense of Zadeh.

We assume that the semantical content of each word in the vocabulary is independent of context. This assumption is not quite necessary, but it simplifies things considerably. It also may not be wholly unreasonable in view of the fact that we operate exclusively within the realms of psychological continua.

The meaning of a verbal assignment statement with n independent variables will be modelled as a $n+1$-dimensional fuzzy relation. The consequence of a verbal assignment statement, i.e. the value of the dependent variable, will be inferred using the rule of fuzzy compositional inference (Zadeh, 1973).

For practical purposes, a fuzzy set will be represented by a discrete collection of points from the universe of discourse with their respective membership-values. In the concrete language of APL, therefore, fuzzy sets will be represented as arrays or (higher order) matrices of membership-values, the structure depending on the dimensionality of the actual fuzzy set.

With respect to the individual words in the vocabulary, it thus becomes natural to interpret primary terms and elementary relations in the form of constant fuzzy sets. The words from these two lexical categories will accordingly be called *fuzzy constants*. The grammatical rules (10) and (12) ensure that hedges always precede their arguments. This is also true of the normalizer "value" (1). The hedges together with "value" are therefore syntactically equivalent, and may be referred to as *monadic semantic operators* since they modify the meaning of what is to follow in an expression. All other words are seen to operate on the combined meaning of what is on each of their sides. These words may correspondingly be referred to as *dyadic semantic operators*.

We are now in the fortunate position that the three syntactical categories, in which the vocabulary can be split, are equivalent to the APL-categories of constants, monadic functions and dyadic functions. A semantic model may therefore be defined by specifying each word from the vocabulary directly as appropriate APL constants, monadic, or dyadic functions. If this has been done, any verbal assignment statement will also automatically be an APL statement.

SEMANTICAL MODELS OF THE INDIVIDUAL WORDS

Primary terms

Models of the meaning of the four primary terms are shown below:

high	$\leftrightarrow$	0	0	0	0	0	0	0·1	0·3	0·7	1	1
low	$\leftrightarrow$	1	1	0·7	0·3	0·1	0	0	0	0	0	0
undefined	$\leftrightarrow$	0	0	0	0	0	0	0	0	0	0	0
unknown	$\leftrightarrow$	1	1	1	1	1	1	1	1	1	1	1

The positions of the elements in the arrays represent corresponding points in the universe of discourse. The numbers represent membership-values of these points.

Elementary relations

A seven-by-seven point model of "higher" is:

$$
\text{higher} \quad \leftrightarrow \quad
\begin{array}{ccccccc}
0{\cdot}1 & 0{\cdot}6 & 0{\cdot}9 & 1 & 1 & 1 & 1 \\
0 & 0{\cdot}1 & 0{\cdot}6 & 0{\cdot}9 & 1 & 1 & 1 \\
0 & 0 & 0{\cdot}1 & 0{\cdot}6 & 0{\cdot}9 & 1 & 1 \\
0 & 0 & 0 & 0{\cdot}1 & 0{\cdot}6 & 0{\cdot}9 & 1 \\
0 & 0 & 0 & 0 & 0{\cdot}1 & 0{\cdot}6 & 1 \\
0 & 0 & 0 & 0 & 0 & 0{\cdot}1 & 1 \\
0 & 0 & 0 & 0 & 0 & 0 & 1
\end{array}
$$

This means that, for instance, the degree to which the position of point 3 is "higher" in the interval than point 1, is 0·9. Thus "higher" is here assumed to be a quite fuzzy concept: we don't say that something is "higher" than another thing unless it really is quite a bit higher. Note also that the degree to which point 7 is higher than anything, is 1·0. This is so because 7 is the highest possible point. The matrix is thus more precisely a model of the concept "higher, if possible". The relations "lower", "similar" and "opposite" are similarly defined. "Equal" is modelled non-fuzzily as the identity matrix.

The normalizer

"Value" operates so as to normalize the meaning of the expression following it in a statement, if this is not identical to "undefined". The normalizing is effected by dividing each component of the fuzzy set by the value of the largest component. According to (1), when a value is assigned to the dependent variable in an assignment statement, it is always ensured that the value is normal. This corresponds to the psychological assumption, that when a linguistic value is assigned to a variable, at least some of the values of the base variable must be fully compatible with this value.

Hedges

The semantics of the individual hedges has been defined according to the general principles and ideas set forth in Zadeh (1972) and Lakoff (1972). For simplicity, hedges are assumed to operate only on membership-values, i.e. their effect is independent of positions of the operand in the universe of discourse. This is also true of the relation hedges which act in a uniform manner on all elements in the relation in question.

Examples of the effects of some of the hedges are:

high	$\leftrightarrow$	0	0	0	0	0	0	0·1	0·3	0·7	1	1
moreorless high	$\leftrightarrow$	0	0	0	0	0	0	0·3	0·5	0·8	1	1
very high	$\leftrightarrow$	0	0	0	0	0	0	0	0·1	0·5	0·9	1
rather high	$\leftrightarrow$	0	0	0	0	0	0	0	0	1	0·2	0
sortof high	$\leftrightarrow$	0	0	0	0	0	0	0·3	1	0·1	0	0

$$
\text{slightly higher} \quad \leftrightarrow \quad
\begin{array}{ccccccc}
0 & 1 & 0{\cdot}1 & 0 & 0 & 0 & 0 \\
0 & 0 & 1 & 0{\cdot}1 & 0 & 0 & 0 \\
0 & 0 & 0 & 1 & 0{\cdot}1 & 0 & 0 \\
0 & 0 & 0 & 0 & 1 & 0{\cdot}1 & 0 \\
0 & 0 & 0 & 0 & 0 & 1 & 0{\cdot}1 \\
0 & 0 & 0 & 0 & 0 & 0 & 1 \\
0 & 0 & 0 & 0 & 0 & 0 & 1
\end{array}
$$

$$
\begin{array}{ccccccc}
0 & 0{\cdot}9 & 1 & 0{\cdot}1 & 0 & 0 & 0 \\
0 & 0 & 0{\cdot}9 & 1 & 0{\cdot}1 & 0 & 0 \\
0 & 0 & 0 & 0{\cdot}9 & 1 & 0{\cdot}1 & 0 \\
\text{somewhat higher} \quad \leftrightarrow \; 0 & 0 & 0 & 0 & 0{\cdot}9 & 1 & 0{\cdot}1 \\
0 & 0 & 0 & 0 & 0 & 0{\cdot}9 & 1 \\
0 & 0 & 0 & 0 & 0 & 0 & 1 \\
0 & 0 & 0 & 0 & 0 & 0 & 1 \\
\end{array}
$$

somewhat higher $\leftrightarrow$

0	0·9	1	0·1	0	0	0
0	0	0·9	1	0·1	0	0
0	0	0	0·9	1	0·1	0
0	0	0	0	0·9	1	0·1
0	0	0	0	0	0·9	1
0	0	0	0	0	0	1
0	0	0	0	0	0	1

considerably higher $\leftrightarrow$

0	0	0·9	1	0	0	0
0	0	0	0·9	1	0	0
0	0	0	0	0·9	1	0
0	0	0	0	0	0·9	1
0	0	0	0	0	0	1
0	0	0	0	0	0	1
0	0	0	0	0	0	1

(For practical purposes, the relations are here reduced to 7-by-7 matrices. All numbers are rounded off to only one decimal.)

Connectives

"And" and "or" are defined in the standard fuzzy set-theoretical way (Bellman & Giertz, 1973). For A and B being either fuzzy sets or truth-values, we have:

$$A \text{ and } B \leftrightarrow A \llcorner B \tag{14}$$
$$A \text{ or } B \quad \leftrightarrow A \ulcorner B$$

where $\ulcorner$ and $\llcorner$ perform, element for element, maximum- and minimum-operations, respectively. "Not" belongs syntactically in the class of hedges and is defined there, also in the standard way, as:

$$\text{not } A \quad \leftrightarrow 1\text{-}A. \tag{16}$$

Relation evaluators

If ER is a relation from the value of X to the value of Y, it is possible to *infer* the value of Y when X is given, by using the rule of fuzzy composition:

$$Y \leftarrow ER \ulcorner.\llcorner X \tag{17}$$

where the APL symbol $\ulcorner.\llcorner$ performs max-min matrix multiplication (i.e. fuzzy composition). Examples of the form (17) are:

$$Y \leftarrow (\text{slightly higher}) \text{ than } X$$
$$Y \leftarrow \text{opposite of } X$$
$$Y \leftarrow \text{similar to } X.$$

It thus becomes natural to ascribe to the three prepositions the semantical act of executng the implied inference. Accordingly,

$$\text{than} \leftrightarrow \text{to} \leftrightarrow \text{of} \leftrightarrow \ulcorner.\llcorner. \tag{18}$$

As an illustration: the value implied by the expression

"(somewhat higher) than rather low"

can now be inferred by executing

$$\text{(somewhat higher)} \ulcorner.\llcorner \text{ rather low}$$

which gives:

$$
0 \quad 1 \quad 0{\cdot}2 \quad 0 \quad 0 \quad 0 \quad 0 \quad \ulcorner.\llcorner
\begin{array}{cccccccc}
0 & 0{\cdot}9 & 1 & 0{\cdot}1 & 0 & 0 & 0 & 0 \\
0 & 0 & 0{\cdot}9 & 1 & 0{\cdot}1 & 0 & 0 & 0 \\
0 & 0 & 0 & 0{\cdot}9 & 1 & 0{\cdot}1 & 0 & 0{\cdot}9 \\
0 & 0 & 0 & 0 & 0{\cdot}9 & 1 & 0{\cdot}1 & 1 \\
0 & 0 & 0 & 0 & 0 & 0{\cdot}9 & 1 & 0{\cdot}2 \\
0 & 0 & 0 & 0 & 0 & 0 & 0{\cdot}1 & 0{\cdot}1 \\
0 & 0 & 0 & 0 & 0 & 0 & 1 & 0
\end{array}
\leftrightarrow
$$

The result, 0 0 0·9 1 0·2 0·1 0 is not far from the meaning of the linguistic value "(sortof low) or (not high) and not low", and might therefore be approximated by this label (see the sub-section headed COMMENT that follows).

Conditional statements
The present semantical definition of "if" has an appearance which deviates from that of Zadeh's. It therefore needs a closer consideration. Assume that a_i, b_i and c_i are values (fuzzy sets) of the linguistic variables A, B and C, $i = 0,1,2, . .$ Zadeh defines the meaning of the *relation*

$$a_1 \text{ if } b_1$$

as follows:

$$(a_1 \, \text{o}.\llcorner \, b_1)\ulcorner(\text{unknown o}.\llcorner \text{ not } b_1) \tag{19}$$

where the APL-function o.$\llcorner$ calculates the minimum-Cartesian product of the two vectors, i.e. $(a_1 \, \text{o}.\llcorner \, b_1) \, [i;j] \leftrightarrow a_1[i]\llcorner b_1[j]$.

More generally, he defines:

$$a_1 \text{ if } b_1, \text{ or } a_2 \text{ if } b_2, \text{ or } . . \text{ or } a_n \text{ if } b_n \tag{20}$$

as

$$(a_1 \, \text{o}.\llcorner \, b_1)\ulcorner . . \ulcorner(a_n \, \text{o}.\llcorner \, b_n)\ulcorner(\text{unknown o}.\llcorner \text{ not } b_1\ulcorner . . \ulcorner b_n). \tag{21}$$

This is a direct generalization of implication in classical logic. It corresponds to the "if b then a, else anything"—connotation of "if". We may, however, also define "if" with an "if b then a, else undefined"-connotation. This will show itself to have some decisive mathematical advantages. (21) now becomes:

$$(a_1 \, \text{o}.\llcorner \, b_1)\ulcorner . . \ulcorner(a_n \, \text{o}.\llcorner \, b_n)\ulcorner(\text{undefined o}.\llcorner \text{not } b_1\ulcorner . . \ulcorner b_n). \tag{22}$$

But this is, according to our definition of "undefined", the same as:

$$(a_1 \, \text{o}.\llcorner \, b_2)\ulcorner . . \ulcorner(a_n \, \text{o}.\llcorner \, b_n). \tag{23}$$

Accordingly, the matrix (23) will be our semantical model of the relation underlying the conditional statement (20).

Now, assume that the value of B has been found to be b_0. What is then the value a_0 of A if (20) is supposed to be valid? By applying the principle of fuzzy compositional inference, we have:

$$a_0 \leftarrow ((a_1 \circ.\llcorner b_1)\ulcorner .. \ulcorner(a_n \circ.\llcorner b_n)) \ulcorner.\llcorner b_0. \tag{24}$$

By virtue of the associative and distributive laws, (24) can be shown to be equivalent to:

$$a_0 \leftarrow (a_1 \llcorner b_1 \ulcorner.\llcorner b_0)\ulcorner ... \ulcorner(a_n \llcorner b_n \ulcorner.\llcorner b_0). \tag{25}$$

Let us now *redefine* "if" so that it becomes semantically equivalent to the minimum operator $\llcorner$. Let us further define the semantics of the word "is" as a performer of fuzzy composition with arrays as arguments; i.e. "is" performs max-min scalar multiplication ($\ulcorner.\llcorner$). (25) can then equivalently be written:

$$a_0 \leftarrow (a_1 \text{ if } b_0 \text{ is } b_1) \text{ or } .. \text{ or } (a_n \text{ if } b_0 \text{ is } b_n). \tag{26}$$

Here, we have achieved an elegant syntact-semantical form. (26) not only is a verbal expression of a relation between the value a_0 of the dependent variable A and the value b_0 of the free variable B, but also an *algorithm* which calculates a_0 as a function of b_0.

We may generalize (26) by allowing A to be dependent on several variables, say B and C. A parallel to (20) would be:

$$(a_1 \text{ if } b_1 \text{ and } c_1) \text{ or } (a_2 \text{ if } b_2 \text{ or } c_2) \tag{27}$$

which again is a fixed relation from B and C to A. Mathematically, (27) would be represented as:

$$(a_1 \circ.\llcorner b_1 \circ.\llcorner c_1)\ulcorner(a_2 \circ.\llcorner b_2 \circ.\ulcorner c_2) \tag{28}$$

whe:e we have modelled conjunction and disjunction between values in *different* universes as $\circ.\llcorner$ and $\circ.\ulcorner$, respectively, the latter symbolizing the maximum-Cartesian product.

If now B and C have the values b_0 and c_0, and by assuming that B and C are *non-interactive* (Zadeh, 1975), a_0 can again be inferred by:

$$a_0 \leftarrow ((a_1 \circ.\llcorner b_1 \circ.\llcorner c_1)\ulcorner(a_2 \circ.\llcorner b_2 \circ.\ulcorner c_2))\ulcorner.\llcorner c_0 \circ.\llcorner b_0 \tag{29}$$

where $\ulcorner.\llcorner$ in this case represents max-min matrix multiplication over two dimensions.
One can also in this case show that (29) is mathematically equivalent to:

$$a_0 \leftarrow (a_1 \llcorner (b_0 \ulcorner.\llcorner b_1)\llcorner c_0 \ulcorner.\llcorner c_1))\ulcorner(a_2 \llcorner(b_0 \ulcorner.\llcorner b_2)\ulcorner(c_0 \ulcorner.\llcorner c_2)). \tag{30}$$

Thus, in the same fashion as before, we can write (30) and therefore (29) in the elegant verbal version:

$$\begin{aligned} a_0 \leftarrow (a_1 \text{ if } (b_0 \text{ is } b_1) \text{ and } c_0 \text{ is } c_1) \text{ or} \\ (a_2 \text{ if } (b_0 \text{ is } b_2) \text{ or } c_0 \text{ is } c_2). \end{aligned} \tag{31}$$

We are now ready to take out the essence of this discussion.

The comparator
When an expression like "b_0 is b_1" is evaluated according to the above definition of "is"

the result is a number between 0 and 1. This number may appropriately be called a *truth-value*, N, since it, in some sense, represents the degree of truth of the statement (compare with rule (6) of the grammar). We now adopt:

$$V_1 \text{ is } V_2 \leftrightarrow V_1 \ulcorner . \llcorner V_2 \tag{32}$$

where V_1 and V_2 are linguistic values in the form of fuzzy sets.

The conditionalizer
The definition of "if" is already clear:

$$V \text{ if } N \leftrightarrow V \llcorner N. \tag{33}$$

According to (4), we will always have a truth-value, N, as the right argument of "if" (the APL-operator $\llcorner$ here establishes a new array with each component equal to the minimum of the number N and the corresponding component of V). It must be noted, however, that implicit in (33) is the "*a if b*, else undefined"-connotation of "if".

COMMENT
We have now outlined a complete semantic model which can be used to effectuate verbal assignment statements. Although the development has been sketchy in nature, it is possible to demonstrate systematically that the present syntactic-semantical system is compatible with Zadeh's fuzzy-set theoretic principles, notably that of fuzzy compositional inference (see Wenstøp, 1975).

What we have achieved, is that verbal assignment statements like,

X←((somewhat lower) than Y) if (U is low) or V is not similar to W

by imposing the semantical model, *also* are algorithms which (on an APL-terminal) automatically computes the appropriate value of X when the values of Y, U and V are known either linguistically or in the form of fuzzy sets. The resulting value of X will have the form of a fuzzy set.

The only thing we lack in this connection, is a function which can label a given fuzzy set, such as X above, with an appropriate grammatical linguistic value. This problem has been called that of *linguistic approximation* by Zadeh. An APL-function, called LABEL, which does this has been implemented. LABEL is an heuristic search routine which develops a label by stepwise building it up from simpler elements by disjuncting them. The fitness criterion in LABEL is the least sum of squares.

OPERATIONAL CHARACTERISTICS OF THE SYNTACTIC-SEMANTIC SYSTEM
Some examples of the working characteristics of the APL-implemented system are presented below. The indented statements are inputs to the machine whereas the machine responses are left-margin justified.

    LABEL SIMILAR TO LOW
MOREORLESS LOW
    LABEL OPPOSITE OF LOW
MOREORLESS HIGH
    LABEL HIGHER THAN LOW
NOT VERY LOW

LABEL (SLIGHTLY HIGHER) THAN LOW
RATHER LOW

LABEL (SLIGHTLY HIGHER) THAN RATHER LOW
SORTOF LOW

LABEL (SOMEWHAT HIGHER) THAN RATHER LOW
(NOT HIGH) AND NOT LOW

LABEL (CONSIDERABLY HIGHER) THAN RATHER LOW
SORTOF HIGH

LABEL (CONSIDERABLY HIGHER) THAN SORTOF LOW
RATHER HIGH

LABEL (NOT LOWER) THAN SORTOF LOW
NOT VERY LOW

LABEL (NOT HIGHER) THAN SORTOF LOW
(MOREORLESS LOW) OR RATHER LOW

LABEL LOWER THAN SORTOF LOW
VERY LOW

LABEL HIGH OR NOT HIGH
UNKNOWN

LABEL HIGH OR NOT LOW
NOT LOW

LABEL HIGH AND LOW
UNDEFINED

LABEL HIGH AND NOT HIGH
(SORTOF HIGH) OR RATHER HIGH

LABEL NOT HIGH OR LOW
(NOT HIGH) AND NOT LOW

LABEL HIGH AND VERY HIGH
VERY HIGH

LABEL MOREORLESS VERY HIGH
HIGH

LABEL (NOT SORTOF HIGH) AND NOT VERY HIGH
NOT MOREORLESS HIGH

LABEL SORTOF VERY HIGH
SORTOF HIGH

An example of illustrative simulation

In his book *Patterns of Industrial Bureaucracy*, Gouldner (1954) reports and discusses the findings of a case study of organizational behavior at a mining company. The data collection method consisted mainly of field interviews with employees who in their own language were allowed to express their views and sentiments about what was going on and why. The situation at the plant was dominated by the effects of an increase of closeness of supervision over the mine workers. This new supervising behavior was brought about by the appointment of a new plant manager.

Gouldner's research team observed an increase of the use of bureaucratic rules and of the level of hostility towards supervisors, and a drop of workers' performance as a result of this increase of closeness of supervision.

Based on evidence from the contents of the interviews, Gouldner induced a model which was intended to explain the general causes and effects of use of bureaucratic rules, and in particular, the course of events which had been observed. The resulting model is verbally formulated (ch. IX, ibid.). Although the variables do have intuitive meaning and their values can be subjectively observed and stated in linguistic terms, the model is not operational since no objective way of measuring them is given. The model is also not deductive since there is no systematic way of deriving its consequences. It only serves to clarify the mechanisms whereby the use of bureaucratic rules is perpetuated, but does not give explicit clues to actual dynamic behavior under given circumstances.

We will here attempt to make Gouldner's model deductive by rephrasing it as a verbal model and employing our semantic model in order to simulate its behavior.

THE MODEL

Figure 1 shows graphically the structure of causal relations between Gouldner's variables.

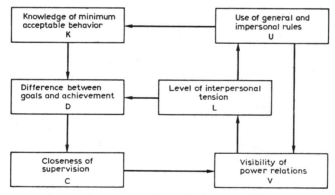

FIG. 1. Structure of causal interrelations in Gouldner's model.

Consider now the following *verbal model:*

(34) $U_t \leftarrow$ value (((somewhat higher) than U_{t-1}) if L_{t-2} is (very high) or rather high) or ((equal to U_{t-1}) if L_{t-2} is not low or very high) or ((slightly lower) than U_{t-1}) if L_{t-2} is low or rather low;

(35) $K_t \leftarrow$ (very similar) to U_t;

(36) $L_t \leftarrow$ (very similar) to V_{t-1};

(37) $D_t \leftarrow$ value ((similar to K_t) if L_t is not low) or (similar to L_t) if L_t is low or (sort-of low) or rather low;

(38) $C_t \leftarrow$ value (((considerably higher) than C_{t-1}) if (D_t is higher than D_{t-1}) and D_t is high) or (equal to C_{t-1}) if ((D_t is high) and D_t is (not higher) than D_{t-1}) or D_t is not high or low) or ((slightly lower) than C_{t-1}) if D_t is low;

(39) $V \leftarrow$ ((opposite of U_t) if C_t is low or rather low) or ((very similar) to C_t) if C_t is not low;
$V_t \leftarrow$ value (V if U_t is (not higher) than U_{t-1}) or ((considerably lower) than V) if U_t is higher than U_{t-1}.

The model is an adaption from Gouldner's own verbal discussion. (34) implies that use of bureaucratic rules is enforced, or new rules are instated, after a delay of two periods if the tension level is high. On the other hand, U decreases slightly when the tension level is low. (35) says that the degree of knowledge of minimum acceptable behavior corresponds to the current use of bureaucratic rules. (37) implies that workers take advantage of their knowledge of minimum acceptable behavior if the level of tension is not low, by restricting output. (38) says that closeness of supervision increases if the performance level is already low and still deteriorating. Supervision is sustained if the current performance level is not satisfactory. It decreases only if performance is satisfactory. (38) thus expresses a typical management reaction pattern. Finally, (39) says that the visibility of power relations are inversely related to U if supervision is low. It is otherwise proportional to supervision. It will, however, be mitigated by increased use of bureaucratic rules.

THE PROBLEM

Consider the following questions: Does our verbal model lead to the same kind of behavior as that actually observed by Gouldner? What are, according to our model, the effects of different supervisory policies (other versions of statement (38)) in different situations?

These questions cannot without considerable efforts be answered on intuitive grounds by inspecting the model. They can be approached, however, by coupling the model with the semantical system and then deriving its implied behavior by simulation.

SIMULATION OF THE VERBAL MODEL

The essence of what we have achieved can be appreciated by noting the following: when the verbal model (34–39) is coupled with the semantic system as outlined above, a new dimension is added to it; it becomes an *algorithm* whereby the values of the dependent variables can be directly calculated, given the necessary initial state values. Moreover, if the semantic system is defined in an APL-workspace, the verbal model (with minor modifications) is *in itself* an APL-program which does the calculations automatically. Each word in the vocabulary is here defined appropriately as a constant or a simple APL-function, bearing the word as its name.

Below, we will report some results from APL-based simulations. All output values will be reported linguistically, using the function LABEL. We note that the structure of the model is such that a state cannot be concluded to be stable, unless it has appeared for four periods in a row. Further, all variables are so chosen that uniformly higher values indicate more unfavourable states.

Simulation 1
Initial state: unfavorable; all state values "sortof high".
Output:

Period 1
USE IS VERY HIGH
TENSION IS RATHER HIGH
DIFFERENCE IS VERY HIGH
SUPERVISION IS VERY HIGH

Period 2
USE IS VERY HIGH
TENSION IS (NOT HIGH) AND NOT LOW
DIFFERENCE IS ATLEAST VERY HIGH
SUPERVISION IS VERY HIGH

This eventually proves to be a stable state. Thus, the situation grew immediately worse, except with regard to tensions between employees which were somewhat reduced.

Simulation 2
Initial state: intermediate; all state values "not moreorless high or low".
Output:

Period 1
USE IS (NOT HIGH) AND NOT LOW
TENSION IS (NOT HIGH) AND NOT LOW
DIFFERENCE IS ATLEAST (NOT HIGH) AND NOT LOW
SUPERVISION IS ATLEAST (NOT HIGH) AND NOT LOW

This pattern shows itself to prevail throughout, with the values becoming gradually more fuzzy:

Period 5
USE IS ATLEAST (NOT HIGH) AND NOT VERY LOW
TENSION IS ATLEAST (NOT VERY HIGH) AND NOT VERY LOW
DIFFERENCE IS ATLEAST (NOT VERY HIGH) AND NOT VERY LOW
SUPERVISION IS ATLEAST (NOT VERY HIGH) AND NOT VERY LOW

Simulation 3
Initial state: favorable; all state values "sortof low".
Output:

Period 1
USE IS VERY LOW
TENSION IS RATHER LOW
DIFFERENCE IS RATHER LOW
SUPERVISION IS VERY LOW

Period 2
USE IS VERY LOW
TENSION IS VERY HIGH
DIFFERENCE IS VERY LOW
SUPERVISION IS VERY LOW

Period 3
USE IS VERY LOW
TENSION IS VERY HIGH
DIFFERENCE IS VERY LOW
SUPERVISION IS VERY LOW

Period 4
USE IS SORTOF LOW
TENSION IS VERY HIGH
DIFFERENCE IS ATLEAST SORTOF LOW
SUPERVISION IS ATLEAST VERY LOW

Period 5
USE IS ATLEAST SORTOF HIGH
TENSION IS ATLEAST (RATHER LOW) OR (SORTOF LOW) OR (NOT
  HIGH) AND NOT VERY LOW
DIFFERENCE IS ATLEAST (RATHER LOW) OR (SORTOF LOW) OR (NOT
  VERY HIGH) AND NOT LOW
SUPERVISION IS ATLEAST VERY LOW

Period 6
USE IS ATLEAST MOREORLESS HIGH
TENSION IS ATLEAST NOT VERY HIGH
DIFFERENCE IS (NOT RATHER HIGH) OR (SORTOF HIGH) OR MOREOR-
  LESS HIGH
SUPERVISION IS ATLEAST (MOREORLESS LOW) OR (NOT HIGH) AND
  NOT VERY LOW

Period 7
USE IS ATLEAST (RATHER HIGH) OR MOREORLESS HIGH
TENSION IS ATLEAST MOREORLESS LOW
DIFFERENCE IS UNKNOWN
VISIBILITY IS UNKNOWN

In this case, the model displays a quite intricate behavior suggestive of underlying oscillatory dynamics. We note for instance that "difference between goals and achievement" starts to rise slowly only after an initial temporary improvement. After seven periods, the values start to become too fuzzy to be informative.

Simulation of other supervisory policies
Statement (38) in the model may be exchanged with other supervisory response-patterns. The model has been simulated with the same three initial states as above where, instead of (38) we had:

$$C_t \leftarrow \text{low};\tag{38a}$$

$$C_t \leftarrow \text{very high}.\tag{38b}$$

Here, closeness of supervision is kept constant irrespective of how the organization behaves. We shall not present those results here, but instead discuss the general findings.

Summary of simulation results

By comparing the results of the nine different simulations indicated above, the following conclusions seemed warranted. First of all, the model is in good correspondence with Gouldner's observations.

Further, high supervision produces high use of bureaucratic rules and low performance no matter what the initial conditions are. These effects appear some times first after a long delay.

Normal supervisory behavior (38) leads to high use of rules starting from a favorable or from an unfavorable state, but does not change an intermediate state.

There is no significant difference between the effects of normal or low supervision, starting from an intermediate or favorable state, but low supervision is the only policy that can change an unfavourable state into a soit-of favorable one.

A favorable state, with all values rather low, is untenable with any of the supervisory policies which were studied.

Finally, it may be that there does not exist any simple supervisory strategy which works well under all conditions.

Conclusions

In order to evaluate the potential usefulness of the concept of verbal models, it is appropriate to consider the following important questions.

First, the semantic problem: Is fuzzy set-theory an adequate basis for semantic interpretations for the purpose of making verbal models deductive?

Secondly, the syntactical problem: Is natural language versatile enough to express complicated mental ideas of causal relations? In other words, may it be that the relatively concise use of everyday language which is permitted here, is too restricted for the purpose of describing interesting properties of organizations?

Finally, the methodological problem: How powerful are deductive verbal models as tools for analyzing organizations?

Based on the experience which was gained in this exercise, we shall proceed to give tentative and preliminary answers to these questions.

FUZZY SET-THEORY AS A PRINCIPLE FOR SEMANTICAL INTERPRETATIONS

Informal evaluation of the operational characteristics of the semantical system seems to indicate that they are in general acceptable. The semantical system appears to be somewhat more precise than what is encountered in normal language usage, but people seem to have few problems in adapting to it and using it effortlessly when it is perceived as a normative standard.

There are indications that the functional properties of the semantic system are rather insensitive to changes in the particular definitions of hedges and primary terms as long as these follow some general principles.

Hence, even under the additional restrictions imposed by the syntax of APL, fuzzy set theory appears here as a promising basis for calculating the meaning of verbal assignment statements.

ADEQUACY OF NATURAL LANGUAGE

In spite of the fact that some successful simulation models have been built, the particular syntactical system, comprising a grammar and a vocabulary, specified in this article, appeared to have some shortcomings. The only way to verbalize more complicated relations between variables, is in the form of lists of if-statements, i.e. "X←(high if Y is low) or (sortof high) if Y is not low". Such lists cannot, however, adequately express ideas of continuous relations because of the discontinuous nature of the premises (low, not low). The practical effect of this, is that, under simulation, conclusions become unduly fuzzy when the values of free variables happen to fall in the boundary region between two values of the premises.

This may indicate a symptomatic limitation on the part of everyday language which makes it less powerful as a medium for formulating essentials of complex relationships.

The situation may be improved, however, by supplying natural language with borrowed mathematical concepts which might be fuzzily used. For example, "the relation R from X to Y has a 'slightly' increasing slope which initially is 'sortof' positive. Y is 'rather low' when X is 'very low' ". This would admittedly allow statements to be less "verbal" in nature, but would at the same time take advantage of the full power of mathematical concepts while preserving the benefits of achieving significance on the cost of precision by retaining the concept of linguistic variables.

PROSPECTS FOR VERBAL MODELS

It seems from our experience that the expected benefits with regard to achieving significance on the cost of precision hold true. In the case of Gouldner's model, for instance, the model may be said to be less objectionable than a corresponding mathematical one. Although its output is imprecise, it still provides important information on which decisions might be made. This evaluation is based on pure intuitive grounds, however, and should be investigated more seriously. One way to go, might be to define formally what is meant by precision and significance, respectively, so that these entities might be quantitatively calculated for different kinds of models. The final test, however, will be to see whether, in practise, verbal models have the right to life or not.

There are, of course, important problems which have to be solved if verbal models are to be employed in empirical research on organizations. First of all, there must exist methods to ensure that the semantical model which is used is representative of actual semantical usage. The way to go here, would be to train people who are involved in the empirical process to adopt to the semantics of the model. Secondly, linguistic values must somehow be measurable. Questionnaires are a natural instrument in this connection. Thus, none of these problems pose insurmountable obstacles. More detailed approaches are discussed in Wenstøp (1975).

The area of applications where verbal models may turn out to be especially powerful, however, is as pedagogical instruments for informal understanding of organizations. Given an APL-based semantical system, it is easy for anyone to analyze consequences of their own ideas about how organizations behave, be it general or particular organizations, by interactive simulation of assignment statements. Since this process takes place at the informal verbal level, unexpected findings might have significant implications.

It would certainly add to the powerfulness of verbal models if one could develop mathematical theories for the behavior which were based on the properties of the fuzzy set-theoretic interpretations of the models, thus making it possible to supplement the technique of simulation with the more powerful method of mathematical analysis. Little has so far been done in this direction, but it might turn out to be a rewarding area.

This paper is based on a doctoral dissertation at the Graduate School of Business Administration, University of California, Berkeley (Wenstøp, 1975). The study was made under a fellowship granted by the Ford Foundation.

References

BELLMAN, R. E. & GIERTZ, M. (1973). On the analytic formalism of the theory of fuzzy sets. *Information Science*, **5**, 149–156.

BOOLE, G. (1854). *The Laws of Thought*. First published by Macmillan (New York: Dover, 1958).

CHOMSKY, N. (1965). *Aspects of the Theory of Syntax*. Cambridge, Mass.: MIT Press.

CYERT, R. M. (1965). Simulation of organizational behavior. In MARCH, J. G. *Handbook of Organizations*. Chicago: Rand McNally.

FORRESTER, J. W. (1961). *Industrial Dynamics*. Cambridge, Mass.: MIT Press.

GARZO, R. & YANOUZAS, J. N. (1967). *Formal Organization. A Systems Approach*. Homewood, Ill.: Dorsey & Irwin.

GILMAN, L. & ROSE, A. J. (1970). *APL 360—An Interactive Approach*. New York: Wiley.

GOULDNER, A. W. (1954). *Patterns of Industrial Bureaucracy*. Glencoe, Ill.: The Free Press.

IVERSON, K. E. (1962). *A Programming Language*. New York: Wiley.

LAKOFF, G. (1972). Hedges: A study in meaning-criteria and the logic of fuzzy concepts. In *Proc. 8th Regional Meeting of Chicago Ling. Soc.* Univ. of Chicago Linguistic Dept.

MARCH, J. G. (1965). *Handbook of Organizations*. Chicago: Rand McNally.

MARCH, J. G. & SIMON, H. A. (1958). *Organizations*. New York: Wiley.

TORGERSON, W. S. (1958). *Theory and Methods of Scaling*. New York: Wiley.

WENSTØP, F. E. (1975). Application of linguistic variables in the analysis of organizations. Doctoral dissertation, Univ. of Calif., Berkeley. To appear as a technical report of The Center for Research in Man. Sci., Univ. of Calif., Berkeley.

ZADEH, L. A. (1965). Fuzzy sets. *Information Control*, **8**, 338–353.

ZADEH, L. A. (1972). A fuzzy-set-theoretical interpretation of linguistic hedges. *Journal of Cybernetics*, **5**, 4–34.

ZADEH, L. A. (1973). Outline of a new approach to the analysis of complex systems and decision processes. *IEEE Transactions on Systems, Man and Cybernetics*, **SMC-3**, 28–44.

ZADEH, L. A. (1975). The concept of a linguistic variable and its application to approximate reasoning—II. *Information Science*, **8**, 301–357.

A general approach to linguistic approximation

F. Eshragh and E. H. Mamdani

Department of Electrical and Electronic Engineering,
Queen Mary College, University of London, U.K.

This paper describes a technique by which a fuzzy subset can be linguistically labelled. The technique involves the separation of a given fuzzy set into a certain number of specific subsets. The labelling is based on assignment of labels to these specific subsets and their concatenation with connectives "AND" and "OR".

The technique allows the user to specify, up to a certain number, his own primary subsets and their respective names. The input subset is also freely specified and properties like normality of input subsets do not constitute any constraint.

1. Introduction

In many "hard" applications of fuzzy logic, works have been concentrated almost entirely on the properties of the theory in relation to policy making in linguistic ways. These linguistic rules are numerically translated and used in, for example, Controller Design. Controllers deal with exact numerical data even when the variables are not exact. However, in "soft" and managerial applications, the Controller of a system demands a more humanistic and linguistic interaction. This would mean a linguistic output as well as input and poses the question of assigning a linguistic label to a given fuzzy subset which has been calculated by a fuzzy algorithm in a system.

This paper describes a system called "LAM5"† for finding a linguistic representation of a value, assigned to a fuzzy variable, from a set of pre-specified primary names and hedges.

The labels are made up of a combination of predetermined linguistic terms connected together by appropriate logical connectives "AND" and/or "OR". The linguistic terms are formed by using hedges or modifiers on primary subsets, provided by the user, within a primitive space. The fuzzy subset, for which a linguistic assignment is required, should naturally belong to the same environment.

In order to achieve a better result, the unknown subset is labelled together with its numerically negated version. The label obtained in this way is then linguistically negated in order to get the correct representation of the original input. In some cases this results in a much shorter label and also improves the semantic acceptability of the label.

The approximation process takes place both before and after linguistic assignment. That is, the subset is initially re-arranged numerically through the processes like monotonisation. Also, numerically equivalent and more suitable linguistic phrases are substituted for less desirable ones. For instance, the label "NOT ABOVE X AND NOT BELOW X" is numerically exactly and semantically approximately equivalent to the linguistic value "X".

† "LAM5" is an abbreviated name for the system—"LA" stands for "Linguistic Approximation" and the last two characters refer to the mark number.

2. Preliminary discussion

As progress in the field of fuzzy set theory and its applications to control, decision-making and approximate reasoning advances further, the need for a more universal means of humanistic interaction between man and machine becomes more apparent. In the control of physical plants such need is not so significant as in say, a Question Answering system.

The problem of linguistic approximation can be systematically defined as a mapping from S, the set of fuzzy subsets in a universe U, into a set of labels, L, which are generated according to a grammar G and a vocabulary V. The task of retrieving such information calls for a heuristic search within the set L. There are many factors which govern the structure of the search. Atomic terms or primary subsets are of considerable importance. The question of generality of the system's applications is closely related to the choice of primary subsets. There have been systems for linguistic approximations which were almost entirely problem dependent (Wenstøp, 1976). This has brought out the question of the user's freedom to choose his own primary subsets. In some cases, this can lead to problems perhaps not completely known to the user. He may specify only two primary subsets in a universe of discourse composed of perhaps 25 elements. Obviously, this would not be very conducive if a close match was required in such a sparse space. Thus, some care should be taken to ensure a reasonable density of subsets within the primary space.

Modifiers, or "Hedges", are of comparable importance in linguistic approximation. They act as the modifiers of the meaning of their operands and thus create more terms which can be used as labels for fuzzy values assigned to a linguistic variable.

Hedges automatically increase the population of the primary space and hence facilitate the search for labels. At the first glance, it appears that a substantial number of hedges would be of great advantage. The mathematical functions which are used to represent the semantic transformation of a composed linguistic term with a hedge should be regarded with extreme caution to ensure a genuine representation.

Humanistic studies appear to support the theoretical position that people manipulate vague concepts as if they are processing them according to rules of fuzzy logic and definitions expressed for hedges (Zadeh, 1977, 1973).

In a paper by Hersh & Caramazza (1976), the transformations which occur when primary subsets are operated upon by "NOT", "VERY" and other hedges, are empirically evaluated. For instance, the fact that the comparison between a negative phrase like "NOT SMALL" and the complement of an affirmative phrase "1-SMALL" indicates a reasonably good fit supports the fuzzy set notion of negation as being the complement of the positive subset.

Vocabulary and grammar should also be borne in mind in the synthesis of a system for linguistic approximation. In order to create a system which is precise and consistent in its behaviour, one has to impose restrictions with regard to the use of certain terms and the order of their composition. The use of natural language should be more precise and consistent than every day language. The use of ambiguous terms like "VERY NOT BIG" and similar should be avoided. A grammar which consists of a finite set of rules would be of advantage when specification of a language structure is concerned. Therefore, it should not be ignored or undervalued.

The consideration of these factors will prove of great value in the design and the use of any system of linguistic approximation.

2.1. SOME DEFINITIONS

Before any further advance, we should look at some definitions which might prove valuable to those readers who are not familiar with some of the terminology used in the description of the technique.

S and Π Curves

S and Π curves are those which simply look like a skewed "S" and "Bell" respectively. S-curves can further be divided into two groups—S^+ and S^- according to the value of the membership function at either end of the spread. "S" and "Π" type curves are further discussed in Appendix 1.

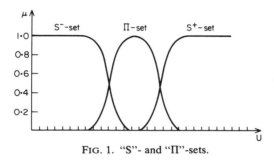

FIG. 1. "S"- and "Π"-sets.

Hedges

Most hedges are fairly well-known to the readers of fuzzy materials. The hedges used in this paper are described in detail in Appendix 2. Here, however, a brief account will be given as one or two hedges might be totally new to some readers.

"NOT" is interpreted as the complementation operator. "VERY" and "MORE OR LESS" act as concentrating and dilating operators of the meaning respectively.

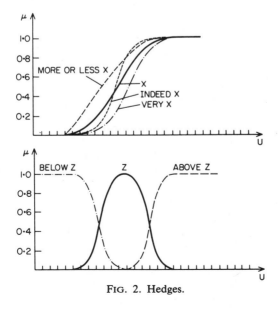

FIG. 2. Hedges.

"INDEED" intensifies the meaning of its operand. Two more hedges are also introduced—"ABOVE" and "BELOW". These are interpreted the same way as "MORE
THAN" and "LESS THAN" in Pappis & Mamdani (1976).

"ABOVE" and "BELOW" create S^+ and S^--types of subsets, respectively, when
operating upon a given Π-type subset. "ABOVE" and "BELOW" can be used with
S^--subsets and S^+-subsets in a restricted manner. That is, we can say "ABOVE
SMALL" or "BELOW BIG" but not "ABOVE BIG" or "BELOW SMALL". Figure
2 describes the effect of different hedges on primary subsets.

3. Technique

The technique employed here enables us to assign a linguistic label to a fairly complex
fuzzy spread by dealing with a relatively simpler task of labelling its segments. For
example, the spread shown in Fig. 3(a) consists of four segments labelled S1–S4. The
dividing points between the segments are called Effective Turning Points "ETP" which
are defined in Appendix 1. Note that normality is not a necessity here.

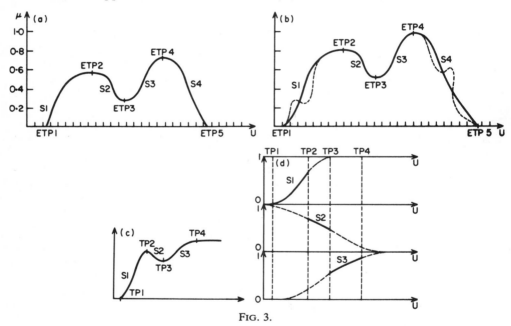

FIG. 3.

Almost every spread can be re-arranged or approximated to look like the one shown
in Fig. 3(a). The advantage here is that, from now on, the labelling is confined only to
those spreads which have well known shape, namely, S^+ and S^- types of subsets (see
Appendix 1).

However, to illustrate the technique more generally, consider the uneven fuzzy
spread shown in Fig. 3(b) (dotted). Initially, the ETP's are located as described in
Appendix 1. Then, the segments between each pair of ETP's are analysed for monotonicity. If needed, the segment is smoothed to eliminate the inherent unevenness in a
segment. The smoothing process is based on fitting a continuous and monotonically
increasing or decreasing curve.

Each segment is then separated. These segments are, naturally, all of either S^+ or S^- type. Now, heuristically, the best label is selected from a repertoire of suitable labels. Using connectives "AND" and "OR", the labels obtained for each segment are appropriately concatenated to form a linguistic statement. This statement can be considered logically and semantically a good representation of the numerical fuzzy subset "X", where upon translation, using semantic and logical rules, this statement yields, exactly or approximately, the original value of the input fuzzy set.

3.1. THE USE OF CONNECTIVES

Consider the subset shown in Fig. 3(c). If we now break the curve at its turning points, marked TP1–TP4, and regard each segment as part of an independent S-type curve, we will have the arrangement shown in Fig. 3(d) where S1, S2 and S3 represent segments corresponding to those in Fig. 3(c).

In order to eliminate the upper dotted sections of segments S1 and S2, we can use the connective "AND" and thus obtain the fuzzy subset "S1 AND S2". This subset can now be combined with the last segment S3. The connective to be used here is "OR" as we would like to eliminate the remaining dotted line. Therefore, the final result will be the "OR"ed combination of two subsets "S1 AND S2" and "S3". Furthermore, brackets can be employed to identify the precedences of the operators.

It can be noted that whenever a pair of consecutive segments form a hill the connective to be used is an "AND" and whenever they form a valley the appropriate connective is "OR". It should also be noted that if the original subset had a reversed appearance, the positioning of the connectives would have been reversed, that is, "(S1 OR S2) AND (S3)" instead of "(S1 AND S2) OR (S3)".

In Fig. 3(b) there are five effective turning points and four segments, namely, S1–S4. If the labels obtained for each segment are called L_1 to L_4 respectively, then the phrase

$$\text{``}(L_1 \text{ AND } L_2) \text{ OR } (L_3 \text{ AND } L_4)\text{''}$$

can be taken as an approximate or in most cases an exact description of the fuzzy subset "X".

At this point, one might question the case where a perfect primary subset of type Π is given and a composite label is returned. The answer lies in the nature of the hedges used. The two possible segments of a Π-type primary subset will be labelled as:

$$\text{``(NOT ABOVE P)''} \quad \text{and} \quad \text{``(NOT BELOW P)''} \text{ respectively.}$$

The composition of these two labels with the connective "AND" would be the answer. But, because of the nature of the hedges "ABOVE" and "BELOW" (see Appendix 2), the phrase:

$$\text{``(NOT ABOVE P) \quad AND \quad (NOT BELOW P)''}$$

is semantically and numerically equivalent to just "P" and hence will automatically be replaced by the latter. The same also applies to

$$\text{``(ABOVE P) \quad OR \quad (BELOW P)''}$$

and

$$\text{``(NOT ABOVE } P_i) \quad \text{AND} \quad \text{(NOT BELOW } P_i)\text{''}$$

which are respectively equivalent to "NOT P" and "P_i AND P_j".

With reference to the segments, there is one more point which must not be left out. It must be noted that the number of segments created is a good measure of approximation. The higher the number of segments the more exact the outcome. But this also has problems associated with it. An excessive number of segments would mean a high number of linguistic terms to be connected together and hence a very long phrase which might not be all that comprehensible. On the other hand, the reduction of the number of segments, to a low value, by excessive approximation, might yield a result which is not acceptable. So, a compromise should be reached. This is left to the user. It is done by asking the user to specify the value of a parameter which governs the number of the effective turning points.

In some cases, the numerically negated version of a given subset provides a better ground for the labelling exercise than the original one. Knowing the fact that a linguistic statement can also be negated, this proposition looks even more attractive and thus it can lead to outcomes which are perhaps more comprehensible and shorter in length.

4. Program structure

Broadly speaking, "LAM5" is a heuristic search program which consists of three phases:

  (i) a generator which generates the search domain for a particular set of primary fuzzy subsets with their given linguistic representations;

 (ii) a search procedure which would by-pass the irrelevant pieces of information in a reasonably efficient manner;

(iii) an evaluation method which would guide the search all the way through.

4.1. GENERATION OF THE SEARCH SPACE

Consider a set of n primary subsets defined over a universe of discourse U of m elements arranged as shown in Fig. 4(a).

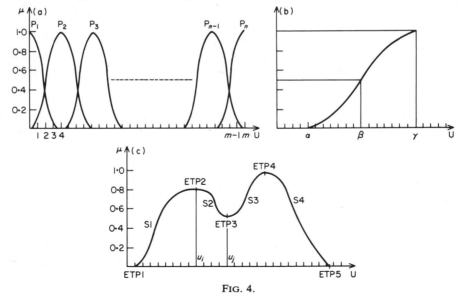

FIG. 4.

Each primary is also given a linguistic representation like "BIG", "NEGATIVE BIG" and etc. Note that the arrangement of the primary subsets, as far as their types and positioning is concerned, is the only restriction. That is to say the first and last primary subsets must be S-type and the rest Π-type. This is usually the case as when a variable takes values on a scale from one extreme end to another, it would have to attain values in the order that is shown in Fig. 3(a).

A collection of labels, which are representative of the S-type subsets, can now be generated from these given subsets. The repertoire of these labels is composed by using six different linguistic modifiers or hedges operated upon the primitive subset (see Appendix 2 for explanation on hedges).

The hedges used are "NOT", "VERY", "MORE OR LESS", "INDEED", "ABOVE" and "BELOW". The main structure of the repertoire is based on the combination of the following arrangement of hedges with every Π-type primary subset (see Appendix 1 for definition of Π-type subset):

ABOVE (BELOW) P_i
MUCH ABOVE (BELOW) P_i
INDEED ABOVE (BELOW) P_i
MORE OR LESS ABOVE (BELOW) P_i $\forall i \in (2, 3, \ldots, n-1)$
VERY MUCH ABOVE (BELOW) P_i
INDEED MUCH ABOVE (BELOW) P_i
NOT BELOW (ABOVE) P_i
NOT MUCH BELOW (ABOVE) P_i
NOT VERY MUCH BELOW (ABOVE) P_i

(See Appendix 2 for the hedge "MUCH". "i" takes integer values from 2 to $n-1$.)

In addition, the following combination of hedges are used in conjunction with the first and the last primary subsets:

ABOVE(BELOW) $P_1(P_n)$
MUCH ABOVE(BELOW) $P_1(P_n)$
INDEED ABOVE(BELOW) $P_1(P_n)$
MORE OR LESS ABOVE(BELOW) $P_1(P_n)$
VERY MUCH ABOVE(BELOW) $P_1(P_n)$
INDEED MUCH ABOVE(BELOW) $P_1(P_n)$
NOT $P_1(P_n)$
NOT VERY $P_1(P_n)$
NOT VERY MUCH $P_1(P_n)$
P_n
VERY $P_n(P_1)$
INDEED $P_n(P_1)$
MORE OR LESS $\times P_n(P_1)$
VERY MUCH $P_n(P_1)$
INDEED VERY $P_n(P_1)$

Note that the terms inside the brackets replace those immediately before them to produce S^--type subsets rather than S^+-type ones.

Thus, the entire collection, basically, consists of two sections. One section contains all labels for S^+-type subsets and the other contains all those for S^--types. This itself provides the first branching point in our search. The next step is to acquire information about the characteristics of the subsets represented by these labels. The simplest way of doing so is to use the parameters used by Zadeh in his works. These parameters, α, β and γ, are points in the universe of discourse at which the compatibility function attains values 0, 0·5 and 1 respectively [Fig. 4(b)].

TABLE 1

Table for S^+-type subsets for four primary subsets

	Rec. no.	Labels	G	p	α	β	γ
GROUP 1	1	ABOVE P1	1	1	1	3	5
	2	MUCH ABOVE P1	2	1	1	3	5
	3	INDEED ABOVE P1	3	1	1	3	5
	4	MORE OR LESS ABOVE P1	4	1	1	2	5
	5	VERY MUCH ABOVE P1	5	1	1	4	5
	6	INDEED MUCH ABOVE P1	6	1	1	3	5
	7	NOT P1	7	1	1	3	5
	8	NOT VERY P1	8	1	1	2	5
	9	NOT VERY MUCH P1	9	1	1	2	5
	10	P4	10	4	6	8	10
	11	VERY P4	11	4	6	9	10
	12	INDEED P4	12	4	6	8	10
	13	MORE OR LESS P4	13	4	6	9	10
	14	VERY MUCH P4	14	4	6	9	10
	15	INDEED VERY P4	15	4	6	9	10
GROUP 2	21	ABOVE P2	21	2	6	8	10
	22	MUCH ABOVE P2	22	2	6	8	10
	23	INDEED ABOVE P2	23	2	6	7	10
	24	MORE OR LESS ABOVE P2	24	2	6	8	10
	25	VERY MUCH ABOVE P2	25	2	6	9	10
	26	INDEED MUCH ABOVE P2	26	2	2	4	6
	27	NOT BELOW P2	27	2	2	4	6
	28	NOT MUCH BELOW P2	28	2	2	3	6
	29	NOT VERY MUCH BELOW P2	29	2	2	4	6
GROUP 3	31	ABOVE P3	31	3	8	10	12
	32	MUCH ABOVE P3	32	3	8	10	12
	33	INDEED ABOVE P3	33	3	8	10	12
	34	MORE OR LESS ABOVE P3	34	3	8	9	12
	35	VERY MUCH ABOVE P3	35	3	8	10	12
	36	INDEED MUCH ABOVE P3	36	3	4	6	8
	37	NOT BELOW P3	37	3	4	5	8
	38	NOT MUCH BELOW P3	38	3	4	4	8
	39	NOT VERY MUCH BELOW P3	39	3	4	3	8

Each label is given a generating number "G" and a primary number "P". "G" would be used to regenerate the information needed about a particular label and "P" is used to identify the primary subset which is used in conjunction with that label. The information acquired for each label is then tabulated and stored permanently in a back up file and referred to when required. The S^+ section of the label information table for a system with a primitive space of four primary subsets, "SMALL", "BIG", "MED$^+$" and "MED$^-$" is as shown in Table 1. The S$^-$ section is identical with the exception that record numbers in the extreme left-hand column start from 101 rather then 1.

As one can see, three groups of labels are created—one for each type of S-shape subsets—one less than the number of primary subsets. The 1st group contains 15 labels and the hedges in each label operate on either the first or the last primary subset. The labels in the remaining groups are related to only one primary subset whose number is indicated in the p column. Each label contains a maximum of four hedges and is preselected so that meaningless arrangements of hedges like "VERY NOT BIG" are excluded. Each hedge name is coded as a single digit integer which will facilitate the retrieval procedure of the information about a label.

4.2. SEARCH PROCEDURE

The search procedure has two main phases. The first phase is exhaustive and the second phase is heuristic. The exhaustive phase takes care of trivial cases. That is, if a given subset shows characteristics similar to those of primary or negated primary subsets, then it will be tested against appropriate types of primary subsets for perfect match. If a perfect match occurs, then the search is terminated. For instance, if a negated normal Π-type set is input then the negated version of all Π-type primary subsets is tested for perfect match before proceeding to the second phase of the search.

If phase I proves unsuccessful, the program enters the second phase. In this phase, the input is appropriately processed and its segments are separated. The set of all the points in the universe of discourse which are covered by the projection of a segment onto the universe of discourse is called the support set of that segment [Fig. 4(c)]. The set $(U_i, U_{i+1}, \ldots U_j)$ is the support set of the segment S$_2$. In the second phase, α, β and γ parameters of a given segment, if they exist, are found. In the case of segment S2, only the parameter β can be found. So, the other two parameters are considered irrelevant and will not have any influence in the search routine. If a segment does not include any one of the three parameters, then that parameter will take a value of $\varnothing$ which indicates irrelevancy and would not be used in the search procedure. To illustrate this point take the following segment x_1, with the support set (5, 6, 7)

$$\mu(5) = 0 \cdot 45 \ \mu(6) = 0 \cdot 72 \ \mu(7) = 0 \cdot 82.$$

The values of α, β and γ would be 0, 5 and 0 respectively.

The next step in this phase is to locate all the labels, amongst those in the appropriate label information file, which have the same α, β and γ points as the unknown subset. In the case of segment S2 in Fig. 3(d), we have to locate labels with only equal β parameters as the other two are irrelevant. When the first of such labels is found, before any attempt is made in finding the next one, the label is more extensively examined.

The distance between the relevant section of the subset, represented by that label, and the segment under test is found. This is done by using the least square technique. If the distance is zero than that label is accepted as the label for that segment, otherwise, the sum of the squares of the distances at all the points in the support set of the segment is noted. If this sum is smaller than a previous one, the new label will be considered as a more suitable one and will replace any one previously found. If the sum is greater than or equal to any previous one, the new result is disregarded and the previous one remains as the best known label and so on.

5. Results

Two sets of results were obtained. The first set takes as its input a set of three primary subsets in a universe of discourse containing ten elements. Their associated names are "LOW", "MEDIUM" or "MED" and "HIGH". The second set of results is related to a set of seven primary subsets in a 14-element universe with the names "NB", "NM", "NS", "ZO", "PS", "PM" and "PB" (see Appendix 3 for details). A fuzzy translator (ESHRAGH—78 "TRAN") was used to translate certain fuzzy linguistic values into

TABLE 2

(a) *Results with three primary subsets*

	Actual input to LAM5	Output from LAM5	
		Direct assignment	Negated assignment
I	HIGH	HIGH	HIGH
II	0·37, 0·71, 0·91, 0·98 LOW	NOT VERY MUCH (0·9)†	INDEED NOT VERY LOW (0·95)
III	ABOVE LOW	NOT LOW	NOT LOW
IV	MEDIUM	MEDIUM	MEDIUM
V	NOT MEDIUM	NOT MEDIUM	NOT MEDIUM
VI	ABOVE MEDIUM AND NOT HIGH	ABOVE MEDIUM AND NOT HIGH	ABOVE MEDIUM AND NOT HIGH
VII	MEDIUM OR HIGH	MEDIUM OR HIGH	MEDIUM OR HIGH
VIII	BELOW HIGH	NOT HIGH	NOT HIGH
IX	BELOW HIGH AND ABOVE LOW	NOT LOW AND NOT HIGH	NOT LOW AND NOT HIGH
X	NOT BELOW HIGH OR NOT ABOVE LOW	LOW OR HIGH	LOW OR HIGH
XI	MEDIUM AND HIGH	MEDIUM AND HIGH	MEDIUM AND HIGH
XII	MEDIUM OR NOT BELOW MEDIUM	BELOW MEDIUM	BELOW MEDIUM
XIII	VERY LOW OR LOW	LOW	LOW
XIV	LOW OR MEDIUM OR HIGH	LOW OR MEDIUM OR HIGH	LOW OR MEDIUM OR HIGH

(b) *Results with seven primary subsets*

	Actual input to LAM5	Output from LAM5	
		Direct	Negated
I	NB OR NM	NB OR NM	NB OR NM
II	NOT NB AND NOT NM	NOT NB AND NOT NM	NOT NB AND NOT NM
III	NOT ABOVE ZO AND NOT BELOW ZO	ZO	ZO
IV	NOT ABOVE ZO AND NOT BELOW PS	ZO AND PS	ZP AND PS
V	NB OR ZO OR PS	NB OR ZO OR PS	NB OR ZO OR PS

† Confidence level assigned to each label. Those without a CL have a CL of 1.

their numerical representation. "TRAN" and "LAM5" are designed compatable and share one input space of primary subsets. In Tables 2(a) and 2(b) are given sets of three fuzzy phrases. The first is the input to the translator and the actual input to "LAM5". The second column gives the output from "LAM5" when the labelling was carried out by analysing the input subset directly. And the third item is the output from "LAM5" when labelling was done by considering the negated version of the input subset and re-negating the final outcome. In both cases, the approximation level was chosen such that maximum accuracy was obtained. That is, every peak was considered to constitute a turning point.

An overall view of the tables would establish that the labels assigned to each input are usually the same for both direct and indirect or negated assignments. This, however, need not be the case when more random cases are involved. In Table 2(a), II is a typical example where two different labels are returned and one usually attains a higher degree of accuracy or confidence level. In the same table, in III, "ABOVE LOW" has been given the label "NOT LOW". The same effect is also evident in Table 2(a), VIII. The reason for this is that "LAM5" attempts to use more well established operators when and where possible. Thus, "ABOVE" or "BELOW" is replaced by "NOT" when operated upon the first and the last primary subsets respectively.

An important point worthy of mention is the absence of any necessity for normalisation of the input subset. Therefore, the assignment of labels to ANDed fuzzy subset, which are usually subnormal by nature, is facilitated. The desirability of this kind of ANDed labels are subject to debate. It is, for instance, meaningless to assign the value "MEDIUM *AND* HIGH" to a variable whereas the label "ABOVE MEDIUM *AND NOT* HIGH" is acceptable.

There are also other interesting points to observe. In Table 2(a), X, we can see that the relatively long label "NOT BELOW HIGH OR NOT ABOVE LOW" is changed to a shorter and more acceptable label "LOW OR HIGH" which is semantically and numerically equivalent to the first one. The same can be noticed in Table 2(b), III and IV.

The system also detects certain equivalent phrases and automatically replaces them by a more suitable one. Item XIII in Table 2(a) is a typical example. "VERY LOW OR LOW" is numerically equivalent to "LOW" and hence it is replaced by the latter.

6. An application of LA

Here, what follows is an exercise in the fuzzy set theory and the concept of fuzzy restrictions. In the second IFAC Round Table on Fuzzy Automata and Decision Processes (1976), the following example was given by Professor Zadeh.

The problem is to find the restriction imposed on the height of Nancy given that:

Ann is very short	①
Nancy is much taller than Ann	②
Gail is quite tall	③
Nancy is not much shorter than Gail	④

The solution is obviously closely dependent on our definitions for SHORT, TALL and the hedges "MUCH", "VERY", "QUITE" and the relations TALLER THAN and

SHORTER THAN. Let us define the atomic terms "SHORT", "MEDIUM" and "TALL" as follows

SHORT	1	1	1	1	0·8	0·4	0	0	0	0
TALL	0	0	0	0	0	0	0·4	0·8	1	1

MEDIUM   (although not used) = NORM(NOT SHORT AND NOT TALL)

Using the notion of restrictions proposed by Zadeh (1975) we have

from 1: Height (Ann) = VERY SHORT
from 3: Height (Gail) = QUITE TALL
from 2 and 4: Height (Nancy) = MUCH TALLER THAN Height (Ann)
AND NOT MUCH SHORTER THAN Height (Gail)   ⑤

"SHORTER THAN" and "TALLER THAN" can be interpreted as "LESS THAN" and "MORE THAN" or "BELOW" and "ABOVE" respectively.

"QUITE" can be regarded as a concentrating or intensifying or a mixture of the two operators. Thus, QUITE can be defined as VERY, INDEED or "INDEED VERY".
From 1, 3 and 5 we have

Height (Nancy) = MUCH TALLER THAN (VERY SHORT) AND
NOT MUCH SHORTER THAN (QUITE TALL)   ⑥

Height (Nancy) can be interpreted as any of the following

I   MUCH ABOVE (VERY SHORT) AND NOT MUCH
     BELOW (VERY TALL)

II   MUCH ABOVE (VERY SHORT) AND NOT BELOW
     (INDEED TALL)

III MUCH ABOVE (VERY SHORT) AND NOT MUCH
     BELOW (INDEED VERY TALL)

where MUCH is interpreted the same way as VERY.
I, II and III above are translated to the following fuzzy subsets

I	0	0	0	0	0	0	0·29	0·87	1·0	1·0
II	0	0	0	0	0	0	0·54	0·99	1·0	1·0
III	0	0	0	0	0	0	0·1	0·93	1·0	1·0

These are fairly simple subsets to label and the results were found to be as follows in Table 3.

TABLE 3

	Direct labelling	Negated or indirect labelling
I	INDEED TALL (0·98)†	INDEED NOT BELOW TALL (0·98)
II	TALL (0·95)	NOT MUCH BELOW TALL (0·97)
III	INDEED TALL (0·95)	INDEED NOT BELOW TALL (0·94)

† Confidence level assigned to each label indicated in brackets.

By considering the labels given in the table above, one can conclude that the predominant labels are

(1) TALL
(2) INDEED TALL
(3) NOT MUCH BELOW TALL

An overall view of the results in (1)–(3) above would confirm some degree of agreement amongst the different items, the common factor being the fact that Nancy is indeed a tall girl.

7. Conclusion

The LAM5 program described here is a vehicle to be used in the study of fuzzy systems. It can serve both "hard", control types and "soft", managerial types of systems. It is constructed upon the idea of separation of fuzzy spreads into an appropriate number of segments with well defined characteristics. The number of segments is a good measure of approximation. The more the number of segments the more exact is the outcome. But it also poses certain problems. Too many segments result in more exact results and lengthy labels whereas fewer segments result in shorter and more approximated ones. The choice is given to the user via the value of a variable which determines the effective turning points. However, when segments are separated they are labelled accordingly. The final answer is a combination of these labels.

All attempts have been made to keep the program as applicable to all types of fuzzy systems as possible. A set of "N" primitive fuzzy subsets can be defined by the user over a universe of discourse of "M" discrete elements. The subsets can be given appropriate names to suit one's particular application. These names are operated upon by certain linguistic modifiers called "hedges" which will create more subsets and thus facilitate the labelling task. Hedges, although very attractive tools in this exercise, can entangle one's mind with the question "how accurate are they in terms of universal human perceptions?" One can be fairly sure of what is generally meant by saying that "A MAN IS OLD" but can one conclusively say that what is understood by the statement "A MAN IS MORE OR LESS OLD" is universal. Psychological works have proved certain points for some of these modifiers but still further work is needed.

Wenstøp (1975) developed a system for linguistic approximation. This was basically the first and none has been reported since. He uses two basic subsets only, "LOW" and "HIGH". A third one is created, namely, "MEDIUM", by the combination "NOT HIGH AND NOT LOW". The system is rather restricted as for the number of primary subsets and their names. This makes his system not very attractive to the general user. Amongst other constraints, normality of the subsets is another one which has its own problems. For example, the fuzzy subset "HIGH AND MED" will never be labelled as "HIGH AND MED".

However, considering these, the results obtained from "LAM5" are quite encouraging and also considering the number of previous attempts and difficulties involved, one can say that "LAM5" has proved workable.

References

ESHRAGH, F. (1978). *Fuzzy Translator Manual.* Fuzzy Working Group, Electrical Engineering Department, Queen Mary College, University of London.

GAINES, B. R. (1976*a*). *Research Notes on Fuzzy Reasoning.* Proceedings of a Workshop at Queen Mary College, University of London.

GAINES, B. R. (1976*b*). Foundation of fuzzy reasoning. *Report No. EES–MMS–FREAS*-76. University of Essex.

HERSH, H. M. & CARAMAZZA, A. (1976). A fuzzy set approach to modifiers and vagueness in natural language. *Journal of Experimental Psychology*, **105**(3).

IFAC Report (1975). *Automatica*, **12**, 1976.

MAMDANI, E. H. (1976). Advances in linguistic synthesis. Queen Mary College, University of London.

PAPPIS, C. P. & MAMDANI, E. H. (1977). A fuzzy logic controller for a traffic junction. *IEEE Transactions on Systems, Man and Cybernetics*.

WENSTØP, F. (1976). Deductive verbal models of organisations. *International Journal of Man–Machine Studies*, **8**, 293–311.

ZADEH, L. A. (1972). A fuzzy set theoretic interpretation of linguistic hedges. *Journal of Cybernetics*, **2**.

ZADEH, L. A. (1973). Outline of a new approach to the analysis of complex systems and decision processes. *IEEE Transactions on Systems, Man and Cybernetics*, **SMC-3**(1).

ZADEH, L. A. (1975*a*). A fuzzy algorithmic approach to the definition of complex or imprecise concepts. University of California, Berkeley.

ZADEH, L. A. (1975). The concept of linguistic variable and its applications to A. R. *Information Sciences*, **8**.

ZADEH, L. A. (1978). The linguistic approach and its application to decision analysis. University of California, Berkeley.

Appendix 1. Definitions

1. FUZZY SUBSET

A fuzzy subset is characterized by a function, μ, called the compatibility function, over a set of elements, called the universe of discourse, U:

$$U = (u_1, u_2, \ldots U_n)$$

$$\mu : U \rightarrow [0, 1].$$

2. SUPPORT SET

The support set of a fuzzy subset is $U' \subseteq U$ such that $\mu(u_i') > 0$ for every u_i' in U'.

3. S AND Π-TYPE SUBSETS

A function μ is called S type if it is monotonically increasing or decreasing. A monotonically increasing one is called S^+-type and decreasing is called S^--type.

A function μ is called Π-type if there exists only one point at which monotonicity changes direction (see Fig. A1).

4. NORMAL SUBSET

A subset is said to be normal if it attains values 0 and 1.

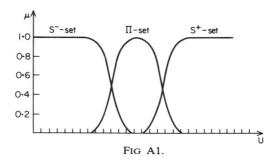

FIG A1.

5. α, β AND γ PARAMETERS

For the representation of the compatibility functions, it is sometimes more convenient to employ standardized functions with adjustable parameters. These functions are called "S" and "Π" functions and one way of defining them is as follows (Zadeh):

$$S(U_i; \alpha, \beta, \gamma) = 0 \qquad\qquad U_i \leq \alpha$$

$$= 2\left(\frac{U_i - \alpha}{\gamma - \alpha}\right)^2 \qquad \alpha \leq U_i \leq \beta$$

$$= 1 - 2\left(\frac{U_i - \gamma}{\gamma - \alpha}\right)^2 \qquad \beta \leq U_i \leq \gamma$$

$$= 1 \qquad\qquad U_i \geq \gamma$$

$$\Pi(U_i: \beta, \gamma) = S\left(U_i; \gamma, \beta, \gamma - \frac{\beta}{2}, \gamma\right) \qquad U_i \leq \gamma$$

$$= 1 - S\left(U_i; \gamma, \gamma + \frac{\beta}{2}, \gamma + \beta\right) \qquad \geq \gamma$$

In $S(V; \alpha, \beta, \gamma)$, the parameter β is the "crossover" point, that is, the value of U_i at which the compatibility function takes the nearest value to 0·5. In "Π", β is the "band width", that is, the distance between the crossover points of Π, where γ is the point at which Π is unity. Thus, given these parameters, one can construct the corresponding normal function.

The reverse process is also useful. That is, given a spread, one can find its parameter. If a subnormal spread is given, some of the parameters might not be definable. This is usually the case when we try to find the γ parameter of an "S" spread which is not normal. Here, one can define γ as the point at which and after which the function takes its maximum value.

6. EFFECTIVE TURNING POINTS (ETP)

ETP's play a very important role in this work. They basically determine the level of approximation involved. Before we can define an "ETP", we must begin by defining primary turning points, PTP, and turning points, "TP".

If $U = (U_1, U_2, \ldots U_n)$ be a universe of discourse containing n discrete elements then, the point with the co-ordinates $[U_i, \mu(U_i)]$ is defined as follows.

I. *PTP*

If one of the following is satisfied:

(a) $[\mu(U_i) > \mu(U_{i-1})] \wedge [\mu(U_i) \geq \mu(U_{i+1})]$
(b) $[\mu(U_i) \geq \mu(U_{i-1})] \wedge [\mu(U_i) > \mu(U_{i+1})]$
(c) $[\mu(U_i) < \mu(U_{i-1})] \wedge [\mu(U_i) \leq \mu(U_{i+1})]$
(d) $[\mu(U_i) \leq \mu(U_{i-1})] \wedge [\mu(U_i) < \mu(U_{i+1})]$

Also $[U_1, \mu(U_1)]$ and $[U_n, \mu(U_n)]$ are each a PTP if we have $\mu(U_1) \neq \mu(U_2)$ and $\mu(U_n) \neq \mu(U_{n-1})$ for U_1 and U_n respectively.

II. *TP*

If one of the following holds:

(a) $[U_i, \mu(U_i)]$ in the first or last PTP
(b) $\sqrt{(\mu(U_i) - \mu(U_j) + (U_i - U_j)^2} \geq K$

where $[U_j, \mu(U_j)]$ is a PTP immediately preceding the PTP $u:, \mu(u_i)$. The value of K is critical. It determines the level of approximation in this work. For example, the following subset:

$$x = 0 \quad 0.2 \quad 0.7 \quad 1 \quad 0.8 \quad 0.65 \quad 0.77 \quad 0.45 \quad 0.1 \quad 0$$

could be approximated to

$$\bar{x} = 0 \quad 0.2 \quad 0.65 \quad 1 \quad 0.98 \quad 0.82 \quad 0.5 \quad 0.27 \quad 0.09 \quad 0$$

The higher the value of K, the higher is the level of approximation (see Fig. A2).

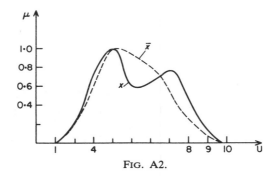

FIG. A2.

III. *ETP*

If either (a) or (b) applies:

(a) $[\mu(U_i) > \mu(U_j)] \quad [\mu(U_i) > \mu(U_k)]$
(b) $[\mu(U_i) < \mu(U_j)] \quad [\mu(U_i) < \mu(U_u)]$

where $[U_j, \mu(U_j)]$ and $[U_k, \mu(U_u)]$ are TP's immediately preceding and following $[U_i, \mu(U_i)]$ respectively.

Note: if PTP, TP and ETP are sets of primary turning points, turning points and effective turning points then,

$$PTP \subset TP \subset ETP.$$

Appendix 2: Hedges

This appendix describes the hedges used in the program "LAM5". There are six basic hedges:

1. NOT
2. VERY (MUCH)
3. INDEED
4. MORE OR LESS
5. ABOVE
6. BELOW

Description of hedges

LET x and y be fuzzy subsets of a universe of discourse U, containing N elements, and have μ_x and μ_y as their compatibility functions defined as follows

$$\mu_x : U \to [0, 1]$$

$$\mu_y : U \to [0, 1]$$

The hedges used here are based on four basic set-theoretic operations; complementation, concentration, dilation and contrast intensification of the meaning of a certain primary subset.

1. COMPLEMENTATION (NOT)

Complementation is a unary operation and is defined by the relation

$$\mu_{not\,x}(U_i) = 1 - \mu_x(U_i) \qquad \forall U_i \in U.$$

2. CONCENTRATION (VERY)

Similar to complementation, concentration is a unary operation. Its effect is to reduce the membership values. The reduction is more significant where the membership values attain lower values. This effect can be described mathematically by the operation of squaring the membership values

$$\mu_{very\,x}(U_i) = \mu_x^2(U_i) \qquad \forall U_i \in U.$$

3. DILATION (MORE OR LESS)

Dilation is another unary operation which has an effect opposite to concentration and is mathematically represented by the relation.

$$\mu_{more\,or\,less\,x}(U_i) = \mu_x^{1/2}(U_i) \qquad \forall U_i \in U.$$

4. CONTRAST INTENSIFICATION (INDEED)

This has the effect of intensifying the meaning and unfuzzyfying the value. It increases the membership values above $0 \cdot 5$ and decreases those below $0 \cdot 5$. Mathematically, it can be represented by the function

$$\mu_{\text{indeed } x}(U_i) = \begin{cases} 2\,\mu_x^2(U_i) & \text{for} \quad 0 \leq \mu_x(U_i) \leq 0.5 \\ 1 - 2\Big[1 - \mu_x(U_i)\Big]^2 & \text{for } 0.5 \leq \mu_x(U_i) \leq 1 \end{cases}$$

$\forall U_i \in U$.

Note that the operations concentration, dilation and intensification are distributive over the union and intersection, that is,

$$\begin{aligned} \text{CON } (A \dotplus B) &= \text{CON}(A) \dotplus \text{CON}(B) \\ \text{DIL } (A \dotplus B) &= \text{DIL}(A) \dotplus \text{DIL}(B) \qquad A \;\&\; B \geq 0. \\ \text{INT } (A \dotplus B) &= \text{INT}(A) \dotplus \text{INT}(B) \end{aligned}$$

5. ABOVE AND BELOW

The effect of ABOVE and BELOW on a Π-type subset can be best described mathematically by

$$\mu_{\text{above } x}(U_i) = \begin{cases} 1 - \mu_x(U_i) & U_i \geq U_{\max} \\ 0 & \text{otherwise} \end{cases}$$

$$\mu_{\text{below } x}(U_i) = \begin{cases} 1 - \mu_x(U_i) & U_i \leq U_{\min} \\ 0 & \text{otherwise} \end{cases}$$

where $U_{\max}(U_{\min})$ is the value of U; where $\mu_x(U_i)$ attains its maximum (minimum) value.

According to the above definitions the following holds

NOT ABOVE X AND NOT BELOW X = X
ABOVE X OR BELOW X   = NOT X.

Appendix 3: Primary subsets

SET 1
LOW
| 0 | 0 | 0 | 0 | 0 | 0 | 0.1 | 0.4 | 0.8 | 1 |

MED
| 0 | 0 | 0.1 | 0.4 | 0.8 | 1 | 0.8 | 0.4 | 0.1 | 0 |

HIGH
| 1 | 0.8 | 0.4 | 0.1 | 0 | 0 | 0 | 0 | 0 | 0 |

SET 2

NB												
1	0·7	0·3	0	0	0	0	0	0	0	0	0	0
NM												
0·3	0·7	1	0·7	0·3	0	0	0	0	0	0	0	0
NS												
0	0	0·3	0·7	1	0·7	0·3	0	0	0	0	0	0
ZO												
0	0	0	0	0·3	0·7	1	0·7	0·3	0	0	0	0
PS												
0	0	0	0	0	0	0·3	0·7	1	0·7	0·3	0	0
PM												
0	0	0	0	0	0	0	0	0·3	0·7	1	0·7	0·3
PB												
0	0	0	0	0	0	0	0	0	0	0·3	0·7	1

MED = MEDIUM
NB = NEGATIVE BIG
NM = NEGATIVE MEDIUM
NS = NEGATIVE SMALL
ZO = ZERO
PS = POSITIVE SMALL
PM = POSITIVE MEDIUM
PB = POSITIVE BIG

On foundations of reasoning with uncertain facts and vague concepts

PETER SCHEFE

Fachbereich Informatik, Universität Hamburg, 2 Hamburg 13, Schlüterstrasse 66–72, Hamburg, West Germany

(Received 15 August 1978, and in revised form 20 April 1979)

"Fuzzy sets theory" and "fuzzy logic" based on the former have become of rapidly increasing interest. The foundations, however, are still disputed. Especially, the definitions of some set operations and logical connectives appear to be somewhat arbitrary. The relations of "fuzziness" to "probability" and "possibility" are not yet clear. This paper contains an outline of a probabilistic foundation of multi-valued ("fuzzy") reasoning. The fundamental concept is "agreement probability". It is shown that some undesirable consequences of "fuzzy logic", e.g. that tautologies of propositional calculus are not preserved can be avoided. A proposal for alternative definitions of "degree of membership" and operations on membership-graded sets is given.

"Fuzziness" is interpreted as a subjectivistic concept, i.e. subjective uncertainty pertaining to the truth of a proposition. An important consequence thereof is that, from a graded agreement associated with a conjecture, an agreement degree pertaining to its negation cannot be computed.

According to this foundation Shortliffe's model of medical diagnosis is reviewed as an application paradigma. There is no fundamental disagreement with Shortliffe's interpretation.

However, Zadeh's "linguistic modelling" is shown to be inadequate. "Fuzziness" of linguistic concepts is interpreted as uncertainty of the applicability of a predicate in a given situation. This leads to the conclusion that the definition of derived concepts, especially, of hedged expressions referring to continuous scales, cannot be modelled using Zadeh's fuzzy set operations. Experimental findings of Hersh & Caramazza support an alternative interpretation.

Particularly, Zadeh's conjecture that truth values can be equated with membership degrees is shown to be inadequate. Alternative interpretations of the linguistic phenomena considered and of the sorites paradox are given. Especially, the meta-linguistic character of the phenomena is emphasized. It is argued that "vagueness" and "uncertainty" should be clearly distinguished as well as "possibility" and "applicability". Suggestions are made how underlying measuring scales and orderings of objects are used in reasoning processes involving vague concepts.

> "Kennen Sie irgenwelche grosse, blonde Frauen?"
> "Da muesste ich nachdenken", sagte ich. "Ich hoffe es. Wie gross?"
> "Grosse halt. Ich weiss nicht, wie gross das ist. Ausser, dass sie fuer einen Kerl, der selber gross ist, gross ist ... sie hatte hellblonde Haare unter ihrem Kopftuch, und zwar viele."
> "Das sagt mir nichts", sagte ich.
>
> Raymond Chandler, *Das hohe Fenster*

1. Introduction

An article dealing with fuzzy sets theory or fuzzy logics, if written some years ago, should have had an introduction to the topic itself. Today, this does not seem to be necessary, at least for a considerable part of the computer science community. Surveys are available now (Gaines, 1976; Gaines & Kohout, 1977). There is growing interest in the topic. So, I assume some familiarity with the terminology of the field.

This paper deals with two issues. The first is a proposal for a "probabilistic" foundation of "fuzzy" reasoning and "fuzzy sets theory" resulting in some non-trivial deviations from the model given by L. Zadeh and used by many other authors. An outline of this is given in sections 2 and 3.1. The motivation for this is mainly formal in nature, i.e. Zadeh's model has some deficiences, which should be avoided.

The second issue is a critical review of Zadeh's "linguistic approach", which can be interpreted both as a general application of fuzzy logic and fuzzy set theory to linguistic phenomena and as a special amplification of the theory itself. This is the content of sections 3.2 through 3.5. Zadeh's theory seems to be essentially originated in the intention to deal with the phenomenon of linguistic vagueness. I am convinced, however, that, firstly, this is not the main application, and, secondly, that Zadeh's model of vagueness is inadequate.

It will be shown that the area of application of "fuzzy" reasoning is "uncertainty of facts". This broadens the horizon for possible applications and interpretations. "Degree of membership" and "degree of agreement" are both interpreted as "degree of certainty" pertaining to a membership or a proposition. Thus, all areas of uncertain knowledge are concerned, i.e. pattern recognition, artificial intelligence, especially question-answering systems or consultation systems, e.g. systems for medical diagnosis, etc.

Zadeh, however, introduces a new notion called "possibility", which is meant to be purely linguistic, i.e. "quite different from that of modal logic" (Zadeh, 1978), and thus pertaining to vagueness only. Vagueness, however, is only a special case of uncertainty, i.e. uncertainty of "linguistic facts". This will be explained in section 3. There exists an essential difference between this point of view and that of Zadeh. Vagueness has to be dealt with metalinguistically. It will be shown that most of the inadequacies of Zadeh's modelling are due to his "linguistic" point of view.

As to the first issue, it has been pointed out that a connection between probability theory and fuzzy logic would be desirable (Lee 1972), and several similarities of probability laws and laws of fuzzy logic and fuzzy sets theory or "possibility theory" have been noted (Terano & Sugeno, 1975; Gaines, 1976; Zadeh, 1978). The main advocate of the whole field, Zadeh, however, still points out the distinctiveness of the two (1978, p. 8).

> To illustrate the difference between probability and possibility by a simple example, consider the statement "Hans ate X eggs for breakfast", with X taking values in $U = \{1, 2, 3, 4, \ldots\}$. We may associate a possibility distribution with X by interpreting $p_i(u)$ as the degree of ease with which Hans can eat u eggs. We may also associate a probability distribution with X by interpreting $P(u)$ as the probability of Hans eating u eggs for breakfast. Assuming that we employ some explicit or implicit criterion for assessing the degree of ease with which Hans can eat u eggs for breakfast, the values of $p_i(u)$ and $P(u)$ might be as shown in Table 1. (Left out here–P.S.)
> We observe that, whereas the possibility that Hans may eat 3 eggs for breakfast is 1, the probability that he may do so might be quite small, e.g. 0·1. Thus, a high degree of possibility

does not imply a high degree of probability, nor does a low degree of probability imply a low degree of possibility. However, if an event is impossible, it is bound to be improbable . . .

Zadeh is right arguing that the "degree of ease" with which Hans can do something has a distribution being quite different from the distribution of the probability that he really does it. But this does not necessarily lead to the conclusion that "possibility" cannot be accounted for in terms of probability theory. In another paper Zadeh (1977) argues:

> From the definition of $P_i(A)$ (possibility measure defined as the supremum of degrees of membership in a fuzzy set—P.S.), it follows at once that the possibility measure of the union of two arbitrary subsets of U is given by
>
> $$P_i(A \vee B) = P_i(A) \bigvee P_i(B)$$
>
> where $\bigvee = \max$. Thus possibility measure does not have the basic additivity property of probability measure, namely,
>
> $$P(A \vee B) = P(A) + P(B) \text{ if A and B are disjoint}$$
>
> where $P(A)$ and $P(B)$ are the probability measures of A and B, respectively, and $+$ is the arithmetic sum.

It is not necessary to get into the formal details here. It is just the type of argument which should be recognizable. If there are two concepts, one having a property which the other does not have, then it can be inferred that one concept cannot be the base concept for the other one. This does not hold. It could be argued, for example, that possibility measure behaves as a probability measure does under the restriction that of two events, say, A, and B, one contains the other. Zadeh (1977, p. 16) also gives a general argument:

> An essential aspect of the concept of possibility is that it does not involve the notion of repeated or replicated experimentation and hence is not statistical in nature.

This argument denies the basic fact that linguistic experience is statistical in nature as well as non-linguistic. People learn most fuzzy concepts in real life situations of communication with considerable statistical variability (Klix, 1976). If Zadeh's argument is directed towards statistical information theory, I agree, because statistical information theory cannot account for meaning. As far as I see, there are no arguments which definitely make it impossible to conceive of a probabilistic base for fuzzy sets theory. There are several reasons to search for such a base:

(1) to relate one theory with another broadens the horizon of people engaged with either of them;
(2) results of one theory can be taken over by the other;
(3) a new theory becomes more consistent, if tied to a well known and well elaborated field.

The third seems to me most urgent, because in fuzzy sets theory, and particularly, in fuzzy logic based on the former, there are deficiencies which have not yet been removed. For example, there is not yet a solution to the problem of tautologies having a degree of truth membership below 1. Zadeh seems to be aware of this, writing (1977, p. 39f):

> A somewhat subtle issue that arises in this connection in PRUF relates to the need for normalizing . . . . As an illustration of this point, suppose that the descriptor middle-aged is defined as
>
> $$\text{middle-aged} = \text{not young and not old} \tag{3.49}$$

Now . . . , the translation of the right-hand member of (3.49) is expressed by

not young and not old → YOUNG' ∧ OLD'

where YOUNG and OLD are the translations (fuzzy sets—P.S.) of young and old, respectively, and ' denotes the complement. Consequently, for some definitions of YOUNG and OLD the definition of middle-aged by (3.49) would result in a subnormal fuzzy set, which would imply that there does not exist any individual who is middle-aged to the degree 1.

What is not expressed here directly, is that the truth value of a tautology depends on the truth values of its parts. To this, normalization could not be a satisfactory answer. I do not know any other answer to this question given by Zadeh. The problem underlying this deficiency is the adequate definition of complementation. I will come back to that.

A general problem is the definition of functions for union intersection, etc. of fuzzy sets as well as combination rules for "or" and "and" in fuzzy logic. There seems to be relatively good agreement concerning the min and max functions for the connectives "and" and "or", respectively. The definition of implication, however, as a base for fuzzy reasoning may still be an open question for most. Gaines (1976, p. 642) resumes his discussion on various systems:

Zadeh (1975, 1976) has suggested that Łukasiewicz' L_1 be taken as the base logic for fuzzification in modelling linguistic truth values. However it is worth emphasizing that whilst this is an important possibility, particularly in view of the wealth of study of this particular MVL, there is inadequate evidence from either theory or practice as yet to discriminate between the different possibilities given above.

The basic assumption underlying my approach is that agreement is "probabilistic in nature". In this respect my approach resembles that taken by Giles (1976) and Gaines (1976 and elsewhere). Giles conceives of an elementary experiment which has as outcome the reaction of a listener to the utterance of an expression, say, "yes" or "no". Giles points out that such an experiment can be dispersive, i.e. the outcome produced by a repetition is not necessarily the same as the outcome of the first experiment (also if the repetition is not under the influence of the foregoing experiment). Gaines derives probabilistic and fuzzy logic from a "model in terms of the responses of a population" (1976, p. 658). He then gets the three interpretations of a frequentists probability model, of a socio-linguistic model, and of a subjective probability model. These interpretations seem to be very useful for possible applications.

But these "statistical" approaches could be misleading, because there are difficulties as to the interpretation of the reactions of speakers. Typically, there will be three proportions of speakers answering "yes", "no", or "don't know", if asked whether a proposition "a" containing a predicate P is true. How shall one deal with these three proportions? Beyond that, the answer "Don't know" has at least two meanings: "a is undeterminable", and "I do not know, whether the predicate P applies or not". These problems (and others) can be avoided, at least at this point, if one simply gives a model of one ideal person. An ideal speaker behaves such that everybody should agree with him. A real person is said to be reasonable if behaving like an ideal person.

That there is a need for modelling of agreement, which can be graded, is rather obvious. People often use hedges to express some degree of agreement with a statement deviating from full agreement, e.g. "I almost agree", "This is not very precise", "rather probable", and even numbers, e.g. "I agree 80%".

For conceiving a theoretical base an axiomatic approach appears most adequate. In a formal model of agreement, no assumptions are made concerning the character of statements, e.g. whether they are theoretical or empirical, analytical or synthetical, etc. General requirements of the model are:

(1) it has to be sound in a formal sense;
(2) it should preserve the laws of "classical" logic;
(3) it should not yield counter-intuitive results.

The basic notion developed in the following sections is that of agreement event probability, for short, agreement probability of a proposition a, $p(a)$. I use the term "agreement probability", because the concept defined as a measure η of Borel sets can be considered as a special case of general probability, and agreements can be considered as events associated with propositions.

2. Foundations of "fuzzy" reasoning

2.1. THE CLASSICAL CASE

The definition of agreement probability of a proposition can be given for the classical case, i.e. for the propositional calculus. Every atomic proposition is associated with an agreement event. In propositional calculus there are two possible outcomes of an agreement experiment, say, "true" and "false". As mentioned above, however, I do not conceive of a frequentist probability model. The axiomatic base of probability is the theory of Boolean algebra. Probability is defined as the norm of a Boolean algebra (see, e.g., Meschkowsky, 1968). A Boolean algebra for the semantics of propositional calculus is quite simple, containing only two events, namely, full agreement represented as {true}, and total lack of agreement represented as { }.

An agreement event associated with an atomic proposition is a "reply" of an ideal listener to an atomic proposition. This can be interpreted in two ways. Firstly, it is the reply of an ideal person to a proposition which is "true". Then, "true" is the certain and "false" is the impossible event. Secondly, the reply to a true or false proposition is represented by the event {true} and { }, respectively. It is worth noting that the refusal is represented as the empty event. This has important consequences for the derivation of combination rules as will be seen. On the other hand, one can also construct an algebra with {false} representing refusal which would lead to symmetric results.

According to the definition of the norm of a Boolean algebra one gets, obviously

$$p(\{\text{true}\}) = 1, \tag{1}$$

$$p(\{\ \}) = 0. \tag{2}$$

Now one can derive the rules for combinations of agreement events from the axioms of the theory of normed Boolean algebras. The agreement probability of the conjunction of two atomic propositions a, b is defined as

$$p(a \wedge b) = p(A \cap B) \tag{3}$$

where A, B denote the agreement events associated with a, b, respectively. Since for every pair (A, B) of agreement events

$$A \subseteq B \quad \text{or} \quad B \subseteq A \quad \text{where A, B} \in (\{\ \}, \{\text{true}\})$$

holds, one gets

$$p(a \wedge b) = \min(p(A),\ p(B)) = \min(p(a), p(b)). \tag{4}$$

Similarly, one gets for disjunction

$$p(a \vee b) = p(A \cup B) = \max (p(a), p(b)).\tag{5}$$

Negation is defined by complementation

$$p(\neg a) = p(\bar{A}) = 1 - p(A) = 1 - p(a).\tag{6}$$

Implication is defined as

$$p(a \supset b) = p(\neg a \vee b) = p(\bar{A} \vee B) = \max (1 - p(a), p(b)).\tag{7}$$

It should be noted that the max function is derived for the implication connective as well, because

$$\bar{A} \subseteq B \quad \text{or} \quad B \subseteq \bar{A}$$

holds.

These results may not be surprising, but it is important to show that the classical propositional calculus is only a special case of probabilistic logic as defined here. Deduction rules will be treated in section 2.3. Extension to first order predicate calculus could be done in a natural way.

2.2 THE "FUZZY" CASE

To get the "fuzzy" case, as I call it tentatively, one has to allow any degree of agreement for an atomic proposition, ranging from total agreement to total lack of agreement. In fuzzy sets theory this set of degrees is represented by the interval of real numbers

$$Z = \{0 \le z \le 1\}, \quad z \in R$$

with R being the set of real numbers. The use of numbers gives rise to the general problem of the mathematical foundation, as Gaines (1976, p. 635) pointed out:

> A difficulty in fuzzy sets theory that becomes a major problem in multivalued logical foundations for set theory is that "the numbers are not available early enough", i.e. set theory is a necessary foundation to the arithmetic that allows us to talk in terms of a "degree of membership" of $0 \cdot 3$.

A variant of this argument is: multi-valued logic is based on bivalent logic. Another question is, whether degrees are just "numbers" or a sort of measure. It seems to me that a multivalued system can only be based on the latter. Thus, I shall define

(1) the notion of "degree of agreement" as a measure of Borel sets,
(2) the connectives in terms of operations on Borel sets,
(3) logical inference in terms of conditional agreement probability, and relate the choice of alternative operators to the notions of dependence/independence in probability theory.

Instead of mapping propositions directly to numbers in the interval $[0, 1] \subset R$ every atomic proposition is mapped to an interval X_a open on the left-hand side and representing a "fuzzy" agreement event:

$$X_a = \{y/0 < y \le x_a\} \quad \text{where } 0 \le x_a \le 1; \quad x_a, y \in R.\tag{8}$$

We then generate a σ-algebra by the sets:

$$X = \{y/0 < y \le x\} \quad \text{where } 0 \le x \le 1; \quad x, y \in R.\tag{9}$$

These sets are measurable. For short, let the set X be denoted by its "head", the supremum of the set itself, say $[x]$.

For example, the set

$$[0 \cdot 6] = (y/0 < y \le 0 \cdot 6)$$

denotes the fuzzy agreement event of degree $0 \cdot 6$.

Obviously, the agreement probability of a proposition a can be defined as;

$$p(a) = \eta(X_a) = x_a - 0 = x_a \tag{10}$$

where η is the Borel–Lebesgue measure. Of course, the axiom of σ-additivity could be replaced by the axiom of finite additivity, if the number of events is finite. In any case, we are allowed to speak of a probability measure, too, because its range is the interval $[0, 1]$. Again, it should be noted that an agreement event comprises every other agreement event with the head of the latter being less than the head of the former. Hence, as in the classical case the rules for conjunction and disjunction become:

$$p(a \wedge b) = \eta([x_a] \cap [x_b]) = \min(x_a, x_b) \tag{11}$$

and

$$p(a \vee b) = \eta([x_a] \cup [x_b]) = \max(x_a, x_b). \tag{12}$$

At this point, one could consider agreement probability as a special case of "ordinary" probability, because of the loss of the additivity property. I prefer this view to that of Terano & Sugeno (1975), who defined a fuzzy measure making weaker assumptions than needed for probability measure, so that the latter can be considered as a special case of the former. Taking over the axioms for probability measures and Boolean algebras has obvious advantages. One can simply refer to well known theorems of the field. Beyond that one has a motivation with stronger intuitive appeal for the "loss of additivity". Expecially, the connection to the classical conception of truth makes it easier to understand what the concept of "fuzziness" is meant to be. It will be shown in the following that taking the agreement-probabilistic generalisation of truth as a base of fuzzy reasoning and fuzzy sets theory one can avoid some undesirable consequences exhibited as yet by that theory.

Negation is defined by complementation corresponding to the classical case. The complement of an agreement event is defined by

$$[\overline{x_a}] = (y/x_a < y \le 1) \quad \text{with } x_a, y \text{ as above.} \tag{13}$$

The complement of the full agreement event is as in the classical case

$$[\overline{1}] = \{ \; \} \tag{14}$$

which is compatible with (13). Of course, then

$$p(\neg a) = \eta([\overline{x_a}]) = 1 - x_a. \tag{15}$$

These outcomes agree with those in the classical case. But defining implication brings out a difference. Rule (7) must be rejected, because an agreement event of a proposition b does not always contain the complement of any other proposition a or vice versa. So one has to adopt the law of probability

$$p(a \supset b) = 1 - p(a) + p(a \wedge b) \tag{16}$$

which leads to

$$p(a \supset b) = 1 - p([x_a]) + p([x_a] \cap [x_b])$$
$$= 1 - x_a + \min(x_a, x_b)$$
$$= \min(1, 1 - x_a + x_b) \tag{17}$$

which resembles the "bounded sum" of Zadeh taken from Łukasiewicz' Alephl (Zadeh, 1977, p. 59).

It is interesting to see that a value of 1 for the implication is compatible with

$$p(b) \geq p(a).$$

The implied proposition b may have a higher agreement probability than the antecedent proposition a. In other words: an implication is true, even if the implied proposition is "more true" than its antecedent. But this should not be surprising, because, in the classical case, it reduces to the fact that something true can be implied by something false. In this case rule (17) yields the same results as rule (7) does. So the former is the more general one.

The definition of implication demonstrates the importance of the definition of complementation. This will be more obvious, if one considers tautologies and contradictions. The rules for the computation of the values of the connectives "or" and "and" in fuzzy sets theory and fuzzy logic do not take into account the fact that an agreement event and its complement can be disjoint so that the min and max functions cannot be applied. These functions can be applied to atomic propositions or to a combination consisting exclusively of complements of atomic propositions but not to a combination of both. This pertains to tautologies and contradictions. For the former we have according to (16):

$$p(\neg a \vee a) = \min(1, 1 + x_a - x_a) = 1. \tag{18}$$

The latter is given according to the definition of the complement:

$$p(a \wedge \neg a) = p([x_a] \cap p[\overline{x_a}]) = 0. \tag{19}$$

Fuzzy logic based on fuzzy sets theory cannot account for such tautologies and contradictions because of the deficiency of the definition of complementation:

$$\bar{F} = \int_u (1 - \mu_F(y))/y$$

which means that for every member of a fuzzy subset F of a reference U the degree of membership for the complement $\bar{F}$ is computed as

$$\mu_{\bar{F}}(y) = 1 - \mu_F(y).$$

If taken as base for the concept of truth, this leads to undesirable consequences, e.g.

$$p(a \wedge \neg a) = \min(p(a), 1 - p(a))$$

with truth membership degrees ranging from 0 to 0·5 dependent on the value of $p(a)$ (see Sanford, 1976). This could be interpreted as "both true and false" being a reply of a listener to certain natural language statements, but this is quite another interpretation, hence it does not solve the problem. (See section 3 for this alternative interpretation.) That Zadeh's fuzzy sets theory has not removed this deficiency is quite in accord with the fact that the definition of the conditional is taken from multivalued logic (see, e.g. Bellman & Zadeh, 1977, p. 128), because it cannot be based on fuzzy sets theory properly.

It should be emphasized that the probabilistic system proposed here is not entirely "truth-functional" in the classical sense. If complements are involved, the agreement probabilities of a compound proposition cannot be derived in a unified fashion from the agreement probabilities of the constituents. It appears to me that it makes no sense to conceive of a "truth-functional" multivalued system. There is some intuitive evidence that truth values cannot be graded. "Truth" pertains to the classical case of absolute certainty. A gradation of agreement leads to uncertainty (see the next sections for that topic).

The agreement-probabilistic model is not constrained to bivalent and infinite-valued systems. One can construct an agreement-probabilistic model of a logic with any number of agreement values. For example, to construct a three-valued logic one introduces three agreement events, { } representing the empty agreement event, {1, 2} representing full agreement, and {1} representing "medium" agreement. Obviously, one gets as agreement values 0, 1 and $\frac{1}{2}$, respectively. The complements are given by:

$$[\bar{1}] = \{2\},$$

$$[\bar{2}] = \{\ \}.$$

The rules for deriving values of compound propositions are just those of infinite-valued logic. The difficulties which Łukasiewicz had in constructing a three-valued logic vanish. Łukasiewicz gave up his attempt, because the tautologies of the classical propositional logic could not be preserved (see Sinowjew, 1968).

The law of the excluded middle need not be given up, however, in a logic with any number of values based on the agreement-probabilistic model. This implies that these values are not interpreted as primary entities, but measures of agreement events represented by Borel sets.

2.3. FUZZY DEDUCTION

The problem of deduction can be studied by considering *modus ponens*. One can conceive of this deduction rule as the tautological conditional:

$$((a \supset b) \wedge a) \Rightarrow b \qquad (20)$$

where "$\Rightarrow$" denotes that the right-hand proposition called "conclusion" can be deduced from the conjunction of propositions called "premises" to the left of the symbol. The validity of this inference scheme is given by the fact that

$$((a \supset b) \wedge a) \supset b \qquad (21)$$

is a tautology. This means that the agreement probability of the scheme is always equal to 1. Under this precondition one can derive the deduction rule in the following way:

$$1 = p(((a \wedge (a \supset b)) \supset b))$$

$$= 1 - p((a \wedge (a \supset b))) + \min(p((a \wedge (a \supset b))), p(b))$$

which leads to

$$p((a \wedge (a \supset b))) = \min (p(a \wedge (a \supset b))), p(b))$$

which leads to

$$p(b) \geq \min (p(a), p(a \supset b)) \tag{22}$$

which means that b can be inferred at least with an agreement probability of the minimum of the agreement probabilities of a and the implication $a \supset b$. We were tacitly assuming so far that the complex propositions involved behave like atomic propositions, i.e. we were assuming:

$$p(a \supset b) = 1.$$

Otherwise we would set:

$$p(b) < p(a).$$

This inference rule, however, seems not to be very interesting, because we have to fix its validity to 1, in order to set a useful measure. What one would like to have is an inference rule which can be ascribed a graded validity.

There is a strong intuitive evidence that the conditional in reasoning with graded agreement is modelled similar to conditional probability. Conditional agreement probability of a proposition b under the condition of agreement to a proposition a is thus defined as:

$$p(b/a) = p(a \wedge b) : p(a). \tag{23}$$

$p(b/a)$ can be interpreted as the agreement degree of proposition b, if one has already agreed with proposition a. From (23) one gets

$$p(b/a) = \min (p(a), p(b)) : p(a). \tag{24}$$

Similar to the behaviour of implication, one has a value of 1 for the conditional, if

$$p(a) \leq p(b).$$

Otherwise one has the interesting equation:

$$p(b) = p(b/a) . p(a) \tag{25}$$

i.e. given the agreement probability of the conditional, $p(b/a)$, and the probability of the antecedent proposition, $p(a)$, one can compute the agreement probability of the consequent, $p(b)$.

There is an important difference between (20) and (25), because the agreement probability of the conclusion in (20) never falls below that of the implication itself. What then about the applicability of the schemes? To answer this remember the fundamental difference of the two schemes. The first is essentially a tautology, hence, the validity of the scheme is fixed to 1. It can only be taken as a model if the inference rule to be modelled is valid. If this is the case, then both inference schemes yield results compatible with each other:

$$\min (p(a), p(a \supset b)) \leq p(b) \leq 1,$$

$$p(a) \leq p(b) \leq 1,$$

respectively. An inference rule with an agreement probability less than 1 can only be modelled by (25).

The rules considered have in common the assumption that the agreement events are dependent on each other. If one allows two agreement events to be not dependent on each other, i.e. that

$$p(b/a) = p(b) \quad \text{and} \quad p(a/b) = p(b)$$

holds, then the rules for conjunction and disjunction are different from (11) and (12), respectively, corresponding to Zadeh's "interactives":

$$p(a \wedge b) = p(a) . p(b) = x_a . x_b \tag{26}$$

$$p(a \vee b) = p(a) + p(b) - p(a) . p(b)$$

$$= x_a + x_b - x_a . x_b. \tag{27}$$

Once more, it seems worth emphasizing that the classical case is just a special case. (26) and (27) are equivalent to the min and max functions, respectively, if the range of degrees is $\{0, 1\}$. Thus, the important difference between dependent and independent propositions vanishes in the classical case. How can one decide, which of the rules should be used in a certain case? This question can only be answered with respect to the domain of application.

The probabilistic model proposed here as well as those referenced are formal, and exact in the sense that they rely on some mathematical base. This does not imply that they can account as yet for all aspects of human reasoning with its real fallacies and "fuzziness".

2.4. INTERPRETATION AND AN EXAMPLE OF APPLICATION

Epistemologically, agreement probability is a subjectivistic concept. This is the theoretical frame for all interpretations and applications. An ideal speaker/listener assigns an agreement degree to a proposition. If this degree is equal to 1 this is interpreted as follows.

It is certain that the conjecture expressed holds.

Note the important point: it is this proposition which can be assigned an agreement degree between 1 and 0, not the conjecture itself, say:

It is to an extent (degree) of 0·6 certain that the conjecture expressed holds.

It is not difficult to understand this sentence in a natural way. Shortliffe (1974) has shown that experts are able to grade their agreement this way. The important consequence thereof is that the negation of the above proposition is:

It is to an extent (degree) of 0·4 not certain that the conjecture expressed holds.

but not as:

It is certain that the conjecture expressed does not hold (is not true) to an extent of 0·4.

This follows from the subjectivistic interpretation. Given an evidence for a conjecture, this cannot be an evidence for the negation of the conjecture, too. (See Shortliffe, 1974, p. 219.)

There is an essential difference between subjective certainty and objective probability: given the probability of an event, say, "A man will die when he is 80 years old", one always knows the probability of the complement, say, "A man man will not die when he is 80 years old". This difference, however, does not lead to the conclusion that reasoning with subjective uncertainty cannot be modelled on a probabilistic base.

Shortliffe is right in arguing against the applicability of "subjective probability" as developed in philosophy (see Shortliffe, 1974, p. 213ff; Kutchera, 1976), because it is inadequate to infer $p(\neg a)$ from $p(a)$, where a is a conjecture.

Shortliffe is right, then, to introduce two "certainty factors", one for the confirmation (MB), and one for the disconfirmation (MD) of a hypothesis combined into one as $CF = MB - MD$. His model of medical reasoning can be taken as a direct interpretation or application of agreement probability. It may be surprising that Shortliffe developes an "approximation technique" arriving at almost the same "combining functions" as defined here, because the way of defining seems to be quite different from that taken here. Shortliffe sets up some "defining criteria", which are intuitively acceptable, e.g. that the order of observations or gathering pieces of evidence should not have an effect on the combined confirmation degree (see p. 235f). To demonstrate the application of agreement probability to medical reasoning, I take an example given by Shortliffe interpreting it in terms of agreement probability theory. Given the rule:

IF: (1) THE STAIN OF THE ORGANISM IS GRAM NEGATIVE,
     AND
     (2) THE MORPHOLOGY OF THE ORGANISM IS ROD, AND
     (3) (A—THE AEROBICITY OF THE ORGANISM IS AEROBIC
     OR B—THE AEROBICITY OF THE ORGANISM IS UNKNOWN)
THEN: THERE IS SUGGESTIVE EVIDENCE (0·6) THAT THE
       CLASS OF THE ORGANISM IS ENTEROBACTERIACEAE

its form is according to Shortliffe:

$$CF'(h, S1 \wedge S2 \wedge (S3 \vee S4)) = X$$

In terms of agreement probability, X is the conditional probability of agreement to hypothesis h, if one has agreed with the combination of the premises. Then, according to Shortliffe's "Function 4":

$$CF(h, S1 \wedge S2 \wedge (S3 \vee S4)) = X \times \max (0, CF(S1 \wedge S2 \wedge (S3 \vee S4), E))$$

and, because of $CF = MB - MD$:

$$MB(h, S1 \wedge S2 \wedge (S3 \vee S4)) = X \times MB(S1 \wedge S2 \wedge (S3 \vee S4), E)$$

where E is some observational evidence. Without loss of generality, we can assume that E is certain; hence:

$$p(h) = X \times p(S1 \wedge S2 \wedge (S3 \vee S4)) \quad \text{where } X = p(h/S1 \wedge S2 \wedge (S3 \vee S4))$$

According to Shortliffe's "Function 1" and "Function 2":

$$MB(S1 \wedge S2 \wedge (S3 \vee S4), E)$$

$$= \min (MB(S1, E), MB(S2, E), (\max (MB(S3, E), MB(S4, E))))$$

corresponding to:

$$p(S1 \wedge S2 \wedge (S3 \vee S4)) = \min (p(S1), p(S2), \max (p(S3), p(S4))).$$

It is interesting to examine Shortliffe's line of argument for the foundation of "Function 1a":

$$MB(h, S1 \wedge S2) = \begin{cases} 0, & \text{if } MD(h, S1 \wedge S2) = 1 \\ MB(h, S1) + MB(h, S2)(1 - MB(h, S1)), & \text{otherwise} \end{cases}$$

which corresponds to definition (27) for independent propositions. Shortliffe argues (p. 240f):

> The assumption implicit in this function includes more than an acceptance of the independence of S1 and S2. The function was conceived purely on intuitive grounds in that it satisfies the four Defining Criteria I have listed. However, some obvious problems are present. For example, the function always causes the MB or MD to increase, regardless of the relationship between new and prior evidence. Yet Salmon has discussed an example from subparticle physics (Salmon, 1973) in which either of two observations taken alone confirm a given hypothesis, but their conjunction disproves the hypothesis absolutely! Our model assumes the absence of such aberrant situations in the field of application for which it is designed . . . . Although we have suggested that perhaps there is a numerical relationship between confirmation and probability, we agree that the challenge for a confirmation quantification scheme is to demonstrate its usefulness within a given context, preferably without sacrificing human intuition regarding what the quantitative nature of confirmation should be . . . we have . . . demonstrated that the technique models the conclusions of the expert from whom the rules were acquired . . . . The most aberrant points, however, are those that represent cases in which pieces of evidence were strongly interrelated for the hypothesis under consideration (termed "conditional non-independence").

Shortliffe's own empirical investigations suggest that the independence of propositions is required for the applicability of the rule considered, i.e. that each symptom or observation gives evidence for the hypothesis independently. The intuitive appeal of this rule is that by each observation pertaining to h the certainty degree of the combination increases. Thus, it seems to be well suited for a set of application cases in medical diagnosis. However, Shortliffe misses the point, if he interprets this combination as a "conjunction", i.e. intersection of agreement events. Rule (27) corresponding to "Function 1a" models the union of agreement events. Its application is adequate, if each observation in isolation gives evidence for a hypothesis independently. The "counter-example" taken from Salmon, however, cannot be modelled by the same operation, because the two observations have a complementary distribution; hence, practically, it is not a counter-example for the validity of the rule under consideration.

It seems to me that Shortliffe has no rule for intersection, because, typically, there is no use of it. For example, intersection could be taken as a model, if there is one symptom, say, headache, co-occurring with both fever and trauma of the cervical vertebra, so that there is no reinforcement for a hypothesis, say, flu.

The problem of decreasing confirmation vanishes if given the right mathematical interpretation. To me, this suggests that a coherent mathematical base is even useful with respect to interpretation and application.

3. Fuzzy sets and linguistic modelling

The main application area for fuzzy sets theory seems to be modelling of "fuzzy" reasoning expressed in natural language. Zadeh at least directs his attention to this topic in many papers. Particularly, he developed the notions of "linguistic variable", and of "linguistic approximation". I shall not report upon that in detail, but instead consider some fundamental aspects of linguistic modelling using fuzzy sets theory.

3.1. FUZZY SETS AND MEMBERSHIP-GRADED SETS

As has been shown, there are deficiencies of fuzzy sets theory if taken as a base for modelling linguistic truth. Especially, the definition of complementation of fuzzy sets leads to some undesirable consequences. So it seems worth-while to remove the deficiency by "redefining" fuzzy sets in terms of agreement probability theory. This means that degree of membership in a set is no longer considered to be a basic, but a derived concept. To construct an "agreement-probabilistic set" A one has to associate with each member y of the reference set U an agreement event pertaining to an atomic proposition, say,

$$y \in A. \tag{28}$$

I call this an atomic membership proposition. Using Zadeh's notation one has:

$$A = \int_u [x_y]/y \tag{29}$$

where $[x_y]$ denotes the agreement event pertaining to (28). This seems to be compatible with Zadeh's concept of a function d_A of the fuzzy set A

$$d_A: U \to [0, 1] \subset R \tag{30}$$

with R being the set of real numbers. It is important, however, to note the difference: Zadeh uses numbers, say x, directly representing degrees of membership; in (29) numbers denote infinite sets, say $[x]$, representing agreement events. Now one can give the definitions of union and intersection of agreement-probabilistic sets, which I shall call membership-graded sets, similar to, but definitely distinct from Zadeh's fuzzy sets:

$$A \cup B = \int_u MAX\,(d_A(y), d_B(y))/y \tag{31}$$

where MAX is a function, which takes as argument the agreement event pertaining to atomic membership propositions and yields as result the agreement event with the head having the higher value. Intersection is defined as:

$$A \cap B = \int_u MIN\,(d_A(y), d_B(y))/y \tag{32}$$

with MIN corresponding to MAX. The complement is given by:

$$\bar{A} = \int_u \overline{d_A(y)}/y \tag{33}$$

where $\overline{d_A(y)}$ denotes the complement of the agreement event $d_A(y)$.

Note the important difference: because membership is not directly associated with a probability $p([x_y])$, but with an agreement event $[x_y]$,

$$(a \in A) \wedge \neg(a \in A) \tag{34}$$

becomes a contradiction as in the classical case. It is easy to show that many of Zadeh's fuzzy algorithms for computing truth values based on fuzzy sets do not comply with this consequence. Especially, the operations of union and intersection cannot be applied according to (31) and (32), if complements are involved. I shall not elaborate on that here.

3.2. PROBABILITY AND POSSIBILITY

How can a membership-graded set be interpreted in comparison with a classical set? There are two interpretations of both. For example, the predicate "murderer" can be applied to a person in a deterministic and in a non-deterministic manner:

$$\text{John is one of the murderers.} \qquad (s1)$$

$$\text{John is one of the possible murderers.} \qquad (s2)$$

The set of murderers can be interpreted as representing facts or possibilities. Thus, in the classical case, one has to draw the distinction between deterministic or factual sets on the one hand, and non-deterministic or possibilistic sets on the other hand. One can ascribe to both sentences (s1) and (s2), which could be interpreted as atomic membership propositions, a graded value of agreement. Thus, a graded-membership set can represent both facts and possibilities as well as a classical set, which can be considered a special case of the former. Tentatively, one may equate these two interpretations with "probability" and "fuzziness", respectively. This is misleading, however, because agreement probability can only be interpreted as (subjective) certainty of an ideal hearer pertaining both to facts and possibilities. On the other hand, it is to be admitted that, firstly, the notion of comparative possibility in modal logics does not seem to be well defined until now (Kutchera, 1976), and, secondly, in many interpretations "possibility" can be equated with "factual uncertainty". Zadeh does not consider this interpretation. As has been mentioned, he claims that "fuzziness" has nothing to do with "possibility" in the sense of modal logic (see Zadeh, 1978). It can be shown easily that this does not hold (see below). Zadeh's concept of "fuzziness" is equated with the concept of "vagueness", and his concept of "possibility" is meant to be purely linguistic.

A degree of possibility whatsoever can be "redefined" as the agreement probability of an atomic membership proposition:

$$\text{Poss}\,(y = u) = p([x_u]) \qquad (35)$$

where $p([x_u])/u \in A$, and A is a label of a membership-graded set. The special aim of Zadeh is to model the meaning of "fuzzy" linguistic concepts using fuzzy sets. (I use this term quite in the sense of Zadeh.) For example, given the scheme:

$$\text{X is an integer}$$

then X represents the possibilistic set of all integers. The possibility of each member has the value 1. However, in the scheme:

$$\text{X is a small integer}$$

the members of X have "fuzzy" degrees of membership "redefined" as graded agreement events:

$$\text{SMALL INTEGER} = ([1]/1, [0\cdot8]/2, [0\cdot6]/3, [0\cdot3]/4) \qquad (36)$$

where all other members of the reference set have associated with them the agreement event { }. Then, for example:

$$\text{Poss } (y = 2) = p([0{\cdot}8]) = 0{\cdot}8$$

and "small" induces the possibility distribution given by (35) and (36). It is the hypothesis of Zadeh that a listener who has this information will assign possibility values to the members of the set of integers, e.g. in terms of agreement probability:

It is to an extent of 0·3 certain that one would agree that 4 is a small integer.

The distinctiveness of the concepts of "possibility" mentioned is given by the different "ontological" status. "Possibility" in the sense of modal logics is related to facts, i.e. assertional; Zadeh's "possibility" is related to linguistic concepts, i.e. definitional. However, the latter can be shown to be only a special case of the former. Consider the sentence "x is less than 3" or "$0 < x < 3$", which induces a set of integers. This can be taken as an axiom in a certain world of discourse. Then, the proposition "$x = 1 \lor x = 2$" becomes a theorem, hence, necessarily true. On the other hand, one cannot deduce "$x = 1$". We only know what "$x = 1$" as well as "$x = 2$" are possibly, but not necessarily true, i.e. contingent propositions. Finally, "$x = 3$" can be proven to be false, hence, to be nessarily false, i.e. impossible in the given world of discourse.

Thus, the formal equivalence of the two notions is obvious. On the other hand, Zadeh does not clearly distinguish between his "linguistic" concept of possibility and the notion of "natural" possibility. The examples he uses to illustrate the difference between "possibility" and "probability" (cited above) are clearly not of the linguistic type.

3.3. FUZZY SETS AND CONTINUOUS SCALES

The use of numbers seems a bit strange, because a real speaker/listener may never use numbers in his answers, but expressions like "not very true", "rather", etc. But where do the numbers come from?

There is at least one answer to this question. Zadeh (1968) himself has equated the probability of a "fuzzy event" with the expectation of the membership function, which inspired Hersh & Caramazza (1976) to design a psycholinguistic experiment for measuring these values. Before examining some of their interesting results several fundamental difficulties concerning the answer to the question raised above, and concerning the interpretation of empirical results should be considered.

The first pertains to the design of an experiment, and the statistical uncertainty involved. For example, it is possible to design an experiment using a method similar to that of the well known "Semantic Differential" of Osgood (Osgood, Suci & Tannenbaum, 1957) to get the agreement probabilities for a sentence, say,

$$190 \text{ cm is large for a man} \tag{s3}$$

in a certain socio-cultural context. Then, one has, of course, only an estimate of the value for a certain population. Another difficulty arises from an uncertainty of our cognition, not only in everyday life, but in science as well. The third difficulty is the "fuzziness" of our linguistic knowledge itself originating both in the statistical nature of communication (see Labov, 1970; Schefe, 1975) and in the uncertainty of cognition. So a real listener will most probably reject a sentence that provides with a precision, which cannot be attained, e.g.:

It is to an extent 0·813 certain that "tall" applies to a height of 180 cm.   (s4)

So this must give rise to the question: how can fuzzy sets theory cope with "fuzziness", if the numbers and functions used in the calculus suggest an arbitrary degree of precision?

One answer could be: it is only aimed at descritive adequacy, the application of a formal system does not imply the conjecture that the numbers used represent a psycho-linguistic reality. Then one has to look for the former.

Consider the natural language sentence:

John is old and not old.   (s5)

If one adopts Zadeh's view of "old" as referring to the label of a fuzzy set, there is one meaning, roughly formalized according to Zadeh's PRUF language:

John is OLD ∧ John is OLD′

with OLD denoting a fuzzy subset of the integer interval [0, 100], and OLD′ denoting its complement. If one adopts the view of probabilistic agreement theory, one has a conjunction of a membership proposition and its negation:

$$(\text{John} \in \text{OLD}) \wedge \neg (\text{John} \in \text{OLD}'')$$

where OLD″ denotes the membership-graded set corresponding to the fuzzy set OLD. This is a contradiction according to the definition of the complement. Perhaps there is a second interpretation implying that the speaker does not refer to facts, but to "linguistic" agreement probabilities, so that the sentence could be paraphrased as:

John can be said to be old as well as he can be said to be not old.   (s6)

This interpretation is clearly metalinguistic in nature. An important consequence thereof is that one need not give up the law of the excluded middle, in order to cope with this interpretation. The speaker expresses that the age in question is a borderline case of the "applicability" of the antonyms "old" and "not old". So, he applies an *ad hoc* definition of "middle-aged". Zadeh's example (cited above), however, seems to be still more obvious. To be "not old and not young" means that neither "old" nor "young" can be applied. This interpretation is supported by the fact that (s5) is less acceptable, and to be "old and young" is rather unacceptable. Zadeh tries to model such "definitions" by directly applying numerical operations on fuzzy sets. But one should be careful about the metalinguistic character of the phenomenon. Looking at the operations in detail one has to realize, too, that an adequate model cannot be achieved. Assuming the standard distribution of fuzzy values given by Zadeh, one establishes for the intersection of the two fuzzy sets a distribution which is not only subnormal but also non-standard (Fig. 1). There is no evidence at all that this computation is useful, if the result must be normalized and standardized. Firstly, this gives rise to the question of closure under the operations defined by Zadeh.

Secondly, it would be a fundamental misunderstanding if the borderline cases of the applicability of antonyms referring to a continuous scale are modelled by overlapping continuous membership functions. "Borderline" is meant to be a case in which the applicability of both antonyms is completely dubious or uncertain, i.e. the certainty

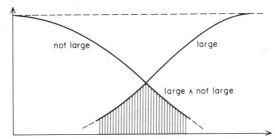

FIG. 1. Intersection of two standard fuzzy sets establishes a subnormal non-standard fuzzy set.

degree of applicability is 0. There may also be cases with a certainty degree between 0 and 1, but it is not useful to assume for both antonyms a degree not equal to 0 at the same point of the scale. It is the same problem we came across earlier: from "*a* is *x* certain" we can infer "*a* is $1 - x$ uncertain", but not "not *a* is $1 - x$ certain". Thus, the intermediate concept cannot be defined by fuzzy set operations. This is supported by the findings of Hersh & Caramazza that the "membership functions" of "small" and of "not large" exhibit a significant difference. That there is some overlapping of the "membership functions" of "small" and "large" is due to the experimental situation. If there is no alternative in a classification experiment with a vague concept, people may extend the applicability range as far as possible covering borderline cases, too. P. Hayes (1974) calls this phenomenon "hysteresis", i.e. "an intermediate heap will be considered small if it began as small and grew, and considered large if it began as large and shrank" (p. 77).

On the other hand, the finding that there is no significant difference between the fuzzy set function representing "not large" and the complement of the fuzzy set representing "large" seems to support Zadeh's proposal for the definition of negation. Again, however, there is another interpretation of the experimental result: "'not large' appears to extend the concept 'small' to include the midrange of the continuum" (Hersh & Caramazza, 1976, p. 265), i.e. to say something is not large means to say that one does not know whether it is really small, or "One cannot say large". Hence, "not large" is less precise than "small", and covers a larger proportion of the continuous scale. Particularly, a "complementary distribution" is induced, because from "It is uncertain whether one can apply 'small'" follows "It is uncertain whether one cannot apply 'small'", and there are symmetric decreasing functions of certainty for both propositions, such that the truth of the former is certain if the opposite is certain to be false. However, there is no "direct" way from a grade of applicability to a grade of applicability of the opposite.

Thirdly, if the new antonym becomes a stable constituent of the current context, then one has to change some parts, if not the whole of the linguistic representation of the continuous scale. The scope of each antonym has to be adjusted to the scopes of the other ones (Fig. 2). If one is asked to classify people according to the scales "young–old", and "young—middle-aged—old", then typically the results will be different. I did not find any discussion on this fundamental process in any of Zadeh's papers.

There should be mentioned another misunderstanding: the uncertainty or "possibility" degrees are uncertain themselves; empirically, this uncertainty is due to the inconsistency of people in classifying objects. This aspect of vagueness could be labeled

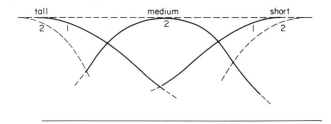

FIG. 2. Antonyms are not modelled by overlapping applicability functions, and change their meanings in different contexts (1, 2).

"statistical vagueness" (Denofsky, 1976). It cannot be accounted for by a simple continuous function, because the function itself is "fuzzy".

The same is true for the modelling of linguistic hedges. Zadeh's proposal to represent hedges as operators on fuzzy sets has some amazing results but cannot be taken as a model seriously. Consider the definition of "very" as a "concentrator" yielding the squares of the fuzzy values operated on. Again, there is neither intuitive nor experimental evidence for this definition. On the contrary, Hersh & Caramazza (1976) found a distribution for the hedged concept involving a displacement (Fig. 3). Attaching a

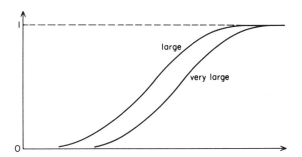

FIG. 3. Fuzzy sets for the representation of "large" and "very large" after Hersh & Caramazza (1976).

hedge to a concept referring to a continuous scale means creating a new antonym. For example, attaching "very" to the concept "old" creates the new antonym "very old" as opposed to "old". Thus "old" can change its meaning in this context. The same pertains to the example supplied by Gaines (1976, p. 656): "He is not just tall but very tall". If a teacher is asked to classify his students according to "good" and "very good", this effect may be still more obvious. Thus, the meaning of hedged expression depends essentially on the set of alternatives involved. The experimental findings of Hersh & Caramazza (1976) support this interpretation, for example, in the case of "very". A displacement is just the result of adding a new member to the set of antonyms referring to a continuous scale. Again, there is no use for a somewhat bulky numerical operation on a fuzzy set. One has only to compute the new midpoint or "saturation point" and assume some standard distribution. For most purposes it may be superfluous to compute such a "possibility distribution". If the compatibility of two pieces of information has to be computed, for example, for the sentences "John is very old" and "John is 60 years old", one has to know, whether or not "60" lies in the interval of the scale covered by "very old" (see Wechsler, 1975; Wahlster, 1977).

The metalinguistic or pragmatic character of communication involving references to continuous scales is also reflected in the findings of Hersh & Caramazza (1976, p. 269) that

> . . . the use of litotes such as *not very* does not imply the complement of the continuum . . . but only some range near the middle of the continuum: For example, to say that someone is *not very tall* is typically interpreted as meaning that he is *rather short or sort of short.*

Hence, "not" does not imply an operation on a fuzzy set, but a metalinguistic statement, say, "You cannot say 'very tall' at all, you cannot say even 'tall', you must say 'rather short' ". One subject in the experiment of Hersh & Caramazza behaved differently as to this concept (see p. 271). It created an antonym "not very small" with a shift on the scale away from "very small". This seems to be a second valid interpretation of the expression "not very small" with stress on "very". There are still other findings of Hersh & Caramazza, which support the "metalinguistic" interpretation and which "invalidate the principle claim that intensifiers and hedges can be described as operators on fuzzy sets", i.e. I do not follow Hersh & Caramazza (1976, p. 273), who just negate the expression cited above.

3.4. CONTINUOUS SCALES AND LINGUISTIC TRUTH

It should be clear that Zadeh's proposal to consider the following sentences as semantically equivalent cannot be accepted in general:

" 'Rahim is honest' is very true."   (s8)

" 'Rahim is very honest' is true. "   (s9)

Even if there is a context, in which these sentences express the same, Zadeh's proposal to equate the truth value of a proposition expressing a membership degree with this membership degree cannot be maintained. Consider the natural language statement similar to that given by Zadeh (see above):

John ate one or two eggs for breakfast.   (s7)

Possible replies are:

This is very probable.   (s8)

This is absolutely possible.   (s9)

This is true but not correct (precise).   (s10)

The answer depends on the knowledge of the replier, i.e. the knowledge of the probability distribution, of the possibility distribution, or the factual situation, respectively. The difference of the third case is that there are two reactions, one concerning the truth value, which is not graded, because it deals with a classical factual proposition, the second concerning the "correctness" or "precision" of the statement. In real communication these different aspects of a statement are often mixed up by speakers, e.g. the answer may be "not quite true". This may not be surprising, because in most cases, if speakers are referring to continuous scales, there are several difficulties. For example, the conjecture:

John is fairly tall   (s11)

could evoke the following replies:

    Of course true, John is very tall.   (s12)

    False, John is just tall, not fairly tall.   (s13)

    Possibly, I just know that he is tall (somebody told me).   (s14)

    I do not know, whether I should say "fairly tall" or "very tall."   (s15)

    I think, he is tall (I saw him only once).   (s16)

    You may be right, but I would say: John is very tall.   (s17)

etc.

The first difficulty is to decide on the value of truth in a borderline case. The second is the variability of the set of antonyms involved in the current context of communication. The third is the difference of the linguistic representations used by speaker and replier. The replier may take this into account or not. The fourth is the difference of knowledge or cognitive abilities. This list may not be exhaustive. Thus, what seems very clear in the case of discrete scales, becomes very hard in the case of continuous scales. There is no evidence that the simple proposal of Zadeh would be a model of this situation. Even if restricted to one speaker, it cannot account for the uncertainty of cognition, of communication and linguistic representation, and the variability resulting from those. Even if this variability is neglected, i.e. an ideal speaker is modelled using a formal database to represent his knowledge, there remain several inconsistencies.

Firstly, although possibility distributions over continuous scales could be described by graded-membership sets, Zadeh's fuzzy set operations union, intersection and complementation cannot be used to describe combinations and definitions of linguistic concepts referring to continuous scales.

Secondly, the procedures given by Zadeh to model linguistic hedges appear to be not only arbitrary but also inconsistent with different samples. The latter is shown, for example, concerning the max-min-product for attaching a hedge to a "fuzzy" concept by Kayser, Bonnet & Jacob (1977). The arbitrariness renders the model useless for any prediction of real linguistic behaviour. Beyond that, experimental findings exhibit that the meaning of "not" is not complementation of a fuzzy set, and hedges can be viewed as a general means for creating *ad hoc* antonyms, which make the information more precise.

Thirdly, Zadeh's conception of linguistic truth in terms of fuzzy sets theory is not valid, because it does not comprise an adequate definition of complementation.

Fourthly, Zadeh's conjecture that truth values of propositions expressing the applicability of a linguistic concept referring to a continuous scale have to be equated with "possibility degrees" of this applicability does not hold. On the contrary, truth values applying to factual propositions are always binary without mentioning that there is a difficulty in the borderline case, when the applicability is absolutely uncertain (but not "middle-true"). Beyond that, speakers can comment on the precision of a statement. This is often mixed up with the comment on truth in the case of continuous scales. The expression "very true", for example, must not be interpreted as indicating a certain degree of truth below 1, but as "true" and "very precise" or the like. This is supported by Hersh & Caramazza (p. 266):

> Intuitively, it appears that the meaning of very large is qualitatively different from very in very British. The former implies an extreme of a continuum, the latter implies a greater emphasis on characteristic features (Lakoff, 1973).

What can be said of "very" in connection with "true", can be transferred to other hedges. For example, in "more or less British" the hedge refers to the presence or absence of certain features, as is the case in "more or less true". Linguistic truth cannot be graded as such. Graded agreements are not "truth"-values, but degrees of certainty pertaining to facts or possibilities.

3.5. ARE THERE "VAGUE INFERENCES"?

The distinctiveness of truth and precision pertaining to a natural language statement has as a consequence that there is no "logic of vagueness". So what about "vague inferences"? I propose, at least, to abandon the term. Logic deals with propositions, which refer to facts or possibilities. Vagueness pertains to descriptions and their adequacy. Thus, vagueness is an intrinsically linguistic concept. Confusion may arise from the fact that natural language statements involving vague descriptive terms are pragmatically ambiguous. Consider the statement:

SHRDLU is a big program.   (s18)

Is this meant to be a description or a factual proposition? It becomes worse if one takes into account another ambiguity: (s18) could be an answer to both questions (s19) and (s20):

What is SHRDLU?   (s19)

What is a big program?   (s20)

(s20) could be part of a conversational test aiming at the definition of the term "big program". This situation is similar to that of Hersh & Caramazza's experiments. The extensional meaning of "big program" could then be made more "precise" by asking the tested person to grade his agreement with statement (s18). Note the important difference: this agreement does not pertain to a factual situation, but to the descriptive adequacy or linguistic applicability of "big program" to SHRDLU. On the other hand, if asked:

Is SHRDLU a big program?   (s21)

he will answer "True", if the applicability is within a certain range. Thus, a formal representation—using the programming language FUZZY (LeFaivre, 1977) as notational device—say,

((BIG-PROGRAM SHRDLU).0·7)

can be interpreted, firstly, as pertaining to the definition of BIG-PROGRAM, secondly, as pertaining to the descriptive adequacy of the predicate "big program" to SHRDLU. The second interpretation can be mixed up with a third one, i.e. taking the attached degree as a degree of uncertainty of the assertion, that SHRDLU is a big program, but this degree does not pertain to the vagueness of the predicate "big". Hence, there can be made no "vague inference" with such assertions using an attached degree.

Somebody may like to have, however, a model of an inference, such as (Wahlster, 1977):

SHRDLU is a very big program.

If a program is big, then it is defective, too.

SHRDLU is a very defective program, too.   (s22)

or perhaps (see Gaines, 1976, p. 624):

Socrates is very healthy.
Healthy men live a long time.
Socrates will live a very long time.   (s23)

But there is no inference with vague concepts. In both cases, there is no factual assertion derived by a logical inference scheme, but by a transformation of the linguistic representation. One could paraphrase (s22) as:

If one can say that a big program is defective
then one can say that a very big program
is very defective.   (s24)

(s23) could be explained and paraphrased similarly. It may be a matter of taste to call such transformations of the linguistic representation of a continuous scale "linguistic inferences" or "vague inferences".

It is possible that in some cases there is a bijective mapping from one measuring scale to another, such that any precisation on one scale corresponds to a precisation on the other scale. Typically, there is a statistical correlation of the underlying measuring variables, i.e. there is uncertainty of factual knowledge involved. There is a subjective and uncertain operation performed on the underlying scales with the result retranslated into vague terms. For example, such vague terms are used for retranslation in Shortliffe's MYCIN system (see example cited above).

Consider the following "vague inference rule":

$$\bigvee x \bigvee y \bigvee z \; near\,(x, y) \wedge near\,(y, z) \Rightarrow near\,(x, z)$$

with a validity of $0 \cdot 7$. If one copes with the special case that all places considered are ordered on a line, one could "infer", for example:

$$near(\text{Bremen}, \text{Hamburg})/0 \cdot 8 \wedge near(\text{Hamburg}, \text{Kiel})/0 \cdot 8 \Rightarrow near(\text{Bremen}, \text{Kiel})/0 \cdot 56$$

using the min function and multiplication according to rule (25). One could verbalize this as:

If Bremen is very near to Hamburg, and Hamburg is very
near to Kiel, then Bremen is fairly near to Kiel.

But this result is counter-intuitive in some contexts, which is due to the general invalidity of "vague inferences" of this sort. What people really can do if given only imprecise information is to get the value or the range of values of the scale referred to by the natural language expression. "Very near", for example, could mean "up to 100 km" (for reaching a place by car for a weekend trip). Then they can get the new range of values for the possible distance of Bremen and Kiel, say, from 20 up to 200 km. From this more imprecise information they can "infer" that Bremen may be fairly near to Kiel as well as it may be rather far from it. Denofsky (1976), concerned exclusively with "near", offers some interesting models of the "transitivity" of "near" using different probabilistic distributions.

There is a similar "inference" given by Bellman & Zadeh (1976):

> X is small
> X and Y are approximately equal
> Then Y is more or less small

Again, the defect is that the "inferred" statement conveys too much precision. Approximately, "more or less small" indicates a range of values away from "very small". Using the vague measuring scales one can only conclude that Y may be "small", "very small" or "more or less small" or the like. Zadeh's numerical operations do not affect the range, but only the "possibility" values within a fixed range. Thus, his retranslation into natural language goes wrong, because "more or less small" does not entail "small" or "very small".

The situation becomes worse if different interpretations of degrees attached to "propositions" are mixed up. Consider a more sophisticated example given by Wahlster (1978): to model the experience of everyday life that

> If x knows y and y knows z, then x may know z, too.

What Wahlster proposes is to infer a degree of possibility of an acquaintance from two degrees of acquaintances using the rule of "fuzzy" logic. As Wahlster concedes, the above inference rule models an experience of everyday life, but he does not conclude that one is concerned with uncertain facts. However, the possibility that x knows z does not depend on the facts that x knows y, and y knows z. Furthermore, nothing can be inferred from degrees of acquaintance, as is done in the above examples. There exists a statistical correlation between the stochastic variable "acquaintance" of two persons measured as frequencies of invitations and the number of common acquaintances or the like. Thus, Wahlster's proposal must be rejected, mainly, because inferences cannot be drawn from the grades pertaining to the definition of a concept referring to a continuous scale. As in the above example, the underlying measures, not the grades of linguistic scales are subject to processing. Beliefs are not constrained to concepts associated with a physical measuring scale. At least, people can give an ordering to objects, to which the concepts are ascribed (Klix, 1976).

Consider another example given by Wahlster (1978), which is used to demonstrate the inferential capabilities of the natural language system HAM-RPM. HAM-RPM is asked, for example:

> Is the parking zone you see to the left tarred?

If it cannot "see" this object, it draws a "vague inference" from its knowledge base, which may contain the following "assertions":

$$((\text{part-of street parking-zone}) . 0 \cdot 9) \tag{a1}$$

$$((\text{subconcept street thoroughfare}) . 1 \cdot 0) \tag{a2}$$

$$((\text{has-property thoroughfare tarred}).0{\cdot}5) \qquad\qquad (\text{a3})$$

From these the following "assertions" are derived:

$$((\text{has-property street tarred}).0{\cdot}5) \qquad\qquad (\text{a4})$$

$$((\text{has-property parking-zone tarred}).0{\cdot}5) \qquad\qquad (\text{a5})$$

What are the possible meanings of the "fuzzy" values? If one assumes the semantic network links to be assertional, it does not seem useful to me, to assume the "fuzzy" values pertaining to possibility. The possibilities should be 1 in each case. If one looks at the inference process, (a1) and (a2) become an implication or a deduction scheme. HAM-RPM applies two inference rules to achieve the goal:

$$(\text{GOAL (has-property parking-zone tarred)})$$

The first derives properties of the subconcept from properties of the superconcept, the second derives properties of a part from properties of the whole. Both inference rules are modelled according to (20) taking the minimum of the "fuzzy" values for the "fuzzy" value attached to the conclusion. Thus, the "fuzzy" values attached to (a1) and (a2) come out to be values of the strength of an implication. The inference of HAM-RPM is clearly not a "vague" inference, as Wahlster calls it, because there is no vagueness of linguistic terms but only uncertainty of factual knowledge involved. It is only the retranslation into natural language, which uses vague terms:

A parking zone is often tarred.

However, the degrees attached cannot be interpreted as certainty degrees either. It is not the subjective belief (that thoroughfares are tarred) which is graded, but it is the probability given as a subjective estimate. Hence, from (a3) one can infer:

$$(\text{has-property thoroughfare not-tarred}).0{\cdot}5$$

Hence, the "inference" as proposed by Wahlster goes wrong. (a1), (a2), and (a3) have to be considered representing independent events, such that:

$$p(\text{a1 a2 a3}) = p(\text{a1}).p(\text{a2}).p(\text{a3}) = 0{\cdot}5.1{\cdot}0.0{\cdot}9$$

i.e.:

$$((\text{has-property parking-zone tarred}).0{\cdot}45)$$

This seems to me the only intuitively possible interpretation, if there is a useful interpretation at all. To finish this section, I would like to consider once more the paradox of the falakros, sorites, etc. There seems to be a straightforward solution by rule (25), similar to that given by Gaines (1976, p. 647). The inference in question is roughly:

> If there is somebody with n hairs, and he is said to be bald, then, if there is somebody else with $n + 1$ hairs, he can be said to be bald, too.

If we ascribe to this inference scheme an agreement probability of 1 as well as to the premises, then, applying the scheme many times, we get the well known paradox. If we concede only a value less than 1 to the inference scheme, we can compute the agreement probability of the conclusions according to (25). The agreement probability diminishes each time the rule is applied, which has some intuitive appeal. However, there is a serious shortcoming of this "solution". Although the agreement probability of the conclusion diminishes, the opposite "full hair" is never asserted to any degree, because, as has been pointed out above, its applicability cannot be inferred from the inapplicability of its antonym.

People know that the invalidity of the conclusion in the falakros paradox is due to the vagueness of the terms involved (Weiss, 1976). The fallacy is recognizable as such, because there is some awareness of linguistic facts, although not everybody can give an account of it. The "facts" are as follows.

The "difference of one hair" cannot be perceived by glancing at somebody's head. Even the perception of one hair would lead to the same problem of continuity. There could be introduced several stages of development from "full hair" to "total baldness" described by hedged expressions. But this partitioning of the continuum is not fine enough to discriminate between recognizable stages of development. But even this ordered set of developmental stages cannot cope with the difference of one hair. Thus, there will always be a borderline case, and variability of behaviour of individuals and populations as to the classification of objects. Thus, the paradox derives from the inadequate interpretation of the "implication", which is meant to indicate that one hair makes no difference as to the applicability of the concept "bald". Thus, the statement is metalinguistic; it does not refer to objects but to the applicability of concepts to objects. Consequently, no inferences in the object language can be drawn from it. This may be considered as a "fuzzy" analogy to the well known paradox of the "lying Cretian".

4. Concluding remarks

The foregoing exposition of an alternative, although not entirely new, foundation of reasoning with graded agreement values is not only motivated from a logician's but also from a linguist's point of view. I can neither accept Zadeh's modelling of truth nor his modelling of "linguistic" reasoning. I do not judge here the soundness of the theory of fuzzy sets, although it appears to me that the concept of "degree of membership" should be explored further.

Zadeh's as well as Shortliffe's models of "fuzzy" reasoning have some formal deficiencies. If the model of agreement probability is taken as a mathematical base the deficiencies indicated above vanish.

Another question is the epistemic interpretation of graded agreement. In this respect I agree with Shortliffe: graded agreement is due to uncertainty, i.e. there is only belief, not knowledge. On the other hand, there is no intuitive reason to conceive of a graded truth value. Truth corresponds epistemologically to the case of total certainty. An important consequence of this interpretation is that, from a graded agreement associated with a conjecture, an agreement degree pertaining to its negation cannot be computed.

I do not deny that "vagueness" is a language universal as proposed by the Prague Linguistic Circle (see Gaines & Kohout, 1977). However, Zadeh's fuzzy-algorithmic approach cannot cope with the complexity of the phenomenon. At least two aspects of vagueness should be distinguished; the inherent vagueness of all classificational terms and expressions referring to continuous scales, and the uncertainty of the meaning of vague terms due to the statistical variability in communication. Things get even more complicated if one takes into account the variability of cognition, especially in socio-cultural contexts. These factors may be the most important for the change of language in time, which is one of the prevailing themes of the Prague Linguistic Circle.

I do not agree with the assumption that reasoning with vague concepts is purely "linguistic". People perform operations on underlying measuring scales or orderings of objects, if they are dealing with complex expressions involving vague concepts. This gives rise to a general awareness of the vagueness or imprecision of most descriptive terms. Thus, it is quite usual in human communication to comment on the precision of statements. This establishes the metalinguistic character of communication with vague terms. The findings of Hersh & Caramazza give strong support to such an interpretation.

Zadeh's approach fails on several grounds, as has been pointed out. I should like to stress one point here. Zadeh does not distinguish "vagueness" and "uncertainty" in a sufficient manner. This confusion may be reinforced by his concept of linguistic "possibility". One should constrain the meaning of this term to the meaning which it has in modal logic. Then it becomes clear that graded agreement pertains to certainty of factual as well as possibilistic propositions. "Degree of possibility" as introduced by Zadeh should be labeled "certainty degree of applicability". Thus, linguistic "uncertainty" corresponding to "vagueness", and factual "uncertainty" can be clearly distinguished. Uncertainty of "applicability" of a predicate is just a special application case of the former. Unfortunately, Zadeh's concept of a fuzzy set lacks the formal properties and his "linguistic" approach does not exhibit the explanatory power to cope with this phenomenon. Even such "nice solutions" as proposed for the sorites paradox must be rejected.

I have to thank Wolfgang Wahlster, who awakened my interest in the field and discussed the topic with me many times. I also thank Wilfried Brauer, Michael Brodie (Toronto), Karl-Juergen Hanssmann, Manfred Kudlek and H.-H. Nagel who made suggestions for the improvement of a preliminary version of this paper.

References

BAUER, H. (1968). *Wahrscheinlichkeitstheorie und Grundzuege der Masstheorie*. Berlin: de Gruyter.

BELLMAN, R. E. & ZADEH, L. A. (1976). Local and fuzzy logics. In DUNN, J. M. & EPSTEIN, G. Eds, *Modern Uses of Multiple-valued Logic*. Dordrecht: D. Reidel, pp. 105–166.

DENOFSKY, M. E. (1976). How near is near? *AI Memo No. 344*. Massachusetts: MIT.

DUDA, R. O., HART, P. E. & NILSSON, N. J. (1976). Subjective Bayesian method for rule-based inference systems. *Technical Note 124*. Stanford Research Institute, Menlo Park. January.

GAINES, B. R. (1976). Foundations of fuzzy reasoning. *International Journal of Man–Machine Studies*, **8**, 623–668.

GAINES, B. R. & KOHOUT, L. J. (1977). The fuzzy decade: a bibliography of fuzzy systems and closely related topics. *International Journal of Man–Machine Studies*, **9**, 1–68.

GOGUEN, J. A. (1974). Concept representation in natural and artificial languages: axioms, extensions and applications for fuzzy sets. *International Journal of Man–Machine Studies*, **6**, 513–561.

HAYES, P. J. (1974). Some problems and non-problems in representation theory. In *AISB Summer Conference, Proceedings*. University of Sussex, pp. 63–79.

HERSH, H. M. & CARAMAZZA, A. (1976). A fuzzy set approach to modifiers and vagueness in natural language. *Journal of Experimental Psychology: General*, **105**, 254–276.

KAYSER, D., BONNET, A. & JACOB, F. (1977). Natural language comprehension based on approximate reasoning. In AKNIM, Y. et al., Eds, Report No. 77-R-016. Knowledge Representation and Approximate Reasoning for Natural Language Comprehension. Centre de Recherche en Informatique de Nancy (France).

KLING, R. (1973). FUZZY PLANNER. Computer inexactness in a procedural problem-solving language. Technical Report No. 168. University of Wisconsin, Computer Science Department.

KLIX, F. (1976). Ueber Grundstrukturen und Funktionsprinzipien kognitiver Prozesse. In KLIX, F., Ed., Psychologische Beitraege zur Analyse kognitiver Prozesse. Berlin: VEB Deutscher Verlag der Wissenschaften, pp. 9–56.

KUTCHERA, F. v. (1976). Einfuehrung in die intensionale Semantik. Berlin: de Gruyter.

LABOV, W. (1970). The study of language in its social context. Studium Generale, 23, 30–87.

LAKOFF, G. (1973). Hedges: a study in meaning criteria and the logic of fuzzy concepts. Journal of Philosophical Logic, 2, 458–508.

LEE, R. C. T. (1972). Fuzzy logic and the resolution principle. Journal of the Association for Computing Machinery, 19, 109–119.

LEFAIVRE, R. A. (1977). FUZZY Reference Manual. Rutgers University, Computer Science Department.

MESCHKOWSKI, H. (1968). Wahrscheinlichkeitsrechnung. Mannheim: Bibliographisches Institut.

OSGOOD, C. E., SUCI, G. & TANNENBAUM, P. H. (1957). The Measurement of Meaning. Urbana: University of Illinois Press.

SANCHEZ, E. (1978). On the possibility qualification in natural languages. Information Sciences, 15, 45–76.

SANFORD, D. H. (1976). Competing semantics of vagueness: many values versus super-truth. Synthese, 33, 195–210.

SCHEFE, P. (1975). Statistische syntaktische Analyse von Fachsprachen. Geoppingen: Kuemmerle.

SHORTLIFFE, E. H. (1974). MYCIN: a rule-based computer program for advising physicians regarding antimicrobial therapy selection. Memo 251, STAN-CS-74-465. Stanford University, AI Laboratory.

SINOWJEW, A. A. (1968). Ueber mehrwertige Logik. Ein Abriss. Berlin (East): VEB Verlag der Wissenschaften.

TERANO, T. & SUGENO, M. (1975). Conditional fuzzy measures and their applications. In ZADEH, L. A., FU, K. S., TANAKA, K. & SHIMURA, M., Eds, Fuzzy Sets and Their Applications to Cognitive Problems. New York: Academic Press, pp. 151–170.

WAHLSTER, W. (1977). Die Repraesentation von vagem Wissen in natuerlichsprachlichen Systemen der kuenstlichen Intelligenz. Bericht IfI-H-B-38/77. Universitaet Hamburg.

WAHLSTER, W. (1978). Die Simulation vager Inferenzen auf unscharfem Wissen: Eine Anwendung der mehrwertigen Programmiersprache FUZZY, HAM-RPM. Bericht No. 5. Universitaet Hamburg, Germanisches Seminar. (Also to appear in: UECKERT, H. & RHENIUS, D., Eds, Komplexe menschliche Informationsverarbeitung. Beitraege zur Tagung "Kognitive Psychologie" in Hamburg. Bern: Huber.)

WECHSLER, H. (1975). Applications of fuzzy logic to medical diagnosis. Proceedings of the 1975 International Symposium on Multiple-Valued Logic. Indiana University, Bloomington, pp. 162–174.

WEISS, S. E. (1976). The sorites fallacy: what difference does a peanut make? Synthese, 33, 253–272.

ZADEH, L. A. (1968). Probability measures of fuzzy events. Journal of Mathematical Analysis and Applications, 23, 421–427.

ZADEH, L. A. (1976). A fuzzy-algorithmic approach to the definition of complex or imprecise concepts. International Journal of Man–Machine Studies, 8, 249–291.

ZADEH, L. A. (1977). PRUF—a meaning representation language for natural languages. Report ERL-M77/61. University of California.

ZADEH, L. A. (1978). Fuzzy sets as a basis for the theory of possibility. Fuzzy Sets and Systems, 1, 3–28.

Part II

Semantics of implication operators and fuzzy relational products

Wyllis Bandler

Department of Mathematics, University of Essex, Colchester CO4 3SQ, U.K.

AND

Ladislav J. Kohout†

University College Hospital Medical School, London W.C.1, U.K. and Man-Machine Sytems Laboratory, Department of Electrical Engineering Science, University of Essex, Colchester CO4 3SQ, U.K.

(*Received May 1979*)

After a brief discussion of the need for *fuzzy relation theory* in practical systems work, the paper explains the new *triangle products of relations* and the sort of results to be expected from them, starting from a crisp situation. The asymmetry of these products, in contrast to correlation, is noted as essential to the investigation of hierarchial dependencies. The panoply of multi-valued implication operators, with which the fuzzification of these products can be accomplished, is presented, and a few of their properties noted. Then, most importantly, a *checklist paradigm* is given, by which entirely new light is thrown upon the semantics of these operators, connecting them, in a unified way, with measures which might be made upon more refined data. Using a well-known psychological test in an actual situation, so that the finer structure is in fact available, a comparison is made between a checklist measure and several of the operator values, showing the interrelationship concretely. Finally, some products and their interpretations are presented, using further real-world data.

1. Motivation: possibility theories: containment of data structures

The difficulties of saying anything meaningful about a system increase enormously with its complexity. The vogue for, and success of, statistical methods are evidence of one way of doing this. Here we are concerned with quite another, the *possibilistic* (Gaines & Kohout, 1975, 1976; Zadeh, 1977; Bandler & Kohout, 1976*b*), rather than the probabilistic way.

In any real-world situation our information about a system is too voluminous and intricate, and needs to be summarized; or it is approximate from the very beginning. A scientist, attempting to analyze such a system, implicitly asserts his belief that a number of significant things can be said about the system—could they only be found! In his attempt to analyze a real-world system, he is working with a model of it, simplified so as to be manageable and comprehensible. The danger of the assumption that this model can always be deterministic has been demonstrated by Gaines (1976).

In general, it can be said that unwarranted structural assumptions imposed on the working model can lead to dangerous artifacts that do not reflect anything that is contained in the real-world data; this leads consequently to totally meaningless results

† Parkinson's Disease Society Research Fellow, Department of Neurology, University College Hospital, London. This opportunity is taken to thank the Society for financial support towards this research.

of the analysis masquerading as "scientific truth". On the other hand, rejecting such strong unwarranted assumptions, we may still be able to provide some meaningful answers to our questions such as: What structural relationships between the individual items of the analyzed data *must* exist? Which ones *may* exist? Which *cannot* exist? Which may exist perhaps *if*...? These modal terms in which we all think, but which we usually rule out in our "scientific discourse", are in fact the proper terms for *possibilistic systems*.

Possibility theory can be *crisp*: any given structure, say, may be utterly (1) or not at all (0) contained in another structure. More attractive and more consonant with summarized data from the real world, however, is *fuzzy* possibilistic theory: here the degree to which X can be contained in Y is (estimated as) some number from 0 to 1 inclusive. This may sound like a probability, but it is not. The quickest way to see this is from the fact that entirely different operations are performed on these *fuzzy degrees* than are performed on probabilities; this reflects, of course, a deeper semantic and epistemological difference, on which there is a large literature, of which Zadeh (1977) and Gaines (1975) are particularly illuminating.

The topic to which this paper is addressed can be formulated as follows: what is the degree of possibility that a data structure (or a family of data structures) A is contained in (implies) the data structure (the family of data structures) B? It is our contention that *fuzzy relation theory* is the proper mathematical implement to be used for the structural analysis of the real-world data. Elsewhere (Bandler & Kohout, 1978*a,b*, 1979*a,b,c*) we have investigated various aspects of this relation theory. These investigations lead us to the following conclusions.

(1) There exist many distinct meaningful ways of defining the containment of one fuzzy structure in another; these depend on the choice of a particular implication operator for the fuzzy power-set theory in hand (Bandler & Kohout, 1978*a*, 1979*b*; Wilmott, 1978, 1979*a*).

(2) The choice of the semantic properties of a particular implication operator depends on some pragmatic consideration (Carnap, 1943) determined by the methodological questions of a particular application.

(3) In the real-world applications we are forced to determine the value of the membership function of the possibility distribution—this necessitates introducing an observer as estimator of the membership function.

Our attempts to deal with the problems raised by the points (1), (2) and (3) above lead us to the formulations presented in this paper.

Sections 2 and 3 of this paper deal with the transition from crisp to fuzzy relational products. Various ways of fuzzification and the reasons for their choice are discussed in section 4—*Panoply of fuzzy implication operators* and section 5—*Contrapositive symmetry*. A useful theoretical construct *"The checklist paradigm"*, through which the action of an observer— estimator of the membership function— can be described, is discussed in sections 6 and 7. In practice, we do not know, or abstract from, the detailed structure of the checklist, hence we cannot specify the exact value of an implication measure but only its bounds (cf. section 6), or we can determine it for the statistically expected situation (cf. section 7). The values so found and the relations among them are of the greatest interest. The checklist paradigm has been motivated by the work of Gaines (1976*a,b,c*) and Giles (1976) on the one hand, and by the concept of a checklist used in psychology (Guilford, 1954; Zuckermann, 1960), on the other hand. Section

8 presents an example of a real-world application of the checklist paradigm on psychological data, and compares the theoretical bounds on implication operators with the empirically obtained values extracted directly from the experimental data of the example. Finally, section 9 demonstrates the use of fuzzy possibilistic theory (and of fuzzy relational products) in the analysis of clinical data—of motivation and psychomotor profiles of patients with Parkinson's disease undergoing a physiotherapy treatment. This example clearly demonstrates that the profile of an individual patient, or a very small group of patients, with not enough data to be analyzed statistically, can be meaningfully analyzed by fuzzy possibilistic methods.

Many insights are inseparable from concreteness; to promote them, we present the entire theoretical apparatus here in terms of the type of data we have mentioned. It is as if this material were the motive for the theoretical constructions. It will be clear, however, that the theory is in fact an extremely general one—indeed, it is to be hoped that the reader will furnish different examples, and employ our methods on quite other material.

The authors are indeted to Dennis J. G. Farlie for helpful verbal communications about contingency tables.

2. Relational products in the crisp case

We are in possession of fuzzy data of a certain kind. Throughout this paper a leading thread is the attempt to deal with these data in a meaningful way. They concern 5 Parkinsonian patients, observed at intervals over a period of 10 weeks at University College Hospital, London by 2 female physiotherapists, under the supervision of one of the authors (Kohout). On each occasion, each of the patients was assessed, independently, by each of the therapists, under 8 headings; we give at least temporarily, the name of *construct* Ci to the positive pole of each of these assessments, and *symptom* $\bar{C}i$ to the negative pole. The actual rating sheet and further details are shown in Fig. 1.

The result, on each occasion t, of the assessment by therapist θa is a relation $R^{(a)}(t)$, given by a matrix of which the ij-component $R_{ij}^{(a)}(t)$ is *the degree to which the construct* Ci *is attributed to the patient* Pj. The inverse $R^{(a)-1}(t)$ of this relation is a relation from patients to constructs where $R_{jm}^{(a)-1}(t)$ is the degree to which (at time t, by therapist a) *patient* Pj *was considered to exemplify construct* Cm.

Given two such relations, $R^{(a)-1}(t)$ and $R^{(a')}(t)$, where therapist a' may or may not be the same as a, we can make 2 extremely interesting comparisons, by forming 2 *triangular products* of the relations. The first of these gives us a relation from patients to patients, defined as follows: the relation $U^{(a,a')}(t) = R^{(a)-1}(t) \lhd R^{(a')}(t)$ has for its jm component $U_{jm}^{(a,a')}(t)$ the *degree to which the attribution (by therapist a) of constructs to Pj implies their attribution (by therapist a') to Pm*. To understand this product, let us assume to begin with that the original data is crisp, that is to say binary: constructs are always attributed either entirely (with value 1) or not at all (with value 0). Then the attribution by a to Pj of construct Ck implies its attribution by a' to Pm, to the degree 0 or 1 given by the classical table for the material implication $R_{jk}^{(a)-1} \rightarrow R_{km}^{(a')}$, namely

$R_{jk}^{(a)-1}$ $\backslash$ $R_{km}^{(a')}$	0	1
0	1	1
1	0	1

Date : 5.10.78   Name :

	3	2	1	0	1	2	3	
almost normal ability		✓						disabled
difficult to cope with		✓						easy to cope with
independent			✓					dependent
cheerful					✓			depressed
almost healthy		✓						very ill
apathetic and unconcerned			✓					interested and exploring
accepting your advice					✓			rejecting your advice
anxious and worried		✓						calm and secure

Date :   Name :

	3	2	1	0	1	2	3	
almost normal ability		✓						disabled
difficult to cope with						✓		easy to cope with
independent			✓					dependent
cheerful		✓						depressed
almost healthy		✓						very ill
apathetic and unconcerned						✓		interested and exploring
accepting your advice		✓						rejecting your advice
anxious and worried			✓					calm and secure

Date :   Name :

		3	2	1	0	1	2	3	
almost normal ability	1	+						−	disabled
difficult to cope with	2	−						+	easy to cope with
independent	3	+						−	dependent
cheerful	7	+						−	depressed
almost healthy	6	+						−	very ill
apathetic and unconcerned	4	−						+	interested and exploring
accepting your advice	5	+						−	rejecting your advice
anxious and worried	8	−						+	calm and secure

List of symptoms	List of constructs
$\bar{C}1$: disabled	C1: almost normal ability
$\bar{C}2$: difficult to cope with	C2: easy to cope with
$\bar{C}3$: dependent	C3: independent
$\bar{C}4$: apathetic and unconcerned	C4: interested and exploring
$\bar{C}5$: rejecting advice	C5: accepting advice
$\bar{C}6$: very ill	C6: almost healthy
$\bar{C}7$: depressed	C7: cheerful
$\bar{C}8$: anxious and worried	C8: calm and secure

FIG. 1. Rating sheet, symptoms and constructs.

The mean value of this over the 8 constructs is plausibly to be taken as the degree we seek, that is, the degree to which attributions by a to Pj imply attributions by a' to Pm. This idea is embodied in the formula

$$(\mathbf{R}^{(a)^{-1}}(t) \lhd \mathbf{R}^{(a')}(t))_{jm} = \frac{1}{N_k} \sum_k (\mathbf{R}_{jk}^{(a)^{-1}}(t) \to \mathbf{R}_{km}^{(a')}(t)).$$

(Elsewhere (Bandler & Kohout, 1978, 1979b) the present authors have considered a harsher criterion, in which the infimum is taken instead of the mean; it is hoped that the reader will agree that the present formulation is more suitable to the actual material.)

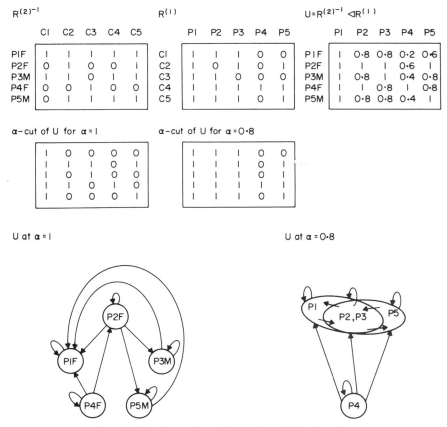

$R^{(2)^{-1}}$	C1	C2	C3	C4	C5
P1F	1	1	1	1	1
P2F	0	1	0	0	1
P3M	1	1	0	1	1
P4F	0	0	1	0	0
P5M	0	1	1	1	1

$R^{(1)}$	P1	P2	P3	P4	P5
C1	1	1	1	0	0
C2	1	0	1	0	1
C3	1	1	0	0	0
C4	1	1	1	1	1
C5	1	1	1	0	1

$U = R^{(2)^{-1}} \lhd R^{(1)}$	P1	P2	P3	P4	P5
P1F	1	0·8	0·8	0·2	0·6
P2F	1	1	1	0·6	1
P3M	1	0·8	1	0·4	0·8
P4F	1	1	0·8	1	0·8
P5M	1	0·8	0·8	0·4	1

α–cut of U for $\alpha = 1$

1	0	0	0	0
1	1	1	0	1
1	0	1	0	0
1	1	0	1	0
1	0	0	0	1

α–cut of U for $\alpha = 0·8$

1	1	1	0	0
1	1	1	0	1
1	1	1	0	1
1	1	1	1	1
1	1	1	0	1

U at $\alpha = 1$

U at $\alpha = 0·8$

FIG. 2. Triangle product with (artificially) Boolean data.

Figure 2 shows (for $t = 22$ September 1978) $R^{(2)^{-1}}$ and $R^{(1)}$, "crispified" from our actual data, and their product $R^{(2)^{-1}} \lhd R^{(1)}$. These are illustrative and not to be taken unduly seriously, although as a matter of fact certain gross features emerge which are also to be found in our more subtle analyses later. Because these calculations are done by hand at this stage, we have reduced the number of constructs from 8 to 5; the "crispification" consisted in α-cuts (see below) at the values 0·7 for $R^{(2)}$ and 0·6 for $R^{(1)}$, near their respective means.

The product $R^{(2)^{-1}} \lhd R^{(1)}$ is, of course, a fuzzy relation from patients to patients; it tells the degree to which $\theta2$'s attributions of good qualities to a patient implies $\theta1$'s attributions to another. To interpret it, one takes α-cuts at various levels (Negoiţă & Ralescu, 1975), that is one temporarily considers values of α and above as being 1, values below α as being 0. Each α-cut is an ordinary crisp relation, of which two are shown in the figure, both as matrices and as diagrams. The salient feature of the top cut at $\alpha = 1$ is that P1F is a universal sink, to whom everybody is related but who is related to no-one but herself; for this relation that means that what $\theta2$ attributes to anyone, $\theta1$ attributes to P1F, but what $\theta2$ attributes to P1F, $\theta1$ need not attribute to anyone else. The other patients all have both ingoing and outcoming arrows, except P4F who, except for a loop to herself, has only outgoings. In the α-cut at $0\cdot8$, near the matrix mean, this patient has become a universal source: whatever good features $\theta2$ finds in her, $\theta1$ finds in everybody. At this α-level, P2F and P3M have fused, in the sense that they occupy identical positions in the network (see Lorrain & White, 1971; Lorrain, 1975; Bandler, 1977), as can be seen from the fact that they have identical rows and identical columns; P1F and P5M are each reciprocally related to them, but not to each other; P4 as we have said is a universal source.

Formed in a similar way, but giving a relation from *constructs to constructs* is the triangle product $R^{(a)} \lhd R^{(a')^{-1}}$, given by

$$(R^{(a)} \lhd R^{(a')^{-1}})_{ik} = \frac{1}{N_j} \sum_j (R^{(a)}_{ij} \to R^{(a')^{-1}}_{jk}).$$

Here the mean is taken over the patients, and the ik-component is *the degree to which the attribution by a of Ci implied (at time t) the attribution by a' of Ck*. To illustrate this, we have kept it to one therapist.

Figure 3 shows $R^{(2)} \lhd R^{(2)^{-1}}$ and 2 interpretative α-cuts and their diagrams.

For $\alpha = 1$, C2 ("easy to cope with") and C5 ("accepting advice") have identical network positions, fusing as the top of a partial order (excluding C3, a total order), with C1 ("almost normal ability") at the bottom, and C4 ("interested and exploring") in between.

According to therapist 2 (at least on that occasion, with those patients, and at this level), "independence" was independent (sic!) of the other constructs, while "ability", via "interest", implied all the others. For $\alpha = 0\cdot8$, the picture is more complicated. Clearly, a rich field awaits this kind of product in investigating the cognitive hierarchy of an observer, or the comparison of those of different observers.

It is clear that there is a scope for this kind of relational product in which the implications are averaged, for one patient, over various times, or over patient-times, that is various patients at various times, or over construct-times (all constructs at all times). Some of these variants will appear later, but first we must tackle the problems (or welcome the opportunities) that appear when it is recognized that the original data is not crisp but fuzzy.

3. Fuzzification of the relational products: introduction of multi-valued implication operators

The previous section has shown 2 kinds of example of a potentially meaningful *triangle product* of relations. Beginning with 2 assumedly crisp relations, we obtained a fuzzy

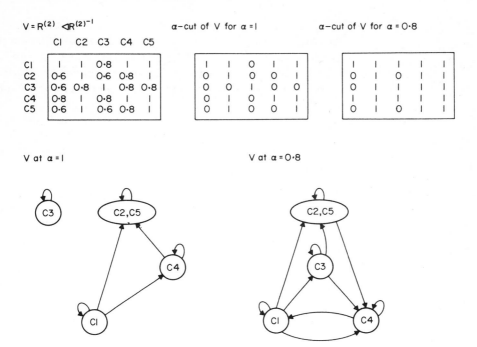

$V = R^{(2)} \lhd R^{(2)^{-1}}$ α−cut of V for α =1   α−cut of V for α = 0·8

	C1	C2	C3	C4	C5
C1	1	1	0·8	1	1
C2	0·6	1	0·6	0·8	1
C3	0·6	0·8	1	0·8	0·8
C4	0·8	1	0·8	1	1
C5	0·6	1	0·6	0·8	1

1	1	0	1	1
0	1	0	0	1
0	0	1	0	0
0	1	0	1	1
0	1	0	0	1

1	1	1	1	1
0	1	0	1	1
0	1	1	1	1
1	1	1	1	1
0	1	0	1	1

V at α = 1   V at α = 0·8

FIG. 3. Another triangle product with the (artificially) Boolean data.

relation in the outcome. Now we must remove the artificial restriction to crisp beginnings; in so doing we will become able to treat what are in fact our original data.

Let us suppose that, in the multi-valued logic of the unit interval $I = [0, 1]$, we have a *fuzzy implication operator* →, which extends the classical material implication which was used in section 2. Such an operation is a mapping from $I \times I$ into I which agrees at the corners $(0, 0)$, $(0, 1)$, $(1, 0)$, $(1, 1)$ with the Boolean one.

Then, whenever R is a fuzzy relation from finite crisp universe U_1 to finite crisp universe U_2, that is, as usually put, a fuzzy subset of $U_1 \times U_2$, and S is a fuzzy relation from U_2 to U_3 (a fuzzy subset of $U_2 \times U_3$), we can construct their triangle product $R \lhd S$, which will be a fuzzy relation from U_1 to U_3 (fuzzy subset of $U_1 \times U_3$) by the formula

$$(R \lhd S)_{ik} = \frac{1}{N_j} \sum_j (R_{ij} \rightarrow S_{jk}). \tag{3.1}$$

This product is entirely different from the usual circlet product of relations, given by the maximin formula

$$(R \circ S)_{ik} = \bigvee_j (R_{ij} \wedge S_{jk}). \tag{3.2}$$

For one thing, the circlet product is symmetric, whereas the triangle product is typically non-symmetric; indeed, this feature of the triangle product is in itself an innovation with important consequences.

Because of the agreement at the crisp corners, this formula will agree with those considered in the previous section whenever the relations R and S happen to be crisp. We are thus dealing with a true generalization. The meaning of the product will not change; that is, indeed, the purpose of the exercise. Where, as is in fact the case, the relations $R^{(a')}$ and $R^{(a)^{-1}}$ are fuzzy to begin with, the triangle products will still bear the interpretations given to them before: $(R^{(a)^{-1}} \triangleleft R^{(a')})_{jm}$ is intended to be *the (mean) degree to which the attribution by a of constructs to Pj implies their attribution by a' to Pm*, and $(R^{(a')} \triangleleft R^{(a)^{-1}})_{ik}$ *the degree to which the attribution by a of Ci implies the attribution by a' of Ck.*

Another, equivalent, way of reading the triangle product is of considerable theoretical importance. The *afterset* $a R$ of $a \in U_1$ is the fuzzy subset of U_2 consisting of those $y \in U_2$ to which a is related, each, of course, with its degree, thus given by its membership function μ_{aR}, with

$$\mu_{aR}(y) = \mu_R(a, y).$$

Similarly, the *foreset* Sc of $c \in U_3$ is the fuzzy subset of U_2 consisting of those $y \in U_2$ which are related to c, each with its degree of intensity, thus with a μ_{Sc} given by

$$\mu_{Sc}(y) = \mu_S(y, c).$$

The *mean degree to which a R is a subset of Sc* is plausibly defined as the *mean degree to which membership in a R implies membership in Sc*,

$$\pi_m(a R \subseteq Sc) = \frac{1}{N_{U_2}} \sum_y (\mu_{aR}(y) \rightarrow \mu_{Sc}(y)).$$

Then it can be seen that this degree is the same as the degree to which a is related to c by $R \triangleleft S$:

$$\pi(a R \subseteq Sc) = \mu_{R \triangleleft S}(a, c).$$

(In the matrix notation,

$$\pi(a_i R \subseteq Sc_k) = (R \triangleleft S)_{ik}.)$$

This fact explains the close connection between fuzzy power-set theory and fuzzy implication operators, which have been investigated together in Bandler & Kohout (1978, 1979b) and Willmott (1978), with "harsh criterion", and in Willmott (1979b) with "mean criterion". It also throws further light on the connection between both of these topics and the triangle product.

Needless to say, in all cases, the actual values of the triangle product-relations, and perhaps the plausibility and the sensitivity with which they support the interpretation which they are designed to bear, will depend upon the particular implication operator which is used to compute them. At first sight (even at second sight), there are surprisingly many distinct fuzzy implication operators with a claim on our attention. To them we must now turn, not with the intention of picking a uniquely well-endowed one for universal use—for there seems to be none such—but with a view to examining and comparing their properties, so that users may know as much as possible about whichever they choose to employ.

4. Panoply of fuzzy implication operators

In Bandler & Kohout (1978, 1979b) the present authors assembled 6 fuzzy implication operators from the multi-valued logic literature (Rescher, 1969; Gaines, 1976) and examined their elementary properties, chiefly from the point of view of fuzzy power-set theory. R. C. Willmott (1978) did the same for a 7th operator which had been put to early use by Zadeh (1973), and an 8th operator of his own invention. These 8, and a certain variant of one of them, are presented in Table 1, in order of increasing fuzziness. Table 2 shows how they look when tabulated for the 11-valued decile set with which our actual calculations all begin. They are certainly remarkably various; almost all they have in common is their agreement at the Boolean corners. (For sources and other comments, see the references just cited.)

Before presenting the operators, it is useful to have the following definition.

4.1. DEFINITION

The *crispness* of $a \in [0, 1]$ is $\kappa a = a \vee (1-a)$. The crispness varies from 0.5 (for $a = 0 \cdot 5$) up to 1 (for $a = 1$ and for $a = 0$).

TABLE 1

Implication operators

1. S #   Standard Sharp

$$a \to_1 b = \begin{cases} 1 & \text{iff } a \neq 1 \text{ or } b = 1 \\ 0 & \text{otherwise.} \end{cases}$$

2. S   Standard Strict

$$a \to_2 b = \begin{cases} 1 & \text{iff } a \leq b \\ 0 & \text{otherwise.} \end{cases}$$

3. S*   Standard Star

$$a \to_3 b = \begin{cases} 1 & \text{iff } a \leq b \\ b & \text{otherwise.} \end{cases}$$

4. G43   Gaines 43

$$a \to_4 b = \min\left(1, \frac{b}{a}\right).$$

4'. G43'   Modified Gaines 43

$$a \to_{4'} b = \min\left(1, \frac{b}{a}, \frac{1-a}{1-b}\right).$$

5. Ł Łukasiewicz

$$a \to_5 b = \min(1, 1-a+b).$$

6. KD   Kleene–Dienes

$$a \to_6 b = (1-a) \vee b.$$

7. EZ   Early Zadeh

$$a \to_7 b = (a \wedge b) \vee (1-a)$$
$$= (a \to_6 b) \wedge \kappa a.$$

8. W Willmott

$$a \to_8 b = ((1-a) \vee b) \wedge (a \vee (1-b) \vee (b \wedge (1-a)))$$
$$= (a \to_7 b) \wedge \kappa b$$
$$= (a \to_6 b) \wedge \kappa a \wedge \kappa b.$$

TABLE 2
Values of the implication operators on the decile set V_{11}

$\longrightarrow_1$ $S^{\#}$

	0	0·1	0·2	0·3	0·4	0·5	0·6	0·7	0·8	0·9	1
0	I	I	I	I	I	I	I	I	I	I	I
0·1	I	I	I	I	I	I	I	I	I	I	I
0·2	I	I	I	I	I	I	I	I	I	I	I
0·3	I	I	I	I	I	I	I	I	I	I	I
0·4	I	I	I	I	I	I	I	I	I	I	I
0·5	I	I	I	I	I	I	I	I	I	I	I
0·6	I	I	I	I	I	I	I	I	I	I	I
0·7	I	I	I	I	I	I	I	I	I	I	I
0·8	I	I	I	I	I	I	I	I	I	I	I
0·9	I	I	I	I	I	I	I	I	I	I	I
I	0	0	0	0	0	0	0	0	0	0	I

$\longrightarrow_2$ S

	0	0·1	0·2	0·3	0·4	0·5	0·6	0·7	0·8	0·9	1
0	I	I	I	I	I	I	I	I	I	I	I
0·1	0	I	I	I	I	I	I	I	I	I	I
0·2	0	0	I	I	I	I	I	I	I	I	I
0·3	0	0	0	I	I	I	I	i	I	I	I
0·4	0	0	0	0	I	I	I	I	I	I	I
0·5	0	0	0	0	0	I	I	I	I	I	I
0·6	0	0	0	0	0	0	I	I	I	I	I
0·7	0	0	0	0	0	0	0	I	I	I	I
0·8	0	0	0	0	0	0	0	0	I	I	I
0·9	0	0	0	0	0	0	0	0	0	I	I
I	0	0	0	0	0	0	0	0	0	0	I

$\longrightarrow_3$ S^{*}

	0	0·1	0·2	0·3	0·4	0·5	0·6	0·7	0·8	0·9	1
0	I	I	I	I	I	I	I	I	I	I	I
0·1	0	I	I	I	I	I	I	I	I	I	I
0·2	0	0·1	I	I	I	I	I	I	I	I	I
0·3	0	0·1	0·2	I	I	I	I	I	I	I	I
0·4	0	0·1	0·2	0·3	I	I	I	I	I	I	I
0·5	0	0·1	0·2	0·3	0·4	I	I	I	I	I	I
0·6	0	0·1	0·2	0·3	0·4	0·5	I	I	I	I	I
0·7	0	0·1	0·2	0·3	0·4	0·5	0·6	I	I	I	I
0·8	0	0·1	0·2	0·3	0·4	0·5	0·6	0·7	I	I	I
0·9	0	0·1	0·2	0·3	0·4	0·5	0·6	0·7	0·8	I	I
I	0	0·1	0·2	0·3	0·4	0·5	0·6	0·7	0·8	0·9	I

$\longrightarrow_4$ $G43$

	0	0·1	0·2	0·3	0·4	0·5	0·6	0·7	0·8	0·9	1
0	I	I	I	I	I	I	I	I	I	I	I
0·1	0	I	I	I	I	I	I	I	I	I	I
0·2	0	0·5	I	I	I	I	I	I	I	I	I
0·3	0	0·33	0·67	I	I	I	I	I	I	I	I
0·4	0	0·25	0·5	0·75	I	I	I	I	I	I	I
0·5	0	0·2	0·4	0·6	0·8	I	I	I	I	I	I
0·6	0	0·17	0·33	0·5	0·67	0·83	I	I	I	I	I
0·7	0	0·14	0·29	0·43	0·57	0·71	0·86	I	I	I	I
0·8	0	0·13	0·25	0·38	0·5	0·63	0·75	0·88	I	I	I
0·9	0	0·11	0·22	0·33	0·44	0·56	0·67	0·78	0·89	I	I
I	0	0·1	0·2	0·3	0·4	0·5	0·6	0·7	0·8	0·9	I

$\longrightarrow_{4'}$ $G43'$

	0	0·1	0·2	0·3	0·4	0·5	0·6	0·7	0·8	0·9	1
0	I	I	I	I	I	I	I	I	I	I	I
0·1	0	I	I	I	I	I	I	I	I	I	I
0·2	0	0·5	I	I	I	I	I	I	I	I	I
0·3	0	0·33	0·67	I	I	I	I	I	I	I	I
0·4	0	0·25	0·5	0·75	I	I	I	I	I	I	I
0·5	0	0·2	0·4	0·6	0·8	I	I	I	I	I	I
0·6	0	0·17	0·33	0·5	0·67	0·8	I	I	I	I	I
0·7	0	0·14	0·29	0·43	0·5	0·6	0·75	I	I	I	I
0·8	0	0·13	0·25	0·29	0·33	0·4	0·5	0·67	I	I	I
0·9	0	0·11	0·13	0·14	0·17	0·2	0·25	0·33	0·5	I	I
I	0	0	0	0	0	0	0	0	0	0	I

$\longrightarrow_5$ $\mathbf{t}$

	0	0·1	0·2	0·3	0·4	0·5	0·6	0·7	0·8	0·9	1
0	I	I	I	I	I	I	I	I	I	I	I
0·1	0·9	I	I	I	I	I	I	I	I	I	I
0·2	0·8	0·9	I	I	I	I	I	I	I	I	I
0·3	0·7	0·8	0·9	I	I	I	I	I	I	I	I
0·4	0·6	0·7	0·8	0·9	I	I	I	I	I	I	I
0·5	0·5	0·6	0·7	0·8	0·9	I	I	I	I	I	I
0·6	0·4	0·5	0·6	0·7	0·8	0·9	I	I	I	I	I
0·7	0·3	0·4	0·5	0·6	0·7	0·8	0·9	I	I	I	I
0·8	0·2	0·3	0·4	0·5	0·6	0·7	0·8	0·9	I	I	I
0·9	0·1	0·2	0·3	0·4	0·5	0·6	0·7	0·8	0·9	I	I
I	0	0·1	0·2	0·3	0·4	0·5	0·6	0·7	0·8	0·9	I

$\longrightarrow_6$ KD

	0	0·1	0·2	0·3	0·4	0·5	0·6	0·7	0·8	0·9	1
0	I	I	I	I	I	I	I	I	I	I	I
0·1	0·9	0·9	0·9	0·9	0·9	0·9	0·9	0·9	0·9	0·9	I
0·2	0·8	0·8	0·8	0·8	0·8	0·8	0·8	0·8	0·8	0·9	I
0·3	0·7	0·7	0·7	0·7	0·7	0·7	0·7	0·7	0·8	0·9	I
0·4	0·6	0·6	0·6	0·6	0·6	0·6	0·6	0·7	0·8	0·9	I
0·5	0·5	0·5	0·5	0·5	0·5	0·5	0·6	0·7	0·8	0·9	I
0·6	0·4	0·4	0·4	0·4	0·4	0·5	0·6	0·7	0·8	0·9	I
0·7	0·3	0·3	0·3	0·3	0·4	0·5	0·6	0·7	0·8	0·9	I
0·8	0·2	0·2	0·2	0·3	0·4	0·5	0·6	0·7	0·8	0·9	I
0·9	0·1	0·1	0·2	0·3	0·4	0·5	0·6	0·7	0·8	0·9	I
I	0	0·1	0·2	0·3	0·4	0·5	0·6	0·7	0·8	0·9	I

$\longrightarrow_7$ EZ

	0	0·1	0·2	0·3	0·4	0·5	0·6	0·7	0·8	0·9	1
0	I	I	I	I	I	I	I	I	I	I	I
0·1	0·9	0·9	0·9	0·9	0·9	0·9	0·9	0·9	0·9	0·9	0·9
0·2	0·8	0·8	0·8	0·8	0·8	0·8	0·8	0·8	0·8	0·8	0·8
0·3	0·7	0·7	0·7	0·7	0·7	0·7	0·7	0·7	0·7	0·7	0·7
0·4	0·6	0·6	0·6	0·6	0·6	0·6	0·6	0·6	0·6	0·6	0·6
0·5	0·5	0·5	0·5	0·5	0·5	0·5	0·5	0·5	0·5	0·5	0·5
0·6	0·4	0·4	0·4	0·4	0·4	0·5	0·6	0·6	0·6	0·6	0·6
0·7	0·3	0·3	0·3	0·3	0·4	0·5	0·6	0·7	0·7	0·7	0·7
0·8	0·2	0·2	0·2	0·3	0·4	0·5	0·6	0·7	0·8	0·8	0·8
0·9	0·1	0·1	0·2	0·3	0·4	0·5	0·6	0·7	0·8	0·9	0·9
I	0	0·1	0·2	0·3	0·4	0·5	0·6	0·7	0·8	0·9	I

$\longrightarrow_8$ W

	0	0·1	0·2	0·3	0·4	0·5	0·6	0·7	0·8	0·9	1
0	I	0·9	0·8	0·7	0·6	0·5	0·6	0·7	0·8	0·9	I
0·1	0·9	0·9	0·8	0·7	0·6	0·5	0·6	0·7	0·8	0·9	0·9
0·2	0·8	0·8	0·8	0·7	0·6	0·5	0·6	0·7	0·8	0·8	0·8
0·3	0·7	0·7	0·7	0·7	0·6	0·5	0·6	0·7	0·7	0·7	0·7
0·4	0·6	0·6	0·6	0·6	0·6	0·5	0·6	0·6	0·6	0·6	0·6
0·5	0·5	0·5	0·5	0·5	0·5	0·5	0·5	0·5	0·5	0·5	0·5
0·6	0·4	0·4	0·4	0·4	0·4	0·5	0·6	0·6	0·6	0·6	0·6
0·7	0·3	0·3	0·3	0·3	0·4	0·5	0·6	0·7	0·7	0·7	0·7
0·8	0·2	0·2	0·2	0·3	0·4	0·5	0·6	0·7	0·8	0·8	0·8
0·9	0·1	0·1	0·2	0·3	0·4	0·5	0·6	0·7	0·8	0·9	0·9
I	0	0·1	0·2	0·3	0·4	0·5	0·6	0·7	0·8	0·9	I

The philosophical preconceptions behind the various operators clearly differ widely. A main division into types occurs between those down to and including 5:Ł and those from 6:KD on, in that all of the former have ones all along the main diagonal, while none of the latter do. This reflects, in the former type, the desire to make the formula "$a \to a$" ("if a then a") into a *strong tautology*, versus the willingness in the latter type to allow it to be only a *moderate tautology* (with designated values when these include those from 0·5 up). The earliest operators 1:S # and 2:S are, indeed, not fuzzy at all, showing at its most extreme the "bootstrap effect" by which crisp conclusions are drawn from fuzzy premisses. This holds, in somewhat less marked degree, all the way through 5:Ł whereas the operators from 6:KD on all demonstrate the *conservation of crispness*: the crispness of any well-formed formula in these systems lies between that of the fuzziest and the crispest atom in its expression (Bandler & Kohout, 1978, 1979*b*; Willmott, 1978).

The motivation of certain of the formulae is notable. The original intention of 4:G43 was to create an implication which, when used in a multiplicative form of *modus ponens* would resolve the *sorites* paradox (Goguen, 1969).

The formula of 6:KD brings over to multi-valued logic the classic equivalence of "if a then b" with "either not-a or b" while 7:EZ non-classically but deliberately equates "if a then b" with "either both a and b or not-a and anything". More on this level of semantics will appear in our discussion of measures in section 6.

Very useful studies of a number of these operators have been made by other writers from various points of view. In particular, there are interesting and detailed examinations of a few of them with regard to inference, in Baldwin (1978), Baldwin & Guild (1978), Baldwin, Guild & Pilsworth (1978), and Baldwin & Pilsworth (1978). A very fruitful comparison of several of them, as they function in the theory and practice of control, has been made by Sembi & Mamdani (1979). The present paper is concerned mostly with the fuzzier of these operators, from 4:G43 onwards, from a semantic standpoint: the meanings of the operators and the differences among them. A very fortunate breakthrough, described in sections 6 and 7, allows us to cast new light on these aspects. Meanwhile, we recapitulate one important elementary semantic result, in the following section.

5. Contrapositive symmetry

In classical logic, the assertion "if a then b" always receives the same value as its contrapositive, "if not-b then not-a". We will say that a fuzzy implication operator $\to$ possesses *contrapositive symmetry*, or is *contrapositively symmetric*, iff

$$(a \to b) = (1 - b) \to (1 - a). \qquad (5.1)$$

In terms of meaning, this would seem a valuable property for an operator to have. Easy calculations give the following result.

5.1. THEOREM

(1) Operators 2:S, 5:Ł and 6:KD possess contrapositive symmetry.
(2) Operators 1:S*, 3:S* and 4:G43 lack it.

Given an operator $\rightarrow_i$ lacking this form of symmetry, it is easy to construct from it one which possesses it. Of the many ways of doing this, 2 stand out because of their use of the typically fuzzy lattice operations. We give them, at least temporarily, the rather barbaric names of *lower contrapositivization* $\rightarrow_{i'}$ and *upper contrapositivization* $\rightarrow_{i''}$, defined respectively by

$$a \rightarrow_{i'} b = (a \rightarrow_i b) \wedge ((1-b) \rightarrow_i (1-a)) \qquad (5.2)$$

$$\text{and } a \rightarrow_{i''} b = (a \rightarrow_i b) \vee ((1-b) \rightarrow_i (1-a)). \qquad (5.3)$$

The operator $4' : G43'$ was deliberately constructed to be the lower contrapositivization of the operator $4 : G43$.

We then discover the following rather interesting relations among our fuzziest operators:

(a) the Willmott operator 8:W is the lower contrapositivization of the Early Zadeh operator 7:EZ;
(b) the Kleene–Dienes operator 6:KD is the upper contrapositivization of the Early Zadeh operator 7:EZ.

Proof of (a)
Writing $\bar{a}$ for $1-a$, etc.

$$\begin{aligned}
(a \rightarrow_7 b) \wedge (\bar{b} \rightarrow_7 \bar{a}) &= ((a \wedge b) \vee \bar{a}) \wedge ((\bar{b} \wedge \bar{a}) \vee b) \\
&= (a \vee \bar{a}) \wedge (b \vee \bar{a}) \wedge (\bar{b} \vee b) \wedge (\bar{a} \vee b) \\
&= (\bar{a} \vee b) \wedge (a \vee \bar{a}) \wedge (b \vee \bar{b}) \\
&= (\bar{a} \vee b) \wedge \kappa a \wedge \kappa b \\
&= a \rightarrow_3 b.
\end{aligned}$$

Proof of (b)

$$\begin{aligned}
(a \rightarrow_7 b) \vee (\bar{b} \rightarrow_7 \bar{a}) &= (a \wedge b) \vee \bar{a} \vee (\bar{b} \wedge \bar{a}) \vee b \\
&= (\bar{a} \vee (\bar{b} \wedge \bar{a})) \vee (b \vee (a \wedge b)) \\
&= \bar{a} \vee b \\
&= a \rightarrow_6 b. \qquad \blacksquare
\end{aligned}$$

The question of contrapositive symmetry will arise again in later sections.

6. The checklist paradigm: measures of implication and their bounds

In this section we develop a paradigm for the assignment of fuzzy values, which throws an entirely fresh light on the meaning of the various implication operators and on the relationship among them. The basic idea goes back to that of "population" as used by Gaines (1976b,c,d; see also Giles, 1976), between probabilistic and possibilistic logics, underlying the one or the other according to its particular nature. In our present paradigm the "population" consists of items in a checklist, and underlies, in a convincing manner, the determination of the fuzzy membership function.

The paradigm is a perfectly general one, but we deliberately present it here specialized to the situation of the Parkinsonian data already mentioned, in order to maximise the concreteness of the illustration.

For any particular construct Ci let us imagine that there is a *checklist* of n sub-constructs or *items*. In many instances, as will be exemplified later, there is actually such a list; in others it is a pure figment. The theory does not hinge on this distinction. For simplicity we describe the use of the checklist as saying "yes" or "no" to each item; the degree to which the construct is assigned is then the total of the "yes" replies divided by n. In actual checklists there are often both "positive" and "negative" items; what we simplistically call here "yes", then means "yes" on positive items but "no" on negative ones. We code "yes" in this adjusted sense as 1, "no" as 0.

Two observers, θr and θs (who may or may not be in fact the same individual), use these checklists for two persons (patients) Pj and Pm, as follows:

$$\theta r \text{ uses the list on } Pj,$$
$$\theta s \text{ uses the list on } Pm.$$

The *fine data* (which it may turn out that we do not know) are then as follows: where $v, w \in \{0, 1\}$,

α_{vw} = the number of items which θr marks v for Pj and θs marks w for Pm.

The *fine data table* is thus the "contingency table" shown in Table 3; to it are attached its row and column totals and the overall total.

TABLE 3

Contingency table of "yes" marks on checklist

Pm $\diagdown$ Pj	0	1	
0	α_{00}	α_{01}	$\alpha_{00} + \alpha_{01} = r_0$
1	α_{10}	α_{11}	$\alpha_{10} + \alpha_{11} = r_1$
	$\alpha_{00} + \alpha_{10} = c_0$	$\alpha_{01} + \alpha_{11} = c_1$	$r_0 + r_1 = c_0 + c_1 = n$

We wish to assign a *measure* to the degree to which θr's saying "yes" to items on the checklist for Pj *implies* θs's saying "yes" to these same items for Pm; in briefer words, a measure of the support these fine data give to the statement "*if yes-j then yes-m*".

In classical logic, "if yes-j then yes-m" is satisfied "by performance" whenever yes-j and yes-m occur together, and "by default" whenever no-j occurs, regardless of the m-answer. Thus all entries support the statement except for α_{10}. Thus if (in our ignorance of any yet finer detail) we weight all items equally, the appropriate *classical measure* of support for the assertion is

$$m_1 = \frac{\alpha_{00} + \alpha_{01} + \alpha_{11}}{\alpha_{00} + \alpha_{01} + \alpha_{10} + \alpha_{11}} = 1 - \frac{\alpha_{10}}{n}. \tag{6.1}$$

Another point of view, worthy of attention, says that only the cases in which an item was checked "yes-j" are relevant, that is, only the cases of satisfaction "by performance". In this view the appropriate measure would be a *performance measure*

$$m_2 = \frac{\alpha_{11}}{\alpha_{10} + \alpha_{11}} = 1 - \frac{\alpha_{10}}{r_1}. \qquad (6.2)$$

Still another point of view wishes to distinguish the proportions of satisfactions "by performance", α_{11}/n, and "by default", r_0/n, and to assign as measure the better of the two, thus

$$m_3 = \frac{\alpha_{11} \vee (\alpha_{00} + \alpha_{01})}{n}. \qquad (6.3)$$

This differs from measure 1 in having $\vee$ in place of one $+$.

Two variations on measure 3 will turn out to be of interest. One is its lower contrapositivization (see section 5):

$$m_4 = m_{3'} = m_3 \wedge \bar{m}_3, \qquad (6.4)$$

where

$$\bar{m}_3 = \frac{\alpha_{00} \vee (\alpha_{01} + \alpha_{11})}{n}.$$

The other arises by taking for the "performance" part the less conservative m_2, giving

$$m_5 = m_2 \vee \frac{r_0}{n} = \frac{\alpha_{11}}{r_1} \vee \frac{\alpha_{00} + \alpha_{01}}{n}. \qquad (6.5)$$

The reader may well imagine other measures with good claims to attention, but the ones mentioned will suffice for present purposes.

Now, very often in practice, by accident or design, we are not given, or do not retain, the four pieces of information in the fine data table, but only its row and column totals, or, what comes to the same thing, the 3 pieces of information r_1, c_1 and n. Indeed, it is very human to summarise the table by the following 2 pieces of information.

6.1. DEFINITION

$$a = r_1/n,$$
$$b = c_1/n.$$

For the present purposes, as we shall see anon, this summary is as good as the 3-bit one.

What can be said about the measures when the amount of information has been reduced to 3 pieces? Besides r_1, c_1 and n (whence of course also $r_0 = n - r_1$, $c_0 = n - c_1$), all we know about the table is that the *cell entries cannot be negative*. Except in very special cases (where r_1 or c_1 is n or 0), this does not allow us to reconstruct the table, but it does allow us to put precise lower and upper bounds on the measures, with extremely enlightening results. In the following lemma, the four conditions $a_{vw} \geq 0$ are all re-expressed as conditions on a single element, the one which figures negatively in all the measures.

6.2. LEMMA

(1) $\max (0, r_1 - c_1) \leq \alpha_{10} \leq \min (r_1, n - c_1),$

whence, in more convenient form,

(2) $\max (-r_1, c_1 - n) \leq -\alpha_{10} \leq \min (0, c_1 - r_1).$

Proof

$0 \leq \alpha_{00},$ so $c_0 - \alpha_{00} \leq c_0,$ that is, $\alpha_{10} \leq c_0,$ that is $\alpha_{10} \leq n - c_1.$

$$0 \leq \alpha_{11} \Rightarrow r_1 - \alpha_{11} \leq r_1 \Rightarrow \alpha_{10} \leq r_1.$$
$$0 \leq \alpha_{10}.$$
$$0 \leq \alpha_{01} \Rightarrow \alpha_{10} - \alpha_{01} \leq \alpha_{10}$$
$$\Rightarrow \alpha_{10} + \alpha_{11} - (\alpha_{11} + \alpha_{01}) \leq \alpha_{10}$$
$$\Rightarrow r_1 - c_1 \leq \alpha_{10}. \qquad \blacksquare$$

We can now bound all our measures by functions (and often very familiar ones!) of the a and b of Definition 6.1.

6.3. THEOREM

(1) The KD-implication and the Ł-implication are respectively the attainable lower and upper bounds of measure 1:

$a \rightarrow_6 b \leq m_1 \leq a \rightarrow_5 b.$

(2) A certain new function of (a, b) and the G43-implication are respectively the attainable lower and upper bounds of measure 2:

$\max \left(0, \dfrac{a + b - 1}{a}\right) \leq m_2 \leq a \rightarrow_4 b.$

(3) Another function of (a, b) and the EZ-implication are respectively the attainable lower and upper bounds of measure 3:

$\max (a + b - 1, 1 - a) \leq m_3 \leq a \rightarrow_7 b.$

(4) Still another function of (a, b) and the W-implication are respectively the attainable lower and upper bounds of measure 4:

$\min (\max (1 - a, a + b - 1), \max (b, 1 - a - b)) \leq m_4 \leq a \rightarrow_8 b.$

(5) Yet another function of (a, b) and one of G43 are respectively the attainable lower and upper bounds of measure 5:

$\max \left(\dfrac{a + b - 1}{a}, 1 - a\right) \leq m_5 \leq (a \rightarrow_4 b) \vee (1 - a).$

Proof

All the assertions follow from Lemma 6.2.

(1) Adding n to all terms in part (2) of the Lemma, and then dividing by n, we have

$\max (n - r_1, c_1) \leq n - \alpha_{10} \leq \min (n, n + c_1 - r_1),$

$$\max \left(1 - \frac{r_1}{n}, \frac{c_1}{n}\right) \leq 1 - \frac{\alpha_{10}}{n} \leq \min \left(1, 1 - \frac{r_1}{n} + \frac{c_1}{n}\right),$$

that is

$$\max (1 - a, b) \leq m_1 \leq \min (1, 1 - a + b).$$

(2) Adding r_1 to part (2) of the Lemma, and then dividing by r_1, we obtain

$$\max (0, r_1 + c_1 - n) \leq r_1 - \alpha_{10} \leq \min (r_1, c_1),$$

$$\max \left(0, \frac{a + b - 1}{a}\right) \leq m_2 \leq \min \left(1, \frac{b}{a}\right).$$

(3) As in (2) above,

$$\max (0, r_1 + c_1 - n) \leq \alpha_{11} \leq \min (r_1, c_1),$$

$$n - r_1 \leq \alpha_{00} + \alpha_{01} \leq n - r_1,$$

hence

$$\max (n - r_1, r_1 + c_1 - n) \leq \alpha_{11} \vee (\alpha_{00} + \alpha_{01}) \leq \max (\min (r_1, c_1), n - r_1),$$

whence, dividing by n,

$$\max (1 - a, a + b - 1) \leq m_3 \leq (a \wedge b) \vee (1 - a).$$

(4) By lower contrapositivization of (3).

(5) Immediate from (2).   ■

The first part of this Theorem is particularly gratifying. It enriches the semantics of the Kleene–Dienes and the Łukasiewicz operators by placing them firmly in the frame— one might say, *as* the frame—of the classical measure m_1. It establishes between these important operators a relationship which we must examine more closely in the following section.

Part (2) of the Theorem furnishes what is perhaps the most convincing semantics for the Gaines 43 operator, as the upper bound of the "by performance" measure m_2. Note that the bounds on this measure are extremely wide apart: while $a \rightarrow_4 b$ is generally quite high, with ones over half of the table, the lower bound is 0 all over the upper left triangle (where $a + b \leq 1$).

Assertion (3) of the Theorem furnishes a fresh and convincing meaning for the Early Zadeh operator, as upper bound of measure 3, which was the greater of 2 conservative measures by "performance" and by "default". The bounds on this measure are very close indeed: in four-fifths of the table they agree, so that there the EZ implication gives the measure exactly. (In fact, the measure and both of the bounds have the "default" value $1 - a$ except in that portion of the table below the middle and to the right of the minor diagonal, where both $a > 1 - a$ and $b > 1 - a$; there the EZ value ascends to min (a, b). The lower bound remains $1 - a$ until $b > 2(1 - a)$, when it becomes $a + b - 1$. The 3 values join again at the edges, where $a = 1$ or $b = 1$, and there they all have the value b.)

Part (4) of the Theorem, similarly, enhances the meaning of the Willmott operator, as upper bound of the lower contrapositivization m_4 of measure m_3. As in part (3), the bounds are very close, although the area of table over which they differ has been doubled by reflection in the minor diagonal.

Part (5) essentially rescues the G43 operator and the appallingly low lower bound discussed under Part (2), giving much closer bounds, capable perhaps of becoming useful operators. But the most interesting and possibly the most significant aspect of measure 5 will appear in the following section.

7. The checklist paradigm continued: values of the measures in the expected case

When only the row and column totals r_i, c_j of the fine data table, as contingency table, are known, the *expected values* for the α_{ij} are $r_i c_j / n$. (These are the mean values of the α_{ij} in the hypergeometric distribution.) With these values, each cell stands in the same proportion to the other in its row (or column), as its whole column (or row) does to the other one:

$$\frac{\alpha_{ij}}{\alpha_{ik}} = \frac{c_j}{c_k}; \qquad \frac{\alpha_{ij}}{\alpha_{hj}} = \frac{r_i}{r_h}. \tag{7.1}$$

The values are shown in Table 4.

TABLE 4

Expected configuration of the table, given the row and column totals

$\dfrac{(n-r_1)(n-c_1)}{n}$	$\dfrac{(n-r_1)c_1}{n}$	$n-r_1$
$\dfrac{r_1(n-c_1)}{n}$	$\dfrac{r_1 c_1}{n}$	r_1
$n-c_1$	c_1	n

What values do the various measures take for this expected configuaration? For the first two measures, this will give their own expected values; for the others (involving max and min) this need not be the case. The following results are immediate consequences of the definitions (6.1) to (6.5) of the measures, and of Table 4.

7.1. THEOREM

The values of the various measures for the expected configuration (Table 4) are:

(1) $m_1 = 1 - a + ab$,
(2) $m_2 = b$,
(3) $m_3 = ab \vee (1 - a)$,
(4) $m_4 = (ab \vee (1 - a)) \wedge ((1 - a)(1 - b) \vee b)$,
(5) $m_5 = a \to_6 b$.

The first result gives us a new implication operator worthy of attention. It stands, as by Theorem 6.3, part (1), it must, between Kleene–Dienes and Łukasiewicz, and may be called and numbered the *KDŁ operator*, $\to_{5.5}$. Perhaps also deserving note is formula 3, standing below 7:EZ, as formula 4 does with respect to 8:W. Formula 2 is not particularly interesting in itself, but is one of the causes of Formula 5, which is of high interest on two counts: it shows the KD operator, not as a lower bound (as in Theorem 6.3, part (1)), but as the value in the expected case of a different but respectable measure, and it links the KD operator with the G43 operator, via Theorem 6.3, part (5).

Returning to measure 1 and the range from KD (through the new KDŁ) to Ł, we have the following pretty result.

7.2. THEOREM

$$(a \rightarrow_5 b) - (a \rightarrow_6 b) = 1 - (\kappa a \vee \kappa b).$$

Proof

$\min (1, 1 - a + b) - \max (1 - a, b)$

$$= \min (1 - (1 - a), 1 - b, 1 - a + b - (1 - a), 1 - a + b - b)$$
$$= \min (a, 1 - b, b, 1 - a)$$
$$= 1 - \max (1 - a, b, 1 - b, a) = 1 - \max (\kappa a, \kappa b). \quad \blacksquare$$

8. A clinical example of the checklist paradigm

Simple, quick and quite revealing is an actual checklist used clinically to assess a patient's anxiety, the A.A.C.L. (Affect Adjective Check List), by Zuckermann (1960), shown in Table 5. The patient is asked to check the adjectives that describe his/her feelings.

TABLE 5

Checklist (A.A.C.L.) for anxiety

C1N	Afraid	C11P	Happy
C2P	Calm	C12N	Upset
C3P	Cheerful	C13N	Worrying
C4N	Desperate	C14P	Steady
C5N	Frightened	C15P	Thoughtful
C6P	Contented	C16N	Terrified
C7N	Nervous	C17P	Secure
C8P	Loving	C18P	Joyful
C9N	Shaky	C19N	Panicky
C10N	Tense	C20P	Pleasant
		C21N	Fearful

Of the 21 adjectives, 11 (marked N) are negative, representing some anxiety feelings, while 10 (marked P) are positive, representing freedom from anxiety. Since the object is to assess a symptom, rather than the corresponding positive construct, the scoring is the opposite to that described at the beginning of section 6. The conventional scoring method is to count the negative adjectives checked plus the positive adjectives unchecked: the resultant score ranges from 0 (no anxiety) to 21 (extreme anxiety); we convert these to fuzzy membership values by dividing by 21.

Using actual clinical data, we can illustrate the measures and implication operators discussed in the previous sections. In Table 6 are shown the responses and scores of the

TABLE 6

Patient P3M's response (upper lines) and scores (lower lines) at 4 times

Time	IN	2P	3P	4N	5N	6P	7N	8P	9N	10N	11P	12N	13N	14P	15P	16N	17P	18P	19N	20P	21N	Conventional score total:Σ	Relative score $\sigma=\frac{\Sigma}{21}$
T1		X	X					X		X					X		X		X				
						+1				+1	+1			+1			+1					5	0·238
T4		X	X					X		X		X			X		X		X				
						+1				+1				+1			+1					4	0·190
T7								X	X	X					X				X				
		+1	+1			+1				+1	+1	+1		+1			+1	+1				9	0·429
T9		X	X					X	X			X			X		X		X				
						+1				+1				+1			+1					4	0·190

Parkinsonian patient P3M, on 4 occasions during and after the 10-week period of physiotherapeutic treatment. Here we have the fine data needed to calculate the exact implication measures between any 2 of these response-sets, for we know precisely which items were scored in each case. Thus we can fill in the contingency tables completely, as is done for 2 pairs of times in parts (a) and (b) of Table 7.

These are accompanied by the various measures of the degree to which the anxiety of the patient at one time implied his anxiety at the other time. Note that, when the times as well as the observer and the patient are the same, in (b), so that the table has diagonal form, measures 1, 2 and 5 are trivially and necessarily 1, but not the other two measures.

Part (c) of Table 7 shows, at time T6, the contingency table and the measures for the degree to which the anxious condition of patient P5 is a subset of the condition of P20; otherwise put, the extent to which the condition of the latter includes or comprises that of the former. Part (d) shows the opposite implication or inclusion. These 2 parts demonstrate very nicely the inherent *non-symmetry* of implication: none of the measures are alike in the 2 situations. This is, of course, in complete contrast with measures of correlation, in which the directional distinction is blurred beyond recovery. The superior sensitivity of the implication measures should be apparent.

Restricting attention to measure m_1, Table 8 shows its actual value, its bounds 6 : KD and 5 : Ł, and its expected value 5·5 : KDŁ, for various pairs of patient-times. There is no claim that the pairs are a "representative sample" (whatever that might mean in this instance) of our data, although they have been chosen in what might be described as a "semi-random manner", mostly prior to calculation. They do suffice, at any rate, to show that almost the whole range between the limits on m_1 is in fact occupied.

There is a tendency to deviate towards the Ł end rather than the KD end, but it would be premature to make anything of this. In any event, the examples show that the use of Ł is by no means always justified; we emphasize this point because the acceptance of the scores as representing the degree of anxiety and the use of them on a comparative basis— as is, of course, the intention of the test—amounts to the covert acceptance of the Ł operator: if Pj scores 9 and Pm scores 16 or 17, then the latter is more anxious, that is, his condition is deemed to include that of the former.

This says, in effect, that his 9 "yes" items are among Pm's 16 or 17, and this leads to the Łukasiewicz implication, in either direction. The table shows that this assumption may, indeed, fit the case, as in line 1, or may be very far from the case, as in lines 5 and 6 (which are also shown in Table 7 (c) and (d)).

TABLE 7

Fine-data tables (contingency tables) of anxiety scorings, and values of the implication measures

(a)

	P3T4		
P3TI	0	1	
0	16	0	16
1	1	4	5
	17	4	21

$m_1 = 0.952$
$m_2 = 0.800$
$m_3 = 0.762$ $\bar{m}_3 = 0.762$
$m_4 = 0.762$
$m_5 = 0.800$

P3TI → P3T4

(b)

16	0	16
0	5	5
16	5	21

$m_1 = 1.000$
$m_2 = 1.000$
$m_3 = 0.762$ $\bar{m}_3 = 0.762$
$m_4 = 0.762$
$m_5 = 1.000$

P3TI → P3TI

(c)

2	10	12
2	7	9
4	17	21

$m_1 = 0.905$
$m_2 = 0.778$
$m_3 = 0.571$ $\bar{m}_3 = 0.810$
$m_4 = 0.810$
$m_5 = 0.778$

P5T6 → P20T6

(d)

2	2	4
10	7	17
12	9	21

$m_1 = 0.524$
$m_2 = 0.412$
$m_3 = 0.333$ $\bar{m}_3 = 0.429$
$m_4 = 0.429$
$m_5 = 0.412$

P20T6 → P5T6

Further investigation of the various actual measures, and their comparisons with their corresponding operators, will continue to be made.

9. Use of the operators on real-world data

With added insight into the meaning of the various implication operators, we are now in a position to return to a consideration of their diverse effects upon our original data.

First let us consider the patient-to-patient relation $R^{(1)-1} \lhd R^{(1)}$, of which the jm-component represents the degree to which the constructs attributed by therapist 1 to patient Pj imply their attribution by her to patient Pm; in short, in the opinion of $\theta 1$ at the given time, the degree to which Pj's good attributes are included in those of Pm. *Where the operator used has contrapositive symmetry* (see section 5), this is the same as the degree to which Pm's bad attributes, or symptoms, are included in those of Pj.

Figure 4 shows various α-cuts of this relation when computed with 4 different operators: first 7 : EZ and 8 : W, which in this case gave the same result; then 6 : KD; and finally 5 : Ł. The matrix mean and standard deviation are shown in each case.

Most striking and gratifying is the tendency for all the operators to give, in cuts near their means, networks which are *partial orders*, or which, with the fusion of structurally equivalent elements, become partial orders. These are shown to the right of the networks in Hasse diagram notation, in which arrows are understood to point upwards, and transitivity to give the composite paths (as, e.g. from P4 to P3 and to P1, at the upper right).

The EZ and W operators, which show little at their top 2 cuts, at $\alpha = 0.62$ divide the patients into 2 "comparability classes"; in one of these P1 is better off than P5, in the other, both P2 and P3 are better than P4, although not comparable with one another. (The identical picture is presented by the Ł operator at $\alpha = 1$.) At $\alpha = 0.60$ the classes

TABLE 8

The first measure, its bounds, and its expected value, for various patients and times, on the anxiety checklist

Line	(1) $X \to Y$	(2) $r_1 = \Sigma_X$	(3) $c_1 = \Sigma_Y$	(4) $n - \alpha_{00}$	(5) $a = \frac{(2)}{21}$	(6) $b = \frac{(3)}{21}$	(7) $m_1 = \frac{(4)}{21}$	(8) $a \to b$ 6: KD	(8) 5.5: KDŁ	(8) 5: Ł	(9) Absolute differences Ł$-m_1$	(9) m_1-KDŁ	(9) m_1-KD	(10) Range Ł$-$KD	(11) Norm. diff. (9)/(10) Ł$-m_1$ (%)	(11) m_1-KDŁ (%)	(11) m_1-KD (%)
1	P5T7 → P5T6	16	9	14	0·762	0·429	0·667	0·429	0·565	0·667	0	0·102	0·238	0·238	0	42·9	100
2	P20T6 → P3T1	17	5	7	0·810	0·238	0·333	0·238	0·383	0·428	0·095	−0·050	0·095	0·190	50	−26·3	50
3	P3T1 → P5T6	5	9	20	0·238	0·429	0·952	0·762	0·864	1	0·048	0·088	0·190	0·238	20·2	37	79·8
4	P5T6 → P3T1	9	5	16	0·429	0·238	0·762	0·571	0·673	0·809	0·047	0·089	0·191	0·238	19·7	37·4	79·8
5	P20T6 → P5T6	17	9	11	0·810	0·429	0·524	0·429	0·537	0·619	0·095	−0·013	0·095	0·190	50	−6·8	50
6	P5T6 → P20T6	9	17	19	0·429	0·810	0·905	0·810	0·918	1	0·095	−0·013	0·095	0·190	50	−6·8	50
7	P18T1 → P5T7	11	16	20	0·542	0·726	0·952	0·726	0·875	1	0·048	0·096	0·226	0·274	17·5	28	82·5
8	P18T1 → P5T6	11	9	15	0·524	0·429	0·714	0·476	0·701	0·905	0·191	0·013	0·238	0·429	44·5	3	55·5
9	P20T6 → P18T1	17	11	13	0·810	0·524	0·619	0·524	0·614	0·714	0·095	−0·005	0·095	0·190	50	2·6	50
10	P20T3 → P20T6	6	17	19	0·286	0·810	0·905	0·810	0·946	1	0·095	−0·041	0·095	0·190	50	−21·6	50
11	P20T3 → P3T1	6	5	16	0·286	0·238	0·762	0·714	0·782	0·952	0·190	−0·020	0·048	0·238	79·8	−8·4	20·2

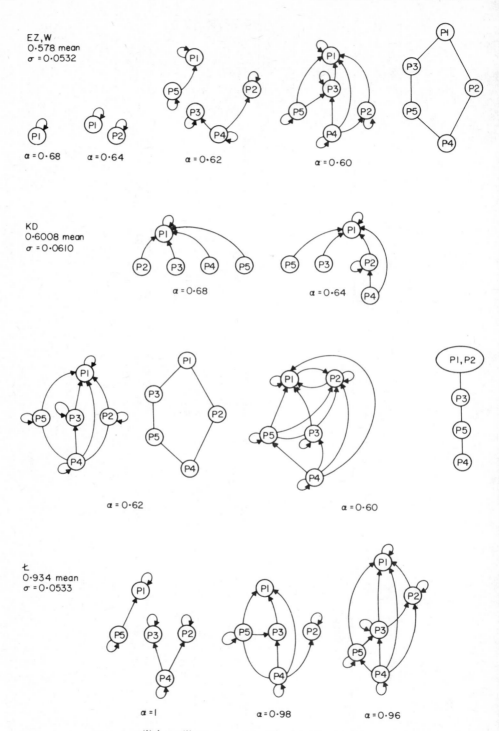

FIG. 4. $R^{(1)-1} \lhd R^{(1)}$. Various operators and various α-cuts.

are brought together in a partial order, in which P4 is worst off, bettered on the one hand by P5 then P3, then P1, and on the other hand by P2 and then P1. Since the W operator has contrapositive symmetry, this diagram may be read in the opposite direction for symptoms: those of P1 are also suffered by P2 and P3, etc.

The KD operator shows a different picture at its higher cuts, but accords with the one just described at $\alpha = 0.62$. At a still lower level, $\alpha = 0.60$, it produces a fusion of the conditions of P1 and P2, at the top of a total order. The Ł operator shows a recognizably similar picture, although at the cuts shown it does not reach a partial order.

Both KD and Ł, after a certain initial reluctance, show P2 comparable not only with P4 and P1, but with P3 (and eventually with P5), whereas EZ and W, as far as we have descended, leave P2 uncompared with P3 and P5. (Of course, if one cuts low enough, everyone will be not only comparable, but undistinguishable!) A casual observer of the treatment class might well notice qualitative similarities between P2 and P4 on one hand, and between P3 and P5 on the other, with a qualitative difference, although a quantitative similarity, between P2 and the pair P3, P5. The latter, for example, both experienced sudden freezings of movement, interfering with their performance in class. At the time in question, P4's mood of anxiety and depression was worse than that of any other patient in the group, and P1, P3, P5, P4 all had qualitatively (but not quantitatively) similar difficulty with their balance.

Next we digress from the original product examples, to examine the *time-to-time* relation of the condition of patient P3M, as judged by $\theta 2$; here the implication values have been averaged over all the 8 constructs: those having to do with the manageability in a class (C1, C2, C3), with the patient's motivation (C4, C5) and with his physical and emotional state (C6, C7, C8). (Note that semantic overlap among the types is frequent and intentional.) Compare all this with Table 8 and its discussion. Figure 5 shows first the top α-cut ($\alpha = 0.88$) for the S operator, then the top cuts (at $\alpha = 0.67$, 0.8, 1 respectively) and cuts near the means for the KD operator, the new KDŁ operators, and the Ł operator.

The top-level cuts all show T2→T4 and T3→T4; on the checklist paradigm this would indicate independence from the fine structure. The cuts near the means also show a certain amount of agreement, justifying the assertion that: *regardless of the fine checklist data*, P3M had been at his best at times T4 and T5, and at his worst at T3. This corresponds very well with other evidence (other tests and records, and one of the authors' personal observations); indeed, there had been a notable slump in the patient's state (shared by other patients and even by the therapists) at time T3.

The construct-to-construct product $R^{(1)} \lhd R^{(1)^{-1}}$ occupies Fig. 6. An arrow from construct Ci to construct Cj means that, at the given α-level, the one implied the other in the cognitive structure of therapist 1, averaged over these patients at this time. Most revealing are the networks based on EZ and W, which happen to come out exactly the same. Reading them as W, by contrapositive symmetry, one need only reverse the arrows to obtain corresponding statements about symptoms. Thus if C3→C1, one can say either "patients that are 'independent' are of 'almost normal ability'", or "patients that are 'disabled' are also 'dependent'". In the highest cut, only construct C4 "interested and exploring" appears; it is evidently central to $\theta 1$'s thinking, as is confirmed by other evidence. As the α-level descends, other constructs appear, until at $\alpha = 0.60$ a partial order is reached, with a fusion of constructs C1 and C3 ("of almost normal ability" and "independent"). These imply C5 ("accepting advice") and then in

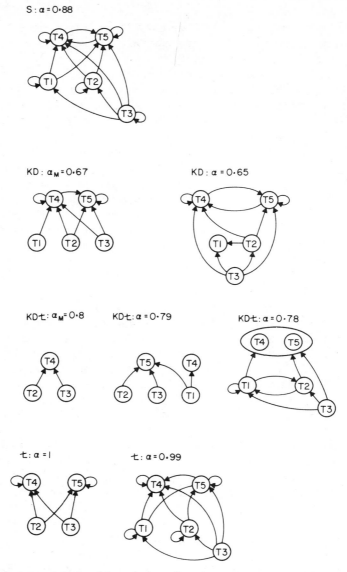

FIG. 5. Implications among the conditions of one patient at 5 different times (patient P3M, assessed by $\theta2$). Various operators and α-cuts.

turn C4 ("interested and exploring") as does also C2 ("easy to cope with") although there is no connection between C1–C3 and C2. (This last indicates a patient with a good score on "ability" or "independence" but not on "easy to cope with", and another with the opposite constellation.) Read symptom-wise, from the top down, $\bar{C}4$ ("apathetic and unconcerned") implies every woe, via $\bar{C}5$ ("rejecting advice").

The other therapist $\theta2$ presents a somewhat different point of view, in Fig. 7. In the first place, the product $R^{(2)} \triangleleft R^{(2)-1}$ using EZ is not identical with that based on W.

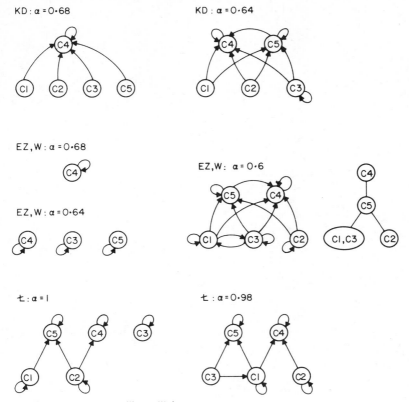

FIG. 6. $R^{(1)} \lhd R^{(1)^{-1}}$. Various operators and α-cuts.

Where they differ, we are not justified in exchanging statements using positive constructs with those using symptoms, as we were before. Whereas $\theta 1$ viewed the situation through C4, "interested and exploring", and C5, "accepting advice", with only a late appearance of C2, this therapist's view is founded on the implication C2 → C5: "patients who are easy to cope with are accepting (my) advice." This appears in all the highest α-cuts, and of course continues further down, where it is joined by C2 → C4, "patients who are easy to cope with are interested and exploring". For EZ at $\alpha = 0.66$, her view is a partial order with C2 "easy to cope with" implying on the one hand the fused pair C4, C5, and on the other C1, "almost normal ability", while C3 "independent" neither implies nor is implied by anything else.

It looks as if $\theta 2$ is perhaps less discriminating than $\theta 1$, and over-fond of the "personal" construct C2. This hypothesis is confirmed by examining $R^{(1)} \lhd R^{(2)^{-1}}$, which shows how the use of each construct by $\theta 1$ implies the use of each construct by $\theta 2$. Figure 8 shows this relation, computed with the KD operator, at 2 α-levels. The upper cut shows immediately that when $\theta 1$ uses any of the concepts C1 ("almost normal ability"), C3 ("independent"), C5 ("accepting advice") or C2 itself ("easy to cope with"), $\theta 2$ uses only C2, "easy to cope with". The other cut shows also $\theta 2$'s tendency to substitute for various distinctions made by $\theta 1$, the construct C5 ("accepting (my) advice").

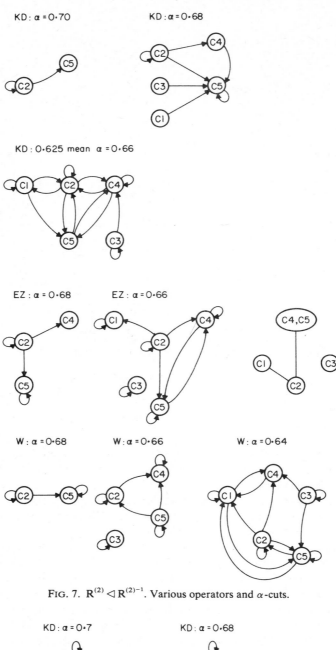

FIG. 7. $R^{(2)} \lhd R^{(2)-1}$. Various operators and α-cuts.

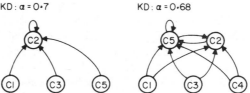

FIG. 8. $R^{(1)} \lhd R^{(2)-1}$. KD operator; two α-cuts.

References

BALDWIN, J. F. (1978). Fuzzy logic and approximate reasoning for mixed input arguments. *Report No. EM/FS 4*. Department of Engineering Mathematics, University of Bristol.

BALDWIN, J. F. & GUILD, N. C. F. (1978). Feasible algorithms for approximate reasoning using a fuzzy logic. *Report No. EM/FS 8*. Department of Engineering Mathematics, University of Bristol.

BALDWIN, J. F., GUILD, N. C. F. & PILSWORTH, B. W. (1978). Improved logic for fuzzy controllers. *Report No. EM/FS 5*. Department of Engineering Mathematics, University of Bristol.

BALDWIN, J. F. & PILSWORTH, B. W. (1978). Axiomatic approach to implication for approximate reasoning using a fuzzy logic. *Report No. EM/FS 9*. Department of Engineering Mathematics, University of Bristol.

BANDLER, W. (1977). Some esomathematical uses of category theory. In KLIR, G. J., Ed., *Applied Systems Research*. New York: Plenum Press (1978), pp. 243–255.

BANDLER, W. & KOHOUT, L. J. (1978a). Fuzzy relational products and fuzzy implication operators. *Report No. FRP-1*, Department of Mathematics, University of Essex, Colchester. Presented at the Workshop on Fuzzy Reasoning—Theory and Applications, Queen Mary College, London, 15 September 1978.

BANDLER, W. & KOHOUT, L. J. (1978b). Application of fuzzy logics to computer protection structures. *Report No. FRP-3*. Department of Mathematics, University of Essex, Colchester. In *Proceedings of the Ninth International Symposium on Multiple-valued Logic*, Bath, England, 29–31 May 1979. New York: IEEE, 79CH 1408-4C, pp. 200–207.

BANDLER, W. & KOHOUT, L. J. (1979a). The use of new relational products in clinical modelling. *Report No. FRP-4*. Department of Mathematics, University of Essex, Colchester. In *General Systems Research: A Science, a Methodology, a Technology (Proceedings of the 1979 North American Meeting of the S.G.S.R.)*. Louisville, Kentucky: S.G.S.R., pp. 240–246.

BANDLER, W. & KOHOUT, L. J. (1979b). Fuzzy power sets and fuzzy implication operators. *Report No. FRP-7*. Department of Mathematics, University of Essex, Colchester; to appear in *Fuzzy Sets and Systems*.

BANDLER, W. & KOHOUT, L. J. (1979c). Activity structures and their protection. *Report No. FRP-9*. Department of Mathematics, University of Essex, Colchester. In *Improving the Human Condition: Quality and Stability in Solid Systems (Proceedings of the Silver Anniversary International Meeting of the S.G.S.R., London, 20–24 August 1979)*. Louisville, Kentucky: S.G.S.R., pp. 239–244.

CARNAP, R. (1943). *Introduction to Semantics*. Cambridge, Mass.: Harvard University Press.

GAINES, B. R. (1976a). On the complexity of causal models. *IEEE Transactions on Systems, Man and Cybernetics*, **SMC-6**, 56–59.

GAINES, B. R. (1976b). General fuzzy logics. *Proceedings of the 3rd European Meeting on Cybernetics and Systems Research*, Vienna.

GAINES, B. R. (1976c). Foundations of fuzzy reasoning. *International Journal of Man–Machine Studies*, **8**, 623–668.

GAINES, B. R. & KOHOUT, L. J. (1975). Possible automata. *Proceedings of the 1975 International Symposium on Multiple-valued Logic*. New York: IEEE, pp. 183–196.

GAINES, B. R. & KOHOUT, L. J. (1976). The logic of automata. *International Journal of General Systems*, **2**, 191–208.

GILES, R. (1976). Łukasiewicz logic and fuzzy set theory. *International Journal of Man–Machine Studies*, **8**, 313–327.

GOGUEN, J. A. (1969). The logic of inexact concepts. *Synthese*, **19**, 325–373.

GUILFORD, J. P. (1954). *Psychometric Methods*. New York: McGraw–Hill.

LORRAIN, F. (1975). *Réseaux sociaux et classifications sociales: essai sur l'algèbre et la géométrie des structures sociales*. Paris: Hermann.

LORRAIN, F. & WHITE, H. C. (1971). Structural equivalence of individuals in social networks. *Journal of Mathematical Sociology*, **1**, 49–80.

NEGOIŢĂ, C. V. & RALESCU, D. A. (1975). *Applications of Fuzzy Sets to Systems Analysis*. Basel: Birkhäuser.

RESCHER, N. (1969). *Many-valued Logic*. New York: McGraw–Hill.

SEMBI, B. S. & MAMDANI, E. H. (1979), On the nature of implication in fuzzy logic. *Proceedings of the Ninth International Symposium on Multiple-valued Logic*, Bath, England, 29–31 May, 1979. New York: IEEE, 79 CH 1408–4C, No. 143–151.

WILLMOTT, R. (1978). Two fuzzier implication operators in the theory of fuzzy power sets. *Report No. FRP-2*. Department of Mathematics, University of Essex, Colchester; to appear in *Fuzzy Sets and Systems*.

WILLMOTT, R. (1979a). On the transitivity of implication and equivalence in some many-valued logics. *Report No. FRP–5*. Department of Mathematics, University of Essex, Colchester.

WILLMOTT, R. (1979b). Mean measures in fuzzy power-set theory. *Report No. FRP-6*. Department of Mathematics, University of Essex, Colchester.

ZADEH, L. A. (1965). Fuzzy sets. *Information and Control*, **8**, 338–353.

ZADEH, L. A. (1973). Outline of a new approach to the analysis of complex systems and decision processes. *IEEE Transactions on Systems Man and Cybernetics*, **1**, 28–44.

ZADEH, L. A. (1977). Theory of fuzzy sets. In BELZER, J., HOLZMAN, A. & KENT, A., Eds, *Encyclopedia of Computer Science and Technology*. New York: Dekker.

ZUCKERMAN, M. (1960). The development of an Affect Adjective Check List for the measurement of anxiety. *Journal of Consulting Psychology*, **24**, 457–462.

Knowledge acquisition by encoding expert rules versus computer induction from examples: a case study involving soybean pathology

R. S. Michalski and R. L. Chilausky

University of Illinois, Urbana, Illinois 61801, U.S.A.

(*Received 15 June 1979*)

In view of growing interest in the development of knowledge-based computer consulting systems for various problem domains, the problems of knowledge acquisition have special significance. Current methods of knowledge acquisition rely entirely on the direct representation of knowledge of experts, which usually is a very time and effort consuming task. The paper presents results from an experiment to compare the above method of knowledge acquisition with a method based on inductive learning from examples. The comparison was done in the context of developing rules for soybean disease diagnosis and has demonstrated an advantage of the inductively derived rules in performing a testing task (which involved diagnosing a few hundred cases of soybean diseases).

1. Introduction

The amount of diagnostic and therapeutic knowledge existing today in the area of human medicine, animal medicine, pathology of plants, etc. surpasses by far what a single expert can encompass. Also, due to the rapid growth of the above disciplines, it is increasingly difficult for an expert to continually update once acquired knowledge. A prospective solution to this problem is the development of expert computer consulting systems which can interactively provide information, advice, and support in decision-making. Such systems could shorten or improve decision-making by suggesting most likely problems or areas of investigation, by calling attention to information which might be overlooked, by suggesting non-typical cases which are possible within the accumulated evidence, etc. In the area of medicine, several experimental consulting systems have been developed, e.g.:

(a) INTERNIST for general medical diagnosis (Myers & Pople, 1977);
(b) MYCIN for antimicrobial therapy advice (Shortliffe, 1976);
(c) CASNET for disease modelling (Kulikowski, 1977, 1978);
(d) CONSULT I and CONSULT II (Patrick, 1979).

Recently, there has been also developed a consulting system in the area of geology, called "PROSPECTOR", for the purpose of providing consultation about mineral exploration (Duda *et al.*, 1978).

A consulting system consists of a knowledge base and an inference mechanism, which matches the queries of users with rules in the knowledge base in order to compute advice. A knowledge base is a symbolic representation of factual and, as well, judgmental knowledge in the subject domain. In each of the above-mentioned consultation systems, the knowledge base was established by handcrafted encoding of the knowledge of human experts. Such encoding can be a very time consuming task, requiring close collaboration between experts of the subject domain and computer scientists trained as "knowledge engineers". This task can be simplified somewhat by special computer programs which facilitate the debugging, modification and maintenance of the knowledge base (Davis, 1976).

An attractive alternative would be to construct a knowledge base by presenting examples of expert decisions to the system and have the system determine the general rules. This means that a consulting system would have to include a module capable of performing inductive inference. The research on computer inductive inference is still at an early stage of development; however, it is already possible to obtain practical results, if the problem is sufficiently well defined and specialized. The papers (Buchanan & Feigenbaum, 1978; Mitchell, 1977; Hayes-Roth &McDermott, 1978; Dietterich & Michalski, 1979) describe some more recent work in this area.

In this paper, we present the results of applying an inductive computer program to the problem of learning from examples the decision rules for the diagnosis of soybean diseases. Then we contrast these decision rules with the decision rules obtained by direct interrogation of experts in soybean pathology. The results may be somewhat surprising to the reader: in the conclusion we have attempted to explain them.

2. The formalism used for knowledge representation

A good formalism for knowledge representation should have not only adequate operators for representing many different aspects of knowledge of human experts, but also be well suited for implementing inference processes on this knowledge. The latter issue seems to be sometimes neglected by workers in the area of knowledge representation.

One of the basic ways for representing expert knowledge is in the form of decision (or production) rules (Davis, Buchanan & Shortliffe, 1975):[†]

$$\text{CONDITION} \overset{\alpha}{:} :> \text{DECISION} \qquad (1)$$

The interpretation of such a rule is that if a *situation* satisfies CONDITION then infer DECISION. The parameter α denotes the "strength of implication". Typically, the CONDITION is a conjunction of binary statements and the DECISION is some action, decision, or assignment of values to a variables (e.g., in Shortliffe, 1976). In general, the CONDITION can be any description expressed in some formal language.

A *situation* is a description of some object or processes under consideration. For example, in medical diagnosis, a situation may be some observed manifestations or results of tests performed on a patient. In plant pathology, a situation may be a description of symptoms of a diseased plant.

Another way of representing expert knowledge is in the form of a semantic net (Brachman, 1978) whose general form is a labeled graph with nodes representing various conceptual entities and links representing relationships among these entities.

This way of representing knowledge is quite natural for certain problems. The network representation has, however, several drawbacks. First, since everything is interconnected, it is difficult to modify and incrementally update or extend the knowledge base. Also, it is difficult to represent non-binary relationships. For example,

† We use symbol : :> instead of → which is often used here to indicate a difference between the decision assignment operator and the logical implication.

it is difficult to represent a statement indicating that a certain logical product of concepts (associated with various nodes) implies some other concept, and that the "strength of the implication" is so and so. Such statements are, however, very common in human decision processes, and, therefore, a decision rule representation is often preferable. In the study by Duda *et al.* (1978), the initial representation of knowledge is in terms of rules but in the final stage, these rules are incorporated into a so-called partitioned semantic net. Moreover, individual rules can be made to represent individual "chunks" or "modules" of human knowledge, and therefore, it is relatively easy to modify or incrementally build-up the knowledge base. Also, it seems that it is easier to explain to a user the inference process done by a system by listing the involved decision rules, than by showing a part of a network. Knowledge aquisition by learning from examples also seems to be easier to implement using a rule representation.

The accurate encapsulating of knowledge in the form of rules, however, encounters a number of problems. Typically, an expert's knowledge is expressed in terms of imprecise concepts and involves operators that are not well defined. Also, much of this knowledge is accompanied by statements indicating varying degrees of credibility and varying levels of importance assigned to expressed conditions.

In this paper, we use the rule representation of knowledge. The knowledge here involves descriptions of plant conditions indicating one of 15 soybean diseases. The format of the rules is based on the variable-valued logic calculus VL_1 (Michalski, 1974). This calculus was developed for formally representing in a simple, compact and self-explanatory way decision and inference processes involving many-valued variables. Commonly, the variables in such processes have semantically determined value sets, which can differ both in the scope and in the structure relating its elements. For example, "sex" is a 2-valued variable with no structure relating its possible values, "height" or "temperature" of a human being varies in certain range of possible values, and the values constitute a linearly ordered set.

A simple way of characterizing, e.g., a person is by a list of attribute-value pairs, which in VL_1 is written in the form

$$[\text{sex} = \text{male}][\text{height} = \text{medium}][\text{blood-type} = O+]$$

A form in brackets [ ] is called a *selector*, and generally is a relational statement relating a variable to one or more values from its domain. A concatenation of selectors denotes the logical product. VL_1 does not include functions or predicates; in many applications, however, descriptions using only variables are sufficient. (A richer language developed in the same spirit which includes functions, predicates and some other forms is VL_{21} (Michalski, 1978).)

In discussions with experts who are trying to describe their decision processes, in particular diagnostic processes, we observed that they often state a condition for a specific diagnosis as a sequence of observations or symptoms (which can be represented by a conjunction of appropriate selectors). However, these experts often also indicate that certain observations are more important than others. In our experiment, observations have ranged from very important to merely supportive or confirmatory. Therefore, we extended here the concept of a selector as defined in (Michalski, 1974) by adding to it a *weight*. A *weighted selector* S^w is a form:

$$[x_i \# R : W] \tag{2}$$

where x_i is a variable, R, called the *reference*, is a list of one or more values from the value set of this variable, $\#$ stands for one of the relational operators $= \neq \geq \leq > <$, and w is the *weight* of the selector, $w \in [0, 1]$. Is assumed to be 1, if not specified. Before explaining further the weighted selector, we will define some preliminary concepts.

An *event e* is defined as a list of values of an assumed set of variables. For example, assuming the variables: sex, height and blood-type, an event can be

$$e: (\text{male, 5 ft 11 in, A+})$$

An event e is said to *satisfy* a selector S: $[x_i \# R]$ if the value of x_i in e is related by $\#$ to at least one element of R. For example, selector

$$[\text{albumin} = \text{low, medium}]$$

is satisfied by e, if the value of albumin in e is low or medium.

It is easy to see that if the *reference* of a selector has more than one element, the selector is equivalent to a disjunction of selectors with one element references:

$$[x_i \# a, b, \ldots] = [x_i \# a] \vee [x_i \# b] \vee \ldots \tag{3}$$

A selector with a reference consisting of more than one element denotes the so-called *internal disjunction* (disjunction on values of the same variables).

In medical or other applications, the knowledge of values of variables (of tests, observations, etc.) may not be certain. It is usually possible to estimate this uncertainty. Let $D(S, e) \in [0, 1]$ denote the *degree* to which event e satisfies the condition S: $[x_i \# R]$.

Given an event and a weighted selector S^w, the *degree of confirmation of selector S^w by event e* is defined:

$$v(S^w, e) = v(S, e) + (1 - w)(1 - v(S, e)) \tag{4}$$

To explain the idea behind the rule (4), let us assume that in a decision rule, C::>D, the condition, C, is a logical product of selectors, each of which can either be satisfied $v(S, e) = 1$) or not satisfied $v(S, e) = 0$). If the weight of each selector is 1, then, when a single selector is not satisfied, the condition, C, is not satisfied. If, however, the weight ("importance") of this selector is small ($\ll 1$), then one would like to see the effect of not satisfying this selector weakened. Formula (4) provides a means for capturing this property. A product of selectors is called a *term*, and a logical union of terms is called a *disjunctive* VL_1 expression (or *weighted* DVL, expression).

A simple way of expressing decision rules is in the form

$$C :: \overset{\alpha}{>} D \tag{5}$$

where C is a DVL, expression D (DECISION) is a single selector, or a product of selectors, and α measures the "strength" of the implication ($\alpha \in [0, 1]$).

An example of such a rule is the following description of post-necrotic cirrhosis of the liver:
[albumin = low][regeneration: bile ducts & fibrosis: diff or focal = present]
[fat: diff or zonal $\neq$ strongly present][fibrosis: portal or central = absent]
[liver nodules = no]

$$\vee$$

[nausea = no][albumin $\neq$ above normal][regeneration: retic. endo. = absent]

[cells: central or portal, fibrosis: diff or focal = present]
[cells: monos. or epithel. $\neq$ strongly present]
::> [Diagnosis = Postnecrotic Cirrhosis]

(When α is not specified then $\alpha = 1$.)

The above example illustrates the form of inductively-derived decision rules used in this study (section 5 and Appendix 2). Expert-derived rules had somewhat more complex form (section 4 and Appendix 1).

3. Description space

In the case study, 15 soybean diseases were selected as being representative of the nature and scope of the problems which are faced in the diagnosis of plant diseases. The task was to develop a knowledge base which contained sufficient information to diagnose the following subset of soybean diseases:

D1:   *Diaporthe stem canker*
D2:   *Charcoal rot*
D3:   *Rhizoctonia root rot*
D4:   *Phytophthora root rot*
D5:   *Brown stem rot*
D6:   *Powdery mildew*
D7:   *Downy mildew*
D8:   *Brown spot*
D9:   *Bacterial blight*
D10:   *Bacterial pustule*
D11:   *Purple seed stain*
D12:   *Anthracnose*
D13:   *Phyllosticta leaf spot*
D14:   *Alternaria leaf spot*
D15:   *Frog eye leaf spot*

A description space for diagnosing the selected soybean diseases was developed in conference with an expert in soybean pathology. The variables used were 35 plant and environmental descriptors and one decision variable (specifying diagnosis). The intent in selecting the particular descriptors and their associated values was to provide a description space which was sufficient to describe the diseases of soybeans in terms of macro-symptoms, i.e. those symptoms which could be clearly observed with no sophisticated mechanical assistance. The reason is that an Extension Service Field Agent, a farmer, or even a layman should be able to make reliable observations. A descriptor is a function which assigns to the plant or its environment a specific value from the set called the domain of the descriptor. For example, descriptor Time of Occurrence (TOC) specifies for the diseased plant the time of occurrence of the disease in the field. The descriptor Condition of Roots (COR) assigns a value describing the state of the roots of the plant. The domains of these descriptors for this knowledge base were:

D(TOC) = (April, May, June, July, August, September, October)
D(COR) = (Normal, Rotted, Galls or Cysts Present)

TABLE 1
Plant descriptors used in the experiment

	Number of values	Variable
1. *Environmental descriptors*		
1.1 Time of occurrence	(7)	(x_1)
1.2 Plant stand	(2)	(x_2)
1.3 Precipitation	(3)	(x_3)
1.4 Temperature	(3)	(x_4)
1.5 Occurrence of hail	(2)	(x_5)
1.6 Number years crop repeated	(10)	(x_6)
1.7 Damaged area	(4)	(x_7)
2. *Plant global descriptors*		
2.1 Severity	(3)	(x_8)
2.2 Seed treatment	(3)	(x_9)
2.3 Seed germination	(3)	(x_{10})
2.4 Plant height	(2)	(x_{11})
3. *Plant local descriptors*		
3.1 Condition of leaves	(2)	(x_{12})
3.1.1 Leafspots—halos	(3)	(x_{13})
3.1.2 Leafspots—margin	(3)	(x_{14})
3.1.3 Leafspot size	(3)	(x_{15})
3.1.4 Leaf shredding or shot holing	(2)	(x_{16})
3.1.5 Leaf malformation	(2)	(x_{17})
3.1.6 Leaf mildew growth	(3)	(x_{18})
3.2 Condition of stem	(2)	(x_{19})
3.2.1 Presence of lodging	(2)	(x_{20})
3.2.2 Stem cankers	(4)	(x_{21})
3.2.3 Canker lesion color	(4)	(x_{22})
3.2.4 Fruiting pod on stem	(2)	(x_{23})
3.2.5 External decay	(3)	(x_{24})
3.2.6 Mycelium on stem	(2)	(x_{25})
3.2.7 Internal discoloration	(3)	(x_{26})
3.2.8 Sclerotia—internal or external	(2)	(x_{27})
3.3 Condition of fruits—pods	(4)	(x_{28})
3.3.1 Fruit spots	(5)	(x_{29})
3.4 Condition of seed	(2)	(x_{30})
3.4.1 Mold growth	(2)	(x_{31})
3.4.2 Seed discoloration	(2)	(x_{32})
3.4.3 Seed size	(2)	(x_{33})
3.4.4 Seed shrivelling	(2)	(x_{34})
3.5 Condition of roots	(3)	(x_{35})

Table 1 lists the selected 35 descriptors. The number in parentheses following each descriptor indicates the number of possible values the descriptor can take. In addition, there is a decision variable which specifies the diagnosis of a disease from the assumed set of soybean diseases.

Individual diseased plants were described in terms of the above 35 descriptors. Thus, the total description space, (i.e. the set of all possible sequences of values of descriptors) has the size $7 \times 2 \times 3 \times \cdots \times 2 \times 2 \times 3 = $ approx. 3×10^{15} events.

4. Expert-derived decision rules

Diagnostic decision rules for the above-mentioned 15 soybean diseases were obtained from discussions with plant pathologists during several conferences. Approximately 20 hours were required to developed the descriptions for the above 15 diseases. The descriptions of diseases were expressed in the form of modified DVL_1 rules. This modification provided a way to express the statements by experts which indicated different levels of significance for applicable conditions. Significant conditions which must be present in a plant when afflicted by a particular disease are grouped in a term preceded by Q_s; conditions which, although generally present, merely confirm the information which is given by significant conditions are grouped in a term preceded by Q_c. When this representation is used, a sum of these terms constitutes a description of disease.

Additionally, we distinguish a new form of selector, called a *functional* selector, which is defined:

$$[x_i : @fn]$$

where *fn* is a function which assigns a weight to the selector dependent upon the value of the variable x_i, and @ indicates the nature of *fn*. It can be $\uparrow, \downarrow, \cap, \cup$, where $\uparrow(\downarrow)$ indicates that *fn* is monotonically increasing (decreasing) over the domain of x_i and $\cap(\cup)$ indicates that *fn* has the greatest (smallest) weight around some mean and decreases (increases) with the distance from this mean.

For example, in [# years crop repeated: $\uparrow$ER1] the $\uparrow$ indicates that the weight assigned by the function ER1 grows as the number of years the soybean crop is repeated in the same field. The function ER1 can be defined, e.g.:

$$ER1: w = \begin{cases} 1 \cdot 0, & \text{if the crop is repeated 3 or more years} \\ 0 \cdot 8, & \text{if the crop is repeated 2 years} \\ 0 \cdot 7, & \text{if the crop is repeated 1 year} \\ 0 \cdot 2, & \text{if the crop has not been repeated.} \end{cases}$$

which is graphically shown in Fig. 1.

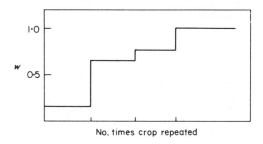

FIG. 1.

TABLE 2

An example of a learning event
(completed questionnaire describing a diseased plant)

Environmental descriptors
    Time of occurrence = July
    Plant stand = normal
    Precipitation = above normal
    Temperature = normal
    Occurrence of hail = no
    Number years crop repeated = 4
    Damaged area = whole fields

Plant global descriptors
    Severity = potentially severe
    Seed treatment = none
    Seed germination = less than 80%
    Plant height = normal

Plant local descriptors
    Condition of leaves = abnormal
        Leafspots—halos = withour yellow halos
        Leafspots—margin = without watersoaked margin
        Leafspot size = greater than 1/8 inch
        Leaf shredding or shot holding = present
        Leaf malformation = absent
        Leaf mildew growth = absent
    Condition of stem = abnormal
        Presence of lodging = no
        Stem cankers = above the second node
        Canker lesion color = brown
        Fruiting bodies on stem = present
        External decay = absent
        Mycelium on stem = absent
        Internal discoloration of stem = none
        Sclerotia—internal or external = absent
    Condition of fruits—pods = normal
        Fruit spots = absent
    Condition of seed = normal
        Mold growth = absent
        Seed discoloration = absent
        Seed size = normal
        Seed shriveling = absent
    Condition of roots = normal

Diagnosis
Diaporthe stem canker( ) *Charcoal rot*( ) *Rhizoctonia root rot*( )
Phytophthora root rot( ) *Brown stem root rot*( ) *Powdery mildew*( )
Downy mildew( ) *Brown spot*(X) *Bacterial blight*( )
Bacterial pustule( ) *Purple seed stain*( ) *Anthracnose*( )
Phyllosticta leaf spot( ) *Alternaria leaf spot*( ) *Frog eye leaf spot*( )

The following is an example of an expert decision rule (describing diaporthe stem canker):

$$Q_s([time = Aug \ldots Spresent][\ precipitation:\uparrow EP][fruiting\ bodies = present]$$
$$[stem\ cankers = above\ second\ node][fruit\ pods = absent])$$
$$+$$
$$Q_c([temperature \geq n][canker\ lesion\ color = brown]$$
$$[\#\ years\ crop\ repeated: \uparrow ER1]$$
$$: : > [Diagnosis = diaporthe\ stem\ canker]$$

The complete set of the expert-derived decision rules and the weight assigning functions are given in Appendix 1.

5. Inductively-derived decision rules

5.1. BACKGROUND INFORMATION

The inductively-derived decision rules were generated by applying the computer program AQ11 (Michalski & Larson, 1978) to a set of events (descriptions of individual diseased plants) with known diagnosis. The events were specified in the form of questionnaires completed by plant pathologists. Table 2 is an example of a completed questionnaire which describes a case of brown spot. All available events (630) were partitioned into a learning and testing set (Table 3).

TABLE 3
Events available for learning and testing

Disease	Learning events	Testing events	Available events
Diaporthe stem canker	10	10	20
Charcoal rot	10	10	20
Rhizoctonia root rot	10	10	20
Phytophthora root rot	40	48	88
Brown stem rot	20	24	44
Powdery mildew	10	10	20
Downy mildew	10	10	20
Brown spot	40	52	92
Bacterial pustule	10	10	20
Bacterial blight	10	10	20
Purple seed stain	10	10	20
Anthracnose	20	24	44
Phyllosticta leaf spot	10	10	20
Alternaria leaf spot	40	51	91
Frog eye leaf spot	40	51	91
Total	290	340	630

Also, rules describing some *a priori* knowledge of the problem were specified. These rules included the following:

1. A description of known relationships among variables, specifically relations stating that if some part of a plant is healthy then all the descriptors which specify the particular

conditions of that part do not apply. For example,

[leaves = normal] ⇒ [leafspots halos = *][leafspots margin = *]
[leafspot size = *][leaf shredding = *]
[leaf malformation = *][leaf mildew growth = *]

where * denotes "does not apply" and ⇒ is the logical implication. Table 4 gives the rules used.

TABLE 4

Rules describing a priori *knowledge*

1. [leaves = normal] ⇒ [leafspots halos = *][leafspots margin = *]
   [leafspot size = *][leaf shredding = *]
   [leaf malformation = *][leaf mildew growth = *]

2. [leafspots halos = absent] ⇒ [leafspots margin = *][leafspot size = *]

3. [stem = normal] ⇒ [presence of lodging = *][stem cankers = *]
   [canker lesion color = *][fruiting bodies on stem = *]
   [external decay of stem = *][mycelium on stem = *]
   [internal discoloration = *]
   [sclerotia internal or external = *]

4. [fruit pods = normal] ⇒ [fruit spots = *]

5. [seed = normal] ⇒ [seed mold growth = *][seed discoloration = *]
   [seed size = *][seed shriveling = *]

2. Definitions of generalization trees which relate to each other the values of structured variables (Michalski & Larson, 1978) from the viewpoint of their generality. Two structured descriptors were used:

DAMAGED AREA

0   Scattered plants
1   Groups of plants in low areas ⟶ 4   Not whole fields
2   Groups of plants in upland areas
3   Whole fields

LEAF SPOTS HALOS

0   Absent
1   With yellow halos ⟶ 3   Present
2   Without yellow halos

The learning events and the above rules were the input to the inductive program AQ11. Before presenting the rules and discussing them, we will briefly describe the basic algorithm underlying the program. (Michalski & Larson, 1978).

5.2. DESCRIPTION OF THE TOP-LEVEL ALGORITHM

Suppose there is given a set of hypothesis, $V = \{V_i\}$, $i = 1, \ldots, m$, and a family of event sets ("facts"), $F = \{F_i\}$, which these hypotheses are supposed to describe. Suppose that for any i, V_i describes correctly only a part of the events from F_i.

The problem is to produce a new set of hypotheses, $V^1 = \{V_i^1\}$, where each V_i^1 describes all events from set F_i, and does not describe events from other event sets F_j, $j \neq i$.

The following solution to this problem is based on an algorithm for determing a *cover*, $C(E_1/E_0)$, of an *event set* E_1 *against* the *event set* E_0. Such a cover can be interpreted as a DVL_1 expression which is satisfied by every event in E_1 and not satisfied by any event in E_0 (or in $E_0 \setminus E_1$, if $E_0 \cap E_1 \neq \phi$). The covering algorithm is based on the effective use "negative events" (i.e. those in E_0), and is especially efficient when the negative examples are expressed as a cover. For the lack of space we have to omit here a review of the covering algorithm, and describe only the process of hypothesis generation which uses the algorithm as the basic book. The algorithm is described in Michalski (1971, 1975). The solution consists of 3 major steps.

Step 1
The first step isolates those facts which are not consistent with the given hypotheses. For each hypothesis, two sets are created:

F^+—a set of events which should be covered by the hypothesis, but are not;
F^-—a set of events which are covered by the hypothesis, but should not be covered.

(An event is said to *be covered* by a hypothesis if the event satisfies the VL_1 formula which represents the hypothesis.) Specifically, this step determines, for each i, $i = 1, 2, \ldots, m$, the sets:[†]

$$F_i^+ = F_i \setminus \tilde{V}_i,$$

$$F_{ij}^- = \tilde{V}_i \cap F_j, \qquad j = 1, 2, \ldots, m; \quad j \neq i.$$

Thus, F_i^+ denotes events which should be covered by V_i but are not, and F_{ij}^- denotes "exception" events, i.e. events in F_j, $j \neq i$, which are covered by V_j, but should not be covered.

Step 2
This step determines, for each i, a generalized formula V_i^- describing all exception events (the union of sets F_{ij}^-, $j = 1, 2, \ldots, m, j \neq i$). This is done by generating, for given i and each j, a cover of F_{ij}^- against the events in the sets $\tilde{V}_i \cup F_i^+$, $i = 1, 2, \ldots, m$:

$$V_{ij}^- = C\left(F_{ij}^- \Big/ \bigvee_{i=1}^{m} (\tilde{V}_i \cup F_i^+)\right)$$

and then taking the logical union of V_{ij}^-:

$$V_i^- = \bigvee_{\substack{j=1 \\ j \neq i}}^{m} V_{ij}^-.$$

The reason for this step is that it is computationally more efficient to use formulas V_i^- than the union of E_{ij}^-, $j = 1, 2, \ldots, m; j \neq i$.

Step 3
New "correct" hypotheses could be obtained now by "subtracting" from each V_i the formula V_i^- and "adding" to it the set F_i^+. To do this however, is difficult. Again, an advantage is taken of the available covering techniques. Namely, the new hypotheses,

---

[†] $\tilde{V}_i$ denotes the set of events covered for formula V_i.

$V_i^1, i = 1, 2, \ldots, m$, are determined as covers:

$$V_i^1 = C\left(F_i \middle/ \bigvee_{\substack{k=1 \\ k \neq i}}^{m} [(\tilde{V}_k \backslash \tilde{V}_k^-) \quad F_k]\right).$$

(The point is that directly simplifying a union of terms is difficult; but subtracting a term from a term or generating a cover of an event set against a formula is easier.)

Step 4

This step determines the final representation of hypotheses V_i^1. The V_i^1 are expressions which are unions of terms. Some terms in a V_i^1 may represent (cover) only a few events in F_i. Such "low weight" terms can be replaced by the events (facts) themselves (since an event takes less memory than a term). (They may also indicate errors in data.)

The rules for the generalization of structured descriptors were applied after the decision rules had been generated.

5.3. THE INDUCTIVELY-DERIVED RULES

AQ11 produced decision rules in which the CONDITION part is a DVL_1 expression involving selectors with $w = 1$. The following is an example of an inductively-derived decision rule (describing *Phytophthora root rot*):

[plant stand < n][precipitation ≥ n][temperature ≤ n][stem = abn]
[plant height = abn][leaves = abn][leaf malformation = abs]   (24, 6, 24)

$\vee$

[time = Ar. .Aug][plant stand = abn][damaged area = low areas]
[plant height = abn][leaves = abn][stem = abn]   (16, 16, 34)
[external decay ≠ firm & dry]
$\Rightarrow$ [Diagnosis = *Phytophthora root rot*]

The complete set of inductively derived decision rules is given in Appendix 2. (AQ11, written in PL/I, took approximately 4 minutes and 30 seconds on an IBM 360/75 to generate the rules.) The triplet of numbers given with each term (a product of selectors) of the rule indicates the performance of that term in covering the learning set of events. The first element of the triplet indicates the number of new events covered by this term (those which were not covered by previously generated terms); the second, the number of events which only this term covered; the third, the number of events which this term covered totally. This triplet provides information about the relative importance of each term to a given decision rule.

The program ESEL (Michalski & Larson, 1978) was used to select the learning events from the set of available events. This program attempts to select the most representative events from each disease set using a "distance" measuring technique. This method of selecting the learning events biases the testing set in some sense since the testing events are those which were not selected by the program. To eliminate this effect one could acquire a distinct set of testing events or select learning events totally randomly. The point of this study was, however, not to test the learning method using a teacher which randomly selects examples, but a "good" teacher which selects representative learning examples. The program ESEL was such a teacher. The selected events were analysed by AQ11 to produce the decision rules.

6. Comparison of the performance of the rules

Both the inductively derived rules and the expert-derived rules were tested using the same testing events (340 cases in total of soybean diseases—Table 3). The experiment involved the application of several inference techniques (Michalski & Chilausky, 1980). Here we present the results which were obtained with the best performing technique for each set of rules.

A. EVALUATION TECHNIQUES USED FOR EXPERT-DERIVED RULES

(Scheme $\langle$P, A, M$\rangle$ as described in Michalski & Chilausky, 1980.)

   (a) Evaluation of a selector:

$$D(S^w) = \begin{cases} 1, & \text{if the value of the variable in the event satisfies the selector,} \\ 1-w, & \text{otherwise.} \end{cases}$$

   (b) Evaluation of a functional selector (i.e. $[x_i: @ fn]$):

$$v(S^w) = \text{value of } fn \text{ for the value of the variable in the event}$$

   (c) Evaluation of a term:

$$v(T) = \sum_i (v(S_i^w)/ \# \text{ of selectors in the term})$$

   where i indexes each selector in the term.

   (d) Evaluation of an expression. Each rule was a sum of two terms, T_s (conditions preceded by Q_s) and T_1 (conditions preceded by Q_1). (In two rules T_1 was empty.) T_s contributed 90% and T_1 contributed 10% to the degree of confirmation of the rule:

$$v(F) = 0.9 \cdot v(T_s) + 0.1 \cdot v(T_c)$$

The coefficients 0.9 and 0.1 were determined experimentally. (When T_1 was empty, the coefficient for T_s was 1.)

B. EVALUATION TECHNIQUES USED FOR THE INDUCTIVELY-DERIVED RULES

(Scheme $\langle$N, A, S$\rangle$ as described in Michalski & Chilausky, 1980.)

   (a) Evaluation of a selector:

$$D(S) = \begin{cases} w, & \text{if the value of the variable in the event satisfies the selector,} \\ -w, & \text{otherwise.} \end{cases}$$

   (The rules consisted of only selectors with $w = 1$.)

   (b) Evaluation of a term:

$$v(T) = \sum_i v(S_i) \Big/ \# \text{ of selectors in the term .}$$

   (c) Evaluation of an expression:
   For $F = T_1 \vee T_2$

$$v(F) = v(T_1) + v(T_2) - v(T_1) \cdot v(T_2)$$

(For the rules which consisted of more than two terms the evaluation was appropriately extended.)

TABLE 5

Confusion matrix summarizing the diagnosis of 340 testing events using expert-derived VL rules

Correct diagnosis	Indecision ratio	Ties	Maximum # of altern	Test cases	Assigned decision															
					D1	D2	D3	D4	D5	D6	D7	D8	D9	D10	D11	D12	D13	D14	D15
Diaporthe stem canker (D1)	1·8	7	3	10	100											40			
Charcoal rot (D2)	1·0	0	1	10		100													
Rhizoctonia root rot (D3)	0·9	0	1	10			90												
Phytophthora root rot (D4)	1·4	18	2	48		27	8	100	2										
Brown stem rot (D5)	0·96	2	3	24					87			4						4	
Powdery mildew (D6)	1·0	0	1	10						100									
Downy mildew (D7)	3·4	10	5	10							80	100	30				30	70	30
Septoria brown spot (D8)	4·9	52	8	52	37						40	100		38		37	90	44	100
Bacterial blight (D9)	2·7	9	4	10							50		100	90			30		
Bacterial pustule (D10)	3·2	9	5	10							10	70	50	100	30		30	20	10
Purple seed stain (D11)	2·1	8	5	10					20		10		10		80			60	30
Anthracnose (D12)	2·1	21	4	24	50				4	4					54	96			
Phyllosticta leaf spot (D13)	4·1	10	6	10							20	100		50			90	80	70
Alternaria leaf spot (D14)	3·1	51	5	51							39	100	20				8	94	69
Frog eye leaf spot (D15)	4·2	51	6	51				4	39		63	100				4	6	100	100

TABLE 6

Confusion matrix summarizing the diagnosis of 340 testing events using inductively-derived VL rules

Correct diagnosis	Indecision ratio	ties	Maximum # of altern	Test cases	Assigned decision														
					D1	D2	D3	D4	D5	D6	D7	D8	D9	D10	D11	D12	D13	D14	D15
Diaporthe stem canker (D1)	2·7	10	3	10	100												100		70
Charcoal rot (D2)	1·0	0	1	10		100													
Rhizoctonia root rot (D3)	2·0	10	2	10			100	100											
Phytophthora root rot (D4)	1·0	0	1	48				100											
Brown stem rot (D5)	1·3	3	5	24				8	100			4						8	8
Powdery mildew (D6)	1·0	0	1	10						100									
Downy mildew (D7)	4·1	10	5	10							100	90					30	90	100
Septoria brown spot (D8)	4·0	52	5	52					10			100					88	100	100
Bacterial blight (D9)	3·2	10	4	10									100	50			10	80	80
Bacterial pustule (D10)	1·6	4	4	10								20		100	10		30		
Purple seed stain (D11)	2·8	7	4	10								40	10		100	10		60	60
Anthracnose (D12)	1·1	2	3	24					8							100			4
Phyllosticta leaf spot (D13)	3·9	10	4	10								100					100	100	90
Alternaria leaf spot (D14)	3·2	51	4	51								100					22	100	100
Frog eye leaf spot (D15)	3·9	51	5	51								100				82	4	100	100

Tables 5 and 6 show the results of testing both sets of rules (expert-derived and inductively derived) to determine the accuracy with which they classified testing cases of plant diseases. The correct diagnoses for testing events were determined by plant pathologists. If two or more rules were satisfied by a testing event (i.e. a description of a sick plant), the event was multiply classified (i.e. assigned a set of alternatives). The labels for the confusion matrices are defined as follows.

Correct diagnosis
The correct diagnosis for the given testing event.

Indecision ratio
The ratio of the number of alternative diagnoses for the events of the given disease over the number of testing events in the set. An increase in the indecision ratio indicates an increase in the average number of alternative diagnoses for the cases of the given disease. A small indecision ratio does not imply correct diagnoses.

Ties
The number of testing events of the disease which were not uniquely diagnosed.

Maximum # of altern
The maximum number of alternatives in diagnosing a case of the given disease.

Test cases
The number of testing events of the given disease.

Assigned decision
Each column under this label gives the percentage of decisions indicating the corresponding disease for the testing events (for which the correct diagnosis is indicated by the label in the row).

Thus, the percent of correctly assigned diagnoses are on the diagonal of each confusion matrix.

TABLE 7
Performance of the rules

Type	% correct diagnosis	% preferred diagnosis	% not diagnosed	Indecision ratio	Threshold
Inductively-derived	100·0	97·6	—	2·64	0·80
Expert-derived	96·2	71·8	2·1	2·90	0·65

Table 7 gives a comparison of the overall performance of the two sets of rules. The rules which satisfied a *criterion of acceptability* were selected as alternative diagnoses. The *criterion of acceptability* was that the degree of confirmation of a rule must be greater than the *THRESHOLD*, and be either maximum or smaller than maximum by no more than *MARGIN OF UNCERTAINTY*. The *THRESHOLD* was 0·65 for the expert-derived rules and 0·8 for the inductively derived rules. The label "% Correct diagnosis" indicates the percentage of cases when the correct disease (according to experts) was one of alternative diagnoses. The *MARGIN OF UNCERTAINTY* was specified as 0·2 for both sets of rules. The label "% Preferred diagnosis" indicates the percentage of cases when the disease which had the highest degree of confirmation was the correct one. Both inductive and expert rules performed well in selecting the correct disease as one of the diagnostic alternatives. However, the inductively derived rules performed better in selecting the correct disease as the preferred diagnosis. The indecision ratio (total decisions over total events) for the two sets of rules were comparable and the number of alternative diagnoses were distributed quite similarly (Tables 5 and 6). Seven cases could not be diagnosed by the expert rules using the given *THRESHOLD*. The *THRESHOLDS* (determined experimentally) were significantly different. This appears to indicate that the inductive rules are "cleaner", i.e. there is less information in them which is non-essential to diagnosis.

7. Conclusion

The comparison of 2 knowledge acquisition techniques indicates that decision rules derived inductively performed somewhat better than the rules derived by representing the knowledge of experts (in the specific context of soybean disease diagnosis). Since this result was contrary to the initial expectations of the authors, the experiment was repeated several times introducing various corrections to the expert-derived rules and the input events and using different inference techniques. The results always had basically the same pattern. There can be several explanations for this outcome.

(1) The information obtained during the conference with the experts was not sufficiently adequate.
(2) Our knowledge representation scheme was not adequate. (It may be interesting to notice here that expert-derived rules were basically single conjunctions of selectors having varying weight, while inductively derived rules were either a single conjunction of unweighted selectors or a logical union of such conjunctions.)
(3) The inference techniques used to evaluate the decision rules were not adequate.
(4) Experts in making diagnoses are not necessarily experts in explaining the process of diagnosis. These functions are different. If this is the case, it means that the reliability of the data describing diagnoses made by experts (i.e. reliability of the learning events) will tend to be better than the diagnostic decision rules which they formulate. This would provide an additional argument for knowledge acquisition by induction from examples.

The major conclusion of this experiment is that the current computer induction techniques can already offer a viable knowledge acquisition method if the problem domain is sufficiently simple and well defined.

The research presented here was supported in part by the National Foundation Grants NSF MCS 76-22940 and NSF MCS 79-06614. The authors would like to thank Professor James Sinclair and Professor Barry Jackobsen, from the Plant Pathology Department of the University of Illinois, for providing the expertise and the data for the experiments reported here, and for their strong interest in this work.

References

BRACHMAN, R. J. (1978). On the epistemological status of semantic networks. *Report No. 3807.* Bolt Beranek and Newman, Inc., Cambridge, Massachusetts, April.

BUCHANAN, B. G. & FEIGENBAUM, E. A. (1978). Dendral and meta-dendral, their applications dimension. *Artificial Intelligence*, **11**, 5–24.

DAVIS, R., BUCHANAN B. & SHORTLIFFE, E. (1975). Production rules as a representation for a knowledge-based consultation program. *Memo AIM-266.* Stanford Artificial Intelligence Laboratory, Stanford, California, October.

DAVIS, R. (1976). Application of meta level knowledge to the construction, maintenance and use of large knowledge bases. *STAN-CS-76-552.* Department of Computer Science, Stanford University, Stanford, California, July.

DIETTERICH, T. G. & MICHALSKI, R. S. (1979). Learning and generalization of characteristic descriptions: evaluation critera and comparative review of selected methods. In *Proceedings of Sixth International Joint Conference on Artificial Intelligence*, Tokyo, Japan, August.

DUDA, R. O. *et al.* (1978). Development of the PROSPECTOR consultation system for mineral exploration. *Final Report.* SRI International, Menlo Park, California, October.

HAYES-ROTH, F. & MCDERMOTT, J. (1978). An inference matching technique for inducing abstractions. *Communications of the ACM*, **21**(5), 401–410.

KULIKOWSKI, C. A. (1977). Problems in the design of knowledge bases for medical consultation. In *Proceedings of 1st Annual Symposium on Computer Applications in Medical Care*, IEEE, New York.

KULIKOWSKI, C. A. (1978). Artificial Intelligence approaches to medical consultation. In *Proceedings of the Fourth Illinois Conference on Medical Information Systems*, May.

MICHALSKI, R. S. (1971). A geometrical model for the synthesis of internal covers. *Report No. 461.* Department of Computer Science, University of Illinois, Urbana, Illinois, June.

MICHALSKI, R. S. (1974). Variable-valued logic: system VL_1. In *Proceedings of Fourth International Symposium on Multiple-Valued Logic*, Morgantown, West Virginia, May.

MICHALSKI, R. S. (1975). Synthesis of optimal and quasi-optimal variable-valued logic formulas. *Proceedings of Fifth Internal Symposium on Multiple-valued Logic*, Indiana University, Bloomington, Indiana.

MICHALSKI, R. S. (1978). Pattern recognition as knowledge-guided computer induction. *Report No. 927.* Department of Computer Science, University of Illinois, Urbana, Illinois.

MICHALSKI, R. S. & LARSON, J. B. (1978). Selection of most representative training examples and incremental generation of VL_1 hypothesis: the underlying methodology and the descriptions of programs ESEL and AQ11. *Report No. 877.* Department of Computer Science, University of Illinois, Urbana, Illinois, May.

MICHALSKI, R. S. & CHILAUSKY, R. L. (1980). An experimental comparison of several many-valued logic inference techniques in the context of computer diagnosis of soybean diseases. *International Journal of Man–Machine Studies*, to appear.

MITCHELL, T. M. (1977). Version spaces: a candidate elimination approach to rule learning. In *5th International Joint Conference on Artificial Intelligence*, Vol. 1, Cambridge, Mass.

MYERS, J. D. & POPLE, H. E. (1977). INTERNIST: A consultative diagnostic program in internal medicine. *Proceedings of the 1st Annual Symposium on Computer Applications in Medical Care*, IEEE, New York.

PATRICK, E. A. (1979). *Decision Analysis in Medicine.* West Palm Beach, Florida: CRC Press.

SHORTLIFFE, E. H. (1976). *Computer-based Medical Consultations: MYCIN.* New York: American Elsevier.

Appendix 1

EXPERT-DERIVED RULES FOR 15 SOYBEAN DISEASES

Q_s indicates significant conditions.

Q_c indicates corroborative conditions.

Abbreviations used: n—normal; abn—abnormal; p—present; abs—absent.

D1: Q_s([time = Aug .. Sep][precipitation: ↑EP]
[stem cankers = above second node][fruiting bodies = p]
[fruit pods = n])

+

Q_c([temperature ≥ n][canker lesion color = brown]
[# years crop repeated: ↑ER1])
       : :> [Diagnosis = *Diaporthe stem canker*]

D2: Q_s([time = Jul . . . Aug][precipitation ≤ n][temperature ≥ n]
[plant growth = abn][leaves = abn][stem = abn][sclerotia = p]
[roots = rotted][internal discoloration = black])

+

Q_c([damaged area = upland areas][severity = severe][seed size < n]
[# years crop repeated: ↑ER2])
       : :> [Diagnosis = *Charcoal rot*]

D3: Q_s([time = May . . . Jun][plant stand < n][temperature < n]
[precipitation < n][leaves = abn][stem = abn]
[canker lesion color = brown][roots = rotted]
([occurrence of hail = no]⇒[stem cankers = below soil line, at or slightly
  above soil line])
([occurrence of hail = yes]⇒[stem cankers = above second node]))

+

Q_c([fruiting bodies = abs][external decay = firm & dry][mycelium = abs])
       : :> [Diagnosis = *Rhizoctonia root rot*]

D4: Q_s([time: ∩ ET][plant stand < n]
([time = Apr . . . Jun]⇒[precipitation = n])
([time = Jul . . . Aug]⇒[precipitation = above n])
([time = Apr]⇒[temperature = above n])
([time = May . . . Aug]⇒[temperature = n])[damaged areas = low areas]
[plant growth = abn][leaves = abn][stem = abn]
[stem cankers = at or slightly above soil line]
([time = May , . . Aug]⇒[canker lesion color = dark brown or black])
[roots = rotted])

+

Q_c([# years crop repeated ≥ 2])
       : :>[Diagnosis = *Phytophthora root rot*]

D5: Q_s([time = Jul . . . Sep][precipitation > n][temperature ≤ n][leaves = abn]
[stem = abn][internal discoloration = brown][lodging = p])

+

Q_c([seed size < n][# years crop repeated: ↑ER3])
       : :> [Diagnosis = *Brown stem rot*]

D6: Q_s([leaves = abn][leaf mildew growth = upper leaf surface])

+

Q_c[time = Aug . . . Sep]
       : :>[Diagnosis = *Powdery mildew*]

D7: Q_s([time = Jun ... Aug][precipitation ≥ n][damaged areas = whole fields]
        [leaves = abn][leafspots halos = no yellow halos]
        [leaf mildew growth = lower leaf surface]
        ([time = Sep ... Oct]⇒[see = abn])[mold growth on seed = p])
                :   :>[Diagnosis = *Downy mildew*]

D8: Q_s([leaves = abn][leafspots halos = p]
        [leafspots watersoaked margin = abs][leafspot size > 1/8 inch])
                                +
        Q_c([time = May, Aug ... Sep][precipitation ≥ n])
                :   :>[Diagnosis = *Brown spot*]

D9: Q_s([time = Apr ... Jun, Aug ... Sep]
        ([time = Apr ... Jun]⇒[precipitation = n, above n])
        ([time = Aug ... Sep]⇒[precipitation⇒above n])
        ([time ≠ Aug]⇒[temperature = n])
        ([time = Aug]⇒[temperature = below n])[leaves = abn]
        [leafspots halos = with yellow halos][leafspots watersoaked margin = p]
        [leafspot size < 1/8 inch][leaf shredding = p])
                :   :>[Diagnosis = *Bacterial blight*]

D10: Q_s([time = Jun ... Aug][precipitation ≥ n][leaves = abn]
        [leafspots halos = no yellow halos][leafspots watersoaked margin = abs]
        [leafspot size < 1/8″][leaf shredding = p])
                                +
        Q_c[# years crop repeated ≥ 1]
                :   :>[Diagnosis = *Bacterial pustule*]

D11: Q_s([time = Sep ... Oct][seed = abn][seed discoloration = p]
        [seed size = smaller than n])
                                +
        Q_c([time = Aug ... Sep][precipitation ≥ n][leaves = abn])
                :   :>[Diagnosis = *Purple seed stain*]

D12: Q_s([time = Aug ...Oct][precipitation ≥ n][stem = abn]
        [canker lesion color = brown][fruiting bodies = p]
        ([time = Sep ... Oct]⇒[seed = abn])
        [fruit spots = abs, brown spots with black specks])
                                +
        Q_c [damaged area = whole fields]
                :   :>[Diagnosis = *Anthracnose*]

D13: Q_s([time = Apr ... Jul][precipitation ≥ n][leaves = abn]
        [leafspots halos = no yellow halos][leafspots watersoaked margin = abs]
        [leafspot size > 1/8 inch][leaf shredding = p])
                                +
        Q_c([damaged area = whole fields][time ≠ Jun]⇒[temperature = n])
        ([time = Jun]⇒[temperature = below n])
                :   :>[Diagnosis = *Phyllosticta leaf spot*]

D14: Q_s([time = Jul .. Oct][leaves = abn][leafspots halos = no yellow halos]
        [leafspots watersoaked margin = abs][leafspot size > 1/8 inch]
        [leaf shredding = abs])

                                    +

        Q_c((([time = Sep . . . Oct]⇒[fruit pods = diseased])
        ([fruit pods = diseased]⇒[fruit spots = colored spots])
        ([seed = abn]⇒[seed discoloration = p]))
                : :>[Diagnosis = *Alternaria leaf spot*]

D15: Q_s([time = Jul . . . Sep][precipitation ≥ n][leaves = abn]
        [leafspots halos = no yellow halos][leafspots watersoaked margin = abs]
        [leafspot size > 1/8 inch])

                                    +

        Q_c((([time = Sep]⇒[fruit spots = colored spots])
        [stem canker = above second node][canker lesion color = tan]
        [fruiting bodies = abs])
                : :>[Diagnosis = *Frog eye leaf spot*]

DEFINITION OF WEIGHT ASSIGNING FUNCTIONS

$$
EP: \begin{cases} 1\cdot0, & \text{if precipitation = above normal} \\ 0\cdot7, & \text{if precipitation = normal} \\ *, & \text{otherwise} \end{cases}
$$

$$
ER1: \begin{cases} 1\cdot0, & \text{if \# years crop repeated} \geq 3 \\ 0\cdot8, & \text{if \# years crop repeated} = 2 \\ 0\cdot7, & \text{if \# years crop repeated} = 1 \\ 0\cdot2, & \text{if crop not repeated} \end{cases}
$$

$$
ER2: \begin{cases} 1\cdot0, & \text{if \# years crop repeated} \geq 2 \\ 0\cdot6, & \text{if \# years crop repeated} = 1 \\ 0\cdot2, & \text{if crop not repeated} \end{cases}
$$

$$
ET: \begin{cases} 1\cdot0, & \text{if time of occurrence = May . . . Jul} \\ 0\cdot7, & \text{if time of occurrence = Apr, Aug} \\ *, & \text{otherwise} \end{cases}
$$

$$
ER3: \begin{cases} 1\cdot0, & \text{if \# years crop repeated} \geq 2 \\ 0\cdot5, & \text{if \# years crop repeated} = 1 \\ 0\cdot1, & \text{if crop not repeated} \end{cases}
$$

Appendix 2

INDUCTIVELY-DERIVED RULES FOR 15 SOYBEAN DISEASES

Abbreviations used: n—normal; abn—abnormal; p—present; abs—absent.

D1:   [time = Jul . . . Oct][precipitation > n][leaf malformation = abs]
        [stem = abn][stem cankers = above second node]   (10, 10, 10)
        [external decay = firm & dry][fruit pods = n]
                : :>[Diagnosis = *Diaporthe stem canker*]

D2:   [leaf malformation = abs][stem = abn]
        [internal discoloration = black]   (10, 10, 10)
                : :>[Diagnosis = *Charcoal rot*]

D3:   [leaves = n][stem = abn][stem cankers = below soil line]
        [canker lesion color = brown]   (9, 9, 9)
                                        ∨
        [leaf malformation = abs][stem = abn]
        [stem cankers = below soil line][canker lesion color = brown]   (1, 1, 1)
        : :>[Diagnosis = *Rhizoctonia root rot*]

D4:   [plant stand > n][precipitation ≥ n][temperature ≤ n]
        [plant height = abn][leaves = abn][leaf malformation = abs]   (24, 6, 24)
        [stem = abn]
                                        ∨
        [time = Apr . . . Aug][plant stand = abn][damaged area = low]
        [plant height = abn][leaves = abn][stem = abn]   (16, 16, 34)
        [external decay = abs, soft and watery]
                : :>[Diagnosis = *Phytophthora root rot*]

D5:   [leaf malformation = abs][stem = abn]
        [internal discoloration = brown]   (13, 13, 13)
                                        ∨
        [leaves = n][stem = abn][internal discoloration = brown]   (7, 7, 7)
                : :>[Diagnosis = *Brown stem rot*]

D6:   [leaves = abn][leaf malformation = abs]
        [leaf mildew growth = on upper leaf surface][roots = n]   (10, 10, 10)
                : :>[Diagnosis = *Powdery mildew*]

D7:   [leafspots halos = p][leaf mildew growth = on lower leaf surface]
        [stem = n][seed mold growth = p]   (10, 10, 10)
                : :>[Diagnosis = *Downy mildew*]

D8:   [precipitation ≥ n][≠ years crop repeated > 1]
        [damaged area ≠ whole fields][leaves = abn]
        [leafspots halos = no yellow halos]
        [leafspots watersoaked margin = abs][leafspot size > 1/8 inch]
        [leaf malformation = abs][roots = n]   (19, 2, 19)
                                        ∨
        [precipitation > n][leaves = abn]
        [leafspots halos = no yellow halos]
        [leafspots watersoaked margin = abs][leafspot size > 1/8 inch]
        [root = n]   (15, 11, 30)
                                        ∨
        [time = Apr . . . Jun][damaged area ≠ whole fields][leaves = abn]
        [leafspots halos = no yellow halos]
        [leafspots watersoaked margin = abs][leafspot size > 1/8 inch]

[leaf shredding = abs][leaf malformation = abs][roots = n]   (6, 6, 12)
    : :>[Diagnosis = *Brown spot*]

D9:   [time = Jun . . . Sep][temperature ≥ n][leaves = abn]
      [leafspots halos = p][leafspots watersoaked margin = p]
      [leafspot size < 1/8 inch][fruit pods = n][roots = n]   (10, 10, 10)
      : :>[Diagnosis = *Bacterial blight*]

D10: [leaves = abn][leafspots halos = with yellow halos]
      [leafspots watersoaked margin = abs][leafspot size < 1/8 inch]
      [stem = n][fruit pods = n]   (7, 6, 7)
V

      [leafspots halos = p][leafspot size < 1/8 inch][stem = n]
      [roots = rotted]   (2, 2, 2)
V

      [time = May][precipitation = n][leaves = abn]
      [leafspots halos = with yellow halos]   (1, 1, 2)
      : :>[Diagnosis = *Bacterial pustule*]

D11: [plant stand = n][precipitation > n][severity = minor]
      [plant height = n][leafspots halos = no yellow halos][seed = abn]
      [seed discoloration = p][seed size = n]   (5, 5, 5)
V

      [leaves = n][seed = abn][seed size = n]   (5, 5, 5)
      : :>[Diagnosis = *Purple seed stain*]

D12: [precipitation > n][leaf malformation = abs][stem = abn]
      [stem cankers = at or slightly above soil line, above second node]
      [seed = abn][roots = n]   (10, 8, 10)
V

      [time = Aug . . . Oct][precipitation > n][leaves = n]
      [stem cankers = above second node][fruit pods = diseased]
      [fruit spots = brown spots with black specks]   (5, 5, 5)
V

      [temperature > n][leafspots halos = abs][leaf malformation = abs]
      [stem = abn][external decay = firm and dry]   (5, 5, 7)
      : :>[Diagnosis = *Anthracnose*]

D13: [time = Jun . . . Jul][precipitation ≤ n][severity = minor]
      [leafspots halos = no yellow halos]
      [leafspots watersoaked margin = abs][stem = n][roots = n]   (6, 5, 6)
V

      [precipitation < n][leaves = abn]
      [leafspots halos = no yellow halos]
      [leafspots watersoaked margin = abs][roots = n]   (3, 3, 4)
V

      [plant stand < n][precipitation = n][occurrence of hail = no]
      [leafspots halos = no yellow halos]
      [leafspots watersoaked margin = abs][stem = n][roots = n]   (1, 1, 1)
      : :>[Diagnosis = *Phyllosticta leaf spot*]

D14: [time = Aug][precipitation > n][seed treatment = none]
      [leaves = abn][leafspots halos = no yellow halos]
      [leafspots watersoaked margin = p][leafspot size > 1/8 inch]
      [leaf mildew growth = abs][stem = n][fruit pods = n]   (8, 5, 8)
                            ∨
      [time = Sep . . . Oct][precipitation > n]
      [damaged area = scattered plants, low areas, whole fields]
      [seed germination ≥ 80%][leaves = abn]
      [leafspots halos = no yellow halos]
      [leafspots watersoaked margin = p][leafspot size > 1/8 inch]
      [stem = n]   (13, 4, 13)
                            ∨
      [time = Aug . . . Oct][damaged area = scattered plants, low areas]
      [seed germination < 80%][plant height = n][leaves = abn]
      [leafspots halos = no yellow halos]
      [leafspots watersoaked margin = p][leafspot size > 1/8 inch]
      [leaf mildew growth = abs][stem = n]   (7, 3, 10)
                            ∨
      [time = Oct][seed germination < 90%][leaves = abn]
      [leafspots halos = no yellow halos]
      [leafspots watersoaked margin = p][leafspot size > 1/8 inch]
      [leaf mildew growth = abs][stem = n]   (4, 2, 7)
                            ∨
      [time = Aug . . .Oct][damaged area = upland areas, whole fields]
      [seed treatment = none, other][seed germination ≥ 80%]
      [leaves = abn][leafspots halos = no yellow halos]
      [leafspots watersoaked margin = p][leafspot size > 1/8 inch]
      [leaf mildew growth = abs][stem = n][fruit pods = n]   (3, 3, 3)
                            ∨
      [occurrence of hail = no][damaged area = scattered plants]
      [severity = potentially severe][seed germination ≥ 80%]
      [leaves = abn][leafspots halos = no yellow halos]
      [leafspots watersoaked margin = p][leafspot size > 1/8 inch]
      [leaf mildew growth = abs][stem = n]   (3, 3, 11)
                            ∨
      [time = Aug . . . Oct][temperature = n][seed treatment = fungicide]
      [seed germination = 80–89%][leaves = abn]
      [leafspots halos = no yellow halos]
      [leafspots watersoaked margin = p][leafspot size > 1/8 inch]
      [leaf mildew growth = abs][stem = n][fruit pods = n]   (1, 1, 6)
                            ∨
      [time = Sep . . . Oct][leaves = abn]
      [leafspots halos = no yellow halos]
      [leafspots watersoaked margin = p][leafspot size > 1/8 inch]
      [leaf shredding = p]   (1, 1, 1)
            : :>[Diagnosis = *Alternaria leaf spot*]

D15: [precipitation ≥ n]
      [damaged area = low areas, upland areas, whole fields]
      [leaves = abn][leafspots halos = no yellow halos]
      [leafspots watersoaked margin = p][leafspot size > 1/8 inch]
      [leaf shredding = abs][leaf mildew growth = abs][stem = abn]
      [roots = n]   (13, 0, 13)
                          V
      [time = Jul . . . Sep][precipitation ≥ n][temperature = n]
      [occurrence of hail = no][damaged area = low areas, whole fields]
      [seed treatment = fungicide][leaves = abn]
      [leafspots halos = no yellow halos]
      [leafspots watersoaked margin = p][leafspot size > 1/8 inch]
      [leaf shredding = abs][leaf malformation = abs][roots = n]   (7, 5, 8)
                          V
      [time = Aug . . . Sep][precipitation ≥ n]
      [damaged area = low areas, upland areas][severity = minor]
      [leaves = abn][leafspots halos = no yellow halos]
      [leafspots watersoaked margin = p][leafspot size > 1/8 inch]
      [leaf shredding = abs][leaf mildew growth = abs][seed = n]
      [roots = n]   (8, 4, 20)
                          V
      [time = Jul . . . Aug][precipitation > n][# years crop repeated ≥ 1]
      [damaged area = scattered plants][seed treatment = none, other]
      [leaves = abn][leafspots halos = no yellow halos]
      [leafspots watersoaked margin = p][leafspot size > 1/8 inch]
      [leaf shredding = abs][leaf mildew growth = abs][roots = n]   (4, 3, 8)
                          V
      [precipitation > n][# years crop repeated ≤ 2]
      [damaged area = scattered plants, upland areas]
      [severity = potentially severe][seed germination < 80%]
      [leaves = abn][leafspots halos = no yellow halos]
      [leafspots watersoaked margin = p][leafspot size > 1/8 inch]
      [leaf mildew growth = abs][roots = n]   (4, 3, 9)
                          V
      [time = Jul][occurrence of hail = yes][leaves = abn]
      [leafspots halos = no yellow halos]
      [leafspots watersoaked margin = p][leafspot size > 1/8 inch]
      [leaf mildew growth = abs][stem = n]   (2, 2, 4)
                          V
      [plant stand = n][precipitation ≥ n][# years crop repeated = 2]
      [leaves = abn][leafspots halos = no yellow halos]
      [leafspots watersoaked margin = p][leafspot size > 1/8 inch]
      [leaf shredding = abs][leaf mildew growth = abs][seed = n]
      [roots = n]   (2, 2, 5)
               : :>[Diagnosis = *Frog eye leaf spot*]

Conversational text input for modifying graphics facial images

Michael L. Rhodes and Allen Klinger

Computer Science Department, University of California at Los Angeles, and Data Structure and Display Co., Los Angeles, California, U.S.A.

(*Received 17 April 1977*)

This paper reports on a text interpretation program for a minicomputer with 8K memory to facilitate modifying line drawings of faces. An interactive language is described that allows conversational dialogues between the user and image modification routines. We present an implementation that retains context during a dialogue and makes possible relational adjustments of facial features. Imprecise feature judgements issued by the user are used to modify images. Ambiguities encountered by the program are resolved by interrogating short term memory buffers and hash table data. Language and hardware features are combined by data structures that interface display processor instructions and requests generated by the interpreted text. Updating these structures is discussed in terms of relationships between structure elements.

1. Introduction

Humans easily recognize faces. We can use verbal descriptions and form mental pictures. Though only a few of us can sketch these visualizations with accuracy, with the help of an artist most can describe our visual memory "pictures" in sufficient detail so that reasonable facsimiles are generated. This paper describes co-operative interactions to use both human recognition and descriptive powers and computer capabilities for generating facial images. A text interpretation program to facilitate this task is described.

The program simplifies communication between user and machine display facilities. It provides a conversational medium to allow a dialogue to be established, where the central processor can logically relate both the display screen contents and user's descriptions. In operation, the user gives descriptions to generate a facial image, and the computer-program serves as an "artist". A sketched interpretation of the description appears on the graphics display. The "artist" is called "SKETCH", a program written for an IMLAC PDS-1 display processor and minicomputer with 8K of 16 bit/word memory. Users can modify the screen contents via the interactive language and, in some cases, teach the machine an interpretation of their descriptions.

The computer inputs are sent as imprecise, subjective feature judgements. Goldstein, Harmon & Lesk (1971) and Harmon (1971) established limits of performance for persons isolating faces from a population using such feature descriptions. Their experiments provide measures of feature reliability for identification, utility for establishing similarities, and sufficiency of sets of features for file retrieval.† Work by Bledsoe (1966) and Sakai, Nagao & Kanade (1972) attempted to sort and classify facial images by working with their features. By contrast, this work allows the use of imprecise feature judgements in *generating facial images*.

---

†Their model predicts that for a population of 4×10^6 only 14 feature descriptors are required to isolate a face; Goldstein *et al.* (1971), p. 757.

The user communicates with SKETCH through a keyboard console in a limited natural language. The machine replies are changes in image displayed or text messages presented on the CRT. Previous work (Gillenson, 1974; Winograd, 1972) was used as a model, but SKETCH was built around a police identification technique (Hopper, 1973). (Details of our implementation are based on a concept relating linguistic variables to numerical codes (Lakoff, 1973; Zadeh, 1965). For an overview of limited natural language computer processing, see Klinger (1973, 1975).)

The language is severely restricted due to the size of the machine but it is sufficiently flexible to be conversational. Command instructions provided allow numerous modifications to facial images. A key contribution is the way SKETCH facilitates processing relational information. Gillenson (1974) cited airline reservation systems as examples of mechanical interaction and Winograd's program for *Understanding Natural Language* (1972) as "intelligent" interaction. SKETCH processes relational phrases concerning faces: this enables interaction like Winograd (1972) with facial images: in its domain, SKETCH is an "intelligent" graphics aid. We can compare commands and display in the sequence of pictures shown in Fig. 1 to demonstrate this.

The first photograph in Fig. 1 shows the introductory frame that begins a user-SKETCH dialogue. The five following pictures illustrate a few typical commands. Photograph 2 shows the HAIR drawn. In photograph 3 a new word, FULLER, is defined and in the subsequent picture the new word is used to enlarge the HAIR. Immediately after the command in photo 4, the command in 5 demonstrates the maintenance of context during the dialogue. Photograph 6 shows the NOSE made wider.

Our purpose is to present the data structures and program organization used for this bridge between language and graphics displays. This is done by focusing on the system; illustrations of its use are also given. In order to describe the SKETCH program, the paper is divided into two main parts. The first section specifies the language, and the second presents data structures used for implementation.

2. Language specification

OVERVIEW

The power of SKETCH depends on how easily and naturally the user can express his modifications to the IMLAC CRT and have them understood. SKETCH can function conversationally because its scope of discourse is very small. Display facilities are also constrained by a finite number of image types, each a facial feature.

Eleven features are in the current language:

FACE	CHIN	JAW
NOSE	EYES	EYEBROWS
HAIRLINE	HAIR	CHEEKLINES
EARS	MOUTH	

Each can be modified in position, size and relative location to other features. All are individually addressable; alterations to one feature may be made relative to another. For instance, eyebrows may be moved closer to the eyes: if this is done the eyebrows will be repositioned relative to the current location of the eyes. Global alterations are also possible where the entire face is subjected to modifications.

SKETCH is modeled on the Penry Facial Identification Technique (Hopper, 1973; Della Riccia, 1973*a*, *b*), also known as Photo-FIT, and Gillenson's interactive program,

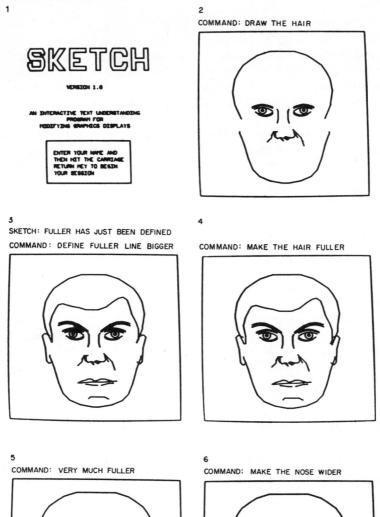

FIG. 1. A series of six photographs showing typical user commands.

WHATSISFACE (1974). The Photo-FIT kit is a police identification aid which consists of transparencies: 162 pairs of eyes, 151 noses, 159 mouths, 112 chin and cheek lines and 261 foreheads with a variety of moustaches, beards, spectacles and headgear. There are over 12,000 million possible combinations of features.

SKETCH enables a similar assembly of faces from features on the display screen, so that a computer could be an aid in the Penry identification process. This gives the investigator added power and convenience, since a single line drawing can be altered in many ways, reducing the number of basic features needed. For instance, we estimate that the 162 pairs of eyes could be realized by 20–25 basic eye templates in the computer display library. The library could be stored on auxiliary storage and accessed via system commands issued by the user.†

WHATSISFACE (Gillenson, 1974) provided 17 basic features for the user to modify while forming the facial image, and involved user communication via analog devices or one-character keyboard symbols; SKETCH adds to this natural discussion between the user and the display processor. However the earlier program possessed superior graphic display capability: hardware facilities for rotational transformation and variable intensity were made available to WHATSISFACE users. No such facilities were available at the IMLAC minicomputer used by SKETCH when it was written.

LANGUAGE DESCRIPTION

Figure 2 describes the SKETCH language in context-free Backus Naur Form notation· Brackets "⟨" and "⟩", are used to distinguish metalinguistic variables defined either in terms of others or in symbol strings. The symbols "|" and ":=" denote "logical-OR" and "defined as", respectively.

The SKETCH syntax has several message structures. The two basic message types allowed are: ⟨DEFINITION PHRASE⟩ and ⟨DESCRIPTION PHRASE⟩. In order for these messages to be interpreted, a carriage return must be hit on the keyboard to begin processing.

WORD ORDER

SKETCH uses sentence normalization in parsing user messages. Only one basic sentence structure must be recognized by the interpreter after normalization has taken place. Normalization does not rearrange the use message, it simply deletes superficial words.

Users are constrained to follow the specified word order in constructing messages. However flexibility is incorporated within each sequence to allow for conversational phrasings of messages. For instance, the following messages have exactly the same meaning for SKETCH:

(1) DRAW EYES LITTLE WIDE
(2) MAKE THE EYES A LITTLE WIDER
(3) DRAW THE EYES JUST A LITTLE WIDER
(4) DRAW EVEN THE EYES A LITTLE WIDER

The essential elements of the message are in (1). DRAW (or MAKE) signals the parser that the ensuing message is a descriptive phrase. The occurrence of EYES as the next non-⟨ARTICLE⟩ signals the parser to expect a message of the form: ⟨COMMAND WORD⟩ ⟨TEMPLATE PHRASE⟩ ⟨MODIFIER PHRASE⟩, ⟨COMMAND WORD⟩ ⟨TEMPLATE PHRASE⟩ ⟨IMBEDDED RELATIONAL PHRASE⟩, or ⟨COMMAND WORD⟩ ⟨TEMPLATE PHRASE⟩.

When LITTLE is encountered, the parser expects a ⟨MODIFIER PHRASE⟩ to complete the message. The word LITTLE by itself is a ⟨DEGREE PART⟩ that is

†Although this is not currently available, the program could support such access at a later time.

```
<USER MESSAGE>:= <USER PHRASE> CARRIAGE RETURN |
            CARRIAGE RETURN
<USER PHRASE>:= <DEFINITION> |<DESCRIPTION PHRASE> |
            <USER PHRASE> AND <USER PHRASE>
<DESCRIPTION PHRASE>:= <COMMAND WORD> <TEMPLATE PHRASE>
            <MODIFIED PHRASE> |<COMMAND WORD>
            <TEMPLATE PHRASE> <IMBEDDED RELATIONAL PHRASE> |
            <SUBSEQUENT COMMAND PHRASE> |REMOVE
            <TEMPLATE PHRASE>
<COMMAND WORD>:= MAKE |DRAW |MOVE |BRING
<IMBEDDED RELATIONAL PHRASE>:= <ARTICLE><IMBEDDED COMMAND> |
            <ARTICLE><IMBEDDED COMMAND><TEMPLATE PHRASE>
<IMBEDDED COMMAND>:= CLOSER |FURTHER
<SUBSEQUENT COMMAND PHRASE>:= <ARTICLE> <VERY> <DEGREE PART>
            <SUBSEQUENT COMMAND>
<SUBSEQUENT COMMAND>:= <ARTICLE><IMBEDDED COMMAND> |
            <ARTICLE><ADD–SUB> |
            <ARTICLE><ADD–SUB><MODIFIER> |
            <ARTICLE><ADD–SUB><IMBEDDED COMMAND>
<DEGREE PART>:= <EMPTY> MUCH |LITTLE
<ADD–SUB>:= MORE |LESS | <EMPTY>
<TEMPLATE PHRASE>:= <ARTICLE><PRONOUN> |<ARTICLE> <TEMPLATE>
<PRONOUN>:= IT |THEM
<MODIFIER PHRASE>:= <ARTICLE> <VERY> <DEGREE PART> <ADD–SUB>
            <IMBEDDED COMMAND>
<ARTICLE>:= A |THE |TO |EVEN |OVER |THAN |BE |SAME |
            AS |JUST |LIKE | <EMPTY> | <ARTICLE> <ARTICLE>
<TEMPLATE>:= FACE |NOSE |HAIRLINE |EARS |CHIN |EYES |
            HAIR |MOUTH |EYEBROWS |JAW |CHEEKLINES
<MODIFIER>:= FAT |WIDE |THIN |BIG |LARGE |SMALL |HIGH
            |LOW |RIGHT |RIGHTWARDS |LEFT |LEFTWARDS |
            TALL |SHORT |UP |DOWN |UPWARDS |DOWNWARDS |
            SLENDER |NORTH |SOUTH |EAST |WEST
<VERY>:= VERY | <EMPTY>
<EMPTY>:=
<DEFINITION>:= DEFINE<ANY WORD> <ARTICLE> <LEXICAL MEMBER> |
            DEFINE <ANY WORD> <ARTICLE> <LEXICAL MEMBER> AND
            <LEXICAL MEMBER>
<LEXICAL MEMBER>:= <COMMAND WORD> |<TEMPLATE> |
            <IMBEDDED COMMAND> |<ADD–SUB> |<PRONOUN> |
            <MODIFIER> |VERY | <ARTICLE>
<ANY WORD>:= ANY ALPHABETIC CHARACTER STRING OF 8 SYMBOLS OR
            LESS NOT CAUSING A HASH COLLISION
```

Fɪɢ. 2. Sketch syntax.

interpreted to be a multiplicative factor of 1/2. This factor is then used as a multiplicand times the standard change associated with EYES when made WIDER. WIDER is a ⟨MODIFIER⟩ that means: "Increase the horizontal stretch lines of the template referenced in the message."

When applied to EYES, WIDER has the effect of increasing the *vertical* but not the horizontal stretch vectors in the EYE display templates. "WIDE EYES" are interpreted "wide open", not "wider in terms of distance between pupils". For most other templates, like NOSE and JAW for instance, WIDE will mean an increase in the actual horizontal stretch vectors of the referenced templates. A command like MOVE THE EYES CLOSER TOGETHER will bring the eyes closer together horizontally (pupil to pupil).

Messages (2), (3) and (4) above are variations of (1) with ⟨ARTICLE⟩s interspersed to achieve a more conversational tone. ⟨ARTICLE⟩s can appear in a variety of places depending on the message construction chosen by the user. If there is room for essential parts of a user's message, then whenever one ⟨ARTICLE⟩ is permitted, the number of ⟨ARTICLE⟩s that can fit in the keyboard queue is allowed. An irregular message like:

DRAW THE JUST EYES THE LIKE EVEN LITTLE WIDE

would appear perfectly acceptable to SKETCH and equivalent to the four messages (1), (2), (3) and (4) seen earlier.

SKETCH expects a sympathetic user who will most likely use common expressions in his commands. Messages which seem nonsensical will interpret to program action if no violation of the language syntax is detected. The user must be careful not to misuse his liberty with ⟨ARTICLE⟩s.

On the other hand, some messages may be sensible but not understood by SKETCH. The user is not expected to ask:

DRAW A LITTLE WIDER THE EYES

since word order is violated. This message will not be understood and the error message processor would reply to the user.

PREDICATE MODIFIERS FOR VARIABLE ADJUSTMENT

The predicate modifiers ⟨VERY⟩⟨DEGREE PART⟩⟨ADD–SUB⟩ form a set of "hedges", or "words whose job it is to make things fuzzier of less fuzzy", Lakoff (1973). Lakoff describes hedges in the context of fuzzy sets (developed by Zadeh, 1965). One such fuzzy set could be the set of all wide pairs of eyes. A degree of membership (real number between 0 and 1) would be attached to each pair of eyes in the fuzzy set indicating just how "WIDE" each pair is considered to be. Any pair of eyes with degree of membership of 0·9 or 1·0 are "WIDE". The membership function for the set of wide pairs of eyes is illustrated in the graph shown in Fig. 3.

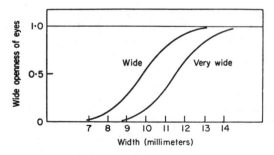

FIG. 3. Membership function for wide pairs of eyes.

Although the "WIDENESS" curves quantify the qualitative text term, the function chosen is subjective. Adding the hedge VERY defines a new set: very wide pairs of eyes. The membership function for this set is also shown in Fig. 3: in effect a shift of values to the right has occurred. Pairs of eyes that were "wide" to degree 0·75 now are only "very wide" to degree 0·25.

The ⟨VERY⟩ ⟨DEGREE PART⟩ and ⟨ADD–SUB⟩ predicate modifiers affect features by causing SKETCH to use new functions to describe membership classes.

(A) DRAW THE EYES WIDE
(1) MAKE THEM VERY MUCH LESS WIDE
(2) DRAW THEM MUCH LESS WIDE
(3) DRAW THE EYES LESS WIDE
(4) MAKE THE EYES A LITTLE LESS WIDE
(5) MAKE THEM A LITTLE MORE WIDE
(6) DRAW THEM WIDER
(7) MAKE THE EYES MUCH WIDER
(8) DRAW THEM VERY MUCH WIDER

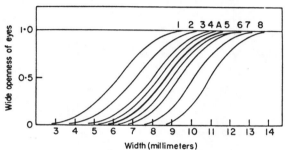

FIG. 4. New membership classes.

Figure 4 illustrates the correspondence between the original membership function for "WIDE EYES" and the various functions resulting from ⟨VERY⟩⟨DEGREE PART⟩ ⟨ADD–SUB⟩ commands. Each numbered modification command is issued in the context of screen (A); the numbered graphs reference the commands listed. The plots show the relative sizes associated command (A) and the new command, when each numbered command immediately follows (A).

In Fig. 5, photographs 8, 9 and 10 show actual display results for commands (A), (2) and (8), respectively. The commands in photographs 9 and 10 were each issued directly following the display shown in photograph 8.

By adjusting a modification in a series of commands the user can reach detail equivalent to 1/2 the resolution of the CRT. The predicate modifiers multiply the standard increment by one of eight factors (–4, –2, –1, –1/2, 1/2, 1, 2, 4). Since each command is relative to the current image, successive modifications are able to reach half of the 1024 screen points in each direction, i.e. EYES could be separated by any amount using a series of commands like:

COMMAND	EFFECTIVE ADJUSTMENT
BRING THE EYES FURTHER APART	CIPD +1(SI)
MUCH MORE	CIPD +2(SI)
A LITTLE BIT LESS	CIPD −1/2(SI)
VERY MUCH LESS	CIPD −4 (SI)
MORE	CIPD +1(SI)

where CIPD = current inter-pupil distance and SI = standard increment for horizontal EYE changes.

The preceding discussion concerns modifications that change feature size. Predicate modifiers can also be used to qualify reposition commands. Increments associated with each template for reposition are the same as the standard value in feature size and shape adjustments.

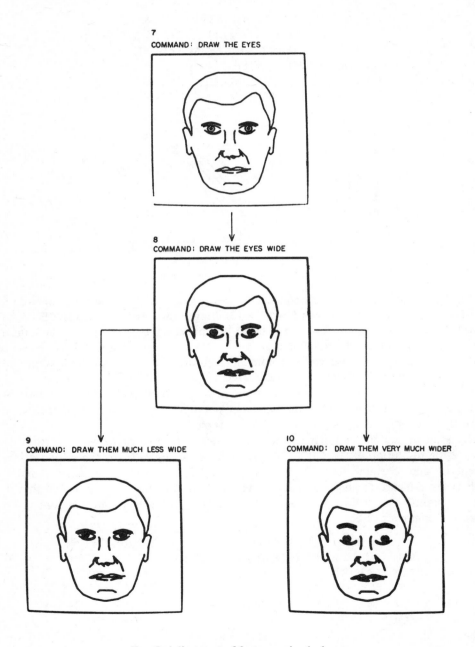

FIG. 5. Adjustment of features using hedges.

DICTIONARY ADDITIONS

The ⟨DEFINITION⟩ phrase allows extensions to the dictionary. For example, the new word TUBBY can be defined to be the same as known words (dictionary members) or a combination of some of them.

DEFINE TUBBY TO BE THE SAME AS FAT AND SHORT

This can also be done in the more natural way:

DEFINE TUBBY LIKE FAT AND SHORT

If we keep only the essential elements in this it becomes:

DEFINE TUBBY FAT AND SHORT

Each message results in a dictionary element with the meaning "combination of FAT and SHORT". Notice the string of ⟨ARTICLE⟩s, "TO BE THE SAME AS" is only used to "naturalize" the user's message. During the interpretive process these ⟨ARTICLE⟩s are stripped from the message and ignored.

3. Sketch implementation

The implementation of SKETCH is best described from the viewpoint of the SKETCH supervisor. Only a few program segments are actually co-ordinated by the supervisor but they represent the brunt of all SKETCH processing. Three logical partitions are made in SKETCH which closely correspond to the program's operational modes: the interpreter section to handle user messages; the message processor to compose messages sent to the user; and the display files to maintain bookkeeping and display processor instructions. Portions of these three partitions are called in sequence by the supervisor.

At the supervisor level SKETCH is uncomplicated. The supervisor simply passes control down a sequence of routines: to invoke any, all its predecessors must have been successfully executed. Whenever a routine is unsuccessful, control is passed to the reply message processor to identify the error and notify the user. If all routines are successful, the supervisor returns to a waiting state for a new user message.

FIG. 6. Photographs 11 and 12. Error message.

Any routine invoked by the supervisor could update one or more of the three program partitions. While a user message is being parsed by an interpretive routine, information is gathered for the reply message processor. A trace is made of the interpreter's flow of control to help locate errors. If an error is encountered, the message processor portion of the program can reply.

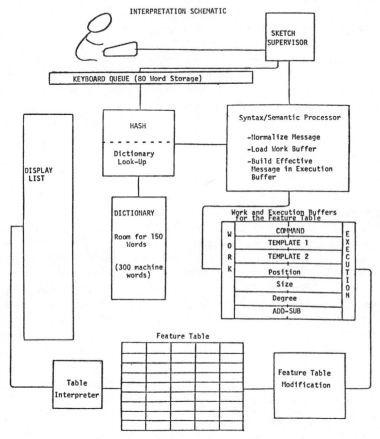

FIG. 7. Program schematic.

In Fig. 6, photograph 11, an error message was sent since SCRATCH in the user message was not in the dictionary. SCRATCH was then defined to be "same as REMOVE". Photograph 12 shows SCRATCH used successfully.

Five program modules are employed by the SKETCH supervisor. Each involves specialized routines for modifying and maintaining specific data structures. The five accomplish the following tasks.

1. Hash-dictionary look-up.
2. Message normalization.
3. Normalized-message processing.
4. Feature table modification.
5. Table interpretation.

The schematic in Fig. 7 illustrates the interconnection of these utility routines and their relevant data structures.

As a user's message is entered on the keyboard, the keyboard queue retains the order and identity of each word for the interpretation phase. Each character is displayed and mispellings can be corrected before sending the message to the interpreter. Once a carriage return key is hit, the supervisor enters the interpretive mode.

The first task undertaken by the supervisor is left to right examination of each word in the user's message. Each word is hashed and the corresponding interpretation is looked up in a dictionary. The hash routine is a very simple one that currently has no collision safeguards but introduces considerable economy of core. If the retrieved interpretation conforms to the semantic restrictions of the language, the next word in the message is then considered. Before hashing the next word, the interpretation of the last is stored in the work buffer. Hash-dictionary look-up continues until either a violation of the language is detected or the keyboard queue is exhausted. At successful conclusion the work buffer will store the relevant information of the user's message.

Alternatives available to the hash look-up routines depend on the message semantics. These alternatives correspond to possibilities in interpreter parse trees. Messages are normalized: they are first filtered for informative elements and then condensed to a standard representation. Message filtering involves ignoring ⟨ARTICLE⟩s and condensation by reducing information in some phrases to more convenient encodings. For example, the predicate modifier phrase, ⟨VERY⟩⟨DEGREE PART⟩⟨ADD–SUB⟩, has a condensed interpretation represented in just two machine words. There are many variations of the standard representation so that the user has a wide range of allowed messages.

The work and table execution buffers are software data structures containing standard representations of user messages. After a message has been normalized and is resident in the work buffer, it is examined again. The second examination yields a message which is given to the table execution buffer and then put into effect. This is called *the effective message*. Indefinite context-sensitive relations appearing in the normalized message of the work buffer are given definite interpretations in the execution buffer. For instance, arguments for ⟨PRONOUNS⟩ are assigned during this type of processing. In addition, ⟨SUBSEQUENT COMMAND PHRASE⟩s that do not reference ⟨TEMPLATE⟩s explicitly are given implicit assignments. Both types of binding interrogate the execution buffer to "remember" which ⟨TEMPLATE⟩s are in context. This contextual information is available since the execution buffer still contains the prior effective message.

The message that is actually executed is a composite of the user's message in the work buffer and information extracted from the execution buffer. Once formed, the effective message is entered into the execution buffer itself and feature table modification can then proceed.

Feature table modification is controlled by the arguments found in the table execution buffer. The encoding of the COMMAND word interpretation selects table modification routines that are candidates for execution. From these candidates POSITION and SIZE isolate the modification to be done while TEMPLATE 1 and TEMPLATE 2 specify features (or records in the feature table) to be addressed.

The table modification procedures respond to relational information encoded in the feature table. This relational information identifies paired features (eyes, ears, eyebrows, etc.) and also controls the incremental changes associated with each feature.

Modifications to the eyes, for instance, are done in smaller increments than those made to a hairline or jaw. Spatial relations such as ears being on the same horizontal are also maintained by the feature table and its traversal routines.

The (feature) table interpreter is the last utility invoked by the SKETCH supervisor. After the feature table is interpreted the supervisor enters a waiting state for subsequent user messages.

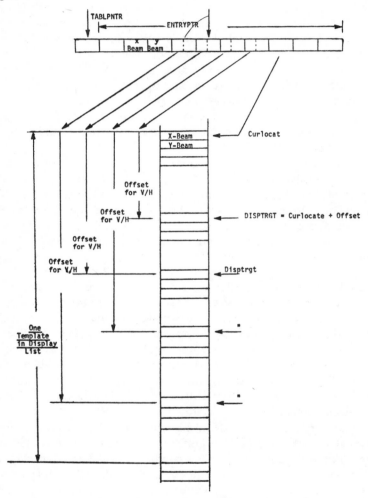

FIG. 8. Pointer fields for each record in the feature table.

All the features listed in the feature table correspond to display list templates. When a change is made to HAIR, for example, the record for HAIR in the feature table is altered then the corresponding display list segment, or template, is modified by the table interpreter. The table interpreter changes the display list to reflect the size and position of templates as specified in the feature table. By using pointers that are elements of the record for each feature, the table interpreter can locate the place in the display list where changes corresponding to record entries should be made.

Figure 8 illustrates the pointer fields in each feature table record. The pointers, TABLPNTR, ENTRYPTR, CURLOCAT and DISPTRGT are all work pointers used by the table interpreter to locate display instructions in the display list. Using the information in the feature table the feature display instruction locations are found and subsequently modified. The type of modification made is also specified in the features table record.

13(A)

13(B)

COMMAND: THE SLASHER SKETCH

FIG. 9. Police sketches and computer image.

4. Conclusion

The SKETCH program is a vehicle for man–machine interaction to generate and modify facial images. We discussed translation from text input to display processor instructions, and how this was accomplished by the program using data structures for modularity and contextual association. The interface of the display processor and mini-computer was discussed in detail.

A variety of structures were used to retain relational information between features and contextual association during a user-SKETCH dialogue. Retention of this data is made possible by encoding relational information for each feature and storing key-words from user messages.

The SKETCH program was designed to be modular so that extensions could be realized by adding new feature display code or by exploiting other display processor hardware features as they become available. Feature rotation or variable beam intensity, for instance, would have their own settings represented in the feature table (see Figs 7 and 8). Changes to these settings could be made through an expanded user language.

The language itself has not been awkward to use but many enhancements have been suggested. Some require minor additional code or simply revisions of existing software. A short tutorial demonstrating typical syntax and listing current lexical entries has been proposed and further suggested enhancements include:

(a) lightpen interaction;

(b) explicit syntax error identification and suggested recovery for users;

(c) access to a large database system for image matching.

The majority of the suggestions are possible only after additional core storage is made available to our mini-computer. The SKETCH program now uses 7·5K of the 8K available.

The quality of the CRT displays depends only on the detail in the facial features addressable by SKETCH. Once a library of features is accessible to the program, accurate sketches of a large number of faces can be made. Figure 9 shows how SKETCH could be used to draw the police suspect sketches published in a newspaper.†

This research was sponsored by the U.S. Department of Justice, Law Enforcement Assistance Administration Graduate Research Fellowship No. 76-NI-99-0062 and the U.S. Air Force Office of Scientific Research, Air Force Systems Command, USAF, under Contract AF-49629-76C-0025. In addition, portions of this research were supported by University of California Grant No. 4-592441-19900-7. The United States Government is authorized to reproduce and distribute reprints for Governmental purposes notwithstanding any copyright notation hereon.

The authors would like to express their appreciation for this support.

References

BLEDSOE, W. (1966). Man–machine facial recognition: report on a large-scale experiment. *Report PRI:22*. Panoramic Research Inc., Palo Alto, Cal.

DELLA RICCIA, G. (1973*a*). Automatic recognition of identi-kit pictures of human faces. *Technical Report MATH-48*. Ben Gurion University, Beer-Sheva, Israel.

DELLA RICCIA, G. (1973*b*). An attempt to identify human faces with only a few available features. *Technical Report MATH-58*. Ben Gurion University, Beer-Sheva, Israel.

GILLENSON, M. L. (1974). The interactive generation of facial images on a CRT using a heuristic strategy. *Ph.D. Dissertation*. Ohio State University, Columbus, Ohio.

GOLDSTEIN, A., HARMON, L. & LESK, A. (1971). Identification of human faces. *Proceedings of the IEEE*, **59** (5), 748–760.

HARMON, L. (1971). Some aspects of recognition of human faces. In O. GRUESSER & R. KLINKE, Eds., *Pattern Recognition in Biological and Technical Systems—Proceedings*. New York: Springer-Verlag.

HOPPER, W. R. (1973). Photo-FIT, the Penry Facial Identification Technique. *Journal of the Forensic Science Society*, **13**, 77–81.

†*Los Angeles Times*, 31 January 1975, p. 1.

KLINGER, A. (1973). Natural language, linguistic processing and speech understanding: recent research and future goals. *Technical Report No. R–1377–ARPA.* The Rand Corporation, Santa Monica, California; *American Journal of Computational Linguistics,* 1975.

KLINGER, A. (1975). Recent computer science research in language processing. *American Journal of Computational Linguistics,* **12** (3), 2–25.

LAKOFF, G. (1973). Hedges: a study in meaning criteria and the logic of fuzzy concepts. *Journal of Philosophical Logic,* **2,** 458–508. Dordrecht, Holland: D. Reidel Publishing Co.

SAKAI, T., NAGAO, M. & KANADE, T. (1972). Computer analysis and classification of photographs of human faces. *Proceedings of the First U.S.A.–Japan Computer Conference,* pp. 55–62.

WINOGRAD, T. (1972). *Understanding Natural Language.* Artificial Intelligence Laboratory, M.I.T., 545 Technology Square, Cambridge, Massachusetts 02139.

ZADEH, I. (1965). Fuzzy sets. *Information and Controls,* **8,** 338–353.

Logical foundations for database systems†

BRIAN R. GAINES

Centre for Man–Computer Studies, Colchester, U.K.

Database systems originated as mechanisms for storing and retrieving information. Codd's relational formalism generalized and made far more flexible the forms of data structure and retrieval specification allowed. However, available implementations of relational databases are in terms of hard, static, deterministic relations; whereas in real-world applications data is often imprecise, inherently dynamic and non-deterministic. In recent years there has been a range of developments concerned with representing and using data that can only be represented in these "softer" terms. Some of the work has been explicitly concerned with database systems, but much of it, whilst highly relevant, has been in other application areas.

This paper classifies and surveys work on a variety of logical systems in the context of its relevance to database systems. The objective is to show through illustrations what can be incorporated into relational database systems to allow for a wider range of real-world requirements and closer man–computer interation. The current state-of-the-art in natural language interaction with databases is illustrated and discussed. The possibility of paradoxes leading to oscillations in database states is demonstrated. The roles of modal, multi-valued and fuzzy logics in databases are described as discussed.

1. Introduction

The emergence of database technologies (Nolan, 1973*a*; Sibley, 1976) as distinct applied sciences of computing during the past decade is one of the most significant features of the transition in computer applications: from "data processing" to "information processing" and perhaps eventually to "knowledge processing". This transition is of key importance to those of us who see the possibility of far closer interaction between people and computers than is being achieved at present—some form of man-machine symbiosis (Licklider, 1968) in which the strengths of each partner mutually compensate for the weaknesses and complement the strengths of the other. The original function of the computer, as a "number cruncher", certainly enables it to compensate for man's weakness in arithmetic and logical power, but it is not a sufficiently strong link to the mainstream activities of the mind to lead to meaningful symbiosis. For that we need an interface into man's world of knowledge.

In discussing how man can cope with the increasing complexity of society, De Bono noted recently:

> "The computer will be to the organisation revolution what steam power was to the industrial revolution. The computer can extend our organizing power in the same way as steam extended our muscle power" (De Bono, 1979, p. 18).

This analogy can be an extremely useful one when we come to consider what it is that we really require of computers in order that they may enter into a close working relationship with man—one that actually gives the "amplification of intelligence" so often

---

† This paper is based on one presented at EUROCOMP 78.

hoped for but not yet achieved. Throughout his extensive studies of the way in which the acquisition of new knowledge can take place Karl Popper (1976) has emphasized the distinct ontological status of the "knowledge" itself as it becomes separate from man and embodies in written records, libraries, etc. I have suggested that the role of the computer in man's world of knowledge, Popper's "World Three", is best seen as analogous to that of engines in the physical world, Popper's "World One":

> "It brings world 3 into the demense of man just as did the steam, internal combustion, and jet engines, world 1. That is, we can move about in, conquer, control and fabricate to our needs the lands and materials of world 3 in a way that makes our previous efforts, all but a few, look feeble" (Gaines, 1978).

Thus, we may think of database technology as the beginning of a process whereby the computer, as a powerful information-processing "engine", begins to be given access to the actual information structures that are of significance to us. Since the cost of computers has, until the recent advent of "personal computers", made it essential to justify their development in terms of commercial applications it has been these that have dominated database developments so far. In common with all such computer-related "technologies", there is no single advance in hardware, software or fundamental concepts, that led to the inception of databases. Indeed, one can see the strongest drive behind them as a purely normative commercial requirement for information storage and retrieval systems suited to the needs of large, complex organisations. The high-level technology of databases is making demands on the lower-level technologies of processors, discs, terminals, operating systems, languages and communications, that are now major forces in determining the directions of commercial development.

Nolan, whose "stage" hypotheses (Nolan, 1973b) have given a highly dynamic and realistic model of the assimilation of data-processing technologies by organizations, has presented a set of possible hypotheses as to the "fifth stage". One hypothesis is that it will be a repetition of the previous four stages but assimilating the new technologies of minis/micros, word-processing and databases. Another hypothesis is that the effect of the new technologies will differ far more according to the organization involved than has happened in previous stages—probably because the new technologies will be far more integrated into the firm. His main hypothesis is, however, that this very integration of the "data resource function" into the firm will form a new stage that will go through the same "learning curves" as did the original assimilation of data processing technology:

> "Hypothesis: Stage V will be acceptance of the reorganization of data processing to appropriately align data resource management functions" (Nolan, 1977).

However, such projections for the "data resource function" are currently far from reality: practical database implementations are still basically straightforward information storage and retrieval systems; the more advanced experiments under the aegis of "artificial intelligence" have produced some dramatic indications of what is to come but are largely expensive showpieces that perform well only in the hands of their designers. Some of the extensions needed to make distributed, dynamic database systems a reality are fairly obvious and well-known, e.g. protection mechanisms, natural language access, and more efficient implementation. Others are not so obvious—problems of information credibility, contradiction, vagueness, structural constraints and internal dynamics. This paper is concerned with some of these non-standard problems that are arising in attempts to make the logic of database systems more closely match that of human practical reasoning. Particular attention is paid to links with developments outside the conventional database literature since many of the problems encountered are truly fundamental and under consideration in other areas of study.

2. Some problems of database dynamics

This paper is concerned with the development of database systems that go beyond present relational databases in coping with the following problems of database dynamics:

(a) *Items in the database that are themselves relations*: e.g. implications imposed by semantic constraints, physical laws or judicial legislation. Such items allow the database to be extended, both positively and negatively, with inferred items that may, or may not, be present—however, the actual extension is wasteful in space, and often impossible in practice, so that "theorem-proving" techniques taking into account the relations must be used for what are apparently straightforward data retrieval or update, requests.

(b) *Action-initiating items in the database*: e.g. such that the entry of an item giving the level of a stock may initiate a re-order process when the value becomes low, or that requests for confidential information are aborted and security action taken if the enquirer has insufficient status.

(c) *Indeterminate or contradictory items in the database*: e.g. not just that an item is, or is not, in the database but that currently no information has been received on it, or contradictory information has been received. Clearly this is also related to the problem of the "credibility" of the information received.

(d) *Vague items in the database*: e.g. that someone's age is specified as not, for example, "25 years", but rather as "between 20 and 30 years", or "about 25 years", or "fairly young". All these are informative statements that would be useful in answering queries or making inferences dependent on the age, but they are a different form of data from that normally considered.

   In the original context of databases as "filing systems" these requirements did not arise. Even in further developments of person-oriented interactive query languages it is possible to neglect them. However, as we move towards dynamic, multi-user, multi-centre database systems, such considerations assume great importance. Is this centre to accept updates from this remote source and give them equal credibility to those from its local controller? When this centre receives information which it passes on to another centre that promptly sends processed data back to the originator, what is the stability of the network (it is easy to invent cases that oscillate wildly!)? And so on—every problem of control and communication ever encountered elsewhere can be essentially reproduced in a database system—we are discussing structures that approach the ultimate generality of system theory and yet are very concrete.

   That the problems mentioned are not highly artificial is best seen through an example conversation. Envision M as a manager and S as an information system and resource controller, eventually to be automated—the line numbers are for later reference:

1	M:	We have a new employee starting tomorrow
2	S:	Name?
3	M:	Peter Grimes
4	S:	Will he work in your division?
5	M:	Yes
6	S:	What section?
7	M:	Either Sales or Distribution
8	S:	Age?
9	M:	Fairly young
10	S:	Own car?
11	M:	Don't know
12	S:	Salary?
13	M:	15,000 for the first 3 months and then 17,500
14	S:	Location?
15	M:	Is 408 very full?
16	S:	Yes
17	M:	What else have we got?
18	S:	319 has room for one more
19	M:	OK
20	S:	I will order a desk and chair
21	M:	How is my staffing now?
22	S:	You have one vacancy in product planning
23	M:	Productivity norms?
24	S:	OK except for L division down 15%
25	M:	Suppose I move Jane from L to G
26	S:	All OK
27	M:	No, that would be a demotion—note that demotions are now allowed
28	S:	You cannot move Jane

FIG. 1. A sample dialogue.

I will discuss the natural language aspects of automating the S side of this conversation later. For the moment note the following points that arise naturally but create difficulties for a standard system:

(a) at line 7 the reply should be single-valued but actually gives two possible alternatives—we cannot treat this as "not information yet" because the data given is actually adequate to answer some queries, e.g. "list staff in Sales or Distribution"—however, we normally would not be able to store this reply or, in a relational database, would have the dual value flagged as an integrity violation;

(b) at line 9 the imprecision of the reply creates a rather worse problem through its vagueness—probably even a human S would have made some rather testy query about this reply—however, it is again an information-bearing reply that should not be ignored if it is the only information currently available—it would enable us to answer an enquiry about "employees not within five years of retirement" without any vagueness since a "fairly young" employee would fall into that class;

(c) line 11 is actually "no information yet"—note that this is quite distinct from "no car", e.g. in response to the query, "which employees do not have their own cars";

(d) line 13 is similar to line 7 in giving two values for a single-valued field but now involves a temporal trigger—it is not our uncertainty about the value but rather its own dynamics that leads to this reply—accepting this reply would involve storing a procedure that changes the salary after 3 months;

(e) line 15 involves imprecision again but this time in the query—note the essential terseness and simplicity of this query conveying exactly the content of the question to be answered—it is *not* the same as the query, "Is there room for one more person

in room 408?'', the literal answer to which might be "yes" when the answer to the
actual query was actually even stronger than "no", e.g. "most certainly not"!;

(f) at line 20 the assignment of the value 319 to the new employee's "location" field
     triggers off an activity on the part of S to order new furniture—such actions
     triggered by changes in the database are actually implicit in the way in which many
     systems are used currently, i.e. programs are run to initiate activities according to
     the state of the database—however, it can lead to interesting problems as the action
     initiated interacts itself with the state of the database;

(g) at line 25 a query is made which involves a counter-factual assertion, "what would
     happen if . . ."—this is a common requirement that is the basis of modelling and
     simulation facilities—in a multi-user dynamic data base system the data entry and
     rollback required may involve very complex processing, particularly if the entry
     itself triggers off other actions—in particular, if temporal data is not stored with
     every item, then requests for future or past data must be treated as counter-factuals,
     e.g. "what will our salary bill per month be in six months time?—what was it this
     time last year?"; at line 27 a constraint is added to the database specifying that
     certain types of change are not allowed—the counter-factual at line 25 is then noted
     to involve a constraint violation at line 28.

And so on—this dialogue is not at all unreasonable and surely resembles what users
have been promised databases will do for them, i.e. allow them to maintain a
straightforward record of the situation of their organization and interact with it in a
simple and natural way. I have avoided the realms of fantasy: the domain of discourse is
very strictly limited and S displays no great "intelligence". The next section gives a brief
model of relational databases leading into the following sections concerning possible
extensions to meet the additional requirements illustrated above.

3. Relational database operation

For the purposes of this paper Codd's relational model of a database is the most useful
because of its basic simplicity and generality. Codd himself (1970, 1974) and Date
(1976) have put the case for a relational model in user terms, and commercially
available systems, such as Tymeshare's FOCUS (1976), demonstrate that the relational
model is also practically realizable. The abstract form of the model is:

—the Cartesian product, P, of a set of a finite set of variable-valued fields, $\{F_i\}$, forms a
   database state support;
—any subset of P, $S_j \subset P$, is a potential *database state*;
—a family of subsets of P, $S \subset 2P$, that are potential states of an actual database is called
   a *database state space*.

These are the standard definitions phrased in a slightly different terminology in order to
bring out the nature of a database as a state-determined machine, or *automaton*, a
particularly important concept in studying database dynamics. Data entry can now be
seen as a process of applying an input to the database automaton causing it to change its
state. A database from which any item may be removed corresponds to a *reversible*
automaton—the potential states of a database correspond to the *reachable* states of the
automaton, and so on (Arbib, 1969).

The problems of database systems may be conveniently classified under three main headings: data retrieval, data entry/modification and system implementation. Considering each in turn:

(1) *Data retrieval* comes first, apparently out of logical order since data entry always precedes it, because it is simplest to consider the problems of accessing databases already established by some means—the problem of retrieval from a *static* database is well-defined and reasonably straightforward to "solve". The main sub-problems are:

    (1a) *inference* of the answers to well-defined queries—this may range from direct data access to complex "theorem-proving";

    (1b) *generation* of well-defined queries from user requests—this may range from a one-to-one translation of requests in a stylized language to the syntactic and semantic analysis of natural language;

    (1c) *protection* of data from unauthorized access—this may range from simple "password" checks to complex information type, value and processing checks.

(2) *Data entry and modification* are often best treated as distinct problems since a purely additive database from which information, once entered, may never be removed or modified comes somewhere between the static case and the fully dynamic one in its complexity and problems. The main sub-problems are:

    (2a) *inference* of the changes to be made in response to well-defined update requests—this may range from simple data storage to complex chains of data dependent modifications;

    (2b) *generation* of well-defined update requests from user requests—again this may range from trivial translation through to natural language "understanding";

    (2c) *integrity* preservation of the database information and structure—this may range from simple checks on authority of data source to complex determinations of the continued correctness of global predicates across the complete data base;

    (2d) *reversal* or "rollback" of modifications is generally required both to take care of error conditions, e.g. and also to allow counter-factual modifications to be made temporarily to the database, for example, for modelling possible changes that have not yet occurred.

(3) *Implementation* of database systems is still a key problem even for the current generation. Only in recent years have the storage costs of high-speed backing stores dropped to a level where it is possible to keep on line substantial amounts of data. To demand also that the data is not only accessible through its storage location but also through its structure and context places additional requirements on the speeds of such mass storage that can multiply the expense up to unrealistic levels. Thus, the efficient implementation of database systems is a major problem and any discussion which ignores this is somewhat unrealistic. However, for much of this paper I will not allow current implementation difficulties to rule out potentially useful techniques—the pace of hardware development and changes in system concept are too rapid for unreasonable pessimism about future implementations (Dolotta, Bernstein, Dickson, France, Rosenblatt, Smith & Steel, 1976). As a temporary developmental strategy this is sound—it is the approach which has lead to

fundamental progress in natural language systems in "artificial intelligence" research—systems which at first appeared as highly expensive research tools have now led to practically useful systems for natural language database retrieval at reasonable cost as will be illustrated in the next section.

4. Natural language interaction

The dialogue of Fig. 1 was in natural colloquial English and that in itself may be seen as a major problem. However, since the linguistic breakthroughs that came first with Weizenbaum's (1967) ELIZA that could maintain conversational niceties without "understanding", and then Winograd's (1972) SHRDLU that could capture much of the deep structure of English through its very "understanding" of a rather narrow domain, there has been a tremendous advance in the linguistic technologies enabling us to coat a core of basically algebraic intercourse between person and computer with the sugar of English language. Actually the significance of this goes far beyond the sweetening of the naïve user's pill—as system designers it is far easier for us to see the weaknesses of our systems when they appear as lack of power to interpret "obvious" English constructions than as algebraic/logical weaknesses. Indeed, since algebraicists and logicians have never come anywhere near expressing the range and variety of semantic structure and reasoning patterns exhibited by people, it would be surprising if an approach based on classical formal structures did not give a mis-match to what people actually require.

Petrick (1976) has given a useful survey of work on natural language based computer systems and some of the arguments for and against its use. The most dramatic demonstrations of the power of current techniques are more recent than his article, and it is worth describing briefly some of the capabilities of Hendrix's (1977) LIFER and Harris's (1977) ROBOT.

LIFER is implemented as a database access system in PDP10 Interlisp and used an augmented finite-state transition network (Woods, 1970; Norman & Rumelhart, 1975) to parse and semantically interpret questions in English. It has language specification functions that allow the transition networks to be constructed automatically from production rules readily comprehended by the specific system designer. These rules are readily modified and tested interactively allowing complex language constructs to be built and tested in a short time. Much of the semantics of the possible values in database fields is imbedded into the networks built by LIFER, e.g. "Gary" and "height" would be treated not just as "nouns" but as "person" and "attribute", respectively. LIFER is fast in operation, parsing, for example, "What is the length of the fastest American sub" in 2000 milliseconds (KL10 processor), and fairly small in size, requiring only 14K words extra over Interlisp itself. Hendrix notes that an extensive language definition for communicating with a fairly large database of 100 fields on 14 files with hundreds of records requires only an additional 33K words including some database access routines. It is particularly good at handling ellipsis where the user omits part of a sentence, e.g.:

```
1    M:   What is the speed of the Kitty Hawk
2    S:   Speed 35 knots
3    M:   Of the Ethan Allen
4    S:   Trying ellipsis: what is the speed of the Ethan Allen
          Speed 30 knots
```

5	M:	Displacement
6	S:	Trying ellipsis: what is the displacement of the Ethan Allen
		Standard-displacement 6900 hundred-tons
7	M:	Length of the fastest Soviet sub
8	S:	Trying ellipsis: what is the length of the fastest Soviet sub
		Length 285 feet/speed 30 knots
9	M:	Who onws the Kiev
10	S:	owns
		Country USSR
11	M:	Who owns the JFK
12	S:	Trying ellipsis: ellipsis failed
		The parser does not expect the word "JFK" to follow "who owns the"
		Options for the next word or meta-symbol are:
		⟨ship-name⟩
13	M:	Define JFK to be like Kennedy
14	S:	Country USA

FIG. 2. Sample dialogue with LIFER (Hendrix, 1977).

This sample shows that the terseness of my invented dialogue of Fig. 1 is fully realistic—computer-based natural language systems can emulate the cryptic style of colloquial English dialogue. At line 10 the Interlisp spelling corrector is used to rectify an error—this illustrates the way in which a standard module (Teitelman, 1975), once it exists, is used routinely by other systems to improve their utility. At line 12 the parse fails but note the excellent diagnostics provided (in technical rather than conversational form in this example) which project to the user what went wrong in readily comprehensible and rectifiable form. At line 13 the user gives an ELIZA-style definition which allows the parse now to be successfully completed.

ROBOT is another natural language enquiry system, this time on an IBM370/155 interfaced to the ADABAS database management system. It has been tested by routine use since January 1977 at Bigelow-Sanford Carpet Co. in connection with their customer and sales files (about 60,000 records). ROBOT is again based on an augmented transition network and Harris notes that it brings five types of information to bear on the translation process.

(1) *The merging of individual English words* is built-in for common words that are independent of the database, e.g. "is", "not", "greater", etc.

(2) *The syntactic structure of English* is represented by an augmented transition network in which each finite-state machine for parsing a syntactic structure is allowed to run, effectively in parallel. Thus ROBOT's parsings are non-deterministic at this level since it will produce all possible analyses.

(3) *Advice from the database administrator* is used to tailor the system to the expected linguistic forms of particular user communities, e.g. definitions of words likely to be used, default information likely to be implied, and navigational information on how the database is structured. Harris calls this "advice" because it can be explicitly overriden by the user in his enquiries.

(4) *The database itself* is used by ROBOT in translating a request to provide information regarding the use of individual words within it, and to help determine when interpretation on an enquiry makes sense with respect to the database.

(5) *The user himself* is the ultimate resort through a clarification dialogue if ROBOT cannot resolve ambiguity in any other way.

The following dialogue with ROBOT illustrates some of these features—the alternative lines given are examples of enquiries that would elicit the same reply:

1	M:	Give me the names of all employees who have jobs working as secretaries in the city of Chicago
1'	M:	Print the names of all the Chicago employees working as secretaries
1"	M:	Who are the Chicago secretaries
1'''	M:	Secretaries in Chicago
2	S:	Print the name of any employee with city = Chicago and job = secretary

The number of records to retrieve is
Reinstedt
Lawler
Mooers
. . . . . .

| 3 | M: | What is the family status of the area managers that live in New York |
| 4 | S: | Request ambiguous. is it: |

Number 1
Print the family status, state and city of any employee with state = NY and job = area manager
Number 2
Print the family status, state and city of any employee with city = New York and job = area manager
Please type the number 1 or the number 2

| 5 | M: | 1 |
| 6 | S: | The number of records to retrieve is 120 |

Married	NY	New York
Married	NY	White Plains
Divorced	NY	White Plains
Married	NY	New York

. . . . . .

| 7 | M: | Los Angeles area managers |
| 8 | S: | Print the name of any employee with job = area manager and city = Los Angeles |

The number of records to retrieve is 14
Atherton
Holzbauer
Needham
. . . . . .

FIG. 3. Sample dialogue with ROBOT (Harris, 1977).

Line 1 of this dialogue is a request in a form where the syntax and semantics of the language make the decoding straightforward even if certain key words are replaced by nonsense words, i.e. the database itself need not be involved until a specific request for information has been formulated. However, at line 1''' the same request is formulated in such a way that knowledge of the structure of English is of little use—the form of the request can only be inferred by using the database itself to determine the nature of the words used. Then the inbuilt "advice" of the administrator must be used to infer the likely objectives of the request.

Harris (1977) and Pruitt (1977), the Data Processing Manager at Bigelow, report a very high degree of acceptance of ROBOT by ordinary users of the database.

"The end user no longer has to think about files and fields in the sense that you and I do. Rather the user properly thinks about information, regardless of the source of that information or how it is stored."

Harris warns against extrapolating the ROBOT dialogue to the assumption that it can cope with arbitrary English conversation. However, within the framework of its own domain of knowledge it does accept a wide range of natural language questions and is properly tolerant of syntactic "errors", ellipsis and so on, as would be any native speaker.

Returning to Fig. 1, I would wish to argue that the use of natural language involved is not beyond currently available computational linguistic technologies. The subtleties in the early part are just those that we are already aware of in programming far more formal dialogues (Gaines & Facey, 1975), e.g. at line 4 S does not ask "Sex?" but infers it from the name "Peter" (using a table look-up rather as in the spelling corrector)—however, since name → sex is not infallible the term "he" is introduced at line 4 to allow M to correct the inference if necessary, and so on—the use of currently available linguistic and dialogue programming techniques can cope with making the conversation in itself acceptable and attractive to the user. The real problems drawn out of Fig. 1 are instead ones of the basic "logic" of the database, rigid concepts of "truth", static views of the world, and so on. It is the actual structures within the database, the forms of information we can store, the patterns of inference available with it, etc., that need radical development. In the following sections I will give some more detailed examples of the problems and related developments.

5. Constraints, possible worlds and modal logics

It would be rare in any real database for the full potential range of database states defined in section 3 to correspond to the actually possible range, i.e. a database state space is a proper *sub-set* of its potential states. If we consider the database as an automaton whose inputs consist themselves of positive and negative sub-sets of P (i.e. items to be added to, and taken from, the database), three types of illegal transitions (subtractions) may be requested:

(1) additions (subtractions) to the state sub-set which lead to an impossible state sub-set such that no further additions (subtractions) can lead to a legal state;
(2) additions such that there exists a unique minimal sub-set of further additions (subtractions) leading to a legal state;
(3) additions (subtractions) such that there exist several incomparable minimal sub-sets of additions (subtractions) leading to a legal state.

The first case is such that for integrity the change must be rejected; the second case allows a unique "completion" of the change that preserves integrity; and the third case may be regarded either as offering a choice of "completion" or as necessitating rejection because of its indeterminacy.

Studies of database "normalization" have been primarily concerned with constraints on the database that lead to case 2, and with the implementation of the database (as a family of projections of the product set P) that automatically enforce the completion of requests. The use of strong and weak functional dependencies between sets of fields to factor the product into a family of projections in *fourth normal form* allows entry and update requests to be treated as single changes in projections that together generate a multiple change in the database state that is legal and preserves integrity (Fagin, 1977a). The normal forms are important because the database projections involved give a simple model of the database structure (as the sum of its projections)—Addis (1977) has pointed out how these projections serve as a "model of the organisation".

Clearly not all constraints on database updates can be expressed in terms of normalization, e.g. it may be that certain combinations of values in fields have been declared illegal for individual reasons that reflect no structural constraints. In the general case we can say that potential database states form a set of "possible worlds", a terminology dating back to Leibnitz but used in recent years to describe a key concept in modelling the semantics of modal logics (Snyder, 1971). What is particularly interesting from this point of view is that logicians commencing with intensional notions of modal concepts such as possibility and necessity, permission and obligation, etc., have arrived in the last decade at semantic systems that are basically extensional using structures of "state-descriptions" that are formally identical to those of database theory. This has enabled many of the fundamendal logical difficulties of formal reasoning with modal concepts to be overcome, so that we now have well-grounded theories for a wide variety of modalities and it is feasible to attempt to formalize many forms of practical reasoning. However, modal logics can also be viewed as a form of constraint analysis of possible worlds, i.e. is this state transition *permitted* (deontic modality), *possible* (alethic modality), *credible* (epistemic modality), etc., and hence are very directly related to the integrity and normalization of databases.

An illustration of this relationship comes, for example, from a comparison of Lewis's (1973) analysis of counter-factual conditionals in philosophical logic and Todd's (1977) analysis of automatic constraint maintenance in databases. Lewis develops a model of the relationships of possible worlds in terms of a partial order of similarity—Todd defines just such a partial order over database states in order to determine the minimal completion of updates necessary to preserve integrity constraints as defined in (2) above. Lewis is concerned to analyse such statements as:
"If kangaroos had no tails, they would topple over"
and notes the problems of considering a possible world satisfying the first clause:

> "We might think it best to confine our attention to worlds where kangaroos have no tails and everything else is as it actually is; but there are no such worlds. Are we to suppose that kangaroos have no tails but their tracks in the sand are as they actually are? Then we shall have to suppose that these tracks are produced in a way quite different from the actual way."

If one replaces his example with:
"If we ship no orders for a week, our cash flow will deteriorate"
the relevance to commercial databases may be more obvious! There are such close links, formal and informal, between the logicians analysis of possible world models for modal logics and current requirements for the constraint analysis of database systems that a mutual interchange of ideas and problems would seem to be very fruitful. We have already indicated some of the relationships in more detail for the Graham & Denning (1972) model of protection structures (Kohout & Gaines, 1976).

Even when the extension of the database system to counter-factual analysis is not required, the concept of possible worlds can be important. The situation at line 7 of the dialogue in Fig. 1 where two possible values are given to a single-valued field is a simpler requirement but leads to similar problems. We cannot put both alternatives in the database without violating the (presumed) constraint that an employee is assigned to one section only. Neither can we simply mark the entries as "possible" since this does not carry the information that at least one of the possibilities must occur and that they cannot both occur together. That is, in modal logic terms, we have to account not only for:

Possible(Sales) **AND Possible**(Distribution)

but also:

Necessary(Sales **OR** Distribution) and
Not Possible(Sales **AND** Distribution)

This is a situation similar to that in automata theory where we might know that an automaton is possibly in each of several states, but with the over-riding constraint that it must be in one, and not more than one, state. We have shown (Gaines & Kohout, 1976) that this type of situation may be represented by a weakened form of probability logic (Rescher, 1969) in which the value 0 means **impossible**, 1 means **necessary**, and intermediate values mean **possible**. The constraint that one and only one of the possibilities must occur is then equivalent to the sum of assigned "probabilities" being 1. In database terms this corresponds to mapping the characteristic function of the relation P not into the two points {0, 1} but into the complete interval [0, 1].

6. Paradoxes, knowledge and action

The close relationships known to exist (Date, 1976; Fagin, 1977b) between databases and systems of logic prompt one to enquire whether the paradoxes of logic may also be found in database operation. Tokuda (1977) has recently pointed out that the axiom of comprehension in naïve set theory that leads to Russell's paradox is implicitly assumed in some of the computing science literature, i.e. we cannot assume that every predicate leads to a well-defined set. Russell's "barber" paradox has a direct representation in terms of a database of information on the person who shaves each individual in a village subject to the constraints that:

(1) if someone does not shave himself he is shaved by the barber;
(2) if someone shaves himself he is not shaved by the barber.

Suppose that items in this database are pairs, (X, Y), representing the relation, "X shaves Y", and let the barber be B. Consider the pair (B, B)—does it belong to the database or not? Starting with no (B, B) in the database and enforcing constraint (1) we have to add (B, B) to preserve integrity. Then applying constraint (2) we find that we have to remove (B, B) to preserve integrity. Thus the net effect of the two constraints is that the state of the database will oscillate between two positions, and an enquirer will sometimes find that "B shaves B", sometimes not. Pinkava (1977) has shown that many classical paradoxes of logic may be represented as oscillations in networks. Clearly, the imposition of a family of constraints can lead to very much more complex autonomous behaviour within the database, basically deriving from the known *inconsistency* of naïve set theory (Frankel, Bar-Hillel & Levy, 1973).

An oscillation in itself may be seen as a local problem that reflects the ambiguous status of certain items of information, i.e. (B, B) should be both in and out of the database (e.g. one resolution of the Russell paradox is to assign this data the truth-value 1/2 (Gaines, 1976b)). However, global problems destroying the integrity of the entire database can arise basically through similar phenomena to those encountered with asynchronous interacting processes, e.g. picking up a supposedly static value not realizing that it is being changed whilst it is being used. If P is an oscillating proposition and Q is *any* other proposition then we can infer that Q is true by a sequence such as:

Examine P—TRUE—hence infer that (P OR Q) is TRUE and put away for later use.

Examine P again—FALSE—hence from (P OR Q) is TRUE infer that Q is TRUE.

Using information within the database itself to determine the form of an update may be viewed as the imposition of an integrity constraint at data entry, and similar phenomena can arise. In general, if we allow entries to a database to be determined, or partially determined, by entries already there, then the entry of one item of information may so change the database that the item should no longer be entered.

Even simpler examples of conflict between the state of a database and data to be entered may arise if we distinguish between entries and updates and validate new entries against the data already entered. Belnap (1976) considers the problem of a real-world database and suggests that the two situations of no information being entered on a particular item, and contradictory information being entered, cannot be avoided. He notes that one cannot represent these situations adequately in a 2-valued logic that only mirrors the truth or falisity of statements, and takes no account of the epistemic state of the database, i.e. one must distinguish "John has a car" is **true** or **false**, from whether "John has a car" is **known** or **unknown**, and one must allow for both "truth" and "falsity" to be known together without the entire logical system for inferences about the database breaking down.

Belnap proposes a 4-valued logic for databases with the values forming the lattice:

Told True and Told False

*   *

*   *

Told True   Told False

*   *

*   *

Not Told

and demonstrates that a simple and consistent logical system may be built on this. In this system the "barber" paradox causes no problems of oscillation because the contradiction involved is acceptable, i.e. (B, B) will be **Told True and Told False** which seems a reasonable resolution of that problem!

Clearly, a move to multi-valued logics does allow more information to be carried about the status of information in a database. However, whilst even a 3-valued logic is known to be adequate to deal with Russell's paradox (Skolem, 1960), there are higher-order paradoxes (corresponding to more complex systems of constraints in this context), that are known to be irresolvable by any finite-valued logic (Chang, 1964; Fenstad, 1964; Maydole, 1975). It is also known that the modelling of modalities, as discussed in the previous section, is not possible in any finite-valued logic (Dugundji, 1940) and even that paradoxes can occur in naïve set theory based on the infinite-valued probability logic (Maydole, 1975) that represents the modal logic S5 (Rescher, 1963). In practice, the significance of a requirement for "infinite-valued" logics is not so unrealistic as it might seem—really it means that the number of values in our logic must be extensible to cope with situations of increasing complexity. That is a common requirement for many fields in a conventional database—in a dynamic real-world situation sooner or later we may run out of bits to represent a possible range of values.

The requirement for more than the 4 values suggested by Belnap will also arise in a real system in other ways—if we have **Told True and Told False**, our next question will probably be "Who told me true and who told me false?"! Indeed, even without contradiction, if we have "**Told True**" for a second time this may well increase the *credibility* of the information actually being true—Giles (1976) has pointed out that conjunction and disjunction are not necessarily idempotent in practical reasoning—we may emphasize the truth of a statement by repeating it. This phenomenon would occur naturally if the database were treated as an *inductive inference* system (Gaines, 1977) in which incoming data was treated as evidence on which to establish truth rather than statements of truth in themselves. It also occurs in these systems of vague reasoning discussed in the next section where all statements are treated as being imprecise so that the precision of knowledge may increase as related information is received. In general, for large multi-user, multi-centric databases some means of carrying information about the epistemic status of the database, its "state of knowledge", seems essential.

A number of systems for the representation and acquisition of "expert" knowledge have used multivalued logics as an intrinsic feature of their computations. Sridharan & Schmidt (1977) in "Believer" use a 3-valued logic with 3 of Belnap's values: **True/False/Unknown**. Isner (1975) in his "understanding" system and Shortliffe (1976) in "MYCIN" both discuss and use many-valued systems. Michalski (1977) has developed a range of quantified variable-valued logics that have been used as the basis of both inductive knowledge acquisition systems and in expert knowledge representation.

The actual imposition of integrity constraints can clearly take place as part of the update routine or as a separate set of processes "woken up" when certain pre-conditions are met within the database. In a complex database system with many possible update paths where integrity constraints may themselves be dynamic variables (as at line 27 of Fig. 1) the use of *data-driven* processes, "demons" or "actors" (Hewitt & Baker, 1977) is attractive. Hendrix (1973) has shown how dynamic processes may be simulated by such data-driven processes and other workers have given a variety of detailed examples of the modelling of physical systems (Reiger & Grinberg, 1976; Lowrance & Friedman, 1977), e.g. the "integrity constraint" that one cannot move through a brick wall is modelled by a process that wakes up when an object comes into contact with the wall and cancels further motion of that object. Smith & Hewitt have suggested that many of the goal-directed activities of the PLANNER system used by Winograd (1972) in implementing SHRDLU may be achieved through simple mechanisms based on data-driven processes, and have proposed a language Plasma (Smith & Hewitt, 1975) based on this. Even in the context of far simpler problems of information access protection (Conway, Maxwell & Morgan, 1972) and languages providing it such as EL1 (Wegbreit, 1974), the detection of access violations is really only practically feasible using hardware mechanisms such as tagged (Feustel, 1973) or descriptor-based (Gaines, Facey, Williamson & Maine, 1974) machines allowing the type of mechanisms that Zelkowitz (1971) has proposed for the IBM360.

It is interesting to note again that philosophical logicians have also treated the problems that arise in reasoning systems determining actions including the types of conflict that lead to oscillations (Rescher, 1967).

7. Imprecision and vagueness

The initial applications of computers were in the exact sciences and comparable commercial areas such as accountancy. Database theory and practice in developing from this, even though it allows for non-numerical data, still requires it to be precise and well-defined. As applications move out of the realms of the accountant and into the less quantitative areas of the firm so also does a requirement for high precision in specifying retrievals and updates of a database become increasingly unnatural. It is possible to argue that precision in itself is always a virtue—a reply to a request for a delivery date that says "soon" would be rated less satisfactory than one that says "in 3 days time"—the latter is more "businesslike".

However, unwarranted precision can itself be highly misleading since actions may be taken based on it—"we will deliver 7 parcels each weighing $15\cdot2$ kilograms at the rear entrance of building 6A on 15th February at 0.03 p.m.", "we will deliver some heavy equipment to your site Saturday evening", and "see you with the goods over the weekend", may each refer to the same event but are clearly not interchangeable, i.e. each conveys an exact meaning that (presumably) properly represents what is to occur. If we prefer the precision of the first statement it is not for its own sake but because the tighter tolerances it implies on the actual situation allow us to plan ahead with greater accuracy and less use of resources. However, if the third statement really represents all that can be said it would be ridiculous to replace it with either of the previous ones. It would be equally ridiculous to say nothing, however, since even the least precise of the three statements does provide a basis for planning and action. A key aspect of executive action is planning under uncertainty and normal language provides a means for imprecision to be clearly and exactly expressed.

In retrieving information from a database the requirement for artificial precision is at least irritating and at worst highly misleading, e.g. the request, "list the young salesmen who have a good selling record for household goods in the north of England", is perfectly comprehensible to a person. Translating it into, "list salesmen under 25 years old who have sold more than £20,000 of goods in the categories . . . to shops in the regions . . .", generates unnecessary work and makes no allowances for the whole spectrum of trade-offs possible, i.e. it will not list the chap of 26 who has made a real killing, or the one of 19 who sold £19,000, etc. The second request is more precise but the first represents far more accurately the actual *meaning* of the retrieval required.

Zadeh (1965, 1976, 1977, 1978a,b) over many years has argued the need for systems engineering to be based on "linguistic reasoning" that accurately reflects the imprecision of most real-life situations, and not the artificially quantitative approaches that form the stereotype in modern "science". He has developed a complete system of *fuzzy logic* that allows imprecise, but practically valid, arguments in everyday reasoning to be translated into computable terms. Over the last decade there have been widespread developments in the foundations of such fuzzy reasoning (Goguen, 1974; Gaines, 1976b) and its applications to problems of control, pattern recognition, linguistics, etc. (Gaines & Kohout, 1977). Recently Zadeh (1978b) has developed a language PRUF which he terms "a meaning representation language for natural languages" that is well-suited to database applications.

The foundation for PRUF is Zadeh's "fuzzy set theory" in which the characteristic function of a set is extended to range throughout the interval [0, 1] instead of taking values only at its end-points. Zadeh terms the value of the characteristic function of a given element of a sub-set its "degree of membership" to that sub-set, and represents imprecise terms as "possibility distributions" of degree of membership to the possible values, i.e. the statement, "Louie is on a high salary" assigns a possibility valuation to each level of salary that Louie might have. Thus such an imprecise statement as an entry to a database can be regarded as corresponding to entering in the database a "fuzzy relation" consisting of a number of possible relations each with a defined degree of membership to being true. Zadeh (1977, 1978a,b) develops in detail an inference system for answering queries about such a fuzzy database.

Clearly, implementing such a fuzzy database by actually storing all the relations generated by an imprecise statement together with their degrees of membership would lead to space problems. It is more realistic to consider storing the original linguistic statement and generating the implied possibility distributions only as required. It is also possible to develop higher level patterns of vague reasoning at the linguistic level that are implied by the possibility distributions but are computationally independent of them—such an approach has proved fruitful in the analysis of fuzzy linguistic controllers (Rutherford, 1979).

8. Summary—the logics of databases

Logics of possibility, induction, imprecision, action, etc., go beyond the classical predicate calculus and are not representable within it. Attempts to do so lead to paradoxes, false inferences and insufficiently rich semantics to express what is required. The common pattern of development for the resolution of these different problems is to go over to *multi-valued* logics allowing a range of "truth-values" in the interval [0, 1] instead of just its two end-points. In terms of Codd's relational model outlined in section 3, this corresponds in the simplest cases to taking the database states not as standard sub-sets of the Cartesian product, P, i.e. mappings to {0, 1}, but instead as mappings from P to the entire interval [0, 1].

However, a number of problems arise:

(1) The multi-valued logics required have to be infinite-valued. This, at first sight, is absurd in computational terms. However, in practice it turns out that it is the extensibility of the truth-values (formally that they be *dense* in [0, 1]) that is required. We wish to be able to place a new truth-value, y, between two old ones, x and z, such that $x < y < z$. Clearly, if on the occasion we have to do this it turns out that the computer word-length is such that there are no values left between x and z then the inference scheme will begin to break down. This is just the way in which the manipulation of floating point reals breaks down and is nothing new computation-ally—indeed it suggests a role for the numerical analyst in areas of theorem-proving that have so far been outside his province!

(2) Actually storing relationships in extensive form is unrealistic when we no longer have available the computational trick of a two-valued world where items mapping

to 1 may be stored and items mapping to 0 left out. However, in many instances it seems far more natural to store the generator of a relation than the extension of it—a person would need a rather large cortex to hold all integers, for example! In practice we have to store some isolated "facts" and much procedural "knowledge" and use the underlying extensional calculus to make inferences combining both.

(3) The logical rules that apply to the multi-dimensional logics generated for different purposes can be very different in their connectives, e.g. the natural logic of possibility is a weakened probability logic whereas that of imprecision and vagueness is Łukasiewicz logic (Gaines, 1975, 1976b). The connectives of one logic are arithmetic operations of addition and subtraction, whereas those of the other are comparisons leading to minimum and maximum, and, even though these may be shown to be related (Gaines, 1976a), they appear quite different. It turns out that in situations where possibility, credibility, imprecision, etc., combine, we require a set of relevant multi-valued logics operating on a *possibility vector*—Gaines (1975) develops such a system for possibility, probability and eventuality.

These considerations leave us with a range of difficult problems to be solved before multi-valued logics may be applied to real database systems. However, only a decade has passed since logicians finally came to grips with the decision procedures of standard modal logics studied since the time of Aristotle. Computational techniques to deal with a range of modal logics are now available, although the problems of mixed modalities are still largely open. Some workers such as Creswell (1973) and Montague (1974) have developed large-scale systems for the logical analysis of natural language. The database as an abstract entity is very closely related to the possible worlds models of modal logics, and as a practical system it is very closely related to the linguistic structures that these logics formalize. I hope this paper will encourage further research into the common problems of database systems, linguistics and philosophical logic.

9. Conclusions

This paper has raised many problems of database dynamics and logic for the next generation of systems and briefly outlines some possible approaches to their solution. This is a fair reflection of the current state-of-the-art where the effort to implement and operate conventional database systems has precluded all but a few explorations of some of the issues raised here. However, the technologies for database support are developing very rapidly indeed and, as has already happened to a large extent with high-level languages, the hardware/software available may soon outstrip current user requirements. We need to think ahead and determine what limitations of current database concepts will prove to be severe restrictions in future applications without paying too much regard to current implementation problems.

I have suggested that the sheer mechanics of natural language communication with databases may prove to be far less of a problem than we have tended to assume— developments such as LIFER and ROBOT are highly encouraging. However, the "world-view" incorporated in the databases driving these systems is highly restricted not so much in the quantity of information stored but in its quality, richness and fitness, compared with that used in comparable human reasoning within an organization. The various sections of this paper illustrate some of the difficulties that may arise and survey some of the techniques currently being investigated to overcome them. As with many of the problems of computing science, and system engineering in general, the solutions themselves seem to present far less difficulty than does the appropriate problem formulation. If we can define what we are trying to achieve then the problem is 90% solved. I hope this paper will encourage wider discussion of the features required in the next generation of databases.

I am grateful for access to related material and discussions on topics treated in this paper with Robin Giles, Joe Goguen, Susan Haack, Larry Harris, Ladislav Kohout, Ebrahim Mamdani, Ryszard Michalski and Lotfi Zadeh.

References

ADDIS, T. R. (1977). An introduction to relational analysis for data-base design. Paper presented at National Conference of Operational Research Society (UG.21), Sept., International Computers Ltd., Stevenage, Herts., U.K.

ARBIB, M. A. (1969). *Theories of Abstract Automata*. Englewood Cliffs, N.J.: Prentice-Hall.

BELNAP, N. D. (1976). How a computer should think. In RYLE, G., Ed., *Contemporary Aspects of Philosophy*. Stockfield: Oriel Press, pp. 30–56.

CHANS, C. C. (1964). Infinite valued logic as a basis for set theory. In BAR-HILLEL, Y., Ed., *Proceedings of 1974 International Congress for Logic, Methodology and Philosophy of Science*. Amsterdam: North-Holland, pp. 93–100.

CODD, E. F. (1970). A relational model of data for large shared data banks. *Communications of the ACM*, **13** (6), 377–387.

CODD, E. F. (1974). The relational approach to data base management: an overview. *IEEE 1974 Texas Conference on Computing Systems* 74-CH0895, 6.1.1–6.1.5.

CONWAY, R. W., MAXWELL, W. L. & MORGAN, H. L. (1972). On the implementation of security measures in information systems. *Communications of the ACM*, **15** (4), 211–220.

CRESSWELL, M. J. (1973). *Logics and Languages*. London: Methuen.

DATE, C. J. (1976). *An Introduction to Database Systems*. Reading, Mass.: Addison-Wesley.

DE BONO, E. (1979). *Future Positive*. London: Maurice Temple Smith.

DOLOTTA, T. A., BERNSTEIN, M. I., DICKSON, R. S., FRANCE, N. A., ROSENBLATT, B. A., SMITH, D. M. & STEEL, T. B. (1976). *Data Processing in 1980–1985*. New York: John Wiley.

DUSUNDJI, J. (1940). Note on a property of matrices for Lewis and Langford's calculi of propositions. *Journal of Symbolic Logic*, **5**, 150–151.

FAGIN, R. (1977a). Multivalued dependencies and a new normal form for relational databases. *ACM Transactions on Database Systems*, **2** (3), 262–278.

FAGIN, R. (1977b). Functional dependencies in a relational database and propositional logic. *IBM Journal of Research and Development*, **21** (6),

FENSTAD, J. E. (1964). On the consistency of the axiom of comprehension in Łukasiewicz infinite valued logic. *Mathematica Scandinavica*, **146**, 65–74.

FEUSTEL, E. A. (1973). On the advantages of a tagged architecture. *IEEE Transactions on Computers*, **C-22**(7), 644.

FOCUS (1976). *Focus Query Language*, California, U.S.A.: Tymshare Inc., June.

FRAENKEL, A. A., BAR-HILLEL, Y. & LEVY, A. (1973). *Foundations of Set Theory*. Amsterdam: North-Holland.

GAINES, B. R. (1976a). Fuzzy reasoning and the logics of uncertainty. *Proceedings of the 6th International Symposium on Multiple-Valued Logic 76CH1111–4C*, May. Utah State University, Logan, Utah, U.S.A., pp. 179–188.

GAINES, B. R. (1976b). Foundations of fuzzy reasoning. *International Journal of Man–Machine Studies*, **8** (6), 623–668.

GAINES, B. R. (1977). System identification, approximation and complexity. *International Journal of General Systems*, **3** (3), 145–174.

GAINES, B. R. (1978). Computers in world three. *Proceedings of the International Conference on Cybernetics and Society IEEE-78CH-1306-0-SMC*, Nov. Tokyo, Japan, pp. 1515–1521.

GAINES, B. R. & FACEY, P. U. (1975). Some experience in interactive system development and application. *Proceedings of the IEEE*, **63**, 155–169.

GAINES, B. R., FACEY, P. U., WILLIAMSON, F. K. & MAINE, J. A. (1974). Design objectives for a descriptor-organized minicomputer. *Proceedings of the European Computing Congress, EUROCOMP 74*, May, pp. 29–45.

GAINES, B. R. & KOHOUT, L. J. (1976). The logic of automata. *International Journal of General Systems*, **2** (4), 191–208.

GAINES, B. R. & KOHOUT, L. J. (1977). The fuzzy decade: a bibliography of fuzzy systems and closely related topics. *International Journal of Man–Machine Studies*, **9** (1), 1–68.

GILES, R. (1976). Łukasiewicz logic and fuzzy set theory. *International Journal of Man–Machine Studies*, **8** (3), 313–327.

GOGUEN, J. A. (1974). Concept representation in natural and artificial languages: axioms, extensions and applications for fuzzy sets. *International Journal of Man–Machine Studies*, **6** (5), 513–561.

GRAHAM, G. S. & DENNING, P. J. (1972). Protection principles and practice. *AFIPS Spring Joint Computer Conference 40*. New Jersey: AFIPS, pp. 417–429.

HARRIS, L. R. (1977). User oriented data base query with the robot natural language query system. *International Journal of Man–Machine Studies*, **9** (6), 697–713.

HENDRIX, G. G. (1973). Modelling simultaneous actions and continuous processes. *Artificial Intelligence*, **4** (3), 145–180.

HENDRIX, G. G. (1977). LIFER: a natural language interface facility. *Proceedings of the Second Berkeley Workshop on Distributed Data Management and Computer Networks TID-4500-R65*, May, pp. 196–201.

HEWITT, C. & BAKER, H. (1977). Laws for communicating parallel processes. In GILCHRIST, B., Ed., *Information Processing 77*. Amsterdam: IFIP, North-Holland, pp. 987–992.

KOHOUT, L. J. & GAINES, B. R. (1976). Protection as a general system problem. *International Journal of General Systems*, **3** (1), 3–23.

ISNER, D. (1975). Understanding "understanding" through representation and reasoning. *Ph.D. thesis* (University Microfilms 75-21,758). University of Pittsburgh, U.S.A.

LEWIS, D. (1973). *Counter-factuals*. Oxford: Basil Blackwell.

LICKLIDER, J. C. R. (1968). Man–computer symbiosis. In ORR, W. D., Ed., *Conversational Computers*. New York: John Wiley.

LOWRANCE, J. D. & FRIEDMAN, D. P. (1977). Hendrix's model for simultaneous actions and continuous processes: an introduction and implementation. *International Journal of Man–Machine Studies*, **9**, (5), 537–581.

MAYDOLE, R. E. (1975). Paradoxes and many-valued set theory. *Journal of Philosophical Logic*, **4**, 269–291.

MICHALSKI, R. S. (1977). Variable–valued logic and its application to pattern recognition and machine learnings. In *Multiple-Valued Logic and Computer Science*. Amsterdam: North-Holland.

MONTAGUE, R. (1974). *Formal Philosophy*. New Haven: Yale University Press.

NOLAN, R. L. (1973*a*). Computer data bases: the future is now. *Harvard Business Review*, 98–114.

NOLAN, R. L. (1973*b*). Managing the computer resource: a stage hypothesis. *Communications of the ACM*, **16** (7), 399–405.

NOLAN, R. L. (1977). Thoughts about the fifth stage.

NORMAN, D. A. & RUMELHART, D. E. (Eds) (1975). *Explorations in Cognition*. San Francisco: W. H. Freeman.

PETRICK, S. R. (1976). On natural language based computer systems. *IBM Journal of Research and Development*, **20** (4), 314–325.

PINKAVA, V. (1977). On the nature of some logical paradoxes. *International Journal of Man–Machine Studies*, **9** (4), 383–398.

POPPER, K. R. (1976). *Unended Quest*. London: Fontana/Collins.

PRUITT, J. (1977). A user's experience with ROBOT. *Proceedings of the Fourth Annual ADABAS Meeting*, April.

RESCHER, N. (1963). A probabilistic approach to modal logic. *Acta Philosophica Fennica*, **16**, 215–226.

RESCHER, N. (Ed.) (1967). *The Logic of Decision and Action*. Pittsburgh: Pennsylvania University of Pittsburgh Press.

RESCHER, N. (1969). *Many-Valued Logic*. New York: McGraw-Hill.

RIESER, C. & GRINBERG, M. (1976). The causal representation and simulation of physical mechanisms. *Computer Science Technical Report Series TR-495*, November. University of Maryland, Virginia, U.S.A.

RUTHERFORD, D. A. (1979). Theoretical and linguistic aspects of the fuzzy logic controller. *Automatica*, to appear.

SHORTLIFFE, E. H. (1976). *Computer-Based Medical Consultations: MYCIN*. Elseveier Computer Science Library (2). New York: Elsevier.

SIBLEY, E. H. (1976). The development of database technology. *ACM Computing Surveys*, **8** (1), 1–5.

SKOLEM, TH. (1960). A set theory based on a certain 3-valued logic. *Mathematica Scandinavia*, **8**, 127–136.

SMITH, B. & HEWITT, C. (1975). *A Plasma Primer*. Artificial Intelligence Laboratory, Massachusetts Institute of Technology, Cambridge, Mass., U.S.A., May.

SNYDER, D. P. (1971). *Modal Logic*. New York: Van Nostrand Co.

SRIDHARAN, N. S. & SCHMIDT, C. F. (1977). Knowledge-directed inference in believer. *Departments of Computer Science and Psychology CBM-TR-75*, January. Rutgers University, New Brunswick, U.S.A.

TEITELMAN, W. (1975). *INTERLISP Reference Manual*. Xerox Palo Alto Research Center, California, U.S.A.

TODD, S. (1977). Automatic constraint maintenance defined relations. In GILCHRIST, B., Ed., *Information Processing 77*. Amsterdam: IFIP, North-Holland, pp. 145–148.

TOKUDA, T. (1977). A question of style in future computing literature. *SIGART News*, **9** (2), 6–7.

WESBREIT, B. (1974). The treatment of data types in EL1. *Communications of the ACM*, **17** (5), 251–264.

WEIZENBAUM, J. (1967). Contextual understanding by computers. *Communications of the ACM*, **10** (8), 474–480.

WINOGRAD, T. (1972). *Understanding Natural Language*. Edinburgh University Press.

WOODS, W. A. (1970). Transition network grammars for natural language analysis. *Communications of the ACM*, **13** (10), 591–606.

ZADEH, L. A. (1965). Fuzzy sets. *Information and Control*, **8**, 338–353.

ZADEH, L. A. (1976). A fuzzy-algorithmic approach to the definition of complex or imprecise concepts. *International Journal of Man–Machine Studies*, **8**, 249–291.

ZADEH, L. A. (1977). A theory of approximate reasoning, *Electronics Research Laboratory Memorandum M77/58*. University of California, Berkeley, California, U.S.A.

ZADEH, L. A. (1978a). Fuzzy sets as a basis for a theory of possibility. *Fuzzy Sets and Systems*, **1** (1), 3–28.

ZADEH, L. A. (1978b). PRUF—a meaning representation language for natural languages. *International Journal of Man–Machine Studies*, **10** (4), 295–460.

ZELKOWITZ, M. (1971). Interupt driven programming. *Communications of the ACM*, **14** (6), 417–418.

Part III

An Experiment in Linguistic Synthesis with a Fuzzy Logic Controller

E. H. MAMDANI AND S. ASSILIAN

Queen Mary College, London University, U.K.

(*Received 2 November 1973*)

This paper describes an experiment on the "linguistic" synthesis of a controller for a model industrial plant (a steam engine). Fuzzy logic is used to convert heuristic control rules stated by a human operator into an automatic control strategy. The experiment was initiated to investigate the possibility of human interaction with a learning controller. However, the control strategy set up linguistically proved to be far better than expected in its own right, and the basic experiment of linguistic control synthesis in a non-learning controller is reported here.

Introduction

Many techniques for the synthesis of automatic controllers will be found in the control literature. The standard textbook approaches, however, all involve quantitative, numeric calculations based on mathematical models of the plant and controller. In recent years there have been many studies of self-organizing, or adaptive, controllers in which the control strategy is not synthesized in advance but is generated by optimization algorithms based on the controller's "experience". Such controllers exhibit some characteristics of human learning and in their more general forms are examples of "artificial intelligence".

However, the capability of self-organization and learning are only two aspects of the many attributes of human intelligence. A different facet, that has not been emulated in control studies, is the ability to comprehend *instructions* and to generate strategies based not on experience but on *a priori* verbal communication. Luria (1961) has given graphic illustrations of the way in which simple perceptual-motor skills are built on verbal foundations in young children. Pask (1971) has emphasized the linguistic nature of many aspects of intelligent behaviour. In artificial intelligence research Winograd (1973) has given an impressive demonstration of the possibility of direct linguistic control of a mechanical arm performing a building task with solid objects. Most control engineers would accept intuitively that the mathematical computations they perform in translating their concept of a control strategy into an automatic controller are far removed from their own approach to the manual performance of the same task, and that there seems to be a fairly direct relationship between the loose linguistic expression of a control strategy and its manual implementation. It was this direct path between a linguistic statement of a control strategy and its implementation that formed the subject of this investigation.

The full richness of linguistic structure exhibited so effectively by Winograd (1972) has no equivalent in the present study since we were primarily concerned with the translation of semantic expressions into control laws, and not with the recognition of the expressions themselves or their manipulation. To the control engineer quantitative languages supporting arithmetic are the natural ones. To support the translation of the vaguer, non-numeric statements that might be made about a control strategy we needed a semi-quantitative calculus. Zadeh's (1973) fuzzy logic seemed to provide a means of expressing linguistic rules in such a form that they might be combined into a coherent control strategy. In the case study reported here we have implemented a controller, a *fuzzy logic controller* based on Zadeh's calculus, and investigated its behaviour in the control of a small steam engine.

The Plant to be Controlled

The plant for which the controller was implemented comprises a steam engine and boiler combination. The model of the plant used has two inputs: heat input to the boiler and throttle opening at the input of the engine cylinder, and two outputs: the steam pressure in the boiler and the speed of the engine. Simple identification tests on the plant proved that it is highly nonlinear with both magnitude and polarity of the input variables. Therefore, the plant possesses different characteristics at different operating points, so that the direct digital controller implemented for comparison purposes had to be retuned (by trial and error) to give the best performance each time the operating point was altered.

The Controller

A fuzzy subset A of a universe of discourse U is characterized by a membership function $\mu: U \rightarrow (0, 1)$ which associates with each element u of U a number $\mu(u)$ in the interval $(0, 1)$ which represents the grade of membership of u in A. The fuzzy set A of $U = u_1, u_2, \ldots, u_n$ will be denoted

$$A = \sum_{i=1}^{n} \mu_A(u_i)/u_i = \sum_i \mu_A(u_i)$$

where Σ stands for union.

Three basic operators that are used in this application are defined next. The union of fuzzy subsets A and B is denoted $A+B$ and is defined by

$$A+B = \sum_i \mu_A(u_i) \vee \mu_B(u_i)$$

where $\vee$ stands for maximum (abbreviated to max). The union corresponds to the connective OR. Similarly, the intersection of A and B is denoted $A \cdot B$ and is defined by

$$A \cdot B = \sum_i \mu_A(u_i) \wedge \mu_B(u_i)$$

where $\wedge$ stands for minimum (abbreviated to min). The intersection corresponds to the connective AND. Finally, the complement of a set A is denoted $7A$ and is defined by

$$7A = \sum_i 1 - \mu_A(u_i)$$

Complementation corresponds to negation, i.e. NOT.

The definition of a fuzzy set permits one to assign values to fuzzy variables. In this application six (four input and two output) fuzzy variables are used:

(1) *PE*—Pressure Error, defined as the difference between the present value of the variable and the set point.

(2) *SE*—Speed Error, defined as in (1).

(3) *CPE*—Change in pressure error, defined as the difference between present *PE* and last (corresponding to last sampling instant).

(4) *CSE*—Change in speed error, defined as in (3).

(5) *HC*—Heat Change (action variable).

(6) *TC*—Throttle Change (action variable).

These variables are quantized into a number of points corresponding to the elements of a universe of discourse, and values to the variables are assigned using seven basic fuzzy subsets (see appendix): (1) *PB*—Positive Big; (2) *PM*—Positive Medium; (3) *PS*—Positive Small; (4) *NO*—Nil; (5) *NS*—Negative Small; (6) *NM*—Negative Medium; (7) *NB*—Negative Big. Using these basic subsets and the three operators defined earlier values such as "Not Positive Big or Medium" can be assigned to the variables. Even more complex values can be computed using linguistic hedges, etc., but in this study no such attempt was made to avoid complications.

The control rules were implemented by using fuzzy conditional statements, for example "*If PE* is *NB then HC* is *PB*". The implied relation between the two fuzzy variables *PE* and *HC* is expressed in terms of the cartesian product of the two subsets NB and PB. The cartesian product of two sets A and B is denoted $A \times B$ and is defined by

$$A \times B = \underset{i}{\Sigma} \underset{j}{\Sigma} \min\{\mu_A(u_i), \mu_B(v_j)\}$$

$$= \underset{ij}{\Sigma} \min u_i v_j \text{ (for short)}$$

where u and v are generic elements of the universes of discourse of A and B respectively. The cartesian product can be conveniently represented by a matrix of m rows and n columns where m and n are the numbers of elements in the universes of A and B respectively. That is, i $= 1, 2, \ldots$, m; $j = 1, 2, \ldots, n$.

Having thus expressed the relation between two fuzzy variables, it can now be used to infer the value of the second variable given a value for the first. For example, "PE is NM. What is HC?" Suppose we denote by R the relation between two variables. Then, if x is the given value of the first variable, the value y of the second variable is inferred by forming the composition $y = x \, 0 \, R$. Composition is interpreted as the max–min product of x and R. Therefore, if $A \times B = R = \underset{ij}{\Sigma} \min u_i v_j$ as defined above, then a subset A' induces a subset B' given by

$$B' = \underset{j}{\Sigma} \max \underset{i}{\min} u_i' \min u_i v_j$$

Relations of higher order than two can be similarly defined. For example, "If A then (if B then C)" is given by the cartesian product $A \times B \times C$. And now given A' and B' the value of C' is inferred to be

$$C' = \underset{k}{\Sigma} \max \underset{ij}{\min} u_i' \, u_i v_j \, 'v_j \, w_k$$

In the present application A' and B' were chosen to be non-fuzzy vectors and with only one element equal to 1, all the rest being 0. In this case the above expression reduces to

$$C' = \underset{k}{\Sigma} \min u_a v_b w_k$$

where a and b indicate the elements at which the vectors A' and B' have the value 1.

Finally, two or more rules can be combined using the connective ELSE, which is interpreted as the max operation, to give an algorithm for the control action. For example,

If A_1 then (If B_1 then C_1)
ELSE If A_2 then (If B_2 then C_2),
    etc.

yields the resultant control action C', given A_1', A_2', B_1', B_2', etc. as

$$C_1 = \max C_1' \; C_2', \text{ etc.}$$
$$= \sum_k \max \{\min u_{a1} \, v_{b1} \, z_k, \min u_{a2} \, v_{b2} \, z_k, \text{ etc.}\}.$$

Therefore more than one rule may contribute to the computation of the control action. This, of course, is because of the fuzzy nature of the rules.

To recapitulate, two algorithms were implemented in this application: one to compute the "heat change" (HC) control action and the other to compute the "throttle change" (TC) control action. Every rule in these algorithms is a relationship between the input variables PE, CPE, SE, CSE (in that order) and either HC or TC. The control actions are computed by presenting values for the input variables to the two algorithms. The input vectors are of course obtained by sampling the states of the steam engine at the sampling instants.

The output of either algorithm is obviously a fuzzy set which assigns grades (of membership) to the possible values of the control fuzzy variable. In order to take a deterministic action one of these values must be chosen, the choice procedure depending on the grades of membership. Various considerations may influence the choice procedure depending on the particular application and in our case effectively that action is taken which has the largest membership grade. It is possible of course that more than one peak or a flat peak is obtained as illustrated below:

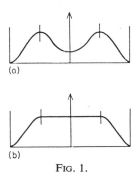

(a)

(b)

FIG. 1.

The particular procedure in our case takes the action indicated by the arrow, which is midway between the two peaks or at the centre of the plateau.

A spread as in (b) indicates the absence of a strong or good set of rules and is not as serious as the spread in (a). The latter indicates the presence of at least two contradictory rules and in such cases it is necessary to locate and modify these rules. This "tuning" process is facilitated in our application by a data-logging procedure which traces the contributing rules for every control action. Apart from resolving contradictions of this type, the above procedure also helps in modifying any weak or bad rules resulting in unacceptable control actions.

It might be useful to note here that it is the rules that are modified and not the seven basic, but subjective, definitions of the values assigned to the variables involved in the rules. Given a simple, say, 14-point universe of discourse, any subjective definition of "positive big" is hardly likely to be too contentious. Stated otherwise, a set of rules is rather insensitive to the definition of an individual fuzzy subset.

Results and Conclusions

The above scheme containing the 24 rules given in the appendix was implemented on the PDP-8 computer and applied to the steam-engine plant. A fixed digital controller was also implemented on the computer and applied to the same plant for the purpose of comparison. With the fixed controller many runs were required to tune the controller for the best performance. This tuning was done by trial and error. Results of many runs with different set points were taken. The quality of control with the fuzzy controller was found to be better each time than the best control obtained by the fixed controller. This is summarized in the figure below.

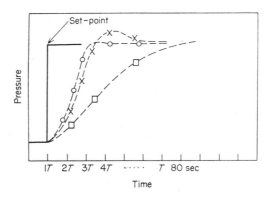

FIG. 2. Fixed controller (DDC algorithm), ×, □; Fuzzy controller, ⊙.

It is difficult to draw many conclusions from a single case study of this kind, apart from the obvious one that it demonstrates the excellent applicability of fuzzy set theory to the design of controllers. Questions may arise as to whether such a deterministic controller represents a non-trivial alternative to other approaches. It is difficult to see any direct relationship between such a controller and any other deterministic controller such as a DDC algorithm or some logic circuit with the same input–output capability. The power of the approach derives from the fact that it is possible to translate into an algorithm an entirely unstructured set of heuristics expressed linguistically.

The only comparable experiment in the literature appears to be that of Gaines (1973, p. 303) who reports a procedure for "priming" an adaptive-threshold-logic-based controller by giving it instructions which it interprets by "mentally rewarding" itself when "imagining" itself carrying out the instructions. Gaines is concerned to demonstrate that learning behaviour shown by human subjects in a series of experiments is also exhibited by a single learning system undergoing the same experiments, and his procedure was put forward as a possible emulation of the effects of instructions on his human subjects. In an earlier paper Gaines & Andreae (1966) propose the use of general-purpose learning controllers as an alternative to classical controller synthesis, and suggest that techniques of *priming* (linguistic communication of an initial control strategy), *coding* (organization of information and control actions to match plant and controller) and *training* (variation of the environment through a sequence of tasks of increasing difficulty) as synthesis techniques appropriate to learning controllers. In terms of this classification we have demonstrated the power of fuzzy logic as a basis for priming and shown that priming alone may be a powerful synthesis technique.

Another way of saying the same thing is that the fuzzy controller has been derived from a fuzzy internal model of the plant identified by the human being. This may suggest a further investigation into a fuzzy identification and control procedure. It would also be interesting to use the approach with other dynamic systems possibly more complex ones (with more input and output variables) where it could be considerably more difficult to specify the rules.

Appendix

The *PE* (Pressure Error) and *SE* (Speed Error) variables are quantized into 13 points, ranging from maximum negative error through zero error to maximum positive error. The zero error is further divided into negative zero error (*NO*—just below the set point) and positive zero error (*PO*—just above the set point). The subjective fuzzy sets defining these values are:

	−6	−5	−4	−3	−2	−1	−0	+0	+1	+2	+3	+4	+5	+6
PB	0	0	0	0	0	0	0	0	0	0	0·1	0·4	0·8	1·0
PM	0	0	0	0	0	0	0	0	0	0·2	0·7	1·0	0·7	0·2
PS	0	0	0	0	0	0	0	0·3	0·8	1·0	0·5	0·1	0	0
PO	0	0	0	0	0	0	0	1·0	0·6	0·1	0	0	0	0
NO	0	0	0	0	0·1	0·6	1·0	0	0	0	0	0	0	0
NS	0	0	0·1	0·5	1·0	0·8	0·3	0	0	0	0	0	0	0
NM	0·2	0·7	1·0	0·7	0·2	0	0	0	0	0	0	0	0	0
NB	1·0	0·8	0·4	0·1	0	0	0	0	0	0	0	0	0	0

The *CPE* (Change in Pressure Error) and *CSE* (Change in Speed Error) variables are similarly quantized without the further division of the zero state. The subjective definitions are:

	−6	−5	−4	−3	−2	−1	0	+1	+2	+3	+4	+5	+6
PB	0	0	0	0	0	0	0	0	0	0·1	0·4	0·8	1·0
PM	0	0	0	0	0	0	0	0	0·2	0·7	1·0	0·7	0·2
PS	0	0	0	0	0	0	0	0·9	1·0	0·7	0·2	0	0
NO	0	0	0	0	0	0·5	1·0	0·5	0	0	0	0	0
NS	0	0	0·2	0·7	1·0	0·9	0	0	0	0	0	0	0
NM	0·2	0·7	1·0	0·7	0·2	0	0	0	0	0	0	0	0
NB	1·0	0·8	0·4	0·1	0	0	0	0	0	0	0	0	0

Apart from the above definitions a further value *ANY* is allowed for all four variables, i.e. *PE, SE, CPE, CSE*. *ANY* has a membership function of 1·0 at every element.

The *HC* (Heat Change) variable is quantized into 15 points ranging from a change of −7 steps through 0 to −+7 steps. The subjective definitions are:

	−7	−6	−5	−4	−3	−2	−1	0	+1	+2	+3	+4	+5	+6	+7
PB	0	0	0	0	0	0	0	0	0	0	0	0·1	0·4	0·8	1·0
PM	0	0	0	0	0	0	0	0	0	0·2	0·7	1·0	0·7	0·2	0
PS	0	0	0	0	0	0	0	0·4	1·0	0·8	0·4	0·1	0	0	0
NO	0	0	0	0	0	0	0·2	1·0	0·2	0	0	0	0	0	0
NS	0	0	0	0·1	0·4	0·8	1·0	0·4	0	0	0	0	0	0	0
NM	0	0·2	0·7	1·0	0·7	0·2	0	0	0	0	0	0	0	0	0
NB	1·0	0·8	0·4	0·1	0	0	0	0	0	0	0	0	0	0	0

Similarly the *TC* (Throttle Change) variable is quantized into 5 points

	−2	−1	0	+1	+2
PB	0	0	0	0·5	1·0
PS	0	0	0·5	1·0	0·5
NO	0	0·5	1·0	0·5	0
NS	0·5	1·0	0·5	0	0
NB	1·0	0·5	0	0	0

The two control action algorithms are given below. These algorithms are based on the non-interactive control principle, i.e. the pressure-heat and speed-throttle loops are separated. Interactive algorithms have also been implemented but these are not discussed in this report.

HEATER ALGORITHM

>   If   *PE = NB*
>   and   *CPE =* not (*NB* or *NM*)
>   and   *SE = ANY*
>   and   *CSE = ANY*
>   then   *HC = PB*

Else

>   If   *PE = NB* or *NM*
>   and   *CPE = NS*
>   and   *SE = ANY*
>   and   *CSE = ANY*
>   then   *HC = PM*

Else

>   If   *PE = NS*
>   and   *CPE = PS* or *NO*
>   and   *SE = ANY*
>   and   *CSE = ANY*
>   then   *HC = PM*

Else

>   If   *PE = NO*
>   and   *CPE = PB* or *PM*
>   and   *SE = ANY*
>   and   *CSE = ANY*
>   then   *HC = PM*

Else
    If $PE = NO$
      and $CPE = NB$ or NM
      and $SE = ANY$
      and $CSE = ANY$
  then $HC = NM$

Else
    If $PE = PO$ or NO
      and $CPE = NO$
      and $SE = ANY$
      and $CSE = ANY$
  then $HC = NO$

Else
    If $PE = PO$
      and $CPE = NB$ or NM
      and $SE = ANY$
      and $CSE = ANY$
  then $HC = PM$

Else
    If $PE = PO$
      and $CPE = PB$ or PM
      and $SE = ANY$
      and $CSE = ANY$
  then $HC = NM$

Else
    If $PE = PS$
      and $CPE = PS$ or NO
      and $SE = ANY$
      and $CSE = ANY$
  then $HC = NM$

Else
    If $PE = PB$ or PM
      and $CPE = NS$
      and $SE = ANY$
      and $CSE = ANY$
  then $HC = NM$

Else

    If $PE = PB$

      and $CPE = $ not $(NB$ or $NM)$

      and $SE = ANY$

      and $CSE = ANY$

  then $HC = NB$

Else

    If $PE = NO$

      and $CPE = PS$

      and $SE = ANY$

      and $CSE = ANY$

  then $HC = PS$

Else

    If $PE = NO$

      and $CPE = NS$

      and $SE = ANY$

      and $CSE = ANY$

  then $HC = NS$

Else

    If $PE = PO$

      and $CPE = NS$

      and $SE = ANY$

      and $CSE = ANY$

  then $HC = PS$

Else

    If $PE = PO$

      and $CPE = PS$

      and $SE = ANY$

      and $CSE = ANY$

  then $HC = NS$

THROTTLE ALGORITHM

    If $PE = ANY$

      and $CPE = ANY$

      and $SE = NB$

      and $CSE = $ not $(NB$ or $NM)$

  then $TC = PB$

Else
    If $PE = ANY$
    and $CPE = ANY$
    and $SE = NM$
    and $CSE = PB$ or PM or PS
  then $TC = PS$

Else
    If $PE = ANY$
    and $CPE = ANY$
    and $SE = NS$
    and $CSE = PB$ or PM
  then $TC = PS$

Else
    If $PE = ANY$
    and $CPE = ANY$
    and $SE = NO$
    and $CSE = PB$
  then $TC = PS$

Else
    If $PE = ANY$
    and $CPE = ANY$
    and $SE = PO$ or NO
    and $CSE = PS$ or NS or NO
  then $TC = NO$

Else
    If $PE = ANY$
    and $CPE = ANY$
    and $SE = PO$
    and $CSE = PB$
  then $TC = NS$

Else
    If $PE = ANY$
    and $CPE = ANY$
    and $SE = PS$
    and $CSE = PB$ or PM
  then $TC = NS$

Else

If $\quad PE = ANY$
  and $\;CPE = ANY$
  and $\quad SE = PM$
  and $\;CSE = PB$ or PM or PS
then $\qquad TC = NS$

Else

If $\quad PE = ANY$
  and $\;CPE = ANY$
  and $\quad SE = PB$
  and $\;CSE = $ not $(NB$ or $NM)$
then $\qquad TC = NB$

References

GAINES, B. R. & ANDREAE, J. H. (1966). A learning machine in the context of the general control problem. *Proc. 3rd Int. IFAC Congress, London.*

GAINES, B. R. (1973). The learning of perceptual-motor skills by men and machines and its relationship to training. *Instructional Science*, 263.

LURIA, A. (1961). *The Role of Speech in the Regulation of Normal and Abnormal Behaviour.* Oxford: Pergamon Press.

PASK, G. (1971). A cybernetic experimental method and its underlying philosophy. *Internatl J. Man–Machine Studies*, **3**, 279.

WINOGRAD, T. (1972). *Understanding Natural Language.* Edinburgh: Edinburgh University Press.

ZADEH, L. A. (1973). Outline of a new approach to the analysis of complex systems and decision processes. *IEEE Trans.* **SMC-3**, 28.

Advances in the linguistic synthesis of fuzzy controllers

E. H. MAMDANI
Queen Mary College,
Mile End Rd, London E.1, U.K.

(*Received 24 April 1976*)

The purpose of this article is to survey the field of application of fuzzy logic in the synthesis of controllers for dynamic plants. A brief tutorial on the method of approach is also included here. Several groups of workers are currently studying various aspects of fuzzy controllers. For each such group a short account is given on the area of investigation undertaken. This along with the list of references provided here should give a broad picture of ongoing research on fuzzy controllers. Although most work is conducted using pilot scale or simulated plants, there are prospects also of an eventual application to a real plant. Some of the problems underlying actual application of fuzzy controllers are mentioned. These principally amount to the use of heuristics in plant controllers and the question of how to obtain an effective set of rules for a given plant. It is proposed that adaptive techniques in linguistic controllers currently being studied may provide a useful possible approach.

1. Introduction

This paper surveys recent developments in the design of control systems using linguistic synthesis based on the rules of fuzzy logic. Since our previous report (Mamdani & Assilian, 1975) there have been a number of significant advances, notably: the validation of the results obtained on a wide variety of plant by researchers at several centres; and the successful transfer of the same linguistic methodology to the level of control policy acquisition and optimization, i.e. to a *learning* control scheme. Whilst all these results have significance in their own right in terms of practical control engineering, we report them here for their possible relevance to human studies of linguistic modification of skilled behaviour, and to computer studies of artificial intelligence (AI). In particular, whilst early studies of machine learning in AI seemed closely related to those of *adaptive controllers* in control engineering, in recent years AI research has become predominantly linguistic. These new results re-establish a bridge between control engineering and AI in terms of linguistic reasoning to the potential mutual benefit of both subject areas.

The true antecedent of the work described here is an outstanding paper by Zadeh (1973) which lays the foundations of what we have termed linguistic synthesis (Mamdani & Assilian, 1975) and which has also been described by Zadeh as Approximate Reasoning (AR). In the 1973 paper Zadeh shows how vague logical statements can be used to construct computational algorithms which may be used to derive inferences (also vague) from vague data. The paper suggests that this method is useful in the treatment of complex humanistic systems. However, it was realized that this method could equally be applied to "hard" systems such as industrial plant controllers. In such cases where a linguistic control protocol can be obtained from a skilled operator of a plant, fuzzy logic, following the approach described by Zadeh can be used to synthesize this protocol.

This method was first applied to control a pilot scale steam-engine using fuzzy logic to interpret linguistic rules which qualitatively express the control strategy. The reader is referred to Mamdani & Assilian (1975) for a fuller description of this work. Prior to that the same steam engine had been used as a vehicle to investigate the practical applicability of artificial intelligence and learning control techniques. However, the results of such techniques did not seem to recommend themselves for industrial applications, see Assilian & Mamdani (1974). An account of this background is given in the doctoral thesis by Assilian (1974). Such AI and pattern recognition methods are principally characterized by their reliance on heureistics and it was easy to see that fuzzy logic was a very appropriate tool with which to implement heuristics. This then was what originally led to the use of fuzzy logic in controller design, even though the first controller did not possess learning ability but was merely a straight description of what should be done to control the plant.

This method was of course non-analytic and the results were consequently presented as a single case study showing what could be done using fuzzy logic. Since then the full potential of this method has gradually become more apparent as more results are obtained by various other researchers applying it. A great deal of more analysis and discussion has taken place during the past year or so. Much of this is yet unpublished and exists at present in the form of internal reports and research memoranda. It is the purpose of this article to survey the results and the ongoing work at various places, the next section briefly reviews the techniques used.

2. The synthesis of a "fuzzy controller"

The purpose of any plant controller is first to relate the state variables to action variables, i.e. to periodically look at the values of the state variables and from the expressed relationships to compute the value of the action variable. Now the controller of a physical system need not itself be physical but may be purely logical. Furthermore where the known relationships are vague and qualitative a fuzzy logic based controller may be constructed to implement the known heuristics. Thus in such a controller the variables are equated to non-fuzzy universes giving the possible range of measurement or action magnitudes. These variables, however, take on linguistic values which are expressed as fuzzy subsets of the universes.

A fuzzy subset F of a universe of discourse $U = \{x\}$ is defined as a mapping $\mu_F(x)$: $U \rightarrow [0,1]$ by which x is assigned a number in $[0,1]$ indicating the extent to which x has the attribute F. Thus, if x is the magnitude of pressure, say, then "small" may be considered as a particular fuzzy value of the variable pressure and each x is assigned a number $\mu_{SMALL}(x) \in [0,1]$ which indicates the extent to which that x is considered to be small.

Given the fuzzy sets A, B of U, the basic operations on A,B are:

    (i) the complement $\overline{A}$ of A, defined by
       $\mu_{\overline{A}}(x) = 1 - \mu_A(x);$
    (ii) the union $A \cup B$ of A and B, defined by
       $\mu_{A \cup B}(x) = \max \{\mu_A(x), \mu_B(x)\};$

(iii) the intersection A ∩B of A and B, defined by
$$\mu_{A \cap B}(x) = \min \{\mu_A(x), \mu_B(x)\}.$$
A fuzzy relation R from $U = \{x\}$ to $V = \{y\}$ is a fuzzy set on the Cartesian product $U \times V$, characterized by a function $\mu_R(x,y)$, by which each pair (x,y) is assigned a number in [0,1] indicating the extent to which the relation R is true for (x,y). There are several ways of constructing $\mu_R(x,y)$. The one used here will be seen later.

Finally given a fuzzy relation R from U to V and a fuzzy subset A of U, a fuzzy subset B of V is inferred, given by the compositional rule of inference:
$$B = A \circ R$$
or
$$\mu_B(y) = \max_x \{\min\{\mu_R(x,y), \mu_A(x)\}\}.$$

A heuristic approach to the control problem was employed, which resulted in a set of linguistic control statements. The above basic ideas of the theory of fuzzy subsets were used for the quantitative interpretation of these instructions as well as the decision-making process.

The fuzzy control instructions for the heat-pressure loop of the steam engine are shown in Fig. 1 and are of the form:

> If E = —ve big OR —ve medium
> and if C = —ve small
> then   H = +ve medium
> else If E = —ve small
> and if C = +ve small
> then   H = +ve medium
> else etc. . . .

Now there are several such rules employed in the control. Each rule is a fuzzy relation between the measurements E,C and the action H. Thus:

$$E = \text{—ve small}; \, C = \text{+ve small}$$

	IF PE = (NB or NM) THEN IF CPE = NS THEN HC = PM
OR	
	IF PE = NS THEN IF CPE = PS THEN HC = PM
OR	
	IF PE = NO THEN IF CPE = (PB or PM) THEN HC = PM
OR	
	IF PE = NO THEN IF CPE = (NB or NM) THEN HC = NM
OR	
	IF PE = PO or NO THEN IF CPE = NO THEN HC = NO
OR	
	IF PE = PO THEN IF CPE = (NB or NM) THEN HC = PM
OR	
	IF PE = PO THEN IF CPE = (PB or PM) THEN HC = NM
OR	
	IF PE = PS THEN IF CPE = (PS or NO) THEN HC = NM
OR	
	IF PE = (PB or PM) THEN IF CPE = NS THEN HC = NM

FIG. 1. Fuzzy control instructions for heat-pressure loop of steam engine. Abbreviations used for linguistic values are: ZE, zero; PZ, positive zero; PS, positive small; PM, positive medium; PB, positive big; similarly for negative values NZ, NS, NM and NB. Change in error negative is taken as movement towards set point and positive as away from it. Other abbreviations are: PE, pressure error; CPE, change in pressure error; HC, heat input change.

is a fuzzy phrase P on the universe of discourse $E \times C$ with grade of membership function:

$$\mu_P(e,c) = \min \{\mu_{-ve\ small}(e),\ \mu_{+ve\ small}(c)\}.$$

The implication "if P then H = +ve medium" is also a fuzzy phrase Q defined on $E \times C \times H$ with grades of membership function:

$$\mu_Q(e,c,h) = \min \{\mu_P(e,c),\ \mu_{+ve\ medium}(h)\}.$$

Finally, two or more fuzzy phrases Q_1, Q_2 connected by "else" form a fuzzy clause S defined as $E \times C \times H$ with grades of membership function:

$$\mu_S(e,c,h) = \max \{\mu_{Q1}(e,c,h),\ \mu_{Q2}(e,c,h) \ldots \text{etc.}\}$$

The control action, as derived from the implementation of a fuzzy clause (i.e. a set of fuzzy implications forming an algorithm) is determined according to the compositional rule of inference as given above. That is, given the set of the actual inputs x and the fuzzy algorithm S, the resultant output is the max–min product xoS. The whole procedure for deciding the control action is explicitly described in Mamdani & Assilian (1975). This work also describes the results that were obtained on the steam engine trials.

Two main conclusions were drawn from this early study using the steam-engine. First, that the results vindicated the approach advocated by Zadeh and demonstrated its potential. The significant nature of this approach is that fuzzy logic can be used to implement heuristics in a fairly straightforward manner. There are other ways of implementing heuristics as well. In particular Gaines (1975) has reanalysed the steam-engine control rules using a form of probability logic obtaining results substantially similar to those obtained using fuzzy logic. The nature of this relationship between stochastic logic, multiple valued logics and fuzzy logic has been investigated at great length by Gaines (1976).

Secondly, it was asserted that the method can easily be applied to many practical industrial situations. This assertion is supported by considering the instance of cement kiln operation. In a book on the subject, Peray & Waddell (1972) list a collection of rules for controlling a kiln. A few examples of these rules are shown in Fig. 2. On comparing this with the steam-engine rules in Fig. 1 it is clear how fuzzy logic can be

Case	Condition	Action to be taken
1	BZ low OX low BE low	When BZ is drastically low: (a) reduce kiln speed; (b) reduce fuel When BZ is slightly low: (c) increase I.D. fan speed; (d) increase fuel rate
2	BZ low OX low BE o.k.	(a) Reduce kiln speed (b) Reduce fuel rate (c) Reduce I.D. fan speed
3	BZ low OX low BE high	(a) Reduce kiln speed (b) Reduce fuel rate (c) Reduce I.D. fan speed

Total of 27 rules

FIG. 2. Some rules for manual control of a lime kiln (Peray & Waddell, 1972). BE, back-end temperature; BZ, burning zone temperature; OX, percentage of oxygen gas in kiln exit gas.

employed in cement kiln control. This potential of employing fuzzy logic to implement control heuristics has been further investigated. In the section below all known investigations on this topic are briefly described.

3. Further trials with a "fuzzy controller"

Below are some brief accounts of further trials with the fuzzy logic control scheme undertaken by other groups working in the area.†

(a) *Delft Technical Highschool, Delft, Holland.* The work was conducted by Professor Van Nauta Lemke and W. J. M. Kickert in the Control Engineering Laboratory DTH. In this research project the control of a warm water plant was investigated. This plant, which was a form of heat exchanger, had poor control properties and so was considered suitable on which to try out a fuzzy controller. The linguistic control algorithm was derived from the experience of a human operator. The results were satisfactory and compared favorably with an optimally tuned PI controller. The fuzzy controller had a faster rise time and after rule modification it was able to achieve a steady-state accuracy equal to that of the PI controller. These results are reported in detail in Kickert & Van Nauta Lemke (1976).

(b) *Danish Technical Highschool, Lyngby, Denmark.* Shortly afterwards Professor P. M. Larsen and Dr J. J. Østergaard began experiments on fuzzy logic control of a pilot heat exchanger process of their own. Apart from different plant characteristics and non-linearities the control problem differed in that it was a two input–two output type with strong cross-coupling.

A particularly interesting aspect of this work was the software implementation of the controller using APL on an IBM/1800 machine. The grammatical structure of APL made it particularly suitable for calculations involving fuzzy sets producing clear and compact programs.

The linguistic protocol was originally derived from common sense and then tuned after successive runs. Although it differed in its finer details from Mamdani and Van Nauta Lemke it gave good results which can be examined in detail in J. J. Østergaard (1976).

(c) *McMaster University, Canada.* Work is being done by Professor N. K. Sinha and the research group in simulation, optimization and control in the Faculty of Engineering, again on a heat exchanger. The findings are not as yet published but the broad conclusions seem to be the same as in most other studies.

(d) *UMIST, Manchester, England.* This work is being carried out by D. A. Rutherford of Control Systems Centre, UMIST (see Rutherford & Bloore, 1975). This is an interesting study as the method, without major modifications, is the first one to be tried on an industrial plant. In cooperation with G. A. Carter and M. J. Hague the controller has been implemented for a sinter making plant at the British Steel Corporation, Middlesborough (Rutherford, 1976; Carter & Hague, 1976).

The control problem was to obtain the most efficient sintering by control of the moisture of the initial raw mix. The efficiency and uniformity of the sintering is monitored by the standard deviation of the permeability of the pre-sintered mix.

†The Workshop on Discrete Systems and Fuzzy Reasoning held at Queen Mary College in January 1976 (Mamdani & Gaines, 1976) covered much of the ongoing work on fuzzy linguistic control together with a range of contributions on fuzzy and multiple-valued logics.

The fuzzy algorithm used was a slightly modified version of the one used by Mamdani & Assilian. The results showed about a 40% reduction in standard deviation over that for manual control. The controller was comparable if not slightly better than a conventional two-term controller. Carter & Hague conclude that the method is particularly useful "where the requirement for little or no plant tuning is matched by a poor knowledge of the plant . . .".

(e) *British Steel Corporation, Battersea, England.* The interest here is the investigation of useful methods for the automatic control of a Basic Oxygen steel making process. This investigation is being undertaken by R. Tong who is at present working as a research associate at Control and Management Systems group, University Engineering Department, Cambridge. The possibilities of using a fuzzy logic controller for such a process are reported in Tong (1976).

(f) *Warren Spring Laboratory, Stevenage, England.* The work was done by P. J. King jointly with W. J. M. Kickert and E. H. Mamdani of Queen Mary College. A pilot scale batch chemical process was used in this study and the controller designed for the temperature control of the process.

A characteristic feature of this process was the large time lag in the response which led to instability when the loop was closed. A model predictor scheme using a fuzzy model of the plant was devised to eliminate this with success. The model was a very crude one consisting of only a few rules which supported the fact that quite satisfactory results can be obtained without having to resort to exact mathematics. The findings are reported in detail in King & Mamdani (1976) and Kickert (1975a).

All these studies have been carried out from a control engineering point of view and the main conclusion from all this is that the method, though unorthodox, needs serious consideration for application to certain difficult plants. The main point to be made here is that the merit of the method does not rest on the use of fuzzy logic but rather the use purely of heuristics for designing a controller. This means that the controller is not deduced from an available model of the plant but is explicitly stated in the form of heuristics. Thus the method is useful for plants which are difficult in the sense that they are difficult to model accurately. Fuzzy logic is suggested as the best tool for implementing these heuristics. The instance of the cement kiln control and the experience with the sinter plant cited above supports this view.

These studies have also indicated two other characteristics of the heuristic controller. One is that in most studies, rules exactly as those of Fig. 1 are applied. This is because the heuristics continue to maintain the "proportional plus integral" nature of the classical controller, only rendering it more flexible (a control engineer might say "making it non-linear"). Second, many studies have found that this type of a controller is more robust to plant parameter changes than a classical controller. The reasons have not been analysed but as suggested by Mamdani (1976) this is merely the consequence of using heuristics. Human experience, which these heuristics amount to, is by nature robust.

4. A question of stability

What concerns many control engineers is how to predict that such a heuristic controller will be stable. Many of those who are investigating this method have not taken the matter seriously or commented on it. This is very likely due to the fact that they have taken it for granted that the fuzzy control method is not an alternative to classical design techniques and that this would be obvious to everyone concerned. However, such apparently is not the case. Control engineering orthodoxy imposes a certain rigid design approach which must include stability analysis. This is assumed to have an important, perhaps sole, bearing on the reliability of the controller. Nevertheless, it should be a simple matter to realize that stability analysis relies on the availability of the mathematical model of the plant but if this were the case then one could possibly deduce the controller in a classical way. As mentioned above, the main advantage of the heuristic controller is that it can be used for plants that are difficult to model.

There is one study, however, which has attempted to investigate this problem. Kickert (1975b) has shown that under certain restrictive assumptions the fuzzy controller can be viewed as a multidimensional (multi-input single output) multi-level relay. Under such conditions one can use describing functions to model the controller. Then along with the model of the system a frequency domain stability analysis can be carried out. Theoretical results of such an analysis accord well with the practical results. However, the method is applicable under very rigid conditions and only with low order systems using low dimensional relay. Thus its practical use is very limited.

A fuzzy controller can be analysed qualitatively to gain assurance that a runaway instability will not occur. The concern of control engineers, on the other hand, is with a rigorous analysis of oscillatory form of instability. Now the best way to do this is to carry out the analysis in the frequency domain and this is what Kickert's work mentioned above amounts to. The conclusion of this work is that frequency domain analysis of fuzzy controllers is not applicable in practical cases. It is the view of this author that the desire for rigorous stability analysis in the frequency domain, even if it were possible, runs counter to the main advantages of the approach which is that it can be used with plants that are difficult to model. A confidence in the quality of control can always be obtained by running it in open-loop with the human operator present to make any changes in its structure to improve its performance. The discussion on stability is irrelevant because it implies that no attempt be made to control difficult processes unless a rigorous theory can be found to design controllers. Thus the main source of discomfort with fuzzy controllers, it may be suggested, is that it elevates heuristics to control plants which some feel ought not to be so controlled.

5. A question of deriving the protocol

The quality of control obtained using the scheme under discussion here is dependent entirely on the clause S (see section 2), assuming, of course, that the sampling rate has been fixed on some rational basis. Hence the various factors affecting S can be used to tune the controller. S is constructed by assuming three more or less arbitrary factors. In fact the choice involved in these factors is governed by the experience of the designer.

In the first place it is necessary to choose appropriate membership functions for the fuzzy subsets involved, such as, medium, small and so on. An assertion in the steam-engine study, and unchallenged since then, is that these functions are not arbitrary and indeed that there is a great deal of objective concensus about the subsets defining these linguistic terms. Thus these subsets should be kept fixed and any change in the membership functions is not the proper way of tuning the controller.

The second arbitrary factor involved is the range of values in the various universes. In all the studies cited a finite set of quantized values is used as the universe. If the universe is formed by quantizing into the same number of levels 0–50 units of measurements instead of 0–100 units, say, then this is equivalent to making the controller twice as sensitive to that measured variable. This form of "gain control" is bound to have a substantial effect on the performance of the controller. It does not affect the linguistic nature of the clause S itself in any way, thus it does not amount to a structural change in the controller. In the classical form of a PI controller this is the only form of tuning that a designer can do.

However, there is a third arbitrary factor which allows a designer to carry out a structural form of tuning in the clause S of a fuzzy controller. This is done by altering the set of rules themselves in the control protocol. Unfortunately this raises the important question of how to derive the best or effective set of control rules (MacVicar-Whelan, 1976). The cement kiln rules of Peray & Waddell notwithstanding, it is the conclusion of most industrial psychologists that a great deal of effort is required to arrive at the protocol used by a skilled operator (see for example, Bainbridge, 1975). Future attempts at practical applications of fuzzy control will no' doubt have to recognize that human factors research has an important bearing on controller design.

The difficulties of obtaining a good protocol to start with can nevertheless be alleviated to some extent in various ways. Firstly it has been realized by most workers that it is not necessary to close the loop with a fuzzy controller nor is it the aim of fuzzy control method to replace the human controller. The use of a fuzzy controller in an advisory capacity can itself be a great help in the control of difficult plants. It is then possible to write the software implementing a fuzzy control algorithm such that the rules can be modified on-line. An example of such a program is the one by Marks (1976). Through such a modification procedure the controller can be made more and more reliable. As confidence increases in the action recommended by it, the result can lead to a more consistent control being applied to the plant than is possible by a human operator. In many industrial plants this consistency is important because it leads to a consistent product obtained from the process.

A second approach being studied by Mamdani & Baaklini (1975) is to automate the modification of rules by introducing a form of adaptive behaviour into the controller. Noting that in a control situation the goal of regulating the plant output about the set-point can be easily stated and assuming that plant input and output are monotonically related, then a fuzzy algorithm can be developed which effectively says that if the output is higher than required, too much input was applied and vice versa. In trials this scheme has worked well and is capable of deriving control policy even when initially started without any rules. Further details of this are also given in Mamdani, Procyk & Baaklini (1976) and Procyk (1976).

6. Concluding remarks

This note has concentrated on the various studies relating to industrial applications of fuzzy control. As is apparent here all workers have approached this method from a very practical view and indeed there is a concensus of opinion among them that the method is practically viable. There have of course been critics of the approach. Although the main discussion has been about the prediction of stability of such a controller, it has been suggested here that the underlying question is whether heuristics should be formally used for controlling certain types of industrial plants.

There is no doubt that heuristics are the best, perhaps only, form of control in humanistic systems. Pappis & Mamdani (1976) have applied fuzzy controller for the control of road traffic junction. It is apparent that fuzzy controller is essentially an extension of decision tables based on fuzzy logic instead of binary valued logic. Thus in numerous humanistic systems decision-making is achieved with a great degree of reliability by implementing heuristics, often using decision tables. There seems little doubt that industrial systems may be similarly controlled using fuzzy decision tables which is what a fuzzy controller amounts to.

There has already been considerable work done in obtaining such heuristics for difficult process plants by human factors researchers and industrial psychologists. In this work fuzzy control methods can have definite applications. Furthermore, with software aids as suggested in section 5 above, and by using hierarchic adaptive controllers the job of implementing heuristics is further simplified.

References

ASSILIAN, S. & MAMDANI, E. H. (1974). Learning Control algorithms in real dynamic systems. In *Proceedings of the 4th International IFAC/IFIP Conference on Digital Computer Applications to Process Control*, Zurich, March.

ASSILIAN, S. (1974). Artificial intelligence in the control of real dynamic systems. Ph.D. Thesis. London University.

BAINBRIDGE, L. (1975). The Process Controller. In SINGLETON, W. T., Ed. *The Study of Real Skills*. London and New York: Academic Press.

CARTER, G. A. & HAGUE, M. J. (1976). Fuzzy Control of Raw Mix Permeability at a Sinter Plant. In MAMDANI & GAINES (1976), op. cit.

GAINES, B. R. (1975). Stochastic and fuzzy logics. *Electronics Letters*, **11**, 188–189.

GAINES, B. R. (1976). Fuzzy reasoning and the logics of uncertainty. *Proceedings of the 6th International Symp. Multiple-Valued Logic*, IEEE 76CH1111-4C, pp. 179–188.

KICKERT, W. J. M. (1975a). Analysis of a fuzzy logic controller. *Internal report*. Queen Mary College, London.

KICKERT, W. J. M. (1975b). Further analysis and application of fuzzy logic control. *Internal report*. Queen Mary College, London.

KICKERT, W. J. M. & VAN NAUTA LEMKE (1976). Application of fuzzy controller in a warm water plant. *Automatica* (to appear).

KING, P. J. & MAMDANI, E. H. (1976). The application of fuzzy control systems to industrial processes. In MANDANI & GAINES (1976), op. cit.

MANDANI, E. H. (1976). Application of fuzzy logic to approximate reasoning using linguistic synthesis. *Proceedings of the 6th International Symp. Multiple-Valued Logic*, IEEE 76CH1111-4C, pp. 196–202.

MACVICAR-WHELAN, P. J. (1976). Fuzzy sets for man–machine interaction. *International Journal of Man–Machine Studies*, **8**, 687–697.

MAMDANI, E. H. & ASSILIAN, S. (1975). An experiment in linguistic synthesis with a fuzzy logic controller. *International Journal of Man–Machine Studies*, **7**, 1–13.

MAMDANI, E. H. & BAAKLINI, N. (1975). Prescriptive method for deriving control policy in a fuzzy-logic controller. *Electronics Letters*, **11**, 625.

MAMDANI, E. H. & GAINES, B. R., Eds (1976). *Discrete Systems and Fuzzy Reasoning, EES-MMS-DSFR-76*. Proceedings of Workshop held at Queen Mary College, University of London, January.

MAMDANI, E. H., PROCYK, T. J. & BAAKLINI, N. (1976). Application of fuzzy logic controller design based on linguistic protocol. In MAMDANI & GAINES (1976), op. cit.

MARKS, P. (1976). A fuzzy logic control software. *Internal report*. Queen Mary College, London.

ØSTERGAARD, J. J. (1976). Fuzzy logic control of a heat exchanger process. *Internal report*. Electric Power Engineering Dept, Danish Technical High School, Lyngby, Denmark.

PAPPIS, C. P. & MAMDANI, E. H. (1976). A fuzzy logic controller for a traffic junction. *Research report*. Department of Electrical Engineering, Queen Mary College, London.

PERAY, K. E. & WADDELL, J. J. (1972). *The Rotary Cement Kiln*. New York: The Chemical Publishing Co.

PROCYK, T. J. (1976). A proposal for a learning system. *Internal report*. Queen Mary College, London.

RUTHERFORD, D. A. & BLOORE, G. C. (1975). The implementation of fuzzy algorithm for control. *Control System Centre Report No. 279*, UMIST, Manchester. To appear in *Proceedings of the IEEE*.

RUTHERFORD, D. A. (1976). The implementation and evaluation of a fuzzy control algorithm for a sinter plant. In MAMDANI & GAINES (1976), op. cit.

TONG, R. M. (1976). An assessment of a fuzzy control algorithm for a non-linear multi-variable system. In MAMDANI & GAINES (1976), op. cit.

ZADEH, L. A. (1973). Outline of a new approach to the analysis of complex systems and decision processes. *IEEE Transactions on Systems Man and Cybernetics*, **SMC-3**, 28–44.

Industrial applications of fuzzy logic control

P. Martin Larsen

Electric Power Engineering Department, Technical University, DK 2800 Lyngby, Denmark

(*Received 23 May 1979*)

Fuzzy logic control projects related to the Technical University of Denmark are presented, and common theoretical and practical problems experienced during their realization are discussed. A detailed description is given of two rotary cement kiln control projects, which resulted in one of the first successful test runs on a full scale industrial process. It is concluded that further investigations are required with respect to the applicability of structural programming, and stability problems in fuzzy control systems.

1. Introduction

The aim of this paper is to present some industrial fuzzy logic control projects related to the Electric Power Engineering Department at the Technical University of Denmark, and to discuss some common theoretical and practical problems experienced during their realization. In 1978 a fuzzy logic controller was operating in closed loop on a rotary cement kiln in Denmark, and to our knowledge that was the first successful test run on a full scale industrial process. On this basis some future aspects and practical problems to be solved are discussed.

In recent years several practical applications of fuzzy logic control on industrial processes have been reported. Mamdani & Assilian (1974) have implemented a controller on a small boiler steam engine by specifying heuristic fuzzy control rules for 2 feedback loops; this process was highly non-linear, but could be approximated by 2 first order lags with time constants and gains varying depending on the operating conditions.

Fuzzy logic control of processes with pure time delay has an inherent tendency to instability, and the control rules in that case will have to include a fuzzy model of the system to predict the future output of the system (King & Mamdani, 1976).

Fuzzy controllers have also been applied to a warm water plant, built in laboratory scale, by Kickert & van Nauta Lemke (1976), and an autopilot for ships has been designed with the aid of fuzzy sets by van Amerongen, van Nauta Lemke & van der Veen (1977) and tested on a simulation model. In both cases the fuzzy controllers perform better than conventional PID or DDC controllers, especially when noise is taken into account.

It is typical for these applications, that they either are simulation studies or pilot plant/laboratory model studies, and that the fuzzy controllers have been directly installed in the control loops. Although the results are promising, the accuracy and the stability problems need to be investigated more deeply.

Due to the quantisation of the input variables the fuzzy controller is not sensitive to small deviations in the controlled variables, and fluctuations and drift have often been experienced. Therefore fuzzy controllers for industrial processes with pure time delays included should primarily be used for supervisory control or combined with conventional analog or digital PID controllers in the internal control loops.

2. Fuzzy logic control research program

The fuzzy logic control research program at the Electric Power Engineering Department was initiated in 1974. In the first project on "Fuzzy logic controllers" Molzen (1975) demonstrated that the programming language APL was very suited for formulation of fuzzy logic algorithms. The fuzzy controller was implemented on an IBM 1800 process computer and connected to a water level control unit in the laboratory; a comparison with a digital PID controller implemented by means of a special process control programming language PROMAC (Holmblad, 1972) did not show any significant improvements in favour of the fuzzy controller.

In 1975 Østergaard investigated "Fuzzy logic control of a heat exchanger process" (Østergaard, 1976) in order to clarify further the practical applicability of fuzzy logic to process control, to evaluate the usefulness of applying APL, and to study the advantages of implementing the APL-programmed controller directly. By using a high level language, such as APL, the amount of time required to solve a given control problem is reduced remarkably, but in cases where the control actions must be very fast a more effective code is often required, i.e. it is necessary to use assembly language.

"Fuzzy logic control of industrial processes" especially related to rotary cement kilns has been investigated by Jensen (1979) during the last 3 years, and test runs in open loop have been executed in March 1978. Fuzzy logic control of rotary cement kilns is now of major interest for the Danish cement factory manufacturer, F. L. Smidth & Co. A/S, and Østergaard is in charge of developing new fuzzy controller systems for the FLS rotary cement kilns. Jensen & Østergaard have concurrently formulated different versions of control strategies for cement kilns and implemented them on separate computer systems connected to the same kiln. These two projects are described in more detail in the next section.

Self-organizing fuzzy controllers have been investigated by Mørkeberg Pedersen (1978) for single input–single output systems based on the principles developed at Queen Mary College (Mamdani & Procyk, 1979). The self-organizing controller was implemented on IBM 1800 and connected to simple simulated processes disturbed by different types of noise. In this preliminary study the noise sensitivity often appeared to be too high. On this basis a new project was recently started up on self-organizing fuzzy controllers for multiple input–multiple output systems.

3. Rotary cement kiln control

In this section, 2 fuzzy logic control projects on a rotary cement kiln are described in details, exclusively quoting information from the works of Jensen (1979) and Østergaard (1979). The description of the cement kiln and the analysis of the operators' performance is rather condensed in this paper; more detailed information on these subjects can be obtained from Umbers & King (1980).

3.1. MEASURED VARIABLES AND CONTROL VARIABLES

The fuzzy logic controllers were installed in Rørdal, Denmark, on a coal-fired wet-process Unax-cooler kiln with a capacity of 1150 tons/day.

The primary control variables of the cement kiln are the coal-feed rate, the air flow, the kiln feed rate and the kiln rotational speed. The kiln feed rate is normally synchronized with the kiln speed in order to obtain an approximately constant filling of material. As the kiln usually operates with constant production, only the coal-feed rate and the air flow are applicable as control variables. Furthermore, the coal-feed rate on the actual kiln is linked with the oxygen percentage of the exhaust gas by means of a PI controller. Therefore the relevant control variables are:

(1) the set point of the oxygen percentage which indirectly controls the coal-feed rate;
(2) the exhaust gas fan louvre damper position which controls the air flow.

The clinker quality, characterized by the free lime content, depends mainly upon the burning zone temperature, which is not available as a reliable measured variable. Therefore the basic idea of the applied control strategies is to use the kiln drive load as an indirect measure of the burning zone temperature in as much as a change of the drive load under normal operating conditions is interpreted as a change in the burning zone temperature in the same direction. (By increasing burning zone temperature the materials will follow the internal side of the kiln further up than before, resulting in a heavier load for the drive motors.) The kiln drive load again is measured indirectly through the armature current of the d.c. drive motors. Therefore the relevant measured variables are:

(1) kiln drive load represented by the motor current, as an indirect measure of the burning zone temperature;
(2) free lime content determined by laboratory analysis as a measure of the clinker quality;
(3) oxygen percentage in the smoke chamber;
(4) temperature in the smoke chamber.

3.2. CONTROL STRATEGIES

The aim of the computerized kiln control system is to automate the routine control strategy of an experienced kiln operator. The applied strategies are based on detailed studies of the process operator experiences which include a qualitative model of influence of the control variables on the measured variables:

(1) if the coal-feed rate is increased, the kiln drive load and the temperature in the smoke chamber will increase, while the oxygen percentage and the free lime content will decrease;
(2) if the air flow is increased, the temperature in the smoke chamber and the free lime content will increase, while the kiln drive load and the oxygen percentage will decrease.

On the basis of thorough discussions with the operators, Jensen defined 75 operating conditions as fuzzy conditional statements of the type:

IF   drive load gradient is   (DL, SL, OK, SH, DH)

AND   drive load is   (DL, SL, OK, SH. DH)
AND   smoke chamber temperature is   (L, OK, H)
THEN   change oxygen percentage   (VN, N, SN, ZN, OK, ZP, SP, P, VP)
PLUS   change air flow   (VN, N, SN, ZN, OK, ZP, SP, P, VP)

The following fuzzy primary terms are used for the measured variables:

(1)   DL = drastically low   (5)   SH = slightly high
(2)   L = low   (6)   H = high
(3)   SL = slightly low   (7)   DH = drastically high
(4)   OK = ok

The following fuzzy primary terms are used for the control variables:

(1)   VN = very negative   (6)   ZP = zero positive
(2)   N = negative   (7)   SP = small positive
(3)   SN = small negative   (8)   P = positive
(4)   ZN = zero negative   (9)   VP = very positive
(5)   OK = ok

The linguistic terms are represented by membership functions with 4 discrete values in the interval $[0; 1]$ associated with 15 discrete values of the scaled variables in the interval $[-1; +1]$.

In order to simplify the implementation of the fuzzy logic controller, Østergaard defined 13 operating conditions as fuzzy conditional statements of the type:

IF   drive load gradient is   (SN, ZE, SP)
AND   drive load is†   (LN, LP)
AND   free lime content   (LO, OK, HI)
THEN   change burning zone temperature   (LN, MN, SN, ZE, SP, MP, LP)

The following fuzzy primary terms are used:

(1)   LP = large   (7)   SN = small negative
(2)   MP = medium positive   (8)   MN = medium negative
(3)   SP = small positive   (9)   LN = large negative
(4)   ZP = zero positive   (10)   HI = high
(5)   ZE = zero   (11)   OK = ok
(6)   ZN = zero negative   (12)   LO = low

The 13 operating conditions are defined by taking only some of the combinations into account, and by including also previous values of the drive load gradient, the latter being calculated from the changes in the drive load. In order to decide whether the oxygen percentage set point or the air flow should be changed, 3 additional fuzzy rules for each operating condition are formulated based on the actual values of the oxygen percentage and the smoke chamber temperature, resulting in 39 control rules.

It was very soon realized by Østergaard, that the control rules developed by Peray & Waddell were not applicable, because the burning zone temperature was not directly accessible for reliable measurement, and because previous states of the cement kiln were not taken into consideration.

---

† Actually the time integral of the load gradient taken from the last time control action was executed.

3.3. FUZZY CONTROLLER HARDWARE AND SOFTWARE

In order to facilitate the design and practical tests of fuzzy logic controllers, Jensen developed a special Fuzzy Controller Design System (FCDS).

The FCDS system includes an interactive design facility which permits modification of the fuzzy controller at the same time as the system is controlling the process. The interactive design facility is obtained by using the APL programming language of which the structure for user-defined functions and variables is extremely suited for implementation of linguistically formulated control strategies.

The FCDS system consists of an IBM 5100 which was the only portable minicomputer available at the start of the system design offering the possibility of APL programming, and a special process interface for communication with the IBM 5100 through its serial asynchronous communication channel. The FCDS system configuration is shown in Fig. 1. The APL compiler is stored in the non-executable read-only

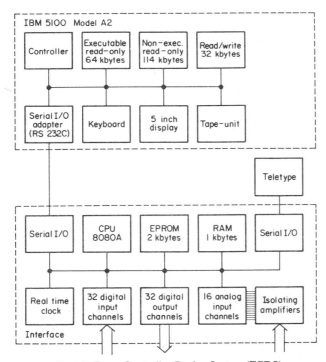

FIG. 1. Fuzzy Controller Design System (FCDS).

storage, and it is transferred to the read-write storage when executed. The executable read-only storage contains programs for bring-up, tests, I/O control and supervision, and APL microprogram routines. The user programs and data are stored in the read–write storage of 32 kbytes, but as the system utilizes 16 kbytes for driver routines for the serial I/O adapter, buffers and working space, only 16 kbytes are available for the user.

The special process interface is microcomputer controlled (Intel 8080A) and includes real time clock, serial I/O (RS 232C standard), digital inputs (4×8 bits) and digital outputs ($2 \times 2 \times 8$ bits). Furthermore, an analog input modul with 16 single-ended channels is included. For hard copy documentation a teletype was provisionally being used, but an IBM 5103 matrix printer will soon be available. The interface software is written in assembler in order to utilize the 2 K EPROM storage most effectively.

Originally, it was the intension to formulate the fuzzy controller linguistically in APL, but it turned out that 20 kbytes read–write storage would be required for this purpose. Therefore, the linguistic formulation unfortunately had to be skipped until the storage could be extended.

The implementation of the fuzzy controller and the associated communication and data-handling programs are based on APL-functions which can be differentiated into utility functions, communication functions, initiation functions, and control functions. The utility functions are used for transformation between different codes for data representation. The communication functions control the exchange of data with the interface. The control functions control the sampling time and determine the controller output; the time, the measured values and the controller outputs are stored on data tape, and the most important variables and applied control rules are printed out on the teletype.

The FLS fuzzy logic controller is being incorporated into the existing FLS-SDR system (Supervision, Dialog and Reporting), which comprises a HP 21 Mx minicomputer with printer, display screen and interface for the acquisition of a total of 2–300 process variables. The SDR system is a plant monitoring device and data concentrator, covering one or more production lines. The minicomputer has a storage of 48 K words of 16 bit of which 38 K are used for SDR functions and data acquisition, and 10 K are available for the fuzzy controllers for 3 kilns. Linguistic formulation of the fuzzy controllers has not been possible, because APL is not available on the HP minicomputer system, and due to the limited storage space the programming has to be as effective as possible utilizing a point structure for the controller rules.

In future SDR systems the storage will be extended, which will permit application of a special interpreter for the fuzzy statements. Such an interpreter is not very fast because the single statements are interpreted each time the program is executed, but that is of minor importance in connection with slow processes such as cement kiln operation.

3.4. PRACTICAL RESULTS

The Fuzzy Controller Design System (FCDS) was tested on the cement kiln in March 1978, but no closed-loop runs were permitted at that time. The control actions and the applied control rules were printed out, and presented for the kiln operator in charge. Some of the control actions were accepted and effectuated manually. The general impression is, that the fuzzy controller recommended control actions earlier, and in smaller steps than the operator was willing to effectuate, but later the operator actually followed the recommended actions resulting, however, in a slight overshoot in the drive load.

The test-runs of the FLS fuzzy control system was started concurrently with the FCDS system in March 1978 and in June they were concluded with a successful 6-days closed-loop operation. In that period 32 major changes in coal feed rate and 3 in air flow were executed, and it was concluded that the fuzzy control was slightly better than control by operator. New FLS fuzzy control systems are now being installed, and the latest experiences show that also a reduction in fuel consumption is obtainable by fuzzy control.

4. Fundamental and practical problems

In the early fuzzy controller applications the fuzzy primary terms were represented by continuous membership functions as exponential expressions, e.g.

$$1 - \exp\left(-\left(\frac{0\cdot5}{\mathrm{abs}(1-x)}\right)^{2\cdot5}\right)$$

for LARGE POSITIVE, which could be directly implemented in APL. However, calculations are very often carried out on fuzzy subsets represented by their membership functions as a whole, and in that case the fuzzy subset must be represented by N discrete values of the membership function, i.e. by a vector with N elements. The number of elements were 15 respectively 11 in the two applications mentioned above; Jensen standardized 4 discrete values of the membership functions $[0, 0\cdot3, 0\cdot7, 1\cdot0]$, whereas Østergaard calculates the values from the exponential expressions. However, the standardized values of the membership functions are altered when hedges are applied. It is interesting that the use of power functions seems to agree with psychophysical observations (Zadeh, 1974; Franksen, 1978).

The number of fuzzy primary terms is necessarily fairly high, but usually the programming is effectuated in a subroutine, where a few basic terms are defined, and by specifying an index the desired position of the maximum can be obtained easily. APL offers the same facilities for rotating the membership function vector.

During the design of the fuzzy logic controllers it is important that the fuzzy control rules are directly accessible for introduction of changes; the same is obvious in the case of self-organizing fuzzy controllers. Therefore it is necessary to operate on vectors for the fuzzy primary terms and for the results of the rules upon each input variable. The result vectors are then combined according to the control rules and applied to the fuzzy primary terms for the output variables in each rule. The combined result can then be implemented in a microcomputer as a decision table. If a complete controller matrix is computed, the rules are not directly accessible, and the computation is very time consuming and very demanding in storage (Mamdani & Procyk, 1979).

5. Future challenges

In the case of slow processes like the cement kiln operation, the response time of the fuzzy controller is no problem today. But the application of APL or special interpreters are problematic in conjunction with faster processes. Therefore structural programming must be further investigated especially with respect to the theoretical background. In this context it is also important to improve the effectiveness of the programming; shortage of storage space prevented Jensen from the intended linguistic formulation of the fuzzy controller in APL as mentioned above.

The stability of fuzzy logic control systems has been investigated by Kickert & Mamdani (1978) by considering the controller as a multilevel relay. However, where large time delays are involved, special measures must be taken. Jensen introduced a time dependant attenuation of the control actions, i.e. the control actions are reduced depending on the time elapsed since the last control action was effectuated. In conjunction with self-organizing fuzzy controllers a delay in reward must be introduced to avoid oscillations around the setpoint (Mamdani & Procyk, 1979). Therefore further investigations of the stability problems of fuzzy control systems must be incorporated in future projects.

The author is greatly indebted to Jensen, Østergaard and other colleagues for their work under the Fuzzy Logic Control Research program, to the F. L. Smidth & Co. A/S for permission to quote the latest development of fuzzy logic controller systems, to E. H. Mamdani for his co-operation and encouragement since the research program was started in 1974, and to the British Council for supporting exchange of researchers between Queen Mary College and the Technical University of Denmark under the Academic Link Scheme.

References

ASSILIAN, S. & MAMDANI, E. H. (1974). Artificial Intelligence in the control of real dynamic systems. *Report*. Queen Mary College, Electrical Engineering Department.

FRANKSEN, O. I. (1978). On fuzzy sets, subjective measurements, and utility. *Workshop on Fuzzy Reasoning—Theory and Applications*. Queen Mary College, September.

HOLMBLAD, L. P. (1972). PROMAC/1800, a real-time macroprogramming language for on-line process control. *Report no. 7201*. Electric Power Engineering Department, Technical University of Denmark.

JENSEN, J. H. (1979). Fuzzy logic control of industrial processes. *Ph.D. thesis*. Electric Power Engineering Department, Technical University of Denmark (to be published).

KICKERT, W. J. M. & MAMDANI, E. H. (1978). Analysis of a fuzzy logic controller. *Fuzzy Sets and Systems*, **1**, 29–44.

KICKERT, W. J. M. & VAN NAUTA LEMKE, H. R. (1976). Application of a fuzzy controller in a warm water plant. *Automatica*, **12**, 301–308.

KING, F. J. & MAMDANI, E. H. (1976). The application of fuzzy control systems to industrial processes. *Proceedings of a Workshop on "Discrete Systems and Fuzzy Reasoning"*, Queen Mary College.

MAMDANI, E. H. & PROCYK, T. J. (1979). A linguistic self-organizing process controller. *Automatica*, **15**, 15–30.

MOLZEN, N. (1975). Fuzzy logic controllers. *M.Sc. thesis* (in Danish). Electric Power Engineering Department, Technical University of Denmark.

MØRKEBERG PEDERSEN, K. (1978). Self-organizing fuzzy controllers. *M.Sc. thesis* (in Danish). Electric Power Engineering Department, Technical University of Denmark.

ØSTERGAARD, J.-J. (1976). Fuzzy logic control of a heat exchange process. *Report no. 7601*. Electric Power Engineering Department, Technical University of Denmark.

ØSTERGAARD, J.-J. (1979). Private communication.

UMBERS, I. G. & KING, P. J. (1980). An analysis of human decision-making in cement kiln control and the implications for automation. *International Journal of Man–Machine Studies*, **12**, 11–23.

VAN AMERONGEN, J., VAN NAUTA LEMKE, H. R. & VAN DER VEEN, J. C. T. (1977). An autopilot for ships designed with fuzzy sets. *Proceedings of 5th IFAC/IFIP International Conference on "Digital Computer Applications to Process Control"*.

ZADEH, L. A. (1973). Outline of a new approach to the analysis of complex systems and decision processes. *IEEE Transactions on Systems, Man and Cybernetics*, **SMC-3**(1), 28–44.

Verbal reports as evidence of the process operator's knowledge

LISANNE BAINBRIDGE

Department of Psychology, University of Reading, Reading RG6 2AL, U.K.

Verbal reports are usually collected with the aim of understanding mental behaviour. As it is not possible to observe mental behaviour directly we cannot test for a correlation between report and behaviour, and cannot assume one. Verbal data cannot therefore be used to test theories of mental behaviour. Verbal data may be produced by a separate report generating process which may give a distorted account. The data can be useful for practical purposes if these distortions are minimal. This paper attempts to assess the conditions in which this is the case. Several methods of obtaining verbal reports are surveyed: system state/action state diagram, questionnaire, interview, static simulation and verbal protocol. Techniques for collecting and analysing the data are described. In each case the small amount of data available on the correlation between reports and observed behaviour are reviewed. The results are not clear. Some verbal data are evidently misleading. Others, however, are sufficiently good to encourage the search for more information about factors affecting their validity.

1. Introduction

Conversation with people operating complex industrial processes suggests that they are using a great deal of mental activity, and knowledge, which cannot be observed directly in their behaviour while doing the task. This paper discusses the verbal report techniques which have been used to access this knowledge. For example, a process operator may describe reasons for his behaviour. What is the status of this report as evidence of his mental processes? There are two separate issues. Firstly, as there is no necessary correlation between verbal reports and mental behaviour, such a report cannot be used to test theories about mental behaviour. Secondly, however, although there is not necessarily a correlation with mental behaviour there may be a correlation between verbal reports and observable behaviour, which can be measured. If we want to use verbal reports as a method of finding out how a man does his job and how he makes his decisions, then we need to know what maximises this correlation with behaviour (the validity of the reports), and what information can be obtained using each reporting technique.

1.1. VERBAL DATA AND THEORY TESTING

As there is no way of observing someone's mental behaviour directly, it is not possible to test whether there is a correlation between what someone thinks and what he says he thinks. Therefore one has to allow for the possibility that there is no correlation between the two, or at least that two types of thinking, or "mental behaviour", may be involved. The process operator's non-verbal behaviour (e.g. his control actions) may be the result of mental behaviour related to his process control task, while his verbal behaviour (what he says) may be the result of separate mental behaviour concerned with the task of generating a report (see Table 1). Therefore we must have two theories, one for the control task, another for report generation. Only control task non-verbal behaviour can be used to test the theory of control task mental behaviour. If verbal behaviour is the result of another type of mental behaviour with different determinants, then when verbal behaviour does not fit a theory of control task mental behaviour one does not have to reject this theory. As the main test for the scientific value of data is that they can be used to reject theories, does this argument imply that verbal data are useless? Many psychologists feel strongly that this is the case. Other investigators, fascinated by the richness of verbal data, are willing to use them but should be aware of their limits.

TABLE 1
Observable and mental behaviour

Mental behaviour		Physical behaviour	
Not observable, so we can only have theories about it		Observable	
Primary (e.g. process control) *task related*	underlies	*non-verbal*	Both observable so correlation can be tested
Report generating	underlies	*verbal*	
	1. Correlations between mental and physical behaviour cannot be tested 2. Observable behaviour can be used only to test theories about mental behaviour underlying the same type of task, see text		

There are three main valid uses for verbal data. First, they can be used as a source of hypotheses about mental behaviour, and so of predictions about non-verbal behaviour, as hypotheses can have any origin. The predictions can then be tested without involving verbal reports. Second, although verbal data cannot be used to test theories on task related thinking, they could logically be used to test theories of verbal report generation. In practice however there are problems. One assumes that the operator's report generation is related in some way to the operator's knowledge of his task. To make predictions about verbal reports one therefore needs theories about both task knowledge and report generation, and if a prediction about verbal behaviour fails it is not possible to distinguish which of the theories involved should be rejected. Third, verbal data may be collected as evidence which correlates sufficiently highly with observable behaviour to be useful for practical purposes. The remainder of this paper is concerned with this. For some practical purposes one can side-step any problems about validity.

For example, if one notes from verbal reports that the process operator uses prediction and complex working memory, one may develop very different working consoles and job aids than one would otherwise. One can then simply compare performance on equipment designed on the basis of observed behaviour with equipment based on inferences from verbal reports, to test which is best.

1.2. VALIDITY OF VERBAL DATA AS REPORTS OF BEHAVIOUR

Although there is not necessarily any correlation between verbal data and the behaviour it is supposed to report, this does not necessarily mean that there is never any such correlation and that all verbal data are completely invalid. Instead, if we want to use verbal data we need to know what factors influence the way verbal reports are produced, so that we can minimize the distortions and maximize the validity of the evidence.

We will find that the validity of verbal reports depends closely on the method of collecting them. Different reporting techniques make it more or less difficult for the person involved to give a report which correlates with his non-verbal behaviour. In this paper we will be concerned primarily with this methodology-validity relation in studies of process control. However we will start by reviewing some other studies on the adequacy of reporting, and will then make some general points about the ways in which verbal reports may be distorted as descriptions of behaviour, and behaviour may be distorted by having to give a report.

1.2.1. Some experimental evidence

There are two main types of experimental evidence, outside the area of process control, which can be mentioned here: "awareness" experiments which test whether someone has to be aware of the influences on his behaviour to learn to respond to them, and "self-perception" studies in which people report what they think are the influences on their behaviour in social situations.

"Awareness" studies are concerned with the question: are conscious processes necessary in the mediation of behaviour, in the link between stimulus and response? In considering the validity of verbal reports, it does not matter whether conscious processes are mediating or parallel, but only whether conscious awareness of the influences on behaviour is available and valid, and the awareness studies have some implications for this. A typical example is reported by Wong et al. (1966). In a verbal conditioning experiment they found that words which had been rewarded by approval from the experimenter were used more frequently. To find whether the children tested were aware of this influence on their behaviour they were asked a series of questions of increasing specificity, e.g. "Did you do anything as a result of my saying 'good'?" These were "recall" type questions, the children had to think of the answer for themselves. Those who were unable to answer any of these questions were given a "recognition" question, a choice of answers: "If I told you I said 'good' every time you used a certain pronoun, which pronoun would you say it was: I, he, she, we, you, they?". Using this question doubled the number of children who were able to report what had happened in the experiment, and only these children showed a change in behaviour. A study by Farber (1963) adds an important further point. He found that about a third of the people who were aware of the experimental influences did not learn. This parallels Cooke's (1965) finding that students controlling a process could report some knowledge about the process which their non-verbal behaviour showed that they did not use in controlling it. This suggests that reportable knowledge is not necessarily used in action.

Ryan (1970, Chap. 7), in a general review of the awareness experiments, comes to the conclusion that studies which have not found evidence of awareness have used inadequate questioning methods. This suggests that recognition questions are the best method for accessing knowledge. Unfortunately they do have limitations. They can only be used at the end of a study, as they give too many clues, so they cannot be used to follow the acquisition of knowledge. For other comments see section 2.2 on questionnaires. Ryan also discusses some important points about experimenter effects in verbal questioning methods. The experimenter, by the social situation which he sets up and the wording he uses, can influence what someone says in an interview. Also, as verbal replies are judged subjectively, the judges' analyses can be biased. Therefore, Ryan comments, it is necessary to use interviewers and judges who do not know the person's performance, with which his replies will be compared. If the evidence is being used in a test of the validity of verbal reports, then interviewers and judges must be non-commital, or cover the range of biases, about the possibility of obtaining useful verbal evidence. Unfortunately there are few if any studies in which such careful controls have been used!

Ryan's conclusion, that one can always find evidence of awareness in learners if adequate questioning methods are used, is in complete contrast to the findings of Nisbett & Wilson (1977), in a review of people's "self-perception" of the influences on their attitudes and judgements. Nisbett & Wilson review studies in which people's behaviour was compared with changes in their environment, to find out objectively which stimuli (aspects of the environment) had an effect on their behaviour. These people also gave verbal reports on what they thought was influencing their behaviour. Nisbett & Wilson conclude that influences on behaviour can change without any change in verbal report, and that when a verbal report does change, it may not mention or may even deny the stimuli which objective measures have shown have an effect, or it may claim that stimuli are effective which behaviour shows are not. These studies thus give experimental support to the point made logically in the previous section, that there is no necessary correlation between behaviour and report.

We have previously mentioned that if there is no such correlation there must be some separate report generating process. Nisbett & Wilson make some suggestions about this. They have found that reports from people actually taking part in an experiment are the same as reports from "observers" who make predictions about the effects of stimuli on behaviour. If this is so, then the possibility of observing one's own mental processes during an experiment does not give any special insights. Nisbett & Wilson propose (p. 248) "that when people are asked to report how a particular stimulus influenced a particular response, they do so not by consulting a memory of the mediating process, but by applying or generating causal theories about the effects of that type of stimulus on that type of response". This analysis is supported by an experiment in which people's reports matched their behaviour when the effective environmental variables were plausible, and not when they were not. This idea is generally similar to Bartlett's (1932) theory in which remembering is done by constructing an appropriate story about what happened, based on general "schemata" of that type of event, rather than on access to exact memories. Nisbett & Wilson suggest that the causal theories (as Bartlett suggests about his schemata) are provided by the culture or by past experience. Nisbett & Wilson suggest that verbal reports will be accurate when influential stimuli are available in memory and plausible, and when there are few plausible but non-influential factors. This provides a way of reconciling their results with those from the "awareness" experiments, as the verbal conditioning experiments present a simple situation in which the effective variables are both salient and plausible.

Nisbett & Wilson conclude (in agreement with Duncker, 1945) that people are conscious of the results of their thinking (in this case their attitudes or judgements) but have no special access to the process of thinking (how they made those judgements). However, they concede (without the same thorough evidence) that an individual does know more than an observer about private facts, not only the results of his thinking but also his focus of attention at a given time, current sensations, emotions, evaluations, plans, intentions and personal history.

If stated reasons for behaviour are based on some "theory" of what is involved, rather than on direct access to thinking, or cognitive processes, we can ask what implications this has for interpreting verbal reports from process operators. We could equate this "theory" with the operator's conscious knowledge of his task, part of what is usually called his "mental model" of the process. This just underlines the problems of interpreting verbal reports which we have already mentioned. We can only investigate the operation of this "theory", used in report generation, by collecting verbal reports and comparing them with non-verbal behaviour to identify the differences.

1.2.2. Types of distortion

If verbal reports are generated by a separate reporting process they may give a distorted and incomplete version of how a task is really done. Smith & Miller (1978) in a reply to Nisbett & Wilson published after first drafts of this paper were written, also comment that the more important research question is *when* self-reports will be veridical. In this section we will review distortions which are common to all methods of verbal reporting. The aim will be to devise reporting techniques which avoid these problems, or at least to keep the problems in mind when interpreting the data. Some of these points are based on observations by people who have collected verbal reports (see, e.g., Leplat & Bisseret, 1965; Rasmussen & Jensen, 1974), others are supported by experimental data.

If parts of the task are done unconsciously, then they are not available for report. The person reporting may say what he genuinely thinks he does, but this may not be what he actually does. Human beings are very good at rationalizing, at making up convincing reasons for their behaviour after the event, presumably making use of "theories" about what is appropriate.

If knowledge is conscious but not verbal it may be misrepresented by having to give a report. Skill involves complex co-ordination of several simultaneous activities, and attempts to impose the sequence of language on this must lead to a description which is disrupted, erroneous or incomplete. Any discriminations may not have simple verbal equivalents. Schuck & Leahy's (1966) study gives an example of the effect of reporting vocabulary. When people fixate luminous figures, parts of the pattern disappear. Schuck & Leahy asked people to report the intact segments, some verbally, others by tracing them on a representation of the figure. The verbal reports contained significantly more "meaningful" intact segments, that is they reported parts which have readily available verbal labels. If the process operator's vocabulary is limited he may not be able to find a translation for all that he knows. His knowledge may therefore appear limited, while actually it is his language which is limited, not his skill.

Having to give a report changes the task situation and may change the way the task is done. Of course one can hardly ask the person reporting whether he thinks that this is happening, as some investigators have done! Having to give a report can make someone self-conscious, so that he may not act in the same way when observing himself as when concentrating solely on the task. The need to give a verbal report may influence the operator, when there are alternative methods of doing a task, to use a method which is easily described. He can for example do a task in a physical rather than a mental way, as this is better fitted to the pace of speech, or do things in sequence rather than doing several things at the same time. He may use a beginner's method (ironically, in some tasks inexperienced workers might give verbal reports more easily, as they are still working in terms of the verbal instructions used in training). Alternatively he could follow the official regulations more closely than usual, as these are in verbal form.

At one level, whether having to give a verbal report influences task behaviour is a simple empirical question. Several studies of problem solving behaviour have measured whether performance time and accuracy are affected by verbalising. Newell & Simon (1972, Chap. 8) report the same solutions, and Dansereau & Gregg (1966) the same solution time, whether problem solving is done silently or while giving a verbal protocol. Gagné & Smith (1962) and Dominowski (1974, Expt. 1) found that performance when asked to give reasons for moves was more efficient. This suggests that verbalising changes the way the task is done, in a useful direction, perhaps by forcing concentration on task components. (Some anecdotal comments after collecting verbal protocols in complex industrial tasks suggest later performance can be influenced in the same way.)

These studies however all involve material which is easy to verbalise. If someone is doing a task in a non-verbal way, and has to give a concurrent verbal report, then he has a second information transforming task, converting non-verbal to verbal material. Peterson (1969) has investigated whether it is possible to do more than one verbal activity at a time. He found little evidence of interference from doing simple verbal tasks, such as emitting an overlearned sequence (e.g. the alphabet), or reproducing input material. However, when people had concurrently to do two verbal tasks involving transformations of inputs, such as addition and anagram solving, performance was only a third to a half of that when each task was done alone. These experiments, in which two different verbal tasks are done, are extreme compared with the verbal reporting situation, which involves related tasks, one verbal and one non-verbal. It does however demonstrate the considerable potential for interference.

Presumably, if inner speech is used in the organisation of behaviour, then any report of this should be much less distorted than reports of non-verbal thinking. Unfortunately, it is not possible to test this, as there is no independent method of testing whether thinking is verbal. For example, Benjafield (1969) has done a study comparing the characteristics of verbal protocols (asking someone to think aloud while doing a task) with those of post-hoc introspection (reporting thoughts from memory after doing the task). He finds that verbal protocols contain significantly more words, fragmentary utterances, pronouns and present tenses. These results are very interesting, and confirm intuitions about this type of data. It is not possible to infer however, as Benjafield does, that these differences imply that verbal protocols make inner speech covert. This would beg several questions about inner speech. One can argue more easily that verbal protocols have these characteristics because the speaker is describing the present under time pressure, when fuller information is available for report than can be extracted from memory.

Whether his thoughts are verbal or non-verbal, someone reporting on them can choose what he makes public, according to the social situation. Different types of social pressure can encourage or discourage undistorted reporting. People in experiments are often very co-operative, and may try to say what they think the experimenter wants to hear. If the person reporting thinks that the listener is superior and perhaps powerful then there are pressures to appear rational, knowledgeable and correct. In the process control situation an experienced operator will talk much more freely and fully if he thinks that his listener knows about the task and will understand what he is talking about.

1.2.3. General points on technique

It is evident from the previous discussion that, to minimise distortion in verbal reports, we should do the study in a social atmosphere which does not constrain what is said, and should access the operator's knowledge in a way in which is natural and parallel to the way he normally accesses it while doing the task: for example, accessing non-verbal knowledge with non-verbal methods, and verbal knowledge using the operator's own language. This implies that different reporting techniques may be most appropriate for different types of knowledge. Process control involves several different types of task, such as control of process dynamics and scheduling, which appear to use different types of cognitive process and background knowledge. Also the nature of the operator's knowledge will depend on the individual and on his experience.

A full investigation of the operator's behaviour and knowledge may require detailed analysis of all possible sources of evidence. When interested in the task rather than the individual, then several operators and foremen should be questioned, as one person may not know all about the plant or the available control strategies. One may not be studying the operator in order to contribute to cognitive processing theory, but as a basis for console and job aid design, performance prediction, training or selection. One can usefully ask which techniques best serve these relatively modest aims, when practical considerations of time and effort may override the need for validity or completeness.

The techniques which will be surveyed in this paper range from simple to complex and time consuming. They include collection of data "off-line"—the operator gives reports from memory when not actually doing the job, in written form or in an interview, and "on-line"—the operator talks while doing the task. With data collected off-line the operator has no feedback about whether the actions he suggests would be successful, while it takes a long time to collect sufficient on-line data about different situations.

All the above discussions emphasise the absolute necessity of validating reports against non-verbal behaviour. In practical situations verbal reports may be used to avoid the large amount of work involved in collecting data by observation, but this cannot be avoided in the initial evaluation of a technique. This paper will discuss the few process control studies in which verbal reports have been compared with actual behaviour, so their validity has been tested. The methodology in these studies will be discussed, rather than what they contribute to our knowledge of process control behaviour. We will not refer to the many papers, in which verbal data have been used as evidence, which do not comment on methodology or validity. We will also survey the types of data which can be obtained using the different techniques. As there are not many relevant studies, our knowledge of the adequacy and potential usefulness of these techniques is very minimal and speculative.

2. Written off-line reports

The two techniques used to obtain written information from process operators off-line have been "system state/action state" diagrams and questionnaires. In both techniques alternative answers are supplied, so replies are constrained to using this vocabulary, perhaps with misleading results. Hopefully these answers should help the operator to recognise the situation tested, but even so he needs imagination to match the situation described on paper with its parallel in the real task.

2.1. SYSTEM STATE/ACTION STATE DIAGRAM

System state/action state (SS/AS) diagrams have been used to investigate control of process dynamics. They provide a way of asking "what action do you make when the process output is behaving in such-and-such a way?" in tabular form. A simple process would involve one controlled variable, e.g. temperature, and one manipulated variable, e.g. heat supplied. A table would be prepared listing potential controlled variable values vertically and rates of change of value horizontally (see p. 147 in Cooke (1965) and Figs A1 and A4 in King & Cininas (1976)). Each pairing of value, and rate of change, represents process output behaviour in a given "state", and defines a "cell" in the table. The operator is asked to enter in each cell what action he would make on the maipulated variable when the controlled variable is behaving in this way.

Cooke (op. cit.) studied a simple laboratory task, and asked the student operators to enter in the table the control setting they would use in each context. King & Cininas (op. cit.) studied industrial operators controlling a much more complicated simulated reaction. This had two controlled variables and five interacting manipulated variables, and the process dynamics changed over time. They asked the operators to quote the size of change in control setting (rather than the new control setting) in each context, as "previous informal discussion with operators indicated they made control changes on an incremental basis". Thus they tried to make sure that the answers required were in the form in which the task was usually done, so that giving an answer did not require unusual mental translations by the operator. King & Cininas used two types of diagram, so they could repeat the test in a different format after a time interval to measure the consistency of the replies. The first form of their diagram included all 7 variables, and was very difficult to comprehend. In the second test, a separate diagram was used for each controlled variable, and only those manipulated variables which could affect it were included. This presupposes that the operators know that these variables are the only appropriate ones. In this case King & Cininas had identified this from the earlier study. Testing for knowledge of interacting variables is still possible, as the interacting manipulated variable will appear in both diagrams. In their second study King & Cininas also tested for knowledge of non-linearities in the process, i.e., that it behaves differently at different periods in the reaction. The operators were asked to fill in separate diagrams for their actions during the beginning, middle and end phases of the reaction.

King & Cininas demonstrate that one can analyse these data to show whether:

(a) manipulated variable changes are different in different phases of the reaction— this can show the operator's knowledge of direct control links in the process, interactions, and non-linearities;

(b) the sizes of these changes are different, e.g. fine, gross, on/off;

(c) the control changes are consistent across the process states in a way which makes sense;

(d) what the operator says is consistent with what he should say if he understands the process.

However, it is only useful to make such analyses if the data are valid and reliable, King & Cininas did not compare the SS/AS reports with actual control behaviour, but did compare the two SS/AS tests, to obtain a measure of reliability. They found that the answers to the two tests did not match, so concluded that the SS/AS is not a reliable tool for investigating control policy. (This assessment does not allow for the problem that the two SS/AS tests used were very different in comprehensibility.)

King & Cininas point out several other basic problems with this technique. The terms used and format of the diagram are restrictive and unnatural; for example the operator's perception of a given process output may depend on a wider context which is not given in the diagram. The operators are constrained to describe proportional control, while their behaviour shows they may use pulsed or on/off control. There is no indication of action timing, which is critical to control success. Overall, the design of the diagram imposes barriers to the accurate description of control strategy.

Cooke (op. cit.) did compare the SS/AS results with actual control behaviour, so was able to make a further range of criticisms of this technique. It was apparently difficult for the operators to imagine the control states and so fill in the diagram. Some students appeared to fill in the table to make a pattern which looked sensible, rather than putting down values actually used. If this is the case then data which is internally consistent and makes sense does not necessarily represent the operator's actual knowledge. The actual control settings used in an experimental trial were compared with settings quoted in an SS/AS diagram filled in immediately after the trial, the agreement was about 50%. "Few of these differences could be attributed to a lack of attention, or poor judgement of system states." Cooke's further studies showed that practised operators controlled by anticipation, while the SS/AS constrains them to describing a feedback strategy.

It had been hoped that the SS/AS technique would allow an operator to report on dynamic control behaviour, whch he can rarely describe verbally (see section 4.2). It appears however that the SS/AS technique has its own problems. It constrains him to perceive and report in numbers, when he may do the task in terms of pointer positions and hand movements. It also constrains him to report on stationary proportional feedback control, when there are many other control policies by which such a task can be done.

The main problem is then that the descriptive vocabulary used in the SS/AS does not necessarily match the terms used by a practised operator in doing the task. An SS/AS can only be devised by assuming that certain distinctions are important in the operator's behaviour, and then testing whether he reacts differentially to these situations. It cannot discover whether there are other discriminations, not embodied in the SS/AS, which better represent his usual behaviour. This technique cannot therefore be used to investigate an unknown control policy.

2.2. QUESTIONNAIRE

This technique uses written questions and answers. Answering can be made easier by providing a vocabulary of possible answers, so the operator simply marks one of them. This of course constrains the vocabulary of replies.

The fullest study available of this technique is by King & Cininas (op. cit.). Operators were asked to read the questionnaire just before a plant run. After the run, they completed the questionnaire in the control room, and several of the operators referred to the control console while doing so. King & Cininas used three distinct ways of asking questions, which are sufficiently interesting to be discussed separately.

2.2.1.

The first type of question attempted to investigate how operators categorised the variable values, e.g.,

(i) What do you consider is a low temperature?

$$50 \quad 51 \quad 52 \quad 53 \quad \ldots \quad \text{etc} \quad \ldots \quad 70.$$

(ii) How much do you turn the caustic valve to turn it up a bit?

$$1 \quad 2 \quad 3 \quad 4 \quad 5 \quad 6 \quad 7 \quad 8 \quad 9 \quad 10 \quad \text{MAX}$$

King & Cininas show that one can use the data collected to identify the sizes of the categories (e.g. "low") used, and whether the assignment of category labels to actual values is consistent across operators. Unfortunately this type of question raises similar problems to those with the SS/AS. It assumes that perception of the process is numerical, and that categories are unchanging in their use. King (personal communication) says however that the answers appeared reasonable, by judgement.

2.2.2.

Drawings of the control knobs were given, and the operator was asked to mark on them the initial control settings he used. This can only be used to investigate the operator's open-loop control. The technique does not require the operator to translate his knowledge into another descriptor but, as the drawing is being used as a memory aid, it is important that it has a 1 : 1 relation with the control panel. One would expect that such pictures would give reasonable access to the operator's knowledge. King (personal communication) says that answers were surprisingly accurately correlated with real behaviour, as assessed by judgement, especially for the better operators.

2.2.3.

The third question type asked which variables affect others, e.g.,

> Which valves control temperature:
> caustic/reactant/recirculation/cooling water/heating?

King & Cininas report that answers to this question type were correct, except for the answers from one poor controller.

These results suggest that these questions form an interesting and useful technique, but rather different conclusions were reached by Broadbent (1977) and Umbers (1976), who did explicitly compare questionnaire and control performance. Broadbent studied housewives who had 6–8 trials at controlling a laboratory scheduling task. Before and after the experiment, questions were asked about the direction of the effect of given directions of change. He reports that there was no correlation between success in answering the final questionnaire and control performance. Also the ability to answer the questions was not reliably improved by experience. It might be encouraging that 3/12 subjects improved at reporting the direct relationships and none deteriorated, but 4 deteriorated in reporting the interacting relationships. Broadbent (personal communication) has since expanded these groups, and found that after training 18/20 people could answer questions about direct relationships perfectly correctly, but they were unable to learn the indirect relationships. Umbers (1976, Chap. 5) gave a questionnaire to students after each of two trials at a simulated industrial control task. Answers to the second questionnaire were more accurate, but there were no clear patterns of correlation with performance.

There are so many differences between the three studies that it is not possible to identify the situations in which questionnaires may give useful information. The tasks were all different, in their control dynamics, the types of decision needed, and the way variable values were displayed, any one of which could affect the controller's mental representation and so its accessibility. The controllers differed considerably in experience with their tasks. Subtle variations in the wording of questions, and the reasoning required to answer them, may affect the ease of imagining the real situation. Umbers (op. cit.) used recall questions, e.g. "What will happen if the 'input rate' is less than the 'hourly send-out'?". Broadbent (personal communication) used recognition questions, e.g., "If t (the time interval between buses) gets longer and f (the parking fee) remains unchanged, will L (the load per 100 buses) get larger/get smaller/stay the same/don't know?" One could suggest that pilot studies on the wording of questions should be used, but this would be difficult in industrial situations with few operators. Finally, both Broadbent and Umbers correlated overall questionnaire score with overall performance score. It might be more appropriate, though much more difficult, to correlate answers to particular questions with detailed aspects of performance which should show that the operator has this knowledge.

Although questionnaires, once developed, would be the quickest method of obtaining information from operators, it is not at present possible to claim that the information so obtained will be valid. There are so many differences between the studies reported above that it is clear that a large amount of future research is necessary before it will be possible to say what questions might be useful in relation to which tasks. It is also not known whether written questions could be asked usefully about process technology or required process behaviour.

2.3. CONCLUSIONS ON WRITTEN TECHNIQUES

As the vocabulary of replies constrains possible answers it is not possible to use these techniques to investigate unknown control behaviour. As these techniques do present known dimensions they might be used either for testing an operator's knowledge, or in training, by making operators aware of the discriminations which can usefully be made. Such uses have not yet been studied.

3. Spoken off-line reports

Two main types of technique have been used for collecting verbal off-line reports; interviews, with spoken questions and free spoken answers, and static simulation, in which the operator works through specific semi-realistic situations, without any time pressure, and makes comments on what he is doing. Methodological issues are concerned with what types of questions can be asked using these techniques, what aids to answering can be given, what types of answer can be obtained, and how valid or reliable these are.

Both techniques for eliciting verbal comments require careful development work. Usually they are preceded by extensive observation, and by open-ended interviews with experienced operators, to find out enough about the task to identify the task aspects which should be investigated further, and to develop the tests. The questions or situations may also be developed by using pilot trials. Although this may lead to a carefully structured set of test situations, it is still valuable to allow all operators an opportunity for spontaneous comment, as the structured format may not have covered all task aspects which they feel are important.

3.1. STRUCTURED INTERVIEW

Structured interviews use spoken questions and answers, in which the questions follow a pre-determined plan but the replies are free. The main evidence on this technique comes from Cuny (1977), who has compared interview data with information obtained from about 60 hours of observation and talking to 4 industrial process operators while they were doing the job.

One problem is to present the questions so that they access the operator's knowledge in the most natural way. Obvious reminders of the working context would be given by doing the interview in the control room or a simulator, but this is not always possible in practice. Kraagt & Landeweerd (1974) used an interviewer who had on-the-job training. Cuny (op. cit.) started his interview programme 3 months after the beginning of his study, by which time the investigators were accepted by the operators. The interviews were in 4 sessions of 2 hours, spaced over several days. He took care that the questions were phrased in the professional language used by the operator being interviewed. The questions were asked in a progressive way, using each later session to refine the discussion and ask for more explanation of points in the previous session; the language of the questions was also revised. In this way both the language and content of the questions depended on the particular operator, attempting to stretch each individual to the limit of his knowledge.

Cuny asked 2 main types of question: about the operator's own behaviour, e.g., "what would you do in such-and-such a situation?", and about the process behaviour, e.g. "why does such-and-such happen?". A range of other question types have been used by other investigators who have not tested the validity of the replies. Kraagt & Landeweerd (op. cit.) asked the operator to give imaginary instructions to an inexperienced operator, to describe difficult situations in which they had been involved, and to make paired comparisons of the importance of different displays. Iosif & Ene (1975), studying malfunction diagnosis, asked operators to assign probabilities to their hypothese about malfunctions. These were compared with probabilities generated by engineers and supervisors, which were taken as the *a priori* probabilities. This may test the adequacy of what is said, but does not test whether what is reported matches the probabilities actually used in malfunction diagnosis.

Cuny is the only writer to have analysed the types of reply, rather than going straight from the interview data to developing a model of the operator's behaviour. He distinguished 6 levels of complexity of reply (to both types of question). The most important distinction was between answers based simply on empirical knowledge (input/output relations), and those including a technical explanation. He did not find any correspondence between the subject of the question and the level of response.

Cuny compared the interview data with observed behaviour by judgement rather than using explicit measures, as the data were complex and there were small numbers of each type. He found that all behaviours observed were mentioned by at least one operator, though not necessarily by the operator observed to have done it. He states that no behaviour as reported was contradicted by behaviour as observed, and so concludes there is no real incompatibility between the two sources of data.

Cuny's comparison of the content of interview data, and observed behaviour, leads him to conclude that interview data are mainly at the level of rules and general principles. In particular, he comments that the verbal replies are more formal and regular, and do not describe the detailed context of real behaviour. The facts are described in a more logical order than they are observed. The operator gives a systemmatic assured description of this sequence, which does not include the hesitancies, uncertainties and retracings found in real behaviour. (Presumably this is because there is no feedback from a real situation). The rather formal description of behaviour does not mention "unofficial" types of behaviour, or cases where the operator decides not to intervene. The description does not cover the compromises imposed on control by particular contexts, e.g. when particular values of relevant variables require a change in the general rule. He does not mention cases where several problems can be dealt with by one intervention, and there is little precision about sizes of changes and their effects.

Cuny's conclusions support the above comments on the incompleteness and probably more official form of verbal reports, but imply that interviews are usefully valid as far as they go. Cuny suggests that both verbal and observation data are required for a full analysis. General control rules are mentioned in the interview, but the quantitative details of which value goes with which are only worked out when actually doing the job, in a particular context, and information about this aspect of the skill is not given in an interview, so must be observed. Interviews may however be the best verbal method for accessing the operator's knowledge of process technology. As discussed in section 4.2, this is not usually mentioned by an operator during his on-line working decisions.

Although Cuny's work suggests that interviews can be a very useful technique, Goillau's (1978) finding gives a reminder that operator comments are not always valid. He studied experienced industrial operators using a new job-aid. Data showed that performance was better with the job-aid, but the operators commented after the trials that it was of no practical use. This suggests the operators were using the information without awareness. One must note that these operators were inexperienced with the equipment, and no special techniques were used to obtain their comments, but this study does show the dangers of assessing new equipment from operator comments rather than performance.

3.2. STATIC SIMULATION

In the static simulation technique, the operator is put in a simulation of the real situation and "talks through" what he would do, without being under time pressure. The simulations are normally relatively simple "paper and pencil" techniques. This method can be considered as an extension of the structured interview (and all the techniques in the previous section can be used to maximise the information obtained), but hopefully it reduces the imagination required of the operator as representations of some of his visual aids are given.

In static simulation, the process behaviour is "frozen", so the operator has time to think things out fully and to describe all his thoughts and inferences. Consequently though, all the objections to verbal data are relevant. One specific problem is that a sequence is necessarily imposed on the operator's behaviour. Another is that his working methods may change when he is not under the stresses of the real situation and its time pressures (through it is possible to introduce some time pressures in a controlled way). Whether or not information about all the operator's knowledge is obtained (of that which can be obtained by this method) depends on the specific situations investigated. Getting a wide sample of types of behaviour is time consuming using this method, although considerably less so than when observing shop-floor behaviour.

Changes in the process over time, and feedback of the results of actions, are intrinsic aspects of control task information which cannot be conveyed by a static simulation technique. Static simulation presents a picture of a situation which does not change until a new picture is introduced. Dynamic simulation aims to represent not only the layout of the information but also the way in which it changes over time, including the effects of the operator's actions. Dynamic simulations are therefore used in "on-line" techniques as, as far as possible, the operator is doing his real task. It might be possible to include dynamic changes in a "static" simulation technique however. This would require much more sophisticated equipment than is usually needed. Variables would change over time in a natural way, but the dynamic simulation would be stopped to allow the operator to comment. This technique has not yet been tried.

Nevertheless the static simulation method has many advantages. Leplat & Bisseret (1965) comment that one can isolate aspects of the work in which one is interested and explicitly monitor the behaviour, compared with the real situation. The subjects can be placed in strictly identical and repeatable situations. This compares with the shop-floor, or with dynamic simulation, in which subjects make different decisions so the final outcomes differ and are difficult to compare. Relatively, the technique is quick and easy to apply. Duncan & Shepherd (1975), who were concerned with training for fault diagnosis, point out that in the real situation the trainee experiences a random sample of faults, and often the experienced operator is too busy to explain.

There are two main categories of static simulation technique, which pose different problems for the operator. In what could be called a simultaneous technique, the operator is given a full display of his information, and then says what he would do. Some investigators prefer to make the operator's sequential use of information more explicit. They give the operator only partial information to start with, and he must request further information as he needs it. Although the operator presumably does obtain information from his displays in sequence, except when he looks at displays together in pattern recognition, this imposed sequence does enforce artificial constraints of timing and search.

Two examples of simultaneous studies with full data can be described. Leplat & Bisseret (op. cit.) investigated the decision-making of air-traffic controllers. They gave a number of flight strips (paper strips with information about individual aircraft) to a controller and asked him to familiarise himself with the situation. They then gave him a new strip, and asked him to describe the steps he would take to check on its safety. This simulation was very natural, as information was given to controllers in that form at that time. From the results Leplat & Bisseret built up a flow diagram representing the controller's decision sequences. They comment that there are considerable problems in testing the validity of such flow diagrams. They assumed that problem solution time was a valid measure of task difficulty, and tested for a correlation between solution time and complexity of path to solution through the flow diagram.

Duncan & Shepherd (op. cit.) used static simulation in training for fault diagnosis, rather than to identify the strategy used. They wanted to put the operator in a situation in which he could develop any adequate strategy, but in a controlled way. They did not want to impose a serial strategy, or to restrict the information available to that used by an experienced operator. They used drawings of the instruments, presented together in a way which preserved instrument design, layout and size. Information not given on the real panel was available on request, as in the real situation. The aim was that the operator could use the same information collecting and processing strategies as in the real situation. They comment that there are great problems in testing for the transfer of strategies, learned in this way, to the real situation.

The investigations using a sequential technique with partial data have also been concerned with fault diagnosis. Iosif (1972) started with a simple "simultaneous" method. He gave 8 variable values to the operator and asked him to say what sequence he used the information in, and what were the possible causes of the malfunction. The results suggested that operators differed in their knowledge of the process, but as not all the potentially relevant information was supplied he developed a sequential technique in which more information was potentially available. He made drawings of all the displays, showing values relevant to some malfunction, then presented one display to the operator. This was either an alarm signal or the value of an output variable, so was assumed to be equivalent to the first signal indicating the malfunction which was noticed by the operator. The operator was asked to say what could cause such an indication, then to ask for new information, saying why, and what he expected the new value to be. He was then given the information requested, and the procedure was repeated. This indicated which data was used, and in what order, though it imposed a strict sequence on the behaviour. Iosif & Ene (1975) have used this type of data to compare the adequacy of different strategies of doing the task, e.g. by comparing the time taken, or the number of solution steps compared with the minimum possible (see also Duncan & Gray, 1975). He compared experienced operators with inexperienced, and looked for gaps in knowledge and the relation of behaviour to hypotheses. All these comparisons were internal to the data obtained, without an external test of their validity.

One might conclude that static simulation is the best, though most time consuming, of the off-line techniques, but unfortunately there has been very little attempt to test the validity of the data obtained. One assumes that this technique puts the operator in the most natural situation, short of the real task, though it constrains him to sequential, conscious behaviour, and in the technique used by Iosif, among others, the operator has to imagine the task situation in order to task for further information. One assumes that

Cuny's comments about the types of information obtained from interviews are also relevant here.

3.3. CONCLUSIONS ON VERBAL OFF-LINE REPORTS

Hopefully one can assume that some information about task knowledge can be obtained using these techniques, although the data may be incomplete and not necessarily entirely related to that used in the real task. Against that, one can comment that if the operator can talk about these things he does have this knowledge somewhere in his head, even if it is not used in doing the task. This suggests the information obtained could give normative data about potential knowledge, which can be compared with normal behaviour and might suggest better ways of tapping this potential. This would have to be done with care, as it is by no means certain what types of knowledge the operator either gives more information about in off-line reports than when doing the task (perhaps process technology and overall aims) or cannot adequately report verbally (perhaps quantitative control and skilled integration of activities), see below.

4. Verbal protocols

Verbal protocols are collected by asking the operator to "think aloud" while he is doing his job, controlling either the real process or a dynamic simulation of it. Hopefully, these verbal reports reflect the constraints and stresses of the natural situation, including feedback about his own actions. The interview technique discussed above may identify gaps in overall knowledge, but cannot identify breakdowns due to cognitive loading, and information on aspects of the task which cause difficulty is important for design purposes. In addition, protocols include some data which allow one to speculate in general about cognitive processes.

Unfortunately, as well as the general problems with verbal data discussed in section 1, several other problems are emphasised by on-line protocols. The operator may not report what is "obvious" to him. He may collect unmentioned information while reporting other activities, which leads to unexplained behaviour later. Most people can think more quickly than they can talk, so only a sample of all their cognitive activity can be reported. The investigator therefore has the same problems, of inferring what lies between the items mentioned in the protocol, as he has when interpreting non-verbal behaviour. There are also some practical difficulties. As real behaviour is being studied, a random sample of process events will be observed. A long period of recording may be necessary to collect a representative sample of activities, though this will depend on the rate of events in a particular process. Protocol collection is not possible if the task itself involves verbal communication. Last, but not least, analysing protocol data is both difficult and time consuming.

Although verbal protocol data are very interesting and appear to be, for some purposes, the most detailed source of information about the operator's cognitive processes, they are still very incomplete. In particular, verbal protocols cannot be used to establish the limits of the operator's knowledge. If something is not mentioned in the protocol this does not prove that the operator does not know it. For this purpose it is necessary to supplement the protocol data with a more direct exploration of the operator's knowledge, e.g. by interview. Protocols then have the unarguable function of acting as a powerful source of hypotheses for guiding this exploration.

As discussed in section 1.1, there can be no ultimate validation of verbal reports as evidence of cognitive processes. It is easier, however, to obtain corroborating evidence for protocols collected from process control than from some other tasks, as the operator is talking about identifiable and changing aspects of the external world. If a simultaneous log has been made of process behaviour and the operator's actions, then the protocol can be checked against the log, to show that the process or actions were as he reported them. Unfortunately, as the data log is very useful in identifying the referents of unclear protocol phrases, this use of the log becomes circular.

4.1. VERBAL PROTOCOL METHODOLOGY

4.1.1. Verbal protocol collection

The operator is asked to "think aloud", using everyday language, and is encouraged by the investigator during silences. His comments are tape-recorded and transcribed. Position of microphones depends on the noise level in the control room and acceptability to the operators. Rasmussen & Jensen (1974) used short tapes which were typed during the session, so that the person recorded could read it at his working position after the session, to correct mistakes and supply further information. The investigator also asked for clarification of weak passages, which can involve the distortions of the interview situation.

As is usual with verbal techniques, the major problem is to ensure that the operator can verbalise without difficulty. It can be useful to record from two operators who are working together to solve a problem, or from an experienced operator guiding a trainee. Maximum communication of thoughts and knowledge, or admission of lack of knowledge, can then be natural aims rather than a source of embarrassment. One might ask however whether people talking to each other report on a different selection of mental processes than an individual would mention when "thinking aloud". A related difficulty can be illustrated from a protocol given by an operator working alone. When there was a slack period in the task, the operator made general comments about his strategy to the investigator. These comments, which might be similar to those obtained in interviews, and can contain fuller knowledge than is mentioned elsewhere, differ in style and content from remarks while doing the job, e.g.:

(i) "If a furnace is making stainless (steel) it's in the reducing period, obviously it's silly, when the metal temperature and the furnace itself is at peak temperature, it's silly to cut that furnace off."

(ii) "I shall have to cut E (furnace) a little bit, it was the last to come on. What's it making by the way, 'stainless' did someone say. Of, that's a bit dicey, I wonder what—I'd be more inclined to—I shall not have to interfere with E then".

The sequences of behaviour, and purpose of behaviour, often are not stated explicitly and have to be induced from the items which are mentioned. The general "interview" type of strategy comments can provide a guide in doing this induction, but then there is no independent check on the validity of either source of evidence on strategy.

Several investigators have not asked operators for an on-going protocol, but have interviewed the operator while doing his job, asking questions about his behaviour after each display observation or action. This has the advantage that on-line performance is observed, and information can be collected which the operator might not have volunteered. The disadvantages are parallel to those in the interview situation, as the operator reports after rather than during his task decisions.

As will be seen in the next section, the detail with which protocols can be analysed is enormously extended if a simultaneous log of plant and operator behaviour is collected. This can be done in several ways but does require a lot more work. An observer can log the display values. A specially instrumented plant can make the log, for example with chart recorders of process variable values, and covers over the displays which the operator has to lift so his sampling can be logged (though this imposes unnatural constraints on his behaviour, by being time consuming and preventing use of peripheral vision or pattern perception). It is easiest to obtain a log when a computer driven simulated plant is available for the investigations.

4.2.1. Verbal protocol analysis

The chief aim of verbal protocol analysis is to identify how the operator makes his task decisions. This sort of detailed information about strategies in particular parts of a task could be very useful in designing interfaces, job aids and training schemes. The analysis requires many complex techniques and a great deal of work. The main aspects will be indicated, but it is not possible to go into full detail here. There are three main analytic problems, which require different techniques: analysing the explicit content, and inferring the implicit content, including how the sequence of behaviour is generated. In most of the techniques, the investigator has to use his own knowledge of the task to interpret what is being said, and infer missing passages. Unless these hypotheses can be supported by evidence from other sections of the protocol then, strictly, several independent judges should be used, and the agreement between their opinions should be measured.

4.1.2.1. Explicit content.

Explicit content of protocol phrases can be analysed by "content analysis". Each phrase is assigned to one from a set of categories of phrase types, and then the number of phrases in each category is counted. The assignment is done using the natural language understanding of judges. In process control studies this technique has been used mainly by Cooke (1965) and Umbers (1976).

The categories of phrase types may be based on, for example, the referents of content words in the phrases, their syntax, or the implied cognitive processes (see next section). There can be no absolute set of these categories or descriptors. A set of categories is required which makes discriminations which are appropriate to the purpose of the study and can be identified reliably by judges. Rasmussen & Jensen (1974) comment that developing a set of analytic categories which can be identified by judges is a major problem. The set can only be developed by iteration, by first generating analytic categories which seem appropriate *a priori* (from a preliminary reading of the protocol), and repeatedly defining and revising these categories by trying to use them to analyse the protocol, until the category definitions and phrase assignments stabilise. This procedure is arduous, as it is very boring but must be done with precision. As the categories have been developed in the process of analysing the data neither the data nor the categories can be justified in terms of each other but some external test is necessary. One test is that the categories can be applied to the data, and with the same results, by judges who were not involved in the development of the categories. Cooke (op. cit.)

found agreement between judges was better than 84%, which is a good measure of reliability. The usual scientific test is that the categories should be applicable to other data. This cannot usually be done at this stage in the development of protocol analysing techniqueŝ. There are too few case studies, from different tasks for which different descriptive categories appear to be most appropriate. Any attempt to integrate these categories into an overview would be entirely speculative at this stage. It will be very interesting if or when independent investigators produce similar sets of categories:

This content analysis is used as a basis for frequency counts. Frequencies can be compared to identify the predominant activities, the proportion of time spent in different activities, and individual differences in these measures. This type of data must be used with caution however, as the verbal protocol frequency does not necessarily reflect the mental activity frequency, but may better reflect the ease of verbalising different activities. The frequency count gives a measure of reported behaviour only.

4.1.2.2. Implicit content. Some aspects of the phrases imply information which is not mentioned in the protocol but can be identified explicitly during the analysis, such as pronominal referents and some cognitive processes. Other types of phrase imply that the operator has background knowledge of some kind, but it is difficult to infer any detail of what this knowledge might be like. It is difficult to make any direct check of the validity of these inferences, they rather have the status of hypotheses for which supporting evidence can accumulate.

The referents of it's, that's and other links between sequences of phrases are identified by the natural language understanding of judges. Doing this requires detailed knowledge of the process, so that the judge can recognise relations in the phrase semantics. Alternatively, these referents can be identified by going through the protocol transcription with the operator, checking on the meaning of unclear passages.

The referents of evaluation words like "low", "too high" can be identified if a simultaneous log of plant values is available. One can then identify the actual value of a variable when the operator uses one of these category words. In simple cases, when the average and range of values do not vary with circumstances, and given a sufficiently large number of instances, one can identify the operator's scale of subjective evaluation (e.g., Bainbridge, 1972, pp. 55, 76). Without a plant log one can at least identify the number of different category words used (e.g. too high, alright, too low are 3 categories), and so the fineness of the operator's evaluations.

Underlying cognitive processes can be identified most easily in two circumstances. Even if the protocol contains only a random sample of the operator's "thoughts", if the same behaviour recurs on several occasions, one will get a different sample of the components of behaviour in each. One can build up a representation of the underlying behaviour by combining this information (e.g. Bainbridge, 1972, p. 117). Process control is an easier task to analyse in this way than many tasks for which protocols have been collected, as the task is naturally cyclic so similar situations recur.

When intervening processing steps are not reported in the protocol, it can be possible to infer them. For example, if the operator says "22 minutes, and I've 8 minutes to go" and one knows that 22 minutes is the time so far in a half-hour, then 8 minutes is the time to go in the half hour, and the operator must have done an unmentioned subtraction (see also Bainbridge, 1972, pp. 117–118). The inference is that the operator could not have said a phrase like this without using this cognitive process, so it can safely be assumed. These inferences are being made via assumptions about underlying cognitive mechanisms. There must of course be many other implicit activities concerned with accessing memories and so on, which would have to be inferred in detail if one was trying to make a complete and functioning model of the operator's behaviour. There are not necessarily any explicit clues about the nature of such mechanisms in the protocol, so the question arises of how deeply it is useful to take these inferences. I take the view that it is most useful, at this stage in our knowledge, to concentrate on describing behaviour at a level at which there are some explicit clues to constrain the range of possible mechanisms suggested, but many people would not agree with this.

The semantics of a phrase may also imply that the operator is referring to wider background knowledge. Take the phrases: "I'll try to run the temperature down to about 400° . . . no trouble, it's far away now." The first phrase implies the operator knows the required process behaviour (400°). The second phrase appears to assess the ease of making such a change, which implies that he has knowledge of how to make both such assessments and such changes. A full protocol analysis ought to detail the types of general knowledge which can be inferred in this way. Unfortunately, although one can infer from the protocol that such knowledge exists, there is very little direct evidence in a protocol about its structure and use. Information about this knowledge can be obtained by following up the protocol study with interviews on these points.

4.1.2.3. Groups and sequences of phrases. In protocols collected from some tasks, each phrase makes little sense when considered alone, and it can be analysed best in the context of a group of phrases. Grouping phrases together can only be done at present by the same sort of intuitive semantic judgements based on natural language understanding as used in identifying pronominal referents. These judgements can be checked by measuring the agreement between several such judges. It may also be necessary for these judges to infer the aim of a sequence of behaviour from its outcomes.

The reasons for choosing one type of behaviour rather than another may not be mentioned in the protocol, particularly if the operator is under time pressure. The basis of this decision can be identified however, if several examples of the same choice, and a plant data log, are available. Say, for example, that behaviour A is sometimes followed by behaviour B and sometimes by C. For each of these occasions one identifies the values of the process variables, and the operator's recent behaviour. One then checks whether any of these are consistently different in the two cases. For example a process variable may always be high when A–B occurs, and low for A–C; the value of this variable is then assumed to be the unmentioned factor determining the choice of behaviour at this point (e.g. Bainbridge, 1972, p. 81).

4.2. TYPES OF DATA OBTAINED

Protocol phrases may be statements about process behaviour or about the operator's decision-making. They can also be questions, statements about remembered events, or evaluations of the operator's own behaviour, so they can reflect some general types of cognitive processing. This section will mention some of the types of information which have been obtained, in particular, data about dynamic control, scheduling decisions, and knowledge of technical aspects of the process. A much wider range of comparative studies will be needed before one can make any definite generalisations.

Several investigators have analysed the operator's dynamic control behaviour, his sampling, his evaluation of process state and awareness of future events, his choice of actions and his conditional statements. The fullest publicly available data on this is in Cooke (1965).

Identifying the referents of evaluation words was discussed in section 4.1.2.2. One can use the wording of these phrases to identify the different ways in which the process state has been described, e.g. numerically or relatively (and to what), and the precision of the statements. Fullest identification of the referents is only possible using a process log. Even then, there may be no explicit evidence on the process of evaluation.

Cooke (op. cit.) has also analysed statements which show awareness of future process behaviour. This appears not only in specific prediction phrases, but also in statements about required changes in process behaviour, or about conditions in which these changes can occur. One can identify the types of prediction and their level of precision. Again the information may not be very specific or detailed.

In similar ways, one can analyse how action and choice of action are described, and what types of reason, if any, are given for those actions. King (1978, Table 4) recorded the rate at which operators sampled the process variables. He compared this with the rate at which the operators mentioned variable values in the protocol. He found that the protocol rate validly represented the actual rate except when the operator was very busy. Unfortunately, if using protocol data when one is unable to collect a plant log, it would be difficult to get an independent definition of when the operator was or was not busy, in order to assess when the protocol sampling rate was a valid representation. One needs to know the actual sampling rate to assess the adequacy of the operator's sampling by comparing it with the rate required by the process. However, if one assumes that task overload would have the same effect on reporting of all variables, one could use the reported rate to identify the relative importance of the variables to the operator. King (op. cit., Table 6) also obtained sufficient numerical comments from his protocols to construct a table (system state/action state diagram) showing how the operator reacted in particular contexts. This was compared with a similar table constructed from the computer log of the operator's behaviour. The differences between reported and actual behaviour were relatively minor, so one assumes that action reports in protocols are valid.

From the operator's conditional statements one can infer what types of knowledge they imply, and analyse what modes of expression are used. These statement types are mainly concerned with the conditions under which process changes will occur, or the conditions which are appropriate for making a given action. The language of the conditionals may be related to the type of process task and the way in which it is being talked about, for example, "If x then y" is used when describing or explaining behaviour in general, but rarely appears in protocols from operators immediately involved in task decisions. Inferences can also be made, from the type of content words used in the conditional statement, about the way the speaker "sees" the process (see below).

Scheduling decisions, that is decisions about how to make best use of several machines, appear to be described in protocols more explicitly than dynamic control decisions are. This might be because these decisions can be based on discrete values and calculations rather than on judgements. The cognitive processes inferred might be likened over simply to a digital computer programme, while the control decisions appear to use more analogue processes and reference to general dynamic "models" or knowledge. However, in some cases, these scheduling decisions are also not described explicitly, and general judgement processes appear to take over, perhaps when the number of factors involved becomes too large. One might hope to identify when this change occurs and so to assess how or when explicit thinking about alternative behaviours breaks down.

The general way in which the operator talks about the process can have implications for the nature of his process knowledge. However, there are several reasons why this evidence must be treated with caution. Cooke (1965) identified the "key concepts", basic to being able to do the task, mentioned in the protocol. He found no relation between the number of concepts mentioned and the quality of control performance. He also found concepts could be stated but not used, or vice versa. This again suggests that more reliable information about knowledge of such concepts could be obtained from observation.

Some unpublished analyses suggest that process behaviour is described differently by operators and engineers, e.g.:

Operator: "we have to go higher up before we can run it up"
Engineer: "we have reduced pressure in the boiler and therefore we have removed water from the economiser".

The operator usually mentioned the behaviour of the process but not its physical components. This might imply that the operator's process knowledge is operational rather than technical, so, for example, he would react to a malfunction by recovering the process state rather than finding the faulty component. However, the operator does mention parts of the process when he is uncertain about appropriate behaviour and asking another operator questions. This might imply that he does have some technical knowledge, but that it is not usually mentioned because it is inappropriate to think or talk at this level of explanation when involved in on-going control, while the engineer is always concerned with diagnosis in terms of design. This suggests that the operator might be able to give technical explanations when not busy, for example in interview situations, see section 2.1. Operators in different plant and industries can have different reponsibilities for maintenance, so it will probably be more useful to generalise about types of task rather than operators *vs.* engineers. Not enough analysis has yet been done to say whether it will be possible to identify the relation between knowledge of process behaviour and knowledge of the physical process, from verbal reports.

5. Conclusions

Although verbal reports can be a poor reflection of what is going on in the speaker's head, if techniques are used with care then verbal data can be both interesting and useful. Different types of cognitive processing can presumably be best reported in different ways, there being some method for giving information about each way of thinking with the minimum of disturbance and unusual mental work. We are far from being clear about either the different types of cognitive processing which exist or the best methods to use! A partly speculative summary of the problems with different techniques and the information which might be obtained from them, is given in Tables 2 and 3.

TABLE 2

Constraints on the data obtainable using given techniques ("perhaps" implies this might be avoided with care in design of technique)

Technique / Constraint	SS/AS diagram	Questionnaire	Interview	Static simulation		On-line interview	Verbal protocol
				Partial data	Full data		
Operator has to imagine	yes	perhaps	perhaps	yes	perhaps	no	no
Vocabulary constrains replies	yes	yes	perhaps	perhaps	perhaps	no	no
Sequence imposed on behaviour	no	yes	yes	yes	perhaps	yes	yes
No real time pressures	yes	yes	yes	yes	yes	no	no
No effects of particular context	yes	yes	yes	perhaps	perhaps	no	no
Encourages rationalisation	yes	yes	yes	yes	yes	yes	yes

TABLE 3

Information which might be obtained using different techniques: see text for fuller discussion. (?: not investigated so far, not possible to make a "definite guess")

Information on: *Technique*	Questionnaire	Interview	Static simulation	On-line interview	Verbal protocol	Observation
General information on which variable affects which	perhaps	yes	yes	yes	perhaps	infer
General information on control strategy	?	yes	yes	yes	perhaps	infer
Numerical information on control strategy	no	no	no	no	perhaps	yes
Technical aspects of process	?	yes	yes	yes	perhaps	perhaps infer
Decision sequences	no	yes	yes	yes	yes	perhaps infer
General types of cognitive processing	no	?	?	?	yes	no
Full range of behaviours	perhaps	yes	perhaps	no	no	no

The technique to use depends on the type of task being done by the operator. In addition, as there is no single purpose of collecting verbal reports, so there is no one ideal technique. For example, techniques in which a vocabulary of answers are given could be useful for testing but not for discovery. A carefully organised interview is probably the best technique to use when time and equipment are limited, as it should give information on general principles of behaviour and plant. If one wanted as full information as possible about the operator's knowledge and cognitive processes, and was working in an ideal world, with no limit to investigating man-hours or equipment (and with certainty that the techniques were valid and successful!) one would use a combination of techniques. Preliminary interviews and observation would indicate the problems and areas of interest. Static simulation with careful interviewing would give information about both general and specific knowledge, while verbal protocols and associated observation would show the details of behaviour in real conditions of complexity and time.

References

BAINBRIDGE, L. (1972). An analysis of a verbal protocol from a process control task. *Unpublished Ph.D. Thesis.* University of Bristol.

BARTLETT, F. C. (1932). *Remembering.* Cambridge University Press.

BENJAFIELD, J. (1969). Evidence that "thinking aloud" constitutes an externalisation of inner speech. *Psychonomic Science,* **15**, 83–84.

BROADBENT, D. E. (1977). Levels, hierarchies and the locus of control. *Quarterly Journal of Experimental Psychology,* **29**, 181–201.

COOKE, J. E. (1965). Human decisions in the control of a slow response system. *Unpublished D.Phil. Thesis.* University of Oxford.

CUNY, X. (1977). Etude de l'activité de regulation dans une situation de conduite de processus. Laboratoire de Psychologie du Travail, 41, rue Gay-Lussac, Paris.

DANSEREAU, D. F. & GREGG, L. W. (1966). An information processing analysis of mental multiplication. *Psychonomic Science,* **6**, 71–72.

DOMINOWSKI, R. L. (1974). How do people discover concepts? In SOLSO, R. L., Ed., *Theories in Cognitive Psychology: The Loyola Symposium.* Lawrence Erlbaum.

DUNCAN, K. D. & GRAY, M. J. (1975). Scoring methods for verification of performance in industrial fault-finding problems. *Journal of Occupational Psychology,* **48**, 93–106.

DUNCAN, K. D. & SHEPHERD, A. (1975). A simulator and training technique for diagnosing plant failures from control panels. *Ergonomics,* **18**, 627–642.

DUNCKER, K. (1945). On problem solving. *Psychological Monographs,* **58**(5) (No. 270).

FARBER, I. E. (1963). The things people say to themselves. *American Psychologist,* **18**, 185–197.

GAGNÉ, R. M. & SMITH, E. C. (1962). A study of the effects of verbalisation on problem solving. *Journal of Experimental Psychology,* **63**, 12–18.

GOILLAU, P. J. (1978). Predictor displays for chemical plant instrumentation. In *The Operator-Instrument Interface.* The Institute of Measurement and Control, Teeside Section.

IOSIF, GH. (1972). Le diagnostic des incidents par les opérateurs de centrales thermiques. *Le Travail Humain,* **25**, 37–48.

IOSIF, GH. & ENE, P. (1975). Diagnosis function in thermo power station operators. *Revue Roumaine des Sciences Sociales—Psychologie,* **19**, 179–197.

KING, P. J. (1978). Performance evaluation and information display in process control. In *The Operator-Instrument Interface.* The Institute of Measurement and Control, Teeside Section.

KING, P. J. & CININAS, A. (1976). Manual Control Strategy Determination using question-naires. *Report No. LR 236 (CON).* Warren Spring Laboratory, Stevenage.

KRAGT, H. & LANDEWEERD, J. A. (1974). Mental skills in process control. In EDWARDS, E. & LEES, F. P., Eds, *The Human Operator In Process Control.* London: Institution of Chemical Engineers.

LEPLAT, J. & BISSERET, A. (1965). Analyse des processue de traitement de l'information chez le contrôleur de la navigation aérienne. *Bulletin du C.E.R.P.*, **1–2**, 51.

NEWELL, A. & SIMON, H. A. (1972). *Human Problem Solving.* Englewood Cliffs, N.J.: Prentice-Hall.

NISBETT, R. E. & WILSON, T. D. (1977). Telling more than we can know: verbal reports on mental processes. *Psychological Review*, **84**, 231–259.

PETERSON, L. R. (1969). Concurrent verbal activity. *Psychological Reviews*, **76**, 376–386.

RASMUSSEN J. & JENSEN, AA. (1974). Mental procedures in real-life tasks: A case study of electronic trouble shooting. *Ergonomics*, **17**, 293–307.

RYAN, T. A. (1970). *Intentional Behaviour: An Approach to Human Motivation.* Ronald Press Co.

SCHUCK, J. R. & LEAHY, W. R. (1966). A comparison of verbal and non-verbal reports of fragmenting visual images. *Perception and Psychophysics*, **1**, 191–192.

SMITH, E. R. & MILLER, F. D. (1978). Limits on perception of cognitive processes: a reply to Nisbett and Wilson. *Psychological Review*, **85**, 355–362.

UMBERS, I. G. (1976). A study of cognitive skills in a complex system. *Unpublished Ph.D. Thesis.* University of Aston.

WONG, R., HARRISON, J. & STOPPER, H. (1966). Intertrial activity, awareness and verbal conditioning of children. *Psychonomic Science* **6**, 55–56.

An analysis of human decision-making in cement kiln control and the implications for automation†

I. G. UMBERS AND P. J. KING

Warren Spring Laboratory, Stevenage, Herts, U.K.

(*Received 25 May 1979*)

This paper describes the investigation into the control skills of cement kiln operators with a view to modelling these skills by a fuzzy algorithm. The operators' strategies were studied by observing and making a detailed record of the operators' behaviour as they controlled the kiln. Analysis of the observational record suggested that many aspects of the operators' control behaviour could be modelled by a threshold logic controller. An improvement to the threshold model was attempted by comparing the operators' performance with the performance produced by a set of prescriptive control rules. Although the prescriptive rules were found to be an inadequate model of the kiln operators, analysis indicated that the rules had the potential to produce better kiln control. The implementation of the prescriptive rules as a fuzzy controller is discussed.

Introduction

Cement kilns are difficult to control because of their time varying non-linear behaviour and the poor quality of measurements available in the severe environment of the cement making process. Consequently, control is usually restricted to a few simple control loops on secondary variables, with the control of primary variables and the selection of operating conditions left as the kiln operator's responsibility. However, it is possible that the concept of automatic regulation as implemented by a fuzzy logic system can provide a better alternative to kiln control. The work outlined in this paper describes an analysis of the cognitive skills of kiln operators and considers how these skills can be modelled by a fuzzy algorithm. The impetus for this investigation came from a desire to evaluate a set of kiln control rules prescribed by Peray & Waddell (1972) with the intention of implementing these rules by a fuzzy control system.

Fuzzy control systems

A schematic of a fuzzy control system (Mamdani, 1974; King & Mamdani, 1977) for a regulation control task is shown in Fig. 1. The fuzzy controller is located in the error channel and consists of a fuzzy relationship or algorithm, relating significant observed variables to the control actions. The form of the decision rules employed depends on the process under control and the heuristics used. In the case of a single input-output

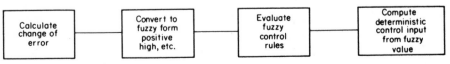

FIG. 1. Fuzzy control system.

369

regulation task it is assumed to be the system error (E) and its rate of change (CE), the result of a control decision being a change in the control valve setting. The control strategy is expressed linguistically as a set of imprecise conditional statements, which form a set of decision rules. For example, a typical rule for a temperature control task could be "if a temperature is high and rising then increase the cooling a lot", where "high" and "rising" are imprecise magnitudes for temperature and rate of change and "increase a lot" is an imprecisely quantified value for the corrective action. This type of formulation for the decision rule structure is similar to the fuzzy algorithm described by Zadeh (1968, 1973) and control system implementation using fuzzy set concepts is claimed to be generally similar to the process operators' approach to control.

The calculation of the control action is composed of the following 4 stages:

    (i) calculate the present error and its rate of change;
    (ii) convert the error values to fuzzy variables;
    (iii) evaluate the decision rules using the compositional rule of inference;
    (iv) calculate the deterministic input required to regulate the process.

The fuzzy logic control system is designed to deal with situations where the available sources of information are inaccurate, subjectively interpreted or uncertain. Several workers have reported successful applications of fuzzy control in the regulation of complex, non-linear processes with measured information of poor quality, e.g. Kickert & Van Naute Lamke (1976), Rutherford (1976), Ostergaard (1976) and Tong (1976).

Plant and process description

CHEMICAL PROCESS

Cement is manufactured by heating a slurry consisting of clay, limestone, sand and iron ore to a temperature that will permit the formation of the complex compounds of cement, dicalcium silicate (C_2S), tricalcium silicate (C_3S), tricalcium aluminate (C_3A) and tetracalcium aluminoferrite (C_4AF). In the first stage of the kilning process the slurry is dried and excess water driven off. In the second stage calcining takes place with the calcium carbonate decomposing to calcium oxide and carbon dioxide. In the final stage burning takes place at between 1250–1450°C and free lime (CaO) combines with the other ingredients to form the cement compounds. The end product of the burning process is referred to as clinker.

CEMENT KILN

The kiln (see Fig. 2) consists of a long steel shell about 130 m in length and 5 m in diameter. The shell is mounted at a slight inclination to the horizontal, and is lined with fire bricks. The shell rotates slowly, at approximately 1 rev/min, and the slurry is fed in at the upper or back end of the kiln. The inclination of the shell and its rotation transports the material through the kiln in about 3 hours 15 mins with a further 45 mins spent in the clinker cooler.

The heat in the kiln is provided by pulverised coal mixed with air, referred to as primary air. The hot combustion gases are sucked through the kiln by an induction fan at the back end of the kiln.

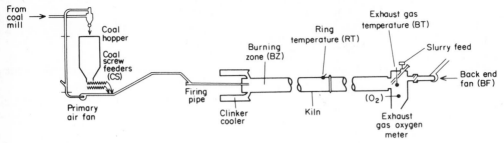

FIG. 2. Schematic diagram of rotary cement kiln.

Task description

PROCESS INFORMATION

The simplified schematic diagram, Fig. 2, shows the 5 main kiln state variables, and the three main control variables. These are:

(i) exhaust gas temperature—back end temperature (BT);
(ii) intermediate gas temperature—ring temperature (RT);
(iii) burning zone temperature (BZ);
(iv) oxygen percentage in exhaust gases (O_2);
(v) litre weight (LW)—indicates clinker quality.

The process is controlled by varying the following:

(i) kiln speed (KS);
(ii) coal feed (CS)—fuel;
(iii) induced draught fan speed (BF).

The relationship between these input variables and the controlled variables is complex, with delays and interactions. The kiln's dynamic response was measured using data obtained from the observers' log following control changes made by the operators. The dynamic responses were all assumed to be represented by a first order lag with a pure time delay, and were determined from the kiln's response to step changes using the "reaction" curve method. This form of representation is a gross simplification because the kiln is subject to random disturbances from several sources which cannot be quantified, and the kiln's response to control inputs is non-linear and extremely variable and depends on the prevailing kiln conditions. The results of several changes were averaged and the resulting transfer functions give an approximate indication of the short term (within 1 hour) response of the kiln. The results are shown in Table 1 and illustrate the relationship between control and observed variables.

OPERATOR INTERFACE

All the instruments were mounted on a central control panel in the kiln control room. The instruments were arranged around a large mimic diagram which occupied the full 9 m length of the panel. Information about the process was displayed in the following ways.

(a) Voltages, currents, damper positions and motor speeds were displayed by means of circular dial meters.

TABLE 1

Kiln dynamic response characteristics

Assumed transfer function, $R(s) = \dfrac{K e^{-\tau_D s} U(s)}{\tau_C s + 1}$

where $R(s)$ = kiln measured variable, $U(s)$ = kiln input variable, K = gain, τ_D = time delay (min), τ_C = time constant (min)

Measured variables	R	Input variables, $U(s)$			
		Coal screw feed CS (r.p.m.)	I.D. fan speed BF (r.p.m.)	Kiln speed spr KS (a)†	(b)
Oxygen, O_2 (%)	K	−0·725	0·069	—	—
	τ_C	11·0	11·4	—	—
	τ_D	4·0	6·1	—	—
Intermediate gas (ring) RT temperature (°C)	K	20·3	−1·76	20	10
	τ_C	22·25	10·6	30	20
	τ_D	9·3	2·0	90	195
Exhaust gas (back end) BT temperature (°C)	K	7·85	0·7	4	2
	τ_C	17·7	11·3	20	20
	τ_D	13·25	5·2	7	195
Litre wt. LW	K	91·8	−16·5	+119·6	
	τ_C	60	—	60	
	τ_D	60	60	120	
Number of responses averaged		20	6	1	

† The temperature response to kiln speed was obtained from only one suitable step response and exhibited a double response. For example the back end temperature responds after a delay of 7 minutes (transfer function a), with a subsequent change after a delay of 195 minutes (transfer function b).

(b) Draughts were displayed on vertical scale meters.

(c) Information on temperatures and oxygen was displayed on horizontal scale meters. Trend information was also provided for these variables on a stamping type of chart recorder.

The kiln was controlled manually from the panel by remote actuation. The controls were of the pistol grip type.

An alarm system was provided for the temperature and consisted of an audible siren, which could be cancelled, and a red flashing light associated with each temperature meter. Lights were also located on the mimic diagram to indicate the running state of important drive motors. An extinguished light indicated that a particular piece of equipment had ceased to function.

TASK OBJECTIVES

There are 4 goals for most process control tasks:

(i) good quality;

   (ii) high quantity;
   (iii) low cost;
   (iv) safe operation.

The control policy adopted by the operators to meet these goals was to run the kiln at the highest level of production at which a steady kiln state could be maintained. If the kiln is not kept at a steady state, product (clinker) quality will fluctuate, and the necessary corrective control actions may demand a temporary reduction in production. The important function of the operator is to detect when the kiln is moving into an unsteady state and to make a suitable corrective action. The skill of the kiln operator lies in performing these two functions effectively. The following section describes how information on the kiln operators' skills was obtained, and how it was analysed.

OBSERVATIONAL STUDY

Method

The chief source of information on the kiln operators' skills was an observational study of their behaviour. Briefly, this consisted of an observer recording the information gathering and control activities of the operators. The control activities were identified as bouts of information sampling frequently culminating in some kind of control action. The direct observations were supplemented by explanations from the operators on what they were doing and why. A complete observational record therefore consisted of a series of events which would be recorded as shown in the example below.

RECORD OF A CONTROL ACTION

8/7 12.50	READ:	$RT = 860$
		$BT = 264$
		$O_2 = 2 \cdot 3$
	OBSERVE:	$BZ = $ same
	ACTION:	$\frac{1}{4}$ turn off coal screw 2
	REASON:	O_2 is a bit low

An important methodological point in making these records is that the observer should develop a system of descriptive terms for describing the activities of the operator (see Umbers, 1976). This has a number of advantages: (i) a consistent description of the operator's behaviour is obtained throughout the observation period, (ii) observational records from several observers will be consistent and directly comparable, (iii) a clear understanding of the types of operator activity is obtained at the outset of the recording period. Several preliminary observational sessions are necessary before a set of descriptive terms can be defined.

In addition to the observations of the operator's behaviour, a log of the 8 main variables (both status and control variables) was made every 15 minutes. This permitted "activity graphs" to be plotted for the period over which an operator's behaviour was observed. Attempts were made to log data using a data logger, however, noise on the signals from the kiln control panel prevented the recording of an accurate log.

Design

The plant was run continuously on a 3×8 hour (morning, afternoon and night) shift system. To obtain a representative sample of behaviour each kiln operator was observed on morning, afternoon and night shifts.

Procedure

It was explained to each operator that the purpose of the observational study was to obtain information on the manual control of cement kilns, with the view to making recommendations for the improvement of kiln control systems. The method of acquiring the necessary information, by recording the details of bouts of activity, was described to them. Although some of the operators were initially apprehensive about the study, by the end of their first shift they appeared to be happy with the situation, and usually described their own behaviour without being prompted by the observer.

ANALYSIS AND RESULTS

Frequency counting

The data obtained from the observational records were initially analysed by counting the frequency of occurrence of certain types of operator behaviour. The analysis provides quantitative information on the relevance of the various state and control variables to the operators' control behaviour. Tables 2 and 3 summarise some of this information.

TABLE 2

Sampling rates for the 4 main kiln state variables

BZ	RT	BT	O_2	
1·8	1·7	1·8	1·9	samples/hr

TABLE 3

Frequency with which control variables were used

Coal screws (CS)	Back end fan (BF)	Kiln speed (KS)
95	15	9

The results show that fuel flow is the most important of the control variables. The information sampling rates are more difficult to interpret since there are two sources of variation which are confounded. Variation in sampling rate can be a function of the importance of a state variable in controlling the kiln, and also a function of the response time of the state variables to a control action. A detailed analysis of the sampling rates shows that they are not constant but seem to depend on the state of the kiln. In 33% of the samples the time between samples was less than 10 min, and in 15% the interval was less than 5 min. The sampling rates tended to increase when the operators were uncertain about the state of the kiln. On several occasions operators were observed making a series of frequent information samples prior to making a control decision. After a control action was made the sampling rates tended to decrease. This distribution of sampling rates is not compatible with the response characteristics of the kiln, but may instead reflect the operators' response to variations in the demand of the control task.

Input/output correlations

The operators' behaviour was analysed to establish a relationship between the state and control variables, by correlating input with output. The aim of the analysis was to obtain a model of the operators' control function. The analysis was carried out on the data from the manual data log, however, the variation in the size of the control actions was negligible, and consequently no evidence was found for the operators behaving as either proportional, integral or rate of change controllers. Examination of the data by eye suggested that the operators were acting as on–off threshold controllers.

The second attempt to find a relationship between state and control variables tested this possibility by correlating the polarity of coal screw control actions with the polarity of the state variable errors. The analysis was restricted to coal screw control actions because the frequency of other actions was too low. The table below shows these correlations for two of the operators. It is apparent from the table that there seems to be some relationship between the polarity of control actions and state variable error. Attempts to improve the correlations were made by combining information from the state variable using an additive procedure.

TABLE 4

Correlations between polarity of state variable error and control actions

		O_2	RT	BT	LW	
Operator	A	0·64*	0·00	0·46*	0·15	* = $p < 0.05$
	B	0·78*	0·43*	0·61*	0·00	Spearman rs

Correlations were not improved by combining information, and the results tended to suggest that the operators do not use all the available state information to make a control action. This was corroborated by the explanations the operators usually gave for making a control action. In most of these explanations the operators only gave the value of one variable as the reason for making a control action, the mean = 1·3 items of information/control action, e.g. they would say that oxygen was high. These results tend to support the hypothesis that the operators behave as threshold controllers; that is, they do not react to a value of a variable until it has reached a predetermined threshold. This would also account for the fact that the operators only act as intermittent controllers making corrective control actions at infrequent intervals (less than 1 per hour).

A THRESHOLD DECISION MODEL

The hypothesis that the kiln operators behave in a similar manner to a threshold controller, was tested by comparing the percentage of control action (CS) polarities correctly predicted by various threshold models. In essence each model had a similar structure: an upper and lower threshold limit was assigned to each measured state variable (RT, BT, O_2 and LW) for each operator. If the value of a variable went outside these limits a control action was predicted. All the logs of the kiln data were treated in this manner so that the predicted control actions could be compared with the actions actually made. When more than one state variable went outside its threshold information was combined according to an additive rule:

$$\text{Polarity of CS action} = BT + RT + O_2 + LW$$

$$(+) = (+) + (0) + (+) + (-)$$

The best performance was achieved by a model whose threshold limits were the interquartile range of the values of the variables observed by the operators. This model predicted correctly 75% of (CS) control actions for all the operators, which is significantly better than chance, $\chi^2 = 11.37$; $p < 0.001$. Performance of this model would probably be improved if burning zone observations could be included; however, there is no objective record of burning zone conditions.

A further test of the model was to compare the reasons given by the model for a control action with those provided by the operators. It was found that out of those control actions where the operators gave reasons, and the model made a correct prediction, i.e. 64·1% of action, the model reasons disagreed with the operators' on 13·4% of control actions. In 17·9% of control actions BZ observation was given as the reason by the operators and could not be compared with the model. In the remaining 32·8% the model agreed with the operators. This agreement between operator and model is encouraging since it suggests that the model has more than face validity:

	Agree	Disagree	BZ obs.	Total
% of correct control actions	32·8	13·4	17·9	64·1

In summary, the threshold model suggests the following about the way in which operators make their decisions. They appear to have a range of values for each variable which they consider to be safe; that is, values within these ranges do not indicate a change in kiln state. When the value of a variable is outside its "safety" range, a change in kiln state is indicated.

The difficulty, however, with the threshold model of decision-making is that it does not adequately deal with situations where more than one variable is outside threshold. The combination rule used in the threshold model places a +, 0 or − in an additive equation depending on the current level of a variable. There is no evidence, however, that the operators in fact behave like this.

Fuzzy logic and kiln control

THRESHOLD CONTROL

The threshold model of the kiln operators provides an adequate description of some of their behaviour. However, a controller based on the threshold model would have a number of shortcomings.

    (i) The threshold model cannot make control actions which require the use of more than 1 control variable.

   (ii) There is no evidence on how state information is combined when several state variables are outside threshold.

  (iii) The threshold levels are difficult to specify and tend to vary over time. The verbal explanations of the operators are characterised by imprecise analogue descriptions of the value of a variable (e.g. high, low, dropped etc.), rather than discrete numerical values which would be expected if the operators behaved like a fixed threshold controller. A model based on fixed thresholds is a simplification of a more complex process in which the operators reflect the poor quality of variable measurement by having a range of thresholds.

(iv) The kiln operators use control strategies which are more complex than those embodied in the threshold model. For example:

OBSERVED BEHAVIOUR		BEHAVIOUR PRESCRIBED BY THRESHOLD MODEL
READ:	RT = gone up	RT = 823
	BT = holding up	
	O_2 = dropped	
OBSERVE:	BZ = bit warm	
ACTION:	BF↓ 5 r.p.m.; CS ↓ $\frac{1}{2}$ turn	CS ↑ $\frac{1}{2}$ turn
REASON:	want to keep heat in front of kiln	RT below minimum threshold

Improvements could be made to the threshold model by carrying out further studies of operator behaviour, but it cannot be certain that a solution would be forthcoming; some control rules may not be accessible to conscious linguistic processes. For example, Bisseret & Girard (1973) in a study of air traffic controllers, found that the controllers were unable to give details on some of their thought processes. In ordinary circumstances where no other sources of data are available, further studies of the operators would be the only way to proceed. However, the Peray & Waddell (1972) control rules present an alternative source of information. The rules represent a prescriptive model of a kiln operator's behaviour, whose validity as an operational model of the kiln operators can be tested by comparing the operators' behaviour with that prescribed by the model. The results of such an assessment may provide further evidence for a better model of the kiln operators. A preliminary examination of the Peray & Waddell rules indicates that there are a number of ways in which a model based on these rules would be an improvement on the threshold model. More specifically, the rules can make (i) multi-variable control actions, and (ii) can combine information from several state variables—2 inadequacies of the threshold model. An additional feature of the rules is that, as Mamdani, Procyk & Baaklini (1976) have observed, they can be readily translated into a fuzzy controller; and furthermore a fuzzy controller would be ideal for dealing with the imprecise linguistic statements that the operators use to describe the state of the kiln—another inadequacy of the threshold model.

AN ASSESSMENT OF THE PERAY & WADDELL CONTROL RULES

The Peray & Waddell rules work by identifying the state of the kiln and prescribing a suitable corrective action, e.g. if oxygen and back end temperature are high and burning zone is alright the recommended control action is to reduce back end fan speed and reduce fuel rate. The method used to identify the kiln state is very similar to the one embodied in the threshold model of the kiln operators; i.e. there is a certain range of "safe" values associated with each state variable, so that when the value of a variable drifts outside these limits a corrective action is initiated. Peray & Waddell consider that there are three state variables of prime importance:

   (i) burning zone temperature;
  (ii) back end temperature;
 (iii) quantity of oxygen in exhaust gases.

Each variable can be above, below or within the allowable range, making 27 possible kiln states. Each kiln state has a prescribed corrective control action associated with it, which uses a combination of kiln speed, back end fan and fuel to achieve the desired correction. Thus, the way in which the Peray & Waddell rules work corresponds very closely with the procedures the operators actually use to control the kiln. To assess the control rules as a model of the kiln operators it is necessary to examine the records of the operators' activities, identify the states of the kiln when control actions were made, and compare the control actions made by the operators with those prescribed by the appropriate control rules. In principle this is straightforward, but in practice there are difficulties in identifying kiln states. The most complete test of the control rules would be to use the range of acceptable values specified for each state variable by Peray & Waddell to identify the state of the kiln. In practice this is unrealistic since the ways in which the measurements of the state variables are made will vary from kiln to kiln, and necessarily the acceptable range of values will vary. Specifically, on the kiln investigated in this study, burning zone temperature was not measured but assessed by the operators looking into the kiln, and the back end temperature was measured much closer to the rear of the kiln than the back end temperature used by Peray & Waddell. For these reasons the kiln state at each control action was identified by using the reasons given by the operators for making a control action. For example, the kiln state identified by the following operator explanation would be back end temperature low; "half a turn on coal screw one as back end temperature has dropped, try to bring it up for the next shift". This means that only the ability of the control rules to make suitable control actions can be assessed. There is also the disadvantage that the identification of the kiln state relies entirely on the operator's explanations, and therefore assumes that the operator's statement is a complete explanation of his behaviour; there is no evidence that in fact the operators give complete explanations for their behaviour. Nevertheless, the results from the comparative analysis of control actions indicates that there is considerable agreement between rules and behaviour. Table 5 shows that in 76 out of 118 control actions the operators gave sufficient explanation to determine the state of the kiln, and that in $61 \cdot 8\%$ of those control actions there was agreement between the rules and the operators' control actions. The probability of a random process obtaining this level of agreement is $p \ll 0 \cdot 001$—using the normal approximation to the binomial

TABLE 5

Agreement between control actions made by operators and those prescribed by Peray & Waddell control rules

	Agree	Disagree	Total	
Frequency	47	29	76	(out of a total of 118 CAs)
Percentage	(61·8)	(38·2)		

distribution. Examination of the control actions where there was disagreement shows that in 15 out of the 29 disagree control actions there is agreement between the coal screw actions, but disagreement over the use of the back end fan. This suggests that response to the back end fan of the kiln in this study may differ from the response assumed by the Peray & Waddell rules. It is possible to make an approximate check on the suitability of the control actions prescribed by the control rules by using the simplified kiln dynamics (Table 1) as a model of the kiln's response to certain control actions.

CONTROL ACTION SUITABILITY

The kiln steady state gain equations were used to construct a set of 3 2-dimensional nomograms showing the effects of coal feed (CS), back end fan (BF) and kiln speed (KS) changes on the measured and observed state variables. With these nomograms it is possible to determine the most suitable corrective control action for a given kiln state. An evaluation of the disagree category control actions, Table 6, shows that the Peray & Waddell control rules would produce more appropriate and comprehensive corrective control actions than the kiln operators.

TABLE 6
Evaluation of "disagree" category control actions

	Both acceptable	Control rules best	Kiln burner best	Total
Frequency	10	18	1	29
Percent	(34·5)	(62·1)	(3·4)	

However, although the rules can be expected to produce better kiln control than the operators, it must be emphasised that the rules do not produce optimum kiln response. The interactions between the control variables means that to obtain the desired response, a complicated juggling of the available control variables is required. Neither the kiln operators nor the rules make full use of the control variables, and therefore, exact kiln control cannot be achieved. The operators are worse in this respect in that they tend to use only one variable (CS) for control, whereas the rules use 2 (CS and BF). The result is that either type of control regime will produce unstable control since any system with more state variables (degrees of freedom) than control variables is inherently unstable. There is, however, a reason for this reluctance to use all 3 control variables, and is that changing kiln speed will produce very long-term changes in the kiln state and the kiln dynamics which are difficult to handle using either automatic or manual control. Consequently, both the operators and the Peray & Waddell control rules tend to reserve their use of the kiln speed to those occasions where large corrective actions are required. The use of a simplified model of system dynamics obviously has its limitations. Nevertheless, although the Peray & Waddell rules are not a complete model of the kiln operators, they are a better basis for an automatic controller than could be obtained with a complete model. Furthermore, the rules can easily be implemented by a fuzzy controller.

The controller would be implemented on a computer. The control action which results from evaluating the rules is deterministic, so that for the same process state (specific values of BZ, BT and O_2), the same control action will always be made unless the rules are altered. The control policy can be implemented directly by evaluating the rules at each sampling interval. This, however, is not computationally efficient, and a considerable saving in on-line computer time can be achieved by extracting the control actions from a precomputed look-up table. In general, the fuzzy logic controller assumes that information is obtained from process measurements. However, the operator's subjective interpretation of process conditions, e.g. burning zone state, could be included with process measurements by providing a suitable data entry terminal through which the operators could specify the observed state of the burning zone. The updating procedure for evaluating the fuzzy logic controller would have to be altered to handle the intermittent manual data entry. This is quite practicable with a fuzzy algorithm since theory does not require regular updating, which is essential in conventional linear digital control policies.

Conclusions

The advantage of a fuzzy controller is that it can implement the imprecise linguistic rules which seem to characterise the explanations given by the operators for their control behaviour. However, the adequacy of a fuzzy controller depends on the adequacy with which the operators can explain their behaviour. The experience from this investigation has shown that even with a detailed study of operator behaviour it is not possible to produce an adequate model of operator behaviour. Furthermore, it was found that certain aspects of the operators' behaviour were not optimum and could be improved. If, however, an exact model of the operators' control behaviour is abandoned it is possible to derive a set of rules which, when implemented by a fuzzy algorithm, should produce satisfactory control. A fuzzy controller is essential to this application since it is the only way in which the imprecise state descriptions, characteristic of Peray & Waddell's rules and the operators' explanations, can be implemented.

References

BISSERET, A. & GIRARD, Y. (1973). The treatment of information by the air traffic controller: a global description of reasoning. *Report 7303-R-37*. Institut de Recherche d'Informatique et d'Automatique.
KICKERT, W. & VAN NAUTE LAMKE, M. (1976). The application of fuzzy set theory to control a warm water process. *Automatica*, **12**, 301–308.
KING, P. J. & MAMDANI, E. H. (1977). The application of fuzzy control systems to industrial processes. *Automatica*, **13**, 235–242.
MAMDANI, E. H. (1974). Application of fuzzy algorithms for the control of a dynamic plant. *Proceedings of the IEE*, **121**(12), 1585–1588.
MAMDANI, E. H., PROCYK, T. & BAAKLINI, N. (1976). Application of fuzzy logic to controller design based on linguistic protocol. *Workshop on Discrete Systems and Fuzzy Reasoning*, Queen Mary College, London.
OSTERGAARD, J. J. (1976). Fuzzy logic control of a heat exchanger process. *Report No. 7601*. Electrical Power Engineering Dept, Technical University of Denmark, Lyngby.
PERAY, K. E. & WADDELL, J. J. (1972). *The Rotary Cement Kiln*. New York: Chemical Publishing Co.

RUTHERFORD, D. A. (1976). The implementation and evaluation of a fuzzy control algorithm for a sinter plant. *Workshop on Discrete Systems and Fuzzy Reasoning*, Queen Mary College, London.

TONG, R. (1976). Some problems with the design and implementation of fuzzy controllers. *Report No. TR127*. Department of Engineering, University of Cambridge.

UMBERS, I. G. (1976). A study of cognitive skills in complex systems. *Unpublished Ph.D. thesis.* University of Aston, Birmingham.

ZADEH, L. A. (1973). Outline of a new approach to the analysis of complex systems and decision processes. *IEEE Transactions on Systems, Man and Cybernetics*, **SMC-3** (1), 28–44.

ZADEH, L. A. (1968). Fuzzy algorithms. *Information and Control*, **12,** 94–102.